I0890018

Commanding Canadians

Studies in Canadian Military History

The Canadian War Museum, Canada's national museum of military history, has a threefold mandate: to remember, to preserve, and to educate. It does so through an interlocking and mutually supporting combination of exhibitions, public programs, and electronic outreach. Military history, military historical scholarship, and the ways in which Canadians see and understand themselves have always been closely intertwined. Studies in Canadian Military History builds on a record of success in forging those links by regular and innovative contributions based on the best modern scholarship. Published by UBC Press in association with the Museum, the series especially encourages the work of new generations of scholars and the investigation of important gaps in the existing historiography, pursuits not always well served by traditional sources of academic support. The results produced feed immediately into future exhibitions, programs, and outreach efforts by the Canadian War Museum. It is a modest goal that they feed into a deeper understanding of our nation's common past as well.

1 John Griffith Armstrong, *The Halifax Explosion and the Royal Canadian Navy: Inquiry and Intrigue*
2 Andrew Richter, *Avoiding Armageddon: Canadian Military Strategy and Nuclear Weapons, 1950-63*
3 William Johnston, *A War of Patrols: Canadian Army Operations in Korea*
4 Julian Gwyn, *Frigates and Foremasts: The North American Squadron in Nova Scotia Waters, 1745-1815*
5 Jeffrey A. Keshen, *Saints, Sinners, and Soldiers: Canada's Second World War*
6 Desmond Morton, *Fight or Pay: Soldiers' Families in the Great War*
7 Douglas E. Delaney, *The Soldiers' General: Bert Hoffmeister at War*
8 Michael Whitby, ed., *Commanding Canadians: The Second World War Diaries of A.F.C. Layard*

Commanding Canadians

The Second World War Diaries of A.F.C. Layard

Edited by Michael Whitby

UBCPress · Vancouver · Toronto

© UBC Press 2005

All rights reserved. No part of this publication may be reproduced, stored in a retrieval system, or transmitted, in any form or by any means, without prior written permission of the publisher, or, in Canada, in the case of photocopying or other reprographic copying, a licence from Access Copyright (Canadian Copyright Licensing Agency), www.accesscopyright.ca.

15 14 13 12 11 10 09 08 07 06 05 5 4 3 2 1

Printed in Canada on acid-free paper.

Library and Archives Canada Cataloguing in Publication

Layard, A.F.C. (Arthur Frank Capel), 1899-1999.
Commanding Canadians : the Second World War diaries of A.F.C. Layard / edited by Michael Whitby.

(Studies in Canadian military history, ISSN 1499-6251)
Includes bibliographical references and index.
ISBN-13: 978-0-7748-1193-4
ISBN-10: 0-7748-1193-5

1. Layard, A.F.C. Arthur Frank Capel), 1899-1999 – Diaries. 2. World War, 1939-1945 – Naval operations – Submarine. 3. World War, 1939-1945 – Naval operations, Canadian. 4. Canada. Royal Canadian Navy – History – World War, 1939-1945. 5. Anti-submarine warfare – Canada – History – 20th century. 6. Great Britain. Royal Navy – Officers – Diaries. 7. World War, 1939-1945 – Personal narratives, British. I. Whitby, Michael J. (Michael Jeffrey), 1954- II. Title. III. Series.

D811.L349 2005 940.54'516'092 C2005-904435-7

Canadä

UBC Press gratefully acknowledges the financial support for our publishing program of the Government of Canada through the Book Publishing Industry Development Program (BPIDP), and of the Canada Council for the Arts, and the British Columbia Arts Council.

Publication of this book has been financially supported by the Canadian War Museum.

Printed and bound in Canada by Friesens
Set in Minion and Helvetica Condensed by Artegraphica Design Co. Ltd.
Copyeditor: Sarah Wight
Proofreader: Gail Copeland
Cartographer: Eric Leinberger
Indexer: Dianne Graves

UBC Press
The University of British Columbia
2029 West Mall
Vancouver, BC V6T 1Z2
604-822-5959 / Fax: 604-822-6083
www.ubcpress.ca

To John Band and Gil Lauzon,
two gentlemen "introduced" to me by Frank Layard,
and whom I am now fortunate to consider friends.

Contents

Maps and Photographs

Maps

Photographs

Acknowledgments

This project would not have seen the light of day without the contributions of many friends, colleagues, and family members. A pleasant reward that made my work much more enjoyable was the fact that, almost to a person, they became captivated by Frank Layard to the extent that he became the subject of the sort of conversations one would have about a close friend.

Two English ladies – my mother, Doris Whitby, and Dianne Graves – helped with the painstaking work of transcribing the diary; Dianne also chased down some contextual odds and ends and compiled the index. Michael Hadley and Marc Milner made invaluable comments on the manuscript and recommended its publication. Alec Douglas, who with Roger Sarty, Bill McAndrew, and Don Graves gave me my formative training as a naval historian, unearthed the diary in the first place, and then with Harry Needham managed support for the project through the Canadian Battle of Normandy Foundation. Bill Glover dispensed reflection from an Edwardian perspective and enjoyed Layardisms – "slight alcoholic remorse" remains the most apropos. Alan Easton, who sailed under Frank Layard in E.G. 9 and who described their complex relationship in *50 North,* perhaps the classic memoir of the Battle of the Atlantic, provided valuable insight and enthusiastic support. "I didn't realize he was thinking like that; he always appeared so confident!" was a common refrain from that dear, elderly gentleman. Richard Mayne, Robert Caldwell, and Jan Drent shared research, while Ginny Tanqueray and Tony Schweppes helped to ease the rigours of writing.

At the institutional level, Matthew Sheldon and Chris Howard Bailey of the Royal Navy Museum in Portsmouth provided friendly advice and a wonderful place to work – where better to research naval history than in a reading room adorned with a complete run of Navy Lists, with a Type 23 frigate moored outside the window, *Victory* through the door, *Mary Rose* down the walk, and *Warrior* around the corner by The Hard! In Australia, David Stevens, Joe Straczek, and John Reeve were affable hosts and provided a terrific forum to present my initial thoughts on Layard at the 2001 King-Hall Naval History Conference, "The Face of Naval Battle," whose proceedings have now been published under that name. Serge Bernier and Steve Harris, director and chief historian respectively at the Directorate of History and Heritage, allowed me to attend that conference, while my former boss Marc Whittingham let me make the detour to Portsmouth, where I first discovered the vast extent, and thus the importance, of the diary. Dean Oliver of the

Canadian War Museum supported and funded publication of the diary for the museum's excellent and much-needed publication series, while Emily Andrew, Camilla Blakeley, Sarah Wight, Ann Macklem, and the friendly, professional staff at UBC Press turned a scruffy manuscript into a handsome volume. Eric Leinberger did an excellent job in preparing the maps.

A few individuals merit special praise. Don Graves, that golden ray of sunshine who will only grudgingly admit he is one of Canada's finest military historians, has been a professional mentor and long-time friend. As well as repeatedly getting me into trouble, he taught me the ropes of the historical craft and more than anyone instilled in me the confidence required of a successful historian. Doug McLean and Malcolm Llewellyn-Jones, practitioners and scholars alike of anti-submarine warfare, graciously shared information and provided wise counsel. Gil Lauzon, a retired US Navy cruiser and destroyer driver with a shrewd understanding of naval professionalism, threw me a lifeline when I was agonizing over the final manuscript amongst myriad crises, acting as a sounding board and posing critical questions that helped to shape the final draft. Raymond Layard – Frank's son and "R." in the diary – not only arranged permission to use the diary, but from the moment I telephoned out of the blue he lent enthusiastic support to the project and provided splendid cheer and hospitality during my trips across the pond. John Trumble Band, who served as Frank Layard's first lieutenant in HMCS *Swansea* and who remained his friend for life, provided insights into Layard's personality and gave steadfast support to the project, always with a gleam in his eye and a smile upon his face.

Finally, my mother and father, veterans of the Royal Navy and Royal Canadian Navy respectively, have "been there" for me in every sense possible; best of all they have suppressed their astonishment that I could ever achieve anything remotely resembling this work! At home, Marina and the irrepressible twins Kaitlynn and Kassandra kept me grounded and ensured that history did not become larger than life. Niki wagged her tail.

Abbreviations

AA	anti-aircraft. Also designates the position directly ahead of a convoy
ACHQ	Area Command Headquarters, a combined maritime command centre located at key bases like Halifax, Plymouth, and Liverpool
ACI	Atlantic convoy instruction
AFI	Admiralty fleet instruction
AFO	Admiralty fleet order
A/S	anti-submarine
A/S P	anti-submarine training evolution
ASW	anti-submarine warfare
BDE	British destroyer escort; RN frigates built in the United States under lend-lease
BEC	British Escort class, anti-submarine vessel built under lend-lease; also known as the Kil class
CAFO	confidential Admiralty fleet orders
Capt. D.	captain (destroyers). A Capt. D. at a shore base handled the administration of destroyers and other vessels while a Capt. D. afloat commanded a destroyer flotilla. (Thus Capt. D17 commanded the 17th destroyer flotilla.)
CAT	Canadian anti-acoustic torpedo gear
CBE	Commander of the British Empire
C-in-C CNA	commander-in-chief, Canadian Northwest Atlantic Command
C-in-C WA	commander-in-chief Western Approaches Command
CNAA	Canadian Naval Administrative Authority
CNMO	Canadian Naval Mission Overseas; RCN headquarters in London
Com. D.	commodore (destroyers)
CS	cruiser squadron; CS 1 would be the officer commanding the 1st Cruiser Squadron
D.	captain (destroyers)
D/C	depth charges
DE	destroyer escort, the American equivalent to a frigate
DF	destroyer flotilla
D/F	direction finding
Derby House	Western Approaches Headquarters in Liverpool

DSC	Distinguished Service Cross
DSO	Distinguished Service Order
(E)	denotes an officer who has qualified as an engineer specialist
EG	escort group
EI	Easy Item search turn
E/S	echo sounder
ETA	estimated time of arrival
FOGMA	flag officer Gibraltar and Mediterranean Approaches
FOIC	flag officer in command
4-striper	officer of the rank of captain
(G) or (g)	gunnery specialist who has passed either the “long” or “short” gunnery course
GEE	RAF radio navigation aid; the naval variant was QH
GMT	Greenwich Mean Time
Gnat	German naval acoustic torpedo
H/F	high frequency
HF/DF	high-frequency direction finding
H/H	hedgehog
HHX	convoy from Halifax to join a New York-UK convoy
HX	convoy from New York to the UK
JW	Arctic convoy from UK to Russia
KMF	fast convoy from the UK to Gibraltar
loran	radio navigation aid
MAC	merchant aircraft carrier
M/F	mid-frequency
MF/DF	mid-frequency direction finding
MID	Mention in Despatches
MKS	slow convoy from Gibraltar to the UK
MOMP	mid-ocean meeting point
(N)	navigation specialist
NCSO	naval control of shipping officer
NEAT	the night attack teacher in Londonderry
No. 1	number one, the first lieutenant or second-in-command of a small ship
NOIC	naval officer in command
NSHQ	Naval Service Headquarters, Ottawa
ON	westbound trans-Atlantic convoy
OOD	officer of the deck
OOW	officer of the watch
PO Tel	Petty Officer (Telegraphist)
PT	physical training

QH	radio navigation device; naval variant of the RAF's GEE system
RAMC	Royal Army Medical Corps
RCNR	Royal Canadian Navy Reserve
RCNVR	Royal Canadian Navy Volunteer Reserve
RDF	radio direction finding or radar
R/T	radio telegraph
R/V	rendezvous
RXC	Canadian-built centimetric radar
S206	personnel evaluation form
SC	slow eastbound trans-Atlantic convoy
SCNO	senior Canadian naval officer
SL	UK-Sierra Leone convoy
S/M	submarine
SNO	senior naval officer
SO	senior officer
SOO	staff officer operations
SS	position directly astern of a convoy
(T)	officer who is a torpedo specialist
TBS	talk between ships: short-range communications system that enabled ships' COs to speak directly with one another
3 striper	an officer of the rank of commander
2 striper	an officer of the rank of lieutenant
2½	an officer of the rank of lieutenant-commander
U/B	U-boat
v.	very
v.g.	very good
VR	volunteer reserve or reservist
V/S	visual signalling
WATU	Western Approaches Tactical Unit, in Liverpool
WESTOMP	western ocean meeting point
W.R.	wardroom
W/T	wireless telegraph

Commanding Canadians

Prologue: Like Cutting Butter

At the end of the first week of November 1942, three armadas steamed resolutely towards the dark shores of French North Africa. These were the ships of Operation Torch, about to launch the second front in the European war. From the open seas of the Atlantic, the American Western Task Force prepared to land soldiers at three sites in French Morocco. Inside the tighter confines of the Mediterranean, two primarily British formations, the Centre and Eastern Task Forces, approached the Barbary coast of Algeria to put troops ashore astride the ports of Oran and Algiers. Each assault area was defended by Vichy French forces, and there was unease among the Allies as to just how stout their resistance might be.

As the Eastern Task Force churned through the darkness towards Algiers, two British destroyers in Force O, the covering force for the assault convoy KMS (A1), left their positions in the screen to go alongside the cruiser HMS *Sheffield*. There, kilometres from shore, *Broke* and *Malcolm* embarked some 686 soldiers from the 3rd Battalion of the US Army's 135th Infantry Regiment. This marked the opening of Operation Terminal, a bold scheme for the two destroyers to penetrate Algiers harbour and land the American troops so as to prevent the French from destroying the vital port facilities or scuttling vessels to block the harbour. Once loaded and heading towards Algiers, *Broke* and *Malcolm* raised the Stars and Stripes to their foremasts, a *ruse de guerre* designed to convince the French, who still had bitter memories of the British attack on their fleet at Oran in July 1940, that it was a wholly American, and thus more acceptable, operation.[1]

War imposes the ultimate stress on those who fight, and in the two destroyers, American soldiers and British sailors wondered what lay ahead. No matter how calm and determined they may have appeared, questions gnawed at their psyches. Would they be frightened? Would they do their unit and comrades proud? Would they survive? We can guess their thoughts, since they are common in anyone facing combat. In one instance, however, we do not have to speculate: we can rely upon a completely forthright, deeply personal account of the thoughts and emotions of a man facing the ultimate test. Lt.-Cdr. Arthur Frank Capel Layard, RN – *Broke*'s commanding officer – kept a detailed personal diary. In bold, neat script he wrote virtually a page a day from the time he entered the Royal Navy as a cadet in 1913 until his retirement in 1947. It is a remarkable document in which, as his account of Operation Terminal demonstrates, he lays bare his soul and shows the human context of great events.

Saturday, 7 November 1942 – At sea

Force O remained cruising at 15 knots in the vicinity of the slow convoy all night and all day. Zigzags and constant alterations of course at 15 knots kept the escort pretty busy. In the forenoon we suddenly got a very good A/S contact and counter attacked.[2] There was a bad balls up in the drill and we dropped our pattern v. late. Quite unable to pick up the echo afterwards and so after searching for a couple of hours we rejoined Force O. At 1800 *Sheffield, Malcolm,* and *Broke* hauled out of line, and while *Sheffield* went slow ahead at 4 knots, *Malcolm* and *Broke* in turn went alongside and embarked our 300 American soldiers apiece. Fancourt and Col. Swenson came on board me.[3] I wasn't v. clever putting my ship alongside and it was nearly dark before the transfer was completed. We then battled along to catch up KMS(A)1.

It was all rather vague what we were supposed to do, but failing other orders we took up screening positions with *Malcolm* astern and us on the Std. Quarter. The convoy was making for Position B when they would launch the attack on B beaches. They arrived there at about 1630 and stopped and lowered boats, and we remained under way in the vicinity waiting for the order to go. All shore lights were on, which was a pleasant surprise and a great navigational aid.

Sunday, 8 November 1942 – At sea/Algiers

Zero hour was 0100 and at about 0130 *Broke* and *Malcolm* (Terminal Four) were ordered to the attack. We shaped course for Cape Matifou keeping 5 miles off Cape Caxian. As we crossed Algiers Bay there was a flicker of search lights from time to time from the Breakwater Forts but no gun fire and no sign of opposition to our landing parties. Matifou Fort to our intense relief showed no signs of life as we passed only about 2 miles off on one S.'ly leg.

We turned to the W. on soundings and R.D.F. [radio direction finding] ranges for the last 6 miles run up to the entrance. As we got nearer the search lights picked us up, and we expected heavy fire to be opened but it was only v. spasmodic and nothing hit us. It was v. blinding, however, and we had to turn up for the entrance on time and soundings and missed it. *Malcolm* astern also missed and we both turned away for another shot. Twice more we tried to find the entrance and failed both times. *Malcolm* 2nd time came under heavy fire and retired with 3 boilers out of action.[4] We then stood well away and decided in spite of only now having ½ our force to have another shot. I had got the position of 2 buoys now taped, both burning dimmed lights. As we rounded the breakwater I felt quite confident and in spite of Fancourt's advice to pull out again I went on to full speed, and sure enough we were right and went slap through the boom like cutting butter. Not much more than machine gun opposition. I put the ship alongside the Quai de Falaise instead of the Q. de Dieppe but it didn't matter much. All our Oerlikons[5] blazing away; God knows what at.

As soon as the brows were out we expected the Americans to stream ashore but there wasn't a move, and we finally almost had to drive them ashore and there was nothing more than dilatory sniping. I was furious and disgusted. We got there at about 0500. The sailors were all a bit worked up and it was difficult to stop them firing at absolutely nothing. I thought there was a rather unpleasant tendency to fall flat every time a rifle went off, and I was delighted to find I didn't want to do it myself. I was simply overjoyed at finding I was able under fire to at least conceal any feelings of fright but of course with so much to do and think about it was comparatively easy not to be windy. I must say when we were being heavily shelled and were sounding the recall I didn't care about it at all. My officers were a *little* disappointing I thought, except Gardner who was as cool as anything and first class. So also were Long, Turner, and Williams, my Canadian R.N.V.R. Subs(E).[6]

When we finally got out [of Algiers harbour] and inspected the damage and took stock we got the [destroyer HMS] *Zetland*'s M.O. [medical officer] on board as Oddie was badly wounded, as was the 1st. Lieutenant, and then with *Zetland* in attendance shaped course for Gib., or rather followed *Z.* as all our charts and navigational instruments had been destroyed by a shell in the chart house. From being a flat calm the wind started to get up, and when in the late afternoon I wanted to transfer the wounded, *Z.* couldn't come alongside and so we had to keep them. Buried the dead just before dark.

I took the precaution to prepare to tow forward before dark, and the Chief seemed quite happy about the flooding situation aft. We'd done a lot of plugging and had the submersible pump going. About midnight, just as I'd laid myself down in my sea cabin for the first time, I got a call from the bridge that the engines had stopped. Found out that they'd lost suction of the forced lubrication pumps. As soon as we lost way we fell away broadside on to the sea, which was quite considerable then, and the weather side being on the holed side we shipped a lot more water and took a very pronounced list. When after about an hour we still couldn't get suction, I signalled *Zetland* to take us in tow and went on the fo'c'sle myself to take charge. Luckily it all ran out clear in the dark, because with our list it was none too easy to work. We towed the remainder of the night quite easily at about 4.5 knots.

Monday, [9 November 1942]

All next day the weather disimproved, and although it was impossible to understand why, the flooding aft increased and the list got worse and worse. After lunch I decided we must get the wounded and some of the surplus American troops over to the *Zetland*, and at about 1500 I ordered *Zetland* to slip the tow and send boats. She used her motor boat and whaler and we had our whaler. It was a frightful job to get the wounded into the boats and across to the *Z.* owing to the sea that was running, and it was obvious the Yanks couldn't go that way as it would be dark long before we'd finished, so *Zetland* was told to try and come alongside with her fo'c'sle to our fo'c'sle. She tried the lee side first but that was not possible and so she came the weather side. About this time the Chief said he couldn't keep steam any longer, because owing to the list they couldn't stand in the boiler rooms any more.

I then had a very difficult decision to make. I first of all decided to abandon ship of all but a small party, and then decided everybody'd better go and we'd return in the morning if she was still afloat. *Z.* came up alongside about 3 times and we jumped for her fo'c'sle. A jolly good bit of work by her Captain.[7] By the time all the boats were hoisted it was dark, and the *Z.* then cruised round the poor old *Broke.* At about 2030 she turned over and sank. I thought when we left she wouldn't last much longer, and I'm glad I made the decision I did. Turned in in the captain's cabin (Lt. Wilkinson [sic] who is an absolutely first class chap) quite exhausted, having had virtually no sleep for 2 days and 2 nights.

Tuesday, [10 November 1942]
Had an excellent breakfast. We are on our way back to Algiers. The more I thought about yesterday the more I felt I hadn't done all that I might have in shoring up and jettisoning more top weight, and I got so depressed that I burst into tears in the captain's cabin. Reaction I suppose.

We got to Algiers at about 1000 and berthed alongside the *Keren* who is being used as an accommodation ship. Crewe-Read[8] is her Captain and he insisted I should use his cabin. All our survivors and wounded were taken on board. It appears that the Americans and the few of our ship's company who were left behind when we pulled out held out for about 1½ [hours] until when the French brought up a couple of tanks they surrendered. About 3 or 4 hours after that again the main landing parties arrived, the town was handed over without a shot and all the prisoners were released again. I'm awfully proud that we did what we set out to do, but I don't believe it had the slightest effect on the operation as there was no attempt to sabotage the port or scuttle the ships in harbour. Pity that there was a useless loss of lives and a good ship.

Six days after Layard resolutely drove *Broke* through the boom at Algiers, he was ushered into the presence of Adm. Sir Andrew Cunningham, the naval commander for Torch, to give a verbal report on Terminal. The legendary "ABC" was a formidable, even ferocious, figure, and Layard's next act was perhaps as courageous as his behaviour under fire. It also testifies to the genuine nature of the man and his diary. "I gave him an account of our little affair," he wrote, "and told him the loss of the ship was due to a bad error of judgement on my part. He seemed v. pleased with what we did at Algiers."[9] Cunningham's final report on Torch echoed this blunt assessment: Layard had performed gallantly under fire but had underestimated the damage to *Broke* and erred in not keeping his damaged ship close by Algiers.[10] Even with this assessment, Layard's performance earned him a Distinguished Service Order "for outstanding zeal and enterprise." "Fancy me getting a D.S.O. It's terrific," a surprised Layard wrote in his diary.[11]

Introduction: An Officer and His Diary

Busting the boom into Algiers harbour marked the most recognized and exciting point of Frank Layard's long naval career. After survivor's leave and a spell of staff duty at the Admiralty, he learned in June 1943 that he had been promoted to the rank of acting commander and was being sent to Canada to command the anti-submarine support group W 10, which was operating as part of the local escort forces out of Halifax under the commander-in-chief, Canadian Northwest Atlantic. Although Layard commanded twelve warships throughout his career – a remarkable achievement matched by only a few officers – W 10 was Layard's first independent formation command, other than a brief stint in command of a destroyer subdivision based in the Irish Free State during the early 1930s.[1] Despite a number of operational snags that prevented the support group from operating as a whole except on a very few occasions, Layard's qualities so impressed senior Canadian officers that they eventually requested that he be appointed senior officer of a new Royal Canadian Navy support group then being formed. The Admiralty agreed, and from January 1944 until past VE Day he commanded E.G. 9, which under his leadership became one of the most effective anti-submarine groups in our navy's history.

This volume covers Layard's Canadian interlude through the medium of his diary. Through Layard's keen eyes we witness signal events such as the invasion of Normandy and the final surrender of Germany's U-boats. We observe both the drudgery of routine naval operations and the trepidation of encounters with the enemy. We experience theatres of war stretching from the northwest Atlantic into the English Channel, and from the Barents Sea to the Gibraltar approaches. We learn how a unit is moulded into an effective fighting force. We gain new insights into the personalities of celebrated British commanders such as Adm. Sir Max Horton and Cmdre. G.W.G. Simpson, and Canadians such as Cdr. J. Douglas "Chummy" Prentice, Cdr. Clarence King, and Lt.-Cdr. Alan Easton. And through a British lens we observe the contrasts and tensions that existed between the RN and the RCN, two vastly different navies. On Layard's final wartime evaluation, Commodore Simpson wrote, "He has led with distinction a difficult team of individualistic Canadian officers."[2] Years later, the frustrations of dealing with Canadians still resonating, Layard commented, "To use a popular expression, 'You can say that again!'"[3]

Layard's diary is also the first comprehensive personal account – British or Canadian – to cover the entire inshore anti-U-boat campaign in European waters.[4] Fought over the final year of the war, the inshore campaign proved both challenging and exasperating for Allied sailors, and forced senior operational commanders to almost recast tried anti-submarine concepts. As in the Battle of the Atlantic, Canadian naval forces proved indispensable. Seven RCN support groups took part in the campaign at one time or another, but Layard's E.G. 9 was the only one there for its duration.[5] Although he cannot speak for the thousand-odd Canadian sailors who scoured shallow inshore waters searching for elusive U-boats, Layard's voice does articulate the many, varied travails associated with a campaign whose unique character can really be understood only through a day-to-day rendition of events.

As important as these insights are, Layard's diary becomes truly remarkable in what it reveals of the daily strain associated with command at sea. As such, it provides a vivid portrait of leadership in war. Layard's remarkable honesty and forthrightness strip away the usual veneer of stoicism and solitude with which most naval commanders – indeed, military leaders of all varieties – surround and protect themselves.[6] The lessons are timeless, and leaders at all levels who consider his example should gain a measure of comfort in knowing that the angst and lack of confidence that marked Layard's personality, and that they perhaps share, are natural and commonplace, and can be overcome. General readers will find a very human story of a man struggling to maintain his way in difficult circumstances and under enormous pressures. His success marks a triumph of the human spirit over adversity, and deserves to be known.

Arthur Frank Capel Layard entered the world on 28 November 1899 at Southwick, near Brighton, England. He was named Arthur after both his father and his mother's brother, who had died of typhoid years earlier. Frank came from his godfather, while Capel had been his mother's maiden name before her mother had inherited a Scottish estate and adopted the family name Carnegy Arbuthnott. Frank, as he became known, was the third child in the family after sisters Margaret – called Peggie – and Katherine. Their father, a tea planter in Ceylon, had brought his family home to England for a vacation before Frank's birth, but they returned to the Far East when he was six months old. In 1906, because there were no quality schools in Ceylon and they did not want to send the children home to England for education as many others did, the entire family returned to England, eventually settling south of London in Tunbridge Wells in a house named "Lanka."

Layard had a typical Edwardian middle-class English upbringing and from his accounts it is obvious that he had a happy childhood. Sports and music filled his days. His relationship with his parents was mixed. "We adored my Mother," he

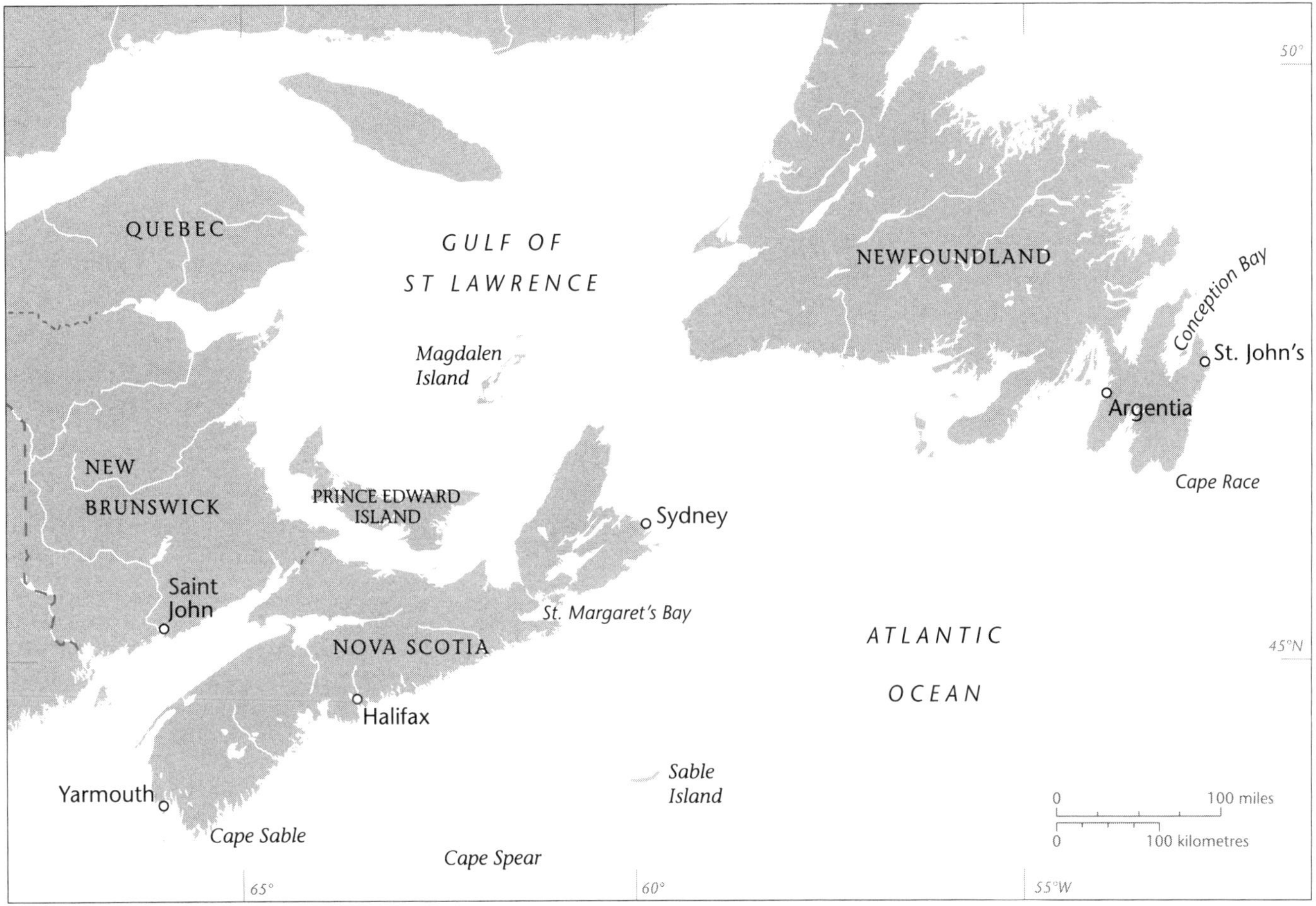

MAP 1 Canadian Northwest Atlantic

0 200 miles
0 200 kilometres
The Shetlands
Lerwick
Orkneys
SCOTLAND
IRELAND
NORTH ATLANTIC OCEAN
U-311, destroyed by Swansea and Matane, 22 April 1944
58°
54°
20°
12°
4°W
50N°
Fair Isle
North Rona
Sulisker
Stack Skerry
Orkneys
Scapa Flow
Switha
Dunnet Head
Pentland Firth
Duncansby Head
Ness Head
Cape Wrath
Butt of Lewis
Thurso
Wick
Loch Eriboll
North Minch
U-309, destroyed by Saint John, 16 February 1945
Hebrides
Little Minch
Loch Ewe
Moray Firth
Kinneard Head
the Skares
Loch Alsh
Aberdeen
SCOTLAND
Barra Head
Tobermory
NORTH SEA
Skerryvore
Methil
May Island
NORTH ATLANTIC OCEAN
Rosyth
Greenock
Glasgow
Edinburgh
56°
Oversay
Lamlash
Firth of Clyde
Inishtrahull
Sheep Haven
Dunagree Point
Horn Head
Rathlin Island
Ailsa Craig
Tory Island
Moville
Foyle

Map 2 The Western Approaches

MAP 3 The English Channel and Bristol Channel

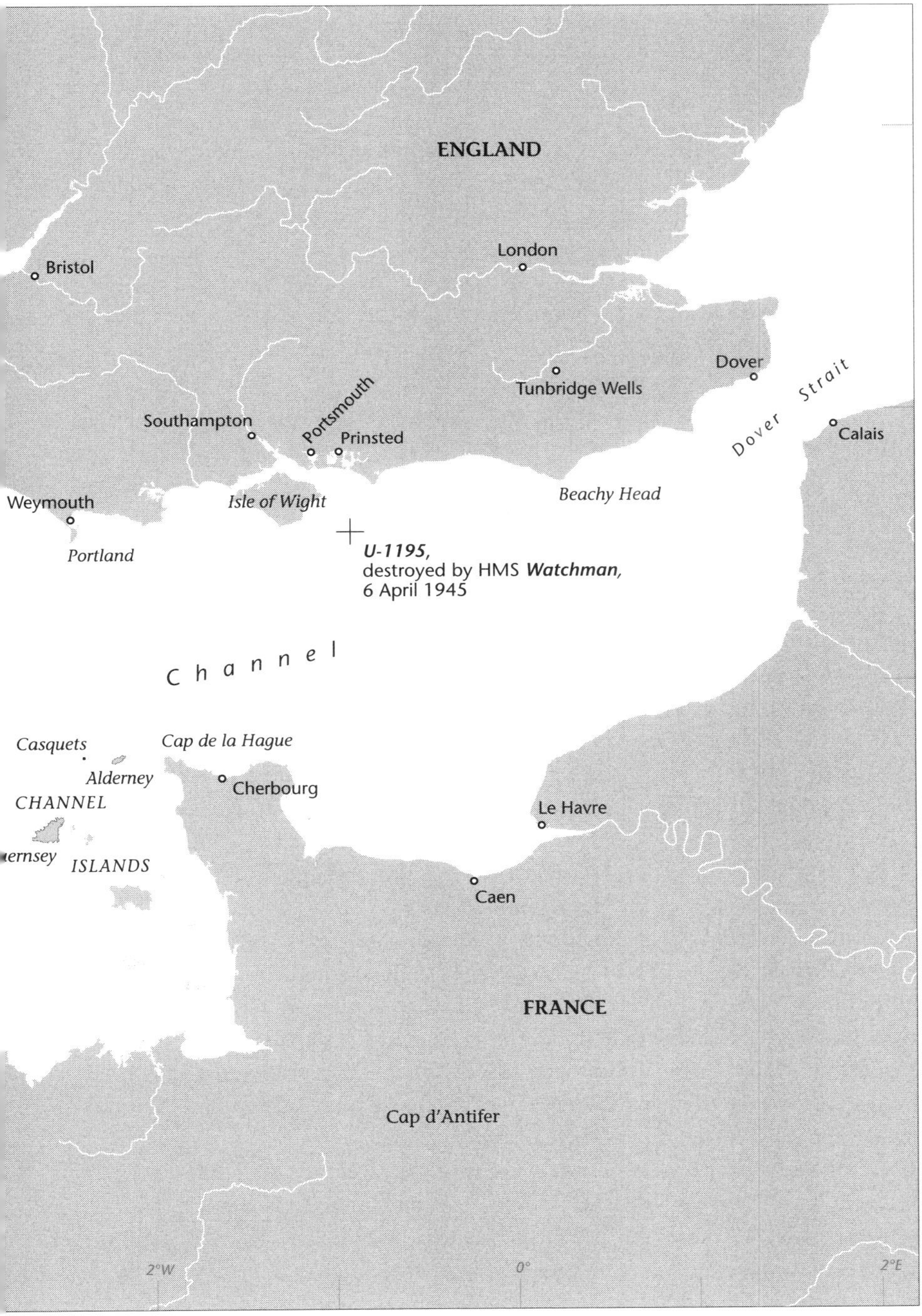
ENGLAND
London
Bristol
Dover
Dover Strait
Tunbridge Wells
Southampton
Portsmouth
Prinsted
Calais
Weymouth
Isle of Wight
Beachy Head
Portland
U-1195,
destroyed by HMS Watchman,
6 April 1945
Channel
Casquets
Cap de la Hague
Alderney
Cherbourg
CHANNEL
Le Havre
ISLANDS
Caen
FRANCE
Cap d'Antifer
2°W
0°
2°E

recalled in later years, "who was in every way a wonderful Mother, but my Father, who took little interest in us, we regarded very much as a stranger."[7] Sadly, Layard's mother died in 1918 and his relationship with his father, who passed away in 1941, remained distant.

In 1913 Layard joined the Royal Navy. The decision was not his; rather, his parents "decided the little man was going into the Navy ... I don't know that anything very much enthused me [about it]," he later explained, "except that in those days the Navy was a great service and it was quite natural to want to belong to it."[8] As his mother recorded in her diary, his departure for the Royal Naval College at Osborne was heart-rending: "Dear Frank went to Osborne today. Arthur took him to Portsmouth. The girls and I saw him off there. He kept up well. Arthur was a little chokey when praying specially for him at family prayers and he shed a few tears then. My heart is very sad at losing him. He has been such a comfort and joy at home these nearly 13 years for which I thank God."[9]

Osborne and the first taste of naval life proved a challenge for Layard, as it did for most cadets. They were, after all, merely boys – during his second term Layard noted in his diary that he barely reached five feet and weighed just six stone, or thirty-eight kilograms, "so I was still very small."[10] He did reasonably well, but his first term lieutenant told him "that as a Cadet Captain I was being too nice."[11] After visiting Osborne for his graduation in June 1914, Mrs. Layard recorded a conversation with his tutor in her diary: "He spoke so nicely of Frank. He said how sorry he was Frank was leaving and that he would be an influence for the good wherever he was. He says he was extremely conscientious and highly developed intellectually and spiritually. His only fear for him is that in after life when he gets thrown in with uncongenial companions he may get depressed and unhappy. He is sure he will have strength for the right, but he fears he may be saddened by contact with evil."[12] Some fifty years later, Layard reflected that upon leaving Osborne, "so too ended what might be termed my age of innocence."[13]

A year at the naval college at Dartmouth followed. The First World War erupted just before his term joined, and since the senior classes had joined the fleet, Dartmouth was quiet and empty. Even better, Layard's entry did not have to endure the hazing associated with being junior classmen. After achieving an overall "Good" rating – "Very Good" in Gunnery, Torpedo and Electric, and Journal; "Fair" in Seamanship, Navigation, and Pilotage – in September 1915 Midshipman Layard joined the Grand Fleet battle cruiser HMS *Indomitable*.[14]

This was a fascinating experience for a young officer, and the high point was his experience in the Battle of Jutland. "Indom" was part of the 3rd Battle Cruiser Squadron attached to Adm. Sir John Jellicoe's main battle fleet. Layard's action station was in the foretop, where he helped measure the angle of deflection for the main armament using a device called the dumaresq. This gave him a spectacular vantage point of the battle: he observed a German torpedo and several shells narrowly miss his ship, caught glimpses of elements of the enemy's High Seas Fleet through the mist, and had "a grim and very sad moment" when they slid past the wreck of the squadron flagship *Invincible,* rent apart by a massive magazine explosion. He was too busy to be frightened but admitted that "I found the noise of our guns most heartening and welcome. It helped to drown out the rumbling noise made by the [German] shells passing over us and the crack of those falling short."[15] Like the rest of the fleet he was deeply disappointed by the outcome of the battle.

Layard left *Indomitable* in December 1917, having passed his sub-lieutenant's exams and been assessed as "a promising young officer."[16] He moved to destroyers and began "one of the best times of my life":

> I had finished with the rules and regulations of the Gun Room. I was a fully fledged officer of the ship, though still very young and inexperienced, with proper duties and responsibilities, and a member of the Ward Room Mess, and I had a cabin to myself and so a bit of privacy when I wanted it ... I was introduced for the first time to flotilla life, which was one of the joys of destroyer service. Everybody knows everybody in the flotilla and you have friends in all the ships, and when in harbour there is always much ship visiting. You take a drink off somebody before lunch and you probably dine out or somebody dines with you in the evening. All this seemed very good to me; after my Gun Room days this was really living.[17]

Layard became a confirmed destroyer man, loving the freedom and increased responsibility that accompanied service in those ships. He saw sea time in two Grand Fleet destroyers, and although most of the duty was routine, his mettle was tested on 26 June 1918 when the destroyer *Wessex* collided with Layard's *Vancouver* while conducting manoeuvres with the 1st Battle Cruiser Squadron.[18] *Vancouver* was split open at the boiler room and five sailors were killed. It was Layard's first experience in handling casualties – some horribly scalded by high-pressure steam – but he held up well, and also helped to jury-rig repairs.[19] At the end of August he was appointed to the destroyer HMS *Sea Bear.* Operations again evolved into a dreary routine, but there was excitement on 30 September when intelligence revealed that the High Seas Fleet might have sailed and the Grand Fleet was put on short notice for sea. "We slipped at 1315 and picked up the 1st BS [Battle Squadron] outside who we were screening ... We were all convinced it was Der Tag."

The climatic battle was not to be, and on 11 November 1918 Layard and the Grand Fleet celebrated the Armistice. In *Sea Bear,* "We waxed excessively convivial over another two bottles of bubbly at dinner. At about 2000 the sirens started sounding again and all the ships switched on searchlights and fired rockets."[20] Besides peace, Layard had a lot to look forward to. He had found his legs as an officer and truly enjoyed navy life, especially in destroyers. The next few years demonstrated the wide variety of experience he could expect to encounter, even in peace. In 1919 three destroyers led by the legendary Cdr. A.B. Cunningham in the cruiser *Curaçao* were despatched to the Baltic to enforce the terms of the Armistice and to support anti-Bolshevik forces. It was Layard's first service outside British waters, and he noted "that it was a great thrill and excitement to visit those foreign places where we were made very welcome."[21] His next posting caused the only significant gap in his diary. In 1919 the RN sent scores of young officers to Cambridge University to make good the education they had lost while serving at sea in the Great War. In a poem about the program Rudyard Kipling pleaded, "Far have they come, much have they braved. Give them their hour of play."[22] Layard obviously played, for during his two years at Cambridge he seldom wrote.

Throughout the 1920s and into 1930, Layard served in the Atlantic, Mediterranean, and Far Eastern Fleets. He was at sea almost the entire time, and his bond to destroyers and flotilla life grew even stronger. In 1930, when serving in the battleship *Emperor of India,* he found himself bored by evolutions involving eight capital ships of the Atlantic Fleet: "At about 0830 we all formed up and proceeded to carry out manoeuvres. I watched from the bridge for a bit, but the simplest turns take so long in big ships that one rather loses interest."[23] Layard showed promise as an officer and managed to survive the heavy cuts of the "Geddes Axe" of the early 1920s, during which hundreds of junior officers, including 40 percent of those in the rank of lieutenant with Layard's seniority, were retired.[24] He recalled years later, "Although I was in the axing zone, I don't remember feeling very worried about it."[25] For reasons undetermined Layard did not specialize as a lieutenant, instead remaining a "salt horse," or general sea officer, but he continued to do well. In 1924 he was appointed first lieutenant of the destroyer *Velox,* and two years later he filled the same position in her sister ship *Verity.*

As Layard's responsibilities grew, however, so did anxiety about his capacity to meet them. Formerly a relatively happy go-lucky junior, he now had to deal with his own lofty, self-imposed expectations. Evidence of this burden is exhibited in an entry from February 1926 when *Verity,* with Layard as "number one," entered Malta to be confronted by the sparkling bright-work of the ships of the Mediterranean Fleet: "We entered Sliema harbour about 1000. Never felt in such a flat spin. Harbour full of 4th and 1st Flotillas all spotless while we are like dung heaps. Everything went wrong. Things got jousted trying to shackle on and everybody was waiting hours in the rain to follow *Keppel*'s orders for spreading awnings. I felt absolutely lost and scared stiff. Don't know how one even competes with all the orders and regulations in this fleet."[26] As was true throughout his career, things were not as bad as they seemed, and Layard performed well as first lieutenant. In fact, when his captain came down with pleurisy while *Verity* was at Hong Kong with the Far Eastern Fleet, Layard was appointed acting commanding officer and brought the ship home to England even though there were qualified officers on station. On 26 August 1930, now a lieutenant-commander, he received the news that all naval officers dream of: "Came down to the ward room and found I had been appointed to the *Wakeful* in command ... Very pleased but a bit frightened all the same. Drank rather a lot of gin on the strength of it."[27]

From September 1930 to December 1934, Layard commanded the destroyers *Wakeful, Vivacious,* and *Walpole* in the Atlantic and Mediterranean Fleets. This catapulted him to lofty status. The Royal Navy was still widely considered to be the finest in the world – certainly other navies looked to it for the way ahead – and to be appointed commanding officer of one of His Majesty's ships was akin to being given a special calling. Layard had to prove he belonged.

If that pressure was not enough, Layard was also under a professional microscope. In 1930 he also entered the dreaded "promotion zone," when he would be either promoted to the rank of commander and be eligible for higher advancement, or passed over to remain in the rank of lieutenant-commander until he quit the service or went on the retirement list.[28] Stephen King-Hall, an officer who endured the experience three years before Layard, recalled the torment associated with that period of an officer's career:

> The drama of the zone was that those who passed out of the zone without being promoted to Commander never were promoted. It was the end of one's upward career. The odds at this time [June 1927-June 1931] were about five to one against any individual being promoted. The promotion selections came out twice a year, in June and December, and the tension and anxiety in a ship as a popular officer approached his last chance was almost unbearable. No one mentioned the subject in front of the victim but the chances were that at age thirty-five or thirty-six an officer was about to face the grim possibility of either starting anew in some other profession or "soldiering on" in jobs of ever decreasing interest until he reached the maximum pensionable age of forty-five. Too often he then "took up farming," commuted half his pension and lost it.[29]

King-Hall made the grade, but Layard's prospects were mixed. In 1933 he attended the prestigious Tactical School in Portsmouth, where he studied alongside such later luminaries as Ian Mansfield, Albert Poland, Thomas Troubridge, Philip Vian, and "Johnnie" Walker. A good result would have given his career a boost, but his comments on the final day of the course suggest that he had failed to sparkle: "Very sorry it's over as it is most interesting and first class value. Finished off the discussion on the exercise. I came in for heavy criticism."[30] It was evaluations of his sea time, however, that were the most important. Layard's annual performance reports – dubbed "S206s" from the number of the evaluation form – are unavailable, but his diary provides a good account of his strengths and weaknesses. As a ship commander he appears to have been average: a fairly good ship handler, but lacking panache. He was a level-headed leader but could never be considered a hard driver, nor did he appear to be at all inspirational. Steady and competent, he lacked the dash and aggressive confidence that characterized the more successful destroyer officers of the day.

As an average officer, and something of an "honest trier," his mistakes probably counted more against him than might otherwise be the case, and two incidents stand out in particular. In October 1931, when the Mediterranean Fleet was on passage to Athens for a port visit, Layard, in *Vivacious* – or "Vivi" as he fondly called her – had "a most humiliating experience":

> I had been detached to exercise with the *Royal Sovereign* and was rejoining the flotilla from ahead to take station in the line astern of *Mackay* [the flotilla leader]. Trying to be too dashing I made an awful balls of it, got too close and instead of turning up in station I went charging through the line, finishing up about ½ a cable [100 yards] on the other side. Up went my pendants "Manoeuvre Badly Executed," and as soon as I was in station Captain D. stopped the flotilla and made to *Vivacious* "Commanding Officer Repair on Board." So I buckled on my sword and I was lowered in the whaler and pulled over to the *Mackay* where I was met by a very angry Captain D. who said I had not only endangered my ship but his as well. I was furious with myself because I had a reputation of being a good ship handler and I was very proud of it, and now I had made a most awful fool of myself.[31]

Another devastating experience occurred in Chatham two years later, when Layard was commanding the *Walpole* and in the final months of the promotion zone: "At about 0815 Commodore D. made a signal saying he was going to walk round *Walpole* and *Wolfhound*. He went to W'Hound first and came to us at about 1000. The ship wasn't looking her best after all those exercises, but that would have been taken into consideration. What absolutely broke my heart was that when we went down to the Petty Officer's Mess it wasn't even cleared up. Towels and caps all over the place. I never thought I should be so badly let down."[32] Though they might seem innocuous to a landsman, these two incidents involved seamanship and discipline, the most basic tenets of command, and could tilt the balance against promotion.

Layard's social reputation may also have affected his career. A bachelor through most of this period, Layard was an ardent party goer whose social calendar was always full. Although shy and retiring in formal situations, he let himself go in the company of fellow officers, and with them and their wives and sweethearts frequented many clubs and social events. Though not a prodigious imbiber of alcohol, he was, nonetheless, a hearty drinker, and his diary is full of references to "boozing." On one occasion, "a chap named Lee-Barber[33] and I nearly got arrested by the police for being a bit rough with the potted plants which were decorating the entrance [of a club]. One of our party who in my diary I refer to as the 'the fat girl' was heard to say 'I do wish they wouldn't always get so drunk.' We weren't drunk of course, just nicely exhilarated with wine."[34] That latter judgment, of course, was subjective, and often the first words in a diary entry were of the nature of "feeling gummy" or "slight alcoholic remorse." Later in life he admitted that in the mid-1920s he became "a much harder drinking type which, although it doesn't seem to have done me much physical harm, probably didn't help my career."[35] One gets the impression that Layard's drinking and socializing largely stemmed from boredom, especially in Malta, where his imbibing seemed to intensify.[36] The fact remains, however, that such a reputation, as well as the professional missteps described earlier, may have made all the difference at a time when promotion lists were short.

Layard's final opportunity to achieve the rank of commander came on 31 December 1934, but on studying the Navy List the day before he saw "no less than 26 of my ½ year [of 85 cadets] have already been promoted so I'm afraid my chances at the end of the year are pretty well nix." That proved accurate. On the day of reckoning, "I rang up the Barracks at 7 o'clock to find out about the promotions and heard I had not been promoted. It is a terrible disappointment when it actually comes although I knew it was more than likely."[37]

Layard was devastated. He thought himself, pure and simply, a failure. After much reflection he decided to stay in the navy but was dismayed at how quickly he was pushed out of the mainstream. Instead of getting another destroyer command or a staff job in Gibraltar as he had requested, he was appointed to the cruiser *Cardiff* as sports officer of the Reserve Fleet.[38] "Feeling terribly depressed," he wrote, "The *Cardiff* is nice enough and as far as I can see a very cheery wardroom, but somehow it seems such an awful come down after commanding one's own ship for the last four years."[39]

Fortunately, Layard's life partner helped to lift the gloom that shrouded his professional life. His career was important to him, but Layard would not have hesitated to say that 13 May 1932 was the most significant day of his life. In Malta in command of *Vivacious*, he had gone ashore for a typical day of sports and socializing:

> I landed at about 1400 and took a taxi to the Sliema Club and played tennis with Ringrose, Thornton and Reep.[40] Very hot and strenuous but very good fun. At times I played quite well. Ringrose brought me back to Valletta and I went on board for dinner. At 2100 much against my will I took the motor boat with No. 1 and the Chief to Sliema and went to the Flotilla ships' company dance at the Queen's Hall. A lot of officers and their women folk were there. It was all very dull until Newsom came along and asked me to come and help him with his party which consisted of Mrs.

> Glasford and a girl friend, Miss Binning.[41] The latter was absolutely grand. Distinctly big, not at all pretty, but most terribly good fun. I quite fell.

The attraction was mutual. Layard and Joan Binning announced their engagement within three weeks, and they married on 3 December 1932 at Brompton Oratory in London.

As the diary makes abundantly clear, Joan became the centre of his life and a crucial factor in his success. She shored up his shaky confidence and provided support and stability that helped him to cope with his various burdens. That role was not unusual for a navy wife, but Layard took it further, enlisting Joan an informal member of his E.G. 9 command team. After his ship *Matane* was glider-bombed in the summer of 1944, for example, Joan accompanied Layard when he visited the wounded in hospital, and she helped compose letters of condolence to the next of kin of those who died.[42] During a layover in Londonderry in January 1945, Layard relied upon his wife to help break the ice with senior Canadian naval officials: "J. arrived on board at 1200 and at about 1230 as per programme Connolly and Capt. Rayner arrived for lunch.[43] We all went over to the *Port Colborne* first for drinks and at about 1315 we returned to the *Saint John* for lunch. Skinner and Shaw of course were there. It was a v. good lunch. J. who was in her usual cracking form helped to keep the party going." Joan was always there for him, and Layard had no hesitation whatsoever in leaning upon her. They were a perfect match, and enjoyed a remarkably successful partnership that endured for almost seven decades.[44]

After only a few months as sports officer in *Cardiff*, Layard returned to Malta, where he commanded the minesweepers *Stoke* and *Harrow* in the Mediterranean Fleet's 2nd Minesweeping Flotilla. He was back in command, although one officer recalled that the professional navy considered minesweeping "the very scrapings of the barrel for the executive branch."[45] Perhaps subscribing to that view, Layard never gave up trying to get another destroyer. When the navy started bringing reserve ships into commission at the height of the Abyssinian crisis in 1935, he pressed Capt. H.T. Baillie-Grohman, Captain D of the 1st Flotilla, for a destroyer command. He said that he would be happy to put Layard's name on the list of prospective COs. "I don't for a moment expect anything will come of it," a doubtful Layard wrote, "but it does seem such a waste of time sitting in the *Stoke* that I thought I might try."[46] His instincts proved correct and he remained in minesweepers until 1936, when he was appointed to the Experimental, or X.P., Department at Whale Island, Portsmouth, the RN's mecca for gunnery. There he did extremely well, exhibiting an understanding of things technical. Although an outsider in the closely knit gunnery world, he became extremely comfortable at "Whaley," which was ironic given earlier complaints in his diary about promotion lists being "gunnery benefits."[47]

After war broke out in September 1939 – "depressingly, depressing" he lamented[48] – Layard persistently requested sea duty but was just as consistently turned down on the basis that the work he was doing at Whale Island was too valuable. Finally, in July 1941, Layard was appointed commanding officer of the old US Navy four-stacker destroyer HMS *Chelsea,* one of fifty ships the RN had acquired in the famous destroyers-for-bases deal. With the exception of eight months ashore in 1943, he was at sea for the rest of the European war.

Layard's experience shows how even the most seasoned officers have difficulty adjusting to the immense challenges of war at sea. *Chelsea* was attached to the Liverpool Escort Force of Western Approaches Command, escorting North Atlantic and Gibraltar convoys in and out of British waters. Within a week of taking over *Chelsea* he met his first convoy – "It quite reminded me of the Grand Fleet at sea in the last war"[49] – and on just his second trip he was horrified to learn that he was to be senior officer of the escort (SOE) of another convoy. He had not been to sea for five years and his preparation for the job of SOE, and indeed for convoy escort work generally, was practically nil. He had received no formal training and did not even have the luxury of a shakedown cruise in his new ship. All he could do was quickly study convoy instructions and tactical manuals, and consult experienced escort commanders in his network of friends and associates. But he even had difficulty in absorbing that information because at the same time, he was relearning how to be captain of a ship. As a result, it is fair to say that Layard was relatively lost during his first few weeks back at sea, and over the next year never really appears to have been comfortable.

Events of August 1942 typified the challenges he encountered. By then Layard had been appointed captain of the destroyer HMS *Broke,* and while at sea with another convoy he was ordered to reinforce S.C. 94, under attack from U-boats in the North Atlantic air gap.[50] Again Layard was dismayed to learn that he had to take over as senior officer. Upon arrival, he found S.C. 94 in complete disarray. After four days of attacks, six merchant ships had been sunk and two escorts damaged in encounters with U-boats. Faced with a tactical situation as murky as the thick fog that shrouded the convoy, unfamiliar with the escorts under his command, and with no opportunity to be briefed by the previous SOE or the convoy commodore, Layard was confronted by what can only be described as a desperate situation.[51] After being with the convoy for only about three hours, in which he handled numerous decisions, Layard took over the bridge:

> It was very dark and when I took over I couldn't really make up my mind where we were. Then suddenly torpedoes were reported passing the ship and I saw one cross the bows from Starboard to Port and then on our Starboard bow appeared the swirl of a U-boat, loud Hydrophone Effect, also reported on the A/S. At that moment some

> ship to the starboard blew 6 blasts. I didn't know where anybody was and I turned towards the U-boat and went on to 20 knots sweating with fear lest I was going to get across the bows of the convoy, for whom I was heading directly, or ram one of the escorts. I was quite unable to concentrate on the U-boat owing to this worry but found myself somehow pointing there. At close range we picked up good echoes and dropped a 14 charge shallow pattern. When it had gone I could only think of how I could turn before getting in among the convoy and had to give up all thought of the U-boat.[52]

This incident illustrates well the nerve-racking test faced by watch keepers and captains of escort vessels manoeuvring in close proximity to a convoy at night while in contact with the enemy. Layard was clearly unnerved, but although he considered his snap attack on the U-boat to have been ineffective, *U-595* was forced to return to base with heavy damage.[53] The attacks on S.C. 94 continued over the next three days, and U-boats sank four more merchant ships. At the end of it all an exhausted Layard despaired at how he had handled the episode: "Looking back on the whole thing I felt I'd made a thorough balls of both the night and the day episodes with which we'd been concerned, and I felt depressed and fed up. There is no doubt about it, I'm not a man of action and when faced with an emergency I just can't compete."[54] Layard was being too hard on himself, but the mental strain associated with such responsibility was clearly immense.

S.C. 94 was just one of many similar episodes, and each time Layard put to sea with a convoy he agonized over the many command decisions to be made: Will I miss the rendezvous? Who should I send out on an anti-shadow sweep, and how far should they go? What's our position? How long should I remain over the contact? Should I join the hunt? Should I break radio silence? Should I stop to rescue survivors? Was the loss of that ship my fault? Layard was surely not the only senior officer to suffer that angst, and his later experience in Algiers harbour in November 1942 confirmed that he was indeed "a man of action" who could make good decisions under fire. Nonetheless, his attitude contrasts strongly with the confidence that oozes through accounts by or of such celebrated escort leaders as Peter Gretton, Donald Macintyre, and Johnnie Walker.[55]

After the loss of *Broke* off Algiers in November 1942, Layard lobbied for another sea appointment. The navy had other ideas, and both his former colleagues at Whale Island and an Admiralty section that Layard dubbed "the strange weapons and devices dept." had designs on his services. The latter won out. From late December 1942 to August 1943 Layard worked in London, out of Room 60 Bank Block at the Admiralty, and lived in "a rather seedy bed sitter in Nottingham Place off Baker Street."[56] This proved an important interlude that saw his self-confidence bolstered by official and public recognition of his performance at Algiers.

When he went up to London to get the "gen" about his new appointment, Layard found he was to be staff officer to Rear-Adm. Edward Renouf, RN, advisor on miscellaneous weapons. Renouf's job, according to Layard's journal, "was to be the go-between between the inventor and the user. To make sure that the [naval] staff was aware of new inventions and to investigate their possible use, and that the inventors and developers were informed of any new and unusual staff requirements." Given his comfort in the world of technology, Layard was a good fit for the job. His main duty was to keep Renouf informed "of all that was actually happening, all that was being planned and about everything that was being invented, developed and tried out." This task took him into the inner sanctum of naval war planning and weapons development:

> My day always started with a visit to the war room, for which I had a special pass, and when I got all the up to date information on the progress of the war at sea, disposition of forces, and reports of current operations and so on. This was of the greatest interest. I also had a special pass into the underground "Citadel" with access to all sections of naval intelligence, including the highly secret U-boat plot, and I was able to obtain information on all photographic reconnaissance. I attended the weekly planning meeting at Combined Operations H.Q. at Richmond Terrace so that I always knew what they were thinking about and doing. I kept in touch with the submarine world at their H.Q. at Swiss Cottage, and with Norway[57] and other old friends of my Whaley days at D.M.W.D. (Weapons and Devices). Other strange departments and organizations from which I obtained interesting information were I.S.R.B. (Interservice Research Bureau) in Baker Street and their research station at Welwyn, and D.S.R. (Director of Scientific Research) in Fanum House, Leicester Square, and the Department of Economic Warfare.[58]

With Layard's insatiable appetite for news and knowledge, exposure to such wide-ranging, sensitive information was a veritable feast.

Although his work was interesting and occasionally demanding, Layard found he had a good amount of time on his hands. He filled it by feeding a new-found fascination with the life of Horatio Nelson. "I got from the library and read every book and every article that had been written about him. I also found and bought for £8 the framed Abbot print which lays in the [Admiralty] dining room and the coloured Baxter print."[59] He gives no explanation for his sudden attraction to the Immortal Memory – perhaps it was because he recognized that he too had passed the test of combat by displaying coolness and effective leadership under fire in Algiers – but whenever things got quiet at work he would devour a few pages of whatever biography was then in his possession.

Throughout his time at the Admiralty, Layard sought another sea appointment. When that was finally granted in June 1943, the news was better than expected. Not only was he appointed senior officer of his own support group, but nearly ten years after being passed over, he received the brass hat of an acting commander.

The only apparent downside was that his group would be based across the North Atlantic at Halifax, which meant "a long separation from home."[60] Mixed blessings aside, the appointment raised the curtain on arguably the most meaningful episode of his long career, one that allowed him ample opportunity to apply the skill, knowledge, and experience he had accumulated as an officer in the Royal Navy. That was service in and alongside the Royal Canadian Navy, the focus of the remainder of this volume.

As MUCH AS THIS VOLUME tells Layard's story, it is also the story of a diary. "A diary is like a confessional," he wrote later in life, "in that all one's sins and omissions are exposed and recorded. Unlike the confessional, however, the good is there as well as the bad and although in life there is much that I regret and am ashamed of, there are also some redeeming features and it is for the reader to form an opinion and to decide whether there is a reasonable balance between the debits and the credits."[61] Layard understood that a good diary does more than simply recount the events of the day; it exposes the innermost feelings and motives of the writer, and therefore provides personal context for historical events. Layard conveys such understanding in his diary, which, in the editor's mind, makes it invaluable to the study of the RCN and the broader war at sea in the last years of the Second World War.

Besides recording his own experience, Layard also seemed to have an eye on posterity. Navy regulations forbade keeping such diaries, so he kept it hidden from others during his service years – Canadian officers who sailed with him recalled often seeing him writing in something, but they were never sure what it was.[62] For years he also kept it from his family, which is not surprising given the mention of several deeply personal matters. As the years passed Layard obviously grasped the historical value of what he had written. Although he did not mention the diary to other historians who interviewed him, in 1987 he revealed its existence to Dr. Alec Douglas, director of history with the Department of National Defence, whom he allowed to copy the sections relevant to Layard's service with the RCN for use in the official Canadian naval history.[63] This photocopy lay in the Directorate of History archives, untouched save by the official historians working on the RCN history and Lt.-Cdr. Doug McLean, who used it as a source for his MA thesis on anti-submarine warfare in the final year of the war.

When I decided to publish portions of the Layard diary in the late 1990s, I was unaware of the precise extent of the document. Investigation led to Layard's son, Raymond, who informed me that his father had donated the diary to the Royal Navy Museum in Portsmouth. Upon visiting that establishment I was startled when more than two dozen annual journals encompassing his entire career spilled out of a grey document box. The challenge then became determining how much of this astonishing document to reproduce. Layard was an engaging writer, and the diary has good narrative flow; therefore excerpting one or two days a week, or a week here and there, was an unattractive option that would lose the continuity of his thought process. I then considered focusing on the periods he commanded ships in both peace and war, but since that covered some twelve warships over some eight years it was too much material for one volume. That left me to concentrate on the period he worked with the Royal Canadian Navy, which, sadly, represents just three slim years of a diary covering more than three decades. Although that period was arguably the most significant of his career, much material remains to be brought to light from other periods, particularly in regard to life in the Royal Navy during the interwar period, and I can only hope that another historian will pursue these angles in the future.

Apart from its utter honesty, the value of the diary lies in both its fullness and its freshness. Through the interwar years to 1941, Layard used a small pocket-sized diary in which he could cram about 200 words a day. In 1943 he changed to a larger daily journal in which he could fit about 300 words per entry. He gave no reason for the change, but it allowed him to be more expansive. Whereas his entries from sea in 1941 are often terse or skimpy, from 1942 they steadily increase in content, until in the last years of the war scarcely a page is not completely full. The diary's freshness stems from its immediacy. As commanding officer of a warship, and especially as senior officer of a support group, Layard had opportunity to slip down to his sea cabin or into the charthouse to enter his thoughts. It appears that he stuck to no particular schedule, but wrote his entries when he went to bed, immediately upon rising, or if he could steal away during the day. There is occasionally some slippage into the next day, but there is no evidence that he ever waited any longer than that. Even his account of breaking through the boom at Algiers appears to have been recorded soon after he took the badly damaged *Broke* out of harbour on 9 November, and then continued intermittently as she slowly foundered. Layard was also true to what he wrote. No matter how revealing or embarrassing an entry, he never crossed out a passage or tore out a page. This trait continued throughout his life. It is obvious that he reread the diary from time to time, particularly when he was writing his informal memoirs, but the only obvious additions are the correction of a mistaken report that a certain officer had died during the war and a reference to mention of himself in another officer's memoirs.[64] Otherwise all is there, as written.

Some diaries are weakened by their self-serving nature. Instead of writing honestly and forthrightly about events, motivations, and consequences, some diarists either colour their accounts to put themselves in a more positive light or simply do not mention adverse events at all. Consider, for example, Cdr. G.R. Miles, RCN, who kept a somewhat sketchy journal during the war. In March 1942, when dozens of his sailors failed to return from leave and delayed his ship's sailing, Miles does not mention it at all but instead blandly describes the more palatable events of the day.[65] In complete contrast, Layard pulls no punches – in this case, self-directed – in his entries of 22 and 23 October 1944, where he describes taking two frigates into Gibraltar to join the remainder of E.G. 9, which had gone in the day previously:

> We got in to Gibraltar and secured alongside the South Mole at about 1145. Captain D.'s staff came down on board to say that ships' companies of the 9th D.F. [i.e., E.G. 9] had been breaking up the town last night and threatening stoppage of all leave if it happened again. Oh these Canadians!
>
> ... After lunch I cleared lower deck and spoke to the sailors about behaviour ashore. I went ashore myself at about 1445 calling in to see *Saint John* on the way. Went up to the Armada Gardens and watched the cricket, and Sammy Boucher gave me some tea in the interval. He also told me that David Abbott was here in the *Enchantress* so at about 1700 I went down on board but on going into his cabin I heard he was turned in and as I could see a Wren officer's hat on his sofa I came to certain conclusions. Went ashore again and walked about to waste time ... Memories of the past. Back to the *Enchantress* at 1815 where I found David and we sat drinking and yarning. Later a Wren officer arrived and we walked along to the Victoria for food and finally came back on board *Swansea*. Beautiful, hot day.
>
> **Monday, 23 October 1944 – Gibraltar/At sea**
>
> I woke up at about 0500 to find I had been violently sick and that my left thumb was dislocated, and with no recollection whatsoever of how I did it. Having first cleaned up the mess I went for the sick berth attendant who tried and failed to put my thumb back. He went for the doctor of the *Stormont* who also tried and failed and so he rang up the Hospital, and I was taken up there and had an X ray and then after considerable delay I was put to bed and finally wheeled into the theatre and given an anaesthetic and the thumb put back while I was out. I didn't come to till about 1400. At about 1630 the doctor of the *Stormont* arrived and said we were sailing at 1900. I then managed to get hold of the Royal Army Medical Corps Colonel who very reluctantly allowed me to get up and I was on board just before 1800. Feeling just a bit groggy and most frightfully ashamed of myself. I know I was alright when I came on board but what happened after I got to the ward room or how many more drinks I had I don't know. No. 1, who was charming, said I did not disgrace myself but I'm not so sure. To think that I should do this, especially after my talk to the sailors. It is so degrading.

That Layard's diary includes these two days in all their embarrassing detail – surely one of the debits he had in mind when musing on diaries – demonstrates that he held nothing back.

As the above entry demonstrates, Layard was a good writer, and that has deterred me from meddling too much with his prose. As much as possible the diary has been presented as written, and the reader is warned that inconsistencies remain that reflect the informal nature of the document. That said, longer entries have been split into paragraphs, "and" has been substituted for Layard's "+," most abbreviations have been spelled out in full, and commas have been inserted to break up some of his phrasing. Spelling has also been corrected, minor punctuation has been standardized, titles, ship's names, and Layard's emphases have been italicized, and all times – except train departure times; one simply cannot tamper with British Rail – have been put into twenty-four-hour service format. Otherwise, the diary remains as written. For the sake of brevity, I have omitted the entries covering Layard's periods of leave at home at Prinsted, though I include the days of his arrival and departure. These entries illuminate the safe haven that Harvest Lodge represented, as well as the burden of returning to war after tranquil days enjoying the company of family and friends or puttering in his garden.

Finally, every editor struggles over how much contextual material to provide to supplement a diary; too much and the stylistic flow is disrupted, too little and certain information is misunderstood. In Layard's case this challenge is complicated by the fact that his Canadian interlude represents just a small portion of a long career. I have attempted to keep intrusions to a minimum but have used notes to identify as many of the people mentioned as possible – not an easy task given that the diarist often misspelled their names – and to explain the relevance of certain events or to clarify Layard's phraseology.

The most important contribution an editor can make to a diary is to provide historical context. With that in mind, I elected to divide the diary into chapters and have provided an introductory essay for each to describe the context of that particular chapter or to expand upon some aspect of Layard's career. This, I hope, will help the reader to understand more fully the people and institutions he served with, the nature of the campaigns he fought in, and the talents and concepts he brought to bear in his service with the Canadians. It is a novel approach, which results in thematic introductions to chronological content, but I believe it is the best way to explain the relevance and importance of various aspects of Layard's career, while still letting the diary speak for itself.

1
One Does Get Tired of Them, September-December 1943

In contrast to the Royal Navy – Layard's navy – with its long, glorious history and rich traditions, the Royal Canadian Navy was a comparative waif. Established only in 1910, the service had built up no fighting heritage in the First World War, and throughout most of the interwar years had struggled not just to survive the fiscal neglect of various Canadian governments but to establish an identity.[1] Only when war clouds threatened on the horizon did the RCN begin to prosper, but even at the outbreak of war its strength was only six River class destroyers and four small minesweepers, while personnel strength stood at a paltry 2,600 officers and men.

The Second World War changed everything. New building programs were approved by Mackenzie King's Liberal government, which saw naval expansion as a way to avoid sending massive land forces overseas and thus sidestep the politically charged issue of conscription. The navy exploded in size and by the time Layard arrived in Canada in September 1943, it boasted more than a hundred warships and about 70,000 men and women in uniform. Moreover, from what had essentially been a coastal defence squadron in the interwar years, by the end of the war the RCN had transformed itself into a dynamic, multirole blue-water navy that fought on virtually every ocean of the world. This staggering achievement had come at a cost. Infrastructure and training simply could not keep pace with the rapid expansion, especially during the first years of the war, and Canada's professional sailors could barely keep their heads above water.[2]

"After dinner we went to see the first showing in Halifax of *Corvette [K]225*, an American made propaganda film of the R.C.N.," Layard wrote soon after arriving in Canada. "Very good but to my mind it depicted something so entirely different from the R.N. as to be almost unrecognisable. But of course the R.C.N. *is* very different."[3] As the senior officer of an RN group serving under RCN operational control out of a Canadian port, Layard was well placed to notice the difference. Among many dissimilarities, the professional immaturity of the staff at the headquarters of Canadian Northwest Atlantic Command (CNA) and in the Halifax dockyard probably jarred Layard the most. He thought the officers at the top were first rate. The commander-in-chief, Rear-Adm. Leonard Murray, RCN – who, like all senior Canadian officers, had plenty of RN training and experience – was an effective leader who stood by the men at sea. Layard was also impressed by Murray's chief of staff, Capt. Roger Bidwell, who was a shrewd and effective administrator, and by such former RN officers as Cdrs. J. Douglas Prentice and William L. Puxley. As Layard would do when he commanded E.G. 9, these officers brought a shrewd, seasoned eye to their job and provided invaluable leadership. Beyond that cadre of effective professionals, and a few others, however, there were simply not enough experienced officers to go around. For Layard, used to working out of long-established shore bases like Chatham, Malta, and Portsmouth, where mature staff and support systems had evolved over decades, the situation at Halifax was muddled and confused. "We started destoring," he complained of one incident, "but had no sooner sent the first lorry load away when the Dockyard woke up to the fact that there was no where to put them so back they all had to come."[4] As will be seen, some British officers reacted poorly to the disarray and developed a fundamental disdain for all things Canadian; ever the professional, Layard managed to rise patiently above the relative chaos.

Halifax – "Slackers" to Canadian sailors – brought its own challenges. The city that lay alongside one of the world's great natural harbours had little to offer Layard. At home in an environment of theatres, clubs, cathedrals, and bookstores, he found Halifax drab and unappealing. Arcane liquor laws that forbade the serving of alcohol in public establishments did not help.[5] Nor did the bitter, cold climate. Two things brought a measure of solace. Although hilly, the city had a number of attractive walking areas, and Layard especially enjoyed striding along the harbourfront to Point Pleasant Park. The second was the company of the Prentice family. Prentice, "Chummy" to Canadians but "Douglas" to Layard, had joined the RN the year before Layard, but he had chosen to retire when he too was passed over for promotion. After a short ranching career in British Columbia, Prentice had joined the RCN at the outbreak of war, and quickly proved to be an invaluable asset for the young navy. When Layard arrived in Halifax, Prentice was serving as Captain D Halifax,[6] and he and his wife, Patricia, provided a nest of hospitality, as well as an outlet for Layard's frustrations.

Layard's adjustment to the Canadian navy and Halifax was not eased by the situation at sea. His new support group, designated W 10, was attached to the Western Escort Force. Organized towards the end of August 1943 by Rear-Admiral Murray as "a supporting group for threatened convoys or particularly large ones," W 10's role was to reinforce the close escort of transatlantic convoys as they transited the Canadian coastal zone.[7] As Layard was to discover, however, W 10 was a support group in name only. Although it nominally included four to six destroyers, including Layard's new command H.M.S. *Salisbury*, the chronic shortage of escorts in the theatre meant that W 10 rarely sailed as a group and was usually deployed in penny-packets to fill gaps in local escort forces.[8] The ships themselves, moreover, were old, worn Town class destroyers similar to *Chelsea*, which Layard had commanded when he returned to sea in 1941.[9] Age and hard service had taken their toll, and the venerable four-stackers had become a maintenance nightmare.

Repair facilities on the east coast were badly overextended, making it difficult to find room for the Towns, and there was a hesitancy to spend scarce time and resources maintaining ships that were clearly on their last legs. The RN had already arranged to take over dozens of British destroyer escorts (BDEs, better known as Captain class frigates), which were being built in American shipyards, and wanted to keep the Towns running only until their crews could transfer to new construction. The RCN was unsure what to do, so the futures of the four-stackers, W 10, and Layard were left hanging.

Layard's arrival in Canada also coincided with the return of the U-boats to the northwest Atlantic. In May 1943 U-boats had suffered enormous losses at the hands of Allied air and naval forces, and in what is now recognized as the turning point of the Battle of the Atlantic, Adm. Karl Dönitz had pulled his forces from the transatlantic shipping routes. By September 1943, new sensors, electronic countermeasures, and weaponry, particularly the acoustic homing torpedo, emboldened him to remount his efforts, and some twenty boats attacked convoy ONS 18/ON 202.[10] Layard learned of the resurgence as he crossed the Atlantic in a destroyer escorting ON 203, the following westbound convoy: "A convoy has been attacked in the Atlantic (the first for months) and everyone is in a flat spin about the acoustic torpedo, which the U-boat is using and which has accounted for no less than 3 escorts."[11] Those reports proved accurate, though the Allies destroyed three U-boats in return. The "flat spin" did not endure, and U-boat losses steadily mounted in the face of effective convoy defences. After losing twenty boats in the North Atlantic between mid-September and early November, Dönitz abandoned wolf pack operations entirely.[12] He now sent only a few U-boats across independently; once in Canada, Layard took part in operations that tried, but failed, to catch those intruders.[13]

Of course, little of this was apparent in September 1943 when Layard arrived at Liverpool to attend the Western Approaches anti-submarine tactical course before heading overseas. The chief of staff's sarcastic greeting – "What have you done to be sent out there?" – set off alarm bells, and after being in Canada for less then a month Layard admitted, "I'm feeling rather depressed about this job. It doesn't seem to be a job at all really, and I can't help feeling I've been had for a sucker by the 2nd Sea Lord's office."[14] Sucker or not, Layard impressed senior Canadian officers during the autumn of 1943 – particularly Bidwell and Prentice – and although the RN may have been willing to jettison him, the RCN, desperately short of seasoned officers, welcomed his experience, skill, and professionalism.

Sunday, 5 September 1943 – Liverpool

Arrived at Lime Street at about 0700. No taxis but eventually got a lift from a Wren in a small navy van to H.M.S. *Mersey*[15] where after some difficulty I got a cabin and some breakfast. Apparently I ought to have asked for accommodation.

At about 0730 I went to Derby House and saw Gardner,[16] who has been put ashore on account of deafness, and fixed up that I should take passage out to Canada in an escort leader that gives me a few days leave after this course. I then walked to the cathedral and found there was a special 4th war anniversary service at 1100, which I attended. A great many people there. F.O.I.C.[17] [flag officer in command] read some prayers, an Air Marshal read the lesson, and the Bishop of Wilkesley preached a good sermon. Among the hymns we sang was "John Brown's Body," which was somewhat unusual. Back to the *Mersey* for lunch. This is really a T124 training depot with a certain amount of spare officers' accommodation. In the p.m. I read and slept in my cabin. Put a call through to J. at 1900, which eventually I got through at 2000. The accommodation here is pretty seedy, but I suppose good enough. Nice sunny day.

Monday, 6 September 1943 – Liverpool

After breakfast I checked in at Derby House at 0900 for the Tactical Course. There are some 25 of us ranging from myself, the only Commander, down to Mids. R.N.V.R. Scott Thomas[18] is one of us. The Director is Capt. Roberts,[19] who is a v. good lecturer but v. theatrical and, of course, would like you to know that he was 75% responsible for the recent defeat of the U-boat in the N. Atlantic. He's probably right and is certainly thought very highly of here. The Deputy, Jerry Cousins,[20] shouts while he lectures so that you are quite stunned. We had a certain number of lectures, and we began the first game where I am S.O. of the escort. I immediately began to feel woolly and helpless, but much as I dislike displaying my ineptitude I'm sure this course is going to be first class value. We lunched at the Derby House canteen and who should Scott and I meet there but Air Commodore Ragg[21] who we knew in the *Vivacious* days at Kyrenia in Cyprus as a Flight Lt. After packing up at 1700 I went to Liver Building about pay and travelling expenses, and then Scott and I had early supper at the *Mersey* and then went out to a cinema and saw some mediocre sort of film.

Tuesday, 7 September 1943 – Liverpool

A lecture and then two hours of the game, which came to an end at lunch time. With a good deal of help from the staff I managed alright as S.O. G.N. Brewer was in the bar at Derby House having just had the *Egret* sunk under him by the new German gliding homing bomb.[22] Sounds most unpleasant. Raymond Blagg[23] was also there, and he took me across to a sandwich bar close by for lunch. In the p.m. more lectures and a summing up of the game. Went to the Derby House canteen for tea and then returned to the Western Approaches Tactical Unit and spent about ¾ hour reading A.C.I.s [Atlantic Convoy Instructions] and thinking about the night attack game we play tomorrow when I am S.O. again of the syndicate.

Back to Derby House and called on Commodore Russell[24] who is Chief of Staff. He greeted me with "What have you done to be sent out there?" which seems to imply it is a God awful job. Collected Gardner from his office and brought him back to the *Mersey* for drinks and dinner. He, Scott, and Marjoribanks sat talking afterwards.

Wednesday, 8 September 1943 – Liverpool

After a bit of preliminary discussion we started in on a night encounter exercise. I was S.O. of our syndicate and had Eardley Wilmott[25] for Staff Officer. Lunch at the canteen and then on with the game until about 1500 when it was summed up. My side didn't do too badly. We then had a short lecture followed by a demonstration on the board of the sort of search operation that support groups are carrying out in the Bay of Biscay, and finally Roberts gave us a few remarks on the new German weapon, the glider bomb.

Scott and I went back to the *Mersey* and shifted and at 1800 it was announced that Italy had surrendered unconditionally. Grand news. Scott and I then went to Derby House and met Ragg and his wife in the Senior Officer's Lounge where we had drinks. There were all the big shots. The A.O.C. [air officer commanding] (Slatter), another Air Commodore, F.O.I.C. (Ritchie), and the Chief of Staff, Russell. Finally the Raggs took Scott and me off to the Bear's Paw for dinner. He is an extremely nice chap, but she is developing into the typical senior officer's wife. They have no children, which is probably her trouble. We walked back to the *Mersey* where we said goodbyes, and Scott told me the tale of his disappointment at being passed over after all the high ups had more or less told him he was a cinch for it.

Thursday, 9 September 1943 – Liverpool

I think one way or another I had a bit too much booze last night and my brain is feeling a bit woolly. On arrival at the Tactical School we were first shown the layout of the big and final game, which covers a period from an hour before sunset to sometime at night. There are 2 convoys, a carrier, and a support group. I am S.O. escort of our convoy. We then withdrew and decided on our policy, what the support group should do, and what the aircraft should do, etc., and then at about 1000 we started the game. I didn't have very much to do, but there was a flood of signals and a lot of plotting to do.

Chavasse and I were bidden to lunch by the C. in C., Admiral Sir Max Horton, at Derby House. Some Captain who was also there told Chavasse he had just been awarded the D.S.O. for some convoy fight which he had conducted successfully some months ago. The conversation at lunch consisted of the C. in C. pumping Chavasse about his new B.D.E.[26] As a result of the lunch we got back to the game rather late. We stopped at about 1630, by which time in the game it was practically dark. Scott and I had tea at the Canteen, and then I returned to the *Mersey* and shifted and listened to the 1800 news. We have made another large scale landing near Naples. In spite of the Armistice we are still meeting fierce opposition from the Germans who are now estimated to have 18-20 divisions in the country. Walked to the Adelphi where I met Raymond and Venetia, and they gave me dinner. They have found a house up here and so will be leaving Little Orchard for good very shortly. Sad.

Friday, 10 September 1943 – Liverpool

A beastly hot day when Liverpool looks its very worst. At the Tactical School we carried on with our game, which today became a night encounter. I didn't have a great deal to do as S.O. of my convoy owing to the brilliant way in which Chavasse's support group rode off the U-boats. We finished at about 1600, and then we were taken down to the Plotting Room at Derby House and shown around. Scott and I then had tea in the Canteen and then I walked back to the *Mersey* and shifted and then went back to Derby House, called for Gardner, and we both caught a train to Crosby. Hector Radford who came out for a short trip with us in the *Broke* had asked us to drinks and supper. It turned out to be quite a big party because in addition to ourselves and Radford's three sisters, there was an R.N.V.R. 2 striper, the old "pilot" on D's staff and his wife, a naval padre, *and* three small children. We had a terrific supper. The table before we started looked rather like the food advertisements in American magazines. Quite a good party. Gardner and I caught the 11:16 back to Liverpool. The news from Italy seems confused, but the Germans seem to be fighting us and the Italians and they claim to have sunk an Italian battleship which was trying to escape from Spezia.[27]

Saturday, 11 September 1943 – Liverpool/Prinsted

I got up early and did my packing before breakfast. It was pouring with rain when I walked to the Tactical School. The whole forenoon was spent summing up the big game, which was most interesting, and at 1200 we broke up. A first class course for which Roberts deserves full marks. Went to Derby House and had several at the bar before having lunch. I then went to the Exchange Station and after waiting some time managed to get a taxi, which I shared with 3 other people who agreed to go to the *Mersey* and pick up my gear and then go to the Lime Street Station. I caught the 1400 train to London and was lucky to get a seat as the train was crammed before it left. Got to Euston just before 1900 and so went to the station restaurant and had dinner and then got a taxi to Waterloo and caught the 8:45 to Havant. Joan met me there with the car, thank God, at 2215 and we drove home. A hot muggy day.

...

Tuesday, 21 September 1943 – Prinsted/Heysham

I was very busy after breakfast doing final packing and some final letter writing. The time flew by and in no time it was 1100 and time to start for the station. Loaded my luggage up into the car and with Gillian and Tich [their dog] we drove to Havant, where I caught the 11:31 to London. Oh these partings!! However, I just can't believe it will be for a long time this time. I am as usual full of remorse at my neglect and impatience with the children. I'm a rotten Father.

Got to London soon after 1300 and after a bit of a wait I got a taxi to Euston, where I found the Heysham train left at 3:00 and not 4:15 as I thought. Had a sandwich and a glass of beer at the Buffet and when the train came along I got a seat. A tedious journey but the train was not crowded and there was a refreshment car where I had dinner and that helped to while away the time. Got to Heysham at about 2130 and then stood endlessly in queues. First to show our identity cards before going on board and again on arrival on board to claim out berth. The lack of organisation and waste of time was infuriating and then the bar was closed. Met Rolph Medley[28] on board and he and I shared a double cabin. He was rather depressing about my new job. The more I hear of it the more ghastly it sounds.

Wednesday, 22 September 1943 – Heysham/Londonderry

We sailed somewhere about midnight after I'd turned in. This is apparently a very inferior type of boat, which has just been put on the run. Turned out and had breakfast before we arrived at Belfast. After endless delays we got ashore at about 0850 and then after further delays I at last got my heavy baggage and caught the 9:30 to Londonderry by the skin of my teeth, where we arrived at about 1230. Rolph M. had an official car to meet him which I shared, and as the *Hotspur* was down at Moville,[29] I went on board R.M.'s ship, the *Saskatchewan,* and he gave me lunch. In the p.m. I walked up to the Operations Room with him and arranged that the 1800 duty boat should take me down to Moville. A convoy has been attacked in the Atlantic (the first for months) and everyone is in a flat spin about the acoustic torpedo, which the U-boat is using and which has accounted for no less than 3 escorts. Details rather sketchy.[30]

Back on board. At 1730 R.M. had a small meeting in his cabin with 2 Fleet Air Arm chaps as he is having one of those new M.A.C. (Merchant Aircraft Carriers) in his next convoy. It is a grain ship with a flat top carrying 4 aircraft. I was forgotten by the 1800 boat and so a special boat was sent for me at about 1945, and I eventually got on board *Hotspur* at Moville at about 2100. Sandy McKillop[31] is Captain. Had lots of drinks in the wardroom and didn't turn in till past midnight. Wrote a letter to J. while on board *Saskatchewan.* God knows when I will hear from her.

Thursday, 23 September 1943 – Moville/At sea

A misty, damp sort of day. We got under way at 1000 and went just outside and anchored in the Bay for HF/DF calibration. We lay broadside on to quite a big swell and rolled our guts out. That took till about 1230, when we weighed and went back and secured to the oiler for a final top up. At about 1445 the whole group, consisting of *Hotspur, Churchill,* and 4 corvettes, weighed and proceeded for the rendezvous. We met the convoy (O.N. 203), consisting of about 63 ships, at about 1630. It was still in the process of forming up and we spent most of the time till dusk passing on the envelopes containing the dope, which we received from the local escort, to the other ships of our group. As it was a bit rough we had to veer it astern every time. There is a gale warning and quite a fresh W.'ly wind and sea. I am using McKillop's cabin aft. Quite interesting to be on the bridge and watch somebody else doing everything.

Friday, 24 September 1943 – At sea

An uneventful day. Moderate wind and head sea, which made us bucket about quite a bit and the upper deck was pretty wet. Not feeling *quite* my best after this long spell ashore. This convoy, which has been attacked, seems still to be surrounded by U-boats. As far as we can make out, 3 escorts have been sunk and one damaged but not more than 4 of the convoy have gone. Spent my time reading, eating, and sleeping, with numerous visits to the bridge to keep in touch with the situation and learn what I can of the duties of the S.O. in these modern times.

Saturday, 25 September 1943 – At sea

Still quite rough, but weather slowly improving. Our support group, consisting of the escort carrier *Tracker* and 4 B.D.E.s, joined up, and *Hotspur* had a busy time stationing them and exchanging information by Coston gun line.[32] McGrath[33] is S.O. in *Tracker* and Chavasse is S.O. of the B.D.E.s. We had a Catalina with us patrolling most of the day. We have been routed rather far N. of the Great Circle track, which has been in use fairly regularly during the last quiet month or two. It certainly looks from the U-boat report as if quite a large number were out again.[34] By the night the wind and sea had gone down altogether. Heard on the wireless that the Russians had taken Smolensk and have reached the Dnieper in several places.

Sunday, 26 September 1943 – At sea

The wind had dropped completely and it was nearly flat calm. At 0900 we dropped back into the convoy to take in oil from one of the tankers. I have never done this, and it was most interesting to watch. The buoyant hose is veered astern by the oiler and picked up by the destroyer. Comparatively simple and quick compared to the old "trough" method. We took in about 80 tons in about an hour. In the p.m. *Tracker* left us. She was told to join another support group. The 4 B.D.E.s, however, remained with us. It blew up again in the evening. We have been routed further north, clear of a large indefinite area thought to contain about 15 U-boats. We had a movie show in the ward room after tea with their 16mm sound projector, which are supplied to all destroyers now.

Monday, 27 September 1943 – At sea

Went on the bridge at about 0700. Quite rough again. Coming aft I met a young sea which completely filled one of my sea boots. Blowing quite hard from the W. all day, but it eased in the p.m. and I managed to get a little exercise in the waist without getting wet. Started to read a life of Elizabeth of Bohemia.

Tuesday, 28 September 1943 – At sea

Patches of rain and fog, and although comparatively calm in the morning it blew up later on from the S.W. and made it v. uncomfortable. Paid intermittent visits to the bridge as usual and did a good deal of reading.

Wednesday, 29 September 1943 – At sea

A most uncomfortable night. Without a rail to my bunk I couldn't sleep, the ship was rolling so heavily, and eventually I had to put my mattress on the deck. Yet another route diversion. We are being kept up in about 60° N. until we reach the longitude of Cape Farewell, about where we shall turn to the south. With considerable difficulty I managed to have a bath before breakfast. Strong wind and pretty uncomfortable all day. Heavy rolling.

Thursday, 30 September 1943 – At sea

Fine bright day, but with a strong N.W.'ly wind and biggish sea making the ship roll heavily and very wet. Pretty cold too as we are now only about 120° S.E. of Cape Farewell. We had our last Liberator out from Iceland in the a.m., and in the p.m. we had the first two from Newfoundland. There had been one or two HF/DF bearings in the night but not very convincing, and the aircraft search in good visibility sighted nothing, and so the opinion is we are not threatened. C. in C. W.A. told our support group to return to Belfast and they parted company at about noon. The Chief put on the steam heating during the day and by dinner time the ward room was very hot. Went up on the bridge to get cool. Wind and sea much reduced by nightfall. Sat up late reading and finishing a thriller by Dorothy Sayers. The convoy turned to 210° at 2200.

Friday, 1 October 1943 – At sea

No wind but still a bit of swell. Overcast with fog patches and coldish. I managed to get in a bit of exercise on the upper deck, which for once was dry. At about 1230 we dropped back and took in oil from one of the tankers. 190 tons in just over an hour!! We then put the Doctor and R.D.F. officer onboard [the corvette HMCS] *Nasturtium* and then resumed our position on the screen. Read A.C.I.s and *Elizabeth of Bohemia.* Convoy doing 9.5 knots course 210° striking south for Newfyjohn [St. John's]. It is rumoured that the 5th Army are in Naples and the Russians are in the outskirts of Kiev. There have been more heavy bombing raids on Germany, including Hanover and a daylight raid on the Ruhr.

Saturday, 2 October 1943 – At sea

A calm day but foggy and damp. Paid numerous visits to the bridge and read, ate, and slept. McKillop came aft to the wardroom in the evening for a drink. Quite like peacetime to see the Captain in the wardroom at sea. Wrote to J. Hope to get it back to her in the *Hotspur* before she returns.

Sunday, 3 October 1943 – At sea

Another day of fog. We had church on the mess deck at about 1030. Read and finished off *A Gap in the Curtain* by Buchan, which I enjoyed. At 1600 the Western Escort Force relieving group appeared out of the fog and took over the convoy from us, and when we had collected our group, which was much facilitated by the fog lifting, we shaped course for St John's. I am beginning to feel a bit windy as the moment of taking over my job draws near. I hope I shall find *Salisbury* in St John's as I don't want to do any more travelling. It blew up again in the evening.

Monday, 4 October 1943 – At sea/St John's/At sea

I turned out and went up on the bridge at 0630. Stayed up there some time. We had picked up the R.D.F. beacon but had some slight trouble avoiding a small coastal convoy. After breakfast I went up again for our entry into harbour. We berthed at the pens in the Naval Dockyard at about 1030 and then put the clocks back to local time, which brought it to 0800. The *Salisbury* is not here. At about 1030 McKillop and I and the Capt. of the *Churchill* went up to the naval offices and I set about trying to find out how to get to the *Salisbury.* It took a very long time as nobody seemed to know where she was. It was eventually decided that I should take passage in the corvette *Collingwood,* sailing for Halifax at 1430. I went back to the *Hotspur* for lunch and then at about 1400 a boat came and took me and my gear to the *Collingwood.* She is one of the R.C.N. corvettes that came over with us. We sailed at 1430 and rendezvoused outside with *Georgetown* and a large Yankee transport which we were escorting. Speed 15 knots, which was just about flat out for us. The Navigator kindly gave me his cabin. The living quarters are appallingly hot and stuffy.

Tuesday, 5 October 1943 – At sea

I got up about 0630 meaning to go up on the bridge but found it raining hard and blowing quite hard from the E. (astern). I had to get some air so I stood in the open under cover and later on washed and shaved. The rain cleared off later on but it continued to blow hard. I read and also paid a visit to the Engine Room. After lunch Pringle[35] (the Captain) showed me round the ship. I noticed all sorts of odds and ends stored in the magazine, entirely contrary to *King's Regulations and Admiralty Instructions,* and also not one single clip on any watertight door. However, I didn't think it was up to me to remark. They are a very nice crowd of officers, all of them R.C.N.V.R., and a good keen and efficient atmosphere about the ship.

Wednesday, 6 October 1943 – At sea/Halifax

I turned out at about 0430 and found that we'd arrived at the outer light vessel, and I stayed upon the bridge until we got into harbour to learn what I could about the approach to Halifax, which I suppose I will be using often in the future. It was a clear night and as it became daylight the sky to the N. became a most beautiful colour. At about 0800 when we berthed it was a most glorious sunny morning. After breakfast I had a bath and at about 0930 I went up to call on [Captain] D., who is Prentice. Puxley is his staff officer. The *Salisbury,* who is at Boston, is due in Saturday. I was given a car to call on the Chief of Staff to the Admiral. It appears they are going to form a support group consisting of six "Four stackers" of which I am to be the S.O. Rather terrifying. I looked in on Pay Commander Johnson,[36] who runs our pay. He was Secretary to D3[37] in our China commission. Back on board *Collingwood* for lunch.

In the p.m. I walked into the town with the intention of finding the graves of Capt. Broke's men of the *Shannon,*[38] but after making many enquiries I couldn't find the grave in the only old cemetery I could find. Eventually got back on board about 1620 having walked my feet quite sore. Not much of a town but rather what I expected. Sat on board and read and had some drinks. At about 1830 a car came for my gear and after collecting Prentice at his office he took me back to his house, having kindly offered to put me up till *Salisbury* arrives. A v. comfortable house and Mrs. P. seems nice. A most lovely day.

Thursday, 7 October 1943 – Halifax

A most comfortable bed. Prentice goes off to work at some unearthly hour. I had breakfast at about 0830 and at about 0915 Mrs. P. took me some of the way to the Dockyard in the car. I went into the shop and bought two travelling photo frames for the pencil drawings of the family and then walked to the Dockyard. Went to Puxley's office and extracted a lot of reading matter, and sat in the C.O.'s waiting room and put in about 3 hours reading. I had a sandwich lunch there and then walked to the Lord Nelson Hotel, where I met Mrs. P. and she drove me home. I then dug out some plain clothes and she and I and the dog went for a walk in what they call "the park," which is really just a bit of wild unspoiled pine forest running down to the water and rather lovely.[39] Had some tea when we got back. Mrs. P. reminds me of Guy Rolfe's cousin Jeanne and also slightly of Peg.

Prentice came home about 1900, and an attractive young woman, wife of some R.C.N.V.R., arrived and after drinks we drove to the Lord Nelson for dinner where we had a v. good lobster but no drink, which is forbidden by law to be sold in any public place. We took the young woman home and then called on the Woodhouses[40] (He is the Admiral's secretary and a brother of the Pay Admiral). Listened to the news and had a drink, and then came home. There has been a fairly sharp raid on London. I can't get over the street and house lights and car head lights, which shining on the trees in the streets look lovely to me.[41] Another nice day.

Friday, 8 October 1943 – Halifax

At about 1000 I went into the town with Mrs. P. in the car where she did some shopping mostly in the market. She then went to some canteen and dropped me at the Dock Yard Gate. After some difficulty I found the *Montgomery* and went on board. Her Captain, a two striper called Hamilton,[42] had asked me on board. I got him to show me round his bridge and we had a long talk about 4 stackers. He is an impressive young man, keen and extremely capable I should say. Here he is as a young 2 striper not only in command but S.O. of a group. It gives me intense inferiority complex when I think he could easily do my job a good deal better than I could. We had some drinks and later on Puxley came on board and we eventually lunched on board.

After I left I went to the War Game room and talked to the chap in charge, an R.N.R. 2½ who I knew before as the Captain of the *Orillia.*[43] I then went home, walking part of the way and going part by tram, and got in about 1700 to find Mrs. P. had retired to bed with a streaming cold, but I sat in her room a bit and talked to her. Prentice came back rather late, and at about 2100 he and I walked to the officer's club where the last command course were giving a farewell party. Drank a good deal of beer and had some snack food but didn't attempt any dancing. Another nice day. Wrote a long letter to J. Feeling v. homesick.

Saturday, 9 October 1943 – Halifax

I heard yesterday that *Salisbury* wouldn't be in till p.m. today so I decided to take some exercise in the a.m. Mrs. P., though much recovered, had work to do so I took the dog Button and went for a walk. It was partly country and partly street, but I had 2 good hours walking anyhow and I posted my letter Air Mail to J. It looked rather like a change in the weather in the a.m. but about midday the sky cleared and the sun blazed out and the p.m. was really hot. After lunch I rang up the Dockyard and heard *Salisbury*'s E.T.A. was about 1630, and so Mrs. P. and I went for a short walk in the park down to the water's edge, and it was really lovely.

I shifted into uniform, had a quick tea and then caught the 1615 tram and went on board the *Salisbury* at about 1700. Started to take over from de St Croix.[44] He is apparently a v. strict disciplinarian, quick tempered and intolerant. He dislikes the R.C.N. and considers them inefficient and has consequently made himself somewhat unpopular, but I think I'm taking over a clean, efficient ship with a good crowd of officers, and I must say it made me feel happier and more confident. I decided to spend one more night with the Prentices and come down with my gear and complete my turnover tomorrow, and so at about 1900 I went up to [Captain] D's office and drove home with him in his car. A giant dinner and fairly early bed.

Sunday, 10 October 1943 – Halifax

We had a rather late breakfast and then we loaded all my gear into the car and Prentice drove me down into the Dockyard. De St. Croix appeared at the office at 1030 and I attended the arrival conference, and then I went down to the ship and officially took over. There was some chance that we might have to go to sea tomorrow but that was cancelled and we are to start our boiler clean. Prentice came on board for a drink before lunch. After lunch and a bit more chat de St. Croix finally stepped ashore at about 1500, and I then unpacked my gear and settled in. My cabin has been enlarged by taking in some of the starboard alley way and so I'm distinctly better off than I was in the *Chelsea,* and I have got my own heads, thank God. I started to read through a mass of stuff. I got an invitation from the Chief (Wilcox)[45] of the *Chelsea* and at about 1830 I walked over to her and had a drink. I have an R.N. 1st Lieutenant, one Black, and the rest of the officers are all R.N.R. or R.N.V.R. except for a Commissioned Engineer R.N.[46] Sat up rather late trying to think of something to say to the sailors tomorrow.

Monday, 11 October 1943 – Halifax

I went round the ship at 0930. We seem to have a very old lot of senior ratings. The coxswain is 48 and the Chief Bos'n's Mate and Chief Stoker are both pensioners. Thumbed through more papers and at 1130 cleared lower deck and spoke to the ship's company. Ogilvie,[47] a 2 striper Captain of the *Leamington,* came to call on me at 1200. In the p.m. I started to work with some group orders. A new support group is being formed of which I am S.O. consisting of *Salisbury, Georgetown, Leamington, Annapolis, Niagara,* and *St Albans.*

The attitude in this ship initiated by the Captain is intensely hostile to the R.C.N. It think it is deplorable and I shall do my best to alter it. We had dinner very late owing to Wilcox being in the Mess and just sticking and sticking. Warmer day again.

Tuesday, 12 October 1943 – Halifax

At 0845 I went with my A/S team for an hour's attack teacher.[48] I'm afraid I wasn't very clever. Went in and talked to Prentice after that about support group tactics. In spite of the very small close escorts in the Western Local, he is keen on keeping the support group on the extended screen.[49] I don't quite agree with him. Got back on board to find we were just moving by tugs to another berth and that took till lunch time. After lunch I went round the A/S department in the ship. Unfortunately I am losing my A/S control officer, who is also Confidential Books officer, which is a curse just as I join. Later on in the p.m. I called on the Engineer Manager in the Dockyard who is a Captain (E), and after talking to No. 1 about the questions of reliefs I went to the Drafting Captain in *Stadacona.*[50] In the dog watches I got down to thinking about support group tactics with the aid of some squared paper, and after dinner I asked Ogilvie to come over and picked his brains a bit.

The papers announced that the *Tirpitz* had been attacked in Alten Fjord by midget Submarines and damaged. That must have been the X craft operation, which was being planned when I was at the Admiralty. A lovely hot sunny day. In Italy the Germans are making a stand on the River Volturno N. of Naples.

Wednesday, 13 October 1943 – Halifax

At 0845 we had another spell on the A/S Attack Teacher and afterwards, after hanging about for quite a bit, I got a car which took me up to the H/Q offices, where I called on the Admiral (Act. Vice Ad. Murray). He was very pleasant. While I was up there I made my number on the S.O.O.[51] and other officers and had a look at the Operations Room. Back on board for lunch and in the p.m. 5 ships of my group – *St Albans, Leamington, Georgetown, Niagara,* and *Salisbury* – had an "exercise" on the Tactical Table. Quite good fun and value. When it was over I had a bit of a discussion on the table with the C.O.s and Briggs on how best to employ our support group in this area. I'm interested to find that the Captain of the *Georgetown,* Lt.-Cdr. Stewart R.N.R., is the late Captain of the *Clare* whom Stephens loathed so heartily.[52] Didn't get back on board till nearly 1800 and then sat down and got on with some more orders. The Portuguese have agreed to lease us naval and air bases in the Azores. That ought to help the battle against U-boats, because by routing our convoys south they will now be able to have continuous shore based air cover.

Thursday, 14 October 1943 – Halifax

Thick fog early on but the sun broke through later on, and it developed into another nice warm sunny day. We were allotted to the night action table. It is a marvellous and realistic training device. Everyone goes – bridge personnel, R.D.F., A/S, W/T, depth charge and gun crews all take part. Excellent value. We didn't do so badly. After that I went to see Prentice and explained my proposals for support group tactics I want circulated to S.O.s of other groups. After lunch I made a final drive at my group orders and gave them to Thomas to get typed.

Soon after 1600 I walked ashore to see our football team play the Norwegians from the *Lincoln.* The ground was up by the Lord Nelson Hotel, which gave me quite a good walk. The standard of football was quite good, but the Lincolns were definitely the stronger side and beat us 1-0. Walked back and wrote my name in the Admiral's Book.

Just as I was going down the hill into the Dockyard I saw an officer ahead of me reeling about frightfully drunk, and so when I got to the gate I told the sentry to send for the Officer of the Guard and detain the drunk. To my surprise and regret who should it turn it out to be but Wilcox, the Chief of the *Chelsea.* Having detained him at the Guard House I went on board *Chelsea* and as the Captain was not on board I told the O.O.D. to deal with the situation. Went on board and wrote to J. Later on the Captain and 1st Lt. of *Chelsea* both came on board. I told them I proposed to take no further action but I requested the Captain to deal with the matter. Very weak of me but I can't run my old Chief in. Why can't these officers refrain from letting their side down?

Friday, 15 October 1943 – Halifax

I saw requestmen and did a lot of paper work, which I continued all through the p.m. At about 1930 I asked the Captain of the *Lincoln* (a Norwegian) LCdr. Monsson over for a drink. A very nice fellow but I thought he was never going and it was nearly 2100 before I got down for dinner.

Saturday, 16 October 1943 – Halifax

A definite change in the weather. Blowing a bit and damp and no sign of sun but still very warm. We had steam once more and I could have a bath. We had yet another game on the Tactical Table, which occupied the whole forenoon. This time my support group was joining a threatened convoy by night, and as we were joining the attack started. We really want a whole day for these sort of games but nevertheless it was most interesting and instructive.

After lunch I walked ashore and went up to the *Stadacona* football ground and watched the *Salisbury* play one of the frigates. They were a bit too good for us. There was an American officer on the touch line who was a most interested spectator. I left before the end and went to Admiralty House (now used as an officer's mess) and had a hair cut. On the way back to the ship I looked in on D.'s operations officer to find out what we were going to do but everything was rather in the air. We'll probably have a job on Monday. Came back and read and wrote two reports. An R.C.N.V.R. 2-striper dined in the mess and to my surprise picked up a bone off his plate in his fingers and proceeded to gnaw it. A very nice chap but strange table manners.

Sunday, 17 October 1943 – Halifax

A damp misty morning. By the midday it was blowing a gale but by evening it was flat calm again. Before inspecting the Divisions[53] I met all the Chiefs and Petty Officers, and after Divisions I read prayers and then talked a bit about the attack on *Tirpitz* by X craft. I had a succession of visitors. First the Flotilla padre, then the Captain of the *Buxton,* and later on Captain D. and Mrs. Prentice and Mrs. Pringle (wife of the Captain of the *Collingwood* and *extremely* attractive). The Prentices took me and Mrs. P. off to lunch and an R.C.N. 2½ who is the Training Officer on D.'s staff and his wife were also there. Quite a nice party. After lunch I got the 2½, whose name I can't remember,[54] to give me a lift in his car. They stopped at their house, which they have recently converted from a stables and I was shown over. Very nice. Then together with their small daughter we drove to the ship and I gave them tea on board. After that I had to deal with our sailing orders for tomorrow and make some signals myself.

At 1900 I went to feed with the Chief of Staff, Capt. Bidwell,[55] who lives in one of the Dockyard houses. His wife is middle aged and unattractive but claims relationship to the Layards. Quite an attractive R.C.N. grass widow[56] staying, but of course I never caught her name. After dinner we went to see the first showing in Halifax of *Corvette [K]225,* an American made propaganda film of the R.C.N. V.g. but to my mind it depicted something so entirely different from the R.N. as to be almost unrecognisable. But of course the R.C.N. *is* very different. We came back and drank beer with the Commodore (Hibbard)[57] and his wife. Flat calm in the evening after blowing a very strong gale at midday.

Monday, 18 October 1943 – Halifax/At sea

Tugs arrived at 0800 and hauled off the ships outside us, and then we slipped and went up to the degaussing range, which is through the Narrows in the inner harbour. A lovely morning, sunny and no wind, for which I was thankful when handling the ship for the first time. How any naval constructor could have designed so unhandy and unmanoeuvrable a type of ship I don't know. When the Degaussing Officer came on board we made about 6 runs over the range, and then as there was some time in hand I dropped the whaler and then hoisted it for exercise, and then proceeded down harbour. At the boom, which we passed at 1130, I overtook the rest of my party, *Lincoln, Hepatica, Digby,* and [illegible], a mixture of destroyers, corvettes, and Bangor class minesweepers, and led them down the channel.

We got to the Halifax Light Vessel at 1400 and then spread in line abreast and did an A/S sweep on a course 110° for 36' and then back again. One of the "monsters," the large fast troop carriers, was expected. This we found afterwards was the *Aquitania,* but we never saw her. I tested out the ship's company by firing a gun and dropping a depth charge, and at about 1800 we went to action stations and fired the close range weapons. On arrival back at the Lt. Vess. at 2000 I sent the remainder into harbour and started on a patrol of about 48 miles perimeter round the entrance channels. The wind started to get up and before long it was blowing hard from just S. of E. It was rather an uncomfortable night and I didn't get much sleep, as we were continually having to mark buoys and alter course.

Tuesday, 19 October 1943 – At sea/Halifax

One of the motor launches who we were relieving on patrol failed to answer the signal telling her to proceed into harbour, and at about 0300 we joined her at one point of the circuit but it wasn't until we'd switched a 10" lamp on to her that we got any life out of her. It was pretty wet on the bridge when we went into the wind and sea. At about 0800 we were told to return to harbour, and after a long wait at the Boom while a lot of ships were coming in we eventually got up harbour and berthed at about 1000, with yet another delay while *Niagara* got her side clear, so I sent for the Captain and gave him a blast.[58]

After lunch I had a stretch off the land and at 1600 I went to a convoy conference only because I'd got the buzz it was coming off. No official signal. I am S.O. of a scratch escort of 4 (only one of my group) taking an H.H.X. tomorrow to MOMP.[59] Then I join up with the escort round the main convoy and go with them as far as WESTOMP and then to St John's. Came back on board and sat down to think out all the information I've got to get to the escorts and various ships in convoy about W/T, HF/DF, R/T, and so on. I can't think why more of this can't be more cut and dried by now, whether or not ships have worked together before. Had a talk with Watson and the P.O. Tel [Petty Officer Telegraphist] about it after dinner and then to bed.

Wednesday, 20 October 1943 – Halifax/At sea

At 1000 the captains of the *St Albans, Fredericton,* and *Summerside* came on board for a short conference, as we are to form the screen of H.H.X. 162 from Halifax to MOMP. Just as we were breaking up the Air Staff Officer of the M.A.C.

ship the *Empire McAndrew* arrived to discuss his flying problems, with result that I was only just able to shift into my seagoing rig in time to shove off at 1120.

Raining hard but not too much wind. Got turned in the harbour quite easily and took my group through the boom. We were an hour ahead of the convoy and had to do a short patrol during that time and then screened the 16 ships down the swept channel. It was misty and raining and beastly until we reached the Halifax Lt. Vess. and then it cleared up and became a lovely evening. The convoy formed up and we took up our screening positions. We went astern for the night.

Thursday, 21 October 1943 – At sea

After a brilliantly clear night it clouded over and started to rain just before daylight. We made contact with the main portion of H.X. 162 at about 0800. As soon as I could I ran up alongside *Richmond* and exchanged information and papers. He, although only an R.N.V.R. 2½, becomes S.O. as I am only a support group S.O. (*Salisbury* and *St Albans*).[60] My two corvettes pushed off after the junction leaving *Richmond, Salisbury, St Albans,* and 2 other corvettes to screen about 65 ships. I spent a long time astern of the convoy after leaving *Richmond* trying to shepherd the 2 portions of it together, and then took station on the port beam. It blew up a bit from the N.W. but nothing much. After dark the wind backed round to the S.W. Very dark until the moon got up at about 0100. Spent quite a bit of time on the bridge. In the night the *St Albans* reported she was experiencing bad flooding forward, was shoring up, and would have to return to harbour, so she left the convoy and we took station astern. My support group is now reduced to one ship – the *Salisbury.*

Friday, 22 October 1943 – At sea

A beautiful fine morning. The M.A.C. ship flew off an aircraft at about 0715. We remained about 12,000 yards astern of the convoy. At about 1030 *Richmond* reported M.A.C. ship's aircraft was one hour overdue and shortly after we intercepted an S.O.S. signal from it saying position unknown and the signal was too weak to D/F. How in this extreme visibility it could lose itself I can't think but apparently it did, tried to make for land, and ran out of petrol. Two other Swordfish went out to search but failed to find it. *Richmond* informed C. in C. and asked for search by shore based aircraft. Otherwise uneventful day. Escort now reduced to 4 ships. Thank God U-boats don't seem to operate in this area because if they did they would do awful slaughter with these tiny escorts. Read, ate, and slept, and took some exercise on the quarter deck.

Saturday, 23 October 1943 – At sea

Another clear fair day. One of the convoy broke down and dropped astern, and after a good deal of signalling, at my suggestion *Richmond* sent a corvette back to stand by her till tugs came out from St John's, and I went up through the convoy and took up screening position on the port bow. We are down to 3 escorts. Weather deteriorated and we had rain squalls and poor visibility, and it looked as if it was going to blow up from the S.E. but it never came to anything. Heard that Admiral Sir Dudley Pound, who has been 1st Sea Lord all the war, has died suddenly.[61]

Sunday, 24 October 1943 – At sea/St John's

At crack of dawn – 0615 – the mid-ocean group were sighted coming to take over at WESTOMP, and by 0700 *Richmond* had completed the turnover and he and I pushed off at 20 knots for St John's. A nice fine day but with a fresh wind from the S.W., which made us pretty wet at 20 knots. At 1500 the coast of Newfoundland hove into sight at max. visibility and we had very little difficulty in hitting the swept channel. Mines have been laid off here recently by a U-boat and two ships have been sunk.[62] We passed the boom at about 1700 and went up to our berth in the pens, where I regret to say I made a balls, had too much way on, couldn't stop, and rammed the wooden wall at the end. The wall didn't look so good afterwards but my bow was quite undamaged, I'm glad to say. The Captain of the *Richmond* came over later on. He is an R.N.V.R. 2½ called Morgan.[63] I'm feeling rather depressed about this job. It doesn't seem to be a job at all really, and I can't help feeling I've been had for a sucker by the 2nd Sea Lord's office. Turned in early.

Monday, 25 October 1943 – St John's

My steward Bamford overslept, so I overslept and wasn't called until 0800. At about 1100 *Richmond* and I shared a car and went up to call on Capt. D. (Rowland)[64] who asked me to lunch. While waiting I went into the Operations Room to find out news and then called on the Commodore. His name is Reid, and he is just about to be relieved by a man called Taylor.[65] I then went to the officer's mess and put off some time until 1230 when I went along to the Commodore's private room and drank gin with him. Rowland and another man arrived later on and took me to lunch at his house. Mrs. R is a weather beaten type and not a bit attractive but very nice.

After lunch Capt. D. drove back to his office and then sent me on down to the Dockyard. I got on board about 1500. Wrote some letters. Heard on the wireless that in an engagement in the Channel the cruiser *Charybdis* and the Hunt class *Limbourne* had been sunk. They announced that Jacky Phipps[66] was in the *Limbourne.* I wonder if Billie's husband Whinney, who was Jack's 1st Lieut. in the *Montrose,* was also with him. We had 2 Canadian naval nurses on board for dinner, and a doctor and his wife appeared later. They were pretty heavy weather.

Damp misty day. Started reading *Clarissa Harlow.* Commodore Stephenson, the little "Tiger" at Tobermory, has died. (This proved quite untrue 12.2.51)[67]

Tuesday, 26 October 1943 – St John's

At 0915 Thomas, Oxley, and I went on to the A/S attack teacher with the A/S team and had some runs. It was raining when we came back. I went round to the *Richmond* before lunch and had a drink with Morgan. I had meant to get some exercise in the p.m. but found it took me all my time till tea to make out my report of collision with the jetty and deal with correspondence, and after tea I had to deal with the case of a man apprehended by the shore patrol last night. No. 1 and I had to interview a whole stream of witnesses. Our sailing orders also arrived for tomorrow, which needed careful study. At about 1900 Mrs. Rowland came on board for a drink and I asked No. 1 to come along to my cabin too. Mrs. R. and I left the ship at about 2015 and we went to an officer's club called "The Crow's Nest," where we had supper.[68] Quite a nice spot. At about 2200 we got a car and I drove Mrs. R. home, and then we went back on board and got involved in my favourite religious cum how-to-improve-the-world sort of discussion in the wardroom before turning in. Very much colder all of a sudden. Rowland was attending some sort of official dinner and so couldn't come on board with his wife. She is very tough, and I'm not sure whether after a whole evening with her I care about the type much.

Wednesday, 27 October 1943 – St John's/At sea

At 0945 *Richmond* and I and both our Navigators got a car up to the Naval Officers' [wardroom] and attended a convoy conference. We are taking 10 ships out of here to join up with ON 207 at WESTOMP and then taking the whole lot on. *Richmond* is S.O. again with his two corvettes and *Salisbury* as support group!! I'm not proud, but really it seems waste of money to pay me as a Commander and always put [me] under the orders of a 2½. Morgan and I walked to Government House and wrote our names in the Walwyns' book,[69] and then I walked back on board. At 1400 we slipped. A pilot took us away from the jetty and turned us round by tug and then I took her out of harbour. A lovely sunny afternoon but a definite nip in the air. We crawled along the swept channel with the merchant ships strung out astern, and the convoy only just got formed up at the end of the channel before dark.

Thursday, 28 October 1943 – At sea

We met O.N. 207 at about 0600 just as it was getting light. It took some time for our little convoy to get their new numbers and form up in the main convoy, and while *Richmond* went on to take S.O. duties from the mid-ocean group I stayed behind and tried to hurry things up. Finally took station on the port bow. A fine day but the Met forecast at St John's was an easterly blow tonight. *Roxborough* joined up with the convoy from St John's with orders to join my group, W 10.

Friday, 29 October 1943 – At sea

It was v. hazy at daylight and rapidly turned into fog. At about 0930, however, it cleared away and what wind there was dropped, and so I made a signal I would take in oil from one of the specially fitted oilers in the convoy. I didn't need the oil but I *did* need the experience in doing it. I felt v. windy about it, because in the first place it was by no means flat calm, and in the second place it scares me stiff to take this ship through the convoy or for that matter anywhere near another ship because she is so unmanoeuvrable. I took a very long time picking up the buffs and getting the stray line and hose inboard, and when slipping the tow finished up by cutting one of the buffs off with my propellers. Not a very clever exhibition but I hope instructive for other occasions. It started to blow up a bit in the night.

Saturday, 30 October 1943 – At sea

The wind (from the W.) and sea got up quickly, and by the morning watch we had to reduce to 8 knots. It was a lovely sunny day with this very strong wind and quite big sea. The convoy from yesterday's 10 knots dropped back to something like 4. We were supposed to reach MOMP at 1700 but were at least 20 hours behind schedule. Additional support consisting of *Columbia* and 3 corvettes arrived in the a.m., but the other group we were supposed to meet at MOMP was of course miles away. I wasn't quite sure what *Richmond* was doing about it all and I don't think he informed C. in C. early enough of our delay. He seemed to intend leaving the convoy as soon as *Lethbridge* and his group arrived, which would probably be about midnight. It struck me that to try and get a new screen formed under bad weather conditions at night was most undesirable, and so I made a signal that W 10 (*Salisbury* and *Roxborough*) would remain with the convoy until daylight. *Lethbridge* made contact eventually at 2300 and from signals received I gather *Richmond* then pushed off. We were stationed 8,000 yards on the port beam of the convoy for the night. Wind went down a lot in the night.

Sunday, 31 October 1943 – At sea/Halifax

I went on the bridge at 0400 and stayed up there. We worked up to the front of the convoy and groped about with some R.D.F. trying to find the *Roxborough,* and at about 0630 just as dawn was breaking we contacted her, told her to follow us, signalled *Columbia* we were leaving, and set course for Halifax. As bad luck would have it the wind, which had almost died down entirely in the night, now started to blow up again and veered round to the N.W. so as to exactly head us. I tried 15 knots but started to take it green over the fo'c'sle and bump badly and had to reduce to 13 kts. The *Roxborough* behaved noticeably better than us in the head sea. I spent a lot of time on the bridge watching the ship, as I wanted to go as fast as I could without breaking things. Towards the end of the forenoon I was able to increase to 14 kts, and after lunch conditions improved so much that we were able to increase to 20. This N.W. wind has quite a nip in it.

We reached the Halifax Lt. Vess. at about 1600 and finally secured alongside *Richmond* at about 1830 just as it was getting dark. Damned cold the last bit. Had a bath on arrival. I made a good alongside, which was a good thing for my reputation. The *Roxborough* berthed outside us and the Captain[70] came over to have a drink. He is a 2½ R.N. ex R.N.R. and rather boring. Turned in fairly early so as to get a good night in.

Monday, 1 November 1943 – Halifax

I attended an arrival conference at Capt. D.'s office at 0930, which was rather a waste of time, and then hung around wasting more time waiting for car to go and see the Admiral, which all C.O.s are expected to do on arrival, only to find out at last that the Admiral was away and us calling was unnecessary. Our sailing orders for tomorrow arrived and I spent some time getting out the necessary signals and group orders. Ogilvie from *Leamington* came over to see me and I dealt with correspondence after lunch, and at 1600 I attended a convoy conference at the naval officers' [mess], at the end of which I was able to discuss what we were going to do with the C.O.s of my group. Went on board feeling thoroughly frosty and so at 1715, as it was too late to go and do some shopping as I meant to do, I went ashore and took a short sharp walk out to the Naval Hospital. A lovely still evening but nippy. I resent spending the whole of my one day in harbour attending conferences and preparing for our next trip to sea.

The three power conference at Moscow (Britain, U.S.A., and Russia) has just finished. Complete agreement and great joy everywhere but I can't gather from the news I've heard *what* was agreed. Still no letter from home. Rolph Medley's suggestion that J. should address her letters care of him was, I'm afraid, a thoroughly bad one.

Tuesday, 2 November 1943 – At sea

My group W 10, consisting of *Salisbury, Roxborough, Leamington,* and *Kenora* (an R.C.N. Bangor) were supposed to sail and pass through the boom at 0430. *Roxborough,* however, had defects and couldn't sail and so after *Leamington* had gone, taking a very long time, tugs had to hold *Roxborough* off to let me out and *I* took a long time to get clear and turn, and so we were ½ hour late at the boom. A lovely night but a grisly hour to sail. I was astonished to hear from No. 1 that Knight, an R.N.V.R. Newfoundlander, was not on board when we sailed. I'm accustomed to men but not officer leave breakers.

At the Halifax Lt. Vess., which we reached at 0730, we spread in line abreast and carried out an A/S sweep to a depth of 36 miles and back. Went to action stations at 1100 and fired off the guns, and I also wrote a letter to J. that I will get transferred to the S.O. Ocean Group to take home to post. As we returned on our sweep we saw the *Mauritania* (who was the cause of our sweep) leaving, but she didn't seem to use the water we'd swept. Back up the swept channel till at the Sambro Lt. Vess. we met our H.H.X. 264 convoy and *Roxborough* coming out, and we spread out alongside them. The Commodore took them right out of the swept channel at one point. On arrival at Halifax Lt. Vess. the convoy formed up, which wasn't completed till after dark. I took night station in position SS astern. Just before midnight an independently routed merchantman just missed the rear of the convoy and nearly hit us. A most lovely sunny day.

Wednesday, 3 November 1943 – At sea

We arrived at MOMP and sighted the main H.X. 264 convoy at about 0800 and were rather far ahead, and so I suggested to the Commodore that ships should be told to act independently and take station in the main convoy. No sooner were our 13 ships all taking action when I got a signal from *Mansfield*, who is S.O. close escort, giving at least 10 of them new numbers, and so I had to chase up after every one and give them their new positions – a great waste of time I feel. I then went ahead and *Mansfield* closed me and I passed over papers and talked to him.[71] It annoyed me that he made no attempt to ask my opinion and then proceeded to station my support group in what I thought to be *most* unsuitable positions. I argued a bit but you can't do much over a loud hailer and signal lamp, and eventually gave in with bad grace. This support group nonsense really is bloody stupid. I wish to God I had a straight forward escort group.

I didn't have my breakfast till nearly lunch time. We seemed to spend our time at *Mansfield*'s direction in moving from position AA right ahead to SS right astern. In the night it blew up quite hard from the S. and then veered to S.W. The Russians are steadily pushing the Germans back and have now cut the Perekop isthmus, which joins the Crimea to the mainland.

Thursday, 4 November 1943 – At sea

The wind eased a lot in the morning and we took up position AA, giving one of the convoy a bottle on the way for burning a stern light in the night visible at least 6 miles. Went back to SS at night fall. At about 0800 the rescue ship *Fastnet* got an HF/DF bearing, which he reported by R/T. From the wording of the report it appeared a long way off and I would personally have done nothing about it, but *Mansfield* told W 10 group to make a search. I detailed *Roxborough* and *Leamington* to go out to 10 miles and was moving across to the port side myself when we got one too, on another bearing, considered on the ground wave but certainly not a first sighting report. However, I dashed out along the bearing at 20 kts to 10 miles. Just as we got there the Chief came up to say he'd got excessive vibration in the port turbine and wanted to stop it as soon as possible. There was no sign of a U-boat on either bearing and so we all returned to our positions on the screen and I had to do the best I could on one engine. As a temporary repair would take about 6 hours stopping and going slow, I think I shall detach tomorrow at WESTOMP and go into St John's with W 9 (*Mansfield*'s group). The rest of the night was beautiful.

Friday, 5 November 1943 – At sea/St John's

At daylight ocean group C 4 arrived to take over the escort and after a certain amount of chat I left the convoy with W 9 group, leaving *Roxborough* and *Leamington* as W 10 remaining in support till daylight 6th. At about 0930 decided to push on ahead independently at my best speed, which with my one engine doing revs for 22 knots worked out at about 16 knots. From being an absolutely flat calm in the morning the wind got up very quickly and by midday was blowing hard from the west, and I was thoroughly worried all the p.m. as to whether we'd be able to follow a N.'ly course with the beam sea. It was of course *perfectly* alright, but there is no doubt bad weather *does* worry me. At about 1600 we got the lee of Newfoundland and there was no further call for anxiety. We turned up into the St. John's swept channel on D/F bearings, one of which was the commercial broadcasting station. At the entrance, which we reached at 2000, a pilot and tugs met us as trying to negotiate the baffle in the entrance in a 4 stacker with only one engine is too risky a job. We berthed alongside the U.S. Army jetty just inside the entrance on the right. Had a very late meal in my cabin and then went down to the wardroom for a drink. I must say there are few pleasures to compare with our first night in after a sea trip. There was a good moon as we came in, but I must say I wouldn't care to negotiate the entrance on a dark night.

Saturday, 6 November 1943 – St John's

A lovely bright sunny day. I went up to the Naval Office and called on [Captain] D. and went down to the Operations Room. W 9 and W 10 will be required probably on Monday to take over an O.N. convoy from *Hotspur*'s group. Monday will be just 5 weeks to the day since their last arrival here when I was on board. *Roxborough* and *Leamington* have left H.X. 264 to hunt a U-boat reported by aircraft S.E. of St John's, but it will take them too long to get there to have any chance of finding it, even supposing it was ever there anyhow. Saw requestmen and went mess deck rounds on return. It is almost impossible to make these crowded mess decks tidy. There is no stowage for the men's gear.

The Capt. of the *Mansfield* came over for a drink, and Capt. D., who happened to be going over to the ship next door, also came into my cabin for a quick gin. Jones (Lt. Comdr. R.N.R.) is quite an elderly man. I told him my views on screening and how I disagreed with his day dispositions. He is a nice chap. After lunch I put on plain clothes and went for walk. I struck out right from the town and more or less circled the huge new American military camp.[72] The country with its pine woods and pretty streams is very much like Scotland. Got back on board soon after 1600 and went through a mass of signals and papers. After dinner I went over to the *Mansfield* and had a whisky and soda with Jones and finally got on to discussing the Roman Catholic Church. The Russians have captured Kiev.

Sunday, 7 November 1943 – St John's

Not a nice day. Overcast, windy, and spots of rain at intervals. Owing to having R.C. Church on board on the stokers' mess deck we didn't go to Divisions till 1000, and then had it on the jetty. I read prayers and addressed a few words to the sailors on pride of ship. Watching their faces there didn't seem to be the slightest response. At about 1130 I walked up to the offices to call on the Commodore but he was at church. Saw Harrison,[73] the Chief Staff Officer, and then went down to Ops where I found out our O.N. convoy, owing to re-routing and weather, has been delayed, and we won't be required to sail till p.m. Tuesday. The Engineers say we must return to Halifax on one engine and I reckon we might just as well do our stuff round the convoy as we can do 15-16 kts. Met Evans[74] – captain of the *Towy* and S.O. of one of the ocean groups. At 1230 *Roxborough* and *Leamington,* who arrived in the morning, came over to see me, and later on Evans arrived too with result that I had a very late lunch. Immediately afterwards I put on plain clothes and set off for a walk. Not very nice as there was a cold wind, which at one time brought a shower of sleet, but when I got into the pine woods it was better. Back on board at 1630 and at 1800 I went over to the *Towy* and took a parcel, which Evans said he would post in England. Capt. D., his wife, and "Egg" Burnett[75] were there too. I think Mrs. D. is rather a grim woman on better acquaintance.

Monday, 8 November 1943 – St John's

A raw cold day. I went over to see Evans in the *Towy* just before lunch to arrange that he should pay duty on the silk stockings I'm sending in a parcel to J. He is a nice chap. After lunch I walked into the town and did some shopping. I bought some stuff for Xmas decorations and I bought a fountain pen for Gillian, and I browsed in a book shop where I found a copy of *Conditions of Peace.* I'm awfully bad at buying presents – don't seem to have any ideas. Back on board for tea. Knight returned on board having been flown up from Halifax and No. 1 brought him in to see me. He had really nothing to say except that he thought we were sailing at 4 p.m. not 4 a.m. Told him to give me his reasons in writing and I would then consider what further action to take.

After dinner Morris from the *Roxborough* suddenly appeared, having just come down from Ops, and said he and *Leamington* had been ordered to raise steam with all despatch and go out and support O.N. 209 who had sighted 2 U-boats yesterday and expected to be attacked tonight. He said they were off in ½ hour's time. V. strange that I shouldn't have been informed. I was then thrown into great uncertainty. Ought I to volunteer to go with them as *Salisbury* is still out of action? I first of all thought there would not be time and of course I dreaded the responsibility, however, I eventually rung up Ops and offered to go, and they rather jumped at it, and so I hurriedly put on my sea kit and a boat came and took me across to *Leamington*, which I decided to make my flag ship. There was an awful delay on account of the difficulty in getting their liberty men back. Eventually still with a few adrift we sailed at about 0030.

Tuesday, 9 November 1943 – At sea

Bright moon light made it quite easy to negotiate the entrance and as soon as we were clear we went on to 22 knots and steered to the N. to intercept. I brought Thomas with me as I thought he'd be useful as an A/S expert, and he and I were given the sickbay – a little dog's hole on the upper deck with two bunks – to live in. The *Leamington* has got an infinitely better bridge, wheel house, and chart house than we have, but the Captain's cabin leaks badly, so I'm one up there in *Salisbury*. We sighted the convoy at about 1030 and ranged up along *Hotspur* to get the dope. They were *not* attacked and he thinks they passed through a U/B patrol without being seen – aircraft keeping the U/Bs down.

We had just taken up our position on the screen when a signal arrived from F.O.N.F. [Flag Officer Newfoundland] telling W 10 to leave the convoy and proceed at high speed to the position where aircraft had made the sighting yesterday and carry out a sweep in the neighbourhood, so we collected *Roxborough* and set off again to the northward at 23 knots. We reached the S.W. end of our area at about 2000 and reduced to 15 knots to sweep across the diagonal. From being a flat calm it started to blow from the S.W., and by midnight it was blowing hard.

A year ago today we were busting the boom at Algiers. I wish there was some one to talk to about it without appearing conceited.

Wednesday, 10 November 1943 – At sea

We altered course to the W. at about 0300 and had to reduce speed first of all to 12 and then to 9 knots on account of the sea. In the course of the day we were told to sweep the area until 1800 and then return to St John's. Our previous orders had mentioned prudent limit of endurance, and so Ogilvie and I had done great calculations about mileage and oil fuel consumption. A very unpleasant forenoon bucketing into this sea. At about 1300 we altered again to the S.E., which brought the sea on to the beam. I wasn't sure whether we'd be able to stick it out and at 1600, after shipping quite a heavy sea right over, we altered to the S. The wind then started to ease and by the time we abandoned the search at 1800 we were able to go on to 15 knots.

This is the anniversary of the day the *Broke* sank. Heard a broadcast by Churchill who hinted at new weapons and methods of attack by the Germans on England, referring presumably to the expected use of these huge long range rocket projectiles.

Thursday, 11 November 1943 – At sea/St John's

Wind and sea dropped, and by 1100 we were going 23 knots back to St. John's. Intercepted signals that an aircraft had sighted and attacked a U-boat about 150 miles S. of Cape Race. In the afternoon I closed *Roxborough* in and gave both ships a few watch drills, firing D/Cs and burning smoke floats, etc. We ran into thick fog at about 1500, which in patches was very thick, but it lifted a bit, thank God, as we approached St John's, which enabled us to find the entrance without much difficulty. We made daylight and secured in the pens at 1730. We've got to go out immediately after oiling to join the party hunting this U/B to the southward. *Roxborough* has unfortunately developed engine room defects and she will have to stay. Considering the flap there seems to be to get us out again, it was funny that it was over 2 hours after arrival before the oiler arrived. We found our A/S dome[76] was leaking and so asked a diver to have a look at it. I felt awfully sleepy, and so after dinner I turned in for a bit. At 2330 I turned out see if the oiling was over but the diver was still holding us up.

Friday, 12 November 1943 – At sea

We sailed at 0030. It was clear in the harbour and at the entrance but thick fog once we got outside. From the end of the swept channel we turned S. and increased to 25 knots. We steamed through thick fog all day. About midday we started to pick up R/T signals from *Montgomery*, who is on the scene as S.O. with about 9 other ships. I don't agree with his dispositions at all. He is still searching round or near the last sighting position. As it is now over 24 hours since that sighting and thick fog all the time, the U-boat may be anywhere up to 150 miles away even if disabled. As E.-S.E. is its most likely course I suggested going off 120 miles in that direction so as to be well placed for interception should it become possible to use aircraft. Shortly before dark I took over S.O., as *Montgomery* had reached prudent limit of endurance and had to leave. I then discovered that *Leamington*'s R/T transmitter was defective and I couldn't get my signals through to the 8 ships that were left. Gave orders for all ships to move to positions on the arc of a circle of 160' radius from the last sighting position.

We had one alarm on a radar contact, which finally turned out to be a rain cloud coming rapidly down on us. The visibility improved a bit in the night.

Saturday, 13 November 1943 – At sea

It was quite clear at daylight, and we were patrolling up and down either side of our position on an arc of a circle 160' radius from the initial datum point. At about 0930 we got a signal from *Timmins* saying she had got a contact and was attacking. I didn't believe it could be a U-Boat, but told the two nearest ships to close and help her to hunt. Owing to our defective W/T we couldn't pass the signal and so we ourselves altered to the N. at 20 knots to close. The fog shut down again and as the forenoon proceeded *Timmins* made more reports of attacks. Owing to differences in dead reckoning, fog, and difficulties in D/Fing we didn't locate her until about 1330, by which time after making her 6th attack she had lost contact. I could get v. little information out of her as to course, speed, and behaviour of target, and still considered she had probably been attacking her own wake or something. It is inconceivable that a submerged U/B would allow itself to come within range of an escort steering a straight line patrol.

Canso arrived just before us but her A/S was out of action. I organized a sweep with *Timmins* and at about 1600 closed and transferred the Doctor to *Canso* to look at a sick officer. Heavy rain squalls about this time. Two aircraft came out and one came into sight at about 1630. A very fine effort in the bad visibility. Our defective R/T made my job much more difficult and I had trouble in passing signals ashore. By dark no sign of the U/B and none of the other ships had joined, so I organised a square patrol with *Timmins* and ordered the rest to return to St John's, as with aircraft searching they could only confuse the issue. A strenuous day. I wish these ships would make certain before saying they've got a U-boat.

Sunday, 14 November 1943 – At sea

I went up on the bridge at about 0400. We were still doing our square patrol and I expected to hear the *Kenora* had joined us, but as there was no news of her I called her up and asked for her position and found she was miles to the westward. Partly my fault for not having told her exactly what we were doing, but I expected her to ask for a D/F bearing if she was in doubt. At 0700 we abandoned the operation, told *Kenora* to proceed to St John's, and set course for Argentia[77] ourselves. The fog lifted and it turned out a lovely sunny day, but towards the evening it clouded once again.

Monday, 15 November 1943 – At sea/Argentia/At sea

I wasn't called as I had asked, but when I went on the bridge at about 0730 we were steaming N. towards Argentia with land in sight to starboard and ahead.

There was a very cold W. wind blowing and going into harbour was a very chilly performance. We secured alongside at about 0900. The Yankee base here is really marvellous. High jetties, buildings, roads, and an aerodrome when 2 or 3 years ago there was literally nothing. Dowler[78] who is the R.N. Capt. D. came on board for a few minutes. I should have liked to have looked round but couldn't as I had no clothes. *Starling*'s famous 2nd Escort Group were in harbour. In their last trip they clocked 2 more U-boats, making 6½ for the group this year. We sailed again at 1330. The wind had gone down a bit, but there was enough sea to make it very wet pushing into it at 17 knots. I am reading and much enjoying *Romney Rye* by George Burrow.

Tuesday, 16 November 1943 – At sea/Halifax

The wind and sea had dropped in the night and we were bowling along at 22 knots, but in the forenoon the wind got up and produced a bit of a head sea, which brought our speed down and made it v. wet indeed and uncomfortable. We arrived at the end of the swept channel at about 1400 and secured alongside *Mansfield,* who was next to *Salisbury* at about 1500. *Was* I glad to get back to my own cabin, have a bath, and get into some clean clothes. It appears that no decision has yet been made about *Salisbury.* The turbine cannot be opened up here and if done will have to be at an American port. As, however, the authorities are very reluctant to spend any more money on these ships, there is a possibility that as they break down seriously they should be paid off. I foresee endless argument before a decision is reached.

Ogilvie came over and had some tea with me, and then we went up to see D. and we talked all round this problem. It looks as if I at any rate will have to move out of *Salisbury.* Back on board. The Doctor had an Army officer on board for dinner and we sat yarning rather late, and what with one thing and another I drank rather too much. *Got my first letter from J!!* As I feared her first letters have obviously been addressed to Rolph Medley and held up in Londonderry, as this one addressed General Post Office refers to earlier ones which I haven't got. An R.N.R. Lieut. (E) Hynes has joined to relieve my chief Comd. Eng. Smith.

Wednesday, 17 November 1943 – Halifax

At 0930 No. 1 and I left the ship and walked up to *Stadacona* and attended a lecture by Capt. Walker, the famous U-boat killer of the *Starling.*[79] *Most* interesting. He talked a bit and then answered questions. After the lecture I went with Capt. D. and Puxley to headquarters where we had a conference with the Chief of Staff on what is to be done with the 4 stackers. It appears the Admiralty wants to pay them off so as to get the crews, of which they are apparently short, and Ottawa is talking of doing the same with the R.C.N. ships. They are now thoroughly unreliable and not worth spending money on. Nothing decided until

Bidwell can contact Ottawa, but it *is* decided that I shall shift over to *Roxborough* as *Salisbury* is out of action. Damnable this chopping and changing.

Went back with Capt. D. and Puxley to the DkYd and had one in the C.O.'s reading room, and then I went back on board for lunch. As No. 1 will be taking over this ship I let him go to the A/S attack teacher in the p.m. and went up to Admiralty House myself for a hair cut. Back on board and spent the dog watches and some time after dinner writing my Report of Proceedings. I hate writing these reports. A damned sweat. At this morning's conference Bidwell said W 10 group – as long as they lasted – would probably be based at St. John's as being nearer the area of U-boat activity. A raw damp day. By a curious twist of fate Capt. Walker's son was lost in one of our submarines on his first cruise.[80]

Thursday, 18 November 1943 – Halifax

There was frost during the night, but it was a most lovely sunny day. At 1000 a car arrived for me and together with a shorthand writer I set off for place called Liverpool to preside at a Court of Enquiry. The distance was about 100 miles, but it was a lovely drive passing through lake and forest scenery at first and then running around bays and sea estuaries. We arrived at about 1245 and after calling on the S.N.O. and R.C.N.V.R. Comdr. the writer and I went to the local hotel and had a very good lunch, and then we went on board the R.C.N. corvette *Alberni* for the Court of Enquiry. The other two members of the board were 2 R.C.N.V.R. Lieuts, and we were investigating the accidental firing of a depth charge thrown into the harbour. It was fairly straight forward but even so being me I took it fearfully seriously, and we didn't finish till after 1600. We finally started back at about 1630 and got back to the ship at 1930. I wrote to J. after dinner.

Friday, 19 November 1943 – Halifax

The new Captain of the *Roxborough* – a Lieut. whose name I can't remember[81] – came over at about 0930. We went together to see D. and had a long wait before we *could* see him. I was shown 2 signals. One from the Admiralty saying if they could have up to 10 British built frigates they could pay off the R.N. 4 stackers between now and Feb. '44. When we saw D. it was agreed that I should not go to *Roxborough* until situation had clarified a bit, but that I should be prepared to go out in an emergency. Went on board and saw requestmen and dealt with a lot of paper work. After lunch I went ashore and first of all saw Puxley about the Chief's [Smith] passage home, then went to [HMS] *Canada*[82] about the same thing, and then set off into the town on a shopping expedition. Bought a very nice but expensive little watch for G., a teddy bear for R., and then walked out to the Prentice home, where I found Mrs. P. who gave me tea and eventually drove me down to the Dockyard, as she was going to a cocktail party on board one of the ships.

The Russians have had a slight reverse, we are being held up in Italy owing to weather and difficult country, and really there are times it looks as if this war might go on for years yet. I was sitting in my cabin before dinner and who should appear but Moffat, my old servant in the *Broke,* now a Leading Seaman in one of our new American built ships.

Saturday, 20 November 1943 – Halifax

I was out on the jetty having a look at the ship when an officer from one of Rolph Medley's ocean group thrust a bag of mail into my hands, and when I opened it I found about ½ doz. letters from J., which was lovely. Her news is that Phyl Garrett[83] was the other evening battered senseless in her house by some unknown man or men and is more or less hanging between life and death. She, J., took the Wren funeral party at Sir Dudley Pound's funeral in London. She has had a letter from Claire saying they have heard that John is a prisoner of war in Java.

I went mess deck rounds and dealt with correspondence. After lunch No. 1, the Doctor (Murphy), and I went ashore and walked to a large football ground near the Lord Nelson to watch a game of American football between 2 Canadian naval teams. It was most interesting as I've always wanted to see it played, but with quite an open mind I do *not* think it such a good game to watch as our rugger, and I'm sure it can't be so good to play. No. 1 and I walked back to the ship and after tea I read. Shifted and went up to the C.O.'s Library in the naval officers' [mess] just before 1900 and presently Prentice, Puxley, and Waterhouse,[84] the new training Commander, came in and we had rather a lot of drinks. Finally, Puxley and I went back with D. to his house for dinner. I felt v. sleepy after dinner. Puxley and I shared a taxi back afterwards. A warm muggy day but foggy at night.

Sunday, 21 November 1943 – Halifax

It poured with rain most of the forenoon. We had to wash out Divisions but I cleared lower deck on the stokers' mess and told the ship's company that the decision hadn't yet been made whether to mend us at an American base or pay us off, and then I read prayers. Had a session in the wardroom with Oxley on the question of charge documents, which seem to be rather a mess. Later on I went over to *Mansfield,* who are having a forenoon do in their ward room, and I had some very good egg nogs. After lunch I put on plain clothes and set off for a walk. It rained a bit to start with but cleared up later. I walked right up along Barrington Street and on until I came to the Park, and I walked round that and came out by the Prentices' house and home past the Lord Nelson. A good 2 hours' walk but mostly on pavements. Back on board for tea, and then I wrote to J. and one or two other letters as the mail was closing in the evening. The Russians have been pushed back quite a bit west of Kiev, and it looks like a big German comeback more than a local counter attack.

Monday, 22 November 1943 – Halifax

A signal has come from the Admiralty to Ottawa asking that *Salisbury* and *Mansfield* should be reduced to care and maintenance, with C. and M. parties provided by the R.C.N. if possible, and that the crews should go to America to man new construction. It remains to be seen what is going to happen to me. I went out calling in the a.m. Found the Commodore Supt. was engaged and so went on to *Stadacona* and called on Commodore Beech.[85] He was No. 1 of the *Versatile* in 1923 when I was No. 2 of the *Velox*. Back to the Dockyard only to find Commodore Hibbard was still engaged, so I left word I called and went back on board and prepared for my Court of Enquiry by plotting courses, etc. After lunch I went up to Capt. D.'s office block and presided over a Court of Enquiry into the collision between a Canadian corvette and an American coast guard cutter. I had 2 R.C.N.R. Lt.Comdrs., Johnson and Easton, on the board with me.[86] We got through the cross questioning of the witnesses fairly quickly but took a long time wording our findings. We finished at about 1830 and I brought both my colleagues down on board for a drink. Sir Oswald and Lady Moseley[87] have been released from detention, where they have been since the war started, on the grounds of ill health, and this has apparently caused a storm of protest in England particularly from the Communists.

Tuesday, 23 November 1943 – Halifax

Went up to D.'s office and saw Puxley, who said they had no news yet but would let me know as soon as anything came through. I went along with our A/S team and did some runs on the table. After lunch the shorthand writer came down and Easton came across and we read through and altered the rough draft of our C. of E. findings. Stayed on board and read. An airman who had done a trip in this ship dined on board, and he and I and No. 1 sat up rather late chewing the rag and I drank too much beer.

Wednesday, 24 November 1943 – Halifax

At 1030 I went up to the *Canada* and saw the Pay Cdr. (Johnson) about paying off and mess savings and then I went to see Seeger[88] and discussed Xmas entertainment for R.N. officers and men. I then went to see D. and he says they are recommending that I take over a new Canadian support group of frigates and corvettes that is being formed. Although I'm not keen about an all Canadian group, because one *does* get tired of them and they are *not* brought up in the same way as us, still if it is to be a mid-ocean group working from Londonderry and St. John's I shall be able to get home sometimes, which will be grand. I went away feeling very bucked. I went ashore at about 1500 and walked up Barrington Street and went to the Capitol cinema and saw a musical thing with Eddie Canter in it which was quite funny. Back on board. No. 1 had asked Puxley on board for dinner, and so instead of going to bed early I sat up talking late again. Berlin has had a terrific pounding 2 nights running. Have just finished reading a collection of short stories of the American underworld of gangsters. *Most* amusing.

Thursday, 25 November 1943 – Halifax

I had an early breakfast as C.O.s and Navigating Officers had been called to attend a lecture at *Kings* (the R.C.N.V.R. officers' training centre) on Loran and transport was coming at 0800. As a matter of fact it didn't come till about 0820. All was well, however, as on arrival at *Kings* they were in the middle of Divisions and the lecture didn't start till about 0900. Loran is a new system of D/F fixing, and the lecture was most interesting. We got back at lunch time. In the p.m. I went up to see D., but he was in session with Bidwell and Menzies [sic][89] from Ottawa. At about 1500 I went ashore and went to the cinema again. It is really rather shame making – two afternoons running – but there was absolutely nothing else to do. I saw a film called *Hers to Hold* with Deanna Durbin, who I think is sweet, and a man called Joseph Cotton – an extremely attractive young man. I came away feeling very sentimental. At dinner No. 1 became v. boring, as he would hold forth on the subject of dress, both officers and men, which we know is bad but he never lets the subject alone. A lovely sunny day. The Germans are still saying "wait for our reprisals on England." I wonder whether this rocket bombardment is coming and just how frightful it will be and whether they really contain up to 10 tons of explosive each.

Friday, 26 November 1943 – Halifax

Another lovely day after frost at night. I saw a large batch of requestmen. Went up to D.'s offices and heard there was now a suggestion that we should steam on one engine to an American port of temperate climate and pay off there to prevent further deterioration. That means we *can't* land our book, stores, and ammunition, which we were all ready to do. At 1200 I went round to the *Georgetown* to see the captain. They are out of action for about a fortnight. After lunch one of D.'s staff officers came to tell me that now it was intended that all R.N. 4 stackers should steam back to the U.K., except *Mansfield* and *Salisbury* who weren't considered fit for the voyage, and we 2 would pay off here. When *will* they make their minds up. I wish to God we could steam across. I'm terrified of finding myself kept out here on the Canadian coast.

I read in the p.m. feeling bored to sobs and after tea I started a letter to J. At about 1800 I went up to Mrs. Bidwell's house in the Dockyard and asked her and Capt. B. to come on board for a drink on Sunday. I stayed and had a drink and talked to her and the children, and then went on to the C.O.'s Library where I met Waterhouse and eventually brought him on board for dinner. He and I and

No. 1 finished up the evening arguing rather heatedly about de St. Croix, who to my mind did a lot of harm out here by his attitude he adopted to the R.C.N.

Saturday, 27 November 1943 – Halifax

Another lovely warm sunny day. At 1100 I attended a conference at which Capt. D. presided at which Operation SALMON (our search for the U-Boat the other day) was discussed. *Montgomery, Georgetown, Leamington,* and most of the corvettes' C.O.s were there. It is still not known what the experts at St John's think after inspecting recorder traces, etc., but I'm still most *curious* about *Timmins*' contact. Did a little drinking in the C.O.'s Library and after lunch I took Knight before D., who gave him a good blast for missing the ship and told me to log him.[90] He ought really to have gone before a disciplinary board. When back on board I shifted into plain clothes and walked out to and round the Halifax park, which did me good as I'm getting a bit gin sodden. Back on board where I finished the thriller I've been reading. This life is getting me down. I wish I knew some people ashore.

Sunday, 28 November 1943 – Halifax

My 44th birthday. It rained in the night but turned out fine and sunny but with a cold wind. We went to Divisions and then I told the ship's company all that was known for certain about their fate. Read a lot of A.F.O.s [Admiralty Fleet Orders] and at 1130 I went down to the wardroom and stood everybody drinks for my birthday. At about 1200 the Doctor brought his Father and sister on board, the Prentices and another woman, the Bidwells and Mrs. Lucas all came down, and we had a very good party on board. The Prentices took me off ashore with them for lunch, picking up Waterhouse on the way. After lunch the Captain and 1st Lieut. of the *Chelsea* arrived, and we all adjourned to the garden and played deck tennis, which in its way gives one quite a bit of exercise. The woman staying with the P.s (a naval wife) came and played too. She is an attractive creature. When we went up to tea there were about 15 or 20 people. The P.s have a standing invitation for anyone to come to tea. I'm not good in these big parties. Eventually I rang up for a taxi, and Waterhouse, Jones (*Mansfield*), and I drove down to the Dockyard and they came on board and had drinks with me.

Monday, 29 November 1943 – Halifax

There are all sorts of rumours that Churchill, Roosevelt, and Stalin are about to meet in Cairo, and there are also rumours of peace feelers from Germany. The first really cold day. A very biting N. wind. I read A.F.O.s and told all officers they had got to start training classes in order to keep the ship's company's interest alive. In the p.m. I walked ashore into town and tried to buy some squash balls but they were not to be had. I also enquired at a tailors, but even here in Canada they are not allowed to make coats with vents. Back on board for tea. At 1845 No. 1 and I got a taxi and went to dinner with the Murphys – the Doctor's people. We had the most enormous meal. They are an extraordinarily nice family.

Tuesday, 30 November 1943 – Halifax

Another cold day. Soon after 0930 I went up to see D. but he was in conference till about 1100, so I got a car and went to the C. in C.'s offices to try and get the latest 4 stacker news. Signals have been cracking backward and forward between C. in C. Northwest Atlantic, N.S.H.Q. Ottawa, and the Admiralty, but nobody seems capable of acting. Nothing but suggestions. Whatever happens to those that can steam back to the U.K., I can't see what is holding up the paying off of *Salisbury* and *Mansfield*, and I got Bidwell to say it could go ahead. He spoke to me about taking over this new support group but it is all somewhat in the air still. Bliss told me while I was there that we'd had heavy losses in destroyers and cruisers in the Med in operations around the Dodecanese. Details unknown but glider bombs suspected.[91]

It started to snow at lunch time and continued up to about 2000, when a slight thaw set in. I made an appointment with Capt. D. at 1600 and ploughed through the wind and snow only to find he had gone out. However, I went around various Dockyard departments trying to whip them up to some sort of activity and interest in our preparations for paying off. Feeling rather sorry for myself in the evening as I've started a cough and a cold is coming on. We should have been able to steam over to U.K. and we would probably all be on leave for Xmas.

Wednesday, 1 December 1943 – Halifax

Had a most uncomfortable night. Coughing and aching and cold. I got the Sick Berth Attendant to take my temperature in the morning but as it was only 99° I got up, but didn't feel fit all day and have got a hacking cough. I don't like the way my colds seem to go to my throat and chest these days. Whole place is deep in snow this morning. No more fell but there was not much thaw. We started destoring, but had no sooner sent the first lorry load away when the Dockyard woke up to the fact that there was no where to put them, so back they all had to come. Paid 2 visits to Capt. D.'s offices. He told me if the Admiralty approve my appointment to this new support group, it was suggested I might go back over the other side for a bit as this group won't be ready for about a month. Yippeee!!!! I started to read *Nicholas Nickleby*. I have now got rid of confidential books and charts and we are to de-ammunition tomorrow, so we are at last getting on with the job.

Thursday, 2 December 1943 – Halifax

I had a good night, but not feeling very bright after breakfast I got the Doctor to look over me and as I had a temperature of rather over 100° I went back to bed and stayed there all day. My temperature was down by the evening. I read a lot. Big local sensation caused by the disappearance of Pay Comdr. Johnson of the *Canada* and his daughter. Evidence points to him having killed his daughter and then committed suicide. Both bodies are expected to be found in the Northwest Arm, from which an empty canoe has already been recovered.[92] Roosevelt, Churchill, and Chiang Kai-shek have had a meeting in Cairo at which they have said that Japan is to be deprived of all territory which she has gained since 1914. Roosevelt and Churchill are reported to be on the way to Persia to meet Stalin.

Friday, 3 December 1943 – Halifax

My temperature was down but the Doctor told me to stay in my bunk until after lunch. We were moved by tugs down to the S. end of the yard and in the p.m. we got out our ammunition. I got up after lunch but stayed in my cabin and read *Nicholas Nickleby* and wrote to J. At 1800 the Capt. of the *Caldwell* came and we had a drink and a chat. I went down to the wardroom for dinner. Warmer day and snow thawing but lots of it still there. V. annoyed and depressed at getting this cold. We are pushing ahead a bit in Italy but it is damned slow work. The body of the Johnson girl has been found in the Northwest Arm with a wound in her head, so now it looks fairly clear that he killed her and then committed suicide.

Saturday, 4 December 1943 – Halifax

Still feeling rather mouldy. I saw requestmen in the a.m. and then walked or rather waded to D.'s office. The slush and melted and melting snow in this Dockyard is indescribable. Signals continue to whiz back and forth between Admiralty, B.A.M.R., and Ottawa about all these 4 stackers, but as far as we are concerned it seems fairly definite that our crew is required at Boston by the 22nd to commission a new B.D.E., and although Halifax haven't yet decided what to do with the "body," I don't think there is likely to be much further change in *our* plans. N.S.H.Q. have asked for me for this new Canadian support group and have suggested I fly home to pick up the latest A/S warfare information at Liverpool, as the group won't be ready before 1st week in January. After lunch I started to feel a bit headachy and so I took a stretch off the land on my bunk. Feel v. sorry for myself after tea with aches and pains and finally went to bed at about 1930. The wardroom had a cocktail party, which unfortunately I didn't feel like facing. I don't know what is the matter with me but it is most unpleasant. A grey beastly day but not cold.

SUNDAY, 5 DECEMBER 1943 – HALIFAX

Feeling better. A horrible dull grey day. There was another short fall of snow. Still thawing and damp. I did not go to Divisions. At about 1100 D. rang up and asked me to come up and hear the latest news and so I bundled up in sea boots and overcoat. There is nothing really very new as regards *Salisbury* and *Mansfield,* but it now looks as if the remaining ships would probably steam across to the U.K. and pay off. Had a drink with D. in C.O.'s library before returning on board for lunch. By the p.m. I was definitely feeling much better than yesterday. Read and snoozed. At tea time I made a signal proposing to pay off on Thursday, keeping back a small retard party for cleaning up. I have been appointed President of a disciplinary court on Tuesday and so I spent quite a bit of the dog watches and after dinner reading the manual on court martial procedure.

MONDAY, 6 DECEMBER 1943 – HALIFAX

A very cold day but it was at least dry and fine. I went up to *Canada* and had quite a satisfactory interview with Seeger, who is prepared to let us have large working party after we pay off to clean up the ship and do final destoring. After tea I went to see Puxley. By ordering everybody into activity continually we are getting on. We are to pay off a.m. Friday. Didn't feel so well again this evening. An R.C.N.V.R. 2½ called Large[93] came down to see me and had lunch. He is to be the Clerk of the Court at tomorrow's Disciplinary Court on an R.C.N.R. Skipper who is charged with running a taxi, having ship's duty free liquor in his house, breaking his open arrest in *Stadacona,* and for grave discrepancies in his mess and canteen accounts. We discussed the matter for a bit and he left me the Circumstantial Letter.

TUESDAY, 7 DECEMBER 1943 – HALIFAX

Had a rotten night, couldn't sleep, aches and pains all over, and I felt sure I was for hospital tomorrow. However, at about 0400 I took 2 aspirins, which put me to sleep and I woke up sweating through everything but feeling much better. As my temperature was only just 99° I felt I had to get up and go to this Disciplinary Court. It was pouring with rain and so I got a motor car and took Knight with me as Officer of the Court. The prisoner pleaded guilty to all charges and the plea was accepted. I considered he ought to have been dismissed [from the service] but the other two members – an A/Lt Comdr R.C.N. and Skipper R.C.N.R. – were more lenient and finally we dipped him 12 months [in seniority], dismissed him his ship, and severely reprimanded him. I was very dissatisfied with the sentence.

After hanging about the C.O.'s library for a bit I eventually got a car to A.C.H.Q. I outlined the result of the board to the C. in C. I then went in to see Roger Bidwell, who told me the Admiralty had approved my going as S.O. E.G. 9, and

C. in C. W.A. had said I must be in Liverpool by Monday 13th, and so arrangements are being made for me to fly on Friday. Got back on board [and] after lunch I turned in on advice from the Doctor. I must be fit for this trip home. It would be just heartbreaking if with this chance of Xmas at home I wasn't well enough to go.

Wednesday, 8 December 1943 – Halifax

I kept to my bed till lunch time. At 1030 tugs arrived and took us over to the Gun Wharf on the Dartmouth side. I had lunch in my cabin and then with the help of Bamford I packed. I had to be very careful how I packed what I was taking with me, as I'm only allowed to take 40 lbs. In the p.m. I rang up Bidwell who told me my seat on tomorrow's train was booked. I tried to get a room for the night at the Nova Scotian but they were full up, and so Bidwell very kindly said he would give me a bed for the night. At about 1800 I went down to the wardroom and had some farewell drinks and then handed the ship over to No. 1. All most delightfully unofficial. Caught the 1915 ferry over to the Dockyard and went with my grips to the Bidwells' house. Found a Lt.Comdr. Stirling (an R.C.N. Signalman)[94] there and later on the Bidwells came in from a drinking party in the *Richmond.* I felt ever so much better in the evening. Don't know if it was the drinks or what.

Thursday, 9 December 1943 – Halifax/Montreal

A staff car arrived to take me to the station. It was very late and I thought I was going to miss the train. However, I just caught it. We pulled out at 0715 and I went straight to the dining car and had breakfast. I am in a carriage, which I suppose corresponds to first class and which at night is made up into upper and lower sleeping bunks. The seats are damned hard. After lunch I sat in what is called a library car, which has much more comfortable chairs. The country we go through is most uninteresting. Flat with mostly pine trees or bushes to look at. The train is not at all crowded and it seems to go awfully slowly with frequent stops. At dinner I sat with a Canadian R.A.M.C. officer with whom I had a good chat. When I went back to my compartment somewhere about 2100 all the bunks were made up and I turned in. The train is awfully hot.

Friday, 10 December 1943 – Montreal

I turned out and had a shave and wash in the smoking room, which has basins. After dressing I went along to the dining car for breakfast. We arrived at Montreal at about 0900, which is 0800 local time. An R.N.V.R. Lt. from N.O.I.C.'s staff met me with a car and took me to the Windsor Hotel, which is about the best in the town and very sumptuous. I kicked my heels there till about 1000 when a car arrived and took me to the N.O.I.C.'s office. I called on the old man, and after a great deal of delay they got on to the chap at the aerodrome who deals with these ferry passages and I gave him my height, weight, etc., and he told me I would be picked up at my hotel at 0800 tomorrow. Back to the Windsor where I booked a room, shifted into a better uniform, and went down to a restaurant in the basement where I had a very good lunch.

In the p.m. I went out and had a look round the shops and bought a few things for J., and then came back to my room, read, and had a nap. At about 1730 I had a bath and then went down to the same restaurant for a drink and then on to a place called the Piccadilly Bar at the Mount Royal Hotel. They are not proper bars, however, and you have to sit at a table to drink. It is something to be able to drink at all in this country. I had dinner at a very nice place called Drury's where I got talking to an Indian Army Colonel also dining by himself. Later on when he left to catch a train I got mixed up for a bit with a very drunk and very boring old Canadian. When I walked home at about 2200 there was quite a bit of snow on the ground and still snowing lightly. Quite a fine city is Montreal. Hearing so much French Canadian spoken is funny as it doesn't sound much like French at all.

Saturday, 11 December 1943 – Montreal

Just after I got up I got a call from the aerodrome saying the plane was delayed and I'd get another call about 1000, and at about 1000 another call came telling me to be ready at 1400. So then I went out. It was very cold with a bit of wind, and after about ½ hour in the streets my ears were so cold I was nearly screaming with pain, so I nipped into Eaton's big store to thaw out and incidentally bought some stockings and a belt for J. and then walked back to the hotel. I found out afterwards that the temperature was 6° below zero. At about that time the ferry service cars arrived at the hotel from the Windsor [sic] and the Mount Royal we picked up about a dozen passengers, some service and some civilian, and drove out to Dorval aerodrome, which is about 15 miles outside the city. On arrival there we had our luggage weighed, signed various forms, and were shown how to put on oxygen masks, and then waited and waited and at about 1630 we were told weather conditions were still not favourable and we couldn't go till tomorrow. Back to the Windsor, where I had a bath and changed and at about 1800 went down to the Embassy restaurant for a drink and then food. I was just turning in really early when I got a phone call from an R.C.N.V.R. Comdr. Campbell who had seen me in the hotel, and I went along to his room for a drink and a chat. Montreal is a fair city.

Sunday, 12 December 1943 – Montreal/In the air

After our postponement the cars came and collected us about 0930 and took us out to Dorval once more. We went through much the same formalities again and at last got aboard our Liberator. It is one which has been specially fitted up with seats and heating and every modern convenience. We took off at about 1200 and climbed up above the snow (it was snowing on the ground) into beautiful bright sunshine. We flew most of the time at 14,000 feet wearing our oxygen masks. A very good sandwich lunch and hot coffee was provided. It was an extremely calm trip and very comfortable. We were up above the clouds most of the time and could not see anything until just before we landed at Gander in Newfoundland, where we arrived at 1600. We spent 2 hours there and had a meal and a wash and took off again a little after 1800 which, of course, is 2300 British Summer Time. We were on oxygen most of the way and for quite a bit were up to 21,000 ft to get above the icing. I read and dozed and ate. Again flat calm and most comfortable. Can't help thinking how ghastly it must be in one of these things over Germany at the mercy of flak and fighters and with 20,000 ft of space to fall through.

Monday, 13 December 1943 – In the air/Liverpool

We touched down at Prestwick [Scotland] at about 0830 after a 9½ hours' trip. I couldn't have been more comfortable. After checking up papers, customs, etc., I had a shave and a wash and then some breakfast. Didn't feel a bit hungry. I tried to fly on to Liverpool but as there was nothing going I was taken to Kilmarnock station in a car and I caught a 1030 train to Liverpool. There was a heavy frost all over the country and I had a long cold wait at Carlisle. Eventually got to Liverpool (Exchange Station) at about 1700 and took a room at the Exchange Hotel. Feeling rather sorry for myself. Perhaps the height and the oxygen is something to do with it. I rang up J. soon after 1800, but as I didn't know my plans we couldn't decide whether or not she should come up. Turned in early.

Tuesday, 14 December 1943 – Liverpool

Feeling very much better I'm glad to say. I went along to the Tactical School and reported to Roberts just before 0900. At 1200 after a lecture the rest of the course went to finish off the first makee train game, and so as I had missed the start yesterday I went over to Derby House and saw the Chief of Staff – MacIntyre.[95] I thought perhaps I could do a bit of the course and also do a bit of discussion with other support group S.O.s, but there don't seem to be any support groups in just now. Lunched at the Derby House officers' canteen and saw Gardner and his wife – now a 3rd officer Ciphering Wren. In the p.m. we had more lectures and a short plotting exercise, after which I went to Liver Building and made some enquiries about ration cards and warrants. Back to the Exchange and rang up J. again, who said she was coming up tomorrow – whoopee!!! At lunch time I met Smitty[96] in the Bar. He has left Whaley and is now Fleet Gunnery Officer up here with an acting brass hat. He came to dinner with me at the Exchange and we had a long chat. He told me Peter Knight had been killed in Sicily a few months ago. I *am* sorry. Poor Bob Knight!![97]

Wednesday, 15 December 1943 – Liverpool

Clocked in at the school at 0900 and after our lecture we started a night battle game. I was bidden to lunch with the C. in C. with a 2½ striper, a 2 striper R.N.R., and a French naval officer who are all doing the course. C. in C. was very affable. Went on with the game in the p.m., summing up, and had one more lecture. I went back to the hotel and shifted and then went along to Lime Street Station to meet J's train due at 6:30. It was ½ hour late and when it came in no J. Met Ragg at the station also waiting to meet his wife on the London train due 7:10, which I now imagine J. is catching. This train is known to be hours late and so we adjourned to the new British Officers Club at the Adelphi and had some drinks. It is a very nice place. As the transportation office was keeping Ragg in touch and there was plenty of time I went back to the Hotel for dinner. Then I got a telephone call from the station, and eventually I found J. waiting for me there at about 2115 having arrived by some unknown train. Anyway we eventually got back to the Hotel and I got J. some sandwiches and drinks in our room. We had a tremendous chat and it was lovely to see her again.

Thursday, 16 December 1943 – Liverpool

I went to school at 0900 and for about 1½ hours we had preliminary discussions and preparations for the big day and night game and then we started to play it. I am in command of one of the support groups, which is about the most interesting command, and have a chief of staff to help me in the plotting. At lunch time met J. at the State Restaurant, but we had to wait such a long time for a table that I had to dash back to my battle before I'd really finished. There was a great deal of activity on the board in the p.m. Went back to the Hotel and met J. for a late tea and at 1830 the Gardners came and had drinks with us. They are a nice couple. Sat about in the lounge before going to bed. This is infinitely more pleasant to stay at than the Adelphi.

Friday, 17 December 1943 – Liverpool

J. caught the 10:00 train to London as she had promised to be home for Gillian's breaking up play. My battle raged all day on the table and finally came to an end at about 1600. Very good value and I think I didn't disgrace myself. I had some tea at Derby House and then rang up S.C.N.O. London from Gardner's office and had a talk with the Signal Officer about one or two W/T points. I went back to the hotel and shifted then after almost ½ hour's wait I caught a tram out to the other side of the town and went to dinner with Speak and his wife.[98] He was with me in *Firedrake* as a Sub R.N.V.R. He is now a Lieut. His wife is American and very pleasant. They gave me a lot of whisky and got me talking much too much, with the result that I missed the last tram and it took me the best part of an hour to walk back to the Hotel.

Saturday, 18 December 1943 – Liverpool/London

Roberts took the whole of the forenoon summing up our game. He is extremely good and it was most interesting. I had an early lunch at the Derby House canteen and then went back to the hotel and tried to get a taxi. After waiting as long as I dared I finally walked with my suit case to Lime Street station and caught the 2:00 train to London. Six of us from the course had reserved a carriage. It was terribly slow and we were 2½ hours late at Euston arriving at 2045. That meant I missed the 10:45 to Havant, so I went to the Euston Hotel and rang up J. to say I couldn't get down and then rang up Lillian to ask if she could give me a bed. Had some sandwiches at the hotel and then tubed to Earl's Court and walked to the Robinsons' House where I was given a camp bed in the drawing room.

Sunday, 19 December 1943 – London/Prinsted

I got up around 0715 and had some breakfast that Lillian had prepared for me over night, and then let myself out and walked to Earl's Court Station. It was raining. Got to Waterloo in good time and caught the 8:27 to Havant. It was a slow train and I didn't arrive till nearly 1045. Found a taxi waiting for me and drove home where I got a very tumultuous welcome from the family. After lunch G. went off to play with the Garretts and J. and I took Raymond for a short walk in his pram. We had some singing after tea and at about 1830 Allan and Dodo and Lola and the Stokes came in for drinks. Very nice to see Allan again, who is now Captain of the Signal School.[99] *Is* it good to be home again and *am* I lucky.

2
Shaking Down, January-March 1944

Support groups played a crucial role on the North Atlantic during 1943, tilting the tactical balance against U-boats by reinforcing close escorts at critical junctures of convoy battles. Like thirsty sailors on a run ashore, senior officers always wanted more, but given the chronic shortage of escorts, the challenge was to find enough ships for support groups without weakening close escort forces. In the summer of 1943, Rear-Adm. L.W. Murray, the commander-in-chief Canadian Northwest Atlantic Command, had scraped enough ships together to form E.G. 9, but was then forced to disband the support group after two of its ships, the destroyer HMCS *St Croix* and the frigate HMS *Itchen,* were sunk in the bitter fight for ONS 18/ON 202. The withdrawal of the U-boats from the North Atlantic in November, however, enabled the Allies to free up escorts, and in December Murray resurrected E.G. 9 and selected Frank Layard as its senior officer.[1]

In all, fifteen warships sailed in E.G. 9 during the fifteen months that Layard commanded the group. Some, like the corvettes *Atholl, Baddeck, North Bay, Frontenac,* and *Owen Sound,* stayed with the group only for its first months, while others, like the frigate *St Pierre,* joined just before the end of the war. In these instances, Layard had little chance to form an impression of either the individual ships or, more importantly, their commanding officers. It was different with the frigates *Matane, Swansea, Saint John, Stormont, Meon, Monnow, Nene, Port Colborne,* and *Loch Alvie.* They made up the core of the group at various times, and their respective commanding officers – Lt.-Cdr. Alan H. Easton, Cdr. Clarence King, Lt.-Cdr. William R. Stacey, Lt.-Cdr. George A. Myra, Lt.-Cdr. St. Clair Balfour, Cdr. Edgar George Skinner, Lt.-Cdr. E.R. Shaw, Lt.-Cdr. C.J. Angus, and Lt.-Cdr. Ernest G. Old – formed Layard's "Band of Brothers." As the reader will appreciate from Layard's comments, this group of Canadian officers was about as far from the idyllic Shakespearean or Nelsonic concepts of professionalism and camaraderie as he could have imagined. That said, E.G. 9's effectiveness was due in large part to their ability and their positive response to his leadership. It is of value, therefore, to take a close look at these officers so as to appreciate what they brought to the group in terms of skill and experience, and to understand what Layard sometimes had to endure.

When considered as a group, their most notable characteristic is that eight of these nine commanding officers belonged to the Royal Canadian Naval Reserve, or RCNR, and were thus professional seamen who had joined the navy from the merchant marine. None were regular force RCN, and *Meon*'s Balfour was the only volunteer reservist, or RCNVR. This reflected a RCN policy that saw the majority of frigate commands go to naval reserve officers. In fact, they commanded forty-three of the navy's seventy frigates, while volunteer reservists commanded twenty-six and regulars just one.[2] The navy's plan was to give its most important small ship commands to its most experienced seamen – regulars, who depended upon promotion, drove destroyers, while VRs commanded most of the late war corvettes – but it was not a policy that Layard welcomed. He was partial to volunteer reservists. "After tea Easton and I walked up to Ops," he wrote in 1944, "where we were told 4 new frigates from Canada are joining this group and all the corvettes are being taken away making an all frigate group. It is a right and logical thing to do I suppose, but I'm damned sorry to lose the corvettes, especially the COs who are really a fine keen bunch of VRs. The NR types I'm likely to get in the frigates probably will be better seamen and more experienced but not half as keen and alive."[3] To his expectations he could have added "unique and individualistic," as, to a man, his NRs liked to do things their own way.

Layard found an early companion in *Matane*'s Easton. In many ways, they were two of a kind; like his senior officer, Easton was soft-spoken, philosophical, introspective, and a keen observer of world affairs. Easton had entered the merchant service in the early 1920s, but over time, he developed an abiding dislike of life at sea, and went ashore in the mid-1930s to work for Bell Telephone in Montreal. When war broke out in 1939, Easton found himself in a difficult situation. He wanted to go to sea, but his strong attachment to life ashore and his young family, and his equally strong abhorrence to life at sea, kept him from enlisting even though he fully understood the grave threat posed by Hitler's Germany. Like so many others, however, when the situation deteriorated in the spring of 1940 with Germany's invasion of Norway, France, and the Low Countries, his sense of duty overcame any personal considerations and he joined the RCNR.[4]

Easton described his war service in *50 North*, which stands as one of the classic memoirs of the Battle of the Atlantic. After a stint in a British cruiser, Easton commanded two RCN corvettes, and *50 North* describes the challenges of command in a strange naval environment while fighting a determined enemy in the grim environment of the North Atlantic, which he grew to despise more then he had in peacetime. These demands took a physical toll. Recalling the eve of an operation later in the war, Easton complained, "I could really raise no enthusiasm for this project. I felt vaguely annoyed that I would have to stay up all night. I was tired and had that gnawing pain. At this time I could no longer keep it away with cocoa or milk or food and it was not only in my stomach, it had reached round to my back, like a pair of interior claws, and gave me pains between the shoulder blades."[5] These ulcers, which were common amongst the captains that fought the war at sea, finally drove Easton ashore in August 1944.

Rather than leading E.G. 9 from his own ship, Layard was initially appointed additional to Easton's frigate HMCS *Matane,* and thus the two officers had to share the bridge. Layard faced this situation a number of times in E.G. 9, and his diary shows that he was rarely comfortable commanding the group from someone else's ship. That discomfort was shared by the captains he sailed with, who had to endure a senior officer looking over their shoulder. "It would be like having a high-powered elderly relative living with you," Easton recalled thinking upon learning that Layard was joining him in *Matane.* "It would be difficult sometimes in drawing the line of responsibility and could be the cause of muddle and perhaps conflicting orders on the bridge; in some cases possibly interference, and that could lead to strained relations between us."[6] Easton steeled himself for a situation that might prove impossible:

> As long as I can remember I had disliked in advance people I was forced to meet – since my mother had taken me to visit her friends whose nice little boys she wanted me to know. But I had been unable to dislike the S.O.
>
> Before we sailed I had spoken to him about our relative positions. We were in his day-cabin, which was next to mine, a kind of office. His dark eyes looked at me gravely. "I hate to say it, sir, but I think we'll both have to be very careful not to foul each other's flags."
>
> His mouth moved very slightly as though he were tasting a small peppermint. Then he said, "I hope very much we won't have any difficulties or differences. But I know what you mean. As a matter of fact I didn't want this job either. I would much rather have remained in command of my own ship."
>
> It was good to hear this, in a way, but it left me wondering if I had not spoken too abruptly. I apologized for having risked spoiling his welcome, but I did want to state my apprehensions clearly at the outset of our relationship. He obviously understood and we let it go at that. But I continued to feel something of a boor for having spoken out. He seemed to be a sensitive chap and I could not help thinking that there might have been no need to bring the matter up at all.[7]

As the diary shows, Layard's discomfort continued, as he wanted to correct the deficiencies he saw in *Matane,* but the two officers grew to enjoy each other's company. When Easton learned in April 1944 that he had been appointed captain of the destroyer HMCS *Saskatchewan* and was reflecting upon leaving a ship and crew he enjoyed, he noted with complete sincerity that "I knew of at least one man who would be pleased: our Commander. He was away on a few days leave in England, and would be delighted when he heard the news. I was glad."[8] Unfortunately, there was a minor dispute in their last days together. By normal custom, Easton wanted to take his steward, P.B. Aucoin, with him to *Saskatchewan,* but the sailor wanted to remain in *Matane.* After wrestling with the decision Layard finally chose not to force the issue by ordering Aucoin to leave, and he stayed in the frigate. Sadly, and this gnawed at Easton for the rest of his life, his former steward was one of two sailors killed when *Matane* was hit by a glider bomb in July 1944.

Although Easton became a close confidant of Layard, Cdr. Clarence King, CO of *Swansea* and second in command of E.G. 9, stoked feelings of anxiety and inadequacy. King was an experienced sailor and warrior, and was probably the RCN's oldest commanding officer. Cmdre. G.W.G. Simpson noted in September 1944 that King's precise birthdate was unknown, but according to RCN records he was born in London, England, on 23 April 1886.[9] He first went to sea in the British merchant service at the age of thirteen and earned his master's certificate twelve years later. King retired from the sea to farm in British Columbia's Okanagan Valley before the First World War erupted but joined the RNR as a sub-lieutenant in July 1916. King served in anti-submarine operations in British waters in motor launches, trawlers, and Q-ships, and was awarded a DSC for his part in an action against a U-boat in May 1917.[10] He returned to farming in the Canadian west in 1919 but, despite being fifty-three years old, volunteered again when duty beckoned twenty years later. King served in the RNR for two years before transferring to the RCNR in January 1942. Later that year, while in command of the corvette HMCS *Oakville,* he rammed and sank *U-94* in the Caribbean, earning a bar to his DSC. He assumed command of *Swansea* in January 1944, and within four months played a role in the destruction of two more U-boats.

Although they never became close, Layard respected King. "He is a nice old boy," he wrote upon meeting him. "To be at sea in small ships at age of 57 isn't too bad."[11] As time passed, King's success in bagging two more U-boats rattled Layard: "I'm beginning to get a slight inferiority complex about King in *Swansea.* What with his actual successes, and one thing and another, I believe he would do my job better than me."[12] That was just Layard's lack of confidence bubbling to the surface; he had a high professional opinion of King and his written evaluations were laudatory. In April 1944 he described him "as an efficient and popular commanding officer" who "has lost none of his dash and possesses the right offensive spirit."[13] When King left E.G. 9 in August 1944 to command his own group, Layard was even more effusive, describing him as "an excellent commanding officer who has maintained a clean, efficient and happy ship. A loyal and dependable divisional officer who on many occasions in my absence has handled the group most ably. For all his years he is fit and extremely alert mentally and full of enthusiasm and vigour."[14] Compliments aside, Layard was relieved by his departure. On 12 August, the day after he drafted King's S206 evaluation form, he wrote in his diary, "I had a C.O.s meeting and we had a long quack about this and that. I must say nice as old King was, I'm damned glad he has gone as I always felt he was slightly antagonistic to me and now it is much easier." Perhaps that was a natural reaction towards an officer whom he pegged as a rival. For his part, King resented leaving a successful group operating on the very front line of the anti-submarine war: "He is keen for action," noted Captain D Newfoundland in his next evaluation, "and was very disappointed at leaving a Support Group to join a Mid-Ocean Group."

While Layard's feelings towards King seem never to have evolved, after a tempestuous beginning he grew to be impressed with *Saint John*'s Lt.-Cr. William R. Stacey. Another old hand, who had been born on 8 July 1901, Stacey rose to become a master mariner with ABC Packers out of Vancouver, British Columbia. After joining the RCNR in September 1939, he served as an examination officer at Esquimalt until appointed to command the minesweeper *Malpeque* in November 1941. Over the next twenty-eight months, *Malpeque* operated out of Sydney and St. John's on local escort duty. This was a difficult time for the RCN, and escorts and especially their COs were pushed to the limit. Stacey responded well and in February 1944 was appointed to command *Saint John*. There, the situation was far from satisfactory. The previous CO and first lieutenant had been relieved in the midst of work-ups, but the final report submitted by the training commander in Halifax credited Stacey and his first lieutenant, Lt. C.G. McIntosh, RCNR, with turning the ship around: "both showed commendable aggressiveness in stamping out the last traces of the previous laxer regime and in establishing an iron-bound routine." Stacey, the report continued, "can be counted on to continue training until *Saint John* attains the maximum efficiency of which she is capable."[15]

Stacey fulfilled those expectations, although Layard was initially unimpressed by his qualities as an officer. On 30 May 1944, shortly after *Saint John* joined E.G. 9, Layard visited the ship and to his "disgust and wrath" found Stacey still asleep at 1015. Later in the morning Layard ordered Stacey to report to *Matane*:

> When he arrived I taxed him with being in bed at 1015, and he said he had been working on the operation orders [for Operation Neptune] until 0200 in the morning, which I believe he genuinely considered entitled him to lie in. I also asked them why his Whaler was hoisted when I made a signal yesterday saying boats were to be exercised under oars and why his Dr. had not been available this forenoon. These R.[C.]N.R. types are hopeless to deal with. When they receive a blast they must always find excuses, and this a.m. Stacey went away thoroughly disgruntled and feeling he'd been v. unjustly treated.

Perhaps he had been, but the conversation reveals the high standards that Layard expected of his officers.

Layard's opinion of Stacey rose sharply as he consistently demonstrated ample professional competence, especially in the destruction of *U-247* in September 1944. In the evaluation he wrote upon Stacey's departure from the group later in the year, Layard showered him with praise: "An efficient, reliable and conscientious officer and an experienced seaman. He has served afloat with distinction for the whole of the war and has proved himself a sound and capable Commanding Officer with a thorough knowledge of his job. He is a man with great determination and will power. I consider that with his knowledge, experience and personality he would make a good senior officer of a group and he is strongly recommended for promotion." Commodore Simpson, commodore D Western Approaches, supported Layard's recommendation, describing Stacey as "an excellent seaman and loyal officer with power of leadership."[16] Although mutual respect had evolved between the two, the Canadian remained his own man. When Layard was forced to transfer to *Saint John* in November 1944, Stacey was given the choice of staying with his ship or taking leave in Canada. Rather than sharing his bridge, he chose the latter.[17]

Layard took the responsibility of evaluating subordinates seriously, and he probably pondered the S206 for Cdr. Edgar George Skinner longer than any other. *Monnow*'s captain was one of the true characters of the Canadian navy. A Newfoundlander born in 1897, "The Old Man of the Sea," as Layard called him, had fought with the Royal Newfoundland Regiment in the First World War. He suffered a serious head wound, but survived the trenches to enter the merchant marine, where he rose to master of both sail and steam vessels. He joined the RCNR in 1929, and in the late 1930s was number one of the RCN's sail training vessel, HMCS *Venture*. He commanded armed yachts, corvettes, a tender, and a destroyer during the Battle of the Atlantic, and in June 1942 was awarded the DSC for his "devotion to duty" and "invaluable service in connection with the escort of convoys during exceptionally severe winter months."[18]

Skinner posed a conundrum for his superiors in that although he completely lacked naval bearing, his ships ultimately performed well. He had more than a few rough edges, but was nonetheless a warrior – Rear-Adm. Leonard Murray described him as having "the guts of the devil."[19] Cmdre. G.O. Stephenson, the legendary Tiger of Tobermory, who commanded Western Approaches' sea training establishment, was unsure what to make of the crusty Newfoundlander. Despite Skinner's considerable experience, Stephenson noted he was "very erratic and gives queer orders which are not always clearly understood or carried out. He has a wonderful faith in his ship, her Officers and men. It is possible that this great faith in them will inspire them, they need inspiration badly."[20]

One would think a staid traditionalist like Layard might have had trouble with Skinner. Instead, he understood, or was at least willing to tolerate, the contradiction posed by Skinner. Layard wrote in his S206:

> This officer acts contrary to nearly every accepted naval standard and custom and yet is a good wartime leader and small ship Commanding officer. He unfortunately knows very little about the Navy and never seems to train and he is intolerant of

> Naval etiquette and custom. He also *will* argue with his senior officers. But he is very jealous of the reputation of his ship and he understands Canadians, and so by his unorthodox methods he achieves efficiency and instills into officers and men a good team spirit and pride of ship. He is a strong personality and is extremely forthright and open. Not an easy man for the Navy officer to get on with but nevertheless he has always been very loyal to me, and I have always had confidence in him.

Commodore Simpson described Skinner as "a personality": "I like Skinner as a keen seaman with offensive spirit and [for being] an obstinate rascal. On the other hand due to his unorthodox methods he is a scourge to my staff and myself and causes more unnecessary paper work than the whole of an entire group. He is too old to learn and at any rate cannot be persuaded that there is anything he does not know."[21] It takes all types to win a war, and Simpson and Layard were willing to put up with Skinner's attitude so long as he ran an effective ship: Layard's comment that "he understands Canadians" seems particularly telling. That said, Skinner proved to be a source of continual exasperation throughout the winter of 1944-5, and Layard's patience sometimes wore thin.

None of the other commanding officers in E.G. 9 had the same impact on Layard as Easton, King, Stacey, or Skinner, though all were solid performers. Layard seems to have been especially impressed by Lt.-Cdr. George A. Myra, RCNR, in *Stormont* and Lt.-Cdr. St. Clair Balfour, RCNVR, in *Meon.* The only one who really seemed to spark a negative reaction was Lt.-Cdr. Ernest G. Old, RCNR, whom Layard rode with in *Loch Alvie* during the winter of 1945. Although he thought him "a nice old boy but rather lazy," Layard disliked his cautious ship handling and thought he drove *Loch Alvie* "like a battleship rather than a frigate."[22] More disconcerting was Old's comportment on the bridge, ranting at his officers when things went awry: "I've come to the conclusion that the real trouble with Old is that he is too old and quite out of sympathy and too intolerant of his young and inexperienced officers. A more friendly and helpful attitude would get much better results."[23]

Two junior officers rounded out Layard's Band of Brothers, and, interestingly, both were young Canadian volunteer reservists. What is startling, given Layard's long service in the Royal Navy and the scorn in which regular officers normally held reservists, is that he considered Lt. John Band to be the finest first lieutenant he had ever had, and Lt. David Kilgour the best navigator of small ships he had ever seen, remarkable praise for two relatively inexperienced officers. Band was a graduate of HMCS *Royal Roads,* who had only two years at sea in the Pacific with the corvette HMCS *Dawson* before becoming first lieutenant of *Swansea* in late 1943. Besides being a good seaman, Band was fastidious in his cleanliness and brought a tone of civility to the wardroom, insisting, for example, that at least one night a week they listen to classical music on the phonograph instead of always playing popular dance tunes.[24] Layard grew exceedingly loyal to Band and was sad to see him go when *Swansea* left the group in late 1944. He tried hard to bring him back as his "flag captain" but the end of the war prevented that from happening. Nevertheless, the two gentleman sailors remained lifelong friends.

Kilgour's contribution was more practical. E.G. 9 spent most of the war operating inshore, where a premium was placed on accurate navigation. But there was more to it than keeping a ship off the rocks. The ability to calculate precise fixes on wrecks and other navigational marks was a key component to the classification of contacts in inshore anti-submarine warfare (see Chapter 4), and a great deal of credit for E.G. 9's success was due to Kilgour's ability. More than anything, however, the young Canadian "pilot" gave Layard a level of comfort that allowed him to focus on the myriad other demands associated with running a group at sea.

For the most part, Layard did well by his Canadian officers. There is no question, however, that as he prepared to head for Canada in January 1944 to assume command of E.G. 9 he felt more than his usual level of trepidation. His first experiences with the Canadians in the fall of 1943 warned that the future would hold many challenges. Even more worrisome was the uncertainty about when he would next see his family. If he stayed in Halifax, as seemed likely, that might not be until the conclusion of a war whose end was not even on the horizon. All in all, there was much to trouble Layard as he fussed over arrangements to return to Canada.

Saturday, 1 January 1944 – Prinsted

I had weekend leave and didn't go to work. A nice sunny morning. I did some edge trimming in the garden. At about 1130 I took Gillian in to Portsmouth where Pay Cdr. Lewis was taking them to the Pantomime. J. and I furious that even on her week end off we couldn't be together, as I had to stick around waiting for a call from S.C.N.O. (London). The call came through at about 1230 saying there was still no news about my air passage but they expected to know and would ring me again on Monday. At lunch I took Tich for a walk on the marshes and came home through Chidham. After tea Raymond and I played the gramophone in the drawing room. He adores it, especially "Tell the Boz," an old Leslie Henson record. J. and G. came home about 1730, J. with a splitting headache. G. absolutely thrilled with the pantomime. The Scott-Moncrieffs had asked us in for a New Year's drink, but J. wasn't feeling good enough and so I went by myself. Most of the village was there. Lloyd, who had just got an O.B.E., and Allan a mention in dispatches. I told Lloyd, who is on Commodore Combined Ops staff, a few things about the Northney Camps[25] that J. had told me. He said they knew most of it but it was damned difficult to get rid of these useless drunken types who are in command of the camps. When I got home I found J. had gone to bed as she was feeling so rotten. Roberts of the Derby House Tactical School has got a C.B.E., I'm glad to see.

...

Tuesday, 4 January 1944 – Prinsted/London/Prinsted

Decided on waking up that I'd go to London, as a personal visit to S.C.N.O. would be more satisfactory than telephoning. I'm getting a bit worried about this delay in getting back to Canada. I caught the 0945 bus to Havant, and while waiting on Havant Station for the 10:30 I went and talked to the Wallaces. On arrival at Waterloo I tubed to Piccadilly and went to the S.C.N.O.'s office. They tell me a "monster" – the *Pasteur* – sails on Saturday direct for Halifax taking about 6 days, and they will get me a passage in her, which is better than waiting indefinitely for this very uncertain air passage. Called on S.C.N.O. himself (Capt. Houghton R.C.N.),[26] who kindly asked me to lunch and took me to the East India Club, in St. James's Square and a very nice club. A good lunch and he seems v. pleasant. I then went for a hair cut and then browsed through several book shops and bought Mahan's *Life of Nelson* at Maggs in Berkeley Square. Back to S.C.N.O.'s for a ration card and then to Waterloo for the 4:45. Met Jim Bird on the platform and travelled down with him. Bussed to Emsworth and walked home from there. After a few minutes with the children I went to join J. at Miss Goldsworthy's drinking party. Quite a big gathering and actually some drink. A cold but nice day. Raymond's 3rd birthday. The Russians have broken through in a big way W. of Kiev, and are within a few miles of the old Polish frontier.

Wednesday, 5 January 1944 – Prinsted

There was quite a hard frost last night. A bright cold sunny day. J. went off to work and at about 0930 I started out for a walk with Tich. I went through W. & E. Ashing and along the back road to Chichester. I have somehow strained a muscle in my left shin and I was rather lame when I got there and so hopped on the first bus I saw and came home. Emily [the nanny] told me the S.C.N.O. had rung me up just after I'd gone out, so I rang back and they told me since I'd been there yesterday they'd found there was no accommodation for me in the *Pasteur*, but Canada House had more or less promised an air passage early next week. I spent most of the p.m. cutting the polygonum down from the garage so that the honeysuckle can spread. I came home for tea and at 1830 we went to drink with Jane. Dock was there.

...

Cdr. Frank Layard, RN, at Scapa Flow on 19 February 1945, the day he left HMCS *Saint John*. Raymond Layard

A reflective Layard on the bridge of HMCS *Swansea*, November 1944. Raymond Layard

The most important day of Frank Layard's life, 3 December 1932. According to a newspaper account, Joan wore a golden gown. RAYMOND LAYARD

BOTTOM: Joan and Tich in the Irish Free State, 1934. RAYMOND LAYARD

FACING PAGE, TOP: The interwar navy put a premium on spit and polish and shiny bright work. Here HMS *Vivacious* lives up to her name in Venice in July 1932. RAYMOND LAYARD

In his younger days Layard was an avid sportsman who played rugby, football, and golf with enthusiasm. Here he proudly displays the trophy won by HMS *Walpole*'s officers and petty officers championship football team in 1934. Raymond Layard

The staff of the Experimental Department at Whale Island before the war. Layard stands behind his friend Bob Knight, who is in civilian attire. Raymond Layard

Layard was well schooled in fleet work. This is the 6th Destroyer Flotilla, with Layard's HMS *Walpole* at the end of the line, manoeuvring at speed during the Atlantic Fleet's 1934 autumn cruise. Raymond Layard

"I wasn't v. clever putting my ship alongside." Layard brings HMS *Broke* alongside the cruiser HMS *Sheffield* on 7 November 1942 to embark 300 American soldiers for the attack on Algiers. RAYMOND LAYARD

Layard leads *Broke*'s survivors ashore at Gibraltar after the attack on Algiers. Captain H.L. St. J. Fancourt, RN, is to Layard's left in the khaki uniform and cap. RAYMOND LAYARD

By 1943, the Town class four stackers were in terrible shape. This is HMS *Mansfield* of W 9 in August 1943. Layard came under her orders a number of times that fall.
DND REA 253-76

Operation "Pub Crawl." Layard descending a rope ladder to attend a briefing onboard the escort carrier HMS *Biter* during a patrol in the North Atlantic off Ireland in April 1944.
RAYMOND LAYARD

The bustling Halifax dockyard in June 1944. For Layard, "Slackers" was truly a foreign port. LAC PA115367

Lt.-Cdr. Alan Easton on *Matane*'s quarterdeck in early 1944. Despite some early unease, Easton became a friend and confidant of Layard's. LAC PA206442

Cdr. Clarence King. An experienced, skilled sailor, whom Layard pegged as a rival. DND L-5356

Monday, 10 January 1944 – Prinsted

J. and I had an early breakfast, and after a very tearful farewell to Gillian we walked to Southbourne Station and caught the 8:30 train. We changed at Bosham into the London train and got to Victoria at 1040. Not quite as fast as the Waterloo route but less crowded. Parked my gear in the cloak room and then bussed to Piccadilly where we first of all went to the bank and then walked to the Pastoria and booked a table for lunch. We then separated and I went to Canada House to get my instructions only to be told that this air passage was off, so I went to the R.C.N. offices, where they said they were v. sorry but aeroplanes were just not flying and they had booked me a passage in the *Queen Elizabeth* sailing the 13th. I put off time in the second hand book shop in the Charing Cross Road, and then met J. for lunch at the Pastoria at 1300. She was surprised and delighted at my news. After a good lunch we went to Swan & Edgars and another big shop looking for a dress for J. but found nothing to her liking. So then we went to the Monseigneur News Cinema and then had tea in a small restaurant in Duke of York Street. We then went back to the R.C.N. office for my embarkation orders and sat a long time while a Wren tried to get me a room in a hotel for tomorrow night but without success. Everywhere is completely booked up, and so finally decided to spend the night at home. At about 1800 I dashed to Victoria, got my things from the cloak room, dashed over to Waterloo where I met J., and we just caught the 6:45 to Havant. From there on to Southbourne and arrived home at about 2100 much to Emily's surprise.

Tuesday, 11 January 1944 – Prinsted

Gillian was v. surprised when I went into her room in the morning. J. went off to work. After ringing up the R.C.N. office in London and telling them to cancel my room I went out and raked the lawn. At 1030 I set out on foot for Emsworth with Tich and almost at once it started to rain. Got the fish and some buns by which time it was so wet that I came back by bus. I then caught another bus to Havant and got my collars back from Chapman's laundry and came home by the next bus. After lunch I played with the children in the drawing room. At about tea time it stopped raining. I shifted into uniform and went out to catch the 1645 bus to Portsmouth but got a lift in a car as far as Havant and bussed on. Met J. at the Queens[27] and at 1800 we went along to the Superintendent's cocktail party. All the Admirals, Commodores, Captains were there, also Allan and Dodo with whom we joined forces afterwards for dinner at the Queens. Allan has got a bar to his D.S.O. and is v. bucked.[28] They gave us a lift home in A.'s official car. Depressing that my last day should have been so wet and depressing.

Wednesday, 12 January 1944 – Prinsted/Glasgow

Early breakfast again, and I was nearly in tears when I bid good bye to J. G. came to Southbourne Station and saw me off in the 8:30 train to Victoria. Oh these partings!! Parked my luggage again in the cloaks and bussed to Piccadilly and got some American money from the Bank and bought a couple of books at Hatchard's and some sandwiches for the train. Then back to Victoria for my gear and taxied to Euston and caught the 1:00 train to Glasgow. Not at all crowded. Read and slept and got v. bored. We arrived at Glasgow 1½ hours late at 2330. Although I'd wired, there was no room for me at the Central so after some supper, which I was lucky to get, I spent a very uncomfortable night on a sofa in the lounge.

Thursday, 13 January to Tuesday, 18 January 1944 – Glasgow/At sea
After a most uncomfortable night I got up and shaved in the public wash place. No time for breakfast, as I had to catch a 0740 train to Gourock in order to be there by 0900 as ordered. On arrival, after a lot of hanging about on the pier with a great many other officers, we all went on board a tug. When it became known that the tug wasn't leaving until 1130, I walked along the pier to where the destroyers were berthed, went on board [the destroyer HMS] *Ambuscade*, and begged a bottle of gin off them as these great monsters are dry. To my great surprise and delight I saw Wallace, who relieved me at the Admiralty, step on board the tug. He is going across to be executive officer of a new escort carrier. An Act. Capt. Currey and a Comd. E. Parker were the other brass hats.[29] We all cursed Sea Transport bitterly in putting us to this maximum discomfort, sleeping in hotel lounges, etc., in order to clock in at 0900 and then keep us waiting till nearly midday. At last we shoved off and arrived alongside the *Queen Elizabeth* in the stream.

I find I am sharing a 12 berth cabin with Wallace, as the ship is never full when westbound. We have a bathroom of our own but only salt water. Not bad really but even so there are some pip squeak civilians with single cabins. Knox Little as a Commodore, Leslie Burgin, and some other minor Cabinet minister are on board. We sailed sometime after dark. I sit at a table with Currey, Wallace, Parker, a 2½ Fleet Air Arm called Callingham, and 2 young Wren officers. Really rather a cheerful party. Meals are in 2 sittings (3 meals) and we are 2nd sitting. There is the 1st class lounge in which we can sit, but only v. uncomfortable upright chairs, otherwise one has to lie on one's bunk. No chairs in the cabins. The deck space for walking about is v. limited and there seems to be no part allotted to officers and one is always being banged out of the way by sailors, soldiers, and airmen, which makes me v. angry. When we got further west 1st class passengers were allowed on the boat and gun decks. Currey also had gin and whisky and he, Wallace, I, and Parker used to meet daily in one cabin for a quick one before lunch and before dinner, and just managed to make our stock last the trip.

We were diverted on to a very N.'ly course and for a part of the time it was v. cold and quite rough, not that a ship this size moves much in the worst weather.

We did about 25 knots most of the way. A retired Commander called Jack is a permanent Naval Staff Officer on board and we had a drink with him one day.[30] The whole ship was stifling hot between decks. On Sunday there was a Church of England service in the lounge, conducted by the ship's American padre. A Canadian read the lesson and a passage; English parson preached. The sermon was v. good and impressed me a lot and later on I spoke to him and went to his cabin and had a talk and aired my views on religion and prayer. Didn't get quite a satisfactory answer out of him, but at his invitation had another talk with him a day or two later. A very nice middle aged man called Allen.

On the last evening or two we organized a card game after dinner with our meal mates. Currey, Wallace, and Parker can all be v. amusing and we laughed a lot. The last evening of all there was a dreadful sort of concert in the lounge, and the climax came when we were all asked to stand and sing "Abide With Me." Read quite a lot.

Wednesday, 19 January 1944 – At sea/New York

Currey, Wallace, Parker, and I just managed to have a drink each before lunch, which absolutely finished our combined stock. After lunch I was up on deck watching our approach to New York. It was cold but not bitter, but unfortunately very misty. The sight of the sky scrapers was certainly most impressive. We berthed at about 1730 and finally got ashore at about 1830. All the naval officers were taken in buses to the Barbizon Plaza Hotel, where there is a permanent small naval staff, a naval club, and a certain number of rooms taken over by the R.N. It acts as an officer's depot for officers landing and passing through.

After a wash and brush up we filled in various forms, got an advance of pay, and then Currey, Wallace, Parker, and I advanced on the bar and proceeded to suck a vast number of whiskies and sodas very quickly. It was obvious from the start that it was going to be one of those evenings. We made the acquaintance of a Yank who was about as bottled as we were and he took us somewhere for food, and then back to his flat of which he was v. proud, and then to the Royal Plaza bar. From there at about 0200 Currey and Parker went home, but Wallace and I, who were now right in our stride, rather like the old 1st Flotilla form, went off with another elderly American – an awfully nice chap – and went on to God knows how many more places including the Stork Club and finally tottered home about 0500. Grand fun but I'm afraid our friends must have paid for nearly everything.

Thursday, 20 January 1944 – New York/Boston

I was awakened by Wallace ringing me up at about 0800. I got up and came down to breakfast feeling fine but definitely not yet sober. Currey joined us for breakfast, and afterwards I hung about in the R.N. Club place waiting for the duty officer to find out what arrangements could be made for my trip to Halifax. I began to wilt badly as the forenoon drew on. Eventually I heard that it was all fixed for me to catch the 1500 train this afternoon. At about 1200 Currey, Wallace, Parker, and I walked to the Royal Plaza Hotel and in the cocktail bar (one of the places we'd been to last night) we met our second host of the evening by appointment for drinks and I had a very much needed horse's neck. Our friend – the one who had taken Wallace and I on the second part of our binge – was an awfully nice elderly American of breeding and, one would imagine, position. After that we returned to the Barbizon Plaza bar, but after another quick one or two the others went off to lunch while I packed my trunk, paid my bill, and took a taxi to the Grand Central Station.

A quick impression is that a much greater part of New York is "smart" than London. Grand Central quite took our breath away. Its magnificence was unbelievable. Picked up my tickets and took my seat in a Pullman car on the 3:00 to Boston. Train was v. hot and I was feeling distinctly ill. Had a very hasty dinner on the train and arrived at Boston at about 2000. Just as I was getting out I got into conversation with a young woman with whom I shared a taxi to the North Station. Then we had a drink together and she v. kindly kept me company until my train left at 2130. On this train I travelled in great comfort in a drawing room all to myself. Quite a mild day and surprisingly no snow on the ground. Left my waistcoat in N.Y. – Damn!!

Friday, 21 January 1944 – Boston/Halifax

A most comfortable night. Got up about 0800 but found there was no breakfast car on the train. We crossed the Canadian border at about 0830, and at 0930 we stopped for about ½ hour when we could get breakfast in the station. Put the clocks on an hour. At Saint John, where we arrived at 1300, a dining car was put on, and after a considerable wait I got some lunch. Read and slept in the p.m. Had dinner at about 1900 and finally arrived at Halifax at 2330. Hoped someone might be meeting me, but as there was no one I went into the Nova Scotian Hotel, where I was luckily able to get a room without booking, had a bath, and went to bed! A lovely mild sunny day. There was snow on the ground and ice on the lakes all along the line in Canada, but it was thawing hard and roads were just slush. Very unusual weather for January.

Saturday, 22 January 1944 – Halifax

After breakfast I rang up Puxley who sent a car for me. I went to Capt. D.'s office and discussed matters. In spite of the delay in my return the group is nothing like ready. It consists of my flag ship the *Matane* and *Swansea,* both frigates, and the corvettes *Baddeck, North Bay, Frontenac, Owen Sound,* and *Atholl.* Later on I went on board *Matane,* who seems to be having a sort of small refit.

The Captain (an R.C.N.R. 2½ called Easton) I've met before and seems quite nice. My quarters are still very incomplete and are being converted from what was a single and double cabin. We discussed a good many things and had a look at the bridge, and later on the Captain of the *Swansea* (a A/Comdr R.C.N.R. called King) came over. The more I think of this business of being S.O. in somebody else's ship the less I like it.[31]

I went up to the C.O.'s Library and met Waterhouse, who took me to lunch at Admiralty House, and then he and I went out by car to St Margaret's Bay where he had about a dozen corvettes and frigates doing their sea training, among them 2 of mine, the *Frontenac* and the *Owen Sound,* which I went on board and had a look at and met the Captains. I'm getting frightened at this idea of trying to run this R.C.N. group.[32] We got back to Halifax soon after 1800 and eventually I went home with Prentice, who is kindly putting me up until I can live in the *Matane.* Waterhouse came to dinner. Still v. mild weather, there is no snow at all in Halifax.

...

Monday, 24 January 1944 – Halifax

A very cold wind and spasmodic snow falls all day, but still damp and slushy under foot. 0830 breakfast and then I caught the 0915 tram to the Dockyard. Went on board *Matane.* Easton took me to the joiner's shop where I looked at the plan of my day cabin and discussed the furniture. Got back to find the Captains of the *Atholl, Baddeck,* and *North Bay* on board, all wavy stripe V.R.s.[33] We had a chat about this and that and a drink. They seem nice and v. keen. Had a sandwich lunch and some drinks at the C.O.'s Library and then went to see the Drafting Captain at *Stadacona* but got no change out of him. I'm not allowed a steward to myself as S.O., which I think is scandalous. I then spent many hours between the Dockyard offices and *Stadacona* trying to find out about my pay, travelling expenses, etc., but nobody seems to know v. much about it.

Caught a tram at about 1715 and got back to the Prentices at about 1800. Did some writing and changed my clothes. Mount-Haes[34] came to dinner again and afterwards I was simply overcome with sleep. The 5th Army have made an advance landing quite close to Rome, which seems to have gone well in its initial stages and may lead to quick developments.

Tuesday, 25 January 1944 – Halifax

Mrs. P. and I caught the 0845 tram, and I went on board the *Matane.* Went to see D. about the officer complement and lunched on board the *Swansea* with King (A/Cdr R.C.N.R.). He is a nice chap. In the p.m. I sat in Easton's cabin with a mooring board and parallel rulers and worked out some attack problems. At about 1715 I met Thomas on board, who is to be my Group A/S and staff officer, and we walked up to see Briggs and arranged to plot some things on the Tactical Board tomorrow. I then set out to walk home. It was freezing hard all day and the roads and pavements are covered with ice. Bright and dry however. Met Ogilvie, who was in the *Leamington* and who is now in a new B.D.E. with a passage crew.[35] At the "Capital" corner I met Mrs. P. and we went the rest of the way home together, partly by tram and partly on foot. After dinner we went to bed fairly early but I sat up writing a long letter to J. There was a bit of a snapping match between the Prentices after dinner, which made me feel v. uncomfortable.

Wednesday, 26 January 1944 – Halifax

A lovely day. Cold but bright and sunny. I caught the 0845 tram and went straight to the Tactical Table in the Dockyard, where with the aid of the Wrens I plotted out some support group problems which I'd been thinking about yesterday. Thomas was there and Easton, King, and the C.O. of the *North Bay.* It was good value, although I don't think I was able to make up my mind on many points I had made in the ward room of the *Matane.* In the p.m. I went through some orders with the P.O. Tel and Yeoman and then got the writer to copy them out. The port HF/DF officer also came down for a chat, then Briggs arrived and we discussed my tactical table problems at some length. This all made me very late and instead of going home and changing as I intended, I had to go to the offices and get a lift with Douglas [Prentice] and Bill Puxley to a small drinking party where we arrived very late. Puxley came back to dinner.

Thursday, 27 January 1944 – Halifax

Sleety rain was falling as I went in to work. Went straight to the Tactical Table, where we had a group game which lasted all the forenoon. Back on board *Matane* for lunch and afterwards I got down to my orders. At about 1600 Puxley rang me up to say the Admiral had expressed a wish to see me, and after waiting a bit I got a car and went to A.C.H.Q. The sleet and a bit of a thaw followed by frost again have made the streets just solid ice in places. Unpleasant driving. The Admiral (Rear-Admiral L.W. Murray R.C.N.) was very pleasant and asked me all about my trip to England and how the group was getting on. Back on board and then up to the offices, where I looked at some of the inspection repairs of ships in my group with a view really to getting ideas for my inspection tomorrow. Met Douglas in the C.O.'s Library later on and drove home with him. The little hill from Tower Road to Franklin Street was a sheet of ice, and we slid down it most of the way broadside on. After I got to bed I spent about an hour roughing out a short speech to make to the ship's company of the *Owen Sound* tomorrow. Feeling v. overwhelmed with the S.O. job.

Friday, 28 January 1944 – Halifax

A car was supposed to pick me up at 0830 but owing to a flat tyre and ice bound streets it didn't arrive till past 0900. Thomas was in it and together we drove rather slowly out to St Margaret's Bay. A lovely sunny morning but with a biting N. wind. We arrived at the pier an hour late and found the *Owen Sound*'s whaler waiting for us, and we pulled off to the ship luckily with the wind astern. Waterhouse had asked me to do her inspection at the end of her 3-week work up period. I first of all inspected the ship's company and then walked round the ship. She is a brand new corvette. I was most impressed at the accommodation and she was beautifully clean throughout. By the time I'd finished that it was 1200 so we got under way to return to Halifax and I had some drinks and lunch in the ward room. At about 1330 I started to put her through her paces at action stations, and we fired all our guns and dropped depth charges and towed forward and shored up and made enemy reports, etc. They were very good. A really good trip.

The sun went in the p.m. and coming up harbour it was damned cold. We passed the boom at 1600 and were then out to the oiling jetty to oil. When we were secured we cleared lower deck and I made my little address to the ship's company, which I really think went down well. Pride in the navy and pride in their ship, and so on. The Captain is a Skipper Lt. called Watson,[36] v. sound, and the 1st Lieut. is excellent. He was in the *Collingwood* when I took passage. A boat came to fetch me and Thomas and I got ashore at 1800. Went to the C.O.'s Library and went home with Douglas. I was terrified at doing this inspection. Afraid of not being able to think of how to put them through the hoop sufficiently.

Saturday, 29 January 1944 – Halifax

Much the same sort of weather. Roads still icy. Went to the Dockyard by tram stopping off and going into Birks about Gillian's watch en route. Went on board and Thomas and I did some work on group orders. At 1130 I went on board the *Frontenac,* as I wanted to speak to the ship's company before they left for Shelburne. Found the Captain[37] in a bit of a spin and rather downhearted about this and that. He wants watching and helping. Cleared lower deck and spoke to the troops. Made my same little speech, which I think goes down well with these raw young R.C.N. sailors.

I then went over to *Atholl.* Her C.O. is a very different type. Confident, efficient, sure of himself, and very nice. Walked round the upper deck, stayed to lunch, and then spoke to the ship's company. I then made one more visit to the *Baddeck* (Brown is Capt.), who may be off to Newfyjohn soon, and met the officers and addressed the sailors. Went back on board feeling rather pleased with myself. Spent the rest of the p.m. up to about 1700 writing out a memo on the acoustic torpedo, in the course of which I thought out a place for a daylight chase, which simplifies things. My cabins are now taking shape and the furniture is going up. At about 1815 Easton and his wife, who is very preg., came on board for a drink and later on King from the *Swansea* and the 2 Prentices. After some drinks we took a taxi to the Lord Nelson where after a bit of a wait we had dinner. It was my party and went quite well I think. Everything went right for me today.

Sunday, 30 January 1944 – Halifax

It was snowing quite hard when I got up. I did not go into the dockyard. Mrs. P. and I went to Church at St. Paul's at 1100. A nice old church and a very nice service. It had stopped snowing but there was about 6 or 7 inches of dry powdery snow lying. Really rather thrilling. Reminded me of Switzerland. Douglas brought Mrs. Bidwell, Mrs. Lucas, and one R.N.R. 2½ back to lunch. Mrs. L., I must say, attracts me rather.[38] At about 1545 I set off and walked to Vernon Street and had tea with the Murphys. Walking not too easy on account of the ice under the snow. The Murphys were very kind and gave me a very good tea and at 1830 I walked back again. Found Ogilvie had arrived and was stopping for supper. Never seem to get to bed early in this house.

Monday, 31 January 1944 – Halifax

Went in as usual by tram. Made out a rough group working up programme at St. Margaret's Bay and then after consulting Capt. D.'s training and gunnery staff I got it typed by his secretary. No sooner had I done this than I was shown a signal saying the group would sail for Newfyjohn on the 6th, have a few days work up, and then take a convoy across. I lunched on board and in the p.m. I went out and wrote my name in the C. in C.'s book and then went to Birks and chose a new watch in place of the defective one I'd given Gillian. Unfortunately I couldn't find such a nice one. Came back to the Dockyard and went to the attack teacher, where *Matane*'s party were doing a run. Then to Capt. D.'s office, where I found a Constructor Captain Harrison[39] from Ottawa who I took down on board to see how my quarters were being fitted out. He also looked at one or two other things. They are being awfully slow on my cabin. Thought out some more orders on group cruising dispositions. Soon after 1800 I went up to the C.O.'s Library and waited for D. He took Sharky Armstrong,[40] the new Capt. of *Stadacona,* back to dinner, which meant another late night as it was past 2300 before he made a move to go.

Tuesday, 1 February 1944 – Halifax

An overcast day with intermittent snowfalls. I went on with key group cruising orders. After lunch I got busy ordering myself mess traps, warm clothing, etc., and looked in to see D. about my steward, and he said he [Prentice] had been ordered to hospital with a bad ear. Back on board and read a whole lot of back signals. Up to the library for a drink and then I went to the hospital where I met Patricia, who had just brought down Douglas' things and was seeing him settled in. She had the car, and after leaving the hospital we went to the cinema and saw *Watch on the Rhine* with Bette Davis. Rather harrowing but very good indeed. Went back home and had a late cold meal. Turned much colder in the evening with a bitter wind and a flurry of snow.

Wednesday, 2 February 1944 – Halifax

I packed up my gear before breakfast as I went to take up residence on board. It was much colder and there was a biting N. wind. Went to the pay offices in the dockyard before going on board and made out a vast number of forms for allotments, marriage allowance, etc. It is still not quite clear what my total pay allowances are to be. Gardiner from the *Atholl* came on board at 1100 and we discussed tactics, etc. Soon after lunch I went ashore and walked up to the travelling expense office in *Stadacona.* The cold and the wind on my face and ears nearly made me scream. I then walked up to the S. end of Barrington St. and did some shopping and eventually met Patricia Prentice in Eaton's, and we bought cushions for my cabin and some things for Joan including a mackintosh.

I then got all my parcels into a taxi and after dropping P. at the hospital I went home, picked up my luggage (all but night things as I find I can't yet live on board and must spend one more night ashore), and brought it down to the ship. Stayed on board till about 1800 and then went ashore. Found Patricia in the same No. 9 tram that I caught. Really did get to bed reasonably early. I don't believe the temperature was much below 15°, but with this strong wind it was Arctic. Got a whole bunch of letters, which have been following me round from the *Salisbury.*

Thursday, 3 February 1944 – Halifax

Another day with the thermometer at about 15° and a strong bitterly cold N. wind. Patricia and I caught the 0845 tram. I got off and went to *Stadacona* expecting to get my travelling allowances only to find the claim had to have D.'s signature first. Walked into the Dockyard and got a harbour craft to take me out to the ship, which was at the swinging buoy adjusting compasses and MF/DF. My cabin, with the carpet down, is now nearly complete. At any rate, being at sea there were no maties working in it and I could use it. I unpacked and got all my books and photos out, and really it will look v. nice when finished.

We slipped the buoy at about 1500. Went outside the boom for gun trials (4" and twin power Oerlikons). Was Arctic on the bridge. There is a lot to be said for this job, because when it is this bloody on the bridge one can go below. There were some defects in the Oerlikons and there were no dockyard or armament representatives on board and the whole thing seemed most improper and casual, and so on return to harbour I made a fairly rude signal about it to C. in C. repeated all round the place. I couldn't feed in my cabin yet and so I suppered in the wardroom. Wrote some letters including a long one to J. and read A.C.I.s. Slept on board in my own cabin. The Americans have launched an attack on the Marshall Islands and have one or two important atolls.

Friday, 4 February 1944 – Halifax

I went to the Dockyard offices about various things. A cold but lovely sunny day and that bitter wind has gone. We slipped at 1200 and went up to Bedford Basin and berthed alongside the ammunition pier so that the HF/DF experts could do some preliminary work on the aerial. It was such a lovely afternoon that I stepped ashore to stretch my legs only to find I was in a large prohibited area of the magazine. However, I managed to find a nice old Corporal of the Canadian Veterans Corps. who was in charge of the guard and who was prepared to accompany me, and we had about a 40 minute walk. We shoved off at about 1700 and berthed again in the dockyard.

I walked up to the offices to find out what I could from Burgess about the other ships in the group and then fed in the wardroom at rather a barbarously early hour, but I can't start feeding in my cabin yet. Apparently my signal had the effect of turning the heat on properly in the Dockyard, which I think is a good thing. There is no doubt about it, this dockyard is scandalously inefficient and the underlings seem to be in charge instead of those at the top. I was very pleased and surprised to get my lost waistcoat returned from the Barbizon Plaza. I walked round the ship in the a.m. before we got under way. These frigates are much more like small big ships than destroyers.

Saturday, 5 February 1944 – Halifax

We slipped at 0830 and went out to the HF/DF calibrating range at Devil's Island, where we anchored and started calibrating. Another lovely day but damned cold. Thermometer at about 5° above. At about 1130 they cleared lower deck, and first of all Easton told the ship's company all about my past career, which was most embarrassing, and then I made my set speech. Read A.C.I.s and spent some time on group orders. We weighed at 1640 having done about 1/3 of the calibration and went back to harbour berthing at about 1800.

Got a message to ring up the Admiral, who said he and Mrs. Murray would *not* be able to come down to our cocktail party but said he would send me tickets for the hockey match. At 1830 the guests for our cocktail party started to arrive. It was Easton's and my party for the higher ups who could come and all the Dockyard officers plus others who had done things for the ship. We had it in the wardroom and at its height you couldn't move. Roger Bidwell, who had just returned to Halifax, was there and I had a talk with him. He is just about to take command of a flat top and is v. thrilled.[41] He *is* a nice man. Patricia Prentice brought down two boxes of groceries for me to take away.

At about 2100 when nearly everyone had gone I broke away and got a lift in a car to the Forum (the ice hockey stadium) and arrived in time to see about ½ of a match between 2 naval sides. It is a most wonderful and exciting game to watch. When the Admiral spotted me he called me over and introduced me to his wife, and after the game I went back to his house with quite a party and had drinks and then walked back on board.

Sunday, 6 February 1944 – Halifax

We slipped at 0830. A very different sort of day. Blowing quite hard from the S.W. and considerably warmer. On arrival at the D/F spot there was no sign of the yacht. However, she eventually hove in sight. In view of the weather we did not anchor but just remained drifting. The HF/DF experts soon came along and said owing to the motion on the yacht they couldn't get reliable readings, and so we packed up and returned to harbour and went straight alongside the oiling jetty. A horrible day. I read and wrote. At about 2030 the *Frontenac* came alongside and Wennberg came over to see me and we talked. We remained at the jetty all night.

Monday, 7 February 1944 – Halifax[42]

A lovely bright cold sunny day. I stepped over to the *Frontenac* at 0800 and she shoved off and berthed at No. 5 jetty. The *Matane* went out at 0830 to continue the D/F calibration. I had breakfast in the *Frontenac* and at about 0930 Wennberg and I went ashore to D.'s office and found one or two Dockyard departments, seeing about his defects. I went to the supply office and had a hate [fit of temper] about some binoculars and at 1100 I got a car and went to A.C.H.Q. and saw Bidwell and talked about the group. I had lunch at the C.O.'s Library and had a yarn with Briggs about escort groups and then had a hair cut at Admiralty House. Then out to see D. in his room in the hospital and talked quite a bit and said goodbye. Nothing to do, so I walked into the town and bought a Moffat New Testament and walked back to the dockyard and sat in the C.O.'s Library.

At 1830 I went on board *Swansea* for a cocktail party. A very good party. In the middle Bidwell took King and me to the side and said there was a U-Boat scare off Newfy and we were going to be sailed at 0800 tomorrow. About an hour later we got a message saying the flap was over and cancel everything. At about 2130 I left the *Swansea* and returned on board *Matane*, who had berthed at about 2000 taking with me Sharky Armstrong and the Gunnery Officer of *Swansea* and his wife. A very nice couple. Stopped up drinking whisky till about midnight. The gunnery officer of the *Swansea* told me there was awful bad feeling between *Swansea* and *Matane* both in the wardroom and on the lower deck.

Tuesday, 8 February 1944 – Halifax

I was so disgusted with the chairs which the Dockyard gave me for my cabin that I made a signal of protest, still without the slightest effect. I must have drunk too much last night because I'm feeling very woolly this morning. I went over to the *Swansea* at 1115 and at 1130 they cleared lower deck and I addressed the sailors. It didn't seem to go down quite so well. Perhaps because I wasn't feeling so well. Stayed and had lunch with King. He is a nice old boy. To be at sea in small ships at the age of 57 isn't bad. Back on board after lunch and thought out our group training and the firing we are going to do on leaving.

At about 1530 I got a message from Bidwell asking me to go and see him. After some delay I got a car and went to A.C.H.Q. He told me that this U-Boat scare is on again. One has been sighted somewhere off Newfyjohn, supposed to be coming E. to the Halifax area and he is going to send us out to do an A/S patrol. While I was up there I visited the plot[43] and saw Stirling about some signal points. When I got back on board I had to cancel and alter a lot of signals. As we are to sail early, the shoots are off. At 2100 the Captains of the *Swansea, Frontenac,* and *Owen Sound* came on board and we discussed the operation and group orders and formations. King stayed on talking rather later.

Wednesday, 9 February 1944 – Halifax/At sea

We slipped at 0800. *Owen Sound* was delayed and so only 3 of us went out. It was 8° below zero and agonizingly cold. Luckily no wind. When the sun got up it got warmer. It was brilliantly sunny all day. When we got clear of the swept channel I did a few "Blue Turns."[44] In the p.m. ships drifted independently and at 2100 after dark we went to night action stations and fired some star shell and burned searchlights. It was warmer in the evening. We did a zigzag at 14 kts. *Frontenac*'s signalling is awful. *North Bay* and *Baddeck,* who were at Newfy, are already out after this U-Boat. I was cold and didn't sleep well.

Thursday, 10 February 1944 – At sea

A very different day. Warmer but overcast, and at about 0930 it started to snow and it didn't stop till nearly night fall. At about 1000 *Swansea* got an A/S contact and started dropping depth charges. Visibility in the snow storm about 2 cables. Our radar operators are about the slowest things in the world, which doesn't help. After *Swansea, Frontenac* got a contact. We were all milling round in the snow storm and I was trying to organise a search. I never believed it was a submarine and when we proceeded to get about 4 very good but definitely non sub echos[45] I was quite certain. Even so it was difficult to make up my mind to leave the area, and I was there till 1500 when I drew stumps and went on, informing C. in C. what I had done. All very good practice for me and the group. Our original orders were altered by signal and we are now told to make for a datum point about 100 miles E. of Newfy instead of patrolling S. of Cape Race. A better night. Slept in my ordinary cabin.

Friday, 11 February 1944 – At sea

Going N. to S/M datum point. Quite a strong W.'ly wind with temperature well below freezing with spray forming ice on guard rails, etc. *Owen Sound* joined up with us at about 1400 and then turned right round to meet *North Bay* and *Baddeck,* who were coming up astern. We met at about 1600 and after sending my message on cruising orders over by Coston gun line we got lined up and turned N. again, the whole group except *Atholl.* Signalling awfully slow and C.O.s have as yet no sense of anticipation, but doubtless it will come. We got a signal at about 1900 ordering us to sweep out a biggish area to the E. of the datum point. It takes a lot of thinking out to get 6 ships spread over about 14 miles manoeuvred round on to different courses but by 2300 we were off on the first leg. We ran through small patches of very thin brash ice. The first I've ever seen. A cold but brilliant moonlight night. Slept in the Chart House,[46] but not well owing to (a) being worried and (b) being cold.

Saturday, 12 February 1944 – At sea

We got to the end of the first E.'ly leg of the sweep at about 0730 and turned S. and then E. for another sweep. The group were very trying and very stupid. I suppose one must realize, however, that this support group work is really much more like destroyer work – manoeuvres, signalling, etc. – and although I've been bred and born to it, those chaps haven't and a lot of training is required. A very clear calm day but rather overcast. At about 1400 we got a signal telling us to abandon search and return to St. John's at best speed. I wasn't sorry as the scent was so stale by now as to leave little hope of finding anything. I expected to arrive at about 0130, but later on I was told to adjust speed to arrive at first light tomorrow and so had to slow down. The glass, which was very high in the morning, started to drop like a stone and by the evening it started to blow from the S.E. with sleet and snow.

Sunday, 13 February 1944 – At sea/St John's/At sea

A horrible night. Sleet, no visibility, and wind, which shifted to the W. increasing to gale force. We weren't quite certain of our position and had been warned to keep clear of some other ships steaming off the end of the swept channel. What with one thing and another I didn't get much sleep. We eventually sighted Cape Spear at about 0745 and made for the entrance. It was blowing like hell. We went in without waiting for the D. (by mistake), but the rest were kept waiting outside quite a while in typical St. John's fashion. Berthed on the S. side but after breakfast there was no hot water for a bath!!

I shaved and dressed and later on Easton and I walked through thick snow to *Avalon II*,[47] where we got a car and called on Capt. D. It seems one U-boat torpedoed a ship just outside the entrance just under their noses the other day.[48] He told us that Walker with E.G. 2 got 3 U-boats in one day quite recently. We then went on to Operations. We are to sail at 1700 this evening and return to Halifax sweeping through certain points. The idea is we will go W. to the Halifax area and so long as these 1 or 2 boats we know to be over this side, E.G. 9 will not leave for the U.K. Went back across the harbour by boat and had lunch in Easton's cabin, then tried to get a little shut eye but had a lot of disturbances. All the group seem to have defects, on account of which our sailing was delayed till nearly 2000, and then we went out without *Swansea* and *Frontenac.* The wind had dropped completely and it was a lovely clear starlit night but v. cold. My patience was almost worn through trying to get my group into cruising order in the dark and I did not get off the bridge till midnight.

Monday, 14 February 1944 – At sea

A fine calm sunny day. I exercised a dummy S/M contact and got the group doing an "Observant" round our smoke float.[49] *Baddeck,* who had been delayed in St. John's, joined up in the p.m. At about 2000 we got a signal saying an aircraft had sighted and attacked a U/B south of Flemish Cap. The position was 420 miles east of us but after some thought I decided to turn the group towards the position, and I made a signal to C. in C. saying I'd turned in anticipation of orders. Went on to 14 knots, which is about the max. station keeping speed of the group.

Tuesday, 15 February 1944 – At sea

Owing to atmospheric conditions my signal had to be repeated and took a long time to get through, with the result that it wasn't till about 0500 that I got C. in C.'s reply telling me to turn back and proceed in accordance with previous instructions for Halifax. Another fine calm day – most of the day – but the glass started to fall like a plummet and in the p.m. the wind started to get up and by dark it was blowing really hard. It altered S.E. and round to the S. At about 2000 it suddenly veered again to the S.E. The glass started to rise and the sky cleared altogether, but the wind and sea increased rather and we had to reduce to 8½ knots. In the small hours *Swansea,* who had joined up with us at about 1330, reported weather damage to the fo'c'sle and fell out of the line. A most unpleasant night. This ship feels more solid and less lively in a heavy sea than a destroyer. We never get any news at sea – nobody seems interested, which is so extraordinary. I want to know what is happening in Italy, as the Germans were making a very strong and determined attack against our small bridge head S. of Rome.

Wednesday, 16 February 1944 – At sea

Glass going up, clear sunny day, but still blowing really hard and quite a big sea. Towards the evening it eased down and we were able to push on again at 12 knots, but we have been frightfully held up by that blow. Had a long discussion with Easton and Westwater,[50] the Signal Officer, on the question of the signal organisation in the ship, and we got it all ironed out I think.

Thursday, 17 February 1944 – At sea

A most perfect calm sunny day. At 1100 just as we sighted the outer swept channel buoy, I closed the group in and did a few manoeuvres at 1½ cables and then led my little squadron into harbour in line ahead. I must say I felt v. proud. We berthed at about 1500 and I had a much needed bath. I gave the captain of the *Stormont*[51] on which we berthed a bottle for having no hands ready to receive us. After tea I wrote to J. Got a letter from Peggie,[52] who still sounds very depressed poor thing. Peter, now 15, is apparently becoming quite the young man.

Gardiner from the *Atholl* came to see me at 1815, and we had a long talk about officers and wardroom life in the R.C.N. It is my opinion that so many R.C.N.R. officers were given commands in the early expansion days that they have given all the V.R. officers much more a merchant service outlook than a naval outlook. Had my supper in my cabin at 1930 and paid a short visit to the wardroom before turning in.

Friday, 18 February 1944 – Halifax

Pouring with rain in the morning and about 20° warmer. I paddled up to Capt. D.'s office hardly able to keep my feet in the melting ice and snow. It seems the group – or as many as can – are to go out tomorrow and look for this elusive U/B which is still thought to be coming to the Halifax area. At 1100 I had a C.O.s meeting on board and went over a lot of points and we had a good chin wag. What with one thing and another we were rather late for lunch, and so Easton and I and a guest of his fed in his cabin. D. rang up to say the Admiral would come down on board tomorrow and invest Easton with his D.S.C. I got a car at 1515 and went up to A.C.H.Q. and saw Laidlaw,[53] who has taken over Bidwell's job. I had a look at the plot and Met, and also saw the Admiral. I gather there is little chance of us getting away over the other side until these 2 U/Bs are either accounted for or move away. To my intense disappointment, I learned that a letter for me addressed c/o Capt. Bidwell had been forwarded to St. John's. Maddening!!

Back on board and after tea I did some writing. At about 1800 Dyer,[54] Capt of the *Kootenay* (ex *Decoy*), who was alongside, came over and asked me to go on board. He is an R.C.N. 2½ who did the Tactical Course with me in Liverpool just before Christmas. Found Easton and one or two others there. Most amusing drinking party. Everybody reminiscing. I got most of them to come back on board *Matane* later on. When they'd gone it was so late I had to feed off sandwiches and coffee. It started to blow in the evening and get much colder. The barometer has done another spectacular dive.

Saturday, 19 February 1944 – Halifax/At sea

A complete change of temperature. A bitter N.W. wind with the thermometer down to 6° above. At 1130 the Admiral came on board and invested Easton with his D.S.C. Hands were at divisions and I read a citation and then the Admiral made a short speech. The other C.O.s of the group, Mrs. Easton and small daughter, and Mrs. Telfer and Mrs. Miller came as guests and after the ceremony there were drinks in the ward room. The Admiral was very affable. Later on I had lunch with Easton and his wife and child in his cabin. A most unattractive little girl of about 3.

Our sailing orders came down in the a.m. ordering us to carry out a Gamma search[55] between 2 points E. of Sable Island. They seem to think this U/B is still on its way W. and it is hoped we may intercept it. We sailed at 1600 with *North Bay, Owen Sound,* and *Frontenac. Baddeck* and *Swansea* unable to sail owing to defects. My God, it was cold in spite of the wind being astern. When we reached the buoy *Matane* went on ahead and did ½ hour burst of full speed, which reckoned by the buoys only gave 17 knots. When at the end of the swept channel we turned E. there was enough sea to throw up quite a bit of spray, and our port side started to freeze up. High glass, clear sky, but no sign of the wind going down; in fact it seemed to freshen. I've never felt such shattering cold before.

London had a really heavy air raid a couple of nights ago. It looks as if our bombing of the rocket emplacements in France had been so effective that failing the secret weapon they have had to revert to ordinary bombing as retaliation.

Sunday, 20 February 1944 – At sea

No improvement in the conditions. Wind as fresh as ever and still shatteringly cold. At about 1300 we arrived on our patrol line and turned to sweep on a Southerly course. The two points are 60 miles apart, which at 10 knots means we turn 180° every 6 hours. As the day wore on it gradually got warmer and the wind died down, thank God. The extreme cold seems to deprive me of all will power. We are pretty severely frozen up on the port side, but we cleared some of the depth charges with a hot water hose. I had a bit of exercise on the upper deck at about 1800. We turned at 1900 and it wasn't long before it was a clear, flat calm night. Had a long talk with Easton about the R.C.N. and the navy in general after dinner.

Monday, 21 February 1944 – At sea

Turned to the southward again at 0100 and back again to the N. at 0700. From being a flat calm in the night the wind sprang up from the S. in the a.m. At 1230 we turned south and at 1500 it started to snow and continued to snow with only a short break up to about midnight. It lay quite thick on board. I spent quite some time reading A.F.O.s and C.A.F.O.s, none of which I've seen since leaving the *Salisbury.* I also read Plutarch's *Lives;* Antony, Cicero, Demetrius, and Demosthenes. Most interesting. I must get the other volumes, as I only have Vol. III in Everyman Edition. Altered N. at 1800 and once more S. at 2300.

Tuesday, 22 February 1944 – At sea

It stopped snowing in the night and the wind shifted through W. to N.W. where it remained blowing quite fresh all day. We turned N. at 0900 and S. for the last time at 1000. At 1430 on reaching the S. point of the sweep we abandoned the Gamma search and started a sweep to the S. and W. through 2 given points and so back to Halifax. The wind went down and it was a glassy night. At 2000 we carried out a short exercise with a dummy radar and A/S contact and all ships doing an Observant round *Matane*'s flares. Very good value, I think, and not at all easy to do on a dark night.

Wednesday, 23 February 1944 – At sea

In the middle of the night we got a signal saying some U.S. Coast Guard cutter had reported attacking a S/M in a position some 250 miles W. of us. So I stopped zig zagging and went on to 14 kts on our 270° course in case we were told to go and have a look. Just before 0700 we got radar pips and found ourselves passing quite close to H.X. 280. A S.E.'ly wind got up v. quickly with a falling glass. Never known such changeable weather. At 1030 I did another dummy contact exercise and carried out creep attack exercise with *North Bay.*[56]

At 1200 I got a completely corrupt message which seemed to imply that our route was altered, and so at 1230 steamed round 180° while waiting to get the signal repeated by *North Bay.* When properly decoded it told us to sweep ahead of H.X. 280 to a certain position before returning to Halifax. As the convoy was by this time some 100 miles away and 9 kts was about the max. we could do into this wind and sea, it was obvious we couldn't do it, and so I made a signal to that effect and asked for further instructions. While waiting for a reply we continued to pound into quite a big sea and gale force S.E. wind. At 1800 came fresh orders to return to Halifax and so rather thankfully we turned our tails to the wind and sea to a course of 320°. Somebody in A.C.H.Q. must have done a pretty phoney bit of plotting, or it must have been obvious they were asking us to do the impossible.

Thursday, 24 February 1944 – At sea/Halifax

Blowing hard all night with the wind shifting to the E. Rain squalls and bad visibility. A very disturbed night as I always feel anxious when approaching land in bad weather, although with D/F and radar and Loran one ought really to feel as safe as houses. I was on the bridge from 0330 until we anchored. It was not easy as we were going very slowly and making a lot of leeway and the lights of buoys and the Sambro Light Vessel could only be seen at 1½ to 2 miles. I should have felt happier if the Captain had fixed the ship occasionally when 2 or more lights were in sight, but he seemed to like to do it all by eye. It was just getting light as we got up to the boom and snowing hard and the visibility was down to about ½ mile. We were ordered to anchor S. of Georges Island till the weather cleared. I was in my bath when at about 1000 we weighed and went alongside in the Dockyard.

Went up to see Capt. D. and had a long chat with him and Puxley. Saw in the paper that London had 4 heavy raids in 5 days, and the battle still rages round the home beach head. Back on board for lunch. We kept on getting contradictory orders. First of all we were to boiler clean, then that was cancelled and we were to remain at short notice, then 4 hrs notice coming to 2 hrs at 0800 tomorrow, and then finally extended notice and boiler clean. Although I had a *Mariner's Mirror*[57] readdressed to the ship by J. there was no letter from her. I put in a little shut eye after lunch and then got down to writing my report of proceedings and some other reports. After my solitary supper I wrote to J. and turned in early. Halifax is feet deep in snow.

Friday, 25 February 1944 – Halifax

At 0930 we had a group arrival conference at Capt. D.'s office, which took a long time. Everybody aired their grievances and it was quite good value. After that we all went up to A.C.H.Q. After rather a long wait we had audience with the Admiral, who said it was the present intention to sail us for C. in C. Western Approach's command on completion of our boiler cleaning about the 2nd or 3rd. That is good news but, of course, something may well happen to alter our plans before that. I was further delayed there because the Admiral wanted me to meet Houghton, the S.O. London, who is over here for a few days. He left before the bombings started but hears his club in St. James's Square has been hit. Back on board for a late lunch.

After lunch I went to eye clinic in the hospital as I'm beginning to think I ought to wear glasses for reading. This was confirmed by the oculist. I feel this is a definite step towards the grave. As I was walking out of *Stadacona*, Mount Haes in a car drove by and stopped and gave me a lift into the middle of the town. Went to the book store and bought another Vol. of Plutarch's *Lives* and then tried to find some white shirts but could find none and so walked back on.

The sides of the streets are heaped feet high with dirty melting snow. They had a terrific fall the night we were making harbour. Wrote to Peggie after tea. After dinner I went ashore and took a tram up Barrington Street and called on Brown (*Baddeck*) and his wife. She is attractive. A nice couple. Talked and had coffee. Walked back at 2300 as all the trams were so full.

Saturday, 26 February 1944 – Halifax

I walked up to the training office and the tactical table and discussed the sort of harbour training I wanted. I then went to the hospital and got my glasses. Yesterday when I complained that my right eye tended to water, the oculist did something to it, which he called cleaning out the tear duct, but the only result is that it has simply poured tears ever since. Back on board for lunch and afterwards I drew out search plans on a mooring board.

We suddenly got a signal to say we were being moved out to a buoy to allow *Iroquois* to berth alongside and then we'd be brought back alongside her. A damned silly idea which stops all work on our boiler cleaning, and so I made a signal of protest and was then told in so many words to stop arguing.[58] While the movement by tugs was going on I went on the upper deck and found fenders over the side, motor boats' gripes blowing away, and there wasn't a single man on deck that I would recognise as a sailor. When we'd berthed again I sent for Carruthers[59] the No. 1 and pointed out those things. I think he was half tight, anyhow it was hard to convince him there was anything wrong. I felt rather disheartened and depressed.

Just as I was going ashore at about 1830 Waterhouse came down to see me. He says 3 or 4 more ships have been hit by Gnats and that the importance of CAT gear[60] is being stressed. I talked to him for a bit and then we went on board the *Valleyfield* next door. A very nice captain[61] and a most cheery ward room. Very different from the rather gloomy, suspicious atmosphere in our ward room.[62] Waterhouse got a staff car, which after taking him to Admiralty House ran me on up Barrington Street and I arrived very late for dinner with the Briggs. I like him and she is a funny fat little thing. Stayed very late talking about this and that and walked back to the Dockyard.

Sunday, 27 February 1944 – Halifax

I definitely drank too much yesterday. I went through the secret and confidential logs after breakfast. I noticed there were no divisions. I was told there was to be a service on board at 1030, and at 1025 a padre came by and said he was sorry he had another service at 1030 and he couldn't do it as ours should have been at 1000. I sent for No. 1, who was in plain clothes, and asked him why this balls and he told me it was the Coxswain's fault and the O.O.D. I really give up when the 1st Lieut. doesn't realize that everything is his responsibility. Soon after 1100 I left the ship and went round to *North Bay* for a drink. Hynes is a nice chap and Watson from *Owen Sound* was there too.

I then walked up to Capt. D.'s office and at about 1300 he took me and Puxley home for lunch. There was another female there. Almost as soon as lunch was over people started coming in for tea. Some of us meanwhile did a bit of snow clearing from the garage approach. After tea played progressive ping pong in the basement and at about 1845 Hynes, who had come for tea, took me off to supper with a couple called Gibson. He is manager of Simpson's store and she is an old childhood friend of Hynes. An excellent supper and a long talk about social conditions and war problems, but I was nearly stifled with the heat of the house. We went back to the Dockyard by tram at about 2230. There has been a most terrific day and night air attack over Germany over the last 2 or 3 days. In one night we lost 79 bombers!! and the Americans lost over 100 by day.

Monday, 28 February 1944 – Halifax

At 1000 I went up to *Stadacona* for a dental appointment and had one small stopping done. Walked down to the Dockyard and went on board *North Bay* and was introduced to the officers, walked round part of the ship, and then made my little address to the ship's company. I have now visited and addressed all ships. Went to the ward room afterwards for a drink and then back on board *Matane* for lunch. In the p.m. I waded through more signal logs and had a hair cut. A very mild day with the snow thawing rapidly, and one flounders through inches of slush and water. At about 1830 Brown and his wife came on board, and soon after 1900 the Briggs arrived and we had drinks in my cabin and then we took a taxi to the Nova Scotian for dinner. A damp drizzle had set in. We had quite a good dinner – it was of course my dinner – and afterwards we went to the cinema and saw a frightfully creepy sort of ghost film. Quite good. After that, somewhat unwillingly, I went back with them all to the Browns' flat and rang up for a taxi which, of course, didn't come, and at last Briggs got a dockyard car for me but by that time it was about 1245. Mrs. Brown is one of the most beautiful creatures I've ever seen and nice too.

Tuesday, 29 February 1944 – Halifax

I went up to D.'s office and saw him and Burgess and then got a car up to A.C.H.Q. and saw Laidlaw. We sail tomorrow for the Azores, where we fuel and then go wherever C. in C. W.A. sends us. Had a look at the plot. Talked to the signal people and then after some waiting I got a car back to the Dockyard. The roads and streets are indescribably mucky as it is still thawing hard. I went to see Hibbard[63] in the *Iroquois*, who is alongside us, and took a gin off him. He has just been to the Azores and so will be able to give my staff useful information. Found letters from J. when I got on board. She seems to have an appalling cold and cough, which I don't like the sound of. After lunch went up to the Tactical Table where we had a convoy battle game. It was quite good value, but a little too ambitious for a somewhat depleted table staff. King in the *Swansea* tells me he has got condenser trouble again and will be delayed about 24 hours. Read a whole lot of new A.F.O.s when I got back on board. At about 1915 the two Prentices and Bill Puxley came on board for a farewell drink. After they'd left I had some sandwiches and coffee. Wrote to J. and then wrote out all the sailing signals, as our steaming signal had arrived from C. in C.

Wednesday, 1 March 1944 – Halifax/At sea

A wet sort of snow was falling. At 0930 I had a C.O.s meeting and discussed a number of points. *Swansea* will *not* now be delayed. We are being sailed direct for the Azores to fuel and then act as ordered by C. in C. Western Approaches. At 1200 we slipped with *Owen Sound, Frontenac,* and *North Bay. Swansea* delayed at last minute and *Atholl* still boiler cleaning. A lousy day and a N.'ly wind freshening all the time. *Swansea* joined up soon after leaving the swept channel. Barometer falling steadily. Thank God we are leaving these coastal waters.

Thursday, 2 March 1944 – At sea

At 0600 we altered to 098° at 13 kts with the wind and sea on the beam. Both getting up. *Baddeck* had to fall out of line in the night to secure D/C. At 0600 I came down to 10 kts, and about ½ hour later *Frontenac* reported the same trouble and I reduced to 8. Really blowing damned hard and a big sea building, snow squalls and virtually about ½ mile visibility. At 0800 I decided to turn into the sea as I was afraid of damaging something if we stood on. *Baddeck* and *Swansea* seem to have lost touch, but we've got them all on R/T. The wind backed a bit but blew [Force] 9-10[64] and the way we plunged made me feel a bit sick. At 1530 we came round to 330° heading the wind. We were icing up quite a bit and by dark R/T communication was getting bad. Wind and sea seemed to ease a bit and at midnight I altered round to 080° at 10 kts and we seemed to ride quite nicely. A relief to get that bitter wind out of our faces on the bridge. A really bloody day. An H.X. convoy somewhere in our vicinity was reported hopelessly scattered. We'd been told to sweep ahead of an S.C. [eastbound] convoy who was well to the E. but there is no hope of getting there after all this delay.

Friday, 3 March 1944 – At sea

By daylight *Frontenac, Owen Sound,* and *North Bay* were in sight but weather deteriorating again. Wind between W. and N.W., Force 8-9 and a very big sea on our quarter. Snow, nil visibility, and icing continuing. At 0800 *Frontenac* reported man over board but picked him up, which was damned lucky in this weather. At 1015 intercepted a signal from an American ship saying she'd sighted a U-Boat about 55 miles to the N. of our position. Debated what to do, but in view of difficulty in getting R/T signals through the perpetual heavy snow and filthy weather decided that I'd stay on my course until or unless ordered to investigate. No orders came. Other ships in the vicinity are talking on [radio frequency] 2410 and R/T traffic is jammed. Managed to shift the group to 2900. At 1300 *Swansea* joined up and a couple of hours later *Frontenac* appeared, and so we are all in touch except *Baddeck.* Between snow squalls there were some nice patches of blue sky between clouds, but the wind blew as hard as ever, ice made R/T signalling worse than ever, and I was in 2 minds whether to heave to again before dark, but didn't. Just before dark we passed about a dozen or so ships all strung out anyway, which was the westbound convoy O.N. 225. Our orders about the S.C. convoy were cancelled and we altered once more to 115° to get on to our original course for the Azores. An anxious and bloody day.

Saturday, 4 March 1944 – At sea

Still a strong W.'ly wind, Force 7-8 and a big following sea. R/T communication becoming much better and temperature is rising. *Swansea,* who was in touch with *Baddeck* where we were not, had been told to home her. We had intercepted 2 bearings, which *Swansea* passed in the night – 021° and 025° – and so when at [illegible] suddenly passed a bearing of 240° I immediately thought it must be a reciprocal. By this time we were again in touch and we homed her all through the p.m. and got a most perplexing situation when *Swansea*'s bearings gave a perfectly good running fix to the S.W. and ours gave an equally good one to the N.E. Eventually decided, as *Swansea*'s was the F.H.4 set,[65] his bearings could not be wrong, and told *Baddeck* to close her bearings but by this time she was some 100 miles away. Infuriating. I blame *Swansea* for not taking more interest and realizing when *Baddeck* passed astern. At 1845 we altered to 101° at 13 kts straight for the Azores. By night the wind and sea dropped completely and the temperature had risen and a certain amount of wet slushy snow falling. I feel with this D/Fing and R/T chatter that we have been making too much noise over the ether and so decided to clamp down on W/T as much as possible.

Sunday, 5 March 1944 – At sea

Everyone 100% more cheerful. Thank God we are out of that shatteringly cold Canadian zone. I can once more stand on the bridge without a cap and comparatively lightly clad. At 0900 we sighted the leading escorts of a large W. bound American convoy and we turned 90° to port to pass down the starboard side of the convoy. At about 1100 I attended prayers and at 1130 the whole group streamed CAT gear (the noise making anti-acoustic torpedo device). No sooner were they out that *North Bay* got an A/S contact and attacked with D/Cs. We went over to investigate and the remainder did an Observant. Not a sign of anything and after a line abreast search to the N.ward we packed up and resumed our 101° course at 1300. Got a good D/F bearing of *Baddeck* at 1630 and again at 2000. At about 2330 *Swansea* reported a radar contact of surface ship, which when she went to investigate faded out at about 1,500 yds, so I turned the group and swept back. I was sure it could be nothing, because to start with it was picked up astern and it was such a light moonlight night that if there had been anything at that close range it must have been visible to the naked eye. At 0020 I turned back again on to our course and proceeded.

Monday, 6 March 1944 – At sea

Baddeck caught up from astern just before daylight, which was a relief. Exercised merchant ship identification procedure in the a.m. At about 1530 got a signal from C. in C. W.A. telling me to send a fuel oil report and, if the group could last till the 18th, to alter course forthwith for S.C. 154, which is to the N. of us. I confirmed that we could do so and at 1000 altered to 045° and detached *Baddeck* to support H.X. 281, also as ordered by C. in C. A beautifully calm fair day, but we are experiencing some difficulty in reading the broadcast signals due to atmospherics. I took plenty of exercise up and down the fo'c'sle deck. It looks as if we're to support this convoy as it passes through a large and somewhat undefined U-boat area. Looked up my A.C.I.s as there are so many things to try and remember. Intercepted signal announcing the kill of a U/B by a support group well to the east of us.

Tuesday, 7 March 1944 – At sea

Put the clocks on an hour at midnight. Had a very vivid but confused dream about Rosemary Leach[66] and woke up feeling how much I'd like to see her again. Fine warm day but overcast. Ordered *Frontenac* and *North Bay* to close and transfer radar officer as *North Bay* reported a defective 271 [radar]. We are having the greatest difficulty in reading broadcasts owing to atmospherics and in fact we are missing a lot. Some we are getting from other ships. At 1630 *Owen Sound* reported he only had 4 days of lubricating oil left and so I ordered him to close *Matane* and we passed over 2 drums using our D/C transfer gear, i.e., a mast rope in both ships. The back handed way in which every possible thing that could be done wrong in *Owen Sound* was done wrong made me hopping mad and we only just finished before dark. On laying off S.C. 154's latest position, course, and speed obtained from *North Bay,* as we'd missed the signal, I found they'd altered to 090° and so at about 1915 we altered round to 080°. I don't like this W/T situation: one doesn't know what important signals are being missed.

Wednesday, 8 March 1944 – At sea

At 0530 we got a radar pip at 10,000 yds on the starboard beam and shortly the huge bulk of the *Queen Elizabeth* became visible. It is the first time I've ever passed one of the monsters at sea. We didn't know we might see her. Presumably one of those signals we missed. E. wind [Force] 4-5 with rain squalls and poor visibility, but it poured all through the day with a rising glass. Atmospherics still bad in the a.m. with more and more signals being dropped. Things improved thank God in the p.m. *Frontenac* reported she wanted a spare valve for her radar. Found out that *North Bay* had one to spare and so after lunch I slowed down while they stopped and transferred the valve by line. From the plot I reckon we will meet the convoy at about 0400 and so at 1430 I slowed down to 12 knots and after dark on account of the brilliant moon I started a zigzag. We have a man on board with a high temperature and so at about 2015 we closed *Swansea* to exchange signals and get advice from the Medical Officer.

On regaining station about 2230 got a signal from C. in C. telling me to detach one ship to stand by *St Laurent* and one freighter from S.C. 154, and as *North Bay* and *Frontenac* both had radar out of action I sent *Owen Sound.* In the middle of all this the wireless office reported having intercepted R/T from C 1 group, who are escorting S.C. 154, suggesting that a U-Boat has been sighted. I banged on to 14 kts but soon it became apparent that the kerfuffle was a false alarm and so I reduced again. Called *Assiniboine* who is S.O. but could get no answer, which is rather funny.

Thursday, 9 March 1944 – At sea

At 0400 I called *Assiniboine* again and again got no reply. This worried me quite a lot as according to the plot we ought to be quite near. Thought of altering but decided to hold on till daylight. At about 0500 we got a radar pip ahead and sure enough there was the convoy and we joined most conveniently just at daylight. We closed *Assiniboine* and chatted and he passed over a lot of bumph, which we in turn had to re-edit and pass to the remainder of the group. The business of passing papers by Coston line is terribly slow even on a flat calm day like this, and it was nearly 0800 before we were able to go ahead from the stern of the convoy and take up our screening position. Sent both corvettes to oil from the escort oilers.

At 1300 C 1 (I don't know who he is by the way)[67] told us oilers were clear and *Matane* and *Swansea* went in to oil. It was the first time Easton had done it and it was a terribly slow business and the arrangements on his fo'c'sle are terrible. The hose burst in the middle of the operation, which made more delay, and finally during the 2nd effort he let the ship fall back too much and the hose pulled away from the deck connection, so at about 1630 we had only managed to get 120 tons. What was worse was that I found out *North Bay* had parted the hose of the other oiler without taking any oil. *Swansea,* who came along after us, had failed even to pick up the buffs before she had to take up night stations. Net result in the whole of our flat calm day 2 ships take about 100 tons each. It is all due to young inexperienced personnel I suppose, but it makes me so angry to see these balls being made. *Matane* took station 7 miles ahead of the leading ships of the close screen. Brilliant full moon all night.

Friday, 10 March 1944 – At sea

Clocks were reversed an hour a midnight. I had a bath before breakfast, a thing I've never done before at sea. The Canadian 271 type radar known as R.X.C. is a bloody awful affair.[68] On a brilliant moonlight night like last night we could see further than the max. radar range, which was only about 4,000 yards from the convoy. Came on the bridge at about 0500. Nothing on the radar and our gyro known to be out and I thought we'd lost the convoy, and got the Captain on the bridge but all was well. It is stupid to get fussed so easily and one ought to rely on one's officers more. At daylight we took position at visibility distance ahead. A very clear but overcast day.

At about 1300 things began to move. *Assiniboine* got 2 HF/DF bearings of U-boats close to and she went out to one and *Forester* to the other, but nothing sighted. In the meantime, *St Laurent,* who was bringing in the straggler *San Francisco* along behind, reported a U-boat on the surface and so *Forester* was sent to support her. We came back on to the main screen. *North Bay* and *Swansea* oiled and were just as slow as us, taking the whole day over it. At about 1700 the convoy made an evasive turn from 005° to 060° and some drizzly rain set in which shut down the visibility a lot. At about 1820 we got an A/S contact and dropped a pattern of charges on it. I think it was definitely fish or something non-sub but we were unable to retain contact, and after sitting on it till the convoy passed, we took up our station again. At 2000 the convoy altered back to 020°. It cleared up again in the first [watch] and we had another clear moonlit night. Before all this kerfuffle started C. in C. had told us to leave S.C. 154 at 0600 tomorrow and support H.X. 281, who is not far to the S.W., provided S.C. 154 is not in contact with the enemy. At about 1800 C 1 sent *Swansea* off to join in the hunt which *Forester* and *St. Laurent* are carrying out. We heard them over the R/T carrying out one attack after another and eventually about 2230 they reported U-boat had surfaced and been sunk and they were picking up survivors.[69] It looked rather as if our convoy might be attacked tonight.

Saturday, 11 March 1944 – At sea

At 0400 the alarm rattlers went and before I got on the bridge depth charges were being dropped, but although it was a good echo and a very good trace we couldn't pick it up again, and after searching round until the convoy was past we were told to take up our station again. At 0730 *Assiniboine* told *Matane* and *North Bay* to search out to a depth of 15 miles along a D/F bearing. A most perfect morning. Not a ruffle, bright sun, and maximum visibility. We went a little beyond 15 miles but saw nothing and so returned to the convoy. I had a yarn with Easton because I know I'm interfering too much and he resents it, but I just can't help it when I see things not being done as I want them. I must say I wish I was in command.

C 1 said he thought he would have to release me as all now seemed quiet, and so at 1800 I collected my flock at the rear of the convoy and set off. Picked up *Swansea,* who was just returning to the convoy, just before dark. It was my intention to operate between S.C. 154 and H.X. 281 during the night and join the latter at daybreak tomorrow. At about 2030 we got a small radar echo ahead at 4,000 yds and went to action stations. I thought the captain made an awful balls of it. He fired starshell set to 4000x when the range was still 4,000, which didn't stand much chance of lighting up anything, and before he knew what it was he stepped aside as an anti acoustic measure and the radar immediately lost touch due to the swing of the ship.[70] When we were headed for the position again there wasn't any sign of anything. Got the other ships on to a new line and did a line abreast search. At 2300 I gave it up and returned to 042°. An overcast night with patches of mist.

Sunday, 12 March 1944 – At sea

At 0500 we turned 180° to sweep back along the line of advance of H.X. 281. Expected from the plot to meet at about 0630. The visibility was very poor with patches of fog, but almost to the dot I got radar contact with the screen and made a head-on meeting. Nice plotting and navigation by the pilot. We closed *Fame* (S.O. B 6), who I found was Bob Currie,[71] and exchanged papers and had a chat. He has got so many escorts (16 with us) that I don't think he knows what to do with them. After leaving *Fame,* transference of the information to the group took an awful lot of time as usual. *Atholl* and *Baddeck,* who have been with this convoy quite a time, joined up with us again. *Atholl* transferred mail to us which she had picked up before leaving Halifax, and to my great joy I got three letters from J. I split them up and sent *Swansea* and the 2nd division to the extended screen on the port bow and took the 1st division up to the Std. bow. We'd no more got there when we received a signal from the C. in C. to detach and head to Lough Foyle, so I turned round and brought my division back in, collected the rest ahead of the convoy and at 1200 set off at 13 knots spread in line abreast. Got a signal saying a Sunderland flying boat had crashed in a position not far from us at 1600. I altered to sweep through the spot only to alter back again at 1945 on receiving a signal to say crew had been picked up. The glass, which had been as steady as a rock at about 30 [millibars] for the last few days, started to fall slowly, and the wind got up from the W and freshened during the night. Wrote to J. and Gillian. We should be at Moville by tomorrow evening.

Monday, 13 March 1944 – At sea/Moville

Blowing hard and quite a big beam sea, which made us roll a lot. We sighted the Irish coast at about 1130, rounded Tory Island at 1330. We got into 2 divisions in line ahead to go through the Inishtrahull narrows and *Swansea* made an awful balls with his division. Arrived off Moville at about 1800 and were given berths at Londonderry but were told not to arrive before 1030 tomorrow, and to complete with oil from the tanker at Moville. I've never seen so many ships anchored at Moville before and of course when we got there we found both sides of the tanker occupied. Somehow or other we all sidled into anchor berths and I made signals to the oiler trying to find out when she would be clear and at about 2130 I went to bed only to be woken up to hear the std side of the oiler was clear and *Matane* and *Frontenac* were going alongside. There was really no need to do so but I turned out. Decided we would stay the night alongside.

3
Overseas, March-May 1944

From its arrival in Londonderry until VE Day, E.G. 9 served in British waters under the operational control of the Royal Navy. Although the group worked under Portsmouth, Plymouth, and Rosyth Commands as well as with the Home Fleet, it operated primarily under Western Approaches Command. It thus became part of the premier anti-submarine organization in European waters, and arguably the most effective of its kind.

Established at the outset of the war in Plymouth, Western Approaches Command was initially responsible for protecting convoys transiting British waters through the southwest approaches of the English Channel and the Irish Sea or north about Ireland. After Germany captured bases in the Bay of Biscay and U-boats pushed out into the North and Central Atlantic, however, shipping eventually required protection across the entire breadth of the North Atlantic, and southward past Gibraltar to Sierra Leone. Working in close cooperation with the Admiralty and the Royal Air Force's Coastal Command, Western Approaches organized convoys and provided escorts over most of these routes. Its primary concern was the Battle of the Atlantic, where the *Kriegsmarine* also concentrated its greatest effort. In February 1941, the command shifted to a new Area Combined Headquarters (ACHQ) at Derby House, Liverpool.[1] "There," in the words of the British official history, "under the direction of a highly skilled staff of both Services, the naval and air sides of the Atlantic battle were fully integrated, and a constant watch was maintained over the whole vast battlefield and over the hundreds of warships, merchantmen and aircraft involved in the unremitting prosecution of the campaign."[2] It was a campaign that the Allies simply could not afford to lose, and Western Approaches was among their most powerful weapons.[3]

Training, technological innovation, experience, effective intelligence, and simply having enough aircraft and escorts were the keys to defeating the U-boats. As the war progressed, Western Approaches drew upon the vast resources and experience of the RN to meet those requirements. Even during the darkest days of the campaign it managed to keep its head above water, and in May 1943, with Coastal Command, Eastern Air Command of the Royal Canadian Air Force, and other Allied navies, it scored the massive successes that forced Dönitz to withdraw his U-boats from the North Atlantic. They returned that September, but as we have seen, the Allies then scored a knockout blow. Credit for the victory is usually accorded to Adm. Max Horton, who brought new vitality and grim determination when he was appointed C-in-C Western Approaches in September 1942, but it seems clear that the victory in May 1943 was the culmination of an evolutionary process.

By the time E.G. 9 joined Western Approaches in the spring of 1944, the command had an experienced cadre of senior officers leading its escort and support groups. Apart from officers in key positions ashore, they were the most important warriors in the Battle of the Atlantic, and the outcome of the battle rested largely upon their shoulders. Some, like Capt. "Johnnie" Walker, achieved legendary status during the battle itself, while others, like Donald Macintyre, Peter Gretton, E.H. Chavasse, and P.W. "Egg" Burnett, earned reputations as skilled escort leaders although largely unknown to the public. A third group, which could be dubbed the "old retreads," included officers like Frank Layard. He, and colleagues such as Martin Evans, A.M. "Sandy" McKillop, and Rolph Medley, were past promotion and either on, or destined for, the retired list. Although their stars would rise no higher in the service, their experience was vast, generally including years of small ship command, and they performed admirably leading often largely untrained escort groups in a difficult battle. Their background, however, was mostly in fleet work. Layard's career demonstrates how little anti-submarine experience they brought to the battle and the steps Western Approaches took to add that component to these officers' otherwise solid foundation of naval experience.

Like the vast majority of professional officers of his generation, prior to the war Layard had only a limited exposure to anti-submarine warfare (ASW). That reflected the specialty's lowly position in the naval hierarchy. Capt. A.J. Baker-Creswell, who earlier called minesweeping "the very scrapings" of the executive barrel, also recalled that the anti-submarine branch was "despised and ignored."[4] The small number of officers who underwent anti-submarine specialist training as lieutenants undertook a dedicated "long" course in the field. Those who chose to specialize in more professionally attractive areas such as gunnery, navigation, or torpedo, and "salt horses" like Layard who did not specialize at all, received only a rudimentary education in undersea warfare. For example, his first command, HMS *Vivacious,* was apparently not equipped with asdic, but that was probably of little consequence as the Mediterranean Fleet devoted little time to ASW, and what it did spend emphasized screening capital ships from attack, not hunting submarines.[5]

Layard soon had to take "pinging," as he dubbed ASW, more seriously. He appears to have become fully aware of asdic and its use on the tactical course in early 1933. "Had a lecture on A/S by Dendy from the A/S School," he wrote. "It's an awfully dull subject."[6] Dull or not, he appreciated its importance, and it is typical of his professionalism that prior to taking command of HMS *Walpole* and joining the Atlantic Fleet later that year, he asked to go out for a day sail with the First Anti-Submarine Flotilla at Portland so he could observe asdic being put through its paces. "We sailed for exercises at 0900," he wrote in his diary. "It was blowing a bit and distinctly cold, although sunny. [The destroyers] *Thruster* and *Salmon* played about all day with a submarine, hunting and attacking her with Asdics. Arliss let me do a couple of attacks myself. It was really quite an instructive day."[7]

The Atlantic Fleet paid more than the usual amount of attention to ASW in 1934, and *Walpole* was involved in a number of screening and hunting evolutions. On passage to the spring cruise just six days after taking over the ship, Layard was concerned enough about ASW that he checked to make certain his asdic set was in fact functioning: "Tried out our A/S set in the dog watches but although the operator assured me it was alright I'm damned if I could hear anything resembling an echo."[8] Before the exercises began Layard attended a briefing for asdic control officers but could only admit, "It is a most defeating subject."[9]

The Sixth Destroyer Flotilla carried out two ASW serials on the spring cruise, both part of a series of fleet evolutions. On 17 May, "We weighed and proceeded at 0800 and did some more sub calibre [shoots]. Then we split up into sub divisions and proceeded E. of May Island, where we met some submarines and did our first A/S exercise. It was the most simple sort of hunt but even so I found it most perplexing, but I certainly learned something." Two weeks later he was not so confident: "In the afternoon there was an A/S exercise. As only 2 submarines were available, all ships could not hunt them so *Vanquisher* and [Layard's] *Walpole* were left to play with [them] ourselves. It was a desperate failure as we never got the ghost of an echo. I just don't understand this ping business."[10]

To learn more about this skill, and perhaps to alleviate his own frustrations, Layard participated in a special evolution on 19 July: "We rendezvoused with *Mackay* and at 0700 took up a screening formation on her for another S/M attack exercise. We had C.P.O. Jenkins (one of the asdic instructors) on board. He was on the Bridge doing A/S control duties and we got marvellous results picking up two S/Ms at 4,000 and 5,000 yds. The conditions it seems were very good but nevertheless it was a most reassuring performance." In September the practice, and worry, paid off and Layard had perhaps his most useful experience:

> At 0920 the 6th D.F. were under way making for a rendezvous for our A/S exercise. At 1000 we were joined by the 1st A/S flotilla and at 1100 we started an endless chain patrol, guarding our imaginary fleet of transports from submarine attack through an imaginary swept channel. It was terribly tedious. We got one submarine and hunted him for ½ hour, and then flushed with success we proceeded to attack 2 non sub echoes of which there were lots. At sunset we formed a line of bearing patrol backwards and forwards all through the night, pinging and burning search lights but no submarine came our way. I was on the bridge all the time and simply overcome with sleepiness. At 0530 when we once more resumed the daylight round about patrol we were sent to a spare position and I got an hour's sleep before once more having to

> take somebody's place. We went on with this exercise all the a.m. and p.m. and at long last at 1700 it was packed up. We managed to get another submarine in the afternoon. When it was over D. led us back to the rest of the Fleet, anchored off Y beach, and then we anchored for the night and I was feeling damned tired. It seems the whole exercise was most successful.[11]

This exercise included many of the facets of ASW that Layard would face during the war: organized hunts, "shipping" to protect, successful attacks, fruitless searching, and long, tiring stretches on the bridge. No matter how successful such exercises were deemed to be, however, they were simply too infrequent to be of great benefit. Certainly, officers like Layard became aware of the challenges of anti-submarine warfare, but his experience confirms that they were not at home with the nuances of the activity. If one can be forgiven a pun, they only had "fleeting" experience in this highly technical form of warfare, and the relative lack of attention to hunting submarines prevented them from being truly expert anti-submarine warriors.

Aware of these shortfalls and recognizing the general need for thorough training, Western Approaches ensured that "retreads" like Layard received the training they required as the Battle of the Atlantic progressed. Layard's experience in the command thus reflects the changes made to raise the level of professionalism in the anti-submarine war. When he returned to sea in *Chelsea* in the summer of 1941 – a low ebb of the campaign – he was given no preparation whatsoever for the convoy war and had to get by on his wits and experience, both dulled by five years ashore. Things improved quickly. When he took over *Broke* in the summer of 1942, the destroyer was sent to HMS *Western Isles,* Western Approaches' main work-up base at Tobermory, Scotland. There, Cmdre. G.O. Stephenson, RNR, the legendary "Tiger of Tobermory," prepared the ship for the rigours of the Atlantic battle by putting the crew through a variety of training evolutions.[12] Layard got off to a rough start when some of his sailors were caught trying to steal a chicken their first time ashore, but he allowed that he soon had the Commodore "purring," a bold assertion from the usually humble diarist. The Tiger regained his ferociousness at the end of the work-ups, telling Layard that "we weren't moving fast enough and he told me I was too kind!! I think it was Scott who made the same remark to me as a Cadet Captain at Osborne 30 years ago."[13]

While *Western Isles* prepared ships and sometimes entire escort groups for the Battle of the Atlantic, the Western Approaches Tactical Unit (WATU) in Liverpool honed the skills of individual group leaders and commanding officers. In a series of lectures and simulations typically lasting five or six days, Capt. Gilbert Roberts and his staff developed, refined, and disseminated the tactics that group commanders and escort captains used against U-boats.[14] Layard took the course twice in 1943 – the second time presumably to familiarize himself with anti-acoustic torpedo tactics – and came away impressed both times: "A first class course for which Roberts deserves full marks," he commented.[15]

One of the great lessons of the Battle of the Atlantic was the importance of continual group training. Effective unit cohesion has been an axiom of naval warfare since before Nelson, and to ensure that escort and support groups remained sharp, Western Approaches included regular group training in its operational cycle. Although schedules varied due to operational requirements, support groups working out of Londonderry usually had seven-to-ten-day layovers between operations in order to give leave and repair defects. Harbour and shore training was carried out while the ships were alongside, and before returning to sea, each group usually underwent a couple of days of group training, including practice against live, "clockwork mouse" submarines. Staff officers often accompanied the ships to critique performances and then submitted reports to Commodore D. at Londonderry.[16]

Finally, to ensure that their forces remained at peak efficiency, Western Approaches' two senior operational commanders met regularly with their group leaders and commanding officers. In "wash-ups" typically held when groups returned to Londonderry following operations or whenever SOs passed through Liverpool, the commander-in-chief, Adm. Sir Max Horton, and his right-hand man, the commodore D. Londonderry, Cmdre. G.W.G. Simpson, put an almost personal stamp on the battle against the U-boats. Both former submariners with formidable personalities, Horton and Simpson digested the lessons of the battle, kept an eye on leadership, and imparted a professional zeal to the men fighting at the sharp end. Simpson had a particular impact on Canadians, as virtually every commanding officer who served in the Mid-Ocean Escort Force or in the support groups deployed in UK waters met with him on a regular basis. Indeed, despite the accolades routinely showered upon Rear-Adm. Leonard Murray and Capt. Douglas Prentice by Canadian naval historians, Simpson probably had the greatest influence on the RCN anti-submarine fleet over the final three years of the war.[17]

Layard seems so awestruck by his audiences with Horton that we do not gain much additional detail to flesh out the portrait of that dynamic wartime leader.[18] "There was nothing particular that he wanted me for," Layard gushed after a meeting in April 1944, "but it is a great thing when these big men take the trouble to meet and know their C.O.s and S.O.s personally. He was very pleasant but I never feel at ease in such company and I think I talked rather a lot of nonsense."[19] We learn more about Simpson. Known as "Shrimp" because of his short stature, the submariner, like Horton, brought the "poacher turned gamekeeper" attribute that was deemed to be an advantage in the fight against the U-boats.[20] Layard's diary emphasizes the professionalism with which Simpson tackled his job, ensuring that his officers were up to scratch, concerning himself with the welfare of the men ashore, and making sure that ships were well maintained. "Just before we slipped,"

Layard noted on one occasion, "the Commodore came on board all ships of the group to impress on us the necessity of anti Gnat tactics as laid down in A.C.I.s."[21] But as much as he was impressed by Simpson, Layard thought he could have done more. Although the commodore reviewed operations with Canadian commanding officers upon their return to harbour, he rarely visited RCN ships, and on one occasion Layard tactfully suggested to Simpson's chief of staff "what a pity it was [the Commodore] didn't try to get to know the Canadian COs better."[22] Another time, he reluctantly went over Simpson's head to Horton to ask if E.G. 9 could do a layover in Plymouth instead of Londonderry so that his sailors could take leave in England and Scotland instead of Northern Ireland, where he thought there was little for them to do but drink. Layard so regretted his disloyalty in that instance that he offered to resign his command; the Commodore "was v. nice and told me not to be a bloody fool or take this too seriously and he did *not* consider it disloyal."[23] We also learn that Simpson had a considerable fondness for alcohol. Many meetings between the two were held over a glass, and in his draft memoirs Layard described Simpson "as a brilliant youngish ex Submariner but my word how he hit the bottle."[24]

Besides benefiting from Western Approaches' leadership and residual expertise, Layard had a first rate anti-submarine platform at his disposal in the River class frigate. Although frigates lacked the responsiveness and manoeuvrability of the "V" and "W" class destroyers Layard so loved from the interwar years, they were far superior to the unwieldy four-stackers *Chelsea* and *Salisbury* he had commanded earlier in the war. Good sea boats with a fair turn of speed and excellent endurance, River class frigates were equipped with the latest anti-submarine sensors and weaponry, including type 144Q asdic, type FH 3 or FH 4 HF/DF, type 761 echo sounders, and hedgehog.[25] They also carried some 200 depth charges, enough for twenty full patterns, which enabled them to take part in extended hunts without having to break off or return to port.[26] One weakness was their Canadian-built RXC centimetric radar, which lacked both performance and reliability – as we have seen, Layard called it "a bloody awful affair" – but in most ships Western Approaches eventually replaced it with superior British sets such as type 271.[27] Later, the Loch class frigate HMCS *Loch Alvie* joined the group, and although its hull proved vulnerable to hard pounding, it was equipped with type 277 radar as well as Squid, the most potent anti-submarine weapon produced during the war.[28]

E.G. 9 had a mixed complement of River class frigates and Flower class corvettes when it arrived overseas in March 1944. Although the Flowers had performed gallantly when they filled the gap during the dark days of the Battle of the Atlantic, they could not hold a candle to frigates in terms of anti-submarine capability. E.G. 9 became an all-frigate group at the end of April 1944, which enabled it to take a giant step forward in terms of capability and cohesion. Likewise, it was some time before the group could fully benefit from all Western Approaches had to offer in terms of training and expertise. In the meantime, experience was a cruel teacher, as the group was immediately thrust into the front lines of the anti-submarine war in European waters: as Layard admitted in the midst of their first patrol, "We live and learn."[29]

Tuesday, 14 March 1944 – Londonderry

I had a very disturbed night, as I was constantly being wakened up by the Officer of the Watch reporting what was happening alongside the oiler. We weighed at 0930 to go up harbour and before we left I managed to sort out the oiling programmes for the rest of the group. I berthed on *Watchman* and as soon as I could I went up to Operations. Apparently the scrum and disorganization at Moville realized but unavoidable. We are required to go out again on the 16th. While I was in Ops the Wren Superintendent of Western Approaches,[30] who is visiting here, came in. My God what a horse faced woman and what an ill fitting overcoat. With her was Lovell Caddy who is Chief Officer, N. Ireland. I tried to contact the Senior Engineering Officer but failed and so went back on board for lunch. At 1230 *Swansea* came alongside us. After lunch King came over and gave us account of the sinking of the U/B. Apparently he came on the scene just as the boat surfaced and took part in a spirited chase and gun action before she was abandoned and sunk. I dealt with my report of proceedings and went on deck to watch *Swansea*'s U/B prisoners being taken ashore. Poor devils, one can't help being sorry for them.

At 1530 I went up to the Commodore's office and saw the Chief of Staff – Selby[31] – the Commodore being away. Then I saw the signals staff and then I sat in the Mess for a bit until [I] heard that Shorto,[32] the senior engineering officer, was in his office and I went to see him. He told me the support groups run for about 3 or 4 weeks and then have about a 10 day period for defects. Back on board to do some more paper work. After supper I walked up to Ops to put a call through to J., but I was told there would be 4 hours delay and so I cancelled the call and went back on board. A damp drizzly day but it was nice to hear the beginnings of bird song.

Wednesday, 15 March 1944 – Londonderry

I tried to get a call through to J. at 0700 but was told no long distance calls before 0900. I went up to Talbot House at about 1000 and called on N.O.I.C. (Capt. Glencross),[33] the Staff Officer Administration, and finally the Commodore, "Shrimp" Simpson, who explained to me the operation we are going out on tomorrow. Back on board for lunch. Signed some papers after lunch and then put on plain clothes and took myself off for a walk. Took a short 2 hours round outside the town and got back by 1600. S.O. C 1 (*Assiniboine*) came to see me at about 1715. He is an R.N.R. Commander and a v. nice chap. At 1800 the Commodore came on board to meet the C.O.s of the group and talk to them. He was most impressive I thought, although one knows he is one of the outstanding personalities of the war. When he left some Canadian press liaison officers appeared and insisted on taking a photograph of me and all the C.O.s sitting round a table studying a chart. I had a late supper with Easton in his cabin. He has been up at the American Hospital all day having his stomach photographed. He thinks he's got one of those ulcers. I hope he isn't going to go sick. Black, who was No. 1 of the *Salisbury* and now captain of the *Rupert,* a Captain class frigate, came to see me after dinner.

I put a call through to J. at about 1700 and it came through unexpectedly at about 1900 and by the time I got to the phone only about a minute of my 6 minutes was left and I hardly had time to say more than hello, so I put another call through and eventually at 2330 I was able to have three minutes. J. says Emily has left owing to health, and so J. is now out of the Wrens looking after the house and children. On the 30th she is taking them both over to her Mother's at Lydney until this 2nd front business breaks, leaving 2 Wren officers to live in the house. Made me home sick hearing her voice. The recent bombing of London sounds pretty grim.

Thursday, 16 March 1944 – Londonderry/At sea

Just before we slipped the Commodore came on board all ships of the group to impress on us the necessity of anti Gnat tactics as laid down in A.C.I.s.[34] In consequence we were rather late slipping – about 0930 instead of 0900. On arrival at Moville, *Atholl* suddenly found he leaked lubricating oil and had to go to the oiler. *Frontenac* just didn't appear, believe delayed by A/S defects, and so as it was getting on we sailed with 4 ships instead of 6. (*Baddeck* was previously known to be unable to sail on account of engine defects.) A lovely day. Sharp but sunny and extreme visibility.

We went to patrol area which is off the N.W. coast of Ireland where it is thought a U-boat working in the W. Approaches for reconnaissance might go for night battery charging.[35] We relieved *Icarus* and his group at 1700 by which time *Atholl* caught up. At 2030, just as it was dark, *North Bay* got an A/S contact. We closed and the remainder did Observant. We were just on a charted non-sub spot and after investigating it some time it was obvious that is what *North Bay* had got, so we formed up and went on with the patrol. Unfortunately *Atholl* in taking up his station went over the spot and picked up the contact and started to plaster it with H/H [hedgehog] and D/Cs, and although I felt that was what had happened, we had to come back and go through the same rigmarole again of Observant until we ourselves had classified it as an unmistakable wreck and then on we went again at 2300. We altered to 180° by E.I. turn[36] at 0100, and I didn't get much sleep as the group got very out of station and I was continually being called up to have their positions reported to me.

Friday, 17 March 1944 – At sea

A somewhat hazy overcast day but still flat calm. At 0430 we sighted Eagle Island Light ahead and altered to 090° and at 0630 we altered to the North again. *Frontenac* had to stop at about 1030 to make good some engine room defect, and I told *Swansea* to stand by him. Went on with the rest up to Tory Island and then altered to 202° to sweep down along the coast. At 1230 we sighted a swamped and abandoned merchant ship life boat which we went alongside and tried to salvage while the rest of the group patrolled round us. It was too heavy to hoist on board, however, even when baled dry, and so after some fruitless efforts we gave it up at about 1430 and went on with our patrol. Crossed the entrance to Donegal Bay and when about 5 miles off the coast turned N. Our area is bounded by a line which runs from Tory Island 60W then 60'S to Eagle Island and the Irish Coast, and so we can never stay on a course longer than about 4 hours, and manoeuvring 6 ships about in line abreast is rather a problem. Received a signal in the night saying we would stay out until the 26th. I think we shall be giddy by that time.

Saturday, 18 March 1944 – At sea

By planning my moves over night and writing out the times of alterations of course for the O.O.W., I remained in my bunk in the chart house all night and just had the alterations reported to me. We had a bit of a blow from the S.S.W. with drizzle and poor visibility. I read a whole lot of secret and confidential Londonderry orders. I am also reading Mahan's *Life of Nelson.* On a S.'ly leg making down towards Eagle Island it was thick enough to make me turn to the E. early and use soundings and radar to find out where we were. After dark it cleared up and the visibility improved.

Sunday, 19 March 1944 – At sea

We steamed up the coast on an 020° course until Tory Is. was 090° and then turned back to 226° at 0110. At 0600 we turned to the N. again and at 0900 just as we were coming around to 090° at the N.W. corner of area we got very mixed up with E.G. 22, another all sloop support group who are operating in Area B just north. Finally sorted ourselves out. On arrival inshore we turned round and went west again and at 1830 turned east once more. A lovely star lit night and very little wind. As we approached Tory Island I detached *Owen Sound* and *North Bay* to pass through Tory Sound and have a radar sweep for a possible lurking U-boat, while we with the 2nd Div. to port passed to the northward of the island just a mile off.

Monday, 20 March 1944 – At sea

Tory Lt. was abeam just over a mile at midnight. Held on to the E.'ward for another ½ hour and then turned to 270° telling *Frontenac* to proceed to Moville for radar repairs. *Owen Sound* and *North Bay* joined up having been around Tory Island and seen nothing in the Sound. At 0215 having got the group on line of bearing and being just about to turn to 205° down the coast we got a radar contact ahead, then some newer ships, and thanks to this lousy R.X.C. set we were practically on top of H.X. 282 coming on opposite course before I had time to pull myself together. I then got flustered and completely wooly brained and instead of quickly turning 180° and getting clear instead I tried to nip across the front of the convoy and got much too close, with the result that navigation lights were switched on all over the place and I got a very rude signal from the S.O. of the escort. I could have kicked myself because if I'd read the situation report more carefully I'd have realized we were going to meet. Finally got my rather scattered group together at about 0330 but I was much too worried and depressed to get much sleep. There is no doubt about it, I'm no good in an emergency. I just lose my head. The thought infuriated and depressed me all day.

We went up and down and backwards and forwards in our area using Blue Turns and Easy Item turns. Thought of going on board one of the corvettes and more or less inspecting her at sea but then quite a bit of wind and sea rose from the W. and so decided not to. E.G. 2, Capt. Walker's group, has just returned to harbour having sunk 6 U-boats in 20 days!!! Incredible.

Tuesday, 21 March 1944 – At sea

Feeling a bit more cheerful. At 0230 we were down by Eagle Island and altered up for Tory on a course 047°. *Frontenac* joined up in the morning watch having completed her radar repairs at Londonderry. At 0815 when up to Tory we altered to 270°. At 1030 the patrolling Sunderland aircraft dropped a smoke marker ahead and carried out exercise homing procedure. We did not go quite according to the book but was good value. *Swansea* and ourselves had just arrived at the spot a bit ahead of the others when *Swansea* reported a contact and proceeded to attack with a 10 charge pattern. We then picked it up, held it, and found it had no movement. Oil was rising from the spot and when we went over it using echo sounding we got a trace of something about 300' feet long and 80' off the bottom. As this position coincided with a plotted non sub it was obviously a wreck and so we left it. Turned S. at about 1300.

At 1630 I carried out some drills. Drop a depth charge, fire a gun, etc., and finally pick up a life buoy with a sea boat. The *Matane* was dreadfully slow and pretty well last in everything. The worst feature was the complete helplessness of Duchesneau the O.O.W.[37] We live and learn, and some more of this drill must be done. Talking to Easton afterwards he pointed out that these war time officers really only know one job, gunnery, navigation, or whatever it is they do. I am amazed to find that hardly a single O.O.W., 1st Lieutenant included, knows how to fix the ship when in sight of land. We were delayed after the drill because *North Bay* had to get medical help from *Swansea* for an injured man. At 1915 when up to Eagle Island we altered first E. and then to 035° to run up to Tory Island. A flat calm day.

Wednesday, 22 March 1944 – At sea

At 0100 we turned round when abreast Tory and steered a diagonal course to the S.W. corner of the area. At 0700 when down by Eagle Island we turned to 300°. Detached *Frontenac,* who was ordered back to Londonderry by signal to join C 1 group, I hope only temporarily. It was a flat calm but overcast day with absolutely extreme visibility. A slow Mediterranean convoy homeward bound passed through our area and was in sight most of the day. I spent most of the forenoon getting out orders for a new type of search which I want to practice in the p.m. I got out some orders, memos, and letters that I want to send off on arrival in harbour.

We were back again at Tory at 1700 and turned to 270° and I carried out two things from the drill table. *Matane* was a little better today. Thomas fitted up a wonderful loud speaker amplifier in the chart house, which is my action plotting position, by which we can hear everything said and reported from the bridge and A/S cabinet and we can even hear the ping of the asdic. At 2000 we got three radar pips ahead at 7,000 yards closing. We were expecting nothing according to the situation report but I wasn't taking any risks this time and turned 180°. The pips turned out to be three British yard minesweepers presumably coming across from America. I wish they'd tell us when things were coming into our area.

Thursday, 23 March 1944 – At sea

At 0100 we turned S. At 0230 the bridge reported a flare in the water to starboard, which we turned to investigate, but before we reached it it had gone out. Think it must have been dropped by an aircraft for measuring drift. Wish they'd chosen some other part of the ocean for their navigation experiments as it disturbs my sleep. Turned west at 0500 and N. at 0700. At 0900 I got each ship to come up alongside and I passed over my new orders on a type of search for a submerged U/B which I made out yesterday. At 1115 we turned E. and at 1130 we picked up an asdic contact which on investigating for some time proved to be the same non sub echo we ran into on Tuesday. Still giving off oil and giving a cracking echo.

Another calm overcast day with extreme visibility. *Baddeck* joined up with the group at 1500, and at 1600 when a few miles off Tory Island we turned to 228°. Almost immediately it was reported that the patrolling aircraft was trying hard to pass an immediate signal to base. We got a D/F bearing of 286° and turned and increased speed. It soon became obvious that there was nothing to it and at 1715 I tried out [a] new "Divisional Outward Sweep," which seemed rather good. At 1830 the two divisions closed and we turned together to 228°. A S.'ly wind sprang up which funnily enough was very chilly. Easton and I had supper together in his cabin.

Friday, 24 March 1944 – At sea

I took the group into the entrance of Donegal Bay and at 0115 sent *Owen Sound* and *North Bay* to sweep right up to St. John's Point Light and took the 2nd Division into Sligo Bay. Found nothing and at 0200 turned round and came out. *Owen Sound* and *North Bay* recalled at 0230 and they rejoined us at daylight. At 0800 we turned to 180°.

At 1120 we intercepted a practice aircraft submarine report which we D/F'd. There was some delay in reporting the bearing, and I didn't get the group around to the course until 1145. The homing procedure on M/F then seemed to break down, although *Swansea* got our bearing. Although we called the plane on R/T we could get no reply. These communications are all-important in this sort of operation and in bowling out mistakes the exercise was good value, but it didn't go on long enough to get us to the spot and begin an A/S search. After a beautifully clear night we had a day of very poor visibility and quite a strong S.'ly wind. At 1600, having run diagonally from the SW corner of the area on our aircraft D/F bearing, we turned S. again and then N. once more. Wrote up some of my report of proceedings including remarks on communications, which seem to leave much to be desired.

Saturday, 25 March 1944 – At sea

The visibility was very poor in the night and we couldn't get a fix on the lights as we went north. Ran out to the west and then back to Tory Island, which we sighted in better visibility, and at 1100 we turned S. down the coast. At 1700 I dropped life buoys and lowered boats. *Matane* again miles last. Discussed the movements for the night very carefully so that we are ready to leave the area at daylight and I made our E.T.A. Moville as 1000 tomorrow. It has been a bit monotonous this sweeping round the area, but to have had 10 days with such continuous good weather was lucky.

Sunday, 26 March 1944 – At sea/Londonderry

My times and courses didn't work out quite as expected and so we had to rather mark time and waste time off Tory. Eventually set course for Inishtrahull at 0600. At about 0900 when off the light we all fired a full hedgehog salvo. When it goes off on the bottom it is a pretty good bang. We arrived at Moville at 1000 and were told not to go up harbour before 1500, so we went to the oiler. *Swansea* came alongside us. At 1130 another signal arrived ordering the group to proceed up to Londonderry forthwith. Sent the corvettes up and *Swansea* slipped at 1300 and we went at about 1330. A most lovely day. Pretty hot sun and trip up the river was delightful.[38]

After tea Easton and I walked up to Ops, where we were told 4 new frigates from Canada are joining this group and all the corvettes are being taken away, making an all frigate group. It is a right and logical thing to do I suppose, but I'm damned sorry to lose the corvettes, especially the C.O.s who are really a fine keen bunch of V.R.s. The N.R. types I'm likely to get in the frigates probably will be better seamen and more experienced but not half as keen and alive. I went into the Ch. of Staff's office to find out about training and courses. The Commodore signalled on arrival that leave to the watch could be given, which is a pity I think, because I was hoping for lots of courses and instruction during this boiler cleaning. Just before leaving the ship I got through almost at once by phone to J. and told her I was coming home on leave.

Easton and I took a bit of a walk round the town before returning. Our ward room were at home to the group, and when we got back we went in and mingled with the crowd. It is a pity that they will get so drunk and noisy. I was finally taken ashore by most of the corvette C.O.s, but as we failed to get anything to eat ashore we all went to the *Atholl* and had an excellent ham and eggs and sat talking.

Monday, 27 March 1944 – Londonderry/Stranraer

Went up to see the Commodore and other officers about this and that, and 1100 there was a group arrival conference at which all defects were discussed and later on training. At the end the Commodore told the corvette captains that they were leaving the group, and sugared the pill a bit by saying it was all on account of the big things that lay ahead. Got back on board for a very late lunch and immediately afterwards got into a car with No. 1 and drove to the station and caught the 2:45 for Larne. Got aboard the steamer, which was v. full, at about 1800 and we sailed about 1930. Had some food on board. No. 1 rather tight and unpleasant. At Stranraer I decided to catch the 1st train (the 10:00 p.m.), which was packed, and I was lucky to get a seat. No sleepers available, although I might have got one on the 2nd train. This travelling is certainly the height of discomfort, but going *on* leave it doesn't matter. Another really lovely warm sunny day.

Tuesday, 28 March 1944 – London/Prinsted

A pretty uncomfortable night but after Crewe the carriage wasn't full. The train was late and didn't get into Euston till about 1030. After waiting for a taxi for a bit I caught the tube to Waterloo only to find next train was the fast train at

12:45, so I parked my suitcases and walked back across Haughford Bridge and went to Norton's and had a hair cut and shave. I then taxied back to Waterloo. Couldn't see much fresh damage from the current air raids on London. Had a bun and a glass of beer in the refreshment room and then caught the 12:45. Got off about 1417 and then bussed home, where I arrived about 1445. Got a tremendous welcome from J. and R. and later on from G. when she returned from school. Walked round the garden, which is looking v. smart and tidy, and looked at all my plants and shrubs. It is heavenly to be home for a day or two, at least I hadn't to start dreading the departure again. J. is doing all cooking and housework and looking after the children, with a few hours daily from a woman from Southbourne. I brought home with me most of the groceries and things that Patricia Prentice got for her in Halifax and they were much appreciated. Another lovely day, but there is quite a drought over here and rain is badly needed.

...

Sunday, 2 April 1944 – Prinsted/London

The clocks went on an hour to double summer time at midnight. I woke up feeling a bit the worn for wear. After a late breakfast I did the drawing room fire, boiler, etc., and then collected in and locked away the silver and other things in the sea chest. Just before lunch R. and I started out for the Scott-Moncrieffs', but he fell down and then insisted on going home, so I went on and took a glass of beer off Allan. After lunch I puttered about, with J. washing up, and packing and starting to count the hours and minutes still left and feeling unhappy and depressed. At about 1545 I walked to the Youngs' with the *Book of British Sports,* which they are going to look after for us, and I talked with Bobby for a bit and then went on to get the washing, but old Mother Faindale was out and so walked home for tea. After tea J., R., and I took a little walk down to the marsh gate and back and then it was time for Raymond's bath and I had to get into my uniform.

At 1900, the dreaded hour of departure, the taxi arrived and I said good bye with my usual aching heart and drove to Havant station meaning to catch the 7:33 but finding unexpectedly there was a fast train at about 7:15 which I caught instead. On arrival at W'loo I taxied to Euston and on enquiring found out there was no sleeper booked for me. Went to the station hotel. Too late for dinner but had sandwiches in the lounge and sat there reading until 2230 when I went back to the station and had a long wait on the platform as the 11:45 didn't come in until 2320. V. crowded but got a corner seat, and after the train started the sleeping berth attendant came along and gave me an unclaimed berth in a 2 berth sleeper. V. much better then sitting up. Am I miserable!! Drizzly rain in the a.m. but quite a nice p.m. Joan takes the family to Lydney to her Mother tomorrow.

Monday, 3 April 1944 – Liverpool/Heysham

Slept like a log. Called at 0700 and had first innings at shaving and dressing while my sleeper mate stayed in bed. On leaving the train I packed my bags in the Officers' Club and then walked to the Adelphi, where I had breakfast and sat about until about 0930, when I walked to Derby House. A wet miserable morning which added to my misery and general unhappiness. I went in to see MacIntyre, the Chief of Staff, and then saw Smitty and the S.O.O. It looks as if the group will only consist of *Matane, Swansea,* and *Stormont* when we sail on the 10th, as the other frigates have been delayed in Canada. The Admiral[39] couldn't see me so I sat about in the Officer's Mess till lunchtime, when the Admiral took me up to his flat and I was greatly honoured by a *tête à tête* lunch. There was nothing particular that he wanted me for, but it is a great thing when these big men take the trouble to meet and know their C.O.s and S.O.s personally. He was v. pleasant but I never feel at ease in such company and I think I talked rather a lot of nonsense.

Made my bow and left after lunch and walked into the town and went to the cinema and saw rather a sloppy film, *Captains Courageous,* then I collected my suitcase and took it to the Exchange Hotel where I had some tea and wrote a letter to J. and eventually caught the 7:15 train to Preston. Arrived there at 2015 and went to the Park Hotel, had dinner, and then caught the 9:47 to Heysham. Arrived Heysham at 2245 and went on board the boat. No berth allotted, but after waiting for ages the unclaimed berths were allocated and I got a double cabin which I shared with a Gunner. The discomfort of travelling on return from leave seems much greater than when going on leave.

Tuesday, 4 April 1944 – Belfast/Londonderry

A hot and stuffy night. Turned out and had breakfast. We ran into a thick fog in the entrance to Belfast Loch, and after creeping along for a bit we anchored. Later on it cleared. We went up harbour but we were about three hours late and we didn't get ashore till nearly 1200. The 1st Lieut. of *Hotspur* and I and a 3rd Officer W.R.N.S. called Baker-Shand took a horse cart to the station and went into the hotel and had drinks and lunch and then caught the 2:00 train to Londonderry. We had a change at Coleraine and from there on it was v. crowded. McKillop got in at Castle Rock and on arrival at Londonderry at 1718 we shared a service car to the dockyard.

On arrival on board I was greeted with the news that I was to take over C.O. of the ship from Easton, as owing to the shortage of C.O.s he was wanted for some destroyer. Well, that is alright, but on top of it Easton says he is getting rid of Carruthers (the 1st Lieut.) on account of drink. I certainly don't want to keep the fellow, but I don't think I can get a new 1st Lieut., and all the other officers in the ship are so young and inexperienced. Sandy McKillop came over at about 1900 and we both went round to the *Hotspur,* where we eventually dined and wined quite heavily, and then we went along to some ship's company dance where we drank a lot of beer and finally got back on board v. late.

Wednesday, 5 April 1944 – Londonderry

Lord what fools we are to drink. Woke up feeling awful and my brain was completely wooly all day. I didn't feel a lot like competing with the problems of taking over command. Went up to the offices about Carruthers and how to get a relief and also enquired about our sea exercises. Back on board I read through a mass of signals. I am making Miller[40] 1st Lieut., but the thought rather frightens me because good as he is his inexperience is vast. In the p.m. I walked along to the Tactical School and had a yarn with Allen[41] about anti-Gnat tactics. When I got back I had the Captain of the *Stormont*[42] over to discuss group orders and tactics. At 1700 I went to see the Commodore and talked about this and that. I told him officially about Carruthers (perhaps I should not have). My group for the moment consists of *Matane, Swansea, Stormont,* and *Owen Sound,* but *Owen Sound* like all the other corvettes will leave soon. Wrote a short, miserable note to J. and went into accounts and other ship's matters with Easton, and at about 1900 I made the signal that I'd taken over command. After dinner I walked over to *North Bay* and said good bye to Hynes, who I am damned sorry to lose. Went to bed feeling harassed, homesick, and unhappy. I am sorry Easton is going (he is getting command of the destroyer HMCS *Saskatchewan*) as we got on v. well together. I wonder how long I will be left in command.

Thursday, 6 April 1944 – Londonderry/Moville

Spent a wakeful night feeling nervous and worried about taking command and mooring the ship. It really is stupid at my age and with my experience. Easton had breakfast with me and then took himself and his gear over to the next ship to await the arrival of the *Saskatchewan.* There was some delay with tugs and pilot and we were the inside one of 4 ships, but eventually we got away at about 0930, hoisted our whaler when in the stream, and proceeded down river. A bit misty early on but it turned into a lovely sunny day. Dropped the pilot at Moville, picked up the HF/DF expert, and went on out and anchored on the calibration range at 1200. The yacht then proceeded to circle us while we had a check calibration on H/F and a calibration on our new MF/DF set. I saw my first batch of requestmen and defaulters after lunch. Mostly drunks and leave breakers. Looking over the side in the clear water it was seen that about 8 feet of our starboard bilge keel had torn away and was standing vertical, and so I made a signal about it asking permission to return up river for a diver to inspect. We didn't finish D/Fing until about 2030 and anchored at Moville just before dark. King from the *Swansea* came over to see me. One of his officers has gone a bit mental and he wants me to take him with me to Derry tomorrow. I had all officers into my cabin and talked to them at 1730, and tomorrow I intend to see the ship's company.

Friday, 7 April 1944 – Moville/Londonderry

We weighed at 0915 when the pilot arrived and proceeded up river to Londonderry. We had to berth in No. 16 berth, which was by no means easy on account of 3 ammunition ships at 17 berth. But for the pilot's advice on how best to make use of the tide I should never have got there. Easton and Gardiner from the *Atholl* came to see me. The former wants to take his steward Aucoin to the *Saskatchewan* in exchange of one already there, which I agreed to, but later on I found Aucoin didn't want to go, so I went over and told Easton who said he'd speak to Aucoin. Later on we found the relief steward seemed a complete dud and Duchesneau our Mess Secretary was very against the exchange. Eventually after a lot of discussion and thought I decided *not* to effect the exchange.

The diver went down to look at our bilge keel at 1530 and by 1800 the bent bit had been cut off. Operations then said we would sail at 0900 tomorrow. We found some rather serious W/T defects, which the base maintenance staff put right for us. After dinner I walked round to the *Saskatchewan,* made my peace with Easton about Aucoin, and sat and talked to him for quite a time. A close muggy day. I feel somehow all in the air. We don't seem to be told what to do until the last minute, and I don't feel quite *au fait* about these exercises tomorrow.

Saturday, 8 April 1944 – Londonderry/Moville

We slipped at 0900 and I had a tug to assist. Dropped the pilot at Moville and then went out to Area R to join the rest of the group, who were exercising with a submarine. A beastly day, blowing quite hard, occasional showers and poor visibility. We got one of the base A/S officers on board from *Owen Sound* and soon after we joined up the S/M came up from his first dip. We put him straight down again and then took the lion's share of the attacking, which, however, was only fair as we'd missed on the first day. It was a damned nuisance as I want this to be a group show exercising, sweeping up, to finding and holding a S/M. Wasn't v. happy about our attacks and just as we started we found there was a defect on the hedgehog circuit. At 1500 our S/M time was up and I took the group off to Area H for high angle firing at a sleeve target. The continual failures we experience in communications are most unsatisfactory. When it was just time to start we were told the practice had been cancelled, so back we came to another area for a low angle shoot. We were the last to fire, and although old Telfer[43] was desperately slow in getting going, the shots certainly seemed to go quite near the target.

Got back to Moville with the group just before dark and we went alongside the oiler. A mass of signals to be made and defects here there and everywhere. At about 2300 we were ready to shove off but found the wind, which was v. strong, was binding us on just as happened once before with me in the *Chelsea*. However, it wasn't quite so bad in this case and we got away after going astern a bit. We then dropped a hook. A most exhausting and worrying day. Quite a time, late as it was, before I got to sleep, I was worrying so much. Got a letter from J.

Sunday, 9 April 1944 – Moville/At sea

We weighed at 0800 and went out for more S/M exercises with a corvette called H.M.S. *Abelia*. Still blowing a bit at first but it developed into a really lovely hot sunny day. Thomas, who had been doing his stuff in the other ships of the group, came on board before we sailed. We had a certain amount of trouble with our A/S recorder but the exercises were excellent value for me and the operators. At 1200 we finished and wasted a lot of time returning to Moville slowly, and we got a signal repeated and decoded which we thought was for the S/M but which was only repeated to it and was for us, telling us to pick up the P.W.T.O. [port watch telegraph officer] at Foxglove. On arriving at the signal station we were given two more signals, one to say the group would be required operationally p.m. today, when I thought we weren't going till tomorrow, and the other saying a letter was being sent out to us. I hung about wasting more time waiting for the boat to collect the swinging officer from *Swansea* and dashed back again to Lough Foyle buoy for a [compass] swing. Had considerable difficulty in interpreting my orders and nearly made a very stupid signal. However, it was sorted out at last. While swinging I had time to scribble a line to J.

Got back to Moville at 1715 and the duty boat took off P.W.T.O. and compass officer and a lot of sea cadets and our mail, and then we just hung about under way until 1800, when we signalled the group to weigh and proceeded out to sea. Moville and the hills and the countryside were looking lovely in the sunshine. We are to rendezvous with the Escort Carrier H.M.S. *Biter* and the 7th E.G. They are at present at sea and have been ordered to sweep an area about 45N and 20W. Another exhausting and trying day. Quite nice to get to sea to have a bit of peace. Passed Tory Island just before midnight and at 0230 put the clocks back 1 hour.

Monday, 10 April 1944 – At sea

Eagle Is. Light was abeam at 0515 and we altered to 220°. Wind and sea started to get up rather quickly, and by 0800 we were pitching heavily and reduced to 12 kts. A wet and uncomfortable day with the wind blowing at Force 6 from the S. I read A.C.I.s on the subject of escort carriers, and I wrote out some new brief group tactics embodying the latest anti-Gnat tactics. After such a long spell of fine weather I find myself feeling a bit queasy with this pitching. I also find myself missing Easton quite a bit. It was nice to have him to talk to and to discuss things with. The situation report showed a homeward bound convoy right in our path, and sure enough at 1830 we sighted them and had to alter course to get out of their way. In spite of the wind, which remained about the same, it was sunny in patches. Reduced to 11 kts at about 1915. Put the clocks back to G.M.T.

Tuesday, 11 April 1944 – At sea

Wind and sea went down completely and it was a lovely day. *Stormont* signalled she had got an HF/DF bearing in the night, which together with a signal from Admiralty reporting a D/F bearing of U/B, made it appear that it wasn't far from us, and so at 1000 I altered to 300° to close the vicinity and made a signal to say what I was doing. Just after lunch (1245), when I was on the bridge, we got an A/S contact which at first seemed good but then we lost it. Then *Stormont* picked it up and lost it, and then we all started getting pings and it certainly pointed to fish or currents but some were so good it was difficult to leave them, especially in view of the D/F bearing and probable proximity of a U/B. It is the most difficult thing in the world to decide when to leave a contact, and finally it wasn't till 1600 that I dragged them all reluctantly away and turned to the S.'ward to rendezvous with *Biter.* The situation report and *Biter*'s signals were very contradictory and confusing. I didn't know which position to take, which of course caused me much anxiety. In the p.m. the weather deteriorated, the wind came up from the N.W., and there was heavy rain from about 1800 till 2200, when it once more cleared up. I spoke to the P.O. Tel in hope to organize some daily news bulletin. I've never been so out of touch with the world and the war as in this ship. Neither officers or men seem in any way interested.

Wednesday, 12 April 1944 – At sea

I started to call *Biter* at 0400 at hourly intervals but didn't get him till past 0800, when he told me to stop transmitting as he was keeping strict R/T silence. Almost simultaneously, however, arrived a signal from him via shore giving his 0730 position, course, and speed, which put him considerably to the W., and I altered to 250° to intercept. Visibility was good although it was starting to blow again from the S. and another gale warning arrived. At about 1315 we sighted *Biter* and the 7th E.G. and closed. I went up to *Biter*'s starboard quarter and talked and exchanged orders by line. L.A.R. Boswell is Captain and is in charge of this operation. It was about 1600 before everything was sorted out and the necessary information had been passed to the rest of the group.

The 7th E.G. formed a close screen and we were stationed with *Owen Sound* at Green[44] 60° and *Swansea* and *Stormont* Red 60°. Course was 000° and at 1900 course was altered to 180°. Just before dark it started to blow quite hard with heavy rain. To my horror, at about 2100 I realized that *Swansea* and *Stormont* had come right round to my side when the Red 180° had been made. Shouldn't have thought it possible that King could have been such a B.F. [bloody fool]. Owing to the rain I couldn't get them to see my light and eventually had to haul over and close them and tell them to go back to their proper station on *Biter*'s starboard bow. The 9th E.G. were to act as striking forces to run out on HF/DF bearings. Just before midnight it cleared up and wind eased.

Thursday, 13 April 1944 – At sea

Biter turned to the N. again at 0700. Our HF/DF got a transmission at 0530 which might have been close but couldn't get a bearing on it and therefore uncertain whether or not to break R/T silence. I did *not* but made a V/S signal to *Biter* when it was light. We remained 6 miles on the Std. bow all day. Fair and sunny but blowing Force 5 from the S.W. and a very big long W.'ly swell. Had a talk with Miller and Telfer to try to get our cruising stations reorganized. At 1400 we started to close with *Owen Sound*, and at 1500 we were given a position on the close screen as *Hoste* and *Grindall* from E.G. 7 were being detached. It was rather fun altering course and taking station on the close screen, and it reminded me of my short spell of fleet work in the *Broke*. Read a whole lot of A.F.O.s. Just before dark we made a big alteration by 2 turns to the S.'ward, which was to be our course for the night. Glass still falling slowly.

Friday, 14 April 1944 – At sea

We had a certain amount of trouble with the station keeping during the night on the close screen, and I spent quite a lot of time on the bridge. At 0700 *Biter* turned to the N. Very little wind all day, only a W.'ly swell still. *Biter* oiled two of the 7th E.G. (*Cygnet* and *Pelican*) while proceeding slowly on her way. At about 1245 *Swansea* on the other side of the screen from us got an A/S contact and counter attacked. *Pelican* was sent to help and they dropped out of sight astern, still in contact but we could listen to their R/T signals. After a 4 hour hunt they brought a U-boat to the surface after a creeping attack and sank it and picked up survivors.[45]

Swansea is certainly doing her stuff. Everybody on board here is desperately jealous – except me. My only reaction is one of fear and doubt whether in similar circumstances I would make a balls of it. We turned round to the S again at about 1900 and *Swansea* and *Pelican* joined before dark. Wind was now from the North, so when *Biter* flew off two aircraft at about 2100 we all had to turn, and we did another turn 2 hours later to fly on again.

Saturday, 15 April 1944 – At sea

At 0430 *Biter* turned into the wind and flew off 2 aircraft. Shortly after we and

Stormont were told to proceed along a bearing to an aircraft contact, but it was negatived almost at once. At 0645 the aircraft flew on again, and at 0715 we all altered to 000° and *Biter* started refuelling *Crane.* It was blowing quite hard from the N. although bright and sunny and a rising glass. At 1200 we got some D/F bearings of a U/B. We were sent out on a bearing with *Stormont* to sweep to a depth of 30 miles. Aircraft were also sent. Nothing seen or heard and at 1415 we were told to rejoin. When we got back at 1530 found *Owen Sound* and *Pelican* missing and heard they had got a contact and dropped astern to investigate. Shortly after we all turned round to the E. and at 1800 sighted the 2 searching ships, which were out of contact. *Biter* got an A/S contact and put us on to it but it proved non-sub. Rejoined the screen and we all steered N. for the night. *Owen Sound* rejoined and *Woodcock* took her place with *Pelican* on the search.

Sunday, 16 April 1944 – At sea

At about 0700 we arrived back at the spot where *Pelican* and *Woodcock* had been sweeping all night and they rejoined. I had just gone down to shave and had my face covered with soap when we got an A/S contact. I dashed up on the bridge and being pretty near to *Biter* we ran in and dropped a pattern, having done which we never regained contact. Not long after *Owen Sound* got another contact about 5 miles away, and we were both left behind searching while the rest returned to the westward. After a bit I collected *Owen Sound* and we went backwards and forwards doing Easy Item turns and finding nothing. I asked if an air search could be carried out to the E. in case (if there was a U/B) the U/B might have surfaced out of sight and got away. Two aircraft were flown off but we never managed to home them on to us. A most lovely warm sunny day.

At 1815 we were told to abandon search and rejoin, which we did about 1915. I went up alongside *Biter* and had a chat and then we took up station on the screen. At about 2000 *Stormont* close to us got a contact and attacked, and *Swansea* and we both got a ping on a contact close by. It was a grand echo and I really thought we'd got a U-boat. *Swansea* attacked with depth charges and after that, although good for a bit, the echo deteriorated. We carried out a hedgehog attack without any result and then lost contact. Eventually as it got dark *Stormont,* who also lost *his* contact, and we were left hunting. After a bit I got an Observant patrol going but never regained contact. Asked for an air patrol but none forthcoming. Awfully difficult to know what to do. After a lapse of time a search with only 2 ships is little use. I found it impossible to make up my mind whether in the first place it was a U/B. Eventually decided to draw stumps and at 0130 set course with *Stormont* to rejoin. This losing contact and doubt is quite infuriating as I never can make decisions without thinking they are wrong ones.

Monday, 17 April 1944 – At sea

We sighted *Biter* at about 0630 and took station on the screen. Just as we arrived *Cygnet* and *Crane* got a contact and dropped out to investigate. According to yesterday's signal *Biter* and 7th E.G. were to return to harbour detaching us for further sweeps at 1000 today. There was a lot of hectic signalling about transference of radar stores and *Swansea*'s prisoners. *Biter* proceeded to circle the two hunting ships at about 10 miles distance, and eventually they rejoined at about 1300 having found nothing, and *Cygnet* transferred some radar stores to us. We expect to be detached at 0400 tomorrow, but another signal altering the area for our search to the N. means we remain with *Biter* a bit longer. During the p.m. we ran into patches of mist and fog but at about 1700 it cleared away. At 2020 we got an A/S contact within the screen, and as it was fairly good I had to dash in and drop a pattern on it. About 3 or 4 minutes after the last charge there was another deep explosion. Probably one of our charges set to safe by mistake. We never regained contact and so there was the usual period of exasperating uncertainty. *Crane* stayed behind to help us. I was of the opinion all the time that it was her wake which we had attacked in the first place, and after about an hour's search I took *Crane* off to rejoin *Biter* at 16 knots. We got back into our position on the screen about midnight.

Tuesday, 18 April 1944 – At sea

I had just finished shaving when the bridge rang down to say *Biter* had made "Operation Pub Crawl" for *Cygnet, Matane,* and *Pelican. Swansea* was also included but had to be negatived as he hadn't got the orders. The three ships went a mile ahead of *Biter* and dropped their whalers with their Captains. I transferred to *Cygnet*'s boat, which also had the Captain of the *Pelican. Biter* stopped and we went alongside and climbed up a jumping ladder about 30' high. Although fairly calm, not my idea of a before breakfast pastime. We went into the Captain's cabin and Boswell came down from the bridge, and we had a quack about the whole operation. It was our unanimous opinion that under present U-boat conditions it was useless for support groups to try and combine the functions of carrier escort and A/S hunting. We all left the *Biter* at about 1000 and *Cygnet*'s boat put us back on board. E.G. 7 is an R.N.R. Cdr. called MacLean,[46] who is doing the job in the absence of Dallison who is sick.

I was quite relieved to find the *Matane* still afloat considering the inexperience of No. 1. Took up our position on the screen until 1200, when our group was detached to carry out a sweep in a new area while *Biter* and the 7th E.G. returned to harbour. In the p.m. the weather deteriorated v. rapidly. It started to blow from the S.W. with a falling glass. At about 1400 *Stormont* got a contact and we all came back and swept about and found nothing, and we'd hardly got formed up again when at 1630 we got a contact. By this time it was blowing hard and A/S conditions were awful, but I eventually decided we were in a non-sub area owing to the number of contacts. Just when I wanted to reform there was heavy rain and visibility fell to about ½ mile, and what with having so many ships with defective radar it was quite a job to collect them together.

Wednesday, 19 April 1944 – At sea

The weather cleared in the night but still blowing strongly from the S.W. I had a good rest and never went on the bridge at all. I had a complete lapse of memory and it wasn't till 0830 that I realized that I had a rendezvous with an aircraft at 1100. We ought to have altered course at 0800 and now we shall be late at the rendezvous. Very stupid of me.

It was a lovely bright sunny day all day, but the Force 7 wind blew steadily in spite of a rising glass. In the p.m. a biggish beam sea made us roll heavily. Our course 203°. At 1100 we started to home a Sunderland aircraft and at 1200 he arrived over us and dropped a container on a parachute with radar spare parts for *Owen Sound* and *Stormont.* After some difficulty *Owen Sound* picked it up, owing to wind and sea. I spent more time and thought on Forms S206 on the commanding officers of the group. At 2400 we altered to 360°. Our patrol area is between 51°54' N. and 16°20' W.

Thursday, 20 April 1944 – At sea

The wind went down in the night, and at 0730 I told *Stormont* to close *Owen Sound* and transfer radar stores by line and he then came up alongside us and I passed him over some A/S fuses. We steamed N. all the a.m. One or two stops to investigate echoes, all of which were fish. I went into the question of secondary steering with the Coxswain. At 1315 we went to General Quarters and fired some bursts of high explosive shells and Oerlikon. At 1400 we altered by E.I. turn to 090°. It started to rain and the visibility started to shut down. With the wind and sea on our starboard side we rolled and listed heavily to port, and I began to be rather worried wondering whether with more than 50% of fuel burned we aren't getting a bit unstable owing to the large amount of recently added top weight. However, the Chief[47] after enquiries informed me that the Ch. Stoker had made a balls and was taking all the oil from the Std. tanks. At 1800 we did an E.I. to 180°. Only about 1 mile visibility. *Stormont*'s radar is now 100% thanks to the spare part dropped by the aircraft, but *Owen Sound* has not yet got hers going even with the new transformer, and *Swansea*'s R.X.C. set is right out. At night and in thick weather I feel rather ham strung as a group.

Friday, 21 April 1944 – At sea

The weather was suitable for boat work in the morning. At 0700 we altered to

010° to run to the N. and at 0830 we stopped and *Stormont* sent Hunt,[48] the radar officer, to *Owen Sound,* and then I closed their whaler and put Thomas into it and he went to *Stormont* about some A/S defect and we then continued on. A beautiful day, calm and sunny, but the light N.W.'ly wind was quite chilly. Walked round the upper deck and talked to the Chief Bos'n's Mate about towing. In the p.m. we got a signal from the C. in C. saying we were to leave our patrol, arriving Lough Foyle p.m. on the 24th, and that we should be required to go out with the *Vindex* a.m. on the 26th as another air striking force. At 1600 the Chief told me he had a defect below and wanted to shut down the steering engine, so for about ½ hour we steered by engines, which in the existing weather conditions was quite easy. At 1730 when the defect was made good we closed *Stormont* and sent a boat over to bring Thomas back. I was glad to see our sea boat get away and pull quite well. At 1900 we turned to 220° to make for the S.W. corner of area. Started to make out my report of proceedings. How I loathe writing reports of any kind.

Saturday, 22 April 1944 – At sea

Not a very nice day with S.W.'ly wind Force 6. We got an HF/DF bearing at 0515 and we weren't certain of distance. I turned the group to the bearing and steamed along it till 1100 but saw and heard nothing. I planned my movements for the night so as to be in the eastern edge by about 0600, when I was going to shape course for Lough Foyle, but a signal arrived ordering us to operate with a Leigh Light Wellington aircraft during the night in another small area, which quite upset my previous plans.

We were just about in the middle of the area, spread out in line abreast, when at 2000 we got an A/S contact to port. It was a cracking echo, and very soon it became obvious that this really was a U-boat. I went slow, meaning to take my time, but the range closed very rapidly and I found myself in to about 300 yds with the bearing going rapidly right and the ship's head swinging as fast as possible to Std. to keep pointed. Suddenly ahead appeared the swirl of the thing, which must have been very shallow. I was still worried that I was going to get so close as to lose contact before ready to attack when the periscope was reported just off the Std. bow. I then got thoroughly rattled and in case he should fire a torpedo or Gnat I reckoned I must go for him. Went full ahead and forgetting we were still in A/S contact dropped a pattern by eye, which as it turned out was a good deal too early. However, we picked him up astern and the other ships were now on the scene. *Swansea* then attacked and although we held him and so did *Stormont* for a time, the A/S conditions, which were never good, suddenly became awful and we simply couldn't get our reverbs out at all and that was the last we heard of him. I started Observant patrol and then a parallel sweep but it was dark soon after losing contact, and if he got away he could make off on the surface. I went through agonies of suspense and worry. What I've always dreaded has happened. We find a U-boat and I make a balls and lose it. It must be admitted the lack of daylight, the bad A/S conditions, and the periscope all made it difficult, but I feel I've let the ship and the group down and feel suicidal with shame.[49]

Sunday, 23 April 1944 – At sea

I had practically no sleep all night while we swept backwards and forwards for this U-boat. At about 0700 a Sunderland arrived to search, and later on two more appeared and I sent them out on various areas to sweep to a depth of 50 miles, but it is too late now. He will be submerged again by daylight. Feeling tired v. depressed and unhappy all day. I feel I have personally let the ship down badly. We continued to search until 1300 and then shaped course for home in accordance with C. in C.'s orders. I sent *Swansea* on ahead as our time in harbour is going to be short anyhow, and he has more defects than the rest of us. We have a stern wind and sea which may help us along. A lovely sunny afternoon. Feeling less depressed and rattled by the evening.

Monday, 24 April 1944 – At sea/Moville

A nice sunny day but a strong W.'ly wind and stern sea, which made us yaw badly about. We sighted Aran Island at about 1630 and Tory Island was abeam at 1800. I must say Kilgour[50] is the best Navigator I've met yet in small ships. Off Inishtrahull we all fired hedgehog which detonated in a very continuing way on the bottom. Arrived at Moville at 2130 and to my surprise were told to proceed up river without oiling. After hanging about off Moville pier for a bit we got pilots and proceeded up in the dark. We were so light with only about 30% fuel left that it is quite difficult to steer. We put the clocks on another hour to summer time, and then it was about 1230 before we secured alongside *Swansea.* After giving the pilot a drink I went to sleep.

Tuesday, 25 April 1944 – Londonderry

Overslept myself badly and didn't come to until 0845. King from *Swansea* and Myra from *Stormont* came over to see me, and then Lucas[51] my new First Lieutenant appeared. He has come from a Canadian Tribal and is a V.R. 2½ with considerable experience, and should be able to take a lot of stuff off my shoulders. As soon as I could get away from paperwork – reports of attack on submarines – loosely reports of proceedings – back signals, etc. I went up to Operations and found that the 3 of us (*Owen Sound* leaves the group for C 2) are to sail at 1400 tomorrow, which is a bit more breathing space then I expected. The Commodore was away, and so I got King and Easton (whose *Saskatchewan* is alongside) over on board for a drink. King from *Swansea* is naturally delighted with his latest U-boat success. I am losing the Chief, Thomas, and Quist. Thomas is to do a long A/S course at *Osprey* and a chap called Cooke[52] is to relieve him. I hate changes.

After lunch I slogged away at confidential reports, but at 1615 after some tea I put on plain clothes and went ashore and walked along the unknown road and around some side roads and back at about 1800. A glorious day in the country, absolutely perfect. Masses of gorse out smelling lovely and all the new leaves coming on the trees. This is the most perfect time of year. Almost exactly two years ago I had the funny party with the Banks and Broomes, when we drove out to Birdstown in unknown rigs.[53] On return on board I shifted into uniform and went on board *Swansea* for a celebration cocktail party and later on brought Watson of the *Owen Sound*, Myra, and Easton back on board for supper. At 1045 when they left I wrote to J., from whom I'd received a lot of letters this morning. Heard from Viola that they had wireless message from K. saying she and George were both well.

...

Friday, 5 May 1944 – Londonderry

We got to Londonderry and secured at 0230. I slept a bit late in the morning. Went up to see Selby (Ch. of Staff) at 1000 and at 1100 there was the usual group conference, which was held the same time as C 1's conference. An awful tedious performance. The Commodore is so damned slow. We're not going to get very much done as we're wanted again on the 14th, which with a couple of days of sea training only gives us a bare week. Found a letter from J. waiting for me. I felt rather fussed in the p.m. about the ship and the group and myself. Went up to the offices again at 1500 and tried to get the gunnery instructions for Telfer – unsuccessfully – and saw Copelin[54] about S206s. Back on board for tea and then I wrote a letter to J. At 1800 I went along to the *Atholl*, who is in harbour. Gardiner was having a small drinking party in his cabin. Prentice was there, having flown from Canada to take command of one of the Canadian destroyer groups.[55] Hynes also from the *North Bay* and Easton. I walked back with the latter and he came on board and had some food with me. I rather unburdened my soul to him about how worried and introspective I am. He is a nice chap. Myra came over later and drank some whiskey with me. Not much of a day.

Saturday, 6 May 1944 – Londonderry

I spent the whole of the a.m. on correspondence and reading A.F.O.s. Had visits and chat with Lee,[56] the base A/S officer, and discussed our failure with U/B. At 1400 No. 1 and I stepped ashore for a walk. We crossed the bridge and took the road and along and up the Foyle and then struck inland and came back along a higher road. A lovely afternoon. Went to the Northern County's Club on return, where we found Hynes, and we all had tea and read the papers. Back on board at about 1730. Shifted and went over to the *Montreal* for drinks at 1815. Finch-Noyes[57] is S.O. but not C.O. Quite a big party. At about 2000 I came back with Easton and two others and we all had dinner in the *Saskatchewan* and I got into a violent argument about religion. Good fun. Heard that the failure in Italy was due largely to venereal disease and to the fact that the American General Mark Clark and a British General ought to have been removed and weren't. Probably just gossip, but it makes me rather tremble for the success of the second front.

Sunday, 7 May 1944 – Londonderry

I had my usual struggle to get breakfast at my proper time. When Aucoin has been ashore it is always about ½ an hour late. I don't believe anybody turns out much before 0900 anyway. Oh for officers who knew what proper Naval routine was. We went to Divisions at 1030. What a performance. No. 1 told me the officers had never been to Divisions before, and the outfits some of the men had the nerve to appear in passed belief. Oh dear, Oh dear, one feels one doesn't know where to begin.

Had another interview with Telfer about his books – Magazine Log, Gunnery Log, etc. – which are all adrift. What am I to do with him? After lunch I read till about 1530. I went ashore with Brown, Cooke, Duchesneau, and 2 from *Swansea* and went to tea at the Wren officers' quarters at Belmont House – the same House incidentally from which I started out with Jackie Broome and the Banks on the wild fancy dress drive in the pony cart. We had a very good tea and the Wrens were very pleasant. Got back on board at about 1800 and wrote Viola and Gillian and had my solitary evening meal and went to bed early.

Monday, 8 May 1944 – Londonderry

Drizzling rain on and off all day. I dealt with some correspondence in the a.m., wandered around the ship down below, talked to the L.S.A. about victualling and had a look at the store room flat aft. I then went ashore and went to the pay office and enquired about my pay. I am told that my Canadian allotments plus dependents allowance, which amounts to nearly £90 a month, should now be all in order.[58] From there I went on into town and had a hair cut and got v. annoyed with the barber, who took too much off round the sides. Soon after I got back on board we were hauled off to allow *Saskatchewan* and *Qu'Appelle* to get out, and then we were berthed inside ship. In the p.m. I walked to the Tactical Table to see Allen but he was busy with a game and so I went on up to Ops. No news of what our next job is to be, with our 3 new ships *Port Colborne, Saint John,* and *Meon,* who I expected today or tomorrow, are coming across with a convoy and can't arrive before Friday or Saturday and then may have to boiler clean. I hear *Valleyfield* (Canadian frigate and S.O. of one of the mid ocean groups) has been sunk by a Gnat.[59] After tea then went to the Tactical Room and fixed up with Allen the sort of game I want for the group on Thursday. Soon after 1800 who should arrive on board to see me but Rex, Miss Goldsworthy's Rex,[60] and we had some gin and a chat. His ship, the *Jed*, is here but just going out to the Far East where most of the R.N. frigates seem to be collecting. I wrote to J. and read and turned in about 2200.

...

Wednesday, 10 May 1944 – Londonderry

We were down in the daily programme for the night action teacher at 1030. We had to get right over to Ebrington Barracks, and when by 0950 nobody had even started to fall in I began to get annoyed. Everything is always left the last minute. Went over by ferry and walked up to the Barracks. An R.N.R. Commander called Gregorie[61] was the N.E.A.T. We had a fairly short run but didn't do very well, on account of my very wild star shell firing which never seemed to be on the right bearing. Got back on board at about 1300 and immediately after lunch Cooke and I caught a bus round to Ebrington again to have a look at *Swansea*'s team in action. I think on the whole they were better then we were. At about 1600 we got a car and drove to the offices to discuss our sea training program for Saturday and then went back on board, finding the ship had been moved once more to No. 10 berth.

We threw a bit of the party in the wardroom in the evening. Gregorie from the night action teacher and about 5 or 6 Wren officers from *Belmont* came down and we had drinks and a buffet supper and then a sing song. The piano playing was a bit primitive but that made little difference. No. 1 was damned funny, he insisted on singing – mostly Gilbert and Sullivan – but without being able to get two true notes in succession. Nobody got drunk, thank God. I thought our guests were never going, and I longed for my bed long before the party was over. A lovely sunny day.

Thursday, 11 May 1944 – Londonderry

The group had the tactical table all the forenoon from 0900. Allen gave us a support group HF/DF sighting problem, which was good value. I'm beginning to get a slight inferiority complex about King in *Swansea*. What with his actual successes and one thing and another, I believe he would do my job better than me. I brought King and Myra back on board and found Capt. Menzies was on board. He is a Director of Personnel at Ottawa and is just about to take command of the *Minotaur*, the first R.C.N. cruiser.[62] Copelin was with him and we drank a lot of gin. Menzies was Capt. D. Saint John's at one time and is an awfully nice fellow. Back to the tactical table at 1400 when we had a night run, also good value. Went back on board at 1700 and got down to some paperwork. I have got to be the President of a Court of Inquiry tomorrow and I had to think about that a bit. Started a letter to J. and finished *A Tale of Two Cities,* which made me feel quite sentimental. Turned in early. We got a signal to say we are to support an S.L. convoy leaving on 14th. Yet another new officer joined – one Lewtas,[63] a gunnery specialist for ships and group duties. If this means I lose Telfer I shall be extremely thankful.

…

Saturday, 13 May 1944 – Londonderry

We slipped at 0800 and proceeded down river with *Swansea* and *Stormont.* My three new frigates, *Saint John, Meon,* and *Port Colborne,* all arrived last night and are boiler cleaning. After dropping the pilot we went to one of the calibration berths and had a check MF/DF run. I also saw requestmen and defaulters. Not feeling *quite* my best this morning. One ought never to dine out the night before going to sea.

At 1030 we rendezvoused with *Stormont* and a submarine and did A/S Ps[64] until 1500. Conditions not v. good but on the whole we had some very good practice. Finished up at 1800 with sending boarding boats' crew to the submarine. There was a bit of a swell running and I thought that one time the boat would be broken up, as Duchesneau took it the weather side of the submarine and then left it without a boat keeper. After that I went back to Moville and went alongside *Swansea* at the oiler. King came over and had a yarn. He had been HF/DF calibrating all day. At about 2100 *Towy* sent a boat, and I and Cooke and Brown all went over and had a conference with S.O. B 3 and his staff. He is a Commander King[65] who I haven't met before. It was luck to have the opportunity for meeting. He is S.O. of the escort of the convoy we're to support. Went down to the wardroom for a drink and met an R.N.V.R. sub who was an Ordinary Seaman with me in the *Broke.* Got back on board at about 2300. Oiling didn't finish until 2330 and then we shoved off and anchored. I was glad to get to bed. The 8th Army are attacking in Italy.

Sunday, 14 May 1944 – Moville/At sea

The group weighed at 0800 and proceeded for exercises. We were all supposed to do A/S Ps, but as 3 is too much of a crowd round 1 submarine I went off on my own up towards Inishtrahull. Chippy[66] was very busy making a target to fire at. When soon after 1000 it was ready, it was put over this side and promptly capsized. We went alongside it and righted it, but over it went again. I think he made the masts and sails too high. We then threw an empty oil drum over the side and did some shooting at it with 4" and Oerlikons. It didn't get quite the range we wanted but was better than nothing. Got back to the S/M area and joined *Swansea* and *Stormont* at about 1215. *Swansea* had one more exercise but I took *Stormont* away and anchored near the calibration berth. At about 1330 *Swansea* anchored close by and I got both C.O.s on board for a short meeting. *Swansea* was having trouble with their new T.B.S. set[67] and Brown went over to see if he could do anything, which rather delayed us. However, we finally weighed at about 1520 and headed for the rendezvous off Oversay. *Towy* and his group were hard on our heels. We joined up with the convoy, which is an S.L. and K.M.S. combined of about 40 ships,[68] at 1800 and took station on the advanced screen ahead. The Loch Ewe and Clyde portions of the convoy were joining up. At about 2000 we got a cracking echo, which was a bit fussing. I was very certain it was a wreck but I brought some charges on it which threw my compass and A/S recorder off. These minol depth charges fairly lift the ship out of the water.[69] We remained in [position] AA for the night.

Monday, 15 May 1944 – At sea

I seemed to have a very disturbed night in spite of the fact that being under the orders of B 3 I ought to be a complete passenger until a threat occurs. This T.B.S. set is a grand thing, and apparently being v. high frequency in short range all previous bans on R/T have been lifted.

We have three escort carriers with the convoy, one of which is *Stalker* with Murray Smith in command. We remained at about 14,000 ahead by night, but during the forenoon I took my group to visibility distance, which was about 13 miles. McDonald, our Radar Artificer, has done something to our R.X.C. sets and it is getting infinitely better results and longer ranges now. He is an excellent man. At about 1400 *Stormont* got a contact, and when went over to look see we ran into an area with a non sub echo almost every square yard. Had to spend some time investigating, however, and *Stormont* dropped some charges before we left it and went on. I informed the S.O., but sure enough when the main screen arrived on the spot they too picked up the same echoes and carried out attacks. Fair sunny day and clouded over towards evening. Glass v. high.

Our carriers only have fighter aircraft on board and will only be used in event of an attack or emergency. They are really only in the convoy as passengers. Read, slept, walked, and sat. At 1600 we put the clocks back an hour.

Tuesday, 16 May 1944 – At sea

Another day of extreme visibility with not a ruffle on the sea but heavy cloud and no sun. At 0850 *Towy* made "identified enemy aircraft in the vicinity" and so we went to A.A. stations. Never saw or heard a thing. One of the carriers flew off a couple of fighters, but when they landed on again and still no more info of the enemy aircraft, we went back to cruising watch. Later on in the forenoon *Stormont* got a contact and attacked, but when we came over to look we picked up 2 or 3 more and classified them all as non sub. Being 12-13 miles ahead by day, one has plenty of opportunity to have a good sniff at these echoes. Put in some shut eye in the p.m. and read a whole lot of A.F.O.s and C.A.F.O.s. We went to General Quarters at 1915 and did a dummy hedgehog attack. While we were closed up *Swansea* reported attacking a contact, so we went over to her and sure enough picked up a very good but different contact ourselves and dropped a pattern on it. They were both non sub, however, and we resumed station. At 2215 we dropped back to our night distance.

Wednesday, 17 May 1944 – At sea

I had a fairly disturbed night. Another calm day with good visibility but very little sun. We got a signal telling us to leave the convoy at 43° N. if not in contact with the enemy and return to Londonderry. Commodore D. was also told to arrange a group exercise for us on return as we would be required again on the 25th. An uneventful day. One or two non sub contacts. At 1900 the convoy turned to 180° and at 1915 I carried out 2 dummy hedgehog attacks. Sometime during the day B 3 detached 2 escorts to bring an oiler over from a home-going convoy over to our convoy, and so at 2210 we closed in to 13,000 yards for the night. At about 2330 one of the main screen reported being in A/S contact with a submarine and attacked with Squid, but finally lost contact and was ordered to resume station. I expected we might be sent to sweep astern but I think the S.O., like me, felt it was probably non sub. Started reading *Oliver Twist.*

Thursday, 18 May 1944 – At sea

At about 0230 we got an A/S contact, which although non sub had to be investigated, and at about 0400 *Stormont* reported Jig [radar contact] and started to fire star shell only to find it was the oiler and her two escorts joining. One way and another a very disturbed night. A little bit more wind from the N.N.E. and not quite so flat calm but lots of sun. An uneventful day. There was some excitement in the dog watches when we sighted a small red buoy, but on closer examination it was some channel marking buoy broken adrift from some port. My new gunnery officer Lewtas is a ball of fire compared with old Telfer – but of course the former is a qualified (g). Heard on the news that we have at last taken Casino in Italy which the Germans have held so stubbornly for so long.

Friday, 19 May 1944 – At sea

An undisturbed night. Nice day with occasional rain. N.'ly wind and slight sea. The carriers flew off fighters, which are to attack the escorts to give the gun layers practice. Two planes made one low run over us but although we kept the Oerlikon guns' crews closed up till 1200 they never came back. I asked permission to detach at 2200, which was approved. At about 2130 we heard *Anguilla* on the close screen report a contact and a bit later on contact. However, S.O. B 3 told me to search astern of the convoy with my group before leaving. As we passed through the convoy we ran into heavy rain squalls. Got my three ships formed up, passed through the datum point and swept to the furthest on position of the supposed course of the submarine. I don't believe for a moment that it was a S/M. At 2330 having detected nothing I told B 3 I was proceeding and altered to 028° 15 knots. It was v. wet and bumpy at that speed into the sea, but I reckoned we could do it without damage. We were in 43° N. and 19°30' W. when we turned back, so we just took the convoy across the dangerous area of the Bay. I wish we could have gone to Gib.

Saturday, 20 May 1944 – At sea

An uncomfortable night. Taking spray over continuously and every now and then a heavy sea and a big bump. Wind and sea eased in the forenoon and I went on to 15.5 knots. A remark at lunch made me think we ought to zig zag and so I started one. It is a nuisance as it reduces our speed made good. At about 1700 I carried out the new drills from my drill table. Fire a gun, depth charge, etc. I was glad to see that *Matane* was first every time, and the bridge got the signals no earlier than the other ships.

I finished *Oliver Twist.* Have come to the conclusion that Dickens the novelist is really rather tedious, but Dickens the portrayer of England a hundred years ago I could read all day. There is too much of the former and too little of the latter in *Oliver Twist.* The evil that he exposes is also seemingly too exaggerated. Flat calm again in the evening.

Sunday, 21 May 1944 – At sea

A quiet night, except for routine calls when the watch was relieved I wasn't disturbed. Went on to 16 knots at about 0800 but at 1300, as it meant the other ships were exceeding 160 revs for station keeping, I reduced ½ knot. When the pilot had got his noon sight I made my E.T.A. signal and defects. Blowing just fresh enough from the N. to make a bit of spray over and spoil my exercise on the upper deck. Rather a chilly day. We put the clocks on to summer time at 1600 and so it didn't get dark till about midnight. Ran into a lot of Irish trawlers at about 2300 and closed and spoke to one to find his nationality. At midnight we altered to 045°.

Monday, 22 May 1944 – At sea/Londonderry

Most of the middle watch I was up fixing the ship with D/F bearings and soundings as we approached land, and finally with the shore lights as they came into sight. Eagle Island was abeam at about 0400. At 0830 we altered round Tory Island

and at 1200 off Inishtrahull we fired hedgehogs and then went in, arriving at Moville at 1330. Embarked pilots at Dunagree Point and went straight up river and berthed at Londonderry at 1530. After giving the pilot some tea I had a bath and read my letters (2 from J.) and then went up to the Commodore's offices and saw Ops and Selby about training and then back on board. At about 1830 I went down to the wardroom for a drink.

I had just finished dinner in my cabin when the Captain of the *Meon* arrived to call. A very nice R.C.N.V.R. 2½ called Balfour.[70] When he left I finished a letter to J. and turned in. My precious night in was disturbed at about midnight by a bloody awful noise of singing, coming I suspect from our wardroom. Before turning in I went on the upper deck (we are inside ship) and watched a stream of drunks reeling back to the ships. The patrol was pretty busy, too, bringing offenders back. Why must these Canadians get so *very* drunk. The advance in Italy continues successfully.

Tuesday, 23 May 1944 – Londonderry

At 1000 I said a few words at a group communications meeting and at 1100 I had a C.O.s meeting on board and tried to explain – not very well – my ideas to the new boys: LtComd. Angus R.C.N.R. in *Port Colborne* and LtComd. Stacey R.C.N.R. in *Saint John*.[71] Almost before we finished Copelin arrived, and shortly afterwards Prentice, and so we drank some gin and discussed slackness and untidiness of troops in harbour. At 1445 King called for me and we walked up to Copelin's office, where there was a meeting to discuss the opening of the rest camp for the sailors somewhere near Fort Rush. The fact is since all long leave has been stopped that there too many sailors milling round in Londonderry with nothing to do but get drunk and break up the place. After a lot of chat it was decided that the Canadian YMCA would run the camp, which is a disused Army camp. I think it should be a good thing, but the details will want careful working out.

It was about 1700 when I got back on board. Had a lot of signals and sea training programmes waiting, and I had to whack out quite a lot of signals to the group. Felt fussed and worried. I'm afraid I haven't the drive for this job and believe in spite of all my R.N. experience that King would make a good but not better job of it. I was sitting in my cabin after dinner when an old Commissioned Gunner T called Guppy[72] came round. He had been in the *Walpole* for short time with me. We talked *and* talked but eventually got rid of him and went to bed.

Wednesday, 24 May 1944 – Londonderry/Moville

We were supposed to slip at 0800, all the group having gone on ahead, but our pilot was late and we didn't get away till only 0830. I picked up the rest of the group, less *Port Colborne* who is calibrating off the Lough Foyle buoy, and proceeded, doing a few full speed maneuvers, to the A.A. firing area where we had an aircraft and sleeve target to fire at. I got very irritated because it took us a long time to contact the aircraft on R/T and then I was made speechless with rage by the whole lack of preparation and supervision during the shoots. Oerlikons opening fire when they liked and blazing away in all the wrong and dangerous directions. When that was over at about 1330 we went to Area P for A/S Ps with a submarine. As five ships around 1 S/M is much too much of a crowd I sent *Swansea* and *Stormont* in to oil, meaning that they should come out after about 3 hours and that two more of us could go in, but they took so long it wasn't worth them coming out at all. From 1400-1900 we, *Meon,* and *Saint John* played with the S/M. The conditions were indescribably poor and we really got practically nothing out of the whole thing. We were supposed to go on till 2000 but at 1900 I decided to pack it up.

As we came in there was a v. strong squall of wind and although it was not very nice went alongside the oiler. I did it really rather nicely although I says it. *Saint John* came alongside us with *Meon* and *Port Colborne* to the other side. The Captains of *Meon* and *Saint John* came over to see me. The Chief came to see me and told me we had a cracked contract steam pipe which had to be mended. We shoved off 2330 as it was getting dark and anchored rather close to mud. We then lowered our motorboat and sent our cracked pipe over to the carrier *Emperor,* who was at anchor and said would try to braze it. Feeling fussed to death, what with the pipe and the boat and the gale blowing and our anchor berths, but perhaps chiefly feeling what an inefficient S.O. I am. I heard E.G. 1 exercising his group on T.B.S. and it made me feel how remarkably lacking in ideas and initiative I am.[73] A very tiring day. Turned in eventually about 0100.

4
The Great Endeavour, May-July 1944

Frank Layard had a keen sense of history, and his diary entry on 6 June – "*The invasion of France started!!*" – indicates his excitement at being involved in the momentous events surrounding the invasion of northwest Europe. Though he and the Canadian sailors under his command would have been keen to participate in the assault itself, they instead found themselves hundreds of kilometres to westward guarding against an eventuality that never became reality. U-boats were considered the principal threat to the shipping that would supply the lodgement won in Normandy on D-Day; indeed, some operational research scientists estimated that at the height of the campaign U-boats might sink as many as twenty-five ships a day.[1] The *Kriegsmarine* had some fifty-eight U-boats ready for anti-invasion operations – thirty-six based in Biscay ports and twenty-two in Norway. To prevent them from entering the Channel in the aftermath of the invasion, or at least to make that prospect unappetizing, planners erected what they hoped would be an "unclimbable fence." Inside the Channel, support groups operating out of Plymouth and Portsmouth were assigned to patrol along the lines Plymouth-Ile de Batz and Portland-Cap de la Hague. Meanwhile, twenty-one Coastal Command maritime patrol squadrons from 19 Group were to cover the area from the south of Ireland into the Bay of Biscay to the extent that any one position would be overflown at least every half-hour around the clock.[2] The most effective defence systems are layered, and under Operation CA, three escort carriers and five Western Approaches support groups, including E.G. 9, formed a trip wire across the western approaches of the Channel to catch U-boats before they could attack the Neptune shipping lanes.[3]

With the exception of a short layover in Londonderry, E.G. 9 patrolled the CA operating area through most of June. It proved to be a frustrating existence. U-boat activity in the area remained low, but numerous contacts and sighting reports had to be chased down. This activity was muddled by poor air-sea co-operation, and Layard's diary seethes at the relentless, and seemingly pointless, toing and froing that is the bane of all commanders.[4] Things did not improve later in the month, when the group operated in the English Channel, and then south in the Bay of Biscay. These moves immersed E.G. 9 in a new type of anti-submarine warfare, now known as the inshore campaign.

Anti-submarine warfare in the relatively shallow, confined waters surrounding the United Kingdom was a stark contrast to the convoy battles in the broad North

Atlantic. When the *U-bootwaffe* moved inshore in an attempt to thwart the transport of materiel to Normandy, instead of searching for convoys over vast transoceanic distances, they learned to lie in wait along the obvious coastal shipping routes, letting convoys come to them. They also took advantage of the physical environment, avoiding detection by lying motionless on the relatively shallow bottom amid the thousands of wrecks that littered the coastal waters, or escaping after attacks by drifting silently away on the powerful currents and tidal rips for which the area is notorious. U-boats also operated independently; *Rudeltaktik* – wolf-pack tactics – were not used, nor was there much occasion for communication between boats at sea and the U-boat command ashore. Schnorchels, which, by the end of the summer, equipped all U-boats deployed to inshore waters, had obviated the need to surface and transformed them more nearly into true submarines. For Allied anti-submarine forces, the impact of this new inshore warfare was staggering. Many of the weapons and tactics that had been decisive to victory in the midocean convoy war – radar, air power, HF/DF, code breaking, and evasive routing – were diminished in effectiveness. Now, surface ships had to pick their way among the myriad wrecks and rock formations that littered the ocean floor, classifying every asdic contact as "sub" or "non-sub," and attacking even those of doubtful origin,[5] all the time subjected to powerful tidal currents. As Layard complained early on, "One just has to attack every echo, and there is *no* way of telling whether he is a submarine on the bottom or not."[6] It was painstaking work, and new search procedures, equipment such as echo-sounders and the navigational device QH, and up-to-date wreck charts emerged as the new war winners.[7]

Frank Layard's diary vividly portrays this dreary battle. E.G. 9 was at the forefront of the inshore campaign for its duration – its only hiatus, if it can be called that, came in October and November 1944 when the group was deployed in a hunt off Gibraltar and then supported a Russian convoy (see Chapter 6). Like others involved in the campaign, Layard found it to be tedious work accompanied by considerable stress. Each anti-submarine contact required numerous command decisions, the dilemma being how much attention to devote to each. "We seemed to get a contact very nearly every ½ hour," he wrote in the midst of one patrol, "Some were known wrecks and others needed investigation, but I had to turn out for every one and fix the ship and decide whether or not to go on. This sort of thing is really exhausting, but on the route between Hartland Point and Trevose Head, where the bottom is littered with wrecks, it happens unceasingly. Contact, investigate, check position, probably attack, examine result, classify ... I shall be thankful to leave this patrol tomorrow and have a spell. It has been a particularly wearing 10 days."[8] Naval authorities tried to deploy escort groups in familiar waters to take advantage of their knowledge of local conditions, and E.G. 9 spent many days patrolling the cluttered waters off the north Cornish coast mentioned above, which grew to become "an old, familiar beat."[9]

Layard was blessed with two attributes that enabled him, if not to master inshore warfare, which nobody really seems to have done, then at least to perform with a fair degree of prowess. One was his appreciation and understanding of new technology, which derived from his time at the Experimental Department at Whale Island and the Miscellaneous Weapons Section at the Admiralty. To aid with navigation in inshore waters, the Royal Navy had adopted the radio-navigation aid QH, which was closely based upon the RAF's GEE system. Receivers on ships triangulated radio waves from a series of beacons located along the British coast and, at virtually the push of a button, gave a position normally accurate to within about 100 yards. The device was a godsend to sailors fighting the inshore anti-submarine war, in which pinpoint navigation was critical, and its impact was probably equivalent to that of HF/DF on the North Atlantic. When contacts were found, the first step was to consult the wreck chart to check whether the contact had already been classified as a known wreck. Then, by plotting a series of fixes, the hunter had to ascertain if the contact had movement, which would indicate that it was a submarine either running slowly or drifting on the current. Unfortunately, those same currents made precise navigation extremely challenging. Layard quickly realized the value of QH. "This Q.H. is a joy and delight," he noted on one occasion, "Had a sniff round a wreck giving off oil on two occasions, on the N.'ly leg and S.'ly leg. Q.H. tells me once it is the same contact and there is no movement."[10] Layard came to rely greatly upon QH, and when he moved to a ship not so equipped or when the group operated north of Ireland or Scotland, where the system was not established until later in the war, he missed the valuable assistance the device gave in classifying contacts. Layard also quickly mastered the use of echo sounders, which helped with the identification of contacts by providing a "trace" or outline of objects on the sea floor in shallow water (see sixth photograph following p. 208).

Layard's long destroyer experience also paid dividends. Support groups manoeuvred in much the same way as destroyer flotillas on fleet duty, albeit slower, steaming in tight, closely choreographed patterns so that their searches were precise and their asdic achieved wide, overlapping coverage. Two evolutions in particular, Gamma searches and Easy Item turns, demonstrate the intricate ballet involved in an anti-submarine hunt. While "Gammaring," as Layard sometimes dubbed it, support groups created an asdic barrier across the estimated line of advance of a U-boat. According to a report prepared by Canadian authorities, "An estimated lane not more than 60 miles in width is established along [the course] a U-boat is expected to pass. A/S vessels are spread in line abreast formation parallel to the U/B's estimated course, and they patrol to and fro across the lane. Distance apart of ships – 3 miles by day, 5 miles by night. Ships zigzag together making good at least 10 knots and they transmit on ASDIC by day and night."[11] To maintain their line-abreast formation, and thus ensure complete asdic coverage, at the end of each swath across the U-boat's estimated path, support groups altered course by Easy Item (EI) turns. Under this search turn, the escort furthest from the direction of the alteration assumed the role of guide of the formation and altered immediately to the new course. The remainder of the ships maintained the original course and altered to the new course when on the beam of the guide.[12]

Performing such manoeuvres at speeds from twelve to fifteen knots while zigzagging, especially at night, put a premium on good ship handling and accurate station keeping. Confidence was a prerequisite to success, and as a sailor with long experience in small ships and fleet manoeuvres, Layard – for once – had plenty. His RCNR commanding officers and RCNVR officers of the watch were another matter entirely. The bulk of their experience was in merchant ships steaming independently at slow speed or on convoy escort duty that featured little formation work: Layard could measure his experience in tight formation manoeuvring in years, they could barely do so in months. This weakness became apparent to Layard in February 1944, when he first carried out searches with the newly formed E.G. 9: "The group were very trying and very stupid. I suppose one must realize, however, that this support group work is really much more like destroyer work – manoeuvres, signalling, etc. – and although I've been bred and born to it, those chaps haven't and a lot of training is required."[13]

Inshore anti-submarine warfare forced an adjustment on everyone, whether seasoned naval professionals like Layard, Macintyre, and Prentice, or inexperienced amateurs like Stacey, Skinner, and Balfour. Despite the many challenges associated with the campaign, E.G. 9 had good success, destroying two U-boats and playing a role in the sinking of a third.[14] While it would be going too far to heap all the credit for that on Layard – Stacey and his anti-submarine crew, for example, were largely responsible for the success against *U-247* on 1 September – support group work in the inshore campaign put a heavy premium on leadership and professional skill. No matter how exasperated he became by the endless slog of trying to detect U-boats under trying conditions, Layard's patience, persistence, and prowess were key factors in E.G. 9's success inshore.

Friday, 26 May 1944 – Moville

No exercise programme for us and so the group remained at anchor. Got a signal from Commodore D. saying the signal telling *Swansea* to go to the assistance of the trawler had taken too long to get through and calling for a report, and so Brown and I studied R/T logs and concocted our report. At 1030 I decided to shift berth as an American merchant ship who came in yesterday was swinging unpleasantly close. We went steaming round the place in all sorts of fancy rigs which annoyed me. Angus from *Port Colborne* lunched on board with No. 1. We are right out of all drink except rum. Rather grim.

I saw a requestmen and defaulters after lunch. Usual crop of drunken and disorderlies apprehended by shore patrol. I made all the group except *Matane* get under way and top up with oil from the oiler. It is an awful sweat, but as I don't know when we shall be required I can't let ships get more than 20 tons down. *Swansea* arrived back from her trawler job at about 1500. Got a signal from C. in C. W.A. saying that 1st, 6th, 9th E.G. and *Emperor* were to sail to arrive Moelfre Bay p.m. tomorrow, and S.O.s were to attend big meeting at Liverpool on the 28th to discuss future operations. Just before 2100 an immediate signal from C. in C. ordering *Emperor* and three ships of E.G. 9 to proceed at once to support an S.L. convoy. I detailed *Swansea, Stormont,* and *Meon,* and there was a hectic time on the bridge with both 10" lamps and Aldis [signal lights] going flat out. They eventually sailed at 2200. I then went down the W.R. and was given hot rum to drink and I'm damned if I didn't stop there talking and arguing till 0200. Speaks well for the rum.

Reading Weekly Intelligence Reports. The Portsmouth area must have had two very unpleasant nights at the end of last month. Bombs at Chichester and Havant, so I'm very glad family were out of Prinsted. Beastly drizzly day.

Saturday, 27 May 1944 – Moville/Moelfre Bay

That rum last night was a mistake. The 6th E.G. weighed and proceeded at 0900 and the remains of the 9th E.G. left at 1000. Not far from the entrance we ran into a flock of gannets all diving madly. A remarkable sight. We went through the Sound of Rathlin. Never been inside that way before. Quite like old times coming down the Irish Sea. Rather chilly day with poorish visibility, which developed into fog at about 1900 just as we were making the Anglesey coast, however, it cleared later on. We anchored in Moelfre Bay near E.G. 6 at about 2100. E.G. 1 (a team of D.E.s) arrived and anchored about an hour later. Last time I was here was in the *Chelsea.*

Sunday, 28 May 1944 – Moelfre Bay/Liverpool/Moelfre Bay

I went over to the *Affleck* at 0730 and at 0745 she sailed for Liverpool. E.G. 5 (Macintyre), E.G. 6 (Comd. Birch R.N.R.) and E.G. 1 (Gwinner),[15] who is captain of the ship, were all on board. The last an Act. Commander but being full of confidence and efficiency having sunk three U-boats on first trip with his group. As we came up the swept channel to the Bar [Light Vessel], it got thicker and thicker and finally we had to anchor for nearly 2 hours, and so instead of getting up to Liverpool at 1045 it was nearly 1300 before we berthed at Prince's Pier. A waiting car took all of us S.O.s to Derby House where we went straight up to the C. in C.'s flat for lunch. A couple of airmen, Peyton-Ward from Coastal Command, and the 2 Chiefs of Staff (MacIntyre and Colridge),[16] were also there.

After lunch there was a big conference in which the Navy and R.A.F. were represented to discuss an operation in which the 6th, 9th, and 1st E.G.s are taking part, with 2nd and 5th in reserve. When it was all over the orders had to be amended and reprinted and the whole of the main operational orders for ships at Moelfre Bay had to be prepared, and so *Affleck* couldn't sail until they were ready. I had some tea at Derby Ho. and then went to Lion Building and got some charts and then, forgetting it was Sunday, tried to do some shopping only to find Gieves shut. Back to Derby Ho. where I kicked my heels in the little officers' mess there. At 1800 I found Birch and went into the bar with him. If only I had J.'s telephone number with me I could have rung her up. Finally, at about nearly 2000, Gwinner, Birch, and I got a car to the *Affleck* with all the orders and bumph but then we had to wait for an officer and we didn't sail to nearly 2200. Gwinner gave us dinner on board.

Monday, 29 May 1944 – Moelfre Bay

Something woke me up at 0230 and I lay awake till nearly 0500 worrying and worrying about the ship and the group and the operation and my inefficiency. Eventually dropped off to sleep. If I let things get me down like this I shall become neurasthenic. A lovely hot sunny day. I went through the operation orders with Brown and the P.O. Tel (Baker) so as to get the communications side clear, and at 1030 the C.O.s of *Saint John* and *Port Colborne* came over and I explained the whole thing to them. Westwater[17] went over to *Affleck* and brought back the sack with the complete Overlord operation orders, which we have been given because although our particular operation is not part of Overlord it is possible that we shall cross the magic line and come under C. in. C. Plymouth.[18]

After lunch I got Brown and Westwater to muster receipt of this mass of stuff and start on the numerous corrections and amendments which have already accumulated. Again then read through the main operation orders, which are of course absorbingly interesting. The *Moorsom* arrived in the p.m. to be temporarily attached to me in the absence of *Swansea* and co. The C.O., who is Stewart[19] (who was in the *Georgetown* in my group in the Western Local), came over to see me and I went through the operation orders and my own group orders. At 1745 I put him back on board his ship and then picked up Gwinner in *Affleck* and we both went on board *Waskesiu* to have a quack with Birch and we had dinner with him. We are slack and sloppy in *Matane*, but I was appalled at what I saw in the *Waskesiu*. The most interesting thing that came out of the evening was the fact that on looking up an A.F.O. we found that Acting Commanders R.N. are senior to confirmed Commanders R.N.R., which makes me S.N.O. Moelfre Bay instead of E.G. 6, who we'd previously thought it to be. Gwinner and I made a call on one of his ships before returning.

Tuesday, 30 May 1944 – Moelfre Bay

Another blazing day. Westwater, Brown, and Cooke hard at work correcting the operation orders. I took the motor boat to *Saint John* at 1015 and to my disgust and wrath I found the Captain still turned in, and so I went straight away on board *Port Colborne* and had a look round them with Angus and went down the wardroom and had a beer and met his officers. Back on board and made to *Saint John* "repair on board." When he arrived I taxed him with being in bed at 1015, and he said he had been working on the operation orders until 0200 in the morning, which I believe he genuinely considered entitled him to lie in. I also asked them why his Whaler was hoisted when I made a signal yesterday saying boats were to be exercised under oars and why his Dr. had not been available this forenoon. These N.R. types are hopeless to deal with. When they receive a blast they must always find excuses and this a.m. Stacey went away thoroughly disgruntled and feeling he'd been v. unjustly treated.

Birch (E.G. 6) came over to see me at about 1130 and 1215 I took him back to the ship and then went on to lunch in the *Affleck* with Gwinner, who gave me cold lobster. How I envy him his self-confident efficiency. A nice chap and v. amusing. Back on board at about 1500 and after tea I did a few corrections myself. The *Monssen* arrived at about 1700 and the C.O. came over to see me and we discussed the operation and my group orders although I don't think he will be working with me. At about 1830 Gwinner came over and drank gin and later on I took him down to the W.R. When he'd gone I had a long talk to No. 1 about my drive to smarten up the appearance of the ship and ship's company.

Wednesday, 31 May 1944 – Moelfre Bay

A change in the weather, overcast and thundery and stuffy with some rain. At 1100 I cleared lower deck at No. 1's request on the subject of dress and appearance. I wonder if really only the big stick is any good. E.G. 6 came over to see me before lunch. In the p.m. I read A.F.O.s while my staff flogged away correcting operations orders. I got v. annoyed again in the morning. I found that we'd landed 98!!! men for beach recreational parties and that our motor boat had a temporary breakdown, and so at about 2000 we still had about 35 men ashore and finally it turned into 4 proper absentees. Sometimes I think No. 1 is mad. The 5th E.G. arrived and anchored about 2200, and so I am now no longer S.O. Moelfre Bay. At about 2230 E.G. 1 arrived alongside with Terry,[20] who was my navigator in the *Chelsea* and now No. 1 of one of the 1st E.G. [ships] Just the same as ever. Got rid of them at about 2330 and turned in. A miserable day of worry and annoyance. I'm fussed about the group. I feel ought to go over and inspect one of these ships and I don't want to. I dread the idea of chucking my weight about. Started to write a letter to J.

Thursday, 1 June 1944 – Moelfre Bay

The *Port Colborne* and *Saint John* went to the oiler to top up at about 0745, and at about 0900 when *Saint John* had finished we weighed went alongside. I let No. 1 do the alongside. I was furious to see that the only ship of the group whose men were not in the rig of the day[21] was the S.O.'s ship. We had finished and were away at 1030 and anchored again and 1100 I went mess deck and store room rounds. Not bad. Two of our absentees returned, but I stopped all further leave to the ship. In the p.m. we went to Action Stations and I watched the D/C party drilling and went round below putting out lights and testing electrical repair parties. I made a signal saying I would walk round *Saint John* and *Port Colborne* on Saturday and Sunday. Altogether feeling much more confident and happier. The carrier *Pursuer* arrived at 1500. At 1800 I went over to see Macintyre in the *Bickerton,* and while I was there Graham (Act. Capt.)[22] of the *Pursuer* arrived but he didn't stay long, and then Macintyre and I went over to *Affleck,* and I finally got back on board about 2000. The W/T coding and cipher staff are working like beavers. The signals are simply flowing in. Another dull cool overcast day.

Friday, 2 June 1944 – Moelfre Bay

Quite a fresh S.W. wind. I inspected the guns at 0930. At 1500 I took an officers' crew away in the whaler under sail. Most of them never been in a service sailing boat before, and as we found it necessary to reef down at one moment I had my hands fairly full.[23] Our last 2 absentees came on board. The S.O.s of all groups were asked to dinner on *Pursuer.* I picked up E.G. 6 and then had about a 3 mile trip where *Pursuer* was anchored. Graham the Captain is an old destroyer type (and a lot younger than me) who I've known before. We discussed the operation a bit. I gave the whole party a lift back. Still no orders to sail.

I wrote to J. At first I wrote very bitterly about the R.C.N. but tore it up and wrote another. Oh! How I hate all this responsibility and worry. *Swansea* and *Meon* arrived from Liverpool at 2100. All three ships of the 2nd Division had developed defects on the way back from escorting *Empress* and had to go to Liverpool for repairs. *Stormont* is still there.

Saturday, 3 June 1944 – Moelfre Bay

At 0930 I went over to inspect *Saint John.* I walked round Divisions first and then upper deck, mess decks, and stores. Rather patchy. Some places, particularly magazines, excellent, but mess decks and some other places were untidy. Books were good. At 1100 I went down to the W.R. after clearing lower deck and giving the sailors a short talk. I came back with Stacey and at 1130 all C.O.s came on board and we had a chat and they all had lunch with me. The 2nd E.G. with the great Walker as S.O. and the *Emperor* arrived, also orders for 3 of my group to act as close screen for *Emperor,* and it rather looks as if the rest of us are going to work with or under E.G. 2. There was an aircraft homing test that all groups were told to take part in. At the end when reports were called for it was the 2 Canadian groups who were all adrift, which annoyed me because it showed my signal had never been properly read. That is so typical. You can never trust a Canadian ship to do anything without being told three times.

There was a never-ending flow of signals. A trawler arrived from Liverpool with the mail, which was a great joy, and I got a letter from J. The wind got up a bit in the course of the p.m. I am still all on edge. I had a talk with No. 1 and told him I was losing heart and reckoned I wasn't the chap for the job. He said he thought they ought to mix these Canadian ships amongst R.N. groups and squadrons, which of course is just what the R.C.N. ships *do* want. At 1900 I went over to *Swansea* to discuss the detailing of ships for *Emperor* and decided to let the three new boys do it, leaving *Matane, Swansea,* and *Stormont* for offensive work. Meant to turn in early but there was a continual flow of signals and orders, some of which we'd missed and had to send to other ships for. Brown is of the greatest assistance and the communication staff are doing magnificently.

Sunday, 4 June 1944 – Moelfre Bay

We were brought to 2 hours' notice in the night. The wind increased a lot and by midday was blowing really hard and we raised steam to insure safety. I cancelled my inspection of *Port Colborne.* At 1030 I read prayers on the mess deck. *Emperor* developed engine defects and left for Belfast, so perhaps I shall take my whole group after all. Still feeling restless and anxious all day. According to the last signal we received, tomorrow would be D Day for the invasion, but this gale must hold things up. The weather started to improve about 1600. *Stormont* arrived in the evening and at 1930 Myra came on board to see me and I think was a bit appalled when I handed him his Operation Neptune orders and showed him how many corrections there were to make. *Port Colborne* annoyed me very much this morning because when told to send boat to a trawler on arrival and collect and distribute stores and correspondence, it took v. nearly 2 hours after the trawler arrived before the boat was away. All I can get out of him was "we had some difficulty getting the boat away." That much was so bloody obvious. Our troops in Italy have taken Rome.

Monday, 5 June 1944 – Moelfre Bay/At sea

Turned in fairly early but had very little peace. All ships here taking part in Operation CA got their orders to sail in the morning, *Emperor*'s escort remaining behind. That had to be dealt with. Then *Swansea* reported HF/DF defects and we had to send our radio artificer over there, and then arrangements to collect from a trawler before sailing. The 1st E.G. sailed at 0600 and the rest of us at intervals, and my reduced party of 3 brought up the rear at 0800 astern of E.G. 2 (the great Walker). The wind had dropped altogether. Our route took us down the Irish Sea and over and through the swept channel along the S. Irish coast. Felt quite homesick when in the distance I saw the entrance to Queenstown.[24]

At 2200 on clearing the channel we formed up on the port wing of the 2nd EG, spread in line abreast on course 160° for our waiting position in 50°30' N. and 7° W. The remaining groups, *Pursuer,* and *Tracker,* are also in waiting positions to the west of us, waiting for orders to move down to the operational area further south. Looks as if we're going to be under the immediate control of E.G. 2.

Tuesday, 6 June 1944 – At sea

The invasion of France started!! The first news came over the German wireless but at 1300 it all came out in our news. Our landings have been on the bit of coast between the Seine and the Cherbourg peninsula. Not much news yet but the P.M. has said in the House that all was going well so far and losses and casualties have been lighter than expected. Enormous preliminary air and sea bombardment had been carried out and the initial assault had taken some 400 ships. No less than 3 *divisions* of air borne troops also been used!! Our first objective is Cherbourg as a port and then the whole of Brittany as far as Nantes, including three of the main U/Boat Biscay ports.

E.G. 2 signaled me that ten ships was too unwieldy, that he proposed to detach *Lochy* and *Loch Killin* to me and that when we were told to start the operation the 2 groups would operate as separate units but we'd be in the same square. In the meantime we patrolled backwards and forwards in our long line abreast formation, turning 180° about every 3 hours so as to remain close to our waiting position. In the evening we started to get aircraft reports of enemy destroyers and enemy ships off Ushant, and in the morning we'd intercepted signals from E.G. 1 and 5 in their waiting positions that they were being shadowed by aircraft. Nothing came our way except occasional rain showers and a fresh N.W. breeze.

D Day was delayed just 24 hours by that gale. I listened to all the news broadcasts in the W/T office. Most exciting. The King spoke at 2100 in the evening. Very good. The immensity of this operation and the planning organization that must have gone before is staggering. Pray God our initial success is maintained.

Wednesday, 7 June 1944 – At sea

The news of the French fighting seems good. We continue to land men and materiel, but they say there is v. hard fighting in progress. We are in the outskirts of Caen. Allied H.Q. are said to be neither optimistic nor pessimistic, indicating that they were always confident of getting the men ashore but the test comes 36 hours later when the Germans can put in heavy counter attacks while we're still weak and short of guns and armour. There were a number of sighting reports by aircraft indicating that a force of German destroyers was at sea off Brest and that a certain number of U-Boats were about off that area.

We continued to cruise up and down, turning about every 2 hours. The N.W. wind eased, I'm glad to say, as apparently conditions on the beaches were not too good account of wind and sea. I plotted all the enemy reports. At 1500 we decoded a signal from C. in C. W.A. telling E.G. 2 and 5, *Pursuer,* and *Tracker* to concentrate in one of the patrol squares at dawn tomorrow. E.G. 1 and 6 are to remain in their present waiting positions and we are to move to the W. to the area vacated by E.G. 5. E.G. 2 pushed off taking *Lochy* and *Loch Killin* with them, and so we're back to our little select 3. The wind dropped and it became a very hot p.m. Having reached our position at about 1850 we patrolled backwards and forwards, turning every 2 hours. One or two aircraft showed up during the day but all identified as friendly. At 2100, however, one remained in sight a long way off near the sun for about 50 minutes. Too far to identify but I thought he was suspicious and reported him as a shadower. *Emperor* with our other 3 ships is on the way and will arrive in this area at 0830 tomorrow.

Thursday, 8 June 1944 – At sea

Another day of waiting going backwards and forwards. Got a signal at about 1115 saying Force 31 had been reported [by the Germans] and that long-range enemy aircraft were very active in the area. On receipt of that we went to 2nd degree of A.A. readiness. About 1400 *Emperor* hove in sight with fighter planes buzzing about, and so we relaxed our precautions a bit. Later on the signal arrived telling us (Force 31), which now only consists of 1st and 9th and *Emperor,* as the 6th have taken place of the 1st as carrier escorts, to proceed to new waiting positions further south, followed shortly after by another signal ordering us to start patrolling in one of the squared areas. This necessitated a certain amount of chat over the T.B.S. between me and E.G. 1 and *Emperor* explaining what we were all going to do, and at 2230 we turned to approach the area we have got to be in by dawn.

Not much news about France except that we have captured Bayeux and that the landings continue. German navy counter attacks expected any time now. Continued to be misty and drizzly.

Friday, 9 June 1944 – At sea

At crack of dawn just as we were slipping into the patrol area *Emperor* came up and told us to close and screen her, as 2 of her own screen were away investigating a contact. We closed her and I told ships off for the screen positions only to be told by *Emperor* that he would follow in my swept water so I had to change everything, get into line abreast again, and set off on a new course. Ships were very bad at taking in signals. V. bad for the temper in the early morning. *Port Colborne* and *Saint John* were away hunting and so we had *Meon* with us, but the other two returned at about 0900 and so we had the whole group sweeping ahead of *Emperor,* which I don't care [for] at all.

At about 1130 we got a very good echo ahead and owing to the carrier I had to rush it and make a counter attack. As it happens the buzzers started to sound for an unknown reason and the D/C pattern was dropped miles early.[25] Regained contact and did a hedgehog attack, after which the most amazing number of dead fish (mostly large cod) came to the surface and the echo then faded out. It had been so good, however, that I kept *Swansea* and *Meon* searching some time and finally did a line abreast sweep to the E. Finally gave up and set off back to the carrier. On the way I'm damned if *Meon* didn't get a contact, which he was certain about at first but *Swansea* and I could get nothing for a long time. Finally, we picked up the v. strong stationary ping and we all H/H'd it and there it still stayed and finally I ran over it slowly with a D/C pattern – still no movement but I once more did a parallel sweep. On the way back again another ping, which I dragged *Meon* off v. reluctantly. I'm sure he thought he had a U-boat but the fact is there are a lot of bottom echoes in this 60 fathom water.

At about 1900 I finally sent *Meon* back to *Emperor* and got *Stormont* in exchange and set off to join the E.G. 1, with whom I'd agreed to tack on to for the night in the new area allocated. It was quite a business maneuvering my 3 into position. I must say sometimes I feel like saying on return, "Please get somebody to take my place I can't make the grade." I feel my wooly handling of situations must lose me the confidence of all the group.

From signals intercepted there was an engagement in the Channel in the night between a division of our Tribals and some German destroyers. One Narvik class sunk, one ran ashore, and one set on fire and one escaped. Minor damage to ours.[26]

Saturday, 10 June 1944 – At sea

When dawn came I broke away from E.G. 1 and set off in an independent patrol in a part of the area allotted to Force 31. We learned that *Tracker* had been in collision with *Teme* in the night and at 1930 we saw *Teme* in tow of *Outremont* with her mast pushed sideways. At about 0800 we got a signal telling us to form an additional screen for *Tracker* (at least that is how I read it but it was extremely badly worded), so we went off to look for *Tracker.* Just then the visibility, which had been extreme, deteriorated and became rainy and misty. Eventually we came up with her at about 1100 and after waiting astern and asking for orders he told us to rejoin *Emperor.* I then contacted *Emperor* on T.B.S., who said in view of a later signal from C. in C. telling *Emperor* and *Pursuer* to return to base, he didn't want me either. As my services were refused with thanks by everyone I pushed off to continue to patrol in our allotted area, informing C. in C. what I was doing. *Stormont* got another of those cracking bottom echoes and threw a hedgehog pattern at it, but I was wise in my appreciation after yesterday's experience, classified non sub after a short investigation, and ordered the party on.

At 1500 a signal from C. in C. to join *Tracker* forthwith with all despatch, so off we went again. I got a position, course, and speed from *Tracker* and I found we were nearly 60' away with a long stern chase. However, the sea was like the mill pond, and we went on to 17 knots. She was bound for Belfast for repairs after her bang with *Teme* and was making for the S. Irish swept channel, and it wasn't until she was about 20 miles from it when we caught her up at about 2200. By then we'd decoded another signal telling the 1st and 9th E.G. to return to Derry for layover period, and no sooner had we taken up screening positions around *Tracker* than she told us to proceed on ahead which we did at 15 knots. Order and counter-order all day.

Sunday, 11 June 1944 – At sea

As we left the swept channel at about 0530 it started to get foggy and at times in the a.m. it got v. thick. We came all the way up the Welsh coast, past Bardsey and past Holyhead and the Skerries, without seeing anything but navigating with extreme accuracy by radar. At about 1200 just after passing the Skerries it cleared and we had good visibility except for occasional heavy rain squalls for the rest of the run. Tide was with us through the N. Channel but we met a v. cold N.W.'ly wind.

I saw my 4 Moelfre Bay leave breakers as defaulters. I look upon their offence as quite deliberate and quite inexcusable, and I propose to punish them with cells.

We arrived off Dunagree Pt. at 2105, embarked pilots, and came up river. The pilot was rather slow and we were not secured until 2330. I've never seen Londonderry so empty of ships.

Monday, 12 June 1944 – Londonderry

Had great difficulty in waking up. I was busy after breakfast seeing requestmen, signing warrants, etc., and at 1100 there was the usual group conference. We're only getting 3 days just to wash through the boilers, as we are urgently required again. We're giving 24 hours leave to each watch and there is no training program. After the C.O.s went back on board *Port Colborne* for a drink. After lunch I had an interview with Telfer and told him I was going to discharge him as being additional to complement, and I had to tell him the reason he was going was because he was the least useful of all the officers. Poor chap, he doesn't want to leave the ship at all and I hate having to do this. Went up to see Copelin and asked him to arrange with London for Telfer's appointment.

Back on board, shifted, and went for short walk. Finished up at the Club for tea. Saw in the Birthday honours list in an old *Times* that Renouf[27] had got a C.B.E. Read a lot of papers. Listened to the 6:00 news. We are making progress in France and seem to have got our beach head really fully established and are beating back strong enemy counter attacks. An airman who was on board this forenoon said we had reached positions which we had not expected to reach until D+30, and that casualties have been much lower than expected. Back on board. Gave Telfer and No. 1 some gin and after dinner struggled with flimsies and confidential reports on Telfer. No letter from J. The mails are probably all at Liverpool. In Italy our troops are ½ way to Florence now. Churchill was over visiting the French front yesterday.

Tuesday, 13 June 1944 – Londonderry

I spent a profitable 2 hours after breakfast dealing with correspondence and about 1100 I went up to see the Commodore. King in the *Swansea* feels on reading the account of his first U-boat action that too little credit has been given the *Swansea,* and I rather agree. The Commodore, however, said he had been put in for his fair share of honours.[28] Had a talk about Canadians in general.

On return I went on board *Swansea* and had a drink in the ward room, and later on in King's cabin. Immediately after lunch I went off with 4 other officers and a party of ratings to an aircraft identification lecture. Browsed in a book shop on my way back and then had a little shut eye in my cabin till tea time. Started a letter to J. At about 1730 I went over to *Saint John* to have a drink with Stacey, who was celebrating his Mentioned in Despatches.[29] On return on board I felt I needed company, and so I asked Westwater and Lewtas who were on board to come for a drink. Finished my letter after dinner and then No. 1 asked me to go down to the W.R. where he had some guests, a Mr. McCluskey and his wife and another man and woman. They were quite amusing and we did a bit of singing but I thought they were never going. Awful stickers. It was damned near 0100 before I got to bed. This hot rum drinking is a menace, but it is all we have to drink in the W.R.

Wednesday, 14 June 1944 – Londonderry

Slight alcoholic remorse. That hot rum is a bad drink. I went up to Ops and to the cypher office. To my joy I got two letters from J. She and Raymond are now at Lanka.[30] They are now nearer home if and when they decide to return, and I'm glad some of the family have a chance to see R. After lunch I had a few moments shut eye in my cabin and then decided to go ashore for a walk, but first of all Cooke came along with the report of proceedings, which wanted considerable alteration, and then one of the base A/S officers arrived, and so I didn't get ashore until 1500.

Meant to walk out in the up-river direction but on arrival at the centre of the town I decided to walk round the walls, which I did, and I also went into the Cathedral to look. Nothing very much to it. Built in about 1650. I then went to the club for tea and read the *Times*. Back on board about 1800. I had asked the Commodore down for a drink but he couldn't make it, but Copelin came and we discussed the R.C.N. Wrote to J. after dinner and turned in nicely early. Beginning to feel frightened and worried about our next trip. We are evidently returning to the same general area that we were in before and relieving E.G. 1. Wrote a short letter to K. wishing her many happy returns of the 17th.

Thursday, 15 June 1944 – Londonderry/At sea

At 0700 we were moved by tugs to No. 4 berth to be ranged for degaussing. The rest of the group proceeded down river to oil, except *Meon* who went off to Liverpool to pick up a new generator. A grim morning with fairly steady rain. At 1030 we left No. 4 under our own steam and proceeded down as far as Lisahally, where we went alongside the American oiling jetty. While we were there I saw defaulters, which consisted of the usual ½ dozen drunks and disorderlies picked up by the naval patrol. At 1300 we shoved off and arrived at Moville at 1400, where we picked up the other 4 ships and proceeded to sea and the Irish Channel at 15 kts. Visibility was variable but improved in the evening. We were off Anglesey at about midnight. It was given out on the news that American Super Fortresses had bombed Japan – no details.[31] A chilly day. One of our sailors died in hospital as a result of being thrown from a horse on to his head in Derry.

Friday, 16 June 1944 – At sea

We got down the last of the swept channel buoys at about 0600 and turned to starboard and arrived at the beginning of [the swept channel] Q2L 58 at 0730. Visibility towards the Irish coast was poor and we couldn't get a fix. Later on we sighted Balleycotton Light and at 1200 we turned to the S. and spread in line abreast. From rather a chilly morning it became a really hot afternoon. We expected to sight E.G. 1 and E.G. 15 at about 2100 and they actually hove in sight at 2115. On our arrival E.G. 1 pushed off and we took station on starboard wing of E.G. 15, who are doing a gamma search between 49°55' and 49°05' along 7°30' W. An enormous spate of signals came through and all lamps were busy till nearly dark. Majendie[32] is E.G. 15. The Americans are more than ½ way across the neck of the Cherbourg peninsula.

Saturday, 17 June 1944 – At sea

K.'s 46th birthday. We turned to 180° by blue turn at 0040 and N. again at 0445. Back again to S. at 0930. I went mess deck rounds. Disappointed to find that there is hardly a corner I can walk into without finding dirt. At 1400 just as we were turning once again *Saint John* got a contact which he seemed unable to classify, and so I sent for *Port Colborne* to help him. I finally turned back myself. Found they had an excellent echo off some stationary object on the bottom.

Saint John did the D/C and H/H attack and we did a H/H. Still no movement or oil or anything, so decided either wreck or rock and pushed off to catch up the rest. I must say in the shallow water (60 fath.) the possibility of the U-boat sitting on the bottom makes it hard to classify a good stationary echo. At about 1830 we got a signal from C. in C. telling us to stop this Gamma search, and giving E.G. 15 and E.G. 9 different areas to sweep in. Thank God we can be on our own at last. Soon after 1930 *Meon* joined up from Liverpool and so for the first time the whole group is out together. After she had joined we moved over into the N.E. half of square JB and started our patrol. A lovely sunny day and flat calm. Heard on the news that the King had been over to the beach head in France.

Sunday, 18 June 1944 – At sea

C. in C. W.A. made a signal turning over all forces who were taking part in Operation CA to C. in C. Plymouth. We reached the S.E. end of our patrol at 0215 and turned to 315°. At 0500 on receipt of a signal from an aircraft that she had detected a disappearing target in a position only about 15 miles away, we altered course to 000° to close. There was nothing there of course, and we spent the whole day sweeping round in Easy Item turns trying to cover the furthest on points. I was expecting by the evening to be given some definite orders, but although all the other groups were mentioned in the night situation signal we were completely ignored, so I started a N. and S. patrol for the night.

Monday, 19 June 1944 – At sea

We turned at 0130 at the S. limit of our patrol. The U-boats suddenly seemed to wake up and there were quite a number of aircraft sightings. The nearest one to us was nearly 90 miles to the W., which I didn't think was for us to go to unless specially ordered. Just before 0400 we sighted 2 aircraft flares and turned to investigate astern. Just after turning we got an A/S contact and there was about an hour of feverish activity trying to hold the echo, control the group in the dark, and deal with a spate of signals which came in from aircraft and shore authorities.

It soon became apparent that someone was expecting us to go to the aircraft sightings 90 miles away, as aircraft were told to home, relief aircraft were sent out, and we were given their call signs. The issue was then further confused by another contact rather nearer with signals about homing *also* addressed to us. I got completely bewildered and rattled. At 0515 when the A/S contact was proved bogus I started off at 17 kts to the W. At 0700 I changed my mind and decided I ought to go to the nearer position and altered to the E. and got hot and rattled and miserable. Arrived on the scene about 0930 to find E.G. 15 already there and requiring no assistance as he was quite convinced the original sightings were quite bogus and so I turned round again and homed on the W.'ly aircraft who was now about 90 miles off. Felt I'd made an ass of myself.

We got good homing signals up to about 1400 when the aircraft had to leave. The whole thing is damned stupid because by now the submarine might be anywhere. At about 1530 just as we must have been getting very near the spot, I'm damned if we didn't hear another aircraft making a sighting report only about 35 miles to the N.'ward so we turned to the original H/F bearing and then pushed up the M/F homing and it all worked just according to A.F.I.s. As we were approaching *Stormont* got a contact and we all had to stop. Eventually I had to leave him and *Swansea* behind to classify while I pushed on with the rest. Found aircraft circling the original marker at about 1830 and started a sweep to the S.E. At about 1900 we picked up a good ping which although in other ways looked much like those other bottom echoes *did* have some movement according to plot. *Meon* who closed did a H/H attack, and thereafter the echo faded right out. I couldn't possibly leave it, however, so put all the other ships on Observant and finally formed up for a parallel sweep, all in fading light and finally pitch darkness. Oh, how I hate these contacts which you cannot say definitely are sub or non sub and which although you want to leave you can't.

Tuesday, 20 June 1944 – At sea

Reported what I was doing to C. in C. and searched all through the night. Found nothing nor was there a single aircraft sighting. In the morning I found myself somewhere near the rather vague aircraft sighting and so went to have a look only to be told by C. in C. that the position was in error and I should return to the scene of my last night contact. Got in some much needed sleep in the p.m. We were nearing the old position at about 1700 when *Saint John* reported an object on the bottom giving a ping and an echo sounder trace not unlike a submarine, so over I went with the whole group. *Could* I make up my mind? It was made much more difficult by continually losing contact. We threw H/H at it and then a D/C pattern but it wasn't until 2045 that I finally decided to leave it and classify it as a rock or pinnacle. All my indecision is deplorable. Owing to all that delay I decided to push on to 15 knots and turned to 090° to try and get to the possible submarine's furthest on circle by dark. Just before 2400 we got an aircraft sighting report but in a position 85-90 miles away to W., and I decided to take no action and turned to the S. to start a N. and S. patrol for the night. The Americans have got right up the Cherbourg peninsula and are in the suburbs of Cherbourg itself.

Wednesday, 21 June 1944 – At sea/Falmouth

Another night of awful doubt and sorrow. After much indecision I decided to take no action on the U/B report to the W., and then of course control tells the aircraft to home me and I wonder am I right, and then comes a late report from the aircraft saying U/B is disabled and then I know I'm wrong and I must go and so alter to the W. By this time it is 0120 and I've lost nearly 1½ hours. Shortly after C. in C. comes up and asks where I am and what I'm doing. Due to night effect the homing signals are almost impossible to D/F. By plot my course should be well S. of W., and yet such bearings as I *can* get and which the other ships are passing all indicate a course N. of W. At about 0500 I had to make another difficult decision and altered drastically to the S. as per plot, but about ½ hour later the situation was clarified by the aircraft saying his original position was made a whole degree of latitude wrong. This showed him by plot and bearing to the N. and so I altered back. The aircraft then had to return to base. Expecting the possibility of the damaged U/B on the surface we prepared to board and I anxiously thought out how best to deal with the situation, anti-Gnat tactics, etc. When at 0900 we reached the estimate position there was not a thing in sight and so we turned to sweep to the E. About an hour later received a signal from C. in C. saying the group was to proceed to Falmouth forthwith to fuel and so for once we were heading in the right direction and so just went on to 16 knots.

Quite a fresh N.W. wind and enough sea to make us bump a bit. The Bishop was abeam just before 4 and when off the Lizard[33] we were told to fuel in 2 halves, so I left the 2nd Div. on patrol and went in with the 1st Div. We were secured by about 2030 and when I inquired if the Admiral wanted to see me the answer was yes and so I had to put on a white-collar. A car was sent but on arrival I found I wasn't wanted at all. However, I did see the Chief of Staff and the Admiral,[34] both of whom were most kind and said we needn't sail till 0600, though in fact the oiling would be finished earlier. The base staff also rallied around and worked all night on some A/S defects. I went to bed as early as I could. The Chief of Staff told me that this wind was holding up the unloading of supplies in France badly and that they were very much behind schedule in this matter.[35]

Thursday, 22 June 1944 – Falmouth/At sea

We sailed at 0600. Feeling much refreshed by my 6½ hours in bed. On arrival off the Lizard I signalled *Swansea* to go in with his division and I started to patrol in the area allotted to us about 20' south of the Lizard. Nothing happened until 1320 when we got a good contact, which we ran over and held as we ran out, and which the plot reported had movement although there was no doppler. Turned round to attack, but the echo, which was cracking at long-range, faded as we came in and we did not fire. Then there was quite an interval before *Port Colborne* picked it up and attacked twice with hedgehog. There was an exciting moment when some time after the H/H explosion a large water disturbance was seen and I was expecting to see a conning tower any moment, but nothing appeared. We all continued to plaster the echo, which now had no movement, and I was getting doubtful when an aircraft sighting report came through of a U/B on the surface not more than 10 miles away. Decided to take *Saint John* and the *Port Colborne.*

As the aircraft didn't home I had to go to the plotted position, which finally worked out as only 11 miles away. On arrival there was not a sign of anything, and back I went to *Port Colborne* who had then lost contact. Started to search when at last our aircraft started to home. He was obviously very close and finally his datum and our datum was plotted not more than 5 miles apart, which was of course obviously absurd. I must say these aircraft are very difficult to work with. They won't stay over the spot and home, and they won't listen out on R/T. Started another search but of course found nothing. U/Bs are certainly coming into the Channel, but even the great Walker doesn't seem to be able to find them and so far they have done no damage.[36]

Friday, 23 June 1944 – At sea

Chased after more non subs in the night. *Swansea* and the 2nd Division arrived in the area at 0100 and I told them to act independently during the night, and at 0630 we all formed up together and carried on sweeping our area to the S. of Lizard to the Wolf.[37] A lovely warm sunny day. Wind has gone down. At about 1030 we got a contact and stopped and looked at it and attacked and ran over with echo sounder. I got very annoyed because I allowed myself to be dissuaded by Cooke from going on much earlier and leaving what was obviously a rock. It was nearly 1200 before we abandoned the investigation. In the p.m. *Port Colborne* got a contact. This time I stayed behind with the 1st Div. and let the 2nd Div. go on and caught up later after classifying non sub. These contacts with rocks and wrecks are maddening because in this depth they could all be submarines sitting on the bottom.

No more excitement for a bit and managed to dictate some of the diary of events, which will have to be sent in at Plymouth, to the writer. At about 2230 I was shown a signal ordering new patrol areas for the night and giving us a position nearly 60 miles away. Just at this minute of course *Port Colborne* gets a contact and holds us up, and then there is a correction to the signal which can't be deciphered and has to be got from *Swansea.* One W/T and Coder is awful. Signals are either missed or take twice as long to reach the bridge as they ought. Eventually we were able to get off the mark at 2400, but I had to signal C. in C. and tell him we were going to be late arriving. I got v. fussed and rattled.

Saturday, 24 June 1944 – At sea

We had an exciting trip to our area at 17 kts dodging other escorts. Our new area takes us right up to the French coast near Ile de Batz. The 1st time we came down to the S. end of our beat it was dark and we altered round on time and radar but the next time in the p.m. we came plainly in sight of land and didn't turn round till the light house was about 12 miles off. What a change when one can approach within sight of France without so much as the single shell or bomb, when one thinks of the time when our own coastal waters were swarming with German aircraft. In view of the proximity of the enemy coast I went to Defence Watch instead of Cruising Watch, but it seems there is no need to.[38]

Later on when we were going N. we got some HF/DF bearings of a U-boat, which although unlikely suggested it *might* be between us and the land astern. Anyhow turned round on spec and luckily just then a Liberator flew overhead and I asked him to sweep in front of me up to the land. He eventually reported a large oil patch and later on that he had attacked a possible periscope. We arrived on the scene at about 1830 and there certainly was a v. big oil patch on a glassy sea. Our aircraft had gone but 2 others were circling. Having swept through the oil and found nothing, I was doing an E.I. turn when the aircraft said they had picked up contact (presumably with one of these new gadgets)[39] and so back we came, and shortly *Swansea* gained a contact and attacked, and *Meon, Stormont,* and I all had a go. I could see no movement but the other ships reported there was. The explosions certainly brought up a lot more oil but nothing else, and I was quite certain there was no U-boat there. Later I think we shifted to another stationary contact. We stuck around to dark and then searched the vicinity but found nothing. Quite exciting for a time. Perfect hot day.

Sunday, 25 June 1944 – At sea

I had as usual v. little sleep in the night. Two or three aircraft sightings which had to be plotted. We started to go for one but then heard E.G. 14 was after it already. We came S. in the morning and at about 0900 when 10 miles off Ile de Batz we turned round again and shortly after Easy Itemed to 090° into our Eastern square. At about 1345 when coming W. again an aircraft was seen dropping markers and D/Cs on our port beam, and so we closed to investigate and he said he'd seen a suspicious oil patch. I'm tired of these oil patches.

As we arrived on the spot *Stormont* signalled he had intercepted an aircraft report of an enemy destroyer off the Ile de Batz steaming very close in shore.[40] I didn't really know what to do. The position we'd closed to was only about 10-12 miles off Sept Iles. Eventually I decided to leave *Swansea* and 2 to search and take the other two close in shore to see if I could see anything of the destroyer. What to do if I did sight it I wasn't at all sure, with our pop gun 4".[41] Closed to within 5 miles of Sept Iles and as the visibility was good we could plainly see if anything was creeping up close in shore that there was not a thing to be seen, and so we patrolled to and fro for a bit. After an hour I thought it was time to go in case the Germans whistled up some bombers and so, *Swansea* and co. having found nothing good, we pushed off to N.'ward. It really is remarkable one can remain an hour close off the enemy post unmolested. We then continued our patrol. The visibility shut down and a thin drizzle started. Apart from some radar pips which were identified as friendly adjacent escorts nothing transpired.

MONDAY, 26 JUNE 1944 – AT SEA/PLYMOUTH

At 0600 we left patrol and shaped course for Plymouth. It was raining and the visibility was down to about 2 miles. However, we found the way all right. Plymouth Sound and Dockyard simply packed with ships. Went alongside No. 2 Wharf with *Saint John* outside us.

I had a bath and then called on Capt. D., one Morice[42] who I've never met before and who doesn't seem particularly helpful. At about 1515 I had a car to take me to A.C.H.Q., where I saw Evans who is operating these support groups, and got a lot of interesting information from him. He reckons that in spite of the few known killings the U-boats in the Channel have done so little that if we can keep the air and surface pressure up a bit longer he may call all his U-boats off altogether. It seems there is no way of telling a U-boat on the bottom, and even if you do kill them, there will be nothing much more than oil to show, which of course may come just as well from a wreck. He showed me some photographs of this snorkel which the U-boats are using. I gather my decisions when looking further W. about not going to contacts 90 miles away were not v. popular.

While in his office rang up J. at Tunbridge Wells. She and R. go back to Prinsted tomorrow. I gather they have been getting some of these new Flying Bombs dropping in T. Wells. From A.C.H.Q. I got a car and went on board *Swansea* who is berthed in the S. yard. Talked to King and later I got another car back to the ship. Wrote to J. I was just thinking of going really early to bed when the Captain of a destroyer alongside came over and kept me up till 2300 much to my disgust. The Americans have taken Cherbourg.

TUESDAY, 27 JUNE 1944 – PLYMOUTH

No absentees and no drunks! Marvelous. I saw requestmen at 0930 and at 1000 I had a car to take me to write my name in the Admiral Superintendent's book, then in the C. in C.'s book, and finally to the Gunnery School at the Barracks where I expected to find Butler as Captain. He had left and Orr Ewing[43] had taken his place but was out. I got the car to drop me in the Dockyard and walked round a bit. The *Anson* and an American battleship are here. The rest are all small ships. Back on board soon after 1100. At about 1145 Admiral Reid R.C.N.[44] came on board and after a chat in my cabin I took him down to the wardroom. King from *Swansea* and Stacey from *Saint John* came over to meet him. He is the Canadian representative in Washington, over here to have a look around. King stayed to lunch.

At about 1530 No. 1 and I went ashore, caught a bus into Plymouth, and then I had a hair cut and bought some books and walked onto the Hoe. At about 1630 I met No. 1, who by then had collected a taxi, and drove out to the Moorland Hotel at Yelverton. From there we set out for a grand walk of about three hours and dropped into the golf links club house for a drink and then back to the Moorland Hotel for dinner. Lots of Americans there. Our taxi came for us again at 2030 and got back on board at 2100 and after a drink I wrote to J. and Gillian and then turned in.

Wednesday, 28 June 1944 – Plymouth

A foul day, rainy and blowing. Guns came along at about 0800 to say our ammunition hadn't arrived, he having gone ashore yesterday and taken no steps to hasten it. Got a car at 0930 and went to A.C.H.Q. and saw Evans to get any last-minute news, which was practically nil, and then went on board *Swansea* and had a brief C.O.s meeting and found *Port Colborne* and *Stormont* would not be ready to sail at 1200 owing to uncompleted defects. It is also doubtful if we will get our ammunition in time now. Went up to Capt. D.'s office to see if they could give me the time of completion for *Port Colborne* and *Stormont* and rang up A.C.H.Q. to report delay. Result was sailing was postponed for two hours till 1400. At 1400 *Stormont* reported still not ready, and as she was outside ship it meant *Swansea* and *Port Colborne* couldn't get out either.

We had to have a tug to help us get away from the wall on account of the wind. Left harbour with *Saint John* and *Meon*. Blowing quite hard from the S. with rain and v. poor visibility. However when we got about 5 or 6 miles S. of the Eddystone[45] it improved. We turned E. at 15 knots to get to our patrol area, which is between Portland and the Channel Islands. Got a good A/S contact on the way and spent an hour plastering it. We found *Swansea* and *Port Colborne* were not far behind and so at 2145 I turned round, and we all joined up before dark and were able to start on to a N. and S. course for the night. Another A/S contact in the middle watch and more H/H and D/C attacks. One just has to attack every echo, and there is *no* way of telling whether he is a submarine on the bottom or not.

Thursday, 29 June 1944 – At sea

I spent a good deal of the middle [watch] on the bridge investigating A/S contacts. We turned to the S. and went about 12 miles off Alderney, which has shore batteries, [and] we turned N. again at about 0700. The day produced the usual infuriating crop of echoes which one could not classify. At about 1430 *Port Colborne* attacked a contact with H/H and produced a monumental explosion. We all dashed up thinking a U-boat had blown up in some way, only to find that the only evidence we were able to pick up clearly showed it was not German and was obviously a wreck carrying ammunition. Very disappointing. *Port Colborne* suffered considerable damage and I sent her into Portland for repairs.

We had hardly got going again when another contact was obtained by *Saint John*, and we went over to help and dropped D/Cs on it and ran over it with echo sounder and finally assessed it as a pinnacle rock. We turned to the S. and when about 10 miles N. of the Casquets[46] we altered to the S.W. and ran on down towards Guernsey. At 2300 just as I was about to turn 180° I saw gun flashes on Guernsey and although we were about 15 miles away, and therefore probably out of range, I turned away and made smoke. Nothing was seen to fall anywhere near us. We then turned back on our tracks to make up towards Portland during the night. *Stormont,* who was delayed sailing owing to defects, joined up at about 1300.

Friday, 30 June 1944 – At sea

There are no alarms in the night but I was kept up quite a bit over the navigation. What with tides and funny results from land echoes by radar, it seems impossible to predict where one will be the few hours ahead. We spent the night and day doing Blue and Easy Item turns in our rather restricted area and everlastingly investigating echoes. Attacking some and leaving others alone until I could nearly scream. I think after another 10 days of this I shall be qualifying for a lunatic asylum. Showers but at times the visibility was extreme. Starting to blow fresh from the S. When in sight of the Cherbourg peninsula we could hear the thud of guns, see flashes and large columns of smoke.

Saturday, 1 July 1944 – At sea

We nearly had a collision with *Saint John* while investigating a non sub echo. At 0115 *Swansea* reported sighting a snorkel and we saw her firing Oerlikon. The rest of us closed, and while *Swansea* swept around in the vicinity the rest of us did an Observant patrol without the sign of an echo. At about 0300 we formed up for a parallel sweep to the S. towards Alderney. When 10 miles off we turned to 270° by Blue turn and saw a great number of flashes from Alderney. Presumably firing at us but nothing reached. We then turned to sweep to the N. At 0530 *Saint John* reported a ground wave U-boat transmission bearing 254° and so, thinking it might be our fellow surfaced and talking, I altered to the bearing. The visibility was poor and at times under one mile and so little hope of air reconnaissance. Any 0830 I started a N. and S. patrol about 30 miles to the W. of the datum point, but after hearing that *Saint John*'s signal was plotted somewhere in 4° W. by the Admiralty I turned E. again at 1300 back to the scene of the sighting and having swept through it again I resumed our normal patrol. I suppose *Swansea did* see this snorkel, but it is extraordinary that we are unable to gain A/S contract. From the lack of interest ashore it seems they don't believe my signals. In the evening it was thoroughly damp and foggy.

Sunday, 2 July 1944 – At sea

An uneventful night but I was kept up quite a bit for navigational reasons. A lousy day of almost continuous drizzle and fog. We paddled back and forth on a N. and S. line most of the day but in the p.m. made a cast to the east with the worst result. *Saint John* found an oil slick and a ping, which I couldn't drag him off although I was damned certain from its position that it was *Port Colborne*'s wreck. *Meon* joined *Saint John* and started reporting that the S/M was moving W. at 1½ knots, quite forgetting that the E.'ly tide running at the time would make a stationary target appear to move W. At last we got away and set off to a new position off the Cherbourg Peninsula to start a Gamma search on a line from Cap de la Hague to Portland. We had the south half of this patrol and E.G. 3 the northern half. The poor visibility and strong tides made it very difficult to fix ourselves accurately even with radar. It poured with rain all night and was quite bloody.

Monday, 3 July 1944 – At sea

A worrying night dealing with the navigational problem. After an unpromising morning it cleared up and turned out a lovely day. Quite uneventful. Hardly a "Queen" [asdic contact] all day, while we heard the 3rd E.G. just north of us reporting contacts about every ½ hour (All non sub). Sent Cooke over to *Stormont* to deal with an A/S defect in the a.m. and got him back at 1600. Now that it is getting on towards Spring[47] the tides here are very strong, and I made a signal asking if I could be detached to Portland or Portsmouth to complete the fixing of this new type of navigation fixing set (like Loran), which was started when in Plymouth and not finished. In reply were told to return to Plymouth. I had hoped perhaps it might be Portsmouth and could see J.

Just before dark when quite near the coast we got a good contact and *Saint John, Meon,* and we spent till after midnight looking at it and dropping patterns of D/Cs on it. Eventually decided it was a wreck and set off after *Swansea* and *Stormont,* who had continued the patrol.

The Russians have made what appears to be a major breakthrough on a large front near Minsk. In Normandy the Americans have advanced a bit, having mopped up the whole of the Cherbourg peninsula, but the British troops still seem to be pinned down everywhere by very stubborn German defence, particularly around Caen.

Tuesday, 4 July 1944 – At sea/Plymouth

We joined up with *Swansea* and *Stormont* at about 0100 and at 0130 turned to the S. and I went down to my sea cabin. At about 0215 I was told Cap de la Hague was 12 miles off, but the bearing seemed a bit wrong. Went up and started to plot our position and turned to the N. to bring the bearing right before going off on our N.'ly patrol again. At about 0300 just as we turned to 338° an absolute blaze of glory went up all round *Swansea.* Star shell, gun flashes, and God knows what. I signalled full speed to the group and crossed my fingers. I realized I'd made an awful mistake and that the radar had been on Alderney instead of Cap de la Hague and that the German batteries had opened up on *Swansea,* who couldn't have been more than 6 or 7 thousand yards off. Thank God she wasn't hit, but for a short time she was under very heavy fire. I made a signal deeply regretting my mistake. The mental agony while it lasted was intense.

At 0600 I turned the group over to *Swansea* and set course for Plymouth at 17 kts. Spent most of the a.m. dictating my report of proceedings to Helpburn, the Leading Writer. Arrived at Plymouth at about 1230 but were kept waiting about in the Hamoaze for quite a bit while some big Yankee ships came down. Eventually berthed alongside at about 1400 and I had a bath. Miller heard he was the father of a son, and so at about 1600 I went down to the wardroom and celebrated with beer!! At 1645 I got a car and went to A.C.H.Q. Apparently they had been told this job would only take three hours. Now that they hear it will take 24 they are wild and would never have brought us in had they known. *Port Colborne* has gone to Belfast for repairs. I feel I haven't slept for days, and so after supper I went to bed at 2030 and was asleep by 2100. Got a letter from P. from Australia.

Wednesday, 5 July 1944 – Plymouth/At sea

I slept until 0730 and could have done more still. At about 0930 I walked to a public telephone in the Dockyard and phoned J. Suggested she should come to Londonderry on the 10th, but I don't know whether the travel ban to Ireland has been lifted yet, but oh Gee, it would be grand if she could be there for our 4 days in. This Q.H. outfit is taking longer to fit than first expected, and instead of 1300 as our time forecasted, it wasn't till 1500 that we eventually slipped. As soon as we were clear of the boom we went on to 160 revs and after clearing the swept channel set course to rejoin the group in the same old area. Saw a strange object in the water which on closer examination proved to be a collapsed small captive balloon. We pulled it on board and continued. Joined the group at about 2200 and passed over some mail to all ships before taking station in the middle of the line. A most beautiful night. Light as day with a full moon and clear sky.

This Q.H. navigation device is certainly marvellous, but even with it the navigation problem of spring tides and one sort of alarm and another was sufficient to keep me up most of the night. Following promotions: to Captain, Currey who went out to America with me and Ted LeMesurier and Stephen Roskill. To Commander, Gwinner (E.G. 1).

Thursday, 6 July 1944 – At sea

An entirely uneventful night. This Q.H. is a joy and delight. Had a sniff round a wreck giving off oil on two occasions, on the N.'ly leg and S.'ly leg. Q.H. tells me once it is the same contact and there is no movement. At about 1830 I detached *Meon* and *Stormont* to Portland to replenish H/H and D/C ammunition and at the same time got a signal from C. in C. telling the 9th E.G. to shift to a patrol further west. Shan't be sorry to see the last of Cap de la Hague and Alderney.

Arrived at the nearest end of our new patrol at 2230 and turned to a course 236°. The early part of the night was much disturbed by mysterious flares, star shell, and corrupt aircraft sighting reports.

Friday, 7 July 1944 – At sea

The latter part of the night was reasonably undisturbed. *Meon* and *Stormont* joined at about 1030, and I detached *Saint John* and *Swansea* to Plymouth to replenish the H/Hs and D/Cs. At the same time the group were told to shift to yet another area further west, just north of Ushant. Altered to the new course and increased to 16 kts. It started to blow quite hard from the S.W. and very soon quite a choppy sea got up, so much so that at 1700 I reduced to 13 kts as we were getting so wet. At about 1800 just as I reached the N.E. corner of our area we got an A/S contact which seemed pretty good, but the sea and wind made conditions difficult. Both other ships eventually gained contact and we all attacked with hedgehog and depth charges. No results at all. The conditions were not easy and I reckon after 4 or 5 D/C patterns and 3 H/Hs we must have got near enough to a stationary target to damage it. At about 2015 I gave it up and went on. *Meon* said he thought we *had* something there. I *don't* think, so but perhaps I should have left 2 ships a bit longer to watch it. How *can* one make up one's mind about these damned ground contacts? *Saint John* rejoined having been told by C. in C. Plymouth not to come in to reammunition. *Swansea* had got in on account of a defect. Our area is only 20 miles square, which means a lot of altering course and not much sleep. Wind and sea went down towards night fall.

Saturday, 8 July 1944 – At sea

A beautiful hot sunny day. I went mess deck rounds and was glad to see a big improvement. At about 1330 we got a lovely echo which reverberated round the whole ship and attacked with H/H and D/Cs, and so did *Meon* and *St. John,* and absolutely nothing happened. No oil, no fish, and the echo remained. There was a trace on the echo sounder which indicated a rock. Very disappointing. Gave it up and went on at about 1545. *Swansea* joined up at about 1700.

About 2000 we got a signal from C. in C. Plymouth altering all the dispositions of the groups and giving us an area just S. of Ushant and right off the entrance to Brest. Earlier on we had intercepted signals from 2 aircraft saying they had sunk U-boats in the northern part of the Bay. The fact that we are now able to operate right off the enemy's doorstep without any interference brings home most forcibly the decline of Germany's might. Even so, I must say it, our area felt a bit too close considering we had no supporting forces anywhere near us. We arrived in the area at 2200. Ushant Light House itself visible and later on its light was exhibited. We rather wondered why. According to the news we have launched a major offensive against Caen.

Sunday, 9 July 1944 – At sea

At about 0300 we intercepted an aircraft sighting report which was a good 60 miles away but which I decided to close. Almost as soon as we started I realized E.G. 5 was closer and so was not surprised to be told to return to patrol. In spite of our close proximity to Brest nothing happened, and at 0730 in accordance with instructions we left patrol and made for Plymouth. It started to blow quite a bit from the west and the visibility shut down. We arrived off the breakwater at 1630 as ordered and found an American depot ship just leaving, which we were to escort as far as The Smalls.[48] Off Falmouth we were told to pick up 2 more ships. I had no idea who was supposed to be in charge of the whole proceedings. I expected the Yankee to act as [a] sort of Commodore and I would just organize the screen and conform. However, he seemed to expect me to do everything. Result, considerable confusion.

We started off the trip at 16 kts but one of the 2 new ships reported 14 was her maximum. Rounding Land's End the wind increased a lot and we ran into a pretty heavy sea, and the next thing that happened we had to reduce to 12, and then just before dark our lame duck hove to and reported her landing craft were all breaking adrift. Told *Meon* and *Saint John* to stand by her and went on with *Swansea* and *Stormont* with the other two. A big beam sea and rolling like hell. Spent nearly the whole night on the bridge as our compass seemed most unreliable, and we spent our time trying to keep accurately ahead of the ships we were screening and also dodging shipping coming in the opposite direction. At midnight we were halfway between Longships and Trevose Head. Our offensive in Normandy has begun and we have captured Caen.

Monday, 10 July 1944 – At sea

Having spent nearly the whole night on the bridge, we found ourselves coming up inside Lundy Island as dawn was breaking at about 0500. Still blowing hard from the west. *Meon* from astern reported more trouble from his ship, and my two were asking permission to push on at full speed 18 kts, which I couldn't possibly maintain in this weather. I eventually told them to go on ahead and as we turned to the W. we reduced to 12 knots. As we approached The Smalls to my surprise I saw *Saint John* coming up from the port quarter and further in the distance *Meon* and his "headache." We took the shortcut inside Grassmother but it was obvious we couldn't possibly make Londonderry till tomorrow morning and so we went on to 15 knots and remained at that speed. I got some much-needed sleep in the a.m. *Meon,* after leaving her ship at The Smalls, came up from astern and detached to Liverpool for some repair job, and the rest of us went on up the Irish Sea. Raw chilly day blowing from the N.W. as progressed. Passed the Skerries at about 1600. I am hoping against hope that my wife will be able to get to Londonderry for the short layover period, as I'm tired and depressed and need my wife.

Tuesday, 11 July 1944 – Londonderry

We had a very strong tide against us in the North Channel and arrived at Moville at 0500, picked up pilots, and came on up harbour and secured Londonderry at 0730. After breakfast I had a bath and then walked up to the Tactical School for the group conference at 1000 only to find that the time should have been signalled 1100. There is no peace or rest, because immediately on arrival we got full information about this newly formed rest camp and they want to know immediately how many are going from each ship, and officers and duty men have to be detailed. The conference came off at 1100. We have got a bare 4 days and so very little can be done. Heard that Myra, Capt. of the *Stormont,* had got his ½ stripe. Joan is *not* here, which is bitterly disappointing, but I gather there is no possibility of civilians being allowed passage across to Ireland yet. I was tied to my desk all the p.m. with correspondence. Who should come over to see me at about 1830 but Grieve and Lt.(E) Garner,[49] who was my Chief in the *Walpole.* They're both now in the *Highlander.*

Wednesday, 12 July 1944 – Londonderry

I went ashore at about 1030 and visited the Pay Office, had a hair cut, and went to see Copelin and Lee. Back on board and went over to *Stormont* to celebrate Myra's ½ stripe, met an R.C.N.V.R. Captain Cross who is over from Ottawa.[50] He is Reserve Officers personnel at NSHQ. King, who was over in *Saint John,* came back on board for lunch with me. When he had gone I began to feel fussed. There seems such a hell of a lot to be done. I have decided to hold an examination in the group for Petty Officers and Leading Seaman tomorrow, and time is very short for making the arrangements. Then to add to my worries the Chief of Staff rang up and asked why no officers attended a lecture given by the Commodore yesterday just after we arrived in. Life is really very grim, and the short spells in harbour are absolutely no rest or relaxation what ever.

I had arranged to go ashore for dinner with No. 1 and at about 1900 he came along to my cabin for a drink and in the course of conversation he said what a very happy ship and group this was. How much I was liked by C.O.s and all, and what a disaster it would be if I left. I don't think he would say so if he did not mean it. It cheered me no end, just as I was feeling in the depths and wondering whether the other C.O.s had any confidence in me at all and whether I was fit to hold this job down. We finally decided to feed on board. At about 2130 Captain Cross came on board and we talked about Stacey and King, both of whom are disgruntled about their seniority. Later on went over to *Saint John,* where we found Stacey and King, and we all went to the ward room and started a sing song which went on till nearly 0200.

Thursday, 13 July 1944 – Londonderry

I spent the whole forenoon examining men for Petty Officer and Leading Seaman and went on with it for about an hour after lunch. My board consisted of Myra and Band[51] (No. 1 of *Swansea*). The former was very slow and so while waiting for him to finish off walked along to the R.N. Pay Office to try and get the Pay Capt. to approve the issue of overalls to our ship's company. From there I went to Operations and found we were sailing early Saturday, and then back on board. When at about 1700 Myra at last finished we compared marks and filled in the exam forms. We examined 11 and Stacey's board in *Saint John* examined another 15 or so. Thank God that's over. Next time if we can get some leave and a longer time in we won't have it hanging over us.

At about 1830 I went round to the *Ottawa* to see Prentice, who has just come in with his group. He reckons he got a U-boat in the Channel.[52] Listening to him and hearing what he has done makes me feel once more most inefficient. He is having a good deal of trouble and having to read endless numbers of warrants. If I really did my duty and insisted on higher standards and wasn't so kind and tired, I ought probably to be taking much more drastic disciplinary action myself. I eventually stayed to supper.

A slightly better day. We did see the sun for one brief moment. I am making the group paint dark hulls and light upper works and washing out camouflage in order (a) to have everyone alike and (b) to simplify the painting. I think it looks rather nice.

Friday, 14 July 1944 – Londonderry

It rained almost incessantly all day. Although it is our last day in the work never stopped. Defaulters, warrants, reports, S206s for officers, and so it goes on, and I and the writer Helpburn never get away from our desks and typewriters. At 1130 I went over to *Highlander* and had a drink with the Chief (Garner). At 1600 I decided to down tools and went ashore to the Pay Offices, then the club, where I had tea and read the papers, and returned on board at 1830 only to find the Commodore didn't like my suggested punishment on a warrant and I had to ring up and there was a long delay getting it back and reading it. After dinner I wrote to J. and sent a postcard to Gillian and Raymond. No. 1 came along and had a drink and we had a long yarn about behaviour of Canadian ratings ashore. Later on Prentice came over and kept me talking and drinking whiskey till after 2400. A bad thing the night before sailing. Oh dear, back to the anxiety of another period in the Channel after 4 days which has seen no sort of relaxation whatsoever.

5

Exasperation Inshore, July-October 1944

Despite their difficulties in hunting U-boats, it was clear by the midpoint of the summer of 1944 that the war at sea had turned almost completely in the Allies' favour. After receiving news on 20 July of the attempted assassination of Adolf Hitler and that a U-boat had apparently surrendered in the Channel, Adm. Sir Bertram Ramsay, the naval commander for Operation Overlord, wrote in his diary, "I feel that the Germans are cracking."[1] Pressing their advantage to the limit, he and the other Allied naval commanders had begun to deploy their forces right up to the coast of occupied France – even in daylight, something they had rarely risked since the dark days of the summer of 1940. Layard was certainly impressed when E.G. 9 was ordered to operate off Ushant, just miles from the German fortress at Brest. "The fact that we are now able to operate right off the enemy's doorstep without any interference," he wrote on 8 July, "brings home most forcibly the decline of Germany's might." Yet he expressed misgivings: "I must say it, our area felt a bit too close considering we had no supporting forces anywhere near us." That concern proved prophetic. Twelve days later, on the same day that Ramsay wrote of the Germans cracking, *Matane* was badly damaged by a glider bomb while operating close under Ushant.

Having already lost *Broke* under similar circumstances, Layard was determined that *Matane* not suffer the same fate, and his actions to help ensure the survival of the frigate provide a sterling example of leadership under pressure. The glider bomb glanced off *Matane*'s stern quarter before exploding, blowing a large hole in the hull by the engine room. The machinery spaces flooded immediately, but the main engine room bulkheads held, which meant the ship could probably be saved. Despite that, panic overcame certain elements of the crew. "Some of the sailors began to lose their heads," Layard recalled, "and started to get out Carley floats and they lowered the whaler. I remember shouting down from the bridge, 'What the hell is going on down there! First Lieutenant get those bloody floats and boats hoisted in at once.'"[2] With order restored, Layard turned his attention to saving the ship. Normally, the first lieutenant in a small ship was responsible for damage control but, although Layard thought him a good officer, Lt.-Cdr. F.W.T. Lucas, RCNVR, was relatively inexperienced. Moreover, two key members of the damage control team, the engineer officer and the chief engine room artificer, were among the wounded. Layard filled the gap, first supervising the shoring of the engine room bulkheads and then going out on the fo'c'sle to make sure the tow line was secured correctly. He then headed to the bridge, where he remained for the thirty long hours it took to tow the crippled frigate back to Plymouth. In recognition of his skill and leadership in getting their ship home, *Matane*'s sailors saluted Layard with three resounding cheers after he put her safely alongside.[3] Perhaps no higher accolade can be accorded a ship's captain than to be cheered spontaneously by his crew, nor can there be much better validation of the leadership displayed by Frank Layard.

Due to the character of naval warfare and the nature of shipboard life, the quality of leadership practised by a ship's captain is perhaps the key component in forging an effective fighting unit. Warships differ from military and air units in that a warship is not just a fighting platform but also serves as the home for its sailors. Also, more often than not, warships operate well clear of land and their home port, sometimes in inhospitable climates where survival in the water can be measured in minutes; as a result, catastrophic damage suffered either in combat or through accident can have grim consequences. Given these circumstances, sailors look to their captains as the key to their very survival. The high degree of trust required to earn sailors' respect is based not only on a captain's skill as a fighter and seaman but also on his ability to mould a ship's company into a cohesive unit, or, in sailors' parlance, to create a happy ship.

Layard's diary provides a practical, day-to-day primer of effective leadership. Entries from the summer of 1944 demonstrate that even in the midst of momentous events and a gruelling operational tempo he never stopped trying to improve his ship or educate his men. On 17 July, for example, Layard became concerned about his sailors' lack of activity even as the group was patrolling close by the French coast: "I came to the conclusion that we are all living a very inactive and rather an unhealthy life, and so I told No. 1 to get some physical training going. It is funny how much PT is neglected in small ships in war time. At 1630 all the ship's company turned up and they were given some PT and doubling round the upper deck, which I joined in." Layard had not only showed keen interest in his men's welfare but participated in the resulting activity, something which they would notice and approve. Two days later he directed his efforts towards his officers. The divisional system, in which officers were responsible for the well-being of a designated group of ratings, was considered the bedrock of naval discipline. Layard took steps to ensure that this system worked well in *Matane*. On 19 July, he wrote, "After lunch I addressed the officers on the subject of divisional work, which I think is being very neglected." In this instance he was ensuring that the wardroom maintained its connection with the lower deck, encouraging his officers to keep their fingers properly on the pulse of the ship and thus maintain team cohesion. Less conventionally, Layard's teaching even extended to social behaviour. He constantly complained about Canadian sailors drinking to excess and on one occasion noted, "I like to show in these ships that I can drink a lot without getting drunk."[4]

The diary is full of examples of how Layard continually focused attention on improving discipline, morale, and training in both his ship and his group. Many commanding officers did not go to such lengths, but Layard worked hard at being an effective leader, even though such activity, which was overt in its very essence, went against his reserved personality. On 31 May 1944, with the invasion just days away, Layard, not surprisingly, found himself more concerned than usual about his command: "A miserable day of worry and annoyance. I'm fussed about the group. I feel ought to go over and inspect one of these ships and I don't want to. I dread the idea of chucking my weight about." Two days later he overcame his reluctance and initiated a series of inspections, when others might have let matters slide. As summer progressed he became increasingly despairing about his leadership, but he kept plugging away. That perseverance, the ability to rise above personal shortcomings to do the right thing, is perhaps the greatest lesson that Layard provides to prospective leaders, especially those of less dynamic personality.

Layard acquired his professionalism almost by osmosis during his long career in the Royal Navy. From the moment he entered Osborne as a cadet, instructors, superiors, and experienced noncommissioned officers instructed him on what was expected of an officer. And just as young Canadian officers learned from his example, Layard learned the art of leadership from the many officers he served under, which included such legendary figures as Andrew Cunningham, James Somerville, Bertram Ramsay, Henry Rawlings, and Harold Burrough, all of whom distinguished themselves in the Second World War.[5] Not all his superiors provided positive examples, and it is interesting that Layard found fault with most of his commanding officers in destroyers. In fact, his journal reveals a certain irony: although Layard did not enjoy his time in big ships as much as destroyers, he probably learned more about the various aspects of naval professionalism during his big ship time.

Two officers seem to have made a particular impression on Layard. Bertram Ramsay, who achieved extraordinary success as an expeditionary force leader during in the Second World War, was commander, or second-in-command, of the battleship *Benbow* when Layard was a young lieutenant in that ship in the early 1920s. *Benbow* was flagship of the Mediterranean Fleet, and Ramsay was relentless in his zeal to make her the most impressive ship in the fleet. Layard recalled Ramsay's attitude at a gathering of international navies at Constantinople: "The British Flagship must of course be the smartest ship in harbour. The quarterdeck must be spotless, awnings taut, booms and ladders scrubbed and squared off, and boats and boat's crews immaculate. All of this required constant attention and a very sharp look out if one was to avoid an imperial rocket from the "Bloke" (Commander) who always demanded the highest standards of smartness and the strictest attention to duty."[6]

Although he admitted to some fear of Ramsay, as well as a certain dislike of his overbearing personality, when Layard left *Benbow* he described it as "an interesting commission which taught me a lot." Perhaps, the most important lesson that Ramsay instilled in Layard was the importance of taking pride in one's ship.[7] A diary passage from 21 March 1945, when Layard was temporarily riding in the frigate *Loch Alvie,* shows how that attitude remained with him: "At about 1500 we shoved off [from Scapa Flow]. I've never been so ashamed of a ship's company. There were men in khaki trousers, in filthy duffel coats, sea boots, jerseys, mostly smoking and not one man in No. 3s. The R.C.N. [destroyer] *Iroquois* was on the other side of the oiler with every man in rig of the day. Thank God we were only seen by another R.C.N. ship. I felt furious and also despairing because obviously apart from me there wasn't another officer who saw anything wrong with it."

Ramsay demonstrated that a leader could be a strict disciplinarian and still produce results, but Layard's commanding officer in the destroyer *Sea Bear* showed the ramifications of going too far. "Not favourably impressed by C.O.," Layard recorded when he first joined the ship on 1 September 1918. Lt.-Cdr. B.C. Gourley was a martinet with a short fuse, and the diary reveals that officers and ratings alike were subjected to his violent temper. On 11 October: "Woke up to hear the Captain shrieking for the Gunner and telling him to put the Quartermaster under arrest for being away from his place of duty." On 3 November: "The Capt. cussed me because some wine had gone adrift and said I didn't take enough interest." Worse occurred on 5 November 1918 when *Sea Bear* was preparing for sea: "There was a little delay with the capstan and one thing and another on the fo'c'sle and the Captain lost all control of himself and raved about. He struck one man and told me I'd failed in my duty." Layard was exceedingly loyal to his superiors and seldom criticized them in his diary, yet he took a measure of satisfaction in describing how Gourley squirmed when the rating he had struck threatened to submit a formal complaint to the flotilla commander. When he became a CO, Layard could become as frustrated as Gourley if evolutions went awry, but he kept his temper under control. One Canadian officer recalls an incident in *Swansea* when a clearly peeved Layard watched the crew bungle the launch of a boat. His face slowly turned a deep red and he repeatedly muttered "Bloody fools, bloody fools" under his breath. Otherwise, he kept his composure. On other occasions when things went wrong, Layard would stride vigorously back and forth on the bridge, grumbling but under control.[8]

Often, an effective link between captain and crew is limited to a particular ship, but Layard's professional approach to leadership worked in each of the three ships he commanded in E.G. 9. When it became apparent that it would take months to repair the damage the glider bomb had inflicted on *Matane,* Layard transferred to *Swansea,* whose commanding officer, Cdr. Clarence King, was appointed senior officer of the escort group C 5. John Band, *Swansea*'s first lieutenant, recalls that change was immediate. Although *Swansea* was a good, happy ship, Band thought that a certain laxness had developed in King's discipline. At defaulters, for example, he commonly awarded relatively light sentences, and when imposing punishments such as the cancellation of leave, he allowed his sailors to count days at sea towards the time served, which often amounted to no penalty whatsoever. No fools, sailors began to take advantage and discipline suffered. There was a discernible change when Layard took over. Band recalls that the first time he presided over Captain's Defaulters, Layard listened carefully to the charges and then heard the familiar excuses that sailors concoct for their behaviour. Then, quietly but firmly, he doled out punishment strictly according to *King's Regulations and Admiralty Instructions*, the bible of naval discipline. That meant, among other things, that the punishment of confinement to the ship was served when *Swansea* was alongside, not at sea, which imposed a real penalty. After a few sailors had been subjected to this new firmness, Band overheard a sailor observe, "This SOB really knows what he's doing!" The slackness that had crept in under King's regime soon began to disappear.[9]

Layard's firm, consistent leadership style, as well as his obvious fighting ability and seamanship skills – in other words, his overall professionalism – won over all the ships in E.G. 9. After *Saint John* left the group, the frigate's asdic control officer, Lt. J.R. Bradley, RCNVR, sent Layard a letter recounting his conversations with some of the crew: "Since leaving Scapa Flow," he wrote, "large numbers of the ship's company have come to me expressing their admiration for you as captain of the ship, and senior officer of the group. They said that you always made them feel that their job was very important no matter how small it was; that you never forgot about leave and mail whenever opportunity to obtain them presented itself; that you were always concerned about the welfare and safety of the ship. They have expressed their wish to serve with you again."[10]

Godfrey Brewer, a friend of Layard's who served with him in Capt. A.B. Cunningham's 1st Destroyer Flotilla during the mid-1920s, recalled that the fiery flotilla commander, recognized even then as a dynamic leader, had three favourite phrases that he frequently repeated to his young officers: "Intelligent anticipation must be your watchword," "NDBGZ" (no difficulty baffles great zeal), and, echoing Nelson, "Duty is the first business of a sea officer."[11] Although there is no direct evidence that Layard heard these professional pearls of wisdom, he had plenty of contact with Cunningham during that time so it is likely he did. The last phrase in particular – "Duty is the first business of a sea officer" – was a watchword of the Royal Navy, and it certainly captures the kernel of Layard's professional philosophy. As E.G. 9 faced, first, the momentous challenge of an historic event like D-Day, then the drudgery of routine operations that followed, concluding with a terrifying encounter with the enemy, Layard's leadership abilities proved an effective weapon in the group's arsenal.

SATURDAY, 15 JULY 1944 – LONDONDERRY/AT SEA

We slipped at 0730 and proceeded down river with *Swansea* and *Stormont. Saint John* was delayed with condenser trouble. On arrival at Moville we found only one side of the oiler was available, as another oiler was alongside topping up or discharging. As I arrived a corvette was just about to slip alongside as a destroyer escort shoved off, but I told them to keep clear as my group had to oil first. He was obviously furious and replied, "Thank you – we have just been 15 days at sea." *Swansea* came up alongside us and when the 2nd oiler shoved off *Stormont* went on the other side. Although none of us had very much to take in, it seemed to take a very long time. We were supposed to leave the Foyle at 1100 but it wasn't till 1330 that oiling was completed and then the oiler was swung half to wind and half to tide, so that it wasn't too easy to get away.

After a rainy, windy forenoon it turned out calm and fine in the p.m., and the visibility was extreme all the way down the Irish Sea. I don't a bit want to go back to the worries and responsibilities of another month in the Channel, and oh, how I want to get home. There was talk in Derry of the ship returning to Canada to refit at the end of September. I wonder what I shall do. We picked up *Meon* at about 2330 at K2 buoy off the Skerries.

SUNDAY, 16 JULY 1944 – AT SEA

After passing K4 buoy it started to get foggy. It was thick when we reached The Smalls, which we rounded without seeing. The radar operator went mad at about this time, which made it very difficult to navigate and I got in too near to the land and very fussed. However, I eventually picked up the light ship off Milford Haven at about 0830 and for a bit the weather cleared but to shut down again very thick, and we never *saw* the next light ship and passed through the straits inside Lundy Island without seeing a thing. Somewhat anxious work. It cleared a bit again at about 1230 and at 1330 we were able to get a fix on the land at Trevose Head and thought our troubles were over, but not a bit. It shut down quicker than ever, and just when we wanted them particularly badly for rounding Land's End, radar bearings and ranges seemed to go all over the place. However, after another very anxious period we picked up the Wolf by radar, which gave us a good position. Having got round the corner we got into line abreast and steamed S. to our patrol area which had been allotted to us, which is N. and W. of Ushant. Passed quite close by E.G. 1[12] in the fog and heard him chatting on T.B.S., and so I rang him up and congratulated him on the bar to his D.S.O. and his confirmed 3rd stripe. We ran out of the fog towards the end of the 1st watch.

MONDAY, 17 JULY 1944 – AT SEA

A quiet and uneventful night and a quiet and uneventful day. There don't seem to be any wrecks or non subs in this area. A hot, rather muggy day with the wind shifting all round the compass. I maintained N. and S. patrols in the area, shifting the line of advance about 7 miles E. or W. at the end of each leg. I came to the conclusion that we are all living a very inactive and rather an unhealthy life, and so I told No. 1 to get some physical training going. It is funny how much PT is neglected in small ships in war time. At 1630 all the ship's company turned up and they were given some PT and doubling round the upper deck, which I joined in.

We were told that Mosquitoes[13] would be patrolling in our area, and further S. where E.G. 14 was working, as fighter protection at dusk and dawn tomorrow. At about 2100 we intercepted a signal from E.G. 14 saying he was being attacked by enemy aircraft but nothing came our way except our friends the Mosquitoes. Wrote a letter asking for another Steward and another Writer. I think it is time I had my own Steward and if we don't get another Writer Helpburn will go sick from overwork. The Russians are now only 45 miles from the East Prussian border.

Tuesday, 18 July 1944 – At sea

We got 2 signals in the night, one shifting our area slightly to the eastward, which we did quite easily and quickly, but the other seemed somehow a mistake although our decoding was carefully checked and found correct, because it told us to change areas with E.G. 12 by mutual arrangement a.m. today. Well, E.G. 12's area is nearly 160 miles away and anyway is a Gamma search and not an area. At 0700 I made a signal saying I'd arrive at 1800. At 0800 although still very doubtful I turned the group to 064° and went on to 16 knots. At 0900 we got a signal saying for E.G. 12 read E.G. 14, which of course *did* make sense as his area is quite close to us and just W. of Ushant. So we altered back in that direction. At 1130 yet another change of orders, and are told to join E.G. 14 and do a combined sweep of an area very much where we'd been in the night but extending further E. and W. and about 15 miles N. of Ushant.

It was a day of heat, haze, and poor visibility, and it wasn't too easy to find E.G. 14 and get my group where he wanted us, which was on his S. wing. However, at about 1330 we were in position and sweeping to the E. When we reached the end of our beat we turned 180° and swept back. S.O. E.G. 14 is Currie in the *Fame.*[14] He had one "Queen" which took him some time to classify as non sub but otherwise nothing. At about 2000 turned to the E. again and at 2215 until dark we closed up anti-aircraft action stations in case of a repetition of yesterday's evening bombing but nothing came. At dark we opened out to 3 miles, reduced to 8 knots, and continued to sweep to the E. Had huge volunteer PT party exercising in the dog watches. Encouraging.

Wednesday, 19 July 1944 – At sea

At 0200 a signal arrived ordering E.G. 14 and 9 to separate and move to new areas. Ours was slightly to the N. and E. and an Easy Item turn to 60° took us there easily and we started an E. and W. patrol. A mild excitement was started at about 1100 when *Meon* reported an aircraft thought to be hostile. Just then we ran into fog. Later on in the p.m. when it cleared there was no sign of an enemy aircraft but plenty of ours. After lunch I addressed the officers on the subject of divisional work, which I think is being very neglected. At about 1400 we got new orders again. This time to establish a Gamma patrol 26 miles N. from a position 12 miles off the Ile de Batz Light, so we increased speed and moved over to our new position. A glassy calm sea and lovely sunny day.

At about 1600 we saw an aircraft circling close to the sea a long way off and altered to close. It dropped a smoke marker, but as soon as we approached it pushed off and I couldn't raise him by radio or visual signalling. They are sometimes most unhelpful these bloody airmen. We swept through the spot but nothing seen or detected, but we noticed 2 or 3 Spitfires and an old Walrus stooging about in the vicinity as well as our Wellington, and when we got a signal saying look at for survivors reported in this locality it was obvious this was an air searching party. We dashed madly about for a bit but found nothing and still got not the word out of the aircraft, and eventually C. in C. cancelled his signal and so we formed up and started our Gamma search. Then along came an American Liberator who said he'd sighted 2 enemy fishing vessels about 50 miles away near the Channel Islands and would we like to take any action. I first decided it was too far, but finally detached *Swansea* alone to investigate but shortly after on hearing control tell the aircraft to continue his patrol I recalled *Swansea*. After all, one must remember "maintenance of the object," which for us is U-boat hunting, and one mustn't be drawn off to other jobs.

E.G. 14 is gammaring just to the N. of us and together we stretch more or less across the Channel. At 2230 just before dark *Swansea* reported a contact and attacked twice with H/H. We closed with *Stormont* and after sniffing round for a bit decided it was a wreck, as by Q.H. we were exactly on the plotted position of a previously reported wreck. Wonderful thing this Q.H. Continued the patrol at about midnight.

Thursday-Friday, 20-21 July 1944 – At sea

During the a.m. we got orders to shift our patrol area once more. This time back to the Brest area. From sightings and D/Fs they think that a U/B is approaching Brest from the W., arriving either a.m. 21st or more likely 22nd. We have been given an area in the approaches to Brest to patrol, and E.G. 14 are to join us once they have finished topping up with oil at Plymouth. We set off on a 225° course at 16 kts. At 1550 Lewtas, who was Officer of the Watch, reported an unidentified aircraft, which he reckoned was the J.U. 88 or 188, a long way away. *Stormont* also reckoned it was hostile, and so although not certain I reported it has such. From the signal I got back it was obvious shore authorities thought I was talking balls, but they sent us some Mosquitoes just the same. We arrived in our area at about 1800 and reduced speed and started our usual A/S patrol. Considering how close in to Ushant we were I was sorry to see our Mosquitoes leave us at about 1900.

At about 2050 I was in my sea cabin when the 1st Lieutenant asked me to come on the bridge at once. I saw a big explosion astern of *Meon,* which we thought at first was a Gnat, but shortly after we realized it was a bomb, as an aircraft was sighted on our quarter with a little thing underneath it which didn't take long to identify as a glider bomb which had just been detached. By this time we were at action stations and seeing the bomb I rang down full ahead but almost before it could take effect this winged monster was right on top of us, traveling at an incredible speed in about a 70° dive. There was a shattering explosion and a frightful escape of steam and I thought we'd been hit right on "Y" gun[15] and I was expecting to step off into the water any minute, but we still remained afloat. I sent the 1st Lieut. aft, who reported the bomb had just grazed the port side of the ship and exploded on the water, blowing in the side of the engine room which it completely wrecked and flooded, but both bulkheads held.

There we were stopped and helpless. Luckily only 3 planes came over, each with 2 bombs. No other hits but another one landed uncomfortably close to us on our port beam. As soon as it was over (our gunfire was quite useless as the planes remained miles out of range of our pop guns) we were taken in tow by *Meon,* and both doctors from *Swansea* and *Stormont* came over, and in response to our call for help out came our fighters – too late. Our casualties were 3 missing, one of whom was my steward Aucoin, I'm very sorry to say, who I think was just blown to bits, and about a dozen badly burnt from the engine room. Westwater at Y gun got a nasty wound in the foot. Our escape from a direct hit and large casualties was miraculous.

The weather was flat calm, and with bulkheads holding well I was fairly happy. We shored up heavily both engine room bulkheads and hoped no E-boats would come our way. Doctors working hard on these horrible and badly burned cases. In the whole everybody behaved well. I didn't care for the haste with which we got out our Carley floats and lowered our boats, all of which had to be hoisted in again. Anders and the Chief engine room artificer were both casualties, which left the Chief Stoker as senior engine room, and he was magnificent and quite untiring. I thought some of the officers might have done more. Thank God for the diesel dynamo, which provided lights as we were without steam.

At dawn [on 21 July] it was flat calm but still foggy, which was all to the good as we are still only 20 miles N. of Ushant. At 0630 we stopped and *Swansea* sent over a boat with more medical stores including all the blood plasma they had. We then continued slowly on our way. As the day went on it started to blow from the N.E., and although never rough the sea was enough to make me extremely anxious not so much for the bulkheads as for the weakened upper and main deck, which began to work unpleasantly. I jettisoned all our upper deck D/Cs to lighten the after part of the ship. At about 1400 a tug appeared, but as we were going very nicely I told him to stand by, which was just as well as he reported engine defects and said he could only just keep up with us at our 5 knots.

At about 1500 the tow parted and I asked the tug to pass his tow. After several attempts he said the starboard engine had broken down altogether, so I told *Meon* to pass his hawser. He made an awful cock of it, came up to leeward and nearly hit us, and eventually passed over a thing that looked like 2½ [inch cable], which I reckoned wasn't good enough, and so I cast it off and told *Stormont* to come up. He made a first-class evolution of it and we were quickly once more under way but altogether lost a good hour. While this was going on it started to rain and it poured without ceasing until midnight. We sighted the Eddystone at about 2100 and shortly after another tug arrived and towed us the rest of the way to the break water, and from there a Dockyard tug took us up to No. 1 Jetty S. Yard, but he was awfully slow and we didn't get alongside till after 0100. Then Capt. D. and Dockyard constructors came on board to look at us and it was 0230 before I got to be in my sea cabin very, very tired and weary. The ship's company gave me cheers as I left the bridge on getting alongside.

Saturday, 22 July 1944 – Plymouth

Came down to find both my cabins an indescribable mess of bottles, bandages, blankets, and blood, just as they'd been left when the wounded had been taken ashore last night.[16] The doctors of the *Swansea* and *Stormont* worked magnificently until we got in and only one man died on us, although 2 or 3 of the badly burned were only just kept alive. Somewhere round about 1000 King, Myra, and Balfour came on board and I went back with them to Capt. D. where I spoke to Ops. They are dashing out again at 1130 and there are one or two things they must have first. We got a boat from Capt. D. and took the C.O.s back on board their ships and then took me back to *Matane* and then took charts and a part to the T.B.S. back on board *Swansea* and *Meon.*

After lunch I went out to the public call box and rang up J. to see if she could come down, which she said she could, and I then rang up a Mrs. Saxon, who does hospitality business for Canadians, and asked her if she knew of anywhere to stay. In about an hour she rang back and said there wasn't a bed to be had in the town, which was just too grim. A 2½ R.C.N.R. who is the Canadian Administration Authority here came on board at about 1700 and after talking to him about what we want for the troops etc., he ran me ashore and we went round one or two hotels, and at last I got a room in a seedy looking pub called The Duke of Cornwall. However, one can't be choosy. He then came back and had a drink on board. I went to bed at about 2130 after ringing up J. again and telling her to come. The big bit of news is that there has been an attempt on Hitler's life, which was all part of quite a big Army revolt. It has failed, but it shows how the wind is blowing.

Sunday, 23 July 1944 – Plymouth

C.N.A.A. (whatever his name is)[17] brought Capt. Cross (the V.R. man from Ottawa) on board, and we discussed transferring to another ship and what was to be done with the officers. I then got a car and went up to A.C.H.Q. and saw Mallinson,[18] who has taken over from Evans, and I also had a long talk with Caslon,[19] who is Chief of Staff, and finally had an interview with the C. in C. (Leatham). Then I called in at the hospital and enquired after the wounded – all of whom are doing fairly well but quite a number of them are still on the serious list. Then back on board. At 1130 the *Rodney*'s picket boat came for me and I went on board for lunch with Jack Boord, who is the Commander of the ship.[20] The band was playing in the wardroom at lunch, and it was nice to get into a *real* ship again.[21] Jack is pompous but very hospitable. Got back on board at about 1430 and did some work on my report of proceedings.

At 1715 I got a taxi from the Dockyard to the station to meet J. and Raymond, only to be told their train was 1½ hours late. So I walked to the hotel and took possession of our room and then walked about putting off time, and finally back to the station at 1915 just as the train came in. We all had some food and then we put Raymond to bed and then shortly after went to bed ourselves. I am distressed to hear that Raymond has rickets and has to have special treatment, massage, etc., for a year. How lovely it is to see J. again after nearly 4 months.

Monday, 24 July 1944 – Plymouth

C.N.A.A. (Comdr. Weller) picked me up in his car and took me down to the Dockyard. I spent the whole forenoon with a Wren shorthand typist making out or dictating my report of proceedings. Found it a bit difficult as I was feeling somewhat woolly about the brain. Weller appeared back at about 1230 and after having a drink, took me back to my hotel for lunch as he was going to his hotel just opposite anyhow. A nice surprise for J., who wasn't expecting me. After lunch back again to the Dockyard and I spent hours with Capt. D. while he discussed our future and drafted out a signal as to his intentions. He is not a very helpful type.

I didn't get back on board till nearly 1430, when I found J. and Raymond, who had come down to have tea with me. It was a very hot day and my cabins were very stuffy. Raymond was thrilled with the ship, but of course was a bit of a menace as he wouldn't sit still for a minute and had to be watched like a hawk. Later on we went down to the wardroom to meet the officers and have a drink. J. of course was awfully good in spite of all these strange faces. We eventually got a taxi and took No. 1 with us back to the hotel for dinner. J. had to put Raymond to bed and then came down to the bar. No. 1 very chatty and rather gushing. We have come to the conclusion that although the hotel is a bit grim, the management are extremely kind and the food is excellent, and we might have done a great deal worse. A lovely hot, sunny day.

The ship is going to have temporary repairs here and will then be towed to a refit port. 50% of the ship's company will be discharged to *Niobe*[22] as soon as possible. No. 1 is to take over command, and I will go temporarily to the *Meon* when the group comes in on Wednesday.

Tuesday, 25 July 1944 – Plymouth

Weller gave me a lift to the Dockyard again. I made a start on some of the hundred and one things which seem to have to be done, and at 1015 Weller's car arrived for me and 2 officers and, after picking him up, we all went to the barracks where the funeral procession for Stoker Laing and E.R.A. Cole formed up at 1100. While waiting, who should I see but "Ditchy" Ford[23] in my term, who I haven't seen since Cambridge days. It was about 1½ miles to the cemetery. The barracks provided gun trains and firing party, and 2 R.C.N. padres took the service. We had quite a big muster for the ship as mourners. There were spots of rain but, thank God, it held off.

Weller's car took us from the cemetery to the Dockyard gate, where we waited for J. and R. who No. 1 had asked down for lunch. Quite a good party and R. behaved very well, but it is rather a snag having him always with us. After lunch we put him to rest on my bunk and left him in charge of Kilgour, who was Officer of the Day, and J. and I got a car and went up to the hospital to see the wounded. The visit, I think, was a big success and I was delighted to find that they all looked so well. Anderson, poor chap, was a bit gloomy with his badly burned hands and face. Some of the worst are still on the serious list, but all are making satisfactory progress. There are 11 of them up there. J. was a great success. It was raining when we came out but we got a lift to the gate. I meant to send J. and R. away so that I could do some work, but finally got on with writing the flimsies[24] while they were on board and at about 1800 we all went ashore together and, as a taxi was unprocurable, we went home by bus. J. put R. to bed and then we had dinner and afterwards I roughed out some letters of condolence to next of kin before going to bed.

Wednesday, 26 July 1944 – Plymouth

A beastly, wet, rainy, and blowy day. I went down to the Dockyard by bus and madly wrote on flimsies most of the a.m. The rest of the group came in at about 0930 and *Meon* came alongside us, as I'd asked to turn over to her and I thought it was approved, and then a signal arrived saying I was to go to *Swansea. Meon* also had trouble with an officer who has got to be court martialled. I dashed up to the gate at 1200 and met J. and R. and brought them on board, and later on we caught *Rodney*'s boat off to the ship and had lunch with Jack. An awfully good lunch too, finishing up with Devonshire cream!! We left again at 1400 so that I could get back in time to say goodbye to the party who were off to *Niobe*, about 50% of the ship's company in all. Shortly after, I took J. and R. to the gate and then returned on board for more paper work.

At about 1800 I went down to the W.R. and found a party just starting. Four Wrens, all boats crews, and in plain clothes. Very nice girls. J. after putting R. to bed, got a nice receptionist to keep an eye on him, and then came down on board and joined the party, which was awful good fun, with a buffet meal and then the piano and singing, and Cooke and Brown doing some of their funny turns. J. in very good form. We finally got away in a taxi about 2330. Gosh how these few days have flown and now it is nearly all over and in addition to having to part from J. again I've got to start all over again on some new ship. Oh, I'm so *tired* of it all.

Thursday, 27 July 1944 – Plymouth

The dreaded day and moment arrives again. I went to the station with J. and R. They were catching the 10:10 to Portsmouth. I did not wait to see them off but caught a taxi down to the Yard, feeling in the depths of despair. A busy forenoon. I am *not* going to *Meon* now, but to the *Swansea*. King is to do this trip in command and then he is going as S.O. C 3 [sic], relieving Rolph Medley, and I then take over command of *Swansea*. I feel depressed and disheartened and haven't the energy to start all over again in another ship.

At about 1145 Cooke and I got a car and went round to *Swansea* to find out what they wanted in the way of extra men, books, etc. King is very sad at leaving his ship. Back for lunch and most of the p.m. I spent packing. At 1630 I got a car and went to A.C.H.Q. and saw Mallinson and had a talk about signals with a very efficient Wren 2½. Back on board this ship. My cabins are too full of ghosts and J. and associations of the last 2 or 3 days when she spent so much time on board. I had supper in the wardroom and afterwards No. 1 and I signed the A2A and U2A [change of command forms] and he assumed command. Unfortunately, a Confidential Book (the *Handbook of Damage Control*) is missing and so I had to make a report by signal.

Everybody seems gloomy and depressed on board. If only the bomb could have hit any other ship. I am quite overwhelmed how much officers and men seem to have liked me in this ship.[25] The officers presented me and J. with a picture of the ship. The combination of saying goodbye to J. and the thought of having to start all over again in *Swansea* is almost more than I can bear. Rang up J. and heard she was safely home, but the line was very poor and I could hardly hear her. Raymond is a sweet little boy and awfully good and really very little trouble.

Friday, 28 July 1944 – Plymouth/At sea

I had breakfast in the wardroom at 0745. At 0800 C.N.A.A.'s van arrived and Cooke's and my gear was loaded in and at about 0815 we both left the ship. I was cheered once again. It is quite overwhelming. The 2nd signalman came last night and woke me up to say goodbye. I was so overcome with my departure that I never said goodbye personally to No. 1, who of course was at the gangway. It worried me awfully afterwards because he must have felt very hurt. We went round to the North Yard and went on board *Swansea.*

The group sailed at 0930, everyone is very nice here but things naturally are done differently, things work differently and seemingly not quite so well, and I miss terribly the familiar and friendly faces. We went off first of all to an area about midway between Ushant and the Scillies and shifted up to patrol between the Scillies and Lizard before dark. The Americans seem to be attacking in strength in Normandy and have broken well through the German lines in places. The Russians also continue to advance and they are now within 3 miles of Warsaw.

Saturday, 29 July 1944 – At sea

We did a number of turns in the night, which I was up for. I don't really get much assistance from King, who obviously resents my presence. I shall be glad when this trip is over and I can take command, even though it means more work. I put in some work on the S206. We got a signal to shift our patrol a bit to the S. on relief on our present beat by E.G. 3, and at about 1700 we turned S., sighted E.G. 3 coming N., and were in our new area by 1800. At about 1930 a signal arrived telling *Swansea* to detach from the group and return to Plymouth a.m. tomorrow and land King, after which I was to take over command. King very indignant that they have not told him officially where he is going. I must say it is a little inconsiderate to give him so little warning for packing up. A nice day but quite a W.'ly swell, which made us roll about a bit.

Sunday, 30 July 1944 – At sea/Plymouth

At 0400 we detached from the group for Plymouth and I went to bed. We arrived at 1000 and at first were told to anchor, but that was quickly amended to a berth alongside in the North Yard. There was a shower of rain as we came in but on the whole it was a fine but muggy day. King was very busy packing. I have never seen a man with so much gear in war time. He went up to A.C.H.Q. on arrival and was told he had to be in Liverpool a.m. tomorrow. I couldn't do anything and so after lunch I had a bit of shut eye on my bunk. Eventually, somewhere round about 1700 we got the A2As and U2As signed and I took over the contingent account and one thing and another. We have a radar defect which has put us on 8 hours' notice until 0800 tomorrow, which is nice and allows me to give leave.

Weller came on board and at about 1800 I went ashore with him, having said goodbye to King. I thought it would be tactful to get out of the ship as the wardroom are more or less dining King before he goes ashore to catch his night train. Weller took me to the *Matane*, where Brown gave us a lot of gin and then we eventually had food. LeFlufy (the loaned Lieut. [E])[26] was also on board and brought a Wren boats crew down. There are certainly some awfully nice girls running the boats here. Later on, Lucas, Lewtas, Kilgour and the new R.C.N. Chief arrived back. It was nice to be in the old, friendly atmosphere again. Got a car back to *Swansea* at about 2245 and went down to the wardroom for a night cap. I stayed yarning rather late. Papers are all very optimistic about a collapse in Germany before the end of the year. The Americans are advancing in Normandy, and the Russians are within sight of Warsaw, Riga, and about 25 miles from the East Prussian border.

Monday, 31 July 1944 – Plymouth/At sea

We slipped at 0830. The group had moved E. up Channel since we left them, and we joined them at about 1200 about 15' S.E. of Start Point. The first thing we did was to lower our whaler with their mail and let each ship in turn go alongside and pick it up, and then we hoisted our boat. By that time we'd got a signal from C. in C. ordering us to do a zigzag search along a line running roughly N.E. and S.W. We reached the N.E. point at about 1500 and turned to start the search. Had some trouble with fish echoes, but at about 1700 *Saint John* picked up a bottom echo which could not be dismissed. We ran over it with echo sounder and got some sort of trace. We threw hedgehogs at it and dropped depth charges on it with no result whatever, and so eventually at about 2000 I reckoned we'd proved it had to be non-sub and we went on. My steward got me unpacked and my cabin squared off, and I must say it looks awfully nice. I had all officers into my cabin and gave them a short address at 2315. I feel much happier and more at home than I did 24 hours ago.

Tuesday, 1 August 1944 – At sea

At about 0100 I was told by signal to detach 2 ships to investigate a radar contact off the Eddystone, and I sent *Meon* and *Saint John*. At about 0400 *Swansea* and *Stormont* came to the end of our zigzag search line and turned 180° and started back again. In the course of the forenoon a signal arrived ordering us to carry out a Gamma search of 20 miles in our old position up and down from Cap de la Hague to about the centre of the Channel. At about 1330 we turned to the E. to get into our new position and almost at once picked up a contact. Ran over with the echo sounder and found it was definitely something on the bottom, so went to action stations and attacked with H/H, which immediately produced oil. *Meon* and *Saint John* joined up while the attack was in progress and altogether we gave it 2 H/H salvos and 2 10 charge deep D/C patterns, but still nothing but fish and oil, and the echo sounder trace looked nothing like a submarine. Reported I was attacking but thought it probably a wreck.

After 3 hours I finally decided it must be a wreck, as those attacks were accurate and must have killed it had it been a submarine, and at about 1730 we all went on and took up our new Gamma search at about 1900. I reported classifying it as wreck and was very worried when at about 2200 a signal arrived asking on what I'd based my classification and implying they thought I'd left it too soon. I was still further fussed when Cooke reported to me that the paper speed on the echo sounder had been too slow and so the trace, which had influenced my decision quite a bit, was completely meaningless. Infuriating to have to signal that. To think I've done the wrong thing naturally puts me into an absolute lather. Rather a chilly foggy sort of day.

Wednesday, 2 August 1944 – At sea

In the small hours of the morning I was told to send 2 ships back to the scene of our attack and so I sent *Meon* and *Saint John.* I was rather relieved to hear not long after that they had regained contact and oil was still coming up, which means either it *is* a wreck or if a submarine, it is killed, as it would have been away by now otherwise. *Stormont* and *Swansea* continued to patrol up and down. Being nearly Springs the tides are very strong indeed off the Cherbourg peninsula, and indeed right across the Channel in this area, and I'm very frightened of putting the outside ship too close to Alderney again. Thank God for Q.H.

A dull, misty day with quite a bit of wind and sea from the East. Having spent the whole day bombarding and watching our "wreck" and getting nothing more than oil up for their trouble, *Meon* and *Saint John* rejoined at about 1900. We went to anti-aircraft stations at that time and I walked round to look at the organisation. At 2000 E.G. 15, who was patrolling from our N. limit up to Portland, was withdrawn, and we were told to take over the double patrol. It suits me, as a 40-mile patrol is infinitely preferable to 20 miles as it only means ½ as many turns. At 2330 we intercepted a signal saying an airman in a dinghy had been seen not far from us and I detached *Stormont* to look for him.

Thursday, 3 August 1944 – At sea

A most disturbed night what with signals, D/F bearings, and navigation. Just before 0700 *Saint John* got a contact with something on the bottom. By Q.H. it was very close to a plotted non sub, but not quite near enough to ignore and so I went over to help him. Couldn't pick up contact and he kept on losing it. Eventually at about 0830 I decided it *was* the non sub and gave it up and went on with the patrol. A misty and rather chilly day. Q.H. went qa qa just as we got down to the S. end of the patrol, and I really wanted it for the turn and to be sure in bad visibility that we were well clear of Alderney. We went round on radar. It is a sign of how fast things move now when one begins to look on radar as a somewhat inefficient secondary aid. What one would do with neither in this thick weather and with spring tides I can't think.

I went store room rounds and was much impressed with the cleanliness everywhere. Just before 1600 *Saint John* got a contact once more in the same general position as this morning. There are 3 plotted non subs here very close together, and I think we found all 3 and *Saint John* attacked twice. It was almost impossible for me to drag them away, when one would report good echo sounder trace and another oil rising, etc. It wasn't till 1815 that I finally took a strong line and we left the scene. The weather cleared up and it was a most beautiful and brilliant moonlight night and a fairly peaceful one as far as I was concerned. The American break through in Brittany is on quite a big scale, and they have now reached Rennes and are only 60 miles from Nantes. The Russians have crossed the Vistula.

Friday, 4 August 1944 – At sea

We picked up an echo just as I was half through my breakfast. The echo sounder showed a trace on the bottom, but Q.H. fixed as exactly over a plotted non sub at the N. end of our patrol and so without wasting much time on it, we were able to disregard. A hot, sunny, flat calm day. At about 1100 I went gunnery rounds. At 1600 we got a signal telling me to detach our ships [one] at a time to Portland to replenish with fuel and ammunition. Sent *Stormont* in first. I'm blowed if we didn't pick up the same non sub again as we were on this morning. This time it gave a trace and an echo as I have seldom seen or heard, but Q.H. was able definitely to fix it as the plotted non sub. *Stormont* rejoined again about midnight but reported her asdic out of action. She closed, and being bright moonlight, we were able to pass a spare part across to her on a line. Nothing of importance happened but it seemed to be a day of continual small incidents – lights, flares, gunfire, objects in the water, all of which kept me continually running up and down on the bridge.

The American break through in Brittany sounds really good. They have captured Rennes and are within 60 miles of St. Nazaire and look like cutting off the whole of the Brittany peninsula soon with the U/B bases of Brest, Lorient, and St. Nazaire. This should have a big effect on the U-boat warfare in general, and our movements probably too.

Saturday, 5 August 1944 – At sea

Sent *Saint John* into Portland at 0400 but at 0700 on coming N. we found her attacking a contact, which we took over and plotted as one of the many established non subs, and so we quickly left it again. At 0930 we got a signal from E.G. 3 saying, "Presume you are taking action on (some aircraft report)." When, a few minutes later, the report came up it was of a sighting of a conning tower, but the position was much nearer E.G. 3 than us. Shortly after came an order from C. in C. ordering us to go. The position he gave was nearly a degree different in longitude and this was certainly our bird, but through bad decoding we have lost about ½ hour. At about 2000 we stopped, lowered a boat, and sent Cooke over to *Stormont,* where asdic was out of action. Damned annoying – here we are on the tracks of a U/B and only 2 ships to sweep with.

At 1100 I went a very quick mess deck rounds. Quite good. The aircraft homed us on 385 kilocycles. We sighted it at about 1200 and slowed down and swept slowly up to it. When we were nearly up to the flares, we got a contact which seemed fairly good and we attacked with H/H but it was only fish. The whole area was full of fish echoes. *Meon* also attacked a different one. *Rochester,* all on his own, appeared on the scene and later on E.G. 15 with 4 ships. I signalled him suggesting we joined forces, to which he agreed but suggested that as I was on the spot first, I should organise the attack. Not at all what I wanted, however, I formed the whole lot up and went off to the E. for 15 miles, then N. and back W. and S. through the return point again, and then at about 1900 we all got contacts, fish, wrecks, non subs. I thought we would never get on. However we did at last. At about 2100 a signal telling the 2 groups to split and giving them different areas for the night. I was quite pleased with my handling of the situation.

The Americans are reported to be in Brest and close to St. Nazaire and Lorient. Some of the support groups are being ordered down to intercept any attempt by the U-Boats to escape from the two ports. No sign of *Saint John* rejoining. Lovely hot summer day.

Sunday, 6 August 1944 – At sea

The three little nigger boys continued their solitary patrol until about 0900, when Cooke reported from the *Stormont* that their asdic was still out of action but they were still hopeful. I decided, however, that having now been out of action for over 24 hours it was time to get base assistance, and so I recalled Cooke and sent the *Stormont* into Plymouth. "And then there were only two." We continued to stooge up and down. We got one good ping only to find by Q.H. that we were right on another of those plotted non subs. At 1545 we unexpectedly got a signal from C. in C. to join *Saint John,* who had sailed from Portland at 1400 and proceed to Londonderry for lay over. *Saint John* joined at 1630 and we turned to the W. The sea was full of fish echoes and we were constantly stopping and investigating, which delayed us a lot. *Stormont* joined us off the Eddystone and not very far W. from there we passed E.G. 3 searching an area where it is believed a U/B is sitting on the bottom. There certainly was a strong smell of diesel oil in the vicinity and also another peculiar gassy smell. Intercepted a signal from E.G. 2 saying he had sunk a U boat with one of his

Squid-carrying corvettes. The first Squid kill.[27] Arrived off the Lizard just before midnight. Another hot, still day.

Monday, 7 August 1944 – At sea

As we got round Land's End the visibility deteriorated, and by 0300 we were in thick fog. Spent an anxious time navigating by radar, dodging convoys, and trying to keep *Saint John* in the straight and narrow path as her radar was out of action. There were temporary gaps in the fog and one came most opportunely off Lundy Island, when we were beginning to get involved with a convoy. Had another bad moment later on when we nearly rammed the first light ship north of Lundy. The weather cleared quite a bit on reaching the St. Gomer Light Vessel at 0945, and we went through the Grassholm channel, but there were patches of fog all the way up the Irish Sea and we never saw Bardsey Island. I was kept on the go most of the day and didn't get much sleep.

Tuesday, 8 August 1944 – At sea/Londonderry

We ran into a southbound convoy right in the middle of the North Channel. The radar was very slow picking them up, and I had to make some quick and drastic alterations of course. Arrived off Lough Foyle at 0615 and we were told to oil before going up. We wanted to keep our tanks empty for repairs and so we just went alongside *Stormont* to wait for a bit as we were told not to arrive up river before 0830. I had a bath and breakfast. We asked for a pilot but none was available, and so at 0815 we slipped and I went up without one. It is really very easy. We berthed at No. 9. The others all came up later and berthed on us, and at 1500 we had our arrival conference. The whole of Northern Ireland is on a week's holiday and so practically nothing can be done.

Selby took me along to see the Commodore after the meeting as he hadn't attended in person, and when I saw him I realized why. He was awfully tight, having had lunch with the Russian Admiral (there are some Russian M.L.s [motor launches] here doing something or other).[28] The Secretary was tight too and very amusing. In spite of, or perhaps because of, his boozeyness the Commodore was very friendly and gave me a whisky and soda and talked a whole lot of balls. I eventually didn't get back on board until about 1800 and then had to deal with the leave organisation to this rest camp, most of which, thank God, No. 1 had organised. Duchesneau came over to see me and we drank a lot of gin. I found the wardroom were not feeding until about 2000 and so I had dinner down there and then went early to bed. After a spell of lovely weather in the Channel we got here to find it chilly and rainy.

Wednesday, 9 August 1944 – Londonderry

I spent most of the a.m. dictating my report of proceedings to a Wren shorthand typist. In the p.m. Copelin came down and went through of scheme of complement and discussed officers. I hear I am getting Brown and Lewtas back, which means getting rid of the Doctor and Wood. I went back with Copelin to his office and rang up C.N.M.O. in London and spoke to the drafting or officers' appointments chap about Anderson, who wants leave to Canada on compassionate ground, and they told me they would let me have Kilgour in his place. Yet another officer change is Cooke, [who] has been appointed back to Canada, and he has been relieved by a man called Earl.[29]

Came back on board and read and wrote to J. After dinner I went down to the wardroom and found No. 1 and a Wren officer there and I had a drink with them, and finally they persuaded me to go along to a dance with them which had been given in honour of the Russians. It was quite amusing and we struggled hard to talk to these Russian types. Back on board later on for a night cap. Dull, rainy day.

Thursday, 10 August 1944 – Londonderry

Angus from the *Port Colborne* came to see me. He has just arrived from Belfast after his repairs. Later on I went up to the Commodore's office and saw the Signal officer and the Chief of Staff. At about 1200 I went over to the *Regulus* to see the Captain, whose name I don't remember.[30] I met him at the dance last night and he *was* the C.O. of the *Bideford.* I feel as if I'd drunk a good deal too much whisky last night. Went ashore at about 1430 and went for a walk over the bridge, along the Foyle, then up and inland by the golf course and back to Derry. It was close and hot and I sweated out some of last night's drink. Went to the Club on return and had tea and read the papers. Saw in the Times that Hilda Rolfe had had a daughter in Edinburgh. Back on board I gave Cooke a farewell drink in my cabin. He is off tomorrow. He is an awfully nice chap, but I hope Earl will be a better staff officer.

Had a bath and then supper and at 2100 I went over to the *Saint John* by invitation, where they were having a farewell party for the officers of the U.S. destroyer *Nelson,* with whom they'd had an entente. There were a number of women, among whom was one very attractive creature who, it transpired, had come down on board the *Broke* for lunch about 2 years ago when we paid a fleeting visit to Belfast. A good party. I am altering my opinion of Stacey. I like him better the more I see of him.

Friday, 11 August 1944 – Londonderry

I did some correspondence and I went down to the engine room to look at the work they are doing on the condenser. So far they have failed to find the leak. I was going to have a C.O.s meeting but at 1015 they started to move all the ships about and so I postponed it and ordered a car and went to call on the Captain of

Ebrington Barracks, a dugout called Ryan.[31] I arrived in the middle of defaulters and had to wait some time. He is very nice and after a chat, we went to his quarters for a drink and eventually I stopped to lunch. Back on board at about 1500. Read and worked on S206s and flimsies. How I hate doing the latter. Got a letter from J. enclosing Gillian's examination papers. She really has done awfully well and knows a lot for her age. Miss Mackinnon is undoubtedly a good teacher. Went to bed early.

Saturday, 12 August 1944 – Londonderry

I did more work on S206s and walked round the ship to see how the defects were getting on. At 1100 I had a C.O.s meeting and we had a long quack about this and that. I must say, nice as old King was, I'm damned glad he has gone as I always felt he was slightly antagonistic to me and now it is much easier. I went ashore after lunch and walked to Culmore Point and back. A lovely, sunny day but not too hot. Found that in my absence the ship had been shifted from No. 9 berth to No. 17 in the American Dockyard. Felt footsore and well exercised when I got back. Wrote to P., who had sent me an air graph letter asking whether Peter was eligible for the navy special entry. I went down to the wardroom at about 1900 for a drink and at about 2000 I went ashore with the Chief, the Doctor, and Sullivan and had dinner at the Savoy Grill. Jolly good steak. After that we went along to the Officers' Club where I've never been before. There was a dance on and I had a dance with Mrs. Bonnett and a very charming wife of a submariner who I'd met in the *Saint John,* the one who'd been on board the *Broke.* It is an awfully nice club and the whole evening was great fun. I was much embarrassed by the kind things my officers said about me when talking about the R.N. and the R.C.N. Back on board with the Captain and No. 1 of a corvette for a night cap.

...

Monday, 14 August 1944 – Londonderry

I got a car and went to Copelin's office and asked him to ring London about Brown and Lewtas, who haven't yet shown up and who were appointed here days ago, and also about Anderson's compassionate leave. At 1100 we slipped and went down river for an engine trial, or rather to prove to the Base staff that we have a leak in our condenser, which they can't find in harbour. Selby brought his 2 children down and they came out with us. I'm awfully shy and bad with children and never know what to say to them, but I think they enjoyed it although both in turn felt a bit sick. We went as far as Inishtrahull as the testers wanted me to fire a depth charge in order to give the ship a good shake. It was a perfectly still day, and towards the evening it was brilliantly sunny. We got back having shown that there was a leak, at about 1800. I shifted and at 1930 Selby called for me and took me to his house for dinner, and what a dinner. Real sirloin of beef and undercut!!!! Mrs S. is awfully nice and they seem a most devoted couple and happy family. The *Stormont* had a ship's company dance to which I'd been invited and felt I ought to go, so at about 1015 the Selbys ran me down to the Navy Hall. I watched the dancing and drank several glasses of stout which I didn't want a bit, and went away as soon as I could, but even so didn't get back on board till after midnight. Much too late. There is a chance in France of encircling and cutting off a large part of the German Army. General Eisenhower has called for a supreme effort by all services.

Tuesday, 15 August 1944 – Londonderry

I went out into the town in the a.m. Went to Gieves and to the officers' clothing store and bought some shirts and things, and then had a hair cut and then went to a book shop and bought some books for Gillian and Raymond. No. 1 returned from leave. Still no sign of Lewtas and Brown and no answer to my signal asking for compassionate leave for Anderson. Had a certain amount of paper work to attend to. It was a hot, sunny afternoon. I read a book I'd bought on the roads of Britain and tried to get some shut eye, but I was continually disturbed.

At 1800 Bruce prepared for my cocktail party and shortly after and quite unasked, the Squadron Leader from Coastal Command who always attends our conferences arrived with a very attractive W.R.A.F. officer. I thought my invited guests would never come, however, they did eventually. Gregory, the Club Manager, and his wife. He is ex and invalided from the R.N.V.R. Mrs. Jackie Broome and a Mrs. Simmons (wife of a naval officer in Gib). I went very easy on the booze, but the others rather knocked it back and it was well after 2000 before they left. As a matter of fact, we all left together (the Air Force had left before by the way) and went to the Club for more drinks and a very late meal. While feeding, a very nice American naval doctor joined us, obviously a great boy friend of Mrs. S., who by this time was a bit shot away. I had to put in an appearance at a party on board *Stormont* and the Yankee doctor offered to drive me to the ship. Mrs. S. insisted on coming and finally we all 3 went on board *Stormont* at about 2300. It was a stag party but everyone was well shot away and so Margot was made very welcome. I had to stop her drinking any more. I like to show in these ships that I can drink a lot without getting drunk. Eventually got my 2 guests away with their car and went to bed. We have made another landing, this time in the S. of France between Marseilles and Cannes.

Wednesday, 16 August 1944 – Londonderry

This time in, there have been too many parties, too little sleep, and too little exercise and I'm feeling the strain. I went along with my ship's A/S team to the attack teacher and had some practice with the new equipment we've been given this time. I came back and dealt with some last minute correspondence and at about 1215 Capt. Ryan from the Barracks came to return my call. I like him. After lunch I went to a lecture on A/S conditioning in the Channel, which was really rather a waste of time. When I came back I made out all the necessary sailing and W/T signals, as we had got our sailing orders from Commodore D. I also fussed around about Anderson's compassionate leave and at the 11th hour got a decision from C.N.M.O. that he couldn't go until next time in. Got a letter from J. which made me very homesick, and I wrote a last letter to her. I always feel a particular longing for her when the thought of the responsibilities ahead make me feel depressed and frightened. Our condenser trouble is still not quite right and in the middle of the night I was told our sailing would have to be delayed from 0800 to 1000. At my drinking party yesterday, I'd told Mrs. Broome that I would take her small Simon down river with me tomorrow, and in the course of the afternoon he came on board to fix it up. A nice lad of about 13, just going up for Dartmouth.

Thursday, 17 August 1944 – Londonderry/At sea

The group slipped at 0600. *Port Colborne* is taking them on [illegible] following up after calibrating. Simon Broome came on board while I was shaving. The Engineers were ready with our condenser a little earlier than they at first expected and we sailed at 0930. On arrival at Moville we did a burst of full astern from ahead to give the condenser a shake up again, and then went alongside the oiler. The duty boat took the trial engineer officers and Simon off. We finished oiling at 1330 and went out to the calibration berth and anchored and did some check HF/DF calibration. We couldn't go through the whole range, but by 1900 we'd done all that was necessary for the Channel and so we weighed and proceeded at 18 kts. A big battle is being fought in Normandy at the Falaise Gap, where it was hoped to trap a big portion of the German Army, but from latest reports they mostly seem to have escaped. Brown and Lewtas joined from *Matane* at the last moment while we were doing our calibration.

Friday, 18 August 1944 – At sea

As we approached The Smalls it started to get foggy again, but visibility never dropped below 3 miles. This must be the foggiest part of the British Isles, I should think. We rounded The Smalls at about 1000. The visibility remained much the same right down the Cornish coast. At about 1800 we developed A/S trouble, which eventually necessitated slowing down to shift oscillations. Having done which, I'm damned if the spare wasn't also dud. There was then nothing else to be done but run for Falmouth, which I did as fast as I could, but couldn't save daylight and rather groped my way in at 2300. I must say, having got there I rather hoped for a night in, but no luck. The base staff found our testing instruments were all wrong and the oscillations were perfectly alright.

Saturday, 19 August 1944 – At sea

I had about an hour's sleep in my chair and at 0100 it was reported to me that we were all tickety boo and ready to ship. Not very nice this manoeuvring in the pitch dark in a narrow harbour, and just as we were trying to find the boom entrance an absolutely blinding rain storm came down. However, we got out somehow and once clear of the swept channel at the Lizard we shaped course to pick up the group, patrolling in an area about 50' south of the Scillies. We joined up with them at 0825.

At 1420 we got a ping, which proved to be something on the bottom, from our echo sounder. We proceeded to attack with *Stormont* and *Saint John* but without any result after 3 H/H and a D/C attack. No oil, nothing. At 1727 I decided it must be a wreck. Unfortunately, Q.H. doesn't work very well in this area and it wasn't possible to pinpoint it quite, but I made a signal and continued the patrol. In the meantime we'd had a signal ordering us right away down into the Bay of Biscay on relief in this area by E.G. 1. We met him at about 2000 and pushed off towards the first point on our route only to get a signal almost at once to continue attacking our contact. So they don't believe us again. E.G. 1 signalled he would do it but I thought I ought to and so I took *Stormont* back with me and sent the others on. Arrived as near as I could to the spot just after dark (2230) and joined with E.G. 1 and his 2 ships and did a sweep round and couldn't find it. Had a tremendous chat with Gwinner on the T.B.S. I'm sure it was a rock or something, but we didn't plot it accurately enough to pick it up again. Later on C. in C. told me to leave it to E.G. 1 and at midnight *Stormont* and I pushed off. A worrying and exasperating situation. Feel I did the wrong thing but also feel I had good cause to classify non sub.

Sunday, 20 August 1944 – At sea

We overtook the other 3 at about 0430 and I'm blowed if *Port Colborne* didn't open fire with star shell at us, although I should have thought it was obvious who we were. I couldn't for the life of me figure out what sort of formation or zigzag they were doing, but at daylight I took charge and altered for the next position on our route at 16 kts. The patrol area allotted us is right off the entrance to La Pallice, 10 miles off shore.[32] I must say it looks a bit close and lonely, although there is a cruiser cum destroyer force in the neighbourhood. I wonder about the air. It became drizzly and misty as we approached but we managed to get a glimpse of the Rochbonne S.E. buoy, which gave us our position, before turning up on to our patrol. Reached the area and turned to the N.'ward at 2118. Feeling extremely anxious and responsible and rather frightened. We may be alright as A/S ships but are woefully under armed and undertrained to fight surface actions even with M class minesweepers.[33]

A very dark night. There is no Q.H. here, unfortunately, and one feels very lost without it. Reached the N. end of our rectangle at 2325 and turned S. and almost immediately things started to happen. We got HF/DF bearings, which seemed near but sense undetermined, and so I sent the 2nd Div. to search to the S.E. and I took the 1st Div. off to the N.W. While this was on we were told to go to an aircraft sighting some way to the south and right off the mouth of the Gironde. Decided to finish what I was doing, but with a lot of signalling managed to send the 2nd Div. on ahead.

Monday, 21 August 1944 – At sea

At 0200 after a 15' sweep we turned to the aircraft sighting. At 0445 we contacted *Meon* and *Port Colborne* by radar. We were about 12 miles off the mouth of the river as best we could judge, and *Meon* was getting hopelessly tied up with buoys. One couldn't help wondering how many mine fields we were skating over. Went to action stations. We never found anything and couldn't even contact the aircraft. We were told to withdraw to 15 miles from the land by first light and then carried out a sweep to the W. and at 0900 altered again to the N. for our old patrol area. At 1050 all ships reported what they thought was a ground wave U-boat transmission, bearing about 050° and so we altered to the bearing, which eventually brought us in sight of land off the approaches to Rochefort. Very flat land and nothing but towers, steeples, and light houses, and at a distance it was damned difficult to identify what we were looking at. Just then *Saint John* sighted and picked up some aircraft survivors, which was most satisfactory.

The Pilot and I were having great difficulty making up our minds where we were, but at 1300 when 10' off Ile de Ré Light House I reckoned we were near enough and altered out, and at that moment the batteries opened up and *Stormont* was inshore of us and got a very nasty 10 minutes until out of range, being continually straddled by 2 6" guns. My heart was in my mouth as I watched, and I altered to try and lay some smoke as near as possible. By a miracle the ship was undamaged, but one man was unfortunately wounded by a splinter.[34] Once more I feel I should have never gone in so close. That is twice I've nearly lost a ship through stupidity. When the shouting and the tumult had died we moved to a new patrol area a little further south. At 1630 sighted Force 27, *Mauritius* and 2 destroyers.[35] At 2200 we moved to yet another area, this time more off the mouth of the Gironde, the nearest point being about 20' off land. Hot, sunny day.

Tuesday, 22 August 1944 – At sea

Quite a bit of wind and sea in the night, which gradually died down. We reached our new area at 2225 and turned to our patrol course, which we maintained during the night, turning every 2 hours. Force 27 (*Mauritius, Iroquois,* and *Ursa*) passed close astern of us at 0530. On reaching the W. end of our patrol at 1130 we sighted Point de la Combre Light House on the horizon and the line of tall spar buoys leading to the mouth of the Gironde. At 1200 we got orders to go to another patrol area further W., passing through a certain position en route, and at 1230 we altered accordingly. At 1300 Force 26 passed quite close to us, coming N. having swept S. along the French coast to Arcachon Point. At 1500 I reduced while the group radar officer was transferred from *Saint John* to *Meon.*

At 1724 we intercepted an aircraft report of a "disappearing contact" in a position only 8 miles N. of us, and I was just about to alter in that direction when a Liberator flew in and told *Port Colborne* by visual signal that he had a contact 19' to the W. and immediately flew off. Unable to get him on R/T and obtain any further details. However, this was the obvious one to follow up and probably the same as the signalled one, but out for position, so we cracked on speed and went off after it. Just then another Liberator hove in sight, who immediately answered on R/T and was most helpful. He flew ahead but could find no trace of our first friend. It was all terribly vague, but after steaming 20 miles I reduced to 12 and swept on another 15 miles to the furthest on position. This took us over the 100 fathom line and into a host of non sub echoes. At 2130 having turned back, and just before dark, we got a very sharp ping which excited everyone very much and we even attacked with hedgehog, but it was only fish or some non sub and at 2245 we went on. In the mean time we'd been ordered back to the area off the mouth of the Gironde to start patrolling at 0100 tomorrow, but this non sub has delayed us so much that we'll be late.

Cracked on at 16 kts. Force 26 carried out some sort of anti shipping operation further N. off Lorient and sank some minesweepers. What with him and surface patrols, nothing much can move on the French Atlantic coast without being detected, and any evacuation of troops from the beleaguered ports would be quite impossible.

Wednesday, 23 August 1944 – At sea

At 0324 just as we reached our area we got a very good HF/DF bearing ground wave of a U-boat estimated within 30 miles to the N.'ward, and I turned the group and set off along the bearing at 15 kts. By 0600 we'd run 30 miles and were getting a bit close to Oléron Island so I started to turn to the W., but just then got a signal from C. in C. to resume patrol and so turned S. again. Reached the area at 0845 and started a to and fro patrol 047°-227° on a 20 mile leg. At 1105 Cap de la Combre bore 054°18'. At 1114 a signal moving us to an area about 20' further to seaward. At 1301 just as we reached it, *Port Colborne* got an A/S contact, which it lost almost at once in the neighbourhood of quite a big oil slick. It all looked pretty hopeful but after searching till 2000 we found nothing and gave it up.

Feeling very tired at the end of the day. Anxiety and lack of sleep beginning to tell. We heard on the news that Paris had fallen to the French Forces of the Interior and also that Marseilles had been captured by the Allies. Great news!! Another signal saying the Plymouth layover had been delayed to the 28th. *Not* such good news!! It feels as if we'd been on this beat for about a fortnight when, in fact, it is only 3 or 4 days.

A glorious hot day. All the ship's company are getting very brown and sun burned. Backwards and forwards in our area all night. Some ghost radar echoes early on kept me up, but later it was a very peaceful night. There was the glow of a terrific fire – presumably Bordeaux – visible all night, although it must have been 60-70 miles away.

Thursday, 24 August 1944 – At sea

Another beautiful day. It was given out on the news that Bordeaux had been occupied by French and Allied troops, but no details of how they got there. As there was nothing much doing in the A/S contact line, I told ships to be ready to do some gunnery practice at drifting targets. *Saint John* and *Port Colborne* did theirs at 1100. At 1200 our patrol area was shifted about 15 miles to the north and so we moved up there. At 1530 *Meon* and *Stormont* did their gunnery, and finally at 1830 we had our crack. Very good value and the troops enjoyed it. There were aircraft reports all day of a destroyer and 2 submarines and some merchant ships moving about in the entrance of the Gironde, and a Narvik destroyer was reported at La Pallice. At about 1815 about 20 Beaufighters flying very low towards the mouth of the Gironde passed us, presumably going to attack the shipping.

I felt a little isolated and worried with reports of these destroyers, as we are still only 20 miles or so off the Gironde and although there *are* 5 of us our guns are woefully short ranged. A signal saying Force 28 was to be ready to support us, if required, made me a little more nervous. I don't think it is physical fear so much as the dread of being faced with a difficult situation or difficult decision to make. Nothing of course *did* happen, except that just before midnight I had to detach *Port Colborne* and *Meon* to search for aircraft survivors further to the North.[36]

Friday, 25 August 1944 – At sea

At 0530 *Saint John* and *Stormont* got an A/S contact just as we got a very good HF/DF bearing, which our operator estimated to be within 10 miles of us, so leaving the other two we beetled off along the bearing but found nothing out to 15 miles. Having decided it was non sub, the other 2 joined us and we searched up and down and then to the W. Force 28 passed going on their southerly sweep down the coast at 0730. At 0950 *Monnow,* who is the latest addition to our group, arrived and joined up. Her captain is an R.C.N.R. Commander called Skinner and they have just left a C group.[37] They came alongside and we had a chat over loud hailers and I sent over some orders.

At 1105 *Port Colborne* and *Meon,* who had picked up 5 airmen, rejoined. If we can do nothing else we are a very good rescue squad for the R.A.F. After reorganising the group completely we started off on the S.'ly leg of our patrol. At 1415 we were told to shift again yet further W. to an area on the 100 fathom line, and we altered course accordingly. Ran into an absolute spate of non subs and simply couldn't get along at all. Just as it was getting dusk we crossed the 100 fathom line and once more ran into fish and what not, and it was nearly midnight before we moved off together again. Anderson is having a spell of inaccuracy with his star sights and I wasn't too sure how accurate our position was. Another very hot day but not quite so cloudlessly sunny as previously. The Roumanians have accepted peace terms and have now declared war on Germany.

Saturday, 26 August 1944 – At sea

A quiet night on the whole and quite a lot of sleep for me. We carried on up and down the area N. and S. I went mess deck rounds. Very impressed. An enormous improvement from last week. No. 1 certainly is v. good indeed. I believe he is the best I've ever had in spite of the fact that he lacks a certain amount of knowledge. At 1330 we got a signal shifting our patrol area another 40' or so west and so we turned on to a W.'ly course. I sent off the depart signal as presumably we will leave patrol fairly early tomorrow.

At about 1500 a single seater Mustang suddenly appeared over us, did one or two swoops and crashed about 3 miles ahead. When we arrived on the scene there was just an oil patch and a few things floating, but while we were over the spot, the pilot's body came up attached to his parachute. Quite dead, of course. An American, Lieutenant Hausard.[38] We picked him up and at 2000 I read the service and we buried him at sea. Poor devil, right out here he must have been hopelessly lost and presumably tried to ditch near us and nose dived instead.

We reached our area at 1700 and once more started a N. and S. patrol. Blazing hot day.

Sunday, 27 August 1944 – At sea

At 0130 *Monnow* reported a "Jig" [radar contact] at 3 miles which he lost almost at once. One naturally thought of a U-boat which had dived, and so I closed the whole group in on him and we carried out a thorough search of the area but found nothing. At 0450 we intercepted a sighting report from an aircraft in a position about 45' away. As the report was 2 hours stale when we got it and as the aircraft couldn't stay to home, I decided not to go to it. At 0730 however, a Halifax came over and told us there was a marker about 20 miles away marking last night's contact, and so we used it and started to sweep to the W. Sighted 4 Spanish trawlers which we closed and boarded, but as there was absolutely nothing suspicious I let them carry on.

Carried on a bit with our sweep to the W. and then went N. and then E. back to a new area very close to the old one. At 1430 we intercepted a signal saying an aircraft had sighted airmen in a dinghy about 100 miles away, but as there was nobody near, I detached *Monnow* and *Stormont* only to hear later on that a flying boat had done the rescuing. At 2130 when E.G. 15 appeared in the area to relieve us I turned to 335° and pushed off with the group at 15 knots for Plymouth. Glorious day. I visited the engine room and boiler rooms with the Chief at 1700.

Monday, 28 August 1944 – At sea/Plymouth

A restful night, thank God, and an uneventful day. 17 knots all the way. I saw defaulters in the a.m. and requestmen. For once on approaching Plymouth it was good visibility. We got up to the Eddystone at about 1600 but were then stymied by a convoy going west and we had to slow down and go round its stern. Passed through the gate at about 1700. *Swansea* and *Meon* went straight up harbour and berthed at No. 1 wharf, and the remainder went to the oiler in the Sound and remained down there overnight. As soon as we were secured I had a bath. Told the Yeoman to ring up the Duke of Cornwall and find out if J. was staying there but alas she wasn't. I didn't really expect it but hoped nevertheless. Balfour from the *Meon* came over, and as it was No. 1's birthday there was rather a lot of drinking before I went to bed. Anderson left the ship for passage to Canada for compassionate leave and Kilgour relieved him. We have now 3 old Matanes. I shall be very glad to get Kilgour as he is a far better navigator than Anderson.

Tuesday, 29 August 1944 – Plymouth

Raining hard nearly all day. I went to see Capt. D. and then I rang up J. Apparently she had tried to come here but couldn't get a room. I spoke to Gillian and Raymond. All quiet in the Portsmouth area, thank God. J. has bought a bull dog puppy. At 1130 I had a C.O.s meeting and met Comdr. Skinner for the first time from *Monnow.* An old N.R. type and not much of an asset to the group on first sight at any rate. It seems *Port Colborne* was fired on by Force 28 on the night she and *Meon* were looking for survivors in a dinghy. I take a very dim view of that. At 1400 a Wren typist came to my cabin and I dictated my report of proceedings. That took me until about 1630 and then a Captain from D.T.M.[39] came on board and talked about hedgehog and A/S work generally. At 1830 I walked round to the *Rodney,* who was alongside in the basin, and had several drinks with Jack, who is just off on 6 days' leave tomorrow. Back on board and supper, after which I meant to write to J. but instead was lured into the wardroom where there were some Wrens, and I sat drinking whisky till nearly 2400.

Wednesday, 30 August 1944 – Plymouth

At 0945 Brown and I got a car to A.C.H.Q. I saw Mallinson and had a long talk with him about the situation. He thinks the Bay patrols are over now, as all those U-boat bases are about to fall. E.G. 2 is now working from Rosyth and E.G. 5 has gone on a N. Russian convoy; *Bickerton* and one other have, incidentally, been sunk.[40] I complained about *Diadem* and his destroyers firing on *Port Colborne.* Got back on board about 1100 and just before noon Bishop Wells, Chaplain of the Canadian Fleet, a flock of young parsons, and Weller came on board and stayed to lunch. The Bish is a nice old boy. We managed to get rid of him about 1400 and later on I shifted and went ashore. Caught a bus into Plymouth and found it was early closing and so walked about a bit, on to the Hoe and back to the Dockyard mostly along the sea front. It was some exercise anyhow. Creighton from Capt. D.'s office came and had a glass of beer with me at 1800, and in fits and starts I managed to get a letter written to J. I'm glad now she *didn't* come down as I should now only be feeling miserably depressed. After supper I went down to the wardroom, where as usual there were some guests. A nice couple called Stuart and their daughter, who is a nurse, and a friend of Milburn's. A lovely morning, but it clouded over and there were some spots of rain in the p.m. The battle in France is going very well. The Americans S. of Paris are pushing on West, and the British and Canadians have secured bridge heads over the Lower Seine.

Thursday, 31 August 1944 – Plymouth/At sea

Once more the pain and grief of responsibility at sea arrives. I'm finding it more and more difficult to make the necessary effort these days. We slipped nominally at 0830 but owing to delays actually at about 0930. It was blowing quite fresh outside. We formed up and when S. of Eddystone altered to the W. for an area round the Scillies. On the way we got orders to sweep up the convoy route from Lizard to Hartland Point. At 1845 when 5' E. of the Wolf, *Saint John* got an A/S contact which he took a long time to classify, losing it once or twice, and to my annoyance asked that we should come back to do a search. I decided to send *Monnow* on with her division and went back to help *Saint John* with *Port Colborne.* After a sweep we picked up the contact and dropped one charge at 2115 to see if it was fish but it still persisted. What made it difficult was that we could only get the echo from one direction. *Saint John* then attacked with H/H which produced some oil. It was now getting dark and after one more H/H attack we completely lost contact at 2300, and at 2400 I formed the 3 ships up and started to sweep down tide to the W. Wind and sea had dropped by the evening. Quite definitely I haven't the patience for this game.

Friday, 1 September 1944 – At sea

I did an Easy Item to the S. when west of the Wolf and another to the E. to pass S. of the Light and back towards the original contact. At 0210 *Saint John* got another contact about 3' south of the Wolf and attacked and brought up a lot of oil. He also reported very good echo sounder trace, which really *might* be a submarine. We could get absolutely nothing, but the oil was plainly visible in the moonlight. *Saint John* attacked again and then we all lost contact. At about 0600 I started an E. and W. patrol till daylight and got about an hour's much needed sleep.

Came the dawn and there was the oil, rather dispersed now but definitely with a fixed source which was unaffected by tide, but we could get *nothing* on A/S or echo sounder. *Saint John* was getting *something* but nothing good enough to attack. But for the fact that we'd been told by the C. in C. to remain, after I'd reported it, till further orders, I would certainly have given up and gone on as there was a reported wreck plotted only 2 miles away. I made a signal saying I thought further search waste of time.

After lunch I decided we must throw something more at it and had just said I was going to drop charges blindly at end of oil slick when *Saint John* reported having good echo sounder trace. He ran over a 2nd time and dropped a pattern of 5 D/C at 1400 and up came a mass of oil and, after a bit, other stuff. He and I lowered whalers and picked up printed German books, letters, certificates and we picked up clothing with German name marks. Really looks like a kill. Entirely C. in C. and *Saint John,* as if I'd had my way we would have been miles away by now.[41]

Saint John and I dropped 2 10 charge patterns on end of oil slick by eye. While all this was going on, C. in C. had ordered me to join *Monnow* to go to an aircraft sighting N. of Trevose Head and to turn this contact over to E.G. 11. When at 1740 *Assiniboine* appeared, I left *Saint John* with him and took *Port Colborne* off to join *Monnow.* As we started, down came the rain and mist and the wind got up from the S.W. As we came N. *Monnow* informed us that he was in contact with what he thought was a S/M off Trevose Head. We arrived on the scene just after 2100 to find it wasn't as promising as I expected.[42]

Saturday, 2 September 1944 – At sea

Contact was poor and a number of attacks had had no result. However, as I turned to close I got a cracking echo and ran in and did a H/H attack. By the different times of bursts we undoubtedly hit something standing off the bottom. Before we even ran over the explosion objects a mass of oil started bobbing up. Ran out and came in for another attack but missed it with H/H. Very heavy rain and nearly pitch dark by now, and blowing hard. Stopped and tried to identify wreckage but couldn't for certain, however, by the number of fish and a shiny bit of wood and bag of flour I suspect wreck. Left *Meon* and *Stormont* in contact and sent *Monnow* and *Port Colborne* to patrol along the convoy route and went off to search in the vicinity of aircraft sighting as ordered by C. in C. An eventful day.

A quiet night and I got some sleep after midnight. Quite rough. At about 0630 the wind went right round from S.W. to N.W. and blew hard. Glass rising rapidly after a quick drop. At 0900 we closed *Meon* and *Stormont* who were holding the contact. Further attacks had brought up more evidence, and so I left *Meon* to watch it and took *Stormont* off. It really blew very hard from about 1200 to 1500 and with the wind and sea on the beam we rolled quite a bit. Summer, I'm afraid, is over.

At 1100 *Meon* reported getting an echo sounder trace of an object 65 feet high on the bottom. As that couldn't well be a S/M I recalled him and he joined me at 1230. At about 1600 the wind started to ease and at 1845 when we closed the position of the "object" it was fairly calm. We gained contact at once and there was a very big oil slick. At 2045 we dropped 5 D/C, which brought up a lot of War Office gridded maps of France and a packet of Chesterfield cigarettes, which conclusively proved it to be a wreck. Most satisfactory to get positive evidence that one's guess is correct. After that continued patrol. *Monnow* reported at about 0200 that *Port Colborne* had gained contact that they were attacking, but could not classify. Later on he put *Port Colborne* on the contact and continued his patrol.

Sunday, 3 September 1944 – At sea

The Allies are fairly racing ahead in France. The Yanks are into Belgium, and the Canadians and English are into Dieppe and across the Somme. Romania had asked for an armistice with Russia and is now fighting against the Germans.

At 0730 I started to close an aircraft sighting position but later got a signal from C. in C. telling *Monnow* and *Saint John* only to go. Extreme visibility in the early morning, but by noon it had shut right down with rain squalls and rising S.W.'ly wind again. I did a sweep well inshore of the swept channel between Trevose Head and Hartland Point in the a.m. and then returned to the area between T. Head and the minefield and N.W. of the swept channel. Got a signal saying the limits of the minefields were to be strictly observed. Thinking they were of not much importance I have already been through the edge.

Monday, 4 September 1944 – At sea

Blowing quite hard from the S.W. and a misty rainy morning. Sighted *Port Colborne* at 0800, who had lost contact in the night and rather lost himself, which wasn't surprising without Q.H. I ordered him to join me and sent *Meon* off to join *Monnow* and help him with his Q.H. I started to close an aircraft sighting on receipt of the flash report and later on C. in C. came up and told the whole group to close. We were much delayed, as is always the case when you are in a hurry, with non sub echoes to be looked at. We arrived in the sighting position about 15 miles W. of Trevose Head at about 1400 and joined up with the rest of our group. Almost at once *Saint John* got a contact and after spending ages running round I went off with 2 ships and left *Monnow* to continue the investigation. I just daren't pull anyone off a contact now after our recent experience with the U-boat.

At 2030, having turned and swept back, I found *Saint John* with yet another echo about which he was getting very excited, but in this case I was able to plot it by Q.H. as *Port Colborne*'s contact, which had been giving off oil for 48 hours. Having found nothing at the sighting position I am sweeping up and down just off to seaward of the convoy route between Trevose Head and Pendeen. The day improved a lot and was hot and sunny.

Tuesday, 5 September 1944 – At sea

All was quiet until 0145 when *Saint John* got another contact, and as is always the case with *Saint John* it was firm and clear and good. Sent the 2nd Div. to continue the patrol and joined *Saint John* with the 1st Div. It certainly was a good clear echo and we got an echo sounder trace. *Saint John* and I attacked it several times without any apparent effect, but the wind and sea were rising and A/S conditions were becoming too bad for accurate attacks and so at 0500 I sent *Port Colborne* away to join *Monnow* and held contact with *Saint John* until daylight. At 0750 we did one more attack and then, leaving *Saint John* to hold contact until weather improved, I joined the group and continued our 045°-225° patrol. A funny day, bright and sunny but with a stiff S.W. wind and lumpy sea. Between 1400-1600 we were investigating and attacking a contact which was finally classified as non sub. Just before dark *Stormont,* who had taken over the watch on *Saint John*'s contact, reported "Padlock" (Have lost contact) and so we turned back to her position and picked it up again for her with the aid of our Q.H., which is simply invaluable on this job. We remained on the spot until nearly midnight when the group passed again going N.E. and we joined up with them, leaving *Meon* this time as sentry.

Wednesday, 6 September 1944 – At sea

We had hardly gone 2 miles from the contact when I'm damned if we didn't pick up yet another. God how I hate these pings, but one can't disregard them. This was difficult to hold but was definitely not fish, and so once more I sent *Monnow* to continue patrol and took *Port Colborne* with me to investigate. After a great deal of trouble we got right over once or twice and obtained a good echo sounder trace of an object on the bottom, having done which at 0400 I decided to cruise round the contact and wait for daylight to attack and, incidentally, give myself a *little* sleep.

At about 0715 when it was light, the remainder of the group closed (less *Saint John* who I had detached to Falmouth to replenish with H/H and D/C) and we started to attack these 2 contacts which were within 2 miles of each other. *Meon* and *Port Colborne* on the original contact were alright and had an easy job, but our other contact was a fair basket and it wasn't till nearly noon that we got the echo sounder trace again and were certain we were on the right echo. Repeated attacks had practically no effect on either target. A bit of oil from both but that was all, so I buoyed them both and left *Port Colborne* to watch and at 1550 the rest of us started off to patrol again. At about 1700 intercepted an aircraft report of a disappearing radar contact (whatever that means on a day with maximum visibility) only about 15 miles away, and so we all turned to close the position and got in R/T touch with the aircraft. Just as we arrived over the spot C. in C. signalled to send only 2 ships, and so leaving *Monnow* and *Meon* I turned back at about 1945 to return to *Port Colborne. Saint John* rejoined at about 2145 and at 2230 on reaching *Port Colborne* I turned the show over to him and started for Falmouth, as the group had been told to detach one at a time to replenish with ammunition.

Thursday, 7 September 1944 – At sea/Falmouth/At sea

We arrived at Falmouth without incident at 0300 and berthed. Oiling started right away but ammunitioning not till 0700. I turned in on arrival but didn't get the most out of my 3 or 4 hours between the sheets as I was a bit cold. We got a mail and in the paper I see there is to be a "dim out" in future instead of a "black out." The Allies are racing across France and it looks as if the Germans wouldn't stand before their own borders. Brussels, Ghent, and Antwerp are ours, and we are investing Calais, Boulogne, and Dunkirk.

We finished getting in our hedgehogs and depth charges and sailed at 1200. Blowing a bit and chilly but fair and bright. Met the group (less *Meon* and *Monnow* who are still further N.) off Pendeen at 1600 and after sending *Port Colborne* into Falmouth, started to sweep N.E. with *Saint John* and *Stormont.* We'd hardly gone any distance before *Saint John* got contact. Not a good one and very hard to hold, and we went round and round and round, sometimes getting a good echo sounder trace and sometimes missing it. We made one or two attacks of doubtful accuracy and then it started to get dark. God, how I hate this sort of job. Sent *Stormont* off to join the other 2 in supporting a convoy and stayed in contact with *Saint John* and held the target all night. Got very little sleep what with losing and gaining contact, and making innumerable signals to the group and C. in C. Got v. annoyed with No. 1. These O.O.W.s are so damned inaccurate when fixing the ship.

Friday, 8 September 1944 – At sea

Saint John was so insistent on the excellence of his echo sounder trace that I decided to hold on to the contact all night and wait till daylight to attack in case any evidence came up. At 0430 the rest of the group arrived, having escorted a convoy down from Trevose Head. Sent *Monnow* in to Falmouth and the other 3 up to patrol between Trevose Head and Hartland Point. When it got light, *Saint John* and we started to attack but it was awfully difficult to hold contact. At about 0830 *Saint John* sent a boat for their mail and Stacey came over and showed me his echo sounder traces, both for this one and his real U-boat. Later on in the a.m. we got firm hold of the thing and both ships did accurate attacks but not even a whisper of oil.

I had just coded up a signal saying I was leaving it when C. in C. signalled that E.G. 6 was to take over, and at last at 1530 HMCS *Grou* and *Cape Breton* arrived and we pushed off to join our group further N. We met them at about 1915 supporting a S. bound convoy and we joined the screen ahead. We got down to Trevose Head at 2330 and E.G. 6 then took over to support convoy down to Pendeen. I was up on the bridge for a long time while we manoeuvred in the dark to detach from the convoy and get clear. Feeling depressed and oh so tired of this job.

Having got back on to the convoy lane astern of the convoy, we turned N.E. again and swept back towards Hartland and Lundy Island. *Monnow* rejoined from Falmouth in the middle of the kerfuffle, but I did not detach *Meon* as if we leave patrol on the 10th on schedule, she will hardly have time to rejoin before we go.

Saturday, 9 September 1944 – At sea

We seemed to get a contact very nearly every ½ hour. Some were known wrecks and others needed investigation, but I had to turn out for every one and fix the ship and decide whether or not to go on. This sort of thing is really exhausting and on this bit of the route between Hartland Pt. and Trevose Head, where the bottom is littered with wrecks, it happens unceasingly. Contact, investigate, check position, probably attack, examine result, classify. Stopped at about 0830 and transferred mails to *Meon* and *Stormont.* At 1100 we were told to support a N. going convoy, which we joined taking station ahead at 1215. On passing Hartland Point, we detached and turned to the S. to continue patrol. At 1846 we were told to support a south bound convoy as far as the meeting point with a N. bound convoy somewhere between Trevose and Pendeen and then transfer to the N. bound and take it as far as Hartland Point. We met the S. bound convoy at 2000 about half way between Hartland Point and Trevose Head and took station ahead. I shall be thankful to leave this patrol tomorrow and have a spell. It has been a particularly wearing 10 days. We detected the N. bound convoy, supported by E.G. 6, at about 2330 ahead of us.

Sunday, 10 September 1944 – At sea

Spent a worrying hour or so disengaging from our convoy and taking station on the other, getting rather mixed up with E.G. 6 in the process. There is no doubt about it, I'm not good at night manoeuvring. It frightens me. At about 0130 we got settled down ahead of the N. going convoy and took them right up to Hartland Point, where we left them at 0730. Came south with the usual crop of wreck echoes and did an E.I. turn to the N.E. to vary the patrol at 1200. I read prayers and said a word to the sailors. I was wondering when we were going to get a signal to leave patrol when at 1445 C. in C. signalled that 3 ships only were to be detached tomorrow and the other 3 would have to wait till the first 3 returned on patrol. Oh dear, oh dear. I shall have to send the 2nd Div. in first and that means another 4 days for us still. I wrote out a long signal urgently requesting we might boiler clean at Plymouth in order that a few days leave in England could be granted, as it is still denied the R.C.N. from Londonderry and we all badly need leave.[43]

We had to repeat last night's programme. South with our convoy to meeting point and then N. with another. Again an anxious and worrying time milling round between the 2 convoys when they met. A lovely, warm, sunny day. News is still good. The Allies are up to the Moselle, Meuse, and the Albert Canal. Mr. Churchill has gone to Canada for another meeting with Roosevelt.

Monday, 11 September 1944 – At sea

We took the N. bound convoy as far as Hartland Point and then left them at 0530 and turned S. again. At 1130 we all stopped, *Meon* lowered a boat which we closed and transferred Brown, who has got acute toothache and I'm sending him in for dental treatment. All ships of the 1st Div. closed the boat and gave it a mail to land, then the 2nd Div. pushed off for Plymouth and we resumed our patrol. We met a S. bound convoy and took station ahead of it, although we had no particular orders to do so and when nearly at Trevose Head, we got a signal telling us to meet a ship called the *Humboldt* at Hartland Point at 1900 and escort it to Trevose. I was expecting some sort of largish merchant ship, but the only thing that came in sight was a U.S. warship rather like a sloop, and it wasn't till she'd passed that I found out she *was* the *Humboldt.*[44] We then had to get her to slow down to allow us to take station on her as she was going 17 kts. All rather funny. We had a good fast spin anyway to Trevose, where we left her, and shortly after picked up a N. going convoy and took them to Hartland.

Had one exciting moment when we got a bottom contact which we hadn't previously met and I decided to drop depth charges. It was right ahead of the convoy, and by the time we'd run over once the approach course for the attack was directly towards them and I wasn't sure whether we or the convoy would get there first. However, we dropped and went hard over and were alright.

In the evening I really felt dog tired. This patrol has really given me no let up at all and practically no sleep. The Americans are across the German border near Trier and British troops are now in Holland. Lovely day.

Tuesday, 12 September 1944 – At sea

Went back to the scene of last night's attack and picked up contact again at 0700, investigated and classified it as definitely wreck. Gave all officers a short address on damage control. We patrolled up and down the swept channel with just enough contacts between the 3 of us to prevent me getting any rest or sleep in the p.m. At about 1500 we took station ahead of a S. bound convoy which we were told to support to Pendeen. We are then to exchange places with E.G. 11 who are to take over our beat while we patrol Pendeen to Trevose. We passed Trevose at about 2000 and I took the group out 30° on the starboard bow of the convoy where I hoped we'd be quite clear of oncoming traffic during the night.

Soon after we detected a bunch of stuff which must be *Rodney* and her screen right ahead and if anything on starboard bow, putting them entirely on the wrong side of the channel, approaching at 18 kts. I really didn't know which way to go and rather late in the day altered to port and got appallingly mixed up with 2 of E.G. 11's destroyers and had to go full astern. Then for a bit I didn't know where I was and started to get foul of a small N. bound convoy. God knows what happened to *Saint John* and *Port Colborne* in the mix up. Very annoying and very undignified, but I find I am quite incapable of appreciating night situations like that. Eventually when everything had passed, we 3 collected ourselves again ahead of our convoy and soon after midnight when abreast of Pendeen we detached, moved well to seaward, and decided to make our night patrol from that position, clear of all traffic. Lovely day. Le Havre has surrendered.

Wednesday, 13 September 1944 – At sea

An uneventful day patrolling on and to seaward of the convoy route, with about the average number of wrecks and no subs to investigate. We got our nightly task of escorting N. and S. bound convoys in our patrol area. Picked up the N. bound convoy 1915 and turned over to the S. bound convoy at about 2200, this time without incident, thank God.

Found a copy of the Admiralty official booklet on the Mediterranean Fleet covering that awful period of Greece, Crete, and the Malta and Tobruk convoys. When I think I'm complaining of being hard worked on this job it makes me feel v. ashamed and rather yellow.

Thursday, 14 September 1944 – At sea/Plymouth

An uneventful night, but just as I was sitting down to breakfast we got a contact which proved to be something on the bottom and which we and *Port Colborne* proceeded to attack and eventually classified as wreck. We then started to move S. so as to be at the Pendeen end of our patrol when *Monnow* and *Meon* arrived. Went to General Quarters at 1030 and exercised damage control, which was good value. At about 1200 we got another contact, which was maddening just as I was in a hurry to get on. However, I turned round, ran over and found it was something on the bottom and dropped a pattern on it and brought up a mass of fish, which I allowed myself to think was proof of a wreck so I left it and went on. I'm afraid the fact that I wanted badly to get on influenced me. I ought to have investigated and attacked again before classifying and it worried me the rest of the day.

When we got down to Pendeen at about 1400 it became very foggy and we dashed wildly about closing radar contacts which we thought were *Monnow* and *Meon.* Later on the fog lifted and we saw them (*Monnow* had given quite a wrong 1200 position) and closed, exchanged signals and then we and *Saint John* pushed on at 17 kts for Plymouth. Poor old *Port Colborne* had to stay behind until *Stormont,* who had been delayed, arrived back on patrol in about 3 hours time. We made Plymouth at 2000 and berthed just before dark alongside *Prince Robert,*[45] and was I ready for a night in??!!!

Friday, 15 September 1944 – Plymouth

A grand night's sleep but a beastly wet, windy day. Stacey came round to see me at 0930 about his report on *U-247,* and later on he and I walked back through the Dockyard and I went to call on Capt. D. but found he was on leave. Back on board and at 1100 I got a car and went to A.C.H.Q. and saw Mallinson, who tells me we have been given a certain kill. Nothing much has come of my signal except that our next lay over in Londonderry is to be 14 days, which presumably will enable us to give leave. I went to see Caslon, Chief of Staff, who talked about the impossibility of boiler cleaning in here and couldn't understand why there were any leave restrictions from Northern Ireland. I also persuaded him to come down on board *Saint John* tomorrow and say "Well done." I told him I thought the R.N. treated the R.C.N. unfairly – all criticism and no help, and we'd never seen a senior R.N. officer on board.

Got back on board to find all the Port Colbornes in our mess including Angus, the Captain. He is an awfully nice chap but a bit tired I think. Very late lunch and then a bit of shut eye in my chair. Stacey came over again at 1630 to discuss the Chief of Staff's visit and when he'd gone, I wrote some letters. At 1830 I went over to the *Prince Robert* and called on the Captain, one Hope R.C.N.[46] Weller was there and later on I brought them both back for a drink here. After a late supper I wrote and read and then went to bed. The Americans are well over the German border and are ½ way through the Siegfried Line in places.

"The Old Man of the Sea." Cdr. Edgar Skinner being interviewed by a WRCNS reporter in March 1944. LAC PA204643

HMCS *Matane,* Layard's home for most of 1944. The glider bomb that crippled the ship on 20 July 1944 glanced off her hull at the break on the port side. DND GM-465

HMCS *Swansea* photographed from the *Matane* while carrying out a towing evolution in January 1944. Note the prodigious depth charge armament of a River class frigate.
LAC PA206487

The North Atlantic could also be a formidable foe. This is *Swansea* battling heavy seas in January 1944. John Band

"I'm damned sorry to lose the corvettes." The corvette HMCS *Frontenac* exercises with EG 9 in early 1944, before it became an all-frigate group. DND K-506

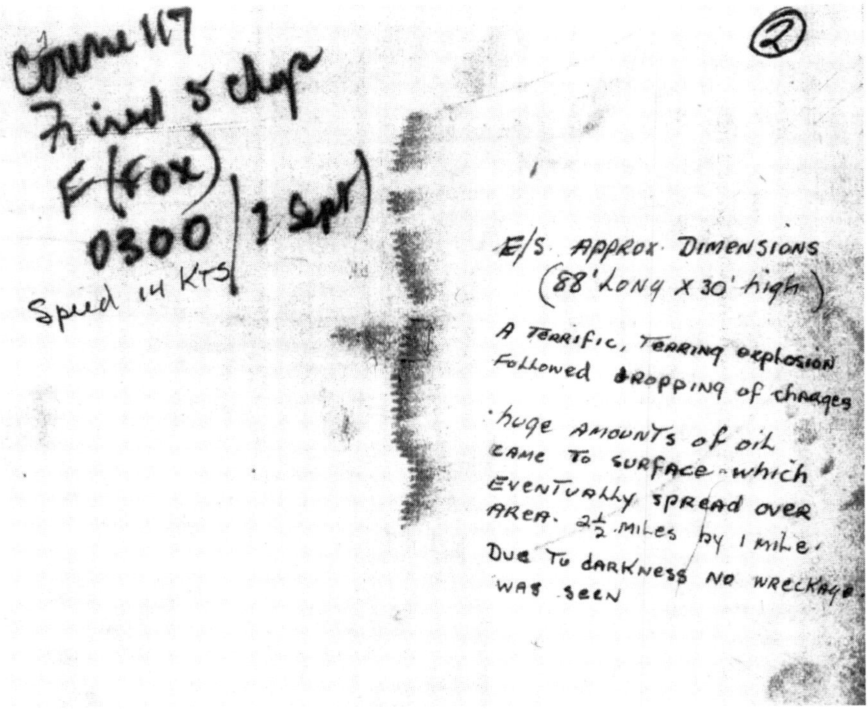

This incredible image is the echo sounder trace of *U-247* lying on the floor of the English Channel before being pulverized by *Saint John* and *Swansea* on 1 September 1944. The exact shape of the U-boat is reproduced, which demonstrates why echo sounders were such invaluable classification tools in the inshore campaign. The notes are *Saint John*'s attack data. PRO ADM 199/1462

Lt.-Cdr. Bill Stacey, right, and Sub-Lt. J.R. Bradley triumphantly display a life raft and uniform jacket from *U-247*. Stacey's persistence was largely responsible for the kill but there is no doubting the skill of Bradley, *Saint John*'s A/S control officer, who also played an instrumental role in the destruction of *U-309* in February 1945. DND PMR-83-1360

Layard and Lt. John Band on *Swansea*'s bridge in the Bay of Biscay, August 1944. John Band

This image of EG 11 attacking a contact in the Bay of Biscay on 18 August 1944 captures both the tactics and character of inshore anti-submarine warfare. In the foreground, HMCS *Kootenay*'s bridge crew times the descent of a hedgehog pattern splashing into the sea ahead of the ship to ascertain the depth of the contact, while HMCS *Ottawa* stands off to hold the target with asdic. The attack resulted in the destruction of *U-621*. DND A-1011

A happy wardroom. Layard's farewell photograph with *Swansea*'s officers on 5 November 1944. Lt. John Band is in the front row to Layard's left, while Lt. David Kilgour is the bearded officer over Band's left shoulder. John Band

HMCS *Saint John*, the last of Layard's twelve commands. LAC PA134503

Layard says goodbye to *Saint John*, 19 February 1945. RAYMOND LAYARD

HMCS *Loch Alvie* in Loch Eriboll with a surrendered U-boat alongside. DND LS-16

Warships operating out of Londonderry, Northern Ireland had to navigate the tight, yet beautiful confines of Lough Foyle. This is the RN frigate HMS *Loch Fada* refuelling at Lisahally after the war. DND O-1538-36

"Relief to have finished with all that worry and responsibility." Frank Layard at Harvest Lodge shortly after the war with Joan, Gillian, and Raymond. RAYMOND LAYARD

Saturday, 16 September 1944 – Plymouth

A lovely day. Angus and I walked round to *Saint John* just before 1000. Caslon (Chief of Staff) and Mallinson came down at 1000. Caslon walked round the ship and then spoke to the ship's company. The ship I thought looked very nice and clean, and I think the visit was a success. When he left we had some coffee with Stacey and then I went to Capt. D.'s office and rang up Londonderry. Spoke first to the Commodore's Secretary and then to the Commodore. It was soon apparent that my signal was *not* favourably looked on. It seems it ought to have been made as a pink signal so that it had less publicity. I talked about this leave question and obviously have entirely different views on the subject. I rang off and went back on board feeling thoroughly depressed. I now see that the signal was foolish but, much worse than that, it was disloyal to the Commodore. Disloyalty is the unforgivable sin in an officer, a thing I've always drilled into young officers and ratings, and now I've done it myself. I feel terribly degraded. Sat down immediately and started to write an official explanation to the Commodore.

After lunch I was going ashore with No. 1 and Earl for a walk when I got a message that the Chief of Staff wanted to see me, so I shifted back into uniform and went up to A.C.H.Q. It was about this leave and my signal. Caslon said C. in C. Western Approaches had taken a very poor view of the signal, but from what he could learn anyone with a reasonable excuse would be granted leave to England, although the orders say next of kin only. I walked back to the Dockyard feeling full of gloom and continued my letter and asked to be relieved of my command. I wrote quite a number of other letters including one pouring out my soul to J. Went down to the wardroom about 2100 and had quite a lot of whisky.

Sunday, 17 September 1944 – Plymouth/At sea

A lovely hot sunny day, but I didn't feel very sunny myself. Still depressed about that signal, and then we have a defect to our refrigeration which we can't get put right, and I don't want to delay sailing. Divisions at 0930. Not badly dressed on the whole. Shortly after 1000 we had stand up church on the *Port Colborne*'s upper deck conducted by our new group chaplain, one Edwards.[47] Seems a nice chap but a bit too long winded. Said goodbye to Lewtas, who has been relieved by a chap called Falconer.[48] Very sorry to lose Lewtas. A good officer and a very nice chap. After that, No. 1 came along to me and said he wanted to leave the ship and he's fed up. The trouble is he is now junior to Falconer, Brown, and Earl and he finds it a bit difficult. However, I smoothed him down by telling him some of my troubles and saying I couldn't spare him. Then I went to *Saint John* and spoke to Stacey for a moment about this leave question.

At 1330 we all slipped and went out and steamed off W. at 16 kts. When off Longships at about 1900 we were told to do a zigzag search between 2 points from W. of the Scillies to about 30'W of Trevose. They are leaving the 2nd Div. to work independently, which is much better in these coastal waters and convoy routes as six ships is too unwieldy a number. Double summer time ended. There has been a very large scale airborne landing in the Rhine delta of Holland.

Monday, 18 September 1944 – At sea

We ran into a tug towing a dredger which, although it was mentioned in the situation report as bound for Falmouth, was so far off the normal route that it was unexpected. I ordered star shell to be fired to illuminate and we fired 3 but they never burst. Wrong elevation on the gun for the long fuse setting. This was at about 0530. Finally used our 20-inch light to illuminate at close range. We reached the end of our patrol line at about 0700 and turned round and zigzagged back again. Extreme visibility but weather reports say there is a depression moving rapidly N.E. towards Iceland and forecasting gales to the W. of Ireland, and so we will probably get the back wash.

At about 1300 it was found that we'd missed a signal which told us to turn W. and proceed at 16 kts until further orders. This was passed to us by *Port Colborne* and we immediately turned. Later, another signal telling us to rendezvous with the Channel portion of an H.X. convoy and support it to the Lizard. This is the first time there has been a channel portion of an Atlantic convoy.[49] Working out courses and speeds we should meet it at 2100, which will be just after dark. At about 1800 we sighted one of the Fleet carriers with destroyer screen and a lot of Avengers and Martlets flying about round it. We sighted the convoy ahead at 2000 and joined up just before dark, which was lucky. Three ships from C 2 group were escorting it and we took up position SS in rear. It is a long time since we were tacked onto an ocean convoy.

Tuesday, 19 September 1944 – At sea

An uneventful night. I ranged up alongside one ship at 0100 and tried to get him to close up but could get absolutely no reply to my signal. There are 35 ships in the convoy and all except about ½ dozen are Liberty ships. This is the first Channel section of an Atlantic convoy going right through to London. We were off the Bishop soon after 0800 and eventually left the convoy at about 1400 when south of the Lizard and proceeded to take up a patrol from Longships to Trevose Head. Got two bottom contacts before reaching the Wolf. We got the second one at 1800 just after we'd plotted the first as a wreck. *Swansea* and *Saint John* proceeded to attack and investigate, while *Port Colborne* went on to support a N. bound convoy. We attacked and attacked without the slightest result and eventually at about 2100 I decided to call it a wreck and pushed on to rejoin *Port Colborne,* who had transferred to the S. going convoy, as per usual nightly orders in this area. The radar operator let us down and before we knew what was happening we nearly hit the *Port Colborne.* How I loathe this night work with meeting and taking station by radar. It puts the wind up me. Got my three ships stationed on the starboard side of the convoy and came south with it to Longships. I'm feeling utterly stale, depressed, and worried. I long to be able to throw the whole thing away and have about 3 weeks' leave. A most lovely hot sunny day with a glassy sea.

Wednesday, 20 September 1944 – At sea

We left the convoy, turned round, and formed up at 0115 and started to sweep back along our patrol. At daylight we were up at Trevose again and turned and came back. Just about midday we got a contact, which on going over with echo sounder proved to be quite a big shoal. Almost at the same time, *Saint John* picked up a ping about 1½ miles off Longships. It was within a mile of a plotted wreck, which we eventually assumed it to be. Feeling all on edge and jumpy. We were given our usual nightly assignment to meet and support a N. going convoy at Longships and transfer to the S. going convoy when met not far S. of Trevose. I had arranged a plan and some fixed screening policy, which I passed to the others by signal this morning, and it worked very well and for once the transfer from one convoy to the other was done without any grey hairs.

A defect to our A/S recorder developed yesterday and we asked permission to go to Falmouth for a new one at daylight tomorrow. The British 2nd Army have made a big advance through Holland with the aid of the airborne troops, who secured several bridges in the line of advance. Another fine, hot day. Received a signal telling us to go to Plymouth with our defect and not Falmouth.

Thursday, 21 September 1944 – At sea/Plymouth/At sea

At about 0400 on arrival off Longships we left the convoy and turned back. At 0600 just as dawn was breaking we left the others and pushed off for Plymouth. Ran into a bit of fog off the Lizard but it soon cleared and turned out another lovely sunny day. Arrived off the breakwater at 1130 and berthed at 1200 alongside a French frigate and I asked the Captain over for a drink. More drink in the wardroom. Just as I was hoping for lunch and to be able to get my head down, Weller arrived and delayed things and so I couldn't get on to my bunk till about 1500. Came to soon after 1700 and found the asdic work would be finished at about 1800.

Listened to the 6 o'clock news. The Allies seem to be up against terrific opposition all along the German front but according to Weller, Admiral Nelles,[50] when he was down here recently, said he thought it would all be over by the end of this month. Went down to the wardroom at 1815 and found the Chief very tight and some pretty steady drinking in progress. We shipped at 1840 and proceeded out of harbour and shaped course W. to rejoin the division off Pendeen. At 2330 when off the Lizard we picked up first a radar and then an A/S contact. Attacked the latter and got an A/S trace of an object on the bottom. Couldn't see result as it was too dark but we could smell oil, and so I decided to hold contact all night and continue attacks at daylight in order to be able to see if there was any result.

Friday, 22 September 1944 – At sea

At about 0200 we were ridden off the contact by two tugs with barges in tow and it took me till 0400 to find it again. I meant to start attacking at about 0700 but I was allowed to sleep on till 0730. By then contact was difficult to hold and it was some time before we could carry out a good echo sounder attack. We were ridden off again, this time by a big American convoy. I had a chat over the T.B.S. with Gwinner, who appeared on the scene with 3 ships of E.G. 1. The attacks brought up nothing but oil, and as the E/S trace was much too big for a U-Boat I classified it as wreck at about 1130 and pushed off to join the division off Pendeen. Hadn't gone far when the inevitable signal from C. in C. received to say "remain in contact until definite evidence." This time I refused to play, signalled my reasons for classification, and went on.

Joined the others at about 1330 and, after transferring mails, continued the patrol. Turned round and came back to Longships in time to meet and screen a large N.'bound convoy at 1600. We remained with it until passed Trevose at 2100, where we met and transferred to the S. going convoy without a great deal of confusion. Feeling much more cheerful somehow today. The news reports the 2nd Army have not yet been able to link up with the airborne troops in and around Arnhem, whose position is now a bit critical. Not such a good day. Colder, windy, and some rain.

Saturday, 23 September 1944 – At sea

At 0330 when back again at Longships we detached from the convoy and turned N.E. again. I made a signal to the 2nd Division to meet me at Trevose Head, and at 0800 they closed me and I transferred mails and then the 2 divisions separated and we each went our own way. A number of small American tugs were passing, towing barges, and the attendant trawler signalled us that one had capsized (one of the tugs). How it could have happened I don't know as only a slight swell was running. At 1320 when back again at Pendeen, we met convoy F.B.C. 90 [France-Bristol Channel coaster] coming N. and although we'd had no signal, I tacked my 3 ships on to it and sure enough, the signal telling us to support it came through shortly after.

In the late afternoon it started to rain and the visibility shut down. At 1530 a Liberator on our port bow reported an oil slick and wreckage and we went over to look, and sure enough there was a big oil patch and 2 Carley floats and a box, which we identified as coming from the tug which capsized this forenoon. The S. bound convoy was late so that we had to go very nearly as far as Hartland

Point with the N. convoy before we met. Transferred to the S. convoy just before dark. Heavy rain squalls and sea and wind rising, and at times in the night the convoy seemed to stand still.

Sunday, 24 September 1944 – At sea

At daylight we were still only half way between Trevose and Pendeen and it was still blowing hard from the N.W. At 0645 some unknown ship flashed at us out of the gloom that she was unable to make headway and was drifting ashore. We went over to investigate and found a large American tug towing a high concrete pontoon affair known as a Phoenix.[51] We stood by and by constant fixing we could see she was just making headway and was going to weather Pendeen Head alright. Another tug and Phoenix with escorting trawler were close by and also just making it. It turned out a nice bright sunny day, but the wind persisted with quite a heavy sea. Crawled along all day with the tow, and at about 1330 *Saint John* and *Port Colborne* were told by C. in C. to join me. But for this we ought to have been on our way with the other division to Londonderry. At about 1400 we passed a big N. bound convoy with E.G. 1 in support and I had a few cracks over the T.B.S. with Gwinner.

At about 1500 it became apparent that the Phoenix was in a poor way. Both reported bad flooding which could not be kept down and increasing. No. 202 was listing to starboard and at 1600 signalled asking that the crew of 7 might be taken off. I tried to lower a boat but didn't like the look of the weather and told the tug to alter course to see if the tow would do better with the sea astern, but the list increased and 202 signalled that the situation was grave, and so I closed and tried to get a Carley Float across and finally lowered my boat too far to leeward and they couldn't pull up. At last I got my stern close enough to get a line and Carley Float over, and we pulled all 7 men over safely and then picked up our boat. A very unpleasant operation, which scared me stiff with that quite big sea running. Shortly after getting the men off the Phoenix ...

Monday, 25 September 1944 – At sea

... fell right over on her beam ends and there remained. The tow by this time had parted and so there was nothing to do, and we expected her to turn right over and sink any moment but she stayed like that and drifted close in shore by Longships. At 1100 we left *Port Colborne* to watch the situation and pushed off for Falmouth to land the survivors. Meanwhile *Saint John* was standing by the other tow, who was doing better and was well on the way to the shelter of Mounts Bay. We arrived Falmouth at 1430 and anchored while a boat was sent and then weighed and went out again. At about 1600 *Saint John* reported the other Phoenix had sunk and all the crew were safe. *Saint John* joined us as we came up to Land's End and at daylight we joined *Port Colborne* off Longships and went close in shore and had a careful search, but there was not a sign of 202 who must have sunk just before going ashore. I reported this and while waiting for orders, we proceeded slowly up towards Trevose.

At 2300 the signal came for us to proceed to Londonderry and off we went at 17 kts. Thick, drizzly weather. Felt tired and depressed and felt I hadn't handled the situation yesterday very well. Had a talk with No. 1 who was fed up with the behaviour and ignorance and uselessness of the other officers. It is a fact that having sent No. 1 away in the boat there wasn't another officer who could lower and hoist it in the sea that was running then. In the evening I had all officers on the bridge and told them they'd got to buck their ideas up. We were up to Bardsey Island by 2030. Clear, fine night.

Tuesday, 26 September 1944 – At sea/Londonderry

At 0400 when off the Mull of Galloway it started to blow, and later on it blew very hard from the N.W. and it held us up quite a lot in the North Channel. We arrived at Lough Foyle at 0915, embarked pilots and went up river. A signal was made giving leave to U.K. to one watch without restrictions at all. My signal, even if unpopular, seems to have had an effect. At 1500 there was a group conference. There is leave from 27th to 4th and then some work up before sailing again on 7th. After the conference I went to see the Commodore who was very nice and told me not to be a bloody fool or take this too seriously and he did *not* consider it disloyal. So that's that, thank God.

Had a talk to C.N.A.A. and Shorto (Comdr E.), and then back on board. Found No. 1 had the whole leave question buttoned up and everything bearing an even strain. At 1900 I went up to the Allied Officers' Club and gave all my C.O.s dinner there and drank a good deal too much. I have got another frigate added to my group – the *Loch Alvie* – with a funny old N.R. 2½ called Old in command.[52] I don't want another as 7 is too many, and I don't want any more of these old men as my C.O.s.

Wednesday, 27 September 1944 – Londonderry

I turned out early and had a very busy forenoon squaring things off before going on leave. Went on board *Monnow* and met all the officers in the wardroom and had some beer with them. Back on board for lunch and at 1400 a car came for me and took me to the station and I caught the 2:30 to Larne. Travelled with Stacey and Old who were both also going on leave. The latter is a nice old boy, but oh, what a talker. We got to Larne at about 1800 and went on board the steamer, and had some food almost at once. We sailed soon after 1830 and had quite a rough passage and everybody was very sick. Arrived Stranraer just after 2100 and got into the train which was v. full. Train left at 2200. These rushed short leaves always give me a feeling of having left undone those things which I ought to have done.

The 2nd Army have been unable to break through to the relief of the airborne troops at Arnhem, who have fought magnificently for about 10 days and all of them have now either been killed, captured, or escaped and broken back into our lines. What a pity. Complete success might have made an enormous difference.

Thursday, 28 September 1944 – London/Prinsted

A pretty uncomfortable night. We got to Euston at about 1030, too late for breakfast, but as I had done very well on Old and Stacey's sandwiches I was alright. Tubed to Leicester Square and then took a taxi to Norton's and had a hair cut and shave and then taxied to Waterloo. Noticed a newly blitzed house just opposite St. James's Palace but nothing else. I gather, however, that the flying bomb while it lasted did enormous damage. Had a glass of beer at the restaurant and then caught the 12:45 to Havant and there I arrived at 1415. J. and Raymond met me with a taxi and we all went home to a very late lunch.

Is it good to be back. Garden looking a bit of wilderness. J. is now keeping 3 ducks and 4 hens and she also has a bulldog puppy – very sweet – known as "Mr. Churchill." Shifted out of uniform after lunch and immediately started in to do a bit of grass mowing. Old Sewell was working in the garden, and J. says he has been awfully good about the vegetables. We bathed Raymond and read to him and put him to bed. His treatment, J. thinks, is doing good. A lovely, sunny day. Gillian has gone to a convent school at Brighton, so unfortunately I've missed her.

6
Deep Open Waters, October-December 1944

A popular maxim says that a change is as good as a rest. After three exasperating months of inshore anti-submarine warfare, in October 1944 Layard and E.G. 9 gained a measure of respite when they found themselves deployed into ocean waters at the southern and northern extremities of the European theatre. It is not that Admiral Horton or Commodore Simpson had any sort of break in mind, as E.G. 9 was just one of a number of support groups patrolling the shallow inshore waters; rather, support groups – the *crème de la crème* of the British and Canadian anti-submarine forces – were being used to bolster operations elsewhere in an effort to take a more offensive posture against the U-boats.[1]

E.G. 9's southward move to the Gibraltar approaches was in response to the actions of a solitary U-boat. *U-1227*, a Type IXC schnorchel boat, had departed Bergen, Norway, on 12 September with orders to patrol the area between Gibraltar and the Azores. While on passage the submarine encountered the westbound convoy ONS 33 about 800 miles west of the British Isles. In what one historian calls "an astonishing display of aggressiveness and boldness," *U-1227*'s commander, *Oberleutnant* Friedrich Altmeier, launched a night surface attack that, not surprisingly, was detected by the escort.[2] A chase ensued under the glare of star shell until Altmeier squeezed off an acoustic homing torpedo that blew the stern off the frigate HMCS *Chebogue*. He then managed to slip away amidst the chaos.[3] Allied naval intelligence organizations knew of *U-1227*'s destination, and the appreciation of the Admiralty's Submarine Tracking Room reveals the quality of their information: "The U-boat is likely to reach Gibraltar in about nine days unless previously found by Azores aircraft or by E.G. 9, which should be on its estimated line of advance by midnight 10th."[4] Once in position, E.G. 9 searched for the marauder with an American hunter-killer group comprising the escort carrier USS *Card* and five destroyer escorts.

Besides placing Layard in a far more familiar ocean environment, the deployment had the additional benefit of getting him back to Gibraltar, his favourite port of call. Throughout his career, "Gib" had served as a refuge from the pressure and formality of bases like Malta and Chatham. Not to stretch an analogy too far, the more relaxed Gibraltar had the same appeal to Layard as destroyer service, while Malta, Chatham, and Portsmouth were more akin to the rigid, "pusser" hierarchy associated with capital ships. He had never had an appointment to Gibraltar, but it was a frequent port of call for the Atlantic and Mediterranean Fleets, and he fell for the place in 1932 when his destroyer *Vivacious* spent two months there on a refit. Shipboard demands were few, so Layard, still a bachelor, let his hair down and took full advantage of a wide range of social and recreational activities in both Gib and southern Spain. Tuesday, 23 February 1932, was typical:

> They flooded the dock but left us there, and brought an oiler in between us and oiled us that way. Another hockey match at 1545 vs. 5th Flotilla. We had only 10 men and were rather badly beaten. Down came the rain just at the end. Really this weather is heartbreaking when one is trying to clean up and paint. I dined with the Wiles and went to another N.O.P. dance. Great fun again in spite of the rain. Barbara Mellor was very sweet. Took the Wiles, Stella Tidd, Mrs. Love, and another chap back on board for ham and eggs. Just after they left at 0315 Martin, Wallace, the Houses, and Mrs. Breed and the Major appeared, so down we went to the wardroom where we found No. 1 and some very shot away submariners and we started circling bars and getting through chairs and God knows what. It was past 0400 before I got to bed. Still pouring with rain.

Layard's attraction to Gibraltar was such that in the dark days after being passed over for promotion he requested a staff position there, only to be disappointed by his appointment to *Cardiff* in the reserve fleet. Returning for a brief layover ten years later, and perhaps overwhelmed by the familiar faces and friendly confines, Layard let his guard down with embarrassing but all too human consequences.

E.G. 9's respite in southern climes lasted scant weeks before they were back in Londonderry. After a short patrol, Layard greeted news that their next operation would be an Arctic convoy to Russia with a succinct "Ugh." His reaction may have related to his sheer dislike of cold weather. On 1 January 1942, as he stood shivering on the bridge of *Broke* awaiting to sail from Iceland, he recalled on old rhyme:

> Cold as the lee of an ice bound shore,
> Cold as the love of an ancient whore.
>
> Cold as a frog in an icy pool,
> Cold as the tip of an Eskimo's tool.
>
> Cold as charity and that's pretty chilly,
> But not half as cold as poor little Willie.

It is more likely that his dismay stemmed from the almost mythic lore that built up around the Murmansk run as the war progressed. Part of this legendary status derived from the challenge posed by the convoys. According to an Admiralty study, the Home Fleet, which was responsible for running the convoys, "had to provide for safety on passage to and from a destination some 2,000 miles distant":

> The route was open to U-boat attack throughout its entire length, was limited to the westward and northward by ice and to the eastward and southward by an enemy-occupied coast, well provided with anchorages whence surface forces could operate at will, and airfields from which aircraft could dominate 1,400 miles of its furthest east, and therefore most vulnerable, waters. The whole route, moreover, including the terminal ports at each end, lay within the end of enemy air reconnaissance, for which he was not lacking in resources, and at two points was crossed by German routine meteorological flights ... Quite apart from enemy interference were the great navigational difficulties in these Arctic waters – strong and uncertain currents; frequent gales, which would disperse the convoys and drive the ships many kilometres from their routes; no sun sights or W/T beacons to enable them to check their positions. And ice, in one form or another, was an ever present menace.[5]

As the First Sea Lord explained to his American counterpart, "The whole thing is a most unsound operation with the dice loaded against us in every direction."[6]

Essentially fleet operations, the Arctic convoys saw some dramatic fighting, including the battles of the Barents Sea and North Cape, and the slaughter of convoy PQ 17.[7] Layard had likely got the flavour of the operations in conversations with his close friend and neighbour Capt. Allan Scott-Moncrieff, who had won a DSO for his actions as a destroyer commander in the long-running battle over PQ 18 in September 1942. Much had changed in the meantime, however, especially with the abandonment of the U-boat campaign in the North Atlantic. Admiral Horton opined in a May 1944 letter to the C-in-C Home Fleet that the Arctic "represented the only prolific area remaining where heavy losses can still be inflicted on both enemy U-boats and long-range aircraft, and this consideration should in no way become secondary in importance to securing the safe and timely arrival of the convoy."[8] As historian Andrew Lambert has demonstrated, Horton wanted to seize the initiative by using the Arctic convoys to mount an offensive against the U-boats. There was some debate on the plan within the Admiralty and the Home Fleet, but the next convoy, JW/RA 59, sailed with two escort carriers and two Western Approaches support groups as part of its screen. Three U-boats were destroyed by escorts or aircraft. The next two convoys had a similar escort and met with equal success, and so in late November 1944 E.G. 9 found itself paired with E.G. 20 as part of the escort for JW/RA 62.

Although Layard had plenty of experience in both fleet and convoy operations, he discovered that the Russian convoys were vastly different. They were faster than the North Atlantic convoys he was used to, they operated in almost perpetual darkness under strict radio silence, escort carriers flew off aircraft from the centre of the formation, causing numerous speed and course changes, and the convoys were opposed by more varied threats – including air attack – each of which called for different defensive schemes. Special North Russian Convoy Instructions gave direction on how to deal with all these factors, but there was still a lot to learn. Layard quickly discovered that station keeping posed the greatest challenge. Support groups like E.G. 9 were stationed about ten miles, or sixteen kilometres, ahead of the forward destroyer screen on either bow of the convoy. "I found that during the long nights," Layard complained, "it was far from easy to keep contact with an outer screen, which was itself faced with the problem of keeping touch with the convoy, and consequently proved a very fluctuating point of contact. The problem became a real headache during alterations of course. Although a very careful plot was kept, there were many times when I was quite uncertain whether I was ahead or on the bow of the convoy."[9] Moreover, information of convoy alterations or speed changes often failed to reach the outlying support groups, raising the dangers of collision or of losing contact. On top of all that, the new German tactic of forming a U-boat barrier off the entrance to Kola Inlet represented a dangerous trip-wire that could ensnare escorts and merchant ships alike. All in all, there was much to be concerned with, and that, perhaps, justified Layard's mournful "Ugh!"

Tuesday, 3 October 1944 – Prinsted/London

We were to have taken R. in to Portsmouth to get the doctor's report on what effect his treatment was having, but being my last day and such a lovely day, we rang up and postponed the visit. I gardened hard, picking some apples among other things and bedding out some hydrangeas which J. had bought. All too soon it was time to change into my uniform. J. and R. were going to sleep with Jane and so at about 1730 we all went round there in the car and we bathed and put R. to bed and then had a drink with Jane, and then J. and I came home again for an early supper. Then we drove to Havant station and I caught the 8:13 to London.

I sometimes wonder if these short leaves are worth while. They are *so* unsettling. I don't know how to go back to the worries, responsibilities, and fears of my job. Oh, for the war to end. There is no doubt about it, I am not a man of action. Got to Waterloo at 2240 and tubed to Euston, where, thank God, I found I had a sleeper to Liverpool on the 11:45.

Wednesday, 4 October 1944 – Liverpool/Londonderry

I didn't sleep very well but at least it was comfortable. Shaved and left the train at Lime Street Station at about 0730 and found a Wren with a car to drive me to the Exchange Hotel, where I had breakfast. At 0900 I went out and had a hair cut and then went to Derby House. It was too early to see the C. in C. but I saw the Chief of Staff (MacIntyre), "Smitty" and Staff Officer (Escorts).[10] I hear *Meon* is leaving the group and is going to Canada to be the S.O.'s ship of a new group with Balfour as S.O.[11] E.G. 9 are expected to go round to the east coast this time to work under C. in C. Rosyth. *Swansea*'s refit date in Canada is Nov. 15, and so I suppose after this next trip I shall be farmed out to another ship temporarily and live in great discomfort.

At about 1130 I had an audience with Max [Horton]. He was extremely nice about my signal and said as long as I realized it was a stupid signal to make all could be forgotten.[12] We had quite a long chat. Think I made some rather stupid remarks about visits from senior R.N. officers. After that I went back to the hotel and at about 1230 a car came for me and drove me to Speke aerodrome, where I caught the 1300 civil plane to Belfast. This trip took about 2 hours and was quite bumpy. On landing I went to the naval offices and got a [travel] warrant on to Londonderry and a car to the station and caught the 3:46 to Derry, where I arrived at 1850 and so on board.

Am depressed. I hear we sail for Moville p.m. tomorrow, so it is going to be an awful rush. No major crises, however, in my absence.

Thursday, 5 October 1944 – Londonderry

I turned out fairly early, feeling homesick and miserable, and got down to a variety of matters that had to be attended to. Went to a radar lecture at 0900, which lasted about an hour, and then I went to Ops. and the Training office and got hold of our sea programme orders for Larne, etc. Then went to see C.N.A.A. about S206s and one thing and another, then walked to Gieves to try on a pair of grey flannel trousers and then back on board to send for all and sundry about our programme. *Monnow* and *Loch Alvie* came to see me and then we all went over to *Meon* to say good bye to Balfour and take a drink off him. *Loch Alvie* came back and had some lunch with me and we talked about group cruising diagrams and group orders, and when he had gone I did the ½ yearly recommends. I am recommending no one but No. 1, who goes in for qualified status and promotion.

A filthy day, raining. The group slipped at 1700-1730. We ran into fog on the way down, which, however, cleared at Moville, where we arrived at about 1900 to find that the tug and target allotted for our night shoot hadn't got the signal and was still anchored. Bonnett,[13] one of the base Gunnery officers, and an awfully nice R.N.V.R. Lieutenant came with us. I formed the group up at the Lough Foyle buoy and went out to the firing area but owing to the delay with the tug we didn't get started on our night shoot until about 2300. Low cloud made the star shell illumination very difficult and most of us never got a round off at all, and all came round for another shoot. Our effort was deplorable. Falconer, the new Gunnery Officer, was pathetic. He just didn't know the first thing and he is supposed to be a qualified little "g" officer.[14] Owing to the difficult cloud conditions all ships came round for ...

Friday, 6 October 1944 – Londonderry

... a second run. Our second effort was no improvement on the first. Ours was the last run, after which we returned and anchored at Moville at 0400. At 0700 *Saint John* and *Stormont* went out for HF/DF calibration, the rest of us weighed at 0815 and first of all did a radar calibration exercise and then with a tug and target we did straddle correction exercise and a day shoot. Again ours was *not* impressive. I got very impatient with the slowness and lack of anticipation shown by all ships while manoeuvring for position and so on. Skinner in *Monnow* is an awful old fool I think.

At the end of that practice, *Swansea, Monnow,* and *Port Colborne* just had time to get into position for a close range A.A. shoot scheduled for 1330, but we were kept hanging about till 1500 before the aircraft appeared. When he *did* come he certainly lost no time and we got the shoot off very quickly and then we made tracks for harbour. At the Lough Foyle buoy we transferred Bonnett to the *Stormont* for another shoot and went in meaning to oil, but found a second oiler alongside *Empire Control* and *Monnow* and *Port Colborne* on the other side, so we anchored. Owing to the slow rate of oiling it was quite a problem to get all ships topped up. Bonnett came back in my cabin. It was eventually not till 2300 that we got alongside the oiler with *Port Colborne* outside us. I went to see the Master, who was very nice and explained that he was giving the ships the oil as fast as he could. A dull, rather hazy day but calm. A tiring day.

Saturday, 7 October 1944 – Larne

Turned out after about 3 hours' sleep and we slipped and the whole group proceeded to sea at 0300, arriving at Larne for group training at 0730 where we anchored. I am rather wondering what awful inefficiencies are going to be brought to light. At about 0915 staff officers from *Philante*[15] came on board each ship, and at 0930 we weighed and proceeded for our first exercise, which was Operation Scabbard with a real bottomed S/M in the area which had to be found.[16] It was rather a farce really because A/S conditions were awful, and even when at last we had to get him to show himself by means of a smoke candle and had buoyed the position with a dan buoy, we couldn't get any sort of a ping and we found 6 ships a bit of a crowd. We had an awfully nice staff officer on board, an R.N.V.R. 2½ called Anderson.

At 1330 the submarine came to the surface. He was fitted with a mock up snorkel, and our next exercise was to see at what radar ranges we could pick up the snorkel when just showing above water. Very dull. Our R.X.C. radar set failed to pick up anything, even at short range. At 1630 we surfaced the submarine, closed the harbour anchorage, and dropped the staff officers, and then the whole group went round to Bangor to top up with oil. We arrived there at 1800 but it was 2330 before we'd all finished and the group got under way and proceeded S. down the Irish Channel. Having expected to be working on the E. coast under C. in C. Rosyth, we have now got entirely different orders to proceed to a position 42°25' N., 22°20' W., which is right out in the Atlantic and not far N. of the Azores. I feel I've almost forgotten what to do in deep open waters.

Sunday, 8 October 1944 – At sea

An uneventful passage down to Irish Sea (so much so that I had a bath before breakfast), except that when we came to where K4 buoy ought to be it was no where to be seen, and so we altered for the swept channel S. of Ireland on dead reckoning. We arrived at the end of the swept channel at 1215 and altered to 230° but at about 1345, Kilgour came to me and said he had discovered that he had laid off the swept channel wrongly and that we were now 11 miles too far to the S. and presumably right in our minefield. As a matter of fact, judging by the number of dan buoys about the sweepers have been busy here and so the risk is probably not that great, but I turned 90° to starboard at once and I was very glad when at 1430 we were once more safely back in the swept channel.

At 1830 we reached the end and turned to our course for our position and formed up in line abreast. It is nice to have some open water ahead instead of having to think of altering course about every 2 hours. At about 2030 *Saint John* and then *Loch Alvie* got contacts, which took some time to investigate before they could be classified non sub. At 2330 *Port Colborne* got a contact and we went back to help. Other ships also got pings and eventually I decided we were in a fish or non sub area and went on, but it was 0130 before we were all formed up again.

Monday, 9 October 1944 – At sea

Our asdic set is giving trouble. At 1115 we picked up an echo at 850 yds with distinct low doppler, but no matter whether we went 10 kts or stopped, it still stayed at the same range. We wasted a couple of hours chasing this thing round before deciding it must be some sort of gremlin in the set. Later *Loch Alvie* reported the same thing. At about 1600 *Monnow* reported asdic trouble, but as our set is still far from right I couldn't let Earl go over. Things improved in both ships later on, thank God. We got a signal that the U-boat which torpedoed the *Chebogue* was estimated to be in the vicinity of the position we were making for and telling us to sweep a certain area. I am feeling fussed and frightened as I feel I shall make a balls of a hunt to destruction, which is what this will probably develop into if we find it. After so many months of shallow water work the group is not well trained in the deep water technique. Mr. Churchill and Mr. Eden have arrived in Moscow for talks with Stalin. Calm but overcast day.

Tuesday, 10 October 1944 – At sea

Feeling more confident. Lots of sleep last night. I saw requestmen and defaulters and at noon we put the clocks back one hour. The Chief Telegraphist informed me that he had found a transformer in one of the sets he doesn't use which would do for *Saint John*'s T.B.S., which has burned out and is out of action, so at about 1330 she came up alongside and we passed a line over to her. When the transformer was ½ way across I'm damned if it didn't drop off. I was furious – just gross carelessness. I then sent *Saint John* ahead to lower a boat into which I put my T.B.S. for her. Later on the radar mechanic dug out yet another transformer, this time a radar spare for our R.X.C. set which he said would do for *Saint John*'s T.B.S., and so she closed again just before 1600. This time we got it safely across and in about an hour's time, *Saint John*'s T.B.S. was working. Thank God we can now get all ships on this line and needn't use R/T (which can be D/F'd) at all. We got a signal from senior British naval officer Azores saying aircraft would be patrolling our area continuously. We had a very sharp wind and rain squall at about 2000 but later on it cleared up. At 2300 I reduced to 11 kts and opened ships out to 3 miles as we had reached the edge of our area. Much warmer in these latitudes (44° N., 20° W.). A week ago was my last day at home. Well, it is something to be no longer able to say, "This time last week."

Wednesday, 11 October 1944 – At sea

At about 0400 on arrival at the middle of the top edge of our area, we turned by Easy Item to 160°. An otherwise uneventful night. We sighted a sailing ship in the forenoon, which I sent *Port Colborne* to investigate. Turned out to be a Portuguese with everything in order. Tried out one of the new anti-Gnat zigzags, which consists of short bursts of high speed and short bursts of low. We did 4 minutes at 15 kts, then altered course 60° and reduced to 7 kts for 5 minutes. At 1500 we altered 90° to port and at 1900 180° to starboard. Our patrol area has been shifted further to the S.E. for the next 24 hours from midnight, and so at 2230 we turned by E.I. to 150° to get into the new area. Really hot weather like the weather we had in the Bay in August.

Thursday, 12 October 1944 – At sea

A quiet night with plenty of sleep for me. At 1000 I told *Saint John, Port Colborne,* and *Stormont* to close and carried out a dummy barrage creep attack to see how communications worked and to test our range finder. It went alright and I only wish it was going to be as easy as that in practice. As I had reached the S. part of our area we did an E.I. turn to 070° and at about 1430 we turned N. again. Got a signal in the evening from an American carrier group (C.T.G. 22.2) who are also operating in our area, giving their movements and intentions. As we have to shift our area yet further S. at midnight they will be clear of us to the N. At 2000 we turned 180° and crossed into our new area at midnight. Hot day.

Friday, 13 October 1944 – At sea

At 0130 I was called and shown an emergency signal from the American Task Force reporting radar and then sonar contact with a submarine shortly after midnight. There was a delay this end in getting the signal through a stupid coding error. I turned to close the position, which was about 100 miles off. It is maddening how long it takes to turn the group when spread out at 3 miles' distance. At 0830 we sighted the carrier, who told us the position of contact was v. different to that reported. It subsequently transpired he had signalled the longitude one degree wrong. Tried to find out what was happening and what was wanted of me but could get no coherent reply.

The carrier U.S.S. *Card* has 2 escorts with her and 3 are away hunting. We soon sighted one, who said he was near the scene of the last contact at 0108 but couldn't tell me where the other 2 were. All v. uncooperative. However, at 1020 *Monnow* got an A/S contact and for 3 hours we bummed round, picking it up and losing it and never sure if we were on the same one. Our set was working abominably or else the conditions were v. poor. I thought once in deep water this uncertainty about classification would end.

At 1310 decided it was all non sub and soon after the 2 hunting destroyer escorts appeared, one of which was S.O. and the carrier told them to join us for "line search" first of all putting me in charge but later at my suggestion making the American S.O., as he knows much more about the situation and the policy of his task group.[17] We swept S. along the U/B's most likely course until we reached his furthest on position at 2100, when we turned and carried out a Gamma search at right angles to his course 25 miles either side of mean point during the night. The Yankee S.O. and I had to discuss the method of carrying out the turns but it all worked v. well, although I don't know how well the mixed group would have handled an emergency. He thinks the U/B was damaged but for the moment it seems to have got away.

Saturday, 14 October 1944 – At sea

Our 8 ships patrolled to and fro during the night and although I fully expected to see something, nothing in fact showed up. I had asked permission to remain in company with the Yanks as it seemed to me if we are both looking for the same U-boat it is most desirable that we should work as one unit. By daylight, however, there had been no reply and so I felt I must comply with the F.O.G.M.A.'s[18] last signal, which was to sweep out a new area from 0800. I signalled this to C.T.G. 22.2 and he recalled his two D.E.s and gave us permission to proceed. I must say I'm rather glad to be on our own as this signalling business is a bit tricky. It appears this U-Boat is steering about S.S.E. at 3 knots and the search area is shifted daily about 80 miles in that direction.

Went mess deck rounds. We are now about 37° N. and 19° W. Hot, sunny day, but wind rising with a tropical storm forecasted in our area at about 1900. At about 1700 we got a signal from F.O.G.M.A. asking *Card* to take us under his orders and form a composite search force. *Card* told us to continue our patrol for the night. At about midnight it started to blow hard from the S.W. when we had just turned to 245°, which conveniently headed the wind and sea. From the news, we seem to be completely stationary all along the W. front and unable to make any headway, which is depressing.

Sunday, 15 October 1944 – At sea

It blew very hard in the middle watch and the sea got up and we had to reduce to 8 kts but it was short lived. The wind veered round to the N.W. and by daylight it had calmed down quite a lot. Got a signal from C.T.G. 22.2 giving us an area to patrol, and all day we patrolled it in a more or less E. and W. direction. A very stuffy, muggy day in spite of the quite fresh wind. Too wet and windy for prayers. Sent off a full report as we are all getting to the 50% mark [of fuel remaining] and some under it, and later on heard 2 ships were coming out from Gib and when they joined about p.m. 18th *Saint John* and *Loch Alvie* were to proceed to Gib to oil. It didn't say what the rest of us were to do.

Monday, 16 October 1944 – At sea

Just before 0200 *Port Colborne* reported a radar contact at 12 miles ahead, which she only held for about 2 minutes and then lost. At first I didn't believe it possible to pick up a U-boat at that range, but *Port Colborne* was so insistent that it could have been that I told her and *Saint John* to proceed ahead and sweep round estimated position of contact while the rest of us advanced at 11 kts. When we came abreast of the contact I brought the other ships round with me and made a thorough search of the area before daylight. Absolutely nothing. We have had and have still got absolutely bloody results from our A/S set this trip with reverbs petering out at about 1,500 yds. Earl assures me it is water conditions and not the set, and all ships seem to be getting rather poor results. I feel a U-Boat could easily escape detection under these conditions.[19]

Having found nothing in the area I swept S.S.E., which seems to be his general direction, to a new furthest on position and then patrolled at right angles. I signalled *Card* about my contact and he closed, but I never saw him or his aircraft. He told me to patrol S.E. of last contact for the night. At 1500 I transferred a sick man to *Stormont* so that their doctor can look after him. A lovely, hot, sunny day. Shirt sleeve weather. At 1900 we took up our night patrol position. We are now right down to about 36°40' N., 19° W., about level with Gibraltar. The Japanese announce a big naval battle off Formosa and claim to have sunk and damaged most of the American fleet. No word one way or the other from Washington, except that the bombing of Formosa by Super Fortresses is in progress.[20]

Tuesday, 17 October 1944 – At sea

All was quiet until 0500 when *Stormont* reported a radar contact at 6,000 [yards] which faded out at 5,000. He thought it was probably atmospherics, but just the same we couldn't neglect it and we swept all round the area until daylight. In spite of the short "sighting" range and excellent A/S conditions, we found absolutely nothing. Our A/S set is back to normal at last, thank God. At about 0730 we turned to the S.E. on the assumption that this elusive U-boat is travelling in that direction at 2.5-3 kts. I signalled *Card* reporting my very doubtful contact and saying failure to make A/S contact in existing conditions was puzzling. He replied that in his opinion now the attacks on the night of 12-13 by his escorts were lethal and that the U/B was sunk. The British authorities won't accept that on the evidence available.[21]

We bummed about all day but found nothing. Hot, stuffy day. At 1400 our sick man was transferred once again, this time to *Saint John* who leaves for Gib tomorrow, as he is seriously ill and should go to hospital. Assumed a N.E. and S.W. patrol for the night about 60 miles S.S.E. of last night's line. At about 2200 we got a signal from Gib saying a Fortress aircraft had reported a long oil slick at about noon in a position about 60 miles W. of us.

Wednesday, 18 October 1944 – At sea

Just after midnight a signal from me to *Card* asking if I should investigate the oil was crossed by a signal from him telling me to do so, and we pushed on to 15 kts. We aimed for a furthest on position assuming a S.E.'ly course and from there, swept up to the reported position and beyond and then back again, and were over the spot at 0700 when it was just light. Nothing seen or heard. Swept the vicinity till about 1000 and then turned E. to rendezvous with 2 B.E.C.s[22] (*Kilmington* and *Kilbirnie*) who are coming out to let 2 of our ships go and fuel. We met them at 1500 and I detached *Loch Alvie* and *Saint John*. Our 2 guests came up alongside and I passed them over some orders and had a chat and then they took up station. Having run dry of all original ideas on the subject of where to patrol for the night, I applied to C.T.G. 22.2 who gave me an area. The night was without incident. I must say coming down into these latitudes takes a month off the winter. It is really hot and we saw flying fish today, which seems quite sub tropical.

Thursday, 19 October 1944 – At sea

F.O.G.M.A. had told us to detach 2 more ships to Gib for fuel today on arrival of *Verity*. I was going in with *Monnow* as we are the lowest in fuel, but *Port Colborne* sent me a signal saying he was suffering the agonies of the damned with neuralgia and asking if he could go in. As we *can* last a bit longer and as it would be unfair to ask him to take over S.O. in that condition, I decided to send him. We steamed last and effected a rendezvous with *Verity* in 35°11' N., 14° W. at about 1730. It is hard to believe she was the first ship I commanded 16 years ago. It was a very good 2 years I spent in her.

After passing her some orders and having a chat, we turned N. to patrol between 35° N. and 36° N. as ordered by "Bloodhound."[23] *Monnow* and *Port Colborne* pushed off and we are now a very motley crew. Just before 2100 *Kilbirnie* reported a small disappearing pip on his radar at 13 miles nearly astern. I felt very sceptical but turned the whole group to close at 15 kts. *Kilbirnie* reported one more fleeting contact at 9 miles. The extreme range and the circumstances seem to me very unlikely. Bloodhound and his escorts were quite close at the time. On arrival near the position I reduced to 7 kts and carried out a very thorough box search covering as far as I could judge all his possible furthest on positions and in spite of good A/S conditions we found nothing. At about 0500 I gave up the search and proceeded N. again. I wish I knew the capabilities of these new radar sets. *Kilbirnie* has an American set.

Friday, 20 October 1944 – At sea

I found it v. difficult to make up my mind on last night's radar contact by *Kilbirnie.* With this American set it is apparently just possible to pick up a S/M at that range, but the circumstances and quick fading of the contact are very unlike what you would expect from a U-boat. I signalled C.T.G. 22.2 giving him the position and saying in my opinion it was non sub. We continued patrolling in the same area. I went Gunnery rounds and was glad to see a big improvement all round. Got a very obscure signal from F.O.G.M.A. saying another ship, the *Hyderabad,* is being sailed to rendezvous with us at 1300 tomorrow but it isn't clear whether on joining *Swansea* and *Stormont* detach. We *must* go as oil fuel is running v. low, but *Stormont* could stay a day or two longer. However, I decided to take her along too and have *Verity* in charge of his mixed bag.

I switched on my wireless at about 1800 and heard the band of the Royal Marines Portsmouth Division conducted by Capt. Vivian Dunn, M.V.O., which made me feel quite homesick. Reading H.V. Morton's *I See Two Englands.* His descriptions of England also give me a terrible longing. I wonder whether if you belong to a vast country like America or Canada, you can ever feel the love for the country itself that you can belonging to a small country like England.

The Americans have landed in the Philippines. The operation is apparently on a very big scale and this claim by the Japs to have won a big naval victory off Formosa seems to be just a complete parcel of lies.

Saturday, 21 October 1944 – At sea

An uneventful night. At about 0900 we turned E. and at 1300 we met the corvette *Hyderabad,* who joined up with *Verity* and his 2 B.E.C.s, and *Swansea* and *Stormont* detached to Gib. We are down to 17% fuel remaining. Quite a fresh N.E. wind, which made it cooler than it's been for some days, however, it didn't stop us doing onto 16 kts. I dictated my report of proceedings to the writer and I also went mess deck rounds.

Sunday, 22 October 1944 – At sea/Gibraltar

I meant to have spoken about yesterday being the anniversary of Trafalgar to the ship's company, but there was no time for prayers as we were at the entrance to the Straits at 0800. We got in to Gibraltar and secured alongside the South Mole at about 1145. Capt. D.'s staff came down on board to say that ships' companies of the 9th D.F.[24] had been breaking up the town last night and threatening stoppage of all leave if it happened again. Oh these Canadians!

We met *Monnow* and *Port Colborne* leaving as we approached and *Loch Alvie* sailed before them. *Saint John* is still here as her defects have not yet been made good. Sammy Boucher is still Capt. D. but he is playing cricket.[25] I went to A.C.H.Q. and had a chat with Tufnell, who was a Snotty in the 6th Flotilla with me.[26] He is going to take us away from C.T.G. 22.2 and bring us in to patrol the entrance to the Straits.

After lunch I cleared lower deck and spoke to the sailors about behaviour ashore. I went ashore myself at about 1445 calling in to see *Saint John* on the way. Went up to the Armada Gardens and watched the cricket, and Sammy Boucher gave me some tea in the interval. He also told me that David Abbott[27] was here in the *Enchantress,* so at about 1700 I went down on board, but on going into his cabin I heard he was turned in and as I could see a Wren officer's hat on his sofa I came to certain conclusions. Went ashore again and walked about to waste time. Passed the N.O.P. and the Bristol and the football grounds. Memories of the past. Back to the *Enchantress* at 1815, where I found David and we sat drinking and yarning. Later a Wren officer arrived and we walked along to the Victoria for food and finally came back on board *Swansea.* Beautiful, hot day.

Monday, 23 October 1944 – Gibraltar/At sea

I woke up at about 0700 to find I had been violently sick and that my left thumb was dislocated, and with no recollection whatsoever of how I did it. Having first cleaned up the mess I went for the sick berth attendant, who tried and failed to put my thumb back. He went for the doctor of the *Stormont,* who also tried and failed, and so he rang up the Hospital, and I was taken up there and had an X ray and then after considerable delay I was put to bed and finally wheeled into the theatre and given an anaesthetic and the thumb put back while I was out. I didn't come to till about 1400. At about 1630 the doctor of the *Stormont* arrived and said we were sailing at 1900. I then managed to get hold of the R.A.M.C. colonel who very reluctantly allowed me to get up and I was on board just before 1800. Feeling just a bit groggy and most frightfully ashamed of myself. I know I was alright when I came on board but what happened after I got to the wardroom or how many more drinks I had I don't know. No. 1, who was charming, said I did not disgrace myself but I'm not so sure. To think that I should do this, especially after my talk to the sailors. It is so degrading.[28]

Swansea and *Saint John* slipped at 1900, leaving *Stormont* behind to dock for a leaky [asdic] dome. No. 1 treated me like a small child and insisted on me doing as little as possible. Just before midnight we got a radar contact just 1,500 yards beyond *Saint John,* who also got it but thought it false. It disappeared after about a minute or two but we closed *Saint John* for a search. Another lovely day.

Tuesday, 24 October 1944 – At sea

I abandoned the search at about 0240 and altered course to join *Monnow, Loch Alvie,* and *Port Colborne,* who were then within radar range patrolling the edge of a large rectangle in the approaches to the Straits. We joined up just as they arrived at the N.E. corner and did an E.I. turn to the west. Uneventful day. Beautiful weather. A signal from Admiralty to F.O.G.M.A. asking him to detach us in time to be back at Londonderry by Nov. 1st.

I'm feeling not quite 100% I think on account of the drug, and oh so terribly ashamed of myself. I feel I must have lost the respect and confidence of all on board because I feel they must know or guess that my accident was because I was tight. Thumb and hand v. swollen and a bit painful. Just before midnight *Monnow* reported a disappearing radar contact, which he thought was a wave or false echo, however, I brought the whole group round and did a thorough search of the area without result.

Wednesday, 25 October 1944 – At sea

Abandoned the search and set off on a N.'ly course up the eastern edge of our patrol. At 0630 just at the crack of dawn, *Port Colborne* reported a disappearing radar contact at 5,000 yds. I didn't believe it was anything but I laid on a very thorough search. There must be some peculiarity of sea or atmosphere round here that gives these funny blips on the radar screen, which fade at once. Abandoned the search at 1200 and continued patrol but reported this one to F.O.G.M.A. We'd hardly been on our way for an hour when *Monnow* got an A/S contact, which at first he said was promising but he kept on losing it. We all came round and had a sniff at it and did Observant and finally after about 1½ hours we classified it as fish and went on. Got a signal later on telling us to leave patrol at 0800 tomorrow and return to Gib for fuel.

Brilliant sunny day again but not so hot on account of a stiff N.'ly breeze. Still feeling ashamed and depressed. I wish I knew how tight I had appeared. I must have got to my cabin from the wardroom alright and then I imagine when undressing (probably when taking my trousers off) I fell over and put my thumb out and got a terrific bruise on my back. I had also been very sick, which is so disgusting. I don't feel I shall ever be able to address the ship's company again or be able to lecture a drunken man.

Thursday, 26 October 1944 – At sea/Gibraltar

An uneventful night. We turned on to an easterly course at 0200 and at the first crack of dawn at about 0630 the African mountains were visible, although they must have been 70-80 miles away. At 0800 we increased speed to 16 kts, left our patrol, and proceeded through the Straits to Gib, where we arrived at about 1300. *Swansea* and *Saint John* went to an oiler alongside the Coaling Pier and the rest to an oiler at the buoys. I went ashore soon after securing. Saw Tufnell at A.C.H.Q., who said we were sailing for Derry at 1400 tomorrow. After hanging about for quite a long time I saw Sammy Boucher who was giving himself rather a long dinner hour. Everyone enquired about my thumb and smiled, and I felt such a fool.

Went off to the ships at the oiler in Capt. D.'s barge and explained that they had to move to the South Mole on completion and then I went back on board. Read and snoozed in my chair. My shame weighs on me so much that I feel I can't take any interest or pleasure in anything. No. 1 came along to my cabin at about 1915 and persuaded me to go ashore with him. We went to the Yacht Club first of all, where later on David Abbott appeared, who assured me I didn't disgrace myself, and finally we went to the Bristol for dinner. I told No. 1 how this matter was weighing on my mind and he promised and assured me that no one on board realized I'd done it in a state of drunkenness, and that even if they did know, it wouldn't make any difference and I wouldn't lose their respect and affection. Felt happier when I got back on board. Lovely day.

Friday, 27 October 1944 – Gibraltar/At sea

I found out this morning that No. 1 late last night in a fit of exuberance had invited the Admiral in my name to come on board for drinks this forenoon. A very good thing, although I did feel that really he [the Admiral] might have done something for me first, considering that he really knew me quite well in the past (Vice Admiral Sir Harold Burrough). I made various signals to the group about slipping and at about 0930 I went ashore to see the Naval Provost Marshal and find out how my Canadians had behaved. I couldn't find him but from all accounts the behaviour was good. Before returning I had a chat with Morris,[29] who is Captain of a radar ship which we were lying alongside.

When I got back on board I found Skinner, Old, and Angus in my cabin and we had a talk about group matters and I made them stay to meet the Admiral, who came by barge at 1230. Sammy Boucher, David Abbott, Tufnell, and one or two others were there too. Burrough was charming and it was a good party. We just had time for lunch before slipping at 1400. We left *Stormont* behind still in dock having her asdic dome fixed.

I got a letter from the Captain of the *Cormorant*[30] complaining about the behaviour of Falconer, who had been abusive and threatening to one of his sentries. Falconer was tight. Having congratulated myself on the good behaviour of the ship's company it is too bad that an officer must disgrace himself and the ship. Sent for him in my cabin at 2000, logged him and stopped his leave and wine bill. He is a useless type. He doesn't know his job and he doesn't know how to behave like a gentleman. We are routed straight back to Derry at 15 kts.

Saturday, 28 October 1944 – At sea

We passed Cape St. Vincent at about 0530. Blowing very fresh from the N., and in spite of a rising glass and cloudless sky, it continued to blow and the sea got up and we had to come down to 12 kts, and even so it was v. wet. Got a signal from C. in C. W.A. to C.N.M.O. suggesting I should be appointed temporarily to *Loch Alvie* when *Swansea* goes to Canada to refit and that Old should remain in command. Oh dear, another new start in a new ship in the difficult position of travelling S.O. I got down to thinking out S206s on the officers.

This head sea is a damned nuisance as it is holding us up badly. Went up to 14 kts again in the 1st watch but had to drop back to 13 later on. At 2300 on reaching 40° N. and 11° W. we turned due north. There has been a very big air naval engagement off the Philippines between the Americans and the Japanese, and the Yanks say the Japs' navy has suffered its greatest defeat. 29 naval ships sunk or damaged including 2 carriers, 2 battleships, and cruisers, and 10 destroyers sunk and 5 battleships damaged. American losses are 1 light and 1 escort carrier, 1 cruiser, and 2 destroyers.

Sunday, 29 October 1944 – At sea

Still blowing hard from the N. and we cannot push on beyond 13 kts and even at that speed every now and then we ship a big one and bump badly. No hope of arriving Lough Foyle before 1st now. I spent most of the forenoon on flimsies and S206s. Borrowed a very good novel (*Random Harvest* by James Hilton) from No. 1 after lunch, which I read hard the rest of the day. After dark the wind and sea went down and we were able by 2200 to push on to 15 kts. A wet and uncomfortable day. Latest figures for the Pacific battle. Of the 60 Jap ships engaged, all but 2 were sunk or damaged. Among the 24 actually sunk are included 4 aircraft carriers, 2 battleships, and 6 heavy cruisers. American losses 1 light aircraft carrier and 5 smaller ships. A tremendous victory for the Yanks, and practically all done by aircraft I believe.[31]

Monday, 30 October 1944 – At sea

We kept up our 15 kts but the wind freshened again in the morning and blew quite hard from the N.N.E., and the ship was very wet all day and I couldn't get any exercise. Again it went down in the evening. Brilliant full moon. Just before 2400 we picked up radar contact of the *King George V*[32] and escort destroyers and had to alter course to clear them. From the situation report, however, I was expecting to meet them and was prepared. We are routed up the W. coast of Ireland.

Tuesday, 31 October 1944 – At sea

A flat calm day at last. I was very worried to get a signal from *Loch Alvie* saying he had developed a leak in his fore magazine and vent and distorted frames as a result of the bumping into head seas in the last day or two. I have only just seen a signal from C. in C. impressing on all the necessity for avoiding unnecessary weather damage now that the winter is on us, so I shall receive an awful blast for not easing down more. The visibility was not too good going up the Irish coast, but at 1700 we were off Eagle Island and turned to 047° to make Tory Island.

Wednesday, 1 November 1944 – At sea

At 0210 shortly after rounding Tory Island, a red flare was sighted on the port bow and shortly after we intercepted a signal from *Affleck* saying a ship had been torpedoed in a position about 15 miles N. of Fanad Light, which presumably explained the flare. E.G. 1 and E.G. 26[33] we know are supporting a convoy through the N.W. approaches. We immediately increased to 16 knots to close the position and I thought, "Hell, just as we are on the doorstep of our lay over we've got this situation to deal with."[34] We arrived at the scene of the action at about 0400. Gwinner in *Affleck* – "Jutland"[35] – was making the T.B.S. red hot with signals and chat but taking charge most ably. It was one of his own D.E.s, the *Whitaker,* which had been torpedoed, but she was still afloat minus her bows. It was bright full moon which helped as we swept the area given us by "Jutland." We attacked a bottom echo at 0530 and brought up a lot of aircraft tyres which proved to be a wreck. Shortly after 0800 we got another bottom contact, which *Swansea* and *Saint John* attacked bringing up lots of oil and masses of fish. *Affleck* came over to look at it later on and we finally defined it as wreck.

At 1330 E.G. 1 formed us all up in line abreast (17 ships) and we carried out a "blitz" attack of the area, dropping 1 charge every minute. Most impressive but without any result. We then did a short sweep close in shore from Fanad Light to Horn Head and then spread for the night sweep. All 3 groups disposed 4 miles apart and ships sweeping between Inishtrahull and Tory Island. After a very clear day it became quite foggy soon after dark and fixing the ship was difficult. Got very little sleep.

Thursday, 2 November 1944 – At sea

At daylight E.G. 1 had thought out a new search scheme, and we were told to split into 2 divisions and carry out 2 Gamma searches. The visibility was variable but mostly thick fog. At about 1200 we intercepted a signal from *Stormont* in the other division reporting a disappearing radar contact and later on a fleeting A/S contact. Knowing *Monnow*'s A/S was out of action, I took *Port Colborne* over to the scene and carried out a thorough search without any success. As a matter of fact *Stormont* later on said he thought his radar pip was a false one.

At 1600 we abandoned the search and returned to our divisional gammas. Shortly afterwards we got a good A/S contact and ran over and got an echo sounder trace. We then attacked with H/H and by the explosions obtained a definite hit. *Saint John,* who was following up, reported oil and bits of wood. The wood, however, was old and water sodden and did not float long. *Swansea* and *Saint John* together carried out 3 more attacks but only oil came up. Eventually at 1800 I classified wreck and took *Saint John* off to our night patrol position, which was the same as last night but with ships only 2 miles apart and *Port Colborne* patrolling close off Sheep Haven entrance in case the U/B had been tying up in there. There was considerable confusion in taking up our station as not only were we late but E.G. 26 was late too, however, we eventually got sorted out and thank God the visibility improved and we could see some shore lights for fixing. At 2122 *Port Colborne* reported gaining A/S contact but she was ...

Friday, 3 November 1944 – At sea/Londonderry

... constantly losing it and it didn't sound v. convincing. However, I told *Monnow* to go over and help, and eventually at 2230 I reckoned I ought to go and settle the matter and so left the line and closed Horn Head. I felt convinced from *Port Colborne*'s reports that the whole thing was bogus in spite of his assurance that there was movement, but soon after arrival I got a ping, which echo sounder showed to be a bottom contact. We attacked with H/H twice and *Port Colborne* once without the smallest result. Finally, on running over in a different direction we got a trace like the Loch Ness monster, 400 yds long, which definitely proved it to be rocks. I then rejoined the patrol line.

At daylight we were detached to Londonderry for our lay over. On arrival at the Lough Foyle buoy there was frightful confusion with order and counter order because the signal station would pass a lot of old cancelled signals. First, we were taking pilots off Dunagree Point, then we were oiling and then we weren't, and eventually we went up river without a pilot and berthed at about 1230. After lunch

I had a bath and went to bed and was awakened at 1600 to say the Commodore wanted to see me at 1630. Got up there and we discussed which ship I was going to, as *Loch Alvie* now is a bit of casualty with her buckled bottom. Thank God it is a weakness of the class and not due to my driving her too hard. Decided I'd go to the *Saint John.* Saw Selby and made enquiries about getting J. over and at 1930 called her up and she said she *could* come. I was just going to bed really early when old Skinner came to see me and we sat drinking whisky till midnight. He is a funny old bird.

Saturday, 4 November 1944 – Londonderry

Stacey came over to see me early and said he thought he would like to be relieved and couldn't I take over the ship instead of coming as travelling S.O. I tried to persuade him to give it a trial, as I don't really want the sweat of taking over a new command, but he was adamant. I dashed round getting the necessary permits and sending off the necessary wires to get J. over and at 1100 we had our conference. I asked the Commodore on board for lunch and told him all about Stacey's request. Luckily Houghton from C.N.M.O. is due here this afternoon, and we think he will be able to help fix the situation. After lunch the Commodore said a few farewell words to the sailors. Hannan and I packed most of the p.m.

At about 1700 I got a message that Houghton was at the Commodore's house and I went up to see him. Explained the situation, said it was in no way a personal matter between Stacey and me as we were very good friends, but told him it would probably be very much easier if Stacey could go on leave and let me take command. Stacey was then sent for and this course was agreed to subject to the Commodore's approval. Took Houghton back on board. He has also settled the question of Brown and Falconer, who, although they are group specialists, are also ship's officers in *Swansea.* I have no wish whatever to keep Falconer and so it was decided to let them both return with the ship.

I got a call through to J. at 1930 and told her about the arrangements for her to travel tomorrow. Hope the weather improves as yesterday and today it has been blowing a gale with increasing rain. Band asked me to go dancing at the Club with Earl, the Canadian Wren officer, and his particular girl friends, the Wrens from Belfast. It was quite a good party. Dinner and then dance but a bloody awful band.

Sunday, 5 November 1944 – Londonderry

A fairly busy forenoon finishing off my packing and getting my gear across to *Saint John* before she was taken into dry dock. At 1130 Houghton and the Commodore came on board, and we got Stacey over and decided that the Commodore would make a signal recommending that I took over command and that Stacey returned to Canada for leave. It means more work for me, but I really think I'd prefer it rather than the added mental strain of dual control in the ship. The wardroom had a farewell cocktail party for the group at 1200 and the Commodore came down for a drink. No. 1 has taken over command.

The *Swansea*, after a last minute delay due to engine room defects which were not complete, slipped at 1600 and went to Lisahally to oil. I went down in her and said goodbye to the ship's company and the officers. I am heartbroken at leaving the ship, I have had nothing but the greatest kindness and support and the things they say about me are most flattering. Band, of course, I am particularly sorry to leave, and I'm so disappointed Joan will not meet him. We had a group of the officers taken on the fo'c'sle and at about 1730 I drove away in a service car with Earl, who I am awfully glad to be taking with me. I drove to the Commodore's house, as he had offered to put me up for the night. He himself was away. Rutherford his secretary entertained me and we had supper with Capt. and Mrs. Glencross, who have the lower flat. He is an old timer and is N.O.I.C. All this farewell business means a lot of drinking. The wind has gone down and so I hope J. has a good crossing.

Monday, 6 November 1944 – Londonderry

It rained on and off all day. I walked down to the deep dock and went on board *Saint John* and did some work on S206s and had lunch on board. Got a car after lunch and went to the Commodore's house and collected my gear and took it to the Melville Hotel, where I'd booked a room, and from there I went to the station to meet J. The Larne train came in at about 1500 but to my dismay no J. However, about ½ hour later she arrived on the Belfast train, which she had caught on the advice of some young R.N.V.R. Lieut. who had looked after her very kindly and efficiently all the way from London. We found the Melville Hotel very cold and dreary, and J. was feeling pretty tired after her long trip. We went very early to bed. God, it's lovely to see her!!

Tuesday, 7 November 1944 – Londonderry

Left the hotel about 0945 and went to Gieves and had a hair cut before going on board. I can't do much in the ship as, of course, Stacey is still occupying the cabin. Went back to the hotel for lunch. Raining again. I wrote to Gillian after lunch. J. has just visited her at her Brighton convent school and says she is looking very pretty but not well. I doubt that G. will ever like boarding school as she will always be homesick. We eventually went out, braving the rain, and bought some tweed and poked about in shops and then had tea in the cinema café. Back to the hotel and after changing we went to the Officers' Club where I had asked all the C.O.s and Earl to dinner so that they could meet J. She was a great success. After dinner, Angus asked us all down on board *Port Colborne* where there was a bit of a party going on. They had just got a set of trap drums for the ship, and the group

Torpedo Officer (Fardell) proved an absolute expert on them and the noise he produced was deafening. J. played the piano. Didn't get to bed till nearly 0130.

Wednesday, 8 November 1944 – Londonderry

I went on board and made a signal to Prentice asking him on board for lunch. J. and Miss Caldwell had been asked by Stacey. Quite a good party and an *excellent* lunch but it went on for ever and by the time we'd got a taxi it was about 1530. Pouring with rain again. J. took Stacey and Earl shopping but I returned to the hotel and finally at last completed the wording of my recommends and inked in the S206s, which was a great weight off my mind. Just as we were preparing to go and drink in the *Qu'Appelle* with Prentice, who should be ushered into our room but Gwinner (E.G. 1) who greeted J. as Lady Macbeth (my R/T call being "Macbeth"). He was in great form. His group are laying over for 48 hours at Lisahally and he was in to do some telephoning. We discussed our little party outside and we gave him a drink at the bar and he then took us in his car to the *Qu'Appelle* before going off himself. A nice chap.

Prentice gave us a drink and then took us over to one of his other destroyers where a party was in progress and then back to the *Qu'Appelle* for some supper. Prentice has had some awfully bad luck in his group, ships bucking down and damaging themselves and now finally one has dragged ashore in Iceland and is a total loss.[36] He has asked to be relieved as he reckons he is too tired a man. Back to the hotel at about 2300.

Thursday, 9 November 1944 – Londonderry

I called in at the gunnery office and also saw the Commodore's Secretary, who said it was approved for me to take over from Stacey, on my way to the ship. Spent about an hour on S206s and period recommends for awards and then walked along to the *Nene,* which is the latest newcomer to my group. Her C.O. is a little 2½ N.R. called Shaw.[37] Talkative but pleasant. I got him to clear lower deck and I spoke to the sailors, and then I had a word with the officers in the ward room and a drink. From there I went on board *Stormont* to see if they had any troubles and had a drink with Myra and then walked back to the hotel for lunch. Showers with some hail all the a.m.

After lunch I rang up for a car and went to Ebrington Barracks to have a look at the fire fighting course which the group is having, but as the first part consisted of seeing a film, it wasn't very interesting, and before the practical could start I got a message that Joe Selby wanted to see me, so I nipped back to the offices where it seemed to me there was nothing he couldn't have told me any other time. Got back to the hotel about 1600 and took J. out for some exercise and fresh air. Having been fine all the early afternoon it had, of course, to rain again while we were out but nothing much. We crossed the bridge and walked up a sort of track on to the upper road and so back. We were so hungry that we had some high tea at about 1800, then changed and went out to dinner with the Bonnetts. Stacey and Miss Caldwell were there too. J. was amused and amazed at Mrs. Bonnett, who really is the world's biggest bore, however, in a way it was an amusing evening.

Friday, 10 November 1944 – Londonderry

Went on board for a short time in the a.m. and did some correspondence and got back to the pub at about 1230. J. and I went down to the bar before lunch where we found Angus and Jeffrey. After lunch it started a fine, misty rain. After a lot of indecision I shifted into plain clothes and took myself out leaving J. resting in our room. I walked out along the Buncrana road and then turned left and came back into the town. It rained harder as I came home and I got rather wet. Persuaded the hotel to give us some tea and later on we shifted and got a taxi to the Officers' Club where, we joined a big party consisting of all the C.O.s, Miss Colborne and Kay Baker the W.R.C.N.S. officers, and Earl. It was the usual Friday night dinner dance with a good band and great fun. J. in great form. It finished at about 0115 and J. and I walked home as taxis were at a premium. Luckily it was only drizzling. This weather is the bottom. I officially took over command of the ship. Everybody says such nice things to J. about me that it is positively embarrassing, but it is nice to think we have such a happy group.

Saturday, 11 November 1944 – Londonderry

Got an official car to take me and a box of stuff the *Swansea* had given me for J. on board. Earl is kindly going to pack it up more seriously and send it home by post. Another dreary, wet day. J. came on board at 1200 complaining of very painful piles. She, I, and Stacey had lunch in my cabin and in the p.m. I left her on board and went up to the offices and rang up *Philante* and talked about our exercises and then walked back to the hotel, did some shopping, and finally back on board for some tea with J. We remained on board as we were being moved out of dock at 1815. J. came on the bridge as we were towed out and berthed at No. 11. By the time that was over it was so late, we had some supper on board. We were both simply craving an early night but were asked to attend a farewell party in the wardroom to Stacey. They were going to present him with a small gift, but the presentation didn't take place till 2300 and so we didn't get away till nearly midnight. A good party but I was feeling terribly weary and more and more depressed as our remaining time together became shorter and shorter. The thought of another spell of worry and responsibility in a new ship is so depressing and frightening.

Sunday, 12 November 1944 – Londonderry

I got a car, had a fairly early breakfast and got all my gear down to the ship. At 0930 all C.O.s and plotting officers went to the tactical table and did some anti Gnat runs. In the end I tried to formulate some cut and dried policy about step asides, CATs, and speed, but really it seemed impossible. Back on board for a few minutes and then I went ashore to the Club, where I met J. looking particularly nice in her red dress. The Selbys arrived a little later to give us lunch. They are very nice. The sun actually shone for a few hours in the middle of the day. Brought J. down on board after lunch to spend the last few hours before we slipped. My 1st Lieut. and Signal officer, who I had had to report as absent from long leave this morning, returned I'm glad to say at about 1400 having missed the boat from England.

We were to have sailed at 1730 but at about 1530 the Chief reported a hot bearing in one of the dynamos, which delayed us. At 1730, however, as we were outside ship we were told to shift berth under our own steam to let the others out and we went down to No. 19 berth outside the *Lanark*. Stacey was on board and went with us as *Lanark* is the ship he is taking passage in. J. eventually dined on board and was able to stay with me till about 2100 when, being ready at last, we slipped and went down river. I left J. in the *Lanark* being entertained by Johnston and S.O. Oh these partings, they just tear one's heart apart. I've been awfully proud to let everyone see J. as she is so marvellously alive and so brim full of personality.

We had a dark and rainy trip down river and went alongside *Loch Alvie* at the oiler. Went to see the Captain of the oiler to try and remain alongside all night, in which I was successful, but there were quite a few other ships asking to come alongside. Got to bed at about 0030. Worried and miserable.

Monday, 13 November 1944 – Moville

I found in the morning, just before shoving off from the oiler at 0800, that all our exercises had been cancelled except the night shoot, so *Loch Alvie* and *Saint John* shoved off and anchored, and the remainder of the group went alongside later on and topped up. I wasn't altogether sorry that the exercises were off, as I had a mass of things to deal with and orders to read and this gave me the opportunity. I also spoke to the ship's company and the officers and I wrote a heartbroken letter to J. Bonnett was on board and he went from ship to ship helping with drills.

At 1500 I went on deck with glasses and watched what I supposed to be the Derry-Larne train passing in the distance and wondered if J. was looking at us and wondering which was the *Saint John.* God, I'm depressed and unhappy.

I took the group out at 1700 for our night shoot, which we started at 1840. Conditions were better than last time but I don't think any of us were v. clever, and *Saint John* I thought was bloody awful. It is damned difficult, however, to illuminate and fire with the same gun. We fired last. It was a long and tedious performance and we did not get back to the anchorage till about 2300. I think J. will have had a fairly calm crossing.

Tuesday, 14 November 1944 – Moville/Larne

I turned out at 0330 and we weighed and proceeded. I near as damn it had a collision with *Loch Alvie.* I hate messing about at this Moville anchorage at night when there are lots of ships there. As we sailed we got a signal to sweep through an area near to the Lough Foyle buoys for a ditched aircraft. In the process we got rather close to E.G. 1 who was also on the same job, which gave me more anxious moments. I don't know why it is, but night work near other ships gives me fits. This search delayed us and we didn't arrive at Larne much before 0900 instead of 0800. By that time it was blowing pretty fresh from the N.N.E. and damned cold.

Staff officers boarded us at once and we split up into 2 groups and went off for A/S Ps right away. It is a long time since we've done this with a moving target and it was good value. Wind increasing all the time. On completion of the forenoon A/S Ps the group joined up for a bottomed S/M exercise, but just as last time we couldn't find it when we swept into the Bay and it was all rather a waste of time. By the end of the exercise at 1730 it was blowing half a gale and so we cancelled the night A/S Ps and closed Larne entrance to land the staff officers, but it was too rough and so we had to take them with us to Moville, where we were told to go and top up with oil before sailing for the Cape Wrath area. We left Larne at about 2000. It was announced that the R.A.F. had sunk the *Tirpitz* in Tromso Fjord by 3 hits with 12,000 lb bombs.

Wednesday, 15 November 1944 – Moville/At sea

The wind eased a lot on our way to Moville and when we arrived there at about 0130, it looked alright for oiling. Both sides of the oiler were empty but she was swung across wind and tide. I got my bows alongside and started to bump rather heavily and so shoved off and told the whole group to anchor for the night and oil in the morning. We then anchored at about 0300 and I turned in for some much needed sleep. At 0800 at day light all ships except *Monnow* and *Saint John* went to the oiler and when, by about 1030, they'd finished, *Monnow* and we went alongside and topped up. We stayed there until the mail arrived from Derry, and at about 1315 the group sailed for Cape Wrath. Cold but calm and fine and v.g. visibility. At about 1700 we got an A/S contact with A/S trace. Difficult to hold but attacked with H/H and D/C without any result, and at 1830 just before dark classified it as non sub and went on. Passage through the Minches was easy although our radar was out of action, as visibility was extreme.

Thursday, 16 November 1944 – At sea

We made rendezvous with E.G. 18 off Cape Wrath at 0815. He passed us some sketchy information and then pushed off. Our area of patrol is from 58° N.-59° N., 4° W.-6°30'W.[38] We have to support all convoys passing through our area and between times carrying out A/S sweeps. We had one or two contacts and at least 6 floating mines, which we sank. Contacts were definitely non sub until one, which we picked up at about 1700 and was difficult to classify. We attacked and brought up a small amount of oil. I considered it to be a wreck but when *Nene,* who was with us, reported movement which I couldn't confirm, I didn't like to leave it. Eventually, after dark I told *Monnow* and *Nene* to hold contact till daylight and continued patrol to the E. with the remainder. Echo sounder trace was rather vague. It didn't look like a U-boat, but on the other hand not big enough to be said to be definitely wreck. Rather cold but calm.

Friday, 17 November 1944 – At sea

We turned round at about 0300 on reaching the eastern limit of our area and swept back, passing *Monnow* and *Nene* at about 0630, still in contact and waiting to attack at daylight. The wind started to get up from the east and by daylight it was blowing hard, which made it hard for the 2 contact keepers to attack. I came back towards them at about 1000 and got a contact myself which seemed good but I lost it, and *Port Colborne* and *Saint John* then did an Observant but found nothing. Meanwhile, *Monnow* and *Nene* had carried out an attack or two, but I felt in the existing weather they couldn't be v. accurate and I was once more in doubt whether I was justified in leaving it yet. Closed the contact myself and satisfied myself that it hadn't moved by Q.H. fix.

I had to be off Loch Ewe to support a leaving convoy at 1800 and so at about 1300 I rather reluctantly classified it as wreck and formed the group up to go south to Loch Ewe entrance. At that very minute *Port Colborne* got a contact with something on the bottom and so I left *Loch Alvie* with him and went on. By now it was blowing v. hard indeed and I was glad to get under the lee of the Scottish coast as we went south. At 1600 *Loch Alvie* reported she had a man requiring a finger amputating, and so I detached *Stormont* to meet her and by closing the land they were able to find smooth enough water to effect the transfer by boat.

Just after dark we detected the convoy inshore of us going north, and I altered to close and told my ships to take up screening positions on either side. The wind, thank God, dropped v. quickly after dark, but what with the weather and the thought of joining up with this convoy after dark, I was almost sick with worry. I have an absolute complex about meeting other ships at night and am very bad at working by radar and plot. The convoy rounded Cape Wrath at about midnight and steered E.

Saturday, 18 November 1944 – At sea

We remained with the convoy until about 0400 when on reaching 4° W. we detached and turned west. At 0645 all ships got a radar contact ahead at about 7 miles, which was lost almost at once. *Monnow* thought it was aircraft and we got I.F.F. response,[39] but all the same I thought it rather suspicious and wondered about a U-boat, and so just as we were coming up to *Port Colborne* and *Loch Alvie* on their all night contact I altered to the N. to do a sweep round the position of the contact. It took a long time to cover a reasonable area and I didn't get back to the contact keepers until about 1100.

According to a previous signal we were due to support an incoming convoy off the Butt of Lewis at 1300, and I was far from sure whether *Port Colborne*'s contact could be left. In this job one always seems to be trying to be in 2 places at once and always trying to make up one's mind when some doubtful contact can be left. However, luckily the convoy was delayed, and so I was able to keep the whole group while I helped *Port Colborne* and *Loch Alvie.* Gained contact and ran over and found by Q.H. that we were back on our old target, which *Monnow* had banged away at last night. Made a number of runs over and at last attacked dropping D/Cs by echo sounder trace. Only a bit of oil to show, and E/S trace being fairly non sub, I decided to leave it at about 1430 and went off to the W.'ward. Just after dark we saw aircraft flares to the N. When, after an interval, about 6 had been dropped, we turned towards. Unable to raise aircraft on R/T. Swept right up to within about 4 miles of Sulisker but found nothing. I think those R.A.F. chaps might make some sort of signal on these occasions so that we know we can disregard. Came back to the Southward and just before midnight we contacted our convoy by radar. Convoy consisted of 1 ship and 4 escorts!! Some convoy. Nice, calm, fine day.

Sunday, 19 November 1944 – At sea

I decided to split the group into 2 divisions and put one div. on either quarter of the convoy and told the S.O. of the close escort to take all four of his ships up ahead. It took a bit of manoeuvring to get into position and again when course was altered to the S. round the Butt of Lewis, but then I was able to get a bit of sleep. At about 0630 we detached on reaching the first Channel buoy at the S. limit of our area, and I formed the group up together and we made to the N.'ward. Fine clear day, but shortly after daylight a fresh N.E. wind got up and made quite a choppy sea. We patrolled our area all day without incident. I read prayers and had a talk to the sailors at 1030.

Port Colborne reported a big condenser leak. Considering in the *Swansea* we ran for months with a perpetual heavy density in our boilers I don't feel very worried about it, but signalled C. in C. saying I thought she ought to return to harbour. Back came an immediate signal saying she was to be sent in forthwith and so at about 1550 I detached her to Londonderry. If a ship breaks down it always seems to be the *Port Colborne.* We had no convoy commitments tonight and so continued to patrol without incident, and I got a fair amount of rest.

Monday, 20 November 1944 – At sea

We were going E. to meet our convoy and were N.E. of Cape Wrath when we got one of these radar contacts, which we held for about 10 minutes and then lost astern of us at about 2½ miles. That was at 0800 just before it got light, so I turned the group and swept back but found absolutely nothing. This delayed us and instead of meeting our convoy (Methil–Loch Ewe) at 0930 in 4°30' W. we met it at about 1030 a bit further W. It was all over the place when we sighted it, with ships strung out and straggling for miles. I got the Commodore to reduce speed to 6 kts and sent *Stormont* off to look after the worst stragglers and formed the rest of the group as a close A/S screen ahead. By slow degrees the convoy closed up. We turned S. round Cape Wrath at about 1300 and eventually arrived off Loch Ewe at 1645, where we detached and turned N. again. Fine clear day. Still a fresh N.'ly wind. Cold. Last night's fall in temperature has put a covering of snow on the highest mountains.

At about 2130 *Stormont* got an A/S contact, which he attacked. I sent *Monnow* to help him and he attacked. Meanwhile I'd fixed the position and was sure they were within a mile of a charted wreck and so I called them off. I opened ships out to 3 miles for the night patrol, with *Stormont* 4 miles astern keeping a listening A/S watch only, as it is believed U-boats will sometimes surface after they hear the sweeping ships pass over.[40]

The French have broken through the Belfort Gap and are advancing rapidly there. The Americans are in the outskirts of Metz.

Tuesday, 21 November 1944 – At sea

Uneventful night. Calm, bright, clear day. At 1100 I dropped a small drifting target and we all fired some practice "Shark" at it.[41] I'm quite impressed with it as a weapon. Picked up the target and turned S. to rendezvous with our next convoy off Loch Ewe. We arrived off the entrance as it left harbour at 1645. Seven ships with a corvette and 2 trawlers as escort bound for Iceland. By the time we'd all gathered round it was pretty well defended. We got a signal telling E.G. 19 to relieve us forthwith and for us to go to Scapa and put ourselves under the orders of C. in C. Home Fleet. That sounds ominously like a North Russian convoy job. Ugh!! Weather forecasts look like coming gales.

Wednesday, 22 November 1944 – At sea/Scapa Flow

I detached *Loch Alvie* at about 0030 to reinforce the screen of a tanker E. bound from Loch Ewe, which sailed at 2300, and the rest of us followed on behind our convoy to the edge of our area and detached at 0415. We rendezvoused with E.G. 19 half way between Cape Wrath and the Butt of Lewis at daylight, and after I had passed over some news and information we pushed off at 15 kts for Scapa. Blowing hard from the S.E. by midday, and on arrival at Scapa at about 1430 it was nearly gale force. I did a very bad alongside the oiler, however, no damage. It started to rain in addition to the wind. Rang up Tubby Hutton, who is Commodore D.[42] and arranged to remain alongside the oilers for the night or at anchor, and to pick up our buoys in daylight tomorrow, when we hope the wind will have dropped. We have never done this buoy business before and I don't propose to start it in the dark with a gale blowing.[43] Had the master of the oiler over for a drink at 1830 and later on took him down to the wardroom to see our small movie.

Thursday, 23 November 1944 – Scapa Flow

As soon as it was reasonably light at 0900 I left the oiler and went to my buoy. The wind had eased but it was still blowing quite hard in gusts from the W., and I couldn't get a good run at the buoy with the result that I over ran it a bit, drifted down on to it, threw the buoy jumper into the water but eventually got the picking up rope on, and without undue delay we got a bridle on too. The rest of the group had considerable difficulty too. I went gunnery rounds.

At 1230 the Commodore's barge came for me and took me ashore. To my surprise I found his youngest boy, aged 6, in the boat and when I got ashore I went to his house or rather hut where Lois was. She has been there since he came ashore when the *Tyne* left for the Far East.[44] Robin Moodie,[45] who is Tubby's staff officer, came to lunch too. Tubby a Commodore is really terrific but just the same as ever. After lunch I went along to his office and got some information. We *are* booked for the next Russian convoy, but we shall have a few days here before the start.

Got back on board at about 1515. We had to slip from our buoy at 1600 and go alongside the *Vindictive,* who is a repair ship, for some refit job on our distiller. Still blowing hard and we had some trouble unshackling. By the time we got alongside the *Vindictive* I was just about tired of going from pillar to post about this harbour in half a gale of wind. Spencer,[46] who is Captain (as Acting Commander) of the *Vindictive,* came to see me at 1730 and I went back and had a drink with him later on. He is still rather a funny little cock sparrow of a man. I am reading again Jeffrey Farnol's *Broad Highway* and I'm rather ashamed to say I'm loving it.

Friday, 24 November 1944 – Scapa Flow

A calm, still day but cold. Thank God. I dictated my report of proceedings to the writer and I went store room rounds. Angus came to see me and at 1230 I went over to the *Vindictive* and had lunch with Spencer. Later on I came back, shifted into plain clothes, and went ashore with Spencer and his Pay Lieutenant for a walk. We plunged about in heather and bogs for about an hour and eventually arrived at the Officers' Club Lyness for tea and then caught a 1700 boat off. Good exercise. Had a drink with Spencer and then came back and had a bath and shifted and wrote a letter to J. At 1915 I went ashore to dinner with the Huttons. Admiral McGrigor, Hugh Browning, and Cdr. Pawlet were there.[47] Pleasant evening. Tubby put me back in his barge.

Saturday, 25 November 1944 – Scapa Flow

Cold, miserable day with showers and a strong N. wind. At 0915 I caught a boat to the A/S trawler with our A/S team and had some runs on the table. At about 1030 I left them at it and went ashore to Com. D.'s offices and saw Moodie about this and that. Eventually got back on board at about 1215. Nobody to receive me. Nobody saw me over the side either. Sent for No. 1[48] and roared him up. Oh, how I miss Band and the *Swansea.*

The full orders for our convoy arrived on board, and after lunch I went through them carefully myself and after tea I got Earl, Panabaker, and Blanchard into my cabin and went through them again.[49] As far as I can see my biggest headache is going to be the fact that I may not use T.B.S. except in emergency. Tried to take a bit of exercise on deck but I was driven off by a cold rain shower. Asked Spencer over to supper and afterwards we went down to the wardroom and saw a very good Mickey Rooney-Judy Garland film on our little movie screen.

Sunday, 26 November 1944 – Scapa Flow

A really lovely, still, sunny day at last. I wanted to go to divisions but so many were out of the ship on church parties that I gave it up. At 1010 I took the boat to the *Greenwich* where, in due course, Com. D.'s barge took all the group C.O.s to the *Kent* for a meeting with C.S.1. (McGrigor) who is in charge of this convoy operation. Quite a big meeting with all the 17th and 6th D.F. C.O.s and a carrier and a cruiser C.O. We left the *Kent* at 1200 and I took all C.O.s back on board *Saint John* for a drink. Later on Tubby, Lois, and Rowley came on board for lunch. They are an awfully nice family. Rowley is a grand little chap. Gosh, I wish I had Tubby's drive and confidence. It is funny that 2 men brought up in exactly the same way should end up so differently. When they had gone I did some work on the operation orders. I also wrote some letters (one to Gillian) and read and took a bit of exercise on deck. Feeling worried and anxious about my ability to handle this operation, or rather our bit of it.

Monday, 27 November 1944 – Scapa Flow

We shoved off from the *Vindictive* at 0900 only to find the oiler's side wasn't clear, and we had to lie off and wait over ½ hour. A very red sunrise, which I hope doesn't foretell another blow. *Nene*, who came alongside outside us, was awfully slow with the result that although we only had 30 or 40 tons to come in to top up, we didn't leave the oiler till 1130, which was the time we were supposed to be alongside the *Demeter* to embark stores for the Army in N. Russia. All the group went alongside in turn. The wind from the S. was steadily increasing and it was damned cold. Every sort of thing got in my way going alongside *Demeter*, with the result that I was slow and we didn't get away again until nearly 1400. We then went up to our buoy and were very slow at shackling on.

I had arranged to go ashore for a walk with Tubby and so immediately I'd rung off the engines I shifted and went ashore. Tubby tells me there is a gale warning and the glass is falling like a stone. Not v. cheering. I wished I hadn't come ashore. However, Tubb, Lois, Rowley and I all went off in the car to the top of Long Hope past Melsetter and then got out and walked along the shore. Blowing hard and damned cold and we mostly had to run to keep warm, but it was rather fun and very good for us. We came back for a late tea at 1700 and I ordered a boat at 1730 but when Tubby ran me down there was no sign of it, and after a lot of hanging about and signalling I was eventually put on board by a drifter. I was getting really worried by now as it was blowing like hell straight up to our buoy from Switha and we only had one bridle. I got steam up at once and set anchor watch. Glass still falling and wind Force 8 or 9 and the cable jerking in a most alarming way. I was constantly up and down to the bridge until 0100, when I lay down on my bunk dressed and had some sleep. At 0400 I went up and the wind had eased a lot and at about 0500 I went to ½ hour's notice. Shortly after that I heard the anchor go and I sprang out of bed and dashed up only to find the fo'c'sle sentry *thought* the cable had parted and without looking to make sure, he let go the anchor.

Tuesday, 28 November 1944 – Scapa Flow

My birthday and the day on which I go on to the retired list. Weather improved all day and there was quite a bit of sun. I got all C.O.s on board for a talk, a birthday drink, and gave them lunch. I'm beginning to feel scared stiff about this next operation. The whole thing practically in darkness. The question of keeping in touch when stationed so far in advance, communications, and so on. My trouble is I always anticipate troubles before they arrive.

I wrote to J. and I read A.C.I.s and I finished off *The Broad Highway*, which I enjoyed immensely. At about 1800 I went into the wardroom and mentioned it was my birthday, and at 2100 I was asked down again and there was a magnificent birthday cake sugared and inscribed. Our Leading Cook is an absolute expert at cakes.

Tubby told me a Canadian officer had left a parcel at his house saying no message and no answer, which when opened proved to contain 2 bottles of whisky.

It put Tubby in a very difficult position.[50] I heard today that all my C.O.s had conspired together as they were so delighted at being asked by Tubby to lunch one day, the first time any serving R.N. officer had taken any notice of them.

Wednesday, 29 November 1944 – Scapa Flow/At sea

I spent a last forenoon reading the orders and reading the new A.C.I.s. I sent Earl round the group with some last minute instructions. At lunch time a radar defect was reported and after a great deal of delay MacDougall,[51] the group radar officer, arrived, and we had to keep him on board when we sailed to finish off. We slipped at 1640 and went out in a blinding rain storm, which, however, was short lived. Glass still rising but quite a stiff W.'ly wind. Once out of the lee of the land, we found quite a big sea running and just off Dunnet Head it was very confused and rather unpleasant. 10 knots was the best we could do and so I remained in line ahead as I couldn't afford the delay of getting into line abreast. *Loch Alvie* in the rough water reported starting up his old leak again in the magazine and so I sent him back. It seems to me with that weak bottom he isn't seaworthy at this time of year. We passed between Stack Skerry and the Nun Rock to intercept and support our convoy, J.W. 62, which had left Loch Ewe earlier this afternoon.

Thursday, 30 November 1944 – At sea

We got in radar touch with the convoy at about 0730 and I took station ahead and spread the group in line abreast. Without the use of T.B.S., as we've been told to maintain complete W/T silence, one feels awfully lost, and visual signalling takes such a time. I was on the bridge most of the night manoeuvring about and getting into position. The day broke fine and clear and we could see the convoy and close screen astern. Still quite rough but wind and sea both went down in the evening. Spent almost the whole p.m. reading signals from *Cygnet*, who is S.O. close escort.[52] The Home Fleet destroyers, carriers, and C.S. 1 haven't joined up yet. Feeling worried to death. The problem of keeping good station at long distances through these interminable nights is a headache, and when to break W/T silence is also another anxiety. We have a bright full moon all through the nights at present which is a great boon. We were up to the level of the Faeroes by midnight. Exercised the watch in the 1st watch and somehow felt happier and more confident.

Friday, 1 December 1944 – At sea

When daylight came at about 1030 (we'd put the clocks on an hour at midnight) we could see Capt. D.6[53] and his C class destroyers coming up to the front of the convoy and it was clear the Home Fleet escort, *Bellona*, and C.S. 1 and his carriers had joined up. We accordingly moved up into our forward position on the starboard bow. The sun was above the horizon for a short time, but it is the last day we shall see it. Clear and excellent visibility and not cold. When it got dark at about 1730 I turned back to close the outer screen and get good radar contact for the night, but even so it was remarkably difficult to hold at times. I don't think our set is too good. Course and speed had to be constantly altered to keep station, and I was always fearful of losing contact, which is an absolute fixation with me when with convoys. All the V/S signalling (no T.B.S. allowed) was very slow. Brilliant moonlight all night.

Saturday, 2 December 1944 – At sea

At about 0800 we had great difficulty in holding contact astern and I got extremely worried. However, all was well and at the first crack of dawn the S. horizon was lighted up and the destroyer screen showed up more or less where they ought to be. Our route had been altered by signal and C.S. 1 made that convoy would alter course at 1200. I started to move across to starboard at 1100 ready for the alteration from N. to 039°. Although the sun never rose there was good daylight from about 1100 to 1500, but almost as soon as it got dark we started to lose ourselves. Contacts faded out astern and I got worried to death and wondered if some alteration of course had been made which I hadn't heard about. Eventually about 2200 we got in touch again but I very much think it is not the group we ought to be ahead of and we've worked over from the starboard bow to ahead of the convoy. However, the relief to be in touch again was tremendous, and we held on like grim death all night. To add to my worries it was raining and bad visibility, and it took hours to get signals for alteration of course and speed by light to the group.

Sunday, 3 December 1944 – At sea

Showery and overcast and windy, but temperature not below 40° which is remarkable at 70° N. The sun never rose but there was light from about 1000 to 1400. We held contact astern all day and I once got into V/S touch and confirmed we were station keeping on the right ship. The Admiral signalled that the convoy would alter course to 065° at 2000 and so we had to go round at about 1845. By aid of the plot we did it quite easily and managed to keep v. good station. Weather cleared and glass rose from 28.8 millibars, to which it had dropped, and it was a fine, moonlit night. Still this gnawing anxiety and terror of doing the wrong thing. The Admiral signalled that when detached, the 2 support groups were to sweep ahead at 14 kts to locate and destroy any U-boats on the track of the convoy.

Monday, 4 December 1944 – At sea

A few hours of watery twilight and that was all. Having held contact well all night we had another alteration to 090° at about, as I estimated, 0700, to be ahead of the convoy when they altered. This time I wasn't so clever and I had some anxious moments getting further and further away as I'd obviously altered too soon. At 1200 E.G. 20 and E.G. 9 were told to proceed in execution of previous orders ahead and finally patrol an area off the entrance to the Kola Inlet until the convoy arrived.[54] There was just enough daylight to assist us in joining forces. E.G. 20 is S.O., thank God.[55] We formed our line and zigzagged at 15 kts. The wind and sea got up in the p.m. and we had to come down to 10 kts. Just before midnight 3 ships got an HF/DF bearing of what was thought to be a ground wave on our starboard bow, and as I was on that wing I took *Monnow* and *Stormont* along down the bearing to investigate.

Tuesday, 5 December 1944 – At sea

After running out to 20 miles along the bearing and finding nothing I rejoined and actually got back into station at about 0500. *Tavy*'s (S.O.) and our ideas of where we are differ by as much as 35 miles. No sights possible and it has to be all by dead reckoning. Strong S.'ly wind blowing and very much colder. Had to start really wrapping up on the bridge. A depressingly short watery bit of daylight between 1000 and 1300. We arrived in our final patrol area at about 1800 and got out CATs and prepared to meet the Gnat menace. A lot of HF/DF bearings, one lot of which cut in to a point beautifully about 24 miles ahead of our line of sweep. At about 0045 as we were approaching the spot I went to action stations.

Wednesday, 6 December 1944 – At sea

On reaching the plotted position there was nothing. I packed up action stations at about 0230 but rang the gongs again almost at once when *Nene* got what sounded like a good A/S contact. *Tavy* left me with my group, less *Port Colborne,* to investigate. Shortly after I got contact myself. However, I classified it as definitely fish. It is funny how bad these other chaps are at classification and what a lot of time we lose in consequence. At about 0500 we set off to rejoin *Tavy* and party and took station at 0800 just as they were in the middle of an E.I. turn and a Quiz [asdic contact], which didn't make it any easier. We then all swept N. and at 0930 we met our convoy again and proceeded to take up our old station, but this time on the other bow. We are so far E. now that the short period of light is between about 0900 and 1300.

From about 1400 life was hell. The convoy was zigging about, there were some false alarm Quizes, and I had to manoeuvre my party about by light. The T.B.S. traffic from the Admiral was terrific. At 1630 we were detached with the White Sea portion, who were taken over by a group of Russian destroyers. By this time, in the pitch dark, I was really rather uncertain where we were. We were told no course or speed and no exact time for detaching. I hoped in time the situation would sort itself out and we'd gain radar contact with our 8 ships. At 1930, however, we got some good HF/DF bearings, fixing a U-boat 17 miles to the W. and turned to close. Nothing when we got there and so we turned back to what I hoped was an intercepting course for the White Sea party, but never got a sniff of them. A really very cold S. wind off the land.

Thursday, 7 December 1944 – At sea

A really bitterly cold day. Came the dawn and no sign of the White Sea portion. I'm pretty sure now they are ahead of us, in which case we can't catch them. Turned round at 1430 so as to make our arrival at Kola Inlet by daylight. Had some difficulty in spite of D/F fixes in figuring out our position, but I'm confident now that convoy is safely past the furthest on position we were told to escort him to. At 1630 we all got HF/DF bearings of a U-boat which I plotted 20 miles to the W., and so we turned and swept up to the position and went to action stations, but we never found a thing. Between then and 0200 we got 3 more U-boat signals, all in a general W.'ly direction in which we were heading anyhow, but not a thing sighted or detected. My sea cabin was bitterly cold. Temperature was never below 22° but the strong S.'ly wind cut like a knife. This is a truly ghastly part of the world at this time of year.

Friday, 8 December 1944 – At sea/Kola Inlet

We arrived off the entrance to Kola Inlet just as dawn was cracking at 0730. Although some lights were showing, which I'd asked for, they seemed altogether different to those shown on the chart, which made it v. difficult to fix the ship. Still v. cold. Kola Inlet is a long, narrow fjord with Murmansk at the top. I wasn't sure if we were supposed to take a pilot, however, as none showed up we went on. There was enough daylight to see comfortably and it was all quite plain sailing. We got orders and counter orders about oiling as we approached, and we were sent 6 or 7 miles up harbour looking for an oiler which wasn't there and we had to turn and come all the way back to where she really was. Eventually secured alongside it at about 1200 and I had a horrible luke warm bath. Angus, who was alongside, came over to see me and we had a drink. After lunch I had a bit of shut eye on my bunk. *Stormont* shoved off when she had finished oiling at about 1600, and *Nene* took her place alongside *Monnow.* The remainder of us are staying alongside for the night.

At about 1700 I was shown a signal from C.S. 1 saying *Stormont* was to go somewhere miles up harbour, collect a lighter from alongside some ship, and tow it back here. The group then had to unload about 40 tons of stores from our oiler (the *Laurelwood*) into the lighter, plus the stores we'd brought from Scapa ourselves. I take an awfully dim view of this, using one of our ships as a tug in a dark, crowded, strange harbour. However, as usual *Stormont* did a difficult job damned well, and by the time he got alongside with his lighter at about 2200 our working parties had got all the stores from the oiler's hold on deck and were able to start putting them into the lighter. I went over to *Stormont* when she had berthed and gave Myra a check up. The whole operation didn't finish until about 0100. That bitter wind stopped, thank God.

Saturday, 9 December 1944 – Kola Inlet

At 0930 we all shoved off and went about 5 miles up harbour and anchored off Muschikov Point. Cold (about 12° of frost) but still, and the short day was bright and clear. We had hardly been anchored an hour when we were all told to weigh and come back and anchor in Vaenga Bay with the remainder of the fleet. Really, what the staff are playing at it is difficult to understand. Their aim seems to be to keep us on the move. We anchored again at about 1245 and immediately after lunch I collected all the C.O.s in our boat and went on board *Campania* for the convoy conference. There was a preliminary meeting for the escorting forces and then the general convoy conference with all the masters of the merchant ships. After the meeting, the Admiral was very nice and apologised profusely for mucking us about so, but apparently all previous arrangements for berthing, stores, etc., have been completely thrown out by the non-cooperation of the Russians. We were offered the chance of going alongside *Bellona* for the night, which personally I should have liked as I could have had a good dinner with Norris,[56] but I reckoned it was a bit hard on the sailors to shift again and so we stayed put.

I am a little too close to *Bulldog* for my complete peace of mind. Made out steaming signals and read and wrote and at 1915 I went down to the wardroom for a drink before having my dinner. We got mail, which *Caesar* had brought up from Scapa, and I got a letter from J.

Sunday, 10 December 1944 – Kola Inlet/At sea

We weighed at 0815 when it was just beginning to get light, and proceeded up the fjord. The ships of the convoy were all moving out at the same time and so I was glad of a little light. On arrival at the entrance off Toros Island at 0845 the Commodore had just arrived there too, and we formed up in line abreast to sweep ahead while the convoy formed up. *Bulldog, Beagle,* and *Westcott* were attached to me. At the conference the Admiral had said the convoy would alter to the N. at a certain position and so I altered my line round accordingly, only to find the convoy standing on another 10 miles or so. I felt badly in need of a bit more information about courses and speeds. No one seems to realize how difficult a job it is for advanced screens when *no* information is forthcoming. Cold S.'ly wind blowing.

At about 1300 (the clocks had been put back 2 hours at noon to A. time) when it began to get dark we took up our night cruising diagram. We are on the port bow this time, and *Tavy* and his group have been told to sweep astern. Almost at once I started to get into difficulties, being unable to identify with certainty the escorts astern and also not knowing whether they were in station or what the convoy speed was. Continuously on the bridge. Very tiring and worrying. There is no doubt from sighting, D/F bearings, etc., that there are quite a number of U-boats hanging round this bit of the N. Russian coast, but the early nights are so dark and so long that we stand a good chance of avoiding them.

Monday, 11 December 1944 – At sea

Spent most of the night on the bridge, groping about trying to keep touch and station on the very elusive escorts astern, with an alteration of course into the bargain. *Stormont*'s radar was broken down and so to add to my commitments I had to keep him in station. The air was full of U-boat transmissions, all ground wave. In my effort not to use T.B.S. I feel perhaps there was too much flashing of signals and too [many] bright lights being shown by the group.

At 0530 we got a signal indicating S/M had sighted the convoy, and at about 0600 *Cassandra* on the port quarter of the convoy reported she had been hit by a torpedo forward. *Tavy* and his group, who were astern, were ordered to close and I rather expected to be sent back to hunt myself, but we were left where we were, ahead. We went to action stations but nothing more happened, although there are was still a mass of near U-boat W/T traffic. It was blowing with quite a bit of sea from the S.S.W. *Cassandra* afloat and can steam stern first.[57]

A few hours of murky twilight. Physically and mentally exhausting. Hoping against hope nothing will be required of us. As the day wore on all U/B signals were being D/F'd astern and there was an aircraft sighting also astern, indicating that we have passed through the main U-boat area. Sent *Stormont* back to the close screen as I can't have him up here for another night with no radar. The convoy has slowed down a lot in this weather. That and radar troubles made it v. difficult to maintain touch.

Tuesday, 12 December 1944 – At sea

A quiet night and I got quite a lot of sleep. Managed to hold contact astern with *Cygnet* on the outer screen but I don't think we were quite where we were supposed to be. I put ships out at 2½ miles and made them zigzag independently, which enables me to make small alterations of course and speed without making signals. At daylight, such as it was, *Stormont* came up from astern and we transferred MacDougall as the weather had calmed down a lot, and in ½ hour he had the set working. He certainly is clever with this radar. We were told to screen ahead, which I think will make station keeping easier.

Shadowing aircraft were reported during the night and at about 1030 we got a report that one of our fighters from the carriers had shot a shadower down. In the p.m. reports of enemy aircraft became more numerous and at 1430 we were ordered to join the close screen for anti-aircraft support.[58] At about 1500 as we were closing in, German torpedo bombers came in to the attack with the last v. dim light. There was a lot of Oerlikon fire from escorts and the convoy did a number of emergency turns. I don't suppose there were more than 8-10 attacking aircraft altogether, and they dropped their torpedoes at long range and nothing was hit as far as I know.[59] Nothing near enough for us to fire at. Quite exciting though.

At about 1600 we were told to assume our station ahead. *Monnow* reported picking up 4 German airmen in a dinghy who we'd seen throwing up flares for some time so at least 1 was shot down.[60] I must say we've rather asked for this, as we are only 60-70 miles off the N. Norway coast on this route. No further alarums or excursions. Quiet and peaceful night.

Wednesday, 13 December 1944 – At sea

As there seemed to be no indications of U-boats in the vicinity I got in CATs at 0800. It wasn't long, however, before D/F reports of U-boats started to come in. Owing to last night's attack the convoy stood on 260° instead of starting to turn south, but at 1330 the convoy altered to 210° in about 70° N. and 7° E. It took a long time to get the signal, which was received v. corrupt, with the result that we were left badly. At the same time we were told to take station on the convoy's port beam and we had a very long way to go with only v. little twilight left. We sort of ranged our way across the front of the convoy. Manoeuvring was v. difficult as the air was simply red hot with reports and orders and one thing and another. There were 2 aircraft sighting reports astern and numerous HF/DF reports, and it looked as if there might be quite a few U/Bs round the convoy. As usual I found it v. difficult to judge when we were in our proper station and I got v. worried about that and the U-boats. C.S. 1 congratulated *Campania* on what appeared to be a certain kill, so one of the aircraft must have done a good attack.[61]

At about 2130 an aircraft reported a contact off the port bow of the convoy and we were told to take station ahead again, sweeping through the bow contact position en route. Nothing found. There were the most beautiful and constantly changing lighting effects in the sky from the Northern lights. We reached our position about 20' ahead at about 0100. This is the only really easy position from which to keep station.

Thursday, 14 December 1944 – At sea

After midnight there were no further submarine reports, and it seemed they had been beaten off and I had some sleep. Day seemed to take an awfully long time to break but having come quite a long way south, when it did come it was much more like daylight and lasted a bit longer, but the sun is still below the horizon. I am reading and enjoying Francis Brett Young's *Island,* a sort of history of England in verse that J. sent me for my birthday. It started to blow up a bit from the S.

To my surprise at about 1500 we got orders to close the convoy to direct T.B.S. touch with the Admiral so that he could pass two signals to us for transmission when we reached 63° N., and shortly afterwards we were told to detach and proceed to the Clyde. I think the latter destination must be a mistake but we can check up on that later on. In the process of turning back I lost *Monnow.* It was getting dark and one of my turning signals must have been missed, but it was light enough to see us and there was no excuse for losing touch whatever. Damned annoying. It eventually transpired that she was in some position S. of the convoy and C.S. 1 told her to join the close screen as we were then some distance ahead. There was quite a bit of a sea by now and 9 knots was the best we could do. What a relief to get away from all that worry and responsibility.

Friday, 15 December 1944 – At sea

An uneventful day. Still blowing hard and 11 knots is all we can do and we are not making good more than 9. I wrote out my report of proceedings for the writer to type. I am not giving a day to day account as I was never on detached service. I am merely making a few general remarks on support groups working with Russian convoys.[62]

Saturday, 16 December 1944 – At sea

It blew harder and harder from the S.E. until it reached Force 8 or 9 with a big sea on the port bow. I was a bit worried at times but although very wet, we rode remarkably well at 10 knots and only v. occasionally took a big one over. Damnably uncomfortable. Hoping for an improvement in the evening, but the barometer continued to fall slowly and steadily and the wind blew just as hard. Got good fixes by Loran by which we were making good about 8 knots. We were about half way across the Faeroes-Shetland gap by 2000. I am developing a cold, a thing I can never remember doing while actually at sea before.

Sunday, 17 December 1944 – At sea

We had a radar alarm at about 0100 – a Jig at about 3,000 yds which at first I thought might be a submarine but which on investigation turned out to be a small trawler. Blew hard all through the night, but as we approached the N. coast of Scotland the sea went down. North Rona was abeam at about 0900, but it wasn't light till about 1000. For a short time about midday, as we were entering the North Minches, the sun came out and the sky cleared and it was really lovely. The first time we've seen the sun since Dec. 1st but alas, it didn't last long. By 1500 it had shut down to about 4 miles' visibility with rain squalls and still blowing like hell from the S.E. As we rounded M1 buoy to head for the narrows, the wind increased to a force I've seldom seen before and even in these comparatively sheltered waters seas were breaking over our fo'c'sle. We got through the narrows without much worry with radar and still some daylight, and shortly after dark the glass started to rise with a bang from the depths of 28.5 millibars to which it had fallen, the wind dropped, and it eventually turned out a calm, bright, starlit night. About time too, after this last 2 or 3 days of continuous gales. Feeling coldy and not too bright.

Monday, 18 December 1944 – At sea/Londonderry

We arrived off Inishtrahull at 0700 and fired off a D/C pattern and a hedgehog pattern. Our H/H wouldn't fire, which annoyed me a lot. There was water in the ripple switch box. After that, while it was still pretty dark, I did an exercise to test out the new step aside procedure against Gnats when approaching a U-boat. I made *Stormont* the U-boat and fired star shell at him, but found so long as I continued to step aside I couldn't close nearer than 6,000 yds. However, it was good value. At about 0900 we packed up and made for the Lough Foyle buoy while I had a shave and breakfast, and we picked up pilots at 1000 and came up river. Just before Culmore Point we ran into dense fog. We groped our way up to Lisahally using radar and secured there for about ½ hour till it lifted. All the other 3 coming up behind us did the same. We finally secured up harbour at about 1300.

After lunch I went up to see Joe Selby, who tells me *Stormont* is going off to Canada for refit tomorrow, and *Port Colborne* is going to Liverpool for her lay over, taking the libertymen from the group to save the rail and boat travel, but that all leave will expire at Liverpool again at 1800 on Boxing Day, which means Xmas Day travelling for all, except those in London. I don't see how I can make it myself. Much too much of a rush both ends.

Went off and had a hair cut and then back on board and read my mail. Angus came over to see me with a man about the leave, and so I went up to see Selby again to see if it could be extended a bit. It seems to me neither the ships at sea or the ships in harbour are getting real Xmas leave this way. Went in to see the Commodore, who was sympathetic but slightly tipsy. Anyhow, back I went to find out particulars of where men were going for their leave and to find out about trains and then I rang the Commodore back, who said the big snag now was Liverpool said they couldn't boiler clean *Port Colborne.* Really, one sometimes envies the Scapa Flow chaps who can't get leave anyway and so have none of these problems. I did some work on reports and at 2100 went over and had a drink with Myra. The news isn't so good. The Germans have put up a counter offensive on the West and have driven the American 1st Army back a long way, and they are still going back.[63]

Tuesday, 19 December 1944 – Londonderry

I was shown a signal in the night cancelling *Port Colborne*'s trip to Liverpool and saying leave was from p.m. 20th to p.m. 27th. That looks much better for me because at any rate it gives me 24 hours more this end to square things up. I had a dental appointment at 0900 and had a tooth stopped. It was down in our sick bay with a portable dental outfit which was brought on board. At 1100 there was a group conference, which for once we managed to get through fairly quickly, and then I went on board *Stormont* who were having a farewell cocktail party in their wardroom. Before I left they cleared lower deck and I said good bye to the ship's companies.

After lunch I saw defaulters, which consisted of the Coxswain, who was drunk on board yesterday forenoon and incapable of steering the ship up harbour. Why do these chaps do these damned stupid things? and just when I want to go on leave. I made out a warrant and sent Blanchard up to Com. D.'s Secretary, and I went into the town and tried on my sports coat and then came back and struggled with correspondence and warrants, etc. I was hoping perhaps to work an air trip to England tomorrow but it didn't materialize. By the time I turned in I felt I'd got most of my work done. Brown arrived back from Canada to resume his group signal duties and he says Falconer is also on the way back. Rainy day. Not much news from France, but this German attack on the American 1st Army front seems to be a very big thing into which they are throwing everything.

Wednesday, 20 December 1944 – Londonderry/London

I got up rather early as I had quite a lot to do, but in the course of the forenoon I got through it all. *Monnow* arrived alongside at 1030 and the Old Man of the Sea[64] came over to see me later on. He said that he told the O.O.W. who lost touch with us just what he thought of him. Skinner eventually had lunch with me and afterwards I shifted and got a car to take me to the station, where I caught the 2:20 to Larne. Angus and one of his officers travelled with me. On going on board at Larne we found the boat v. full and at Stranraer it was an awful struggle to get off and find a seat in the train. In the end we won through but, my God, how I loathe this sort of travelling. We were 6 in the carriage all through the night. The train left Stranraer at 2200.

Thursday, 21 December 1944 – London/Prinsted

I slept really quite well. As we approached London it was foggy and we went slower and slower and eventually didn't get to Euston till just after 1200. As it was so late I had to go straight to C.N.M.O. after waiting ages for a taxi. I found Houghton in, and told him the things I wanted about appointments of officers, but the chap who dealt with air passages had gone to lunch. Tried to get a shave at Nortons but they couldn't manage it so I went to Austin Reeds. There was a frightful mob and I had to wait over ½ hour and it was after 1400 by the time I'd finished my shave. Went straight back to C.N.M.O. and saw a Pay 2½ called Brown about my air passage back to Belfast. He put a call through to the Admiralty but couldn't get on to the right person, so I went out again and tried to get some lunch but it was a bit late, so I sent a wire to J.

Back to C.N.M.O. where I found the Admiralty had said my application for a passage had been forwarded to the American Air Transport people, but [they] hadn't heard the result yet. I couldn't get a car and I couldn't get a taxi but eventually, just as I thought I would miss my train, I got a passage in an R.C.N. Jeep – a most hair raising performance but I just caught the 3:45. Arrived Havant at 1730 and was lucky enough to find a taxi and got home that way. Gillian, who I hadn't seen since March, has grown quite a bit and looking v. pretty. R. was delighted to see me. Was it good to be home but I am already dreading the going away again. Mr. Churchill has also grown a lot.

...

Monday, 25 December 1944 – Prinsted

I vaguely heard the children talking at about 0600 but I didn't go into them until about 0700. They were v. tickled with their presents, although there is awfully little in the way of toys except the most awful rubbish to be had now. I went to 0800 Communion service at Southbourne. There were a lot of people there including the Youngs and Scott-Moncrieffs. There was a hard frost and it was cold, but dry and bright later on. Got back to rather a late breakfast, after which I helped with various chores about the house. At about 1100 J., I, G., and R. all went down to the marshes for a little air and exercise and the children played about with the ice on the puddles and thoroughly enjoyed it. After lunch J. went to bed and had a sleep, and I was hoping to do the same but at the last moment R. said he didn't want to go with G. and play with the Garretts, and so I stayed in the nursery with him and between him and Mr. Churchill I got absolutely no peace. Betty Young looked in for a minute with presents just before tea. Shortly after tea G. and R. paddled off to Jane's, where they are spending the night as is Monique Hayes, so that Jane and we can dine with the Hayes.

I climbed into a dinner jacket and J. put on a dinner dress and at 1830 we went to the Garretts for drinks. It felt v. strange to be in a dinner jacket. Jane was there too and at 1930 she and we left, looked in on the children at Green Meadows and then went over to Wideacre for dinner. A Mrs. Dawson was the other member of the party. We had plenty of good drink and a good meal and thoroughly enjoyed it, and it helped to keep my mind off tomorrow's departure. We didn't get to bed till nearly 0100. A lovely, frosty, moonlight night. The General is a great talker but nice. Lilian I don't mind, but J. thinks her rather a bitch.

7

Wreck to Wreck, Contact to Contact, January-March 1945

Layard and E.G. 9 rejoined the inshore campaign as it entered a new, more intense phase. The *U-bootwaffe* had been slow to recover from the loss of its bases in the Bay of Biscay and the resultant shift of its boats to Norway, with the result that there had been little U-boat activity in British waters over much of the autumn. An Admiralty summary for October 1944 described it as "exceptionally light," and trumpeted that in terms of merchant ship losses, the month was "the LOWEST on record since the War began."[1] November witnessed a "slight increase," but it still saw the second lowest number of merchant ship casualties of the war.[2] German attempts to disrupt shipping carrying supplies to Allied armies in northwest Europe were clearly failing.

The situation changed in December, when the Germans deployed some twenty-eight U-boats towards British inshore waters.[3] One boat sent into the English Channel met with particular success. *U-486* attacked a convoy off Falmouth on 18 December, sinking the 6,100-ton freighter *Silverlaurel.* Over the next ten days the marauder intensified alarm by sinking the frigate HMS *Capel,* two merchant ships, and a landing ship, and damaging another destroyer. The most devastating success came on 24 December off Cherbourg when it sank the troopship *Leopoldville,* taking the lives of some 801 passengers including 785 American soldiers.[4] *U-486* slipped out of the Channel unscathed and made it safely back to Norway.

The score racked up by *U-486* – five merchant ships and two frigates sunk or disabled – caused consternation. The director of the Anti-U-Boat Division, Capt. C.D. Howard-Johnston, dubbed the period "Black Christmas."[5] The Admiralty's immediate response was to send two additional support groups into the Channel. Over the longer term it planned to reinforce the area with two more escort groups, transfer another two groups home from West Africa, and retain fourteen escorts earmarked for the Far East.[6] It also initiated convoys in the Irish Sea and expedited the laying of deep defensive minefields off key focal points such as St. George's Channel. There were doubts, however, that these measures would be enough. The German success in the Channel combined with merchant ship losses in the Irish Sea outdistanced anything the U-boats had achieved inshore through the autumn of 1944. The Anti-U-Boat Division's year-end summary noted that "U-boats have succeeded in gaining, for the time being at least, a great deal of immunity both from air and surface attack. Up till the end of 1944 the balance was still GREATLY in our favour, since they were not taking advantage of this immunity to sink our shipping. Last half of December was, however, a warning."[7] That final thought caused senior officials to take a cold, hard look at the anti-submarine war.

The 25 January 1945 meeting of the powerful Cabinet Anti-U-Boat Warfare Committee chaired by Prime Minister Sir Winston Churchill set the course for the remainder of the anti-submarine campaign in European waters. The First Sea Lord, Admiral of the Fleet Sir Andrew Cunningham, laid out the context in a characteristically blunt manner by stating that since the third week of December, "our successes compare unfavourable with our losses." He warned that the situation might grow even worse: the number of U-boats on patrol was expected to increase from the fifteen or so normally at sea to sixty in February and perhaps even eighty in March and April. Complicating the equation was the anticipated arrival of the new, fast type XXI and XXIII U-boats, which were capable of achieving some fifteen knots submerged. If they operated in numbers in inshore waters or renewed the offensive on the North Atlantic, they could tilt the balance in the war at sea. Cunningham warned that he had "absolutely no spare surface forces" to face the rising U-boat threat. The C-in-C Western Approaches also complained of a paucity of resources. Admiral Horton told the committee he was "stretched to the limit," and that all his support groups had been moved into the Irish Sea or the Channel save one, which was operating under C-in-C Rosyth off northwest Scotland.[8]

Not all present at the meeting shared that gloomy outlook. In the midst of heated discussion, Captain Howard-Johnston advised Churchill that far from posing a serious threat, the U-boats that had penetrated the Channel were "all hiding in terror on the bottom due to our effective countermeasures." That view – probably the most realistic – won out. After some badgering from Churchill, Horton "agreed that the enemy had so far had little success [in the inshore campaign], but felt sure that this was mainly due to the heavy concentration of anti-submarine forces which he had been able to achieve in the comparatively small area of present U-boat operations."[9] Although they were not sinking many U-boats, neither were the U-boats particularly dangerous. In other words, the status quo was acceptable.

The fast type XXI and XXIII U-boats were the unknown factor in the anti-submarine campaign. So long as the *Kriegsmarine* deployed the old, slow type VII or IX boats into limited inshore operational areas, the Allies could cope with the levels of sinkings. There would be trouble only if the fast boats were unleashed into North Atlantic and British waters in numbers. This essentially thrust Allied naval commanders into the role of anxious spectators to a great race, hoping that the American, British, Canadian, and Soviet armies could overrun U-boat bases and building yards, or even force an overall surrender, before the threat posed by new submarines could materialize. Much to their ultimate relief that is precisely what occurred: at VE Day just one type XXI and six type XXIIIs were operational.[10]

Toiling at the sharp end of the campaign, Layard and E.G. 9 had no knowledge of such high-level discussions, but they were affected by new measures tailored to the inshore campaign. With U-boats employing static tactics along well-established shipping routes, Western Approaches increasingly deployed its support groups to reinforce convoys as opposed to patrolling focal points.[11] For E.G. 9 this meant spending much less time on the area searches they had carried out almost exclusively since June. Under the new tactics they stayed in close proximity to a convoy's bow and flanks at night, and in daylight positioned themselves astern as "pouncers," ready to counterattack against any aggressor.[12] When not supporting convoys, they carried out Gamma searches along the shipping lanes or took part in special hunts laid on by Western Approaches. These tactics proved effective. As a postwar RN analysis found, by working in close proximity to convoys, support groups "were able to hunt U-boats to destruction within a short time of their disclosing their presence by attacks."[13] Between December 1944 and the end of the war the policy resulted in twenty-five U-boat kills by ships and aircraft in close support of convoys, compared to eight by independent surface patrols and seven by air patrols.[14]

These changes were backstopped by Admiral Horton's relentless emphasis on training. Even though merchant ship losses remained low, as historian Malcolm Llewellyn-Jones has pointed out, Horton "was failing in his cherished aim of sinking large numbers of U-boats."[15] He wanted a knockout blow, and one way to get that was to improve the "fighting standards by training ... particularly against Schnorchel fitted submarines."[16] Horton also wanted to prepare support groups for the new fast U-boats, whose high submerged speed would complicate tried defensive concepts. Besides working the problem at tactical tables ashore, the submarine HMS *Seraph* was modified to increase its submerged speed, and after being used as a test bed to analyze the threat posed by fast submarines, she was used as a "clockwork mouse" for support groups to hone their skills against.[17] Layard had his first go at *Seraph* in February 1945: "I must say I found it a very difficult thing to attack."[18]

On a long patrol in February, circumstances thrust E.G. 9 into situations where it could put its training to the test against two U-boats. More than anything, the experiences emphasize how support groups had to adjust to vastly different conditions. In the first instance, the group stalked *U-483* in the relatively open waters between the Shetland and Faeroe Islands. The U-boat eventually escaped, and Layard's reluctance to use depth charges or *Loch Alvie*'s Squid elicited criticism from the Admiralty – Layard thought the underwater explosions would cause him to lose asdic contact in the disturbed water.[19] "Having found a U-boat, I had failed to destroy it," Layard lamented after the war, "and I felt angry and depressed at my inefficiency."[20] His confidence was restored a few days later when *Saint John* destroyed *U-309* with surgical precision while operating inshore in close support of a convoy. It proved to be Layard's last U-boat kill, and arguably his most spectacular.

That same February patrol also provided evidence of the toll the inshore campaign was taking on ships. Escorts used depth charges at a prodigious rate, and the powerful explosions in shallow water wreaked havoc on their thin, fragile hulls. Layard led five frigates out of Londonderry on 3 February, yet by the end of the operation only one, *Loch Alvie*, remained operational: *Port Colborne, Saint John*, and *Nene* had been declared unfit for operations, while *Monnow* required docking.[21] As Layard noted in his report of proceedings,

> In recent months the 9th E.G. has been operation [sic] almost entirely in shallow coastal waters making daily and sometimes hourly attacks on bottomed contacts, and the average monthly expenditure of D/Cs and H/H has been equivalent to the normal annual expenditure by ships operating in deep water. This in itself must have brought an unexpectedly heavy strain on ship's hulls and main and auxiliary machinery, but when it is realized how very much greater is the force of concussion from charges exploded on the bottom in 30-50 fathoms of water than is the case with charges, even at shallow settings, dropped in deep water, it is scarcely to be wondered at, if extensive leaks develop. Bearing this in mind D/C attacks in shallow water have never been carried out at less than 15 knots. During one period of 10 days operating off the Cornish Coast, "SAINT JOHN" expended 120 depth charges and 8 patterns of H/H. This was exceptional but it is no exaggeration to say that 60-80 depth charges and 6-8 H/H salvoes were fired monthly over a period of 8 months which started with D-Day on 6th June, 1944.[22]

Layard recommended that more frequent docking and hull inspections be laid on, but the ongoing shortage of anti-submarine vessels made those measures difficult to achieve. As the inshore campaign dragged on through the winter, ships and men alike had to suffer.

Wednesday, 27 December 1944 – Belfast/Londonderry

I woke at about 0600 and lay awake feeling horribly homesick and full of dread of what lay ahead. Caught the 9:00 train, which arrived in Londonderry at 1200, and I got on board for lunch. To my relief I found no particular headaches awaiting me. In the p.m. I went up to the offices. Rang up Larne and talked about our exercises, went to Operations and found out about our sailing time tomorrow, and then saw about some drafting problems and then back on board to read through signals and papers and so on. Wrote a long letter to J.

Thursday, 28 December 1944 – Londonderry/Moville

I woke very early and lay feeling miserable and worried and finally got up and added a P.S. to my letter to J. before having my bath. I put in a good forenoon on signals and paper work, and at 1100 I had a C.O.s meeting and then went over to one of the other groups to see if I could get any information about recent Channel work, as I have a hunch that is where we are going, but didn't find out much. I had just sat down to lunch when Joe Selby came on board and we had some gin and a chat in my cabin. I told him what I thought about the Commodore and what a pity it was he didn't get to know the Canadian C.O.s better.

The group, less *Nene* who had some last minute defect, slipped and went down river at 1315. We went straight to the oiler at Moville, outside *Port Colborne.* It was a lovely bright, frosty day and I took some exercise on the upper deck. Had the Captain of the tanker over for a drink. He is a Norwegian and says the people in Norway are nearly starving. As we took so long to oil and didn't finish till 2100, I decided to stay alongside until we sail at 0345 tomorrow. Had a short yarn with Angus and turned in at about 2200. My responsibilities are hanging heavily on me, as usual, and I'm miserably homesick. This day last week I was just arriving home.

Friday, 29 December 1944 – Moville/Larne/At sea

At 0345 we shoved off from the oiler. It was a most lovely cloudless night with a full moon. *Nene* arrived down in time to sail with us but without oiling. We went round to Larne without incident and anchored shortly after 0800. At 0900 when it began to get light, the staff officers came on board and we split up into 2 groups. *Saint John* and *Port Colborne* worked with one submarine, and *Monnow* and *Nene* with the other, and from 1000 to 1300 we did A/S Ps. Conditions were good and we got good value out of it. There was a damned cold, quite strong, W.'ly wind blowing which made it rather miserable on the bridge. In the p.m. the group concentrated and carried out a bottom submarine exercise. As on both previous occasions we were quite unable to find it – even when it fired smoke candles. That ended at 1700 and at 1800 we started a night A/S P but as only one S/M was available there were too many of us.

At about 2000 we got a signal from Larne telling us to return to the anchorage forthwith and disembark staff officers, and we got orders to proceed at once at best speed to Longships. It seems there is some flap on round the S. Irish coast where several U-boats are believed to be and so no night in and no second day's exercises as was intended.[23] The issue was complicated by *Nene* being 50% short of fuel and *Port Colborne* reporting a serious condenser leak, and I had to ask instructions. We and *Monnow* eventually weighed at 2200 and proceeded south. *Nene* went to Bangor Bay to fuel and *Port Colborne,* having just been told to return to Londonderry, found she could make good the defect herself and followed us about 3 hours later.

Saturday, 30 December 1944 – At sea

A fairly peaceful night coming S. at 16 kts. We reached K4 buoy at about 0930 and we had patches of misty rain and bad visibility as we went round The Smalls, and for quite a bit beyond that. I went mess deck rounds. This ship isn't a patch on *Swansea* down below. We got a signal in the p.m. telling us to relieve 3 escorts who were patrolling Hartland Point to Trevose Head (an old, familiar beat).

We arrived off Lundy Island about 1530 but had to go right down to Trevose Head before finding *Goodall, Antigua,* and *Loch Insh* at about 1700. We very soon started to get contacts, all charted wrecks, the number of which seems to have increased quite a lot since we were here before. *Port Colborne* joined up just after dark and *Nene* in the middle watch. Calm day and bright, moonlit night. The A/S conditions were *too* good. We picked up every single echo up and down the whole course and spent the night identifying their positions by Q.H.

Sunday, 31 December 1944 – At sea

A calm, fine, sunny day. Shortly after daylight, I got a signal telling me to detach 2 ships to patrol between the Scillies and Lizard. I sent *Monnow* and *Nene,* and *Port Colborne* and I continued to cannon from wreck to wreck and contact to contact, in our area. *Port Colborne* annoyed me v. much in the p.m. by hanging around a bottom contact for hours without doing anything and then, without any reason that I could see, classified it non sub. At about 1730, just as we were taking station ahead of a S. bound convoy off Hartland Point, we got a contact. No echo sounder trace but I put down 5 charges for luck, which seemed to disperse it. We parted company with the convoy at Trevose Head and turned N. just after midnight. We got an A/S contact not previously plotted and attacked with H/H and then D/Cs. The latter gave us an awful shaking, and radar and Q.H. came off the board. Eventually got an echo sounder trace which showed it to be non sub. I read prayers and spoke to the ship's company at 1100.

Monday, 1 January 1945 – At sea

Colder day and hazy with no sun. Still an oily calm with perfect A/S conditions – almost too good – and we pick up every single wreck and non sub echo in the area. I didn't get much sleep and during the day, either me or *Port Colborne* seemed to be continually in contact. I read the warrant on the Coxswain depriving him of his medal and badge and I took the opportunity to read the Chiefs and Petty Officers a short lecture on duty.[24] We arrived off Hartland Point at about 1600 and met a S. going convoy. They seem to pass Lundy Island daily at about the same time, crossing a N. going convoy between this and Trevose Head. I took station astern of the convoy this time. At about 2130 we became slightly involved with the N. going convoy as it passed ours. Otherwise it was fairly quiet. We turned round to sweep N. on reaching Trevose Head soon after midnight. I hope to goodness this is the last wartime New Year. I have lost $25 to Commander King, as I bet him the war would be over before the end of last year.

Tuesday, 2 January 1945 – At sea

Soon after we'd turned round we were ordered by signal to proceed to meet an M.K.S. convoy[25] 10' N. of Round Island at 0900 and support it as far as Hartland Point, and so we turned South. We had the inevitable crop of contacts during the night, and we wasted so much time on one of *Port Colborne*'s – a bottom contact which she attacked – that I had to make a signal saying we would be late at the R/V. As it happened the convoy was early and we met some way N. of the rendezvous at about 0730. 15 ships and 3 escorts. I took station ahead until daylight and then took *Port Colborne* with me astern, which seems to be the accepted position for support groups in this shallow water business.

Just after passing Trevose Head at about 1430 we got a contact. Echo sounder trace showed object on the bottom but the echo was difficult to hold. Decided I ought to throw something at it and eventually after a lot of jockeying I fired an H/H pattern which brought up a small amount of oil. Under ordinary circumstances it would have been worth further investigation, but as by now the convoy were almost out of sight I left it and went after them at full speed. I think I was wrong to spend even as much time as I did when my primary duty was protection of the convoy. Caught up with them at about 1700 and at about 1730 we detached on nearing Hartland Point and turned S. to follow behind the usual S. going coastal convoy, which [we] brought up to Trevose Head at about 2300, where we turned N. again. Another flat calm day, but overcast and no sun.

Wednesday, 3 January 1945 – At sea

We had hardly turned to the N. before we received a signal telling us to proceed and screen a floating dock which would be in a position 10' W. of Bishop Rock at 0330. So we turned round and went off in pursuit at 16 kts. We picked it up by radar at about 0430 just off the Bishop. It was in tow of 2 tugs with an escort of 4 trawlers on a southerly course. Destined for the east or Med presumably. We took station one on either bow till daylight, and then I formed a line abreast A/S screen ahead with 5 ships, leaving one trawler astern. The period of flat calm has ended, and it blew quite fresh from the W.S.W. with a slowly falling barometer. We were told to remain with this outfit only as far as 48°30' N., but the choppy sea reduced the speed of the tow considerably and we didn't get there until 2200. We then parted company with *Port Colborne* and shaped course for the Wolf Rock, which were our last instructions. The wind at about 2000 suddenly flew round to the N.

From the news, the German thrust in Belgium seems to have been completely held now, but it has meant giving a bit of ground and releasing some of our pressure on German soil a bit further south.

Thursday, 4 January 1945 – At sea

At about 0430 we received a v. corrupt signal telling us to support an M.K.F. convoy[26] coming from the southward, but lots of repetitions and corrections were required before we could get its position. Eventually about 0530 we got it sorted out and altered to the W. to intercept it as it came up towards the Bishop. It was blowing hard from the N. now with a biggish beam sea, and I had to reduce to 12 kts. At 1000 we turned south and got some D/F bearings of the convoy, which we eventually sighted at 1200. 14 big transports screened by E.G. 5 (*Aylmer* S.O.) and 5 D.E.s.[27] We went to position F. The speed of convoy was down to 11 kts, as escorts were being broken up at higher speeds and the course was slap into the wind and sea. In spite of a rising glass there was no sign of the wind easing, and even at 11 kts it was very wet, bumpy, and unpleasant, with occasional sleety squalls and showers, and one felt one had absolutely nothing in hand. The convoy formed a narrow front just before dark and at 2000 when about 25' W. of the Scillies they altered to 063° for Trevose Head. We got a signal telling *Monnow* and *Nene* to arrive Plymouth for a short lay over tomorrow, which has given them a v. short time out. I didn't expect to go in before the 8th or 9th.

Friday, 5 January 1945 – At sea

The wind and sea eased when we turned and I spent a peaceful night mostly in my sea cabin bunk. We remained with the convoy until we reached Hartland Point at about 0630, when we and *Port Colborne* turned to start our patrol down to Trevose Head once again. In order to exercise Officers of the Watch and the missing watch I gave orders that counter attacks, fire only one charge, were to be carried out on some of these contacts. We had plenty of opportunities, as we were getting echoes as usual up and down the whole length of the patrol. I went store room rounds. The wind has gone down but what there is is cold and from the N. At about 1500 *Kempthorne* and *Keys* passed escorting a ship north, and the former got a contact, which she attacked bringing up oil and wreckage. We closed and identified it with Q.H. as one of the previously plotted wrecks.

We met the daily south going Bristol Channel-Thames convoy off Hartland Point at 1800 and followed it down to Trevose Head. Just as we were turning N. at about 2200 *Port Colborne* got a contact with echo sounder trace where no wreck had previously been plotted and attacked, and we closed later on to have a look see. No visible result from attacks and echo v. difficult to hold, and so eventually at about midnight I got fed up and called it a wreck and went on.

Saturday, 6 January 1945 – At sea

At about 0200 we got another bottom echo not previously plotted and so after looking at it for a bit we gave it 5 charges and then passed on. At about 0500 another contact close in to Hartland Point, on which we spent some time before classifying as non sub. At daylight I sent *Port Colborne* back to look at his last night's contact again and went back to our 0200 echo. It was some time before I could pick it up, but Q.H. put us right over the spot and at last there it was. Ran over with E/S and then attacked with 5 charges. As usual there were some misfires, with in this case rather an alarming hang fire which went off 24 minutes after dropping.

About noon we got a signal to meet a K.M.F. convoy off Lundy and support it as far as 49°30' N. We met it at about 1300. Fourteen large transports ex liners, 14 knots. The escorting group was E.G. 20, S.O. *Tavy,* who was with us with the Russian convoy. We were stationed ahead as far as Trevose Head, and then when the convoy formed on a broad front we joined the remaining escorts as a tight A/S screen ahead. The course was west from Trevose Hd. until 1930 when course was altered to the S. The screen got very ragged on the turn and the S.O. eventually changed to an A.C.I. screening diagram. At 2230 *Tavy* got a contact, which he attacked while the convoy did a step aside and then left us and *Port Colborne* to hold and investigate. Echo sounder showed an object on the bottom which I attacked with H/H and D/Cs and eventually at about 0300 I classified it as wreck and as by then the convoy was miles away we turned back towards the Bishop where we'd been told to meet a home coming M.K.S. convoy and support to Lundy. I signalled C. in C. telling him my contact by E/S was classified non sub. Rather a grey sort of morning but a lovely clear calm p.m. and evening.

Sunday, 7 January 1945 – At sea

On reaching the Bishop at about 0500 we turned to 192° to meet our M.K.S. convoy and at about 0600 *Port Colborne* got a contact which eventually we went over to help him with, as he had an E/S trace. There are 3 plotted wrecks in the vicinity, but as Q.H. is blind in this particular spot it was not possible to pinpoint this contact, and so we had to attack it and as it was not too easy to hold it took us a long time. I had to report to C. in C. what I was doing in case he thought I was with the convoy. At last, at about 0900 after bringing up a lot of fish and nothing else, I classified it as a wreck and went on to meet the convoy, which we sighted shortly afterwards. By the time we'd taken up station astern it was about 1100 and rather too late for prayers, which was a pity as I think a weekly talk to the sailors is a good thing. I walked round the upper deck. Having been a lovely morning it started to blow quite hard from the N.W. and turned very chilly. We followed astern of the convoy without incident up to midnight, altering round the Scillies for Trevose Head and so up the old track to Lundy.

Monday, 8 January 1945 – At sea/Plymouth

At about 0230 we spotted *Monnow* and *Nene* coming up astern. I had to make a long signal giving the position of all the new wrecks we'd found and another signal turning over the patrol duties, and eventually just before 0400 we turned round with *Port Colborne* for Plymouth. We had a sniff at a couple of contacts off the Lizard at about 1100, which I classified (perhaps a little hurriedly) as wrecks. Saw requestmen and defaulters. At about 1300 as we were coming up to the Eddystone we got a contact which I couldn't possibly call a charted wreck as it wasn't within 2 miles of one, and so reluctantly I set to work with *Port Colborne* to attack it. We gave it a pattern of H/H and 3 ten charge patterns and one 5 charge pattern. As nothing but a small wisp of oil came up after that I decided that honour was satisfied and continued on our way. Just as we got contact the weather, which had been bright and sunny, suddenly clouded over with a strong N.'ly wind and flurries of sleet and snow. Damned cold and unpleasant. We passed the breakwater at 1715, which was 2 hours later than intended. Went up harbour and secured alongside the oiler lying opposite the *Defiance* and remained there for the night.

I had a lovely hot bath in which I soaked for some time, and when I had dressed I got Angus over for a drink and he stayed talking for a long time mostly about discipline in the R.C.N. I feel after our talk that I've been awfully weak and have done nothing to buck things up in this group. My popularity, such as it is, has been achieved largely because I haven't faced up to the job of checking the irregularities and bad habits. In fact my old moral weakness. Angus told me it had been announced a day or two ago that Bertie Ramsay (the Supreme Naval Commander for the invasion) had been killed in an aeroplane accident in France.

Tuesday, 9 January 1945 – Plymouth

At 0900 we shoved off from the oiler and berthed on the *Pitcairn* at No. 2 wharf. Still a strong cold N. wind with an occasional flurry of snow. At about 1000 I went to call on Capt. D., who was away on leave and Creighton his staff officer was looking out. While at Flagstaff Steps I looked in on Burrell[28] who is Maintenance Commander. Saw a copy of the promotions. Allan Campbell and Tom Harland have been made Captains, and Wemyss, who is just on retirement, has been promoted to Commander. He is now E.G. 2 and is following in Walker's footsteps, who as a passed over Commander was promoted to Captain. Talbot who was my No. 1 in the *Stoke* in Malta and Waterhouse also promoted.[29] In the Canadian list Band has got his ½ stripe.

Walked back on board and at 1100 I got a car and Earl and I went up to A.C.H.Q. to get the news. There really isn't much. There have been some torpedoings in the Channel, mostly in the Portsmouth area, but not a sign of a U boat to be found. We shall go out for about another 9 or 10 days then back here and finally back to Derry by the 25th. The C. in C. came in while we were there and was v. affable (Admiral Leatham). Back on board for lunch where I found a letter from J.

After lunch I put on plain clothes and went ashore and walked about Devonport and Plymouth looking for a diary without any luck. Went into the Museum and had a look round and had a hair cut and bought a present for R.'s birthday, and then came back on board and wrote to J. It turned out a lovely day but cold. The news is better, with British and American 1st Army, who have all been put under Montgomery's command, attacking the German salient in the Ardennes and making progress, while the Americans in S. are also attacking from that side and squeezing the Germans, who are now definitely on the defensive. The Americans have landed on Luzon in the Philippines, and in Burma we are within 50 miles of Mandalay.

Wednesday, 10 January 1945 – Plymouth/At sea

I spent some of the forenoon writing letters. At 1000 I went out into the Dockyard and rang up J. from a call box and spoke to both G. and R. as well. Oh, to be at home now. I then walked further up the yard and had a look at the *Devonshire* and the *Anson* from the dockside before returning on board. Went over to *Port Colborne* and had a drink with Angus. We had some Wren officers on board for lunch in return for a "do" at the Wrenery for our officers last night. We went to one hour's notice at 1600 and sailed at 1715. The Chief came to me at the very last moment with some story about leaky evaporator coils but, thank God, he managed to borrow some spares from *Port Colborne* and so didn't delay our sailing. This last minute discovery of defects is quite unnecessary if proper tests are carried out in good time.

A cold frosty but fine clear day and although misty in the Sound as we went out at sunset it was clear outside. Our orders were to go to the Lizard and relieve 2 other ships and patrol Lizard to Scillies. We got rather involved with a convoy which we met at about 2100, and later we were delayed investigating contacts, and so we didn't reach the Lizard until after 2300.

Thursday, 11 January 1945 – At sea

I swept up into Penzance Bay to the entrance of Mounts Bay and then turned W. for 4 miles and then out again across the convoy route south, leaving the Wolf to starboard, and then we turned W. towards the Scillies. What with non sub contacts and the navigational necessities in going into the Bay I got v. little sleep during the night. At daylight we were approaching the Scillies and we turned N. and swept close in shore and then E. again back towards the Lizard, which we reached at about 1600. I had just turned N. to have a look into Penzance Bay again when we got a signal to meet and support the Channel section of an H.X. convoy. We were given a rendezvous about 20 miles W. of the Scillies at 0300 tomorrow, and so we turned W. again. From 1800-2000 we were investigating a contact which was v. hard to classify. We dropped a 10 charge pattern finally. I think it was fish.

We'd no sooner made onward than *Port Colborne* got a Quiz [asdic contact]. This is the most exasperating work, for which I haven't the patience. A very cold strong N.E. wind all day. About the coldest we've had so far.

Friday, 12 January 1945 – At sea

We got some very conflicting reports of the whereabouts of our convoy, but somewhere about 0230 we contacted them on radar rather earlier than we expected, only just W. of the Bishop. I was v. doubtful at first if it was *our* convoy and not an M.K.S. which was also due about the same time. It turned out to be ours but in a v. scattered state. We took station on each bow of the leading portion till daylight, when the whole outfit slowed down and the stragglers continually caught up. Still a stiff cold N.E. wind. I hate being ahead of a convoy because one always has to dash at contacts and consider dropping charges although one knows quite well they are probably the usual wreck. When at last we reached the Lizard at about 1600 we were relieved in support by 2 ships from E.G. 19, whose patrol extends from Lizard to the Start.[30] We turned back with *Port Colborne* and swept back to the Scillies. On arriving there shortly before midnight we turned to about 045° to sweep W. of the Wolf. I can't remember how many contacts we had in the mean time.

Saturday, 13 January 1945 – At sea

I was up for a good bit of the middle [watch] while we did E.I. turns and Blue turns near the Wolf. At about 0500 *Port Colborne* got a contact, which we confirmed as bottom contact as her echo sounder was out of action. No plotted wreck here, and as E/S trace was quite inconclusive, I decided to hold it till daylight and then attack. Wind and sea made conditions difficult, and time and again we missed it running over trying to get a classification by E/S trace. We started to attack at 0900 and gave it between us 3 H/H and 2 10 D/C patterns. A little oil was all we got, and eventually at about 1300 I persuaded myself rather against my true judgement that the last E/S trace obtained was definitely non sub. Anyhow I was desperate by then and all patience was exhausted.

Shaped course for Mounts Bay and swept into Penzance Bay where in due course we got an unplotted contact and once more had awful trouble getting good E/S evidence. Eventually after 2 hours we classified it non sub, collected *Port Colborne* who had gone off on her own, and turned S. to get across the traffic route before dark. With *Port Colborne*'s E/S out of action we have to investigate all hers as well as our contacts. A most exhausting day. I never seemed to get off the bridge for more than about ½ hour at a time. From the submarine report today it seems a U-boat is operating in the Irish Sea and has sunk 2 ships off Holyhead.[31] It really seems these snorkelling U boats can operate in these shallow waters and never be found.

Sunday, 14 January 1945 – At sea

Just after midnight *Port Colborne* got a contact which we had to investigate with our E/S. There followed an exhausting 4 hours running backward and forwards from every direction, seldom getting anything at all and never anything conclusive on our E/S. Finally, I told *Port Colborne* to go in and drop a pattern, after which I did one more run over and at last got conclusive evidence that it was a wreck. After that I thankfully abandoned further operations and shaped course eastwards for the Lizard. There had been notice in the situation reports last night of quite a bit of traffic on this part of the coast and I was purposely operating well south of the convoy lanes. At 0800 we met the Channel section of an O.N. convoy west-bound off the Lizard. It was being tracked by 2 ships of another group and we had been told to take over from the Lizard to 7° W. We took station astern just as day broke and had a very peaceful day following them. Still a fresh cold N.W.'ly wind. We arrived at 7° W. just before 1900 and turned back.

Monday, 15 January 1945 – At sea

A quiet fairly undisturbed night. We arrived back off the Lizard at about 0800 and turned round to the W. once more. As soon as it was properly light I turned to 310° to sweep up to the E. of the Wolf. At about 1030 *Port Colborne* got contact and we had to go and investigate it. A bottom contact of indefinite proportions and not previously plotted, so I decided to attack. It was difficult to hold and after 2 H/H attacks we lost it and spent some time bumming round. *Port Colborne* then got off on yet another echo while we at last regained the first one and attacked it again twice. Nothing but fish and a wisp of oil, and so classified it wreck. Went over to *Port Colborne*'s new contact, which the E/S showed to be quite definitely a wreck.

At about 1600, after the best part of 5½ hours' hunting, we moved on but hadn't gone more than a few miles when we were once more in contact. Again not too easy to hold. E/S trace looked quite interesting and so we attacked and got in 1 H/H and 2 D/C patterns before dark. Again nothing but fish and a small amount of oil. Continued to run over for E/S traces after dark and at 2000 classified it as wreck. V. difficult decision and I could see Bradley,[32] my A/S Control Officer, was certain I was leaving a U-boat. How *does* one make an accurate decision on these occasions. I must say I was just about tired out and fed up with this continuous pinging. Later on in the first watch I was involved with alterations of course and yet another Quiz, which after one or two runs was classified fish, and so I really didn't get down to my sea cabin for any rest until about midnight. Fine but still that cold N.E. wind.

Tuesday, 16 January 1945 – At sea

We were told to meet and trail the Channel section of an H.X. convoy from the

Bishop to Lizard. They should have been 12' S. of the Bishop at 0800, but we had to go on west till nearly 1000 before we met them. 30 odd ships. *Vimy* was S.O. escort.[33] Although we are supposed to trail he asked us to take station ahead, which I must say seems a much more sensible place by day from the protection point of view. Flat calm with generally v.g. visibility but with the occasional misty shower. At 1400 *Royal Mount* (an R.C.N. Frigate) on the screen reported "Quiz" and "Hangover" and later on reported he was in contact with a definite S/M. At 1500 I suggested to *Vimy* that I turn back with *Port Colborne* to take over or help, to which he agreed and back we went. We reached the spot at about 1715. The corvette *Arnprior* was also there but they had lost contact. *Royal Mount* reported having dropped 7 D/C and 4 H/H patterns and only got a little oil. He said there was movement, doppler, and faint hydrophone effect. Just before we came up to them we got a contact and ran over and got an E/S trace which looked quite interesting and so we attacked with H/H but absolutely no result. *Port Colborne* then also gained contact about 3 miles away.

Royal Mount came alongside and we talked on the loud hailer.[34] After asking a few questions I'm afraid I don't believe for a moment it was really a submarine. He has no Q.H., and so the tide would give a stationary target apparent movement, and his E/S trace evidence sounds anything but convincing. I certainly can't explain the doppler. Decided to tell him and *Arnprior* to push off as they were wanted for another escort job and at 1800 they left us. I attacked again and *Port Colborne* having classified his contact non sub joined me. I wasn't at all sure about my E/S traces but I was probably influenced by the possibility of a submarine being around and so I decided to hold this contact all night as it was now nearly dark and attack again at daylight. We clicked the spot all night which was grand because I had a peaceful night. Signalled C. in C. what I was doing.

Wednesday, 17 January 1945 – At sea

At about 0800 we started running over the target again for E/S traces. Found it by no means easy to get them and now they really seem to bear no resemblance to a submarine. However, I attacked four times dropping 30 D/C without the slightest result. Told C. in C. first that I was no longer hopeful, and at 1130 I said I was giving it up and proceeding with our patrol and turned towards the Lizard. We had not been on our way 30 minutes when we got a signal to remain with contact until further orders. One might have guessed it!!!

Turned back and in due course gained contact again, but when we fixed by Q.H. it was 2 miles from original position. Dropped a dan buoy and ran back and forth trying to persuade myself it was the old contact but at about 1630 *Port Colborne*, who I'd told to search 2' 040" from me, reported another contact, which on closing I fixed exactly in the right position. He attacked once when I returned to weigh my Dan and then once again in accordance with C. in C.'s signal. I settled down to hold contact all night. Ran over several times and now the object seems to be as long as it is broad with no S/M characteristics. Signalled at 2000 that I was still of the opinion that it was non sub. A perfectly lovely sunny, calm day, but this classification I find difficult and worrying. I never know how to decide whether to remain or leave. The Russians are on the move again in a big way in the E. and have taken Warsaw and are only 15 miles from the German Silesian border.

Thursday, 18 January 1945 – At sea

It started to blow from the W. in the night with a falling glass and A/S conditions steadily worsened. In the morning watch it seemed to me that the contact we were holding was a bit to the N. of the old position, but as I was unable to pick up anything to the S. I concluded it was alright. We lost contact at about 0700 but *Port Colborne* picked it up again. We had been told to leave the contact at day light if there was no further evidence and so at about 0900 I decided to give it up and turned to the E. to sweep towards the Lizard. Wind increasing rapidly and by midday it was blowing Force 8. At 1400 when just E. of the Lizard, we turned round and punched straight into the wind and reduced to 7 knots. A short steep sea with an occasional big one, and we were virtually hove to making good about 3 knots. Could not go any faster without breaking something. The weather cleared in the p.m. and the glass steadied and gradually the wind and sea eased, but I remained at 7 knots as I wanted to delay turning as long as possible. *Monnow* and *Nene* went into Plymouth at 0830 for 30 hours' lay over.

Friday, 19 January 1945 – At sea

Wind and sea eased in the night so that when we were S. of the Bishop at about 0700 we could then turn without much discomfort. Swept slowly back to the Lizard. *Port Colborne* got a contact just before 1200. Owing to the weather it was difficult to get echo sounder results and we had to spend some time on it before we could classify it wreck. We got a signal telling us to rendezvous with *Monnow* and *Nene* off the Eddystone and proceed to meet and support an American C.U. convoy.[35] So our short layover is delayed again.

When just E. of the Lizard we both got contacts. My first E/S trace looked as if my target was off the bottom, which was interesting, and we then lost it temporarily. I started to get v. agitated. How much time should I spend on this thing? It was starting to get dark and unless I pushed on soon I'd be late for my R/V with *Monnow* and *Nene.* It was another of those infuriating instances of apparently 2 contacts within about ¾ mile of each other, and one was never certain whether in fact there were 1 or 2 contacts. Finally, at about 1800 I satisfied myself that the target was stationary and probably non sub and so I went on. We arrived S. of Eddystone at 1930 to the spot where we met the other two and started off to the S.W. to meet our convoy. Quite strange to be a whole group again. More difficult decisions about contacts, whether to spend a long time over careful investigation or push on so as not to be late at our meeting point at daylight. A nice day but cold after yesterday's blow.

Saturday, 20 January 1945 – At sea

It started to blow up again from the E.N.E. in the night and as the last Q.H. fix we could get was at 0430 I wasn't too sure what with wind and tide how much we were set off our course at daylight. I expected to sight the convoy at 0900 and just about that time *Monnow* on the port wing reported she had picked it up on radar. I think they were some way to leeward of this course. It is always a great weight off my mind when a convoy is safely met. We moved over and took station ahead until the American S.O. ("Boss") gave us his requirements, which put us on the close screen. This is a 14 knot convoy with 5 U.S. D.E.s as escorts. Our course for the Start was 044°, which brought the wind and sea on the beam, but even so it was pretty wet at 14 knots. With so little speed in hand we couldn't afford to dawdle about contacts, and in the p.m. we dashed in and counter attacked an echo with 10 charges and as soon as the last ship in the convoy was passed we left the contact and rejoined. My group rather disgraced themselves by being picked up by the U.S. S.O. for being out of station. I was v. impressed by the efficiency and discipline of the convoy and escorts.

At 1830 *Inconstant* and *Assiniboine* joined, and *Saint John* and *Port Colborne* were detached to escort one ship from the convoy to Falmouth. On arrival at D1 buoy at 2140 we led the ship right up to the entrance until the pilot boat was sighted and then turned round, picked up *Port Colborne,* and proceeded down to D3 buoy off the Lizard. Had to make one more counter attack while on the way from Falmouth. Out of 150 we now have only 25 D/Cs remaining. In spite of the wind it was a bright, fine day and a most lovely clear, cloudless night.

Sunday, 21 January 1945 – At sea/Plymouth

We had hardly got clear of the swept channels when we got a signal telling us to meet and trail a T.B.C. convoy[36] due to pass Start Point at 0100, so we set off east at 15 knots. When we were S. of Eddystone we heard that the convoy was using the inshore swept channel and so we turned N. and joined them just W. of Plymouth and trailed them W. till daylight. At about 0830 we turned round and headed for Plymouth where we arrived at 1030 and secured alongside. After I'd had a bath I went over to the *Port Colborne* and had a drink. Got a letter from J. Had a bit of shut eye after lunch and then got to work for a couple of hours on my report of proceedings. Went down to the wardroom at about 1830, where I found Brown alone as Officer of the Day. All the rest were up at one of the Wreneries. I had supper with him in the wardroom and later on went over to the *Port Colborne,* where they were having a bit of a party. I stayed quite late singing at the piano, and then the 1st Lieutenant came over and had a night cap with me. Before I knew what was happening I had about 4 or 5 in my cabin drinking whisky and I didn't get to bed till nearly 0200. A lovely bright but cold day. A smattering of snow on the countryside.

Monday, 22 January 1945 – Plymouth/At sea

Feeling a bit gummy this morning after all that whisky last night. Quite a fall of snow in the night. I went out into the Dockyard and rang up J. but there was no reply. I called on Capt. D. at 1030 and at 1100 Earl, Brown, and I all went up to A.C.H.Q. We had a long talk with Mallinson, who is just going, and I had a word with Beverley,[37] the new Chief of Staff who has relieved Caslon. The *Icarus* got a U-boat yesterday afternoon just off Longships about 2 hours after a ship had been torpedoed there.[38] A few days earlier and it would have been us. There has been another torpedoing in the Irish Sea off Bardsey Island.

We are lying alongside the *Tanatside,* a Hunt destroyer. On my return I went to see the Captain, who is de St. Croix, the great Canadian hater.[39]

We were supposed to sail at 1600, but there was a delay in getting our depth charges and I had to say we wouldn't be ready till 1800. I rang up J. again after lunch and told her to stand by to come to Derry. I read some correspondence which arrived, including a list of exercises which groups are supposed to carry out while at sea. Just one more thing to think about and worry about. We slipped and got through the gate at 1840 just before dark. We have to go back to the Cornish coast and patrol off Trevose Point, but we'd hardly passed Eddystone when we got a signal saying a conning tower had been sighted 12' 220" from Pendeen this morning and ordering us to relieve 3 ships of E.G. 14 now patrolling the area. *Monnow* and *Nene* were ordered to carry out our original patrol. We arrived off the Wolf just before midnight and took over from E.G. 14. Cold, rainy and blowing quite hard from the S.E.

Tuesday, 23 January 1945 – At sea

Carried out a N. and S. patrol between 270° Pendeen 9' and 270° Wolf 6'. We had one alarm in the night with a small radar echo, which we closed and eventually illuminated with star shell to find it was a Bangor class sweeper. The wind went right round to the N. in the morning watch and blew quite fresh all the a.m. Cold and fine. We changed our patrol area at daylight and went closer in shore, and we had not been long on the job before we got a contact close to Longships. Nothing previously charted there and so we attacked. Echo hard to hold and E/S trace difficult to obtain, and so it was one of those v. slow jobs running over and over and trying all courses for the best result. Nothing came of the attacks, but I was still unwilling to leave at 1500 when we got a signal to proceed to another position 5 miles to the N. of Longships where a trawler reported she was attacking a submarine contact. She had by this time lost contact and left the scene, but we sighted some oil and got a ping at the head of it and we and *Port Colborne* both attacked. A great deal of splintered wood came to the surface and a life belt but v. little more oil. At about 1830 I classified it as wreck from evidence and from information from C. in C. that a small coaster had founded in a position under 2 miles away. Wind and sea had died away completely by dark and we returned to our same patrol line as last night. *Port Colborne* caused an alarm in the 1st watch by getting a radar contact and illuminating with star shell and reporting probably snorkel, and all the time it was the unlighted 7 Stones buoy. The Russians are rolling ahead in the E. and are across the Oder in Silesia and within 15 miles of Breslau.

Wednesday, 24 January 1945 – At sea

At 0600 in accordance with C. in C.'s signal we left patrol and proceeded to Londonderry. We picked up *Monnow* and *Nene* just S. of Trevose and all pushed on at 15 knots. Now with U-boats in the Irish Sea one can no longer, I suppose, paddle along happily in line abreast. I remained in line abreast zig zagging, except for one bit when we ran into a snow storm with nil visibility off Pembroke and also while passing the Grassholm swept channel. Before dark we fired some rocket flares, most of which were duds owing to exposure to weather. At 1800 I exercised the group in quickly forming a square search and incidentally exercised my plotters who were damned bad. From the situation report there are no fewer than 8 support groups in the Irish Sea, and as we progressed northwards we met 4 of them. Being a light moonlight night there was not much worry or anxiety.

Thursday, 25 January 1945 – At sea/Londonderry

I seemed to be up most of the middle and morning watch as we were passing up the N. Channel. We arrived at the Lough Foyle buoy at 0930 and embarked pilots and proceeded up river. The whole countryside is covered with snow, and as we went up the temperature dropped to 20 degrees. Damned cold. It was foggy but quite alright until we got to Broomhall when it became very thick indeed, and on the big turn at the Crook the pilot rather lost his bearings, and to add to our embarrassments *Port Colborne* was much too close behind us and we were both backing and filling in this dense fog. I thought at one time we were aground for certain, but at last we got through and secured at No. 11 berth. The river is an amazing sight. Masses of floating ice are coming down from up river and all in among the ships and jetties it is packed tight. More like Halifax than Londonderry.

After lunch I went ashore to fix up about getting J. over, as a special telegram has to be sent authorizing her to travel to N. Ireland. The whole place is covered in hard beaten snow. Back on board for tea and signed a whole lot of papers. *Monnow* and *Nene,* who had secured at Lisahally when I reported how thick it was at the Crook, secured alongside us at about 1600, and later on "The Old Man of the Sea" (Skinner) came over to see me. Having failed to get hold of J. when I rang up in the p.m., I put through another call at about 1900. Apparently the cold and snow all over the country is playing havoc with trains, which are running up to 40 hours late. J. will try to travel tomorrow if the situation improves. I had food on board and then went over to *Monnow* and had some drinks and then to *Port Colborne,* and then just as I was turning in a V.R. commander from N.S.H.Q was brought along by Falconer to see me and we had quite a long quack about the R.C.N.

Friday, 26 January 1945 – Londonderry

A lovely bright sunny day but still damned cold. We had our arrival conferences at 1100. There is leave to the watch from p.m. today to p.m. 2nd. After the conference I went on board *Braithwaite* and had a drink with "Egg" Burnett. Came back on board and after lunch sat down and wrote out some orders for officers forbidding them to lie in in the morning, which I suspect some of them are doing, and telling them to be more strict in their handling of liberty men. This slackness makes me so angry. At about 1430 I went ashore, tried on my coat at the tailor's, and then walked round for a bit before going to the Club, where I read the papers and had tea. Major Goodliffe[40] came in just as I was leaving and I spoke to him. I must try and get out to see them at Birdstown one day.

It was damned cold as I walked back on board after sunset. I shifted into uniform and at about 1800 Skinner and Shaw came to see me, and at about 1845 Elizabeth Vaughan came on board. She had rung me up yesterday and I had suggested a party at the Club. After some drinks in the wardroom, she, I, and Earl went up to the Club on our flat feet as we could not get a taxi and had dinner. There was no dance, which was a pity, however, it was pleasant. Elizabeth is an awfully nice person. Later on we came back on board, where we found a bit of a party in progress in the wardroom which went on forever. Eventually about 0200 I took E. ashore and tried to get a taxi, but we had to walk to the garage and wait there about 20 minutes before at last we could get one. Then I took her back to her quarters over on the Ebrington Barracks side and then back on board and so to bed at about 0400. I wonder whether or not J. was on the way.

Saturday, 27 January 1945 – Londonderry

Colder than ever. Really bitter with nearly 20 degrees of frost. I went at my report of proceedings and at 1040 went up to see the Commodore, who had sent for me to discuss a programme for the visit of the Canadian Naval Minister and Chief of Naval Staff. Elizabeth Vaughan and another Wren officer came down for drinks at 1200 and stayed to lunch. After lunch I finished off my report of proceedings and read a whole lot of signals. Finally at about 1700 I went ashore. I had rung up the route transport officer and found that the Larne boat was late and the train wouldn't arrive here before 1830. Having heard nothing from J., I am presuming she is on the way. I went to the Melville with my little grip, and then having some time to put off I went to the club and read the papers and then walked to the station where I arrived at 1815 to find the train had been in about 15 minutes and no sign of J., so I dashed back to the hotel where I found J. had arrived and was feeling v. sick. Poor darling, she's had a pretty awful journey and now we fetch up at this hotel, which in this weather is absolutely arctic and practically frozen up. After some food J. felt better and we went v. early to bed and piled all our overcoats and a rug on top of us.

Sunday, 28 January 1945 – Londonderry

Colder than ever I think. The hotel is almost unbearable. We had a latish breakfast at about 1000. We walked down to the ship. There is 20 degrees of frost this morning and the ship is about the only place where one can keep warm. I had the C.O.s over to meet J. and have drinks and about 1330 we walked back to the hotel for lunch. The sun was out and it was nice and bright in spite of the cold. After lunch we went out for a bit of exercise and walked round the walls and then went on board again and sat in the warmth of my cabin and I got through some more paper work. Clarkson,[41] who was O.O.D., came and had drinks with us at 1930. I got a car to take me to dinner with the Commodore and dropped J. in the main street to walk back to the Hotel.

The Commodore's dinner was a stag party to meet Angus Macdonald, the Canadian Navy Minister. With him on his tour of inspection is Vice-Admiral Jones who is C.N.S., Mr. Connolly, Parliamentary Secretary, and Capt. Rayner, Director of Plans.[42] All the other local senior officers were there and me and Freeland,[43] the 2 S.O.s of R.C.N. from the harbour. The Minister wore a dressing gown for dinner, which seemed a little peculiar. Jones was shipmates with me in the *Benbow* for a short time. We were both Lieutenant-Commanders in those days!!!! I enjoyed the dinner and had an interesting talk with Pay Capt. Vaughan.[44] J. thinks I should turn over or ask to turn over to the R.C.N. Thought I might sound somebody tonight, but of course I didn't. Not nearly so cold this evening. Looks like a break in the weather.

Monday, 29 January 1945 – Londonderry

There *was* a change in the weather. Much warmer but windy and quite heavy snow, which later turned to rain. I had breakfast at 0800 and got down on board just before 0900. All Canadian ships had to send parties of officers and men to the Navy Hall to listen to an address by the Minister, and I wanted to see our group parties marched away properly. Later on Angus and I followed up in a car. The Minister arrived at the Hall at 1000 and gave quite a good speech followed by a short one by Admiral Jones, and then we all returned on board our ships. J. arrived on board at 1200 and at about 1230 as per programme Connolly and Capt. Rayner arrived for lunch. We all went over to the *Port Colborne* first for drinks and at about 1315 we returned to the *Saint John* for lunch. Skinner and Shaw, of course, were there. It was a v. good lunch. J. who was in her usual cracking form helped to keep the party going. Afterwards I took Connolly up to my cabin and he talked to one of the P.O.s who wanted to know about war gratuities, and then I sounded him on the subject of turning over to the R.C.N. but he couldn't tell me much.[45]

At about 1500 we got rid of our guests but continued to talk to Angus and our officers in the wardroom, and at about 1630 I retired to my cabin quite exhausted and J. had a bath in my bathroom. We then sat about until 1830 when we got a car up to Magee Mess for the Commodore's cocktail party, which was the last thing on the programme for the Canadian party. Then back to the Melville for dinner and then as there was nowhere to sit we went to bed. Pipes are bursting all over the hotel now the thaw has come.

Tuesday, 30 January 1945 – Londonderry

Mild and damp. Very wet and slushy underfoot. After doing some paper work I walked out and went to the Dockyard offices, the tactical room, and the radar instruction place. Incidentally, I found Shaw in the *Nene* still turned in at 1030, which annoyed me a lot. We were shifted by tugs to No. 8 berth. I went ashore for lunch and in the p.m. J. and I did some shopping and then went on board for tea, and I rang up first the Commodore and then Elizabeth Vaughan and asked them to dinner at the club tomorrow. The ice coming down the river on the ebb now that the thaw has really set in is quite remarkable. At about 1700 J. and I went ashore again and went to a cinema. Nothing special but quite amusing. Back to the hotel for dinner. There was a scene when a Dental Lieutenant and 2 sick Bay Stewards were run in and reported to *Ferret*[46] for bad behaviour in the lounge. I had previously had to pull him up for his language at dinner. The Russians are now close to Breslau and are in the outskirts of Konigsberg and have taken nearly all E. Prussia.

Wednesday, 31 January 1945 – Londonderry

I went on board as usual at about 0900 and did a few things. At about 1030 I walked us up to Operations. We are off on Saturday p.m. for a couple of days' training at the new *Philante* base in Loch Alsh, as the Irish Sea now has too many U-boats in it. The new Captain of the *Ferret* (Captain Stanley)[47] came to call at about 1200 and we had some drinks and a chat, and when he had left I went ashore for lunch. At lunch time it started to rain and it poured without ceasing for the next 12 hours. J. stayed in, but I went out and first of all brought back the frock she had bought this morning, having given some coupons for it, and then I went to the station and waited a long time for the Belfast train and met Elizabeth Vaughan and took her to her Wrenery in a taxi and told her about the arrangements this evening. Then I went back to the hotel, picked up J., and went on board where we had tea and J. read and I wrote letters. I tried to have a bath later on but there was no hot water. Elizabeth arrived on board about 1900 and we went down to the wardroom for drinks, and then we took Brown along with us to the club, where we met the Selbys at 2000, and gave them all dinner, and afterwards we all came back again on board and had a most amusing sing song in the wardroom. I was delighted to show off my officers to Selby. They were all most sober and most amusing. We left at about 2345. A v.g. evening.

Thursday, 1 February 1945 – Londonderry

Port Colborne went off early in the morning to dock at Belfast. I went on board at about 0900. I sent for the Captain of the *Nene* who had to explain why he was turned in the day before yesterday at 1030. He denied that he was. I walked out in to the town later on and got my coat from the tailor's, which was v. nice, and I also had a hair cut. *Loch Alvie* arrived back from her repair job at Liverpool with presumably a new and strengthened bottom. I went ashore for lunch and just about that time it started to rain. After lunch I took J. on board and left her in my cabin darning my socks while I went along to the tactical room and saw Allan about our game on Saturday and one or two other things. I looked in on *Loch Alvie* on the way back, but old Old was turned in and I didn't want to disturb him.

Back on board, by which time it had cleared up completely, and so I put on plain clothes plus my smart new sports coat and took myself for a short sharp walk leaving J. on board still. I went out on the Buncrana road and back by the American camp and the dog track. Quite exhausted after about an hour's walk. I'm fat and unhealthy these days. At about 1830 I shifted into uniform and we walked back to the hotel for dinner and we went early to bed. The Russians are now about 45 miles from Berlin. This recent cold spell has been the hardest for 40 years, with temperatures below zero in S. Wales. It must have been just about down to zero on the ground at times here. There has been heavy snow in some parts too and throughout the country traffic has been hopelessly dislocated. Now with the thaw thousands of pipes have burst and the Forces are having to help provide plumbers.

Friday, 2 February 1945 – Londonderry

Walked down on board the ship at No. 8 berth. Went up to Operations to get the latest I could on the U-boat situation. So far in rather over a month about ½ dozen merchant ships and 3 or 4 escort vessels have been torpedoed in the Irish Sea, and 2 U-boats have been sunk there. I had a C.O.s meeting at 1130 and discussed the game tomorrow among other things. When they had gone I shifted into plain clothes and went ashore for lunch, and after sitting about in the lounge till about 1430 we went out, meaning to go for a little walk, but as it was showery we contented ourselves with shopping, which gave us quite a bit of walking anyway. We had some tea in a tea shop and then went back to the hotel where J. shifted. About 1800 we taxied to the ship just in time to get on board before she was shifted to No. 10 berth.

I shifted into uniform and then with great trouble we got a taxi and went to drink with the Selbys, which was fun. From there we went to the club for the dinner dance, and we had a party with Earl and Kay Baker. It was a good deal more noisy and riotous than last time, and the band was v. poor we thought. However, it was v. amusing. When it finished I was persuaded much against my better judgement to go down on board *Saint John,* where we had some eggs and steaks cooked for us. The result was we didn't get back to the hotel until 0230 and so much for my last night in. Deep depression, of course, setting in at the same time, not to mention worry and nerves. Oh dear, oh dear, I sometimes feel I can't go on competing any longer.

Saturday, 3 February 1945 – Londonderry/At sea

In spite of getting to bed so late, I awoke at 0600 and lay thinking and worrying and dreading what lay ahead. Got on board about 0850 and after putting a few essential things in train I went along to the tactical room, where we played a game to investigate the problem of trying to catch the fast submarine, which is reported to be able to do 12-15 knots submerged. I don't know that we came to any very definite conclusion except that with only 5 ships it is almost an impossible problem. Got back on board at about 1230 and found J. on board. I gave her lunch and then went ashore with her, picked up her luggage at the hotel, and went to the station and saw her off in the 2:20 for Larne. These partings are quite unbearable, and the prospect of future responsibilities makes it all worse. Got back on board and signed papers, wrote, and read new General Orders.

It turned into a thoroughly bloody afternoon. Blowing quite hard and raining. Poor J. I hope the crossing isn't too bad. The group slipped at 1730 and we, *Nene,* and *Monnow* went to the oiling berth at Lisahally while *Loch Alvie* went down to Moville. I expected to have all finished oiling by about 2200, but at 2000 I heard *Monnow* couldn't start until we'd finished, with the result she wouldn't complete until midnight. I had about 2 hours' much needed sleep before slipping. Quite miserable and depressed beyond measure.

Sunday, 4 February 1945 – At sea/Loch Alsh

The 3 of us slipped from Lisahally at midnight and went down river, picked up *Loch Alvie,* and sailed from Lough Foyle at 0130. The weather improved and the wind eased and rain stopped, but it suddenly became a bit misty as we were leaving the Foyle, which was a bit unpleasant. Owing to the slow oiling we are going to be unable to arrive at Loch Alsh at 0930. I managed to get a few hours sleep as I wasn't called to the bridge much, but nevertheless on arrival I felt tired and short of sleep. Worry and depression is always tiring. The final part of the trip through the Sound of Sleat and the narrow Kyle Rhea into Loch Alsh was rather lovely.

On arrival at 1100 we secured to buoys. It was flat calm and a lovely sunny morning – luckily – as we were *not* clever at picking up the buoy. As soon as we were secured a boat arrived and all C.O.s attended a conference in *Philante.* The *Somaliland* – a Colony class frigate – is attached to us temporarily for these exercises. At the end of the meeting we returned to our ships, snatched some lunch, and slipped and went out for exercises. Owing to our late arrival the programme was delayed, and we didn't start the first exercises with the *Seraph* – the fast submarine – until 1515. She has this fast underwater speed which the new U-boats are expected to have – up to 15 knots in bursts – and I must say I found it a very difficult thing to attack.

After about an hour in the centre of the ring we returned and let another ship have a crack. That exercise lasted 2 hours, and we were supposed to have a splash target shoot afterwards but it was too late and the light was going so it was cancelled. We got back to our buoys at about 1930 in pitch darkness. Luckily it was again calm or I don't know where we would have ended up. Had some dinner and retired early to bed for a good night's rest. Expect J. will be doing the same after her tiring journey.

Monday, 5 February 1945 – Loch Alsh

I woke at 0600 to hear it blowing. Rang for the O.O.D. and went out on deck but it wasn't anything to worry about. Staff officers came on board at 0900. I cleared lower deck and spoke to the ship's company on the mess deck as it was raining and wet on deck. We slipped at 0915 and went out for further exercises. Wet and misty when we started, but it cleared up later but remained showery and a bit blowy all day. Our first exercise, which started at 1100, was another A/S P with *Seraph* with the ships which hadn't had a go yesterday doing the attacking while the rest of us patrolled around. *Port Colborne* joined us just as we reached the exercise area. It was rather dull, but good practice plotting ourselves on the square patrol.

At 1400 we started the next exercise, which was sighting and chasing a U/B on the surface. This didn't go altogether according to plan, and soon after diving it suddenly broke surface rather unpleasantly close to me. Finally at 1630 we had a day shoot at a towed Pattern VI target. Ours wasn't spectacular but *so* much better than on previous occasions that I was quite pleased. We all returned independently and we arrived at our buoy just before dark. It was blowing a bit and owing to the slowness in getting the boat away I blew right over the buoy before we could get the wire on, and so I had to back away and come in again. With my stern to wind I held the ship long enough to get shackled on. Another lovely long night in.

Tuesday, 6 February 1945 – Loch Alsh/At sea

The base boat called at 0830 to take me and staff to a conference in *Philante.* Nobody was ready, no gangway out, and I was kept waiting. I flew off the handle and bit everybody hard. This habit of leaving everything to the last moment is infuriating. All the C.O.s were at the meeting, and we discussed the training and analysed the *Seraph* attacks with the aid of his track charts. Back on board again at about 1100. We slipped in two lots, the 1st 3 at 1200 and we, *Port Colborne,* and *Somaliland* at 1230. We started an A/S P in Area A, just beyond the narrows, at 1300 and went on till 1530. Fairly successful. When that was over we joined the others in Area B to the N. and formed our long line, which just about stretched across the loch, and did two runs firing at a splash target towed by a small motor launch. Rather good fun.

It had been flat calm all day, but there was a gale warning and at about 1600 it started to blow up a bit with rain and thick mist and I began to foresee an anxious time navigating through the Minches. By the time the target boat had collected all the staff officers from all ships it was nearly 1800. We had been told on completion to proceed to Moville and fuel. Thank God soon after we started N. (we couldn't go via the Kyles of Loch Alsh after dark) the rain and mist lifted. We rounded Troddy in the narrow part of the Minches at about 1945. Blowing quite hard with rain squalls and variable visibility. I seemed to be on the bridge most of the night as there were trawlers and things to dodge, but no convoy, thank God. We got into line abreast at about 2300 when clear of the Narrows.

Wednesday, 7 February 1945 – At sea/Moville/At sea

Coming S. towards Skerryvore in the middle watch the visibility wasn't too good, and the radar had me completely foxed trying to fit by it. Eventually found I was a bit too close to Skerryvore and in pulling out I had to pass over a shallow patch, which as there was quite a sea running gave me some misgivings, but all was well. We were well behind our E.T.A. as wind and sea had slowed us down to about 9 knots. On altering to 166° at Skerryvore, I increased speed to 14 knots. Wind continued to blow hard and backed to W. with quite a big beam sea. We arrived at Lough Foyle buoy at 1030 and went to the oilers. As bad luck would have it they were swung across wind, which was against the tide, making a choppy sea. I got alongside the lee side with *Loch Alvie* outside me. We were alright, but the 2 on the weather side were working rather unpleasantly. Later on when the flood tide eased we swung to the wind, but it was blowing really hard although bright and sunny and I was afraid we'd part our lines. *Somaliland* detached himself from us on arrival. We shoved off from the oiler at about 1600 and anchored, and after an hour or two the wind eased.

Feeling desperately reluctant to start this next operational period. I sometimes feel I really can't take this worry and responsibility any longer. At about 1845 our sailing orders came through, and we weighed and proceeded at 2015 and relieved E.G. 18 patrol just outside. Sweeping between Inishtrahull and Rathlin (a U/B believed to be trying to get into the Irish Sea).[48] Spent rest of the night on the bridge, as the area being fairly small means frequent alterations, and there were in addition one or two ships to be avoided. Telegram from J. saying she got home safely.

Thursday, 8 February 1945 – At sea

I didn't get much sleep, as we were continually turning and without GEE one has to be very careful of the navigation. At about 1030 *Monnow* got an A/S contact, which she quickly lost but reckoned was promising, and so we all closed in on her and began one after another to get contacts also, all of which were non sub. After forming up for a line abreast sweep, *Monnow* got contact again and attacked with H/H and then lost it again. Again he claimed it had movement, doppler, and hydrophone effect, but I must say I feel v. doubtful, as we were continually getting good non sub echoes off fish in the vicinity. In view of his report, however, I started an organised search only to get a signal from C. in C. ordering me to investigate the report of a snorkel by an aircraft just S. of the Lough Foyle buoy. Left *Loch Alvie* and *Nene* with *Monnow* to continue the search and went off with *Port Colborne* after the snorkel. A most unlikely place for a U/B to be.

We arrived on the spot at about 1430, swept all round it, and then closed in shore right along to Benbane Point without finding anything. At about 1730 I gave it up and went off to join *Monnow* and the others, who were now patrolling N. and S. just E. of Rathlin Island, having been north to regain contact. Had a little difficulty in finding them and eventually joined up at about 1930.

At about 2100 we got a signal to proceed forthwith to Cape Wrath via the Minches and put ourselves under the C. in C. Rosyth's orders. So off we went. I'm glad as I dislike intensely the idea of working in the Irish Sea supporting convoys with narrow waters, a lot of night convoy work, and no GEE. The weather, which had been flat calm since about 1400, started to blow up from the S.W. just before midnight as we were approaching Skerryvore.

Friday, 9 February 1945 – At sea

Visibility was good enough to give us a good run through the Narrows and we passed Troddy just before 0800. Shortly after we got a signal from C. in C. Rosyth to establish a Gamma search between the Faeroes and Shetlands.

E.G. 10[49] is also on the way there, and between the 2 of us our patrols will stretch across the Faeroes Channel between the 100 fathom lines. The U-boat situation report places 10-14 between Shetlands and Norway, and I suppose this patrol is to try and intercept them going west. It was blowing hard from the W. and I was afraid when we got clear of the land N. of Cape Wrath that it would produce a v. unpleasant beam sea. It was not so, however, and the wind and sea eased later and we were able to maintain 15 knots comfortably. I felt very nervous and anxious indeed and quite weighed down with my responsibilities.

In the dog watches we intercepted an aircraft reporting he had attacked a definite submarine. I estimated E.G. 10 must be nearer, as our position wasn't far from the S. end of his patrol, and therefore I did nothing and was glad to hear later on that my guess was right and E.G. 10 was on the spot. We finally reached our patrol line near the N. point at 2300 and turned to 143° to start our patrol. Dark but a fine calm night. The British and Canadian armies are staging an offensive on the Western front.[50]

Saturday, 10 February 1945 – At sea

At about 0300 we got a report from an aircraft saying he was attacking a submarine in a position about 30 miles from us. Experienced the usual doubt and uncertainty whether I should go, as E.G. 10 would also be about the same distance. Eventually at 0315 I set the E.I. turn (90°) in motion and signalled E.G. 10 asking if I should go, to which he replied yes. Had the usual difficulty in getting into R/T touch with the aircraft and got no homing signals. However, eventually we sighted the flares on the port bow and altered towards, reduced speed, and got out CATs. We were over the datum at 0530 and I then swept 235° – his most probable course – to his furthest on and then altered to cover if possible the arc 270°-180° from datum, but nothing found. At 1000 several aircraft came to help and I sent them out on Lizard patrols in the Western semicircle from datum to a depth of 30 miles. At 1030 I was told by C. in C. if not in contact to resume Gamma patrol, and so altered to the N.E. for the line. One sometimes feels a bit dubious about these aircraft reports.

At 1300 I had to detach *Port Colborne* to Scapa with serious distiller trouble, which meant she was unable to make enough water to keep going. We sighted E.G. 10 about this time as we both arrived at the middle of the Gamma together, and he turned S.E. and I turned N.W. I slipped on some cocoa on the bridge last night and fell against an Oerlikon locker and gave my hip the hell of a bruise. At 1800 there was another U/B report from an aircraft further to the W., which from the distance might have been the same one as we looked for. As the distance to the new contact was 95 miles I took no action and nor did E.G. 10, in fact C. in C. expressly told him not to.

Sunday, 11 February 1945 – At sea

I had quite a lot of sleep as the night was uneventful. Read prayers at 1030 and we continued to stooge up and down our Gamma patrol without incident, except for considerable delay investigating and attacking a fish echo at about midday, until at about 1530 we saw an aircraft some way ahead drop a depth charge and so we increased speed to close. In the mean time he came up on R/T and reported he was over an oil patch and so I told him to stay and mark it until I could come up and sweep through it. It transpired there were 2 patches and the oil seemed to come from grease on the surface. There was nothing to be found in the vicinity, but on the off chance that it had come from a U-boat I set off to sweep S.W. from the oil to a depth of 20 miles.

At 1915, just as *Monnow* had reported her radar out of action, *Nene* got an A/S contact which she said looked good, and we joined her, picked up contact, and shortly classified it as submarine having pronounced movement and doppler. Shortly after 2000, after a stern chase with the U/B going 4-6 knots, we did our first H/H attack but with absolutely no result. Shortly after *Nene* attacked – again nothing. We then lost contact for a short time but picked it up and held it for quite a time in order to let *Nene* get well into contact. It was none too easy to hold and I was afraid of losing it after attacking. Carried out another H/H attack at 2113 and to my great disappointment still no result. The trouble was he was too deep, but I was v. loath to drop D/Cs for fear of losing him afterwards. I might just as well, however, as sure enough we and *Nene did* lose him after that attack. Can't think how *Nene* managed to lose contact. *Monnow* without radar wasn't much use on the Observant. I formed the group up and swept W. to furthest on and then N. and S., but never gained contact again. It really is disappointing and depressing beyond measure. I feel more than ever how useless and inefficient I am, and how my own ship and the group must be losing confidence in me. Conditions were *not* easy.[51]

Monday, 12 February 1945 – At sea

E.G. 10 came up from the S. to help us. We contacted shortly after midnight and we carried out Gamma searches at his direction, and later on in the day at C. in C.'s direction, well to the W. of our point of contact to try and interrupt him if he went W. or S.W. We were quite unsuccessful. Feeling depressed and short of sleep. At 1830 at orders from C. in C. we turned W. to rendezvous with E.G. 10 for a combined sweep westwards, subsequently dividing into separate groups for a Gamma on the Greenwich meridian between 61° and 62° N., which is N.E. of the Shetlands. It blew up after dark from the S.E.

Tuesday, 13 February 1945 – At sea

We rendezvoused with E.G. 10 at about 0100 and took station on his port beam and swept to Position A. On arrival there at about 0200 the whole party altered to 070° for Position B, which was about 30' E. of the Shetlands. At B we split and made our 2 ways towards our new Gamma searches between 61° and 62° N. on the Greenwich meridian. Blowing quite hard from the S.E. with a steep head sea, and even at 9 knots we bumped quite badly and were v. wet. Just as we were passing N. of Muckle Flugga we got orders to abandon our patrol forthwith to proceed to the vicinity of Kinneard Hind and wait for further orders and so we turned S.

The wind proceeded to do v. funny things, backing 16 points and then settling in the S.W. The S.E. swell persisted for quite a long time and prevented any high speed. We arrived abreast Fair Isle at 1900 just at dark. None of the Orkney lights were burning, but with radar and Q.H., lights are really hardly necessary. Still feeling ashamed and furious about missing that submarine. Heard on the news that Churchill, Roosevelt, and Stalin meeting at some Black Sea port had come to complete agreement on the post war fate of Germany, on the return of Poland, and post war European problems in general.[52]

Wednesday, 14 February 1945 – At sea

On turning S. at Auskerry we went into line abreast. We were expecting to meet 2 small groups of ships and, of course, as bad luck would have it we must meet one just at No. 35 buoy where we wanted to alter course, and in consequence we got a bit involved and I got v. fussed. *How* I hate meeting and passing things at night. We pushed on S. down the swept channel and eventually met our convoy at about 0500. We very nearly passed by without identifying it. Turned round and I took up station astern. There are only 3 ships, so what with their own 2 trawlers and the 4 of us they are doing pretty well. At daylight they were straggling v. badly and I was constantly trying to get them closed up. We were told to detach at Duncansby Head, which we reached at about 0300. We then passed N. of the Skerries, turned N. again and made for Lerwick to meet and support a small convoy of 3 ships from Lerwick to Aberdeen. We eventually met them off Fair Isle and took station on the beams and quarters. E.G. 10 reported at about 1600 that he was hunting a submerged U-boat, and about 2 hours later he reported losing contact after 2 Squid and 3 unsuccessful H/H attacks. It shows that even experts like "Egg" Burnett can drop their catches. It is gratifying personally, but disturbing that it should be so difficult to hold these fellows.

Thursday, 15 February 1945 – At sea

At about 0100 we picked up a contact, which after one or two runs over we identified as a plotted wreck. *Monnow* also gained contact close by, which he said gave hydrophone effect and which he claimed was definite Beggar [submarine contact]. Went over and picked up the echo, which as far as we could see was just a bottom contact. I felt sure *Monnow* was talking nonsense and my echo sounder traces showed very definitely non sub, however, when some one reports "definite Beggar" one can't be too sure and so decided to hold it all night and attack at daylight, letting *Loch Alvie* and *Nene* go on with the convoy. Reported to C. in C. and at about 0600 snatched about an hour's sleep. At about 0800 was told to rejoin, but decided to attack just when it transpired our contact was about 1,000 yards from *Monnow*. This put another complexion on the matter as I couldn't bring any E/S trace evidence to bear and so, as *Monnow* was still v. positive and sure he had a U-boat, I stayed another 2 hours while he attacked with absolutely no result. Quite sure there was nothing myself. At last I dragged him off, and we started off at 16 knots to meet *Loch Alvie* and *Nene* coming N. after leaving the convoy at Aberdeen.

A lovely sunny, sharp day. I went gunnery rounds and at about 1200 we got a contact which we attacked and classified as wreck. We eventually met the other 2 coming N. at about 1600 near No. 32 buoy and immediately turned N. to make for Cape Wrath to meet and support a Loch Ewe-Methil convoy. We passed through the Pentland Firth just after dark but all lights were on and it was v. easy. Blanchard (my Navigator), who impressed me so much on first joining, is now getting lazy and rather sulky. We went to General Quarters at 1630 and exercised damage control afterwards.

Friday, 16 February 1945 – At sea

Just before midnight the 3 other ships all passed in HF/DF bearings thought to be near ground wave, and so I turned to the bearing, which was 060°, and swept back for 25 miles but without result and so round we went back for Cape Wrath. We made radar contact with our convoy N. of C. Wrath at about 0400 and took station in each quarter till daylight, after which we took station ahead. It was misty and blowing a bit from the S.E. as we went through the Pentland Firth.

At about 1430 when between No. 34 and 33 buoys we got an A/S contact while screening on the starboard bow of the convoy. We altered towards, ran over, and got an echo sounder trace, and as by Q.H. there was no plotted wreck in the vicinity, I decided to give it a pattern and so we dropped 5 which immediately brought quite a bit of oil to the surface so rather unwillingly, as I wanted to get on with the convoy, I returned and attacked again. After the 3rd attack I was just saying, "I don't think this is anything, do you?" when on steaming through the oil and explosion kerfuffle we saw a lot of splintered wood work and some paper, which on fishing out of the water proved to be bits of a German signal log!!!!

We lowered a boat and also picked up an aluminium flask and a tube of sorts marked in German "Medical Stores Kiel." All this was most exciting and seemed to indicate that we were on a U-boat. Hoisted the whaler and carried out 2 or 3 more attacks before dark but nothing more came up except a great deal of diesel oil and splintered wood. I recalled *Nene* from the convoy and the two of us held contact all night. The whole thing seems such a complete fluke, but at last one of the hundreds of contacts we've obtained and investigated and attacked in coastal waters has proved to be the thing we've been looking for.

Saturday, 17 February 1945 – At sea/Scapa Flow

At daylight we started in to renew our attacks on the submarine, but in spite of pattern after pattern of D/C and H/H the only thing we could bring up except oil and wood was some torn bits of French charts of the Caribbean with the German Kriegsmarine stamp on them. I can't believe that after about 70 D/Cs and 5 H/H salvos it is possible that the S/M is still alive, but all the same the lack of more evidence is disappointing. E/S traces latterly suggested that the object had broken up a bit. C. in C. Rosyth told us to turn the contact over to *Monnow* and *Loch Alvie* and proceed to Scapa with our evidence. *Monnow* and *Loch Alvie* arrived on the scene at about 1700 and after some delay in getting contact I pushed off for Scapa at 1730, arriving about 2000. Went right alongside the oiler *Danmark* and when secured I proceeded to drink too much rum and ginger ale in the wardroom before turning in. But still it was a bit of an occasion. I don't know what the experts will say, but I don't see that it can be but a U-boat and I think we killed it.[53]

Sunday, 18 February 1945 – Scapa Flow

We shoved off from the oiler at 0830 and went alongside *Scorpion,* who was alongside *Vindictive,* as all this depth charging has caused considerable leaks in many compartments and something must be done about it. At about 1030 I went ashore to see Tubby Hutton, and as I left the ship I heard we were to go into dock at 1400. When I got to Commodore D.'s office I found he was at church, but I saw Moodie[54] and while I was there a call came from the constructors saying our damage was so extensive that it would take a fortnight to put it right and the dock couldn't be spared all that time, the ship was definitely non operational and must proceed with caution to whatever refitting yard was available. I then rang Rosyth Ops and told them the story. They said it was up to me whether I moved over to another ship, and I asked them if they could possibly give us another night in harbour. Went back on board wondering whether, as only 3 ships are now left, Skinner couldn't take charge for the next 10 days and let me go in *Saint John* to the refitting port and then turn over in comfort to *Matane* and perhaps get a little leave.

Went on board *Vindictive* at 1200 and had a drink with Spencer and eventually stayed to lunch. At 1415 Tubby came alongside in his barge with Lois and Rowley, having been lunching in *Cavalier,* and took me ashore. We went along to Tubby's office and made various signals about *Saint John* and tried to ring Derby House to see what they thought about me personally, but everybody was out so arranged to call back later on. Tubby, Lois, Rowley, and I then all went off in the car to "Derflinger Bay."[55] When we got out walked up alongside a burn for some distance and then came back and so home for tea. Spencer and his dentist, and later on "Sloppy" Williams[56] and another, also arrived for tea.

At about 1800 I went over to Tubby's office and rang up Colville[57] at Derby House who rather implied he thought I ought to transfer but would ask the Chief of Staff later on and phone me back. The barge put me back on board and almost at once I went over to *Vindictive* for supper. McMullen,[58] who is Capt. of the *Scorpion,* was there. Spencer took his guests to the movies afterwards, but I went back on board and wrote some letters. Got a message from Colville at about 2300 saying I was to transfer forthwith. I shall go to *Nene,* but my God, the thought fills me with the utmost gloom. I'm just about fed up with all this moving.

Monday, 19 February 1945 – Scapa Flow

We shoved off from the *Vindictive* at 0800 and went to No. 29 buoy. Immediately after breakfast I started in to pack and to make out flimsies. Sent for Shaw from the *Nene* and discussed my transfer and who I should bring. At 1130 I cleared lower deck and said a few farewell words to the troops. After lunch we had a series of photographs taken, and I went on with clearing up paper work. At about 1600 I was asked to come after to the quarter deck, where all the sailors were assembled, and they presented me with one of the beautiful scale models of the ship which have been made in the ship. Very touching how kind and friendly these Canadians are.

Shortly after that I took the boat and went over to *Monnow* to see how the "Old Man of the Sea" was, as I had a feeling he was a bit disgruntled about one or two things while we were at sea last time, but he seemed in really good heart. I had drinks and finally dined in the wardroom when I got back. After dinner some Wrens arrived on board but I broke away fairly soon and went to my cabin and wrote to Viola. Got a letter from Peggie who says [her husband] John is in a prisoners' camp in Formosa. Also heard from Band, who still wants to come back to me. If, as I believe, I am going to be appointed to *Matane* additional[59] I shall ask for him to come as my Flag Captain. The Americans have given Tokyo a 1500 bomber raid operational from a huge carrier task force, and they have also landed on Iwo Jima in the Bonin Islands only 600 miles from Japan.

Tuesday, 20 February 1945 – Scapa Flow/At sea

I was called at 0600, finished my packing, had an early breakfast, and at 0730 together with Brown and Earl and our gear I transferred by boat to *Nene.* Earl's relief was here when we got in, but I decided to hold on to Earl just for this trip. We slipped and proceeded at 0800. It seems v. strange being S.O. in somebody else's ship again and I *don't* like it. However, little Shaw with all his boring habits is most conscientious, and I can confidently rely on him to have us in the right place. With all this wreck work I miss Q.H. badly and have to rely on *Monnow* to check all contacts.

We have been told to proceed to Aberdeen and meet and support a convoy sailing at 1700. A really lovely day but cold. We were delayed once or twice on contacts, one of which was our old friend the U-boat. So he is still down there. Just as we joined up with the convoy (2 ships and 3 escorting trawlers) *Monnow* got a Quiz [asdic contact], which he attacked twice. A small amount of light oil came up, but A/S conditions were bad and it took us (we'd gone over to help) a long time to classify. At last we got a definite non sub trace and set off to catch up the convoy and finally rejoined station at 2115. From what we've seen I don't think the A/S team here is nearly up to the standard of *Saint John* or *Swansea*. From what Colville said from Derby Ho. when I rang him up I gather S.O.s are all going to be appointed additional, and so assuming that will happen when I go to *Matane,* I made a signal to Com. D. Western Approaches asking that N.S.H.Q. be requested to appoint Band in command.

Wednesday, 21 February 1945 – At sea

An uneventful night following astern of the convoy. At about 0400 it clouded over and started to blow, which was expected from a gale warning. By the morning it was blowing quite hard from the S.W. with rain and bad visibility. *Nene* and *Loch Alvie* went to ahead screening positions at daylight. I must say having a "Flag Captain" takes a lot of work off my shoulders, and little Shaw, whatever his faults, is conscientious to a degree and does the navigation most accurately. I dislike being out of touch with the bridge, however, while I am in my cabin.

At about 1230 we got a signal telling us to have leave the convoy at Sumburgh Head (S. point of Shetlands) and carry out a sweep of the Orkneys to Dunnet Head and then W. to a point mid way between Cape Wrath and the Butt of Lewis and then N.E. again. As we were already past Sumburgh Head we turned round and then altered to 255° and passed between Fair Isle and Shetlands. It wasn't really blowing hard but there was quite a steep head wind, and we couldn't make good more than about 8 knots. It cleared up and the wind eased in the late p.m. but increased again as we turned to the southward at about 2130. Wrote some of my report of proceedings.

Thursday, 22 February 1945 – At sea/Scapa Flow

An uneventful night. In spite of a rising glass and a clearing sky the wind continued strong from the W. by S. with quite a big sea. We reached Position A., which was N. of Dunnet Head, at about 0230 and turned to the west for Position B. 10 knots was the best we could do and even then we were bumping a bit and only making good about 8½. There didn't seem much for me to do with little Shaw being most efficient and painstaking about the navigation. At about 1230, much to our surprise, we got a signal telling us to proceed to Scapa and that we would be sailed again a.m. tomorrow. Can't think what that is for unless we are going to do some sort of operation with the Home Fleet and have been sent in to get orders. Anyhow we pushed on at 15 knots and were just approaching Dunnet Head when *Monnow* got a Quiz, and although it was fairly near a plotted wreck it wasn't quite near enough to disregard at once. However, after 2 attacks I finally reckoned it was a wreck and we went on. Arrived Scapa at 1900 and went to the oiler. I had reported leaks in *Nene* and *Monnow* and so on completion at about 2130 we both went alongside *Greenwich* for examination.

Friday, 23 February 1945 – Scapa Flow/At sea

Shaw informed me while I was having my bath that the constructors had had a look at his leaks and certified him unfit for operations. This is like the 10 little nigger boys. *Monnow* is alright at present but her leaks will get progressively worse with more depth charging, and really it seems she ought to be docked before things get any worse. Went ashore at about 1030 and rang up Rosyth from Tubby's office and told Gibson[60] I would transfer to *Loch Alvie* ready to sail p.m., but that I really thought *Monnow* ought to go in dock before she got any worse, but I think he is desperate for ships and will have to use the 2 of us now left. Saw Tubby himself afterwards, and he drafted out a signal reporting *Nene*'s condition and backing up my recommendation about *Monnow*. Looked in on Lois before going back on board. Had a drink with Skinner before lunch. He is rather an old fool, and always seems to think the whole navy is conspiring to do him down and that the whole navy should be run entirely to suit *Monnow*.

I took all my gear and myself over to *Monnow* after lunch, as *Nene* had to go to an oiler and pump out some tanks. At 1400 *Loch Alvie* came alongside *Monnow* and I transferred over to her. I'm afraid *Nene* isn't much of a ship and never will be with Shaw in command. He is a complete non entity and has absolutely no personality and commands no respect whatever and his officers are dirty and slovenly in appearance. What I saw of it, the ship was not too clean. We sailed at 1800 and went S. to meet a convoy leaving Methil at 2030. First *Loch Alvie* then *Monnow* got a Quiz, which had to be investigated and attacked. Both finally classified wreck. Oh, how I hate being an onlooker on the bridge and how I hate being without Q.H. Old is a nice old boy but rather lazy.

Saturday, 24 February 1945 – At sea

We spent a long time investigating a contact of *Monnow*'s just after midnight. After 2 attacks and much time, *Monnow* suddenly discovered it was in the same position as one he had previously classified as wreck. God, was I angry. You might just as well not have Q.H. if you don't use it and keep a record of all non subs.

We met our convoy, E.N. 77, at about 0600 well S. of Aberdeen. 9 ships and escorting trawlers bound for Belfast from Methil. Gale warnings all day and a falling glass and rising S.W. wind, but it remained fine and clear. I went mess deck rounds with the Captain. She is very clean and I must say the Loch class with their slightly extra beam and headroom have considerably more room everywhere.[61] They are awfully well laid out ships. It is a great pity that the wide spacing of frames gives them an inherent weakness.

Blowing hard by sunset. The wind later on veered to the W. and the weather deteriorated generally. When supporting these coastal convoys I always feel I'm being a bit officious in trying to run the trawler S.O. too much, but I always feel unless I do something most of these trawlers will do nothing.

SUNDAY, 25 FEBRUARY 1945 – AT SEA

The convoy formed single line preparatory to going through the Pentland Firth at about 0100. We thought some of these 7 knot ships were going to find the passage in present weather conditions a bit difficult, and sure enough 2 turned back, 2 had to seek shelter – one at Thurso and one in Scapa – and only 5, 1 trawler, *Monnow,* and us finally got through the Firth. The tide was with us, but the westerly wind and swell made very heavy seas and it was none too pleasant. Dunnet Head was abeam at 0330, and once clear of the race the seas were not so big. At daylight we turned round to see if we could locate any of the 4 missing ships and the one escort, but found nothing and so turned W. again and slowly caught up to the convoy. We heard later all 4 stragglers and the trawler *Polka* were at Scapa waiting for the storm to die down before continuing.

The glass rose slowly and the wind died slowly, but it was pretty rough all the way to Cape Wrath with rain squalls and a cold wind. We turned S. at about 2000 down the Minches, and at about 2300 we located the N. coming Loch Ewe-Methil convoy to which we'd been told to transfer and so we moved over and joined it (W.N. 76). I read Norway's latest novel, *Pastoral,* in the wardroom and enjoyed it v. much. A v. uncomfortable day.

MONDAY, 26 FEBRUARY 1945 – AT SEA

Still blowing quite fresh but now it is astern of us. I went on the bridge at about 0415 and was very annoyed to find the Officer of the Watch seemed to have no idea of what was going on, how many trawler escorts there were, or what positions they were in. I couldn't really get the Captain much interested in these shortcomings and so I went angrily back to bed for an hour or so.

We passed Dunnet Head at 0615 and were through the Pentland Firth by about 0745. Then on down the swept channel with Quizes about every 2 hours, most of which were quickly identified as wrecks. *Monnow* had a bit of a bombardment of one at about 1300, and at 1830 just as the light was fading we got one which gave rather a promising E/S trace and I brought *Monnow* back to help. It was v. difficult to hold. We attacked twice with absolutely no result and after spending nearly 2 hours on the spot I gave it up and chased after the convoy.

I've come to the conclusion that the real trouble with Old is that he is too old and quite out of sympathy and too intolerant of his young and inexperienced officers. A more friendly and helpful attitude would get much better results. Finished *Pastoral.* Enjoyed it a lot.

Tuesday, 27 February 1945 – At sea/Methil/At sea

Arrived off May Island at about 0240 and altered up for the Forth. At about 0400 in accordance with our signalled instructions we anchored in Methil Roads and had a good 3 hours sleep in peace. In the morning I made a signal to C. in C. asking if there was time for me to pay a visit to A.C.H.Q. and if so for transport to be arranged. I signalled both ships to exercise whalers under oars and sail in the forenoon. Had occasion to speak to Radcliffe[62] (the 1st Lieut.) about his dress, which in harbour was overall trousers and a sweat rag round his neck. When I told Old about it he made haste to show me his standing orders, which completely covered this particular point. What *is* the use of voluminous orders if you don't see them carried out.

A drifter came to take me ashore at 1120 and when I got ashore at Methil at about 1200 a car was waiting and took me to A.C.H.Q. at Pitrivie, where we arrived at about 1245 having driven like hell. I went into the Officers' Mess where I met Gibson, who runs the A/S support groups. Ruck-Keene was also there.[63] He is Capt. D. Rosyth. After lunch Gibson took me over to the Operations room, where I meet the Chief of Staff and one or two others and finally had a short interview with the C. in C., Jock Whitworth.[64] Went back to Methil by car arriving about 1600. We are going to escort the escort carrier *Ravager* to Scapa, and on my way off to the ship I went on board *Ravager* and saw the Captain (one Faulkner)[65] and discussed the trip. Had a drink with Old and an early supper, and we weighed at 1915. Went out ahead of *Ravager* and took up screening positions on each bow passing May Island. Clear night and brilliant full moon. Cracked along at 15 knots.

Wednesday, 28 February 1945 – At sea

A peaceful night without the usual crop of contacts. I think we ignored one or two that seemed to be stationary, because if we drop back to investigate or attack we never catch up again. A lovely early morning but the day rapidly deteriorated, and by noon it was blowing a full gale from the S.W. We rendezvoused with *Campania* and *Cavalier* in the Pentland Firth in accordance with signalled instructions, and the 2 carriers with us and the destroyer screening proceeded to the Clyde. When we turned S.W. down the Minches I had to ask *Ravager* to reduce from 15 to 12 and later on to 10 kts as were bumping heavily in the short choppy sea. We got into the Narrows soon after dark, but in spite of rain and bad visibility there was no great difficulty as the lights showed up fairly well and there was always radar. We went into line ahead for the narrow bit and then took up screening stations again. The wind eased and veered to the W., and at about 2200 we were able to push on at 15 knots again. Got a nice farewell signal from C. in C. Rosyth thanking us and saying we'd sunk our U-boat.

Thursday, 1 March 1945 – At sea/Londonderry

We rounded Skerryvore at 0430 and the wind, which had gone round to the N.W., was now astern. Still blowing quite hard. *Ravager* kept us with him as far as Ailsa Craig and then told us to shove off, and so at about 1230 we turned round and made for Londonderry. We went through Rathlin Sound as it offered a bit more shelter from the N.W. wind. Arrived Lough Foyle at about 1630 and went to the oiler. Old let the pilot, who we picked up at Dunagree Point, take the ship alongside, and it took ages because he did it as though he was handling a battleship rather than a frigate. *Monnow* also went to the oiler to pump out oil prior to docking tomorrow. I had a bath, and then Old and I had a drink, and then we went down to the wardroom for food. We had been told to remain at Moville until daylight tomorrow, but on asking if we could proceed up after oiling it was approved and we finally got up river at about 2200. The general offensive is going well on the Western front though, by Russian standards, slowly. The Americans are now within 6 miles of Cologne. A year ago today we left Halifax to operate on this side.

Friday, 2 March 1945 – Londonderry

I went up to the offices at about 1030 and found out about this and that. Among other things the *Matane* has developed more engine trouble and won't be ready for about 6 weeks, and so I have no immediate home or ship in view. The group conference was at 1100 in Selby's office. Skinner, the bloody old fool, brought up some asdic defect, the facts of which he didn't know, and got the Commodore's goat and the meeting was pretty electric. When it was over I had a long talk with Simpson and some v. strong gins.

In the p.m. Skinner came on board and I tried to show him how and why he was always getting up against R.N. senior officers. I might just as well talk to a blank wall. He is pig headed and he's determined the R.N. has a down on him. I tried to write some letters but couldn't in the dog watches. Feeling fed up and depressed. I see no hope of getting out of this hopeless and uncomfortable state of living in somebody else's ship with nowhere to put my clothes and books and things, and I haven't the guts to say I won't stand for it.

At about 1900 I went down to the mess (Old has gone on leave) and found Skinner there. He and I eventually went to the Savoy for dinner and then went along to the Officers' Club, where we did a great deal of drinking, and finally drifted down on board *Monnow* and then *Loch Alvie,* where the party lasted till the small hours. Some Fleet Air Arm types sang a most amusing song called "Sylvester." Drank much too much. Lovely sunny spring day.

Saturday, 3 March 1945 – Londonderry

Feeling a little below par this morning. I did a bit of paper work and then walked up to the offices and saw Selby and I also had a talk with the Commodore about Skinner. Walked into the town and bought a book and then back on board for lunch. At about 1400 I put on plain clothes and went for a walk and finished up for tea at the Club, where I read the papers. Back on board in time to write to J., and then at 1900 Hearn,[66] Flavelle,[67] Brown, MacDougall, Earl, and No. 1 (Radcliffe) all met me in the wardroom and after some drinks we went ashore to dinner at the Savoy. It was a farewell dinner to Earl. Afterwards we came back on board, and they produced 2 Wrens and we had the movies in the wardroom. The party – quite quiet – lasted till about 0100 and I was simply longing for my bed. A warm day but a little rain in the evening.

Sunday, 4 March 1945 – Londonderry

Feeling very jaded after 2 late nights. I walked to the Cathedral for the 1015 naval service. Rather an uninspiring sort of performance. After lunch I shifted into plain clothes and mounted the ship's bicycle (an American type) and set off to bicycle to Birdstown House to see the Goodliffes. I nearly turned back after about ¼ hr because it started to rain and I had quite a strong head wind along the Buncrana Road, but then the rain stopped and I went on. I went rather a round about way and so didn't get to the house until about 1600. There must be something wrong with the bicycle. I've never known such hard work trying to shove it along and I arrived hot and exhausted. They gave me tea. The daughter, son in law, and family are there. After tea we sat talking, and finally I had a cocktail before starting off again at about 1845. Thank God it was mostly down hill but it is about 7 or 8 miles and I was v. tired of my steed by the time I got back on board. I paid a fleeting visit to the wardroom after a scratch meal. Hearn, my new Staffy, had a most ghastly-looking, common, little blonde down there. I hope that is not his type of woman in general. Got to bed at about 2130.

Monday, 5 March 1945 – Londonderry

Worked on S206s for the *Saint John* officers. At 1100 I got a car and went to Ebrington Barracks and called on Capt. Stanley. After lunch I read, and at 1530 I went up to see Joe Selby and to make out a combined report for the C. in C. on the efficiency of the group. I was glad to see that we got quite a good report from *Philante* for our 3 days at Loch Alsh. They said the group was rather above the average. At about 1830 McLaron,[68] who is temporary S.O. of C 5 group, came over and had a drink and eventually stayed and had some food. Afterwards I went back with him on board the *Runnymede* and sat talking and drinking till about 2330. Got a long letter from J. Completed my S206s, thank God, and now it only remains to do the recommends and the honours for our U-boat. The Americans are fighting in Cologne now.

Tuesday, 6 March 1945 – Londonderry

I wrote out fair copies of all the S206s and sent them off, and that is a great weight off my mind. I got a signal from C. in C. congratulating me on being mentioned in dispatches. I am delighted. I suppose it is for my part in *Saint John*'s submarine off the Wolf Rock. I really feel I've earned a mention as it has been quite a slog since D-Day.

At 1430 the Commodore called for me and drove me to Ebrington Barracks to discuss with Stanley the organisation of a Court Martial on that Dentist who was so objectionable in the Melville Hotel one evening when J. and I were staying there. I am required as a witness. When the Commodore dropped me opposite No. 11 berth the *Loch Alvie* was in mid stream on her way to No. 16 berth, and so I took myself to the Club where I met the Goodliffes again and had tea with them and later brought them down on board for a drink. They are awfully nice. Had a filthy meal in the wardroom at 1900 and later on saw a movie down there. Wrote to J. and told her of my mention. Cologne has fallen to the Americans, and the Germans are in full retreat across the Rhine almost all along the line.

Wednesday, 7 March 1945 – Londonderry

Wrote my recommendations for awards for our U-boat in the Moray Firth. I then walked out into the town and had a hair cut. On my way home I met a Canadian sailor in a narrow part of the pavement who made no effort to move, and so I stopped and said, "Who is going to get out of the way – you or I?" He said, "Well, as you are carrying a cane I guess perhaps I'd better." Christ, there are times when I never want to see another Canadian.

Got back to find I was bidden to a meeting at the Commodore's office at 1200. When I got there I found the other S.O.s, the Provost Marshal, and Joe Selby. The Commodore talked about dress and appearance of ships companies, smuggling, and officers and men going ashore together. I came away feeling depressed. I feel in spite of my R.N. training I've managed to make no impression on this appalling sloppiness and lack of discipline in my group. My popularity has been obtained largely because I haven't been anything like hard enough or Prussian enough, which is the only way to eradicate these awful habits.

I said goodbye to Earl after lunch. I'm more than sorry to lose him. He is such a damned nice chap as well as being a first class staff officer. Shifted into plain clothes and went for a walk. I walked right up to the old round fort at Mount Greenan and back home a different way, and arrived back quite exhausted after walking for about 4 hours. Put a call through to J. and got through to her at about 2100. Feeling v. homesick and depressed. Anyhow, if I'd taken leave it would have been my last day at home and I would be feeling even more depressed. A nice fine day with quite a bit of sunshine.

Thursday, 8 March 1945 – Londonderry

I sent for No. 1 of the *Monnow* and told him about our meeting yesterday and told him to buck things up. At 1000 I got a car and drove to Ebrington Barracks and first of all went to see Wilson the Drafting Officer and then went to see the training officer about the runs we shall do on Saturday. When I got back I found the ship had moved to No. 11 berth. On my way across the inside ship I stopped off and took a drink off the Captain, a V.R. 2½ by the name of McArthur.[69] After lunch I wrote some letters and read, and at about 1630 I went ashore meaning to go for a short walk but got stuck in a book shop for so long that it didn't seem worth while, so I went back to the Club and read the *Times*. Back on board at 1830 expecting Carne[70] down for a drink but later on I heard my message had never got to him. Had a late rather scratch meal in the wardroom, and just as I was finishing in walked Stacey who I'd heard was on his way. We had a long chat. It seems the *Matane* was in an awful state when he arrived. She may be ready in 6 weeks. He has heard nothing about his decoration yet, so perhaps my M.I.D. is *not* for *Saint John*'s U-boat off the Wolf. I've come to the conclusion that Stacey is well worth a brass hat and command of a group, considering the other types who are getting it, and I shall recommend him.

Friday, 9 March 1945 – Londonderry

Went along to the A/S table with the *Loch Alvie* team and did some runs with a fast submarine. Back on board at 1100, when Stacey came over to see me again and we both went up to the Commodore's office and first of all enquired about awards. I'm beginning to think now that my "mention" was not for *Saint John*'s U-boat but for something else, as none of them have yet got anything.

We then went in to see the Commodore and talk about Stacey's future, as he wants to get back to *Saint John*. It seems probable that I am being relieved for good sometime next month, which is rather surprising but I'm not sorry. Told the Commodore I was going to recommend Stacey for promotion. Stacey came back and had lunch with me on board, and all the p.m. I was doing more confidential reports. As Old was coming back from leave today I decided to clear out of his cabin and asked the Commodore if he could give me a bed and at 1800 went up to his house with a suit case. Rutherford, his Secretary, and I had some beer in the Magee Mess before dinner. The Americans are now across the Rhine in one place.

Saturday, 10 March 1945 – Londonderry

I got down on board soon after 0900 and at 0945 I got a car and went round to Ebrington Barracks to be there for *Monnow*'s "Neat" (Night Action Teacher). I sat in the control room and made some signals as S.O. It was quite a good run (radar contact was surfaced U-boat, closing, and after diving picking up A/S contact). The thing I still find hardest of all to make up my mind about is the best and proper anti Gnat procedure.

Got a car round to the other side when we'd finished and went to the Commodore's offices about S206s and awards, and then down to the *Loch Alvie* for lunch. After lunch Old and I walked to the ferry and went over to Ebrington for *Loch Alvie*'s Neat, which was also quite good, the A/S being particularly so. Back by ferry and on board for tea and then up to the Commodore's house. I got hold of a Wren typist and got the whole of the honours and awards done. It appears *Saint John*'s previous awards are *not* out yet. That took me till past 1800, and then I went down on board *Monnow* and saw Skinner about the S206s he had sent in for his officers. They were all 7s and 8s, and I told him I thought they were too high.[71] After a bit of argument he agreed to write them down a bit. My God, he makes me impatient at times. Back to the Commodore's house for dinner. Capt. Glencross was the only one in for the meal. Wrote a letter to J. before turning in. A busy and very rushed day.

Sunday, 11 March 1945 – Moville

I was supposed to be called at 0600 but no call came. However, luckily I woke. A car came for me at 0645 and took me down to the ship, and we slipped at 0700. I must say it is rather pleasant to be able to shave and wash and breakfast while somebody else takes the ship down. On arrival at Moville we dropped the pilot and went straight off for Position H for our anti-aircraft shoot. Just before reaching the position we joined up with *Hallowell* and a corvette from C 1 group, and we put ourselves under C 1's (in *Hallowell*) orders as we were acting as a private ship. After the usual endless delays the aircraft appeared and flew round a bit and then reported he couldn't stream his drogue, and so the exercise had to be cancelled. That was about 1200, and we all then set off to close the tug and target for our day shoot. When we got there we found ships milling around in all directions, and it seemed to me C 1 was very bad at taking charge and getting the practices going. However, eventually we had our turn and did a radar straddle correction shoot first, then our proper run, and finally we closed and fired 3 sharks. It was all quite good. We then went in and alongside the oiler to top up. We expected to do a night shoot, but while alongside it was cancelled and we were told to sail at 0100 for the Clyde to pick up the ship we are escorting to Iceland and attend a preliminary conference. Rather a cold wind but fine.

Monday, 12 March 1945 – Moville/Greenock/At sea

The ship weighed at 0100, but I lay snugly in my bunk and didn't stir until about 0630, when I went on the bridge and found we were passing Ailsa Craig. A travelling S.O. gets some compensation for his discomforts. We passed the gate at about 0940 and went alongside the oiler off Greenock. At 1115 a boat came and Old, I, Brown, and Hearn went ashore. After a bit of a wait a car arrived and took us first of all to Capt. D.'s office, where I caught a fleeting glimpse of Ely,[72] who was with me at the Admiralty. We were then taken on to N.C.S.O.'s office at Gourock, where we met the Captain of the *Tamarva,* who we are escorting to Reykjavik, and we discussed the route and various other points. Old had been asked to lunch with F.O.I.C. and although I angled blatantly for an invitation to the Flag Lieutenant over the telephone there was nothing doing. However, we all went along to the Admiral's office to see Operations, and as it was then pretty late Brown and Hearn and I got a car to an officers' club where we had lunch. While we were drinking our coffee I got a message that the Admiral would like us all to go along and have a glass of port with him, so back we went to his house. He is a most amusing old boy called Hill and he was most apologetic at not asking us to lunch.[73]

We eventually went off to the ship in his barge, No. 1 having taken her from the oiler and anchored her in our absence. Wrote a last letter to J. and read. Just before we were going to weigh I heard the A/S training motor was defective and we should have to get a new one from shore. I hurriedly made signals saying we would be delayed and waited impatiently for the boat to return from shore. As it happened we were only delayed ½ hour, but it meant *Tamarva* and we got mixed up with a slow convoy as we went through the gate. However, we then forged ahead at 15 knots and met *Monnow* off Ailsa Craig at about 2240. We took up screening positions on either bow and steered for the North Channel from the Clyde Light Ship.

Tuesday, 13 March 1945 – At sea

I was on the bridge until about 0130 and then turned in on the chart house settee. When off Oversay at about 0300 we started zig zagging. Our route took us west, south of Barra Head and not through the Minches. An uneventful day. Calm but inclined to be foggy. We pushed along at 14.5 knots zig zagging. I read some Admiralty Fleet Orders and Weekly Intelligence Reports and took a bit of exercise on the upper deck. The clocks went back an hour at 2000.

Wednesday, 14 March 1945 – At sea

I slept on the settee in the chart house, which wasn't v. comfortable, but I got in quite a lot of sleep as there was no occasion for me to go on the bridge. A calm day but foggy with some rain later on. An aircraft arrived soon after dawn to support us, but when the fog shut down he left. Loran was the greatest assistance as we had no chance for sights.

Thursday, 15 March 1945 – At sea/Reykjavik

Another fairly undisturbed night. This unaccustomed idleness at sea is v. strange. An aircraft arrived again to support us and we made a bit of a balls of homing it. It started to blow from the E. and we had an Elijah warning,[74] but it never blew more than about 5 but it turned much colder. It was still misty up to about 1300 when it cleared. We eventually sighted the very snow capped Iceland mountains at about 1500 at some 35 miles. Loran is no good just to the W. of Iceland, and we were for some time a little in doubt as to our position. The Iceland coast is an extremely difficult one to identify or pick out on the chart. Even as early as this the twilight is beginning to stretch out a lot in these northern latitudes. We arrived and anchored off Reykjavik at about 2030 in the v. last glimmerings of light. Flat calm but cold.

Rather attractive to see the town completely lit up, and before the light went the snow capped hills silhouetted in the west looked lovely. Old and I had a drink before turning in. He gets awfully mad with his officers and men, but apart from barking at them he takes no disciplinary or other corrective action. Put the clocks back another hour on anchoring but found later on that the local time was G.M.T.

Friday, 16 March 1945 – Reykjavik/At sea

We weighed at 0630 and went alongside the oiler with *Monnow* on the other side. We saw the *Skeena* on the rocks. She dragged ashore in a gale a few months ago and became a total loss. Skinner came over and spent most of the forenoon talking to me and Old. On our return she [*Monnow*] has been told to break off for Londonderry while we go on to the Clyde, and later on she meets *Assiniboine* escorting *Canton* to the Clyde. It seems funny to split us up like that and Skinner thinks he is going back to Canada. Wishful thinking.

We returned to the anchorage at about 1130. A perfect day. Sunny and quite calm. The background of snowy mountains looks v. fine. Sent Brown in shore to explain our aircraft homing failure. I took some exercise on the upper deck and read a bit. There was apparently a red hot rumour that the Germans had asked for an armistice on the W. front, which we had refused. *Loch Alvie* and *Monnow* weighed at 1850 and went out slowly and waited for *Tamarva* at No. 7 buoy, and when she had dropped her pilot we took up our old screening positions on either bow at 15 knots. Our return route is the exact reverse of our previous route. The *Tamarva* brought stores and troops and is taking troops back again to the U.K.

Saturday, 17 March 1945 – At sea

It blew up in the night and by daylight there was a strong S.E. wind and quite big sea, so that when at 0730 we altered course to 110° we had to reduce to 12 knots. Things improved later, however, and at about 1200 we went on to 13 and by 1600 we were back to 15 kts.

We had good air cover the whole day. I must say I take my hat off to these airmen. They seem to fly even when the best part of a gale is blowing and when the visibility is down to zero. The U-boat report this evening gives quite an alarming estimate of the number round the coasts of Great Britain.[75] We've heard of a couple of torpedoings since we left the Clyde, but no sort of a blitz has taken place yet. An uncomfortable sort of day with rain and seas coming over the bridge and rather cold.

Sunday, 18 March 1945 – At sea

The wind remained fresh and fluctuated between S.E. and S.S.W. with enough sea to make it wet and wobbly on board but we didn't have to slow down. We had air cover all day. I wrote out a group anti Gnat policy. Read *The Newcomers.* Had an Officer of the Watch drill at about 1900 which *Loch Alvie* made an awful balls of. The Captain got so angry with his officers that I thought I'd better have the bridge. I shall be glad when this trip is over. Although the chances of being torpedoed are fairly remote, it would be horrible if the *Tamarva* got it with all those troops, and if one of us got it I think the other one would have to leave him and go on with the trooper. Furthermore, if we got contact with a U-boat we couldn't stay behind and hunt it. All difficult decisions.

Monday, 19 March 1945 – At sea/Greenock

A lousy day. Strong S.'ly wind, cold and rainy. However, it cleared up in the late evening. We were abreast Barra Head at about 1100 and off Inishtrahull at 1700 and up to the Clyde Light Vessel at 2200. On arrival there I detached *Monnow* to Belfast, where she is to wait and later sail to rendezvous with *Assiniboine* escorting *Canton* to the Clyde. Skinner thinks he is going back to Canada but I v. much doubt it, although their date is mid April, in view of the state of the group. We proceeded on up the Clyde with orders to oil and then proceed to Scapa and escort the U.S.S. *Pioneer* to Belfast. I bitterly resent the fact that I am here to the great discomfort of myself and Old when I have so little to do that I might easily be on leave. Glad to have got the *Tamarva* safely in. The old French destroyer *Mistral* passed us at Ailsa Craig and I got a signal from Smeeton[76] (my 1st Lieut. in *Chelsea*), who is now in command.

Tuesday, 20 March 1945 – At sea

I turned out on approaching the boom. We went alongside the oiler at 0230 and a boat came and I sent Brown ashore to Ops and then turned in. I was on the bridge when we slipped again at 0630 and proceeded for Scapa. A really v. idle day. We cracked along at 16 knots zig zagging with CAT out. We got a contact off Rathlin Island and wasted quite a lot of time on what I thought was obviously non sub. They are *not* good at classifying in this ship. We rounded Skerryvore at about 1630. Still blowing a bit from the W. but when we turned to the northward it was dry enough to get some exercise on the upper deck.

Wednesday, 21 March 1945 – At sea/Scapa Flow

I slept in the Captain's cabin. Turned in shortly after we passed Ness Head, and the next time I came on the bridge at about 0330 we were approaching Cape Wrath. I had a bath before breakfast and at about 0830 we arrived at Scapa and went alongside the *Danmark.* Misty, drizzly rain. The Chief reported a condenser leak just as we arrived and said he wanted about 5 hours to open up and make good. V. annoying as I imagined we were required to sail almost at once. However, we reported it and started to get on with repairs as soon as we were alongside the oiler. The telephone from *Danmark* was broken down and we got no orders, which was v. funny. At 1300 we reported defect made good and at last got through by phone to hear we were probably not sailing till tomorrow and in the mean time we were to go to a buoy.

At about 1500 we shoved off. I've never been so ashamed in my life at the appearance of the ship's company. There were men in khaki trousers, in filthy duffel coats, sea boats, jerseys, mostly smoking, and not one man in No. 3's. The R.C.N. Tribal *Iroquois* was on the other side of the oiler with every man in the rig of the day. Thank God we were only seen by another R.C.N. ship. I felt furious and also despairing, because obviously apart from me there wasn't another officer who saw anything wrong with it. I told Old that it was a bloody disgrace and spent a long time walking up and down after we had secured trying to think out what to do about it. My God, if it had been my own ship. Oh God, these reserve officers. How does one ever teach them? Had some gin in the wardroom at 1800 and felt better. Got orders to sail at 0700 tomorrow with *Iroquois* and the carrier *Premier* and not the U.S. carrier that we expected.

Thursday, 22 March 1945 – Scapa Flow/At sea

Owing to a wrongly read signal we were turned out about an hour too early. We eventually slipped at 0600 and followed *Iroquois* out and met *Premier* coming out of Hoxa Gate. We took station one on each bow and set off for the Clyde at 16 kts, which was just about flat out for us to keep station. We'd hardly cleared the Pentland Firth before it started to blow from the S. and we got a gale warning.

At a matter of fact it never came to much more than a Force 5-6 wind and we did not have to ease down, but it was v. wet and rather bumpy. Our route took us down outside the Hebrides. Nothing much for me to do. From the news it looks as if the British are about to make a big scale attack to cross the Rhine in the north.

Friday, 23 March 1945 – At sea/Greenock

I only turned out once in the night. It felt in my cabin as if the sea was getting up, as we seemed to be pounding rather. I found a cloudless lovely night but still quite a hard S. wind blowing and choppy sea. At 0630 we sighted red and white flares away to the westward, and the only thing I could think of was the same sort of distress signal sent up by the German airmen from their dinghy during our N. Russian convoy. Sure enough about 1½ hours later we intercepted a signal from *Thetford Mines* saying she was picking up survivors in very much the same position. I think this U-boat must have been damaged in an aircraft attack reported yesterday and probably sank or scuttled herself.[77] A bright sunny day, but still blowing hard from the S.E. The *Premier* detached us at about 1215 when off Lamlash, and we turned round for Londonderry.

In the p.m. I got the Chief (Lt(E) Scott R.N.V.R.) to take me round his department, and then I took a bit of exercise as we were passing through Rathlin Sound. We were due at Lough Foyle at 1700 and just before 1600 we got a signal saying our destination should read Greenock and not Londonderry and so back we had to turn. Really it's a bit 'ard to bugger us about like this. We eventually arrived at the gate at 2100 and went alongside the oiler and then anchored at about 2300. Wrote to J. I suppose we won't get any mail now.

Saturday, 24 March 1945 – Greenock

A lovely warm sunny spring day. Old and I went ashore at about 0945 and got a car up to Capt. D.'s office and called on him. This going round with 2 and sometimes only 1 ship seems to me so ridiculous that I asked Capt. D. (Jauncey)[78] if he thought Derby House would approve of me missing our next short trip to Belfast and back so that I could go to Dunstaffnage and have a look at the *Matane.* I then rang up Dunstaffnage and spoke to the Chief Constructor who said the ship expected to leave on the 31st, that Stacey was still in command, that all was going well, and it didn't really seem much point in my going over. By this time Jauncey had rung up Com. D. Londonderry who said it was up to Derby House. Having raised this hare I then said I wasn't going. Felt rather a fool.

Saw and had a long talk with Ely, whose wife has been v. ill. Old and I then got a car to take us up to *Niobe,* where we called on the Captain, a V.R. 4-striper called Hunter[79] and a v. nice fellow. I was most impressed with the smartness of the whole place. Old says the new C.O. seems to have revolutionised the place, which certainly had a v. bad name. We lunched there and then got a car back to the town meaning to do some shopping but found everything shut till 1430. Caught a boat off at 1430. Feeling awfully depressed. Old is so nice but I hate to feel that in harbour I am keeping him out of his cabin. I don't think I should be expected to put up with this discomfort when my presence is so really unnecessary. Looked at the movies in the wardroom after supper. The British advance across the Rhine has started.

Sunday, 25 March 1945 – Greenock/At sea

I was going to walk round the ship's company at divisions but as it was raining hard at 0945 we had to call it off. A boat came alongside at 1015 and took Old and me and my Staff ashore and we were met by a car and taken to a conference with *Monnow* (who arrived last night) and the troopers we are escorting to Belfast. From N.C.S.O.'s we went to Ops at F.O.I.C.'s to get the latest news. We heard there that *New Glasgow,* which is exercising off the Foyle, had rammed a U-boat quite by chance and quite unintentionally. They then sunk it, and we think it is the survivors from it that *Thetford Mines* picked up the day before yesterday.[80]

Raining hard as we came back on board. I read and walked the deck in the rain in the p.m. Feeling fed up and disgruntled. The offensive in the W. seems to be going well, the Germans and their communications having been completely pulverised by our air forces. We weighed at 1730 and together with *Monnow* and our 2 troopers sailed for Belfast. Weather cleared completely and it was a beautiful still, moonlit night. Quite cold.

Monday, 26 March 1945 – Belfast/At sea/Greenock

I did not turn in until our arrival at Belfast at 0100. We anchored in the bay for the night. At about 0730 we weighed, met *Mounsey* (a D.E.) off the entrance, and the 2 of us escorted a light fleet carrier, the *Pioneer,* to the Clyde. A lovely sunny calm day. Just as we were coming up to the Clyde Light Vessel we got a contact right ahead of the carrier, which we were unable to attack until she had passed. As she was so near home I decided to stop and thoroughly investigate this thing, which was undoubtedly something on the bottom. We attacked with Squid several times and after a good number of runs over with echo sounder we finally got a trace over 300 feet long, which proved to be a wreck, and so we left it and proceeded on up the Clyde.

We secured alongside the oiler at about 1600 and got a mail with 2 letters from J. and one from Gillian. On completing oiling we secured alongside *Mounsey* at a buoy. I wrote to Gillian and had a drink with Old before supper. The acting C.O. (in fact the 1st Lieut.) a South African 2-striper, came over to call at about 1930. Got a letter from Band, which made me feel v. homesick for the *Swansea.* That really was a happy time compared to this bloody awful existence. *Monnow* on arrival at Belfast last night went off to Barrow to pick up and escort a submarine to the Clyde. The offensive on the W. front is going well, and the Allies are streaming across the Rhine in a number of places.

Tuesday, 27 March 1945 – Greenock

A misty damp and rather cold day. I spent the forenoon dealing with correspondence. Two of the *Saint John* officers want qualified status and I don't think I can recommend them. At 1200 I went over to the *Mistral* and saw Smeeton and had a long talk with him. The *Mistral* is a gunnery training ship. Back on board for a late lunch. From being emergency ship at ½ hour's notice we reverted to 4 hours' notice at noon and so granted leave. I read, wrote letters, and worked at my report of proceedings. It rained quite hard in the p.m.

Got another long letter from Band – just after I'd posted one back to him – saying he was still trying to get back to the group and that a new ship was being sent over to relieve the *Saint John.* At that rate it looks as if *Monnow* might go back to Canada when *Matane* rejoins, after perhaps one more trip, and that will be the moment for me to leave.

Our advance in the West still goes on rapidly. It *must* all end soon now and then 2 or 3 years more fighting in the Far East. I suppose I shall have to do my duty and go out there if required. Smeeton was v. interesting on the subject of morale among the lower deck after long periods abroad without leave. I think it is going to be v. hard indeed to keep our Armies, Navies, and Air Forces up to scratch for another 2 years so far from home and leave.

8
Oasis of Comfort and Happiness, March-May 1945

Frank Layard was an old salt in a young sailor's game. After sitting down for a glass of gin with two fellow destroyer captains in September 1942 he complained, "When I hear these young 2½ stripers talk I realize what an awful old cup of tea I am by comparison."[1] Old, and increasingly worn out. In 1944 Layard spent 211 days at sea, almost two out of three, and the weight of command exacted a severe toll.[2] On each of those days, Layard had to make dozens of command decisions involving the running of his ship or the direction of his group. On those days that E.G. 9 prosecuted asdic contacts, other, more complex concerns were added to the burden, some potentially involving life and death. Whether hunting U-boats or steaming routinely, Layard spent as much as sixteen to eighteen hours on the bridge on some days. During that time he had to remain alert, ready for any eventuality. Meals, often taken on the bridge, were rushed affairs. For rest, he retired either to the small chart house at the back of the bridge or to his cramped sea cabin one deck below. Sleep would be fitful at best, his ear always tuned to activity on the bridge, his body feeling any fluctuation in engine revolutions or movement of the ship, and his troubled conscience reminding him that inexperienced officers had control of the ship. This existence was not conducive to vitality or stability.

To some, this strain became overwhelming. One escort officer, Cdr. D.A. Rayner, RNVR, who had been at sea almost continuously since the outbreak of war, described the effects well. When his corvette nearly went aground due to a steering failure in late 1944, Rayner found himself shaking uncontrollably on the bridge. "Well," he said to himself after getting his ship safely alongside in Londonderry, "'this is it – you are round the bend.' It was true. I could no longer trust my own body to obey orders. Catching sight of myself in the glass made me pause. There had been a time when people ashore had said, 'You look very young to be a Commander,' but they hadn't been saying that recently. There wasn't any reason why they should. The candle was burned out."[3] Rayner immediately requested a shore appointment. Similarly, in November 1944 Layard's colleague Cdr. Douglas Prentice asked to be relieved of command of E.G. 11 because he thought fatigue was beginning to affect his judgment.[4] In March 1945 another veteran Canadian officer, Cdr. E.T. Simmons, RCNVR, was replaced as SO of E.G. 26 due to illness brought on by exhaustion.[5] In yet other examples, Alan Easton went ashore because of ulcers, and in July 1944 Capt. F.J. Walker died suddenly of cerebral thrombosis brought on by strain and exhaustion. There were many others.

Pressure and fatigue also pushed Layard to the limit. The winter of 1944-5 – "The Last Cruel Winter," historian Doug McLean has called it[6] – took a severe toll; not only did Layard beat himself up more than usual but he expressed more than his habitual angst about going to sea. On 2 February 1945 he had agonized in his diary, "Deep depression of course setting in ... not to mention worry and nerves. Oh dear, oh dear, I sometimes feel I can't go on competing anymore." The war, moreover, seemed as if it might last forever. On 19 April 1945 – three weeks before the European war actually ended – he wrote, "It is obvious there is going to be no order to stop fighting, and the Germans will continue to resist until every square mile is ours and that includes Norway, and so it is still a long time before we can celebrate V.[E.] day." But even that would not be the end: "then 2 or 3 years more fighting in the Far East. I suppose I shall have to do my duty and go out there if required."[7]

Layard recognized the strain he was under, but it was his wife Joan who pushed him to seek relief. At her prodding he asked Canadian authorities about being replaced but, interestingly, he did not harp on the issue in his diary as he did when bothered by other matters.[8] Moreover, he took the matter of his relief up with a Canadian civilian authority instead of an officer in the chain of command. One is thus left with the impression that he was prepared to stick it out, and his comments about the continuing role he might have to play in the war bear that out. So how did he carry on? What got him through? And that question applies to his entire war experience, as an officer lacking confidence and full of self-doubt. Many officers under similar stress suffered medical problems either during or after the war, but Layard remained in excellent health throughout the war, and went on to live a long, active life. The ulcers and other ailments that ravaged other commanding officers who suffered tension and anxiety left him alone.[9] Why?

A number of mechanisms and lifestyle choices bolstered Layard's confidence or provided diversions that gave him respite from the pressure. He had, for example, a vast network of fellow officers whom he knew through past service, and he took every opportunity to tap into it, especially during his first days back at sea earlier in the war. These included well-known officers such as Jackie Broome, R.M. "Tubby" Hutton, Allan Scott-Moncrieff, J.A. "Bez" McCoy,[10] and Sammy Boucher, all of whom rose to the rank of captain and beyond. Whether it was exchanging gin in each other's cabins or going on runs ashore, he relied upon his colleagues to give him the "gen" and to share their experiences. "Got back on board at about 1330," he wrote before taking *Chelsea* to sea for the first time in July 1941. "Read more orders and instructions in the p.m. and at about 1800 Pug arrived on board and we had a long quack and he gave me what hints and tips he could."[11] Although he was often in awe of the accomplishments and temperament of his friends and colleagues, their common experience probably told him that *he* was performing to expectations.

He largely lost contact with that network while he served with the RCN, but another mechanism then provided an outlet. Ironically, although Canadians and the RCN habitually aggravated Layard, and thus added to his strain, the challenge they represented also seemed to steel his backbone. On an almost "us versus them" level, he seemed not only determined to teach but also to better Canadians. One can sense his grim resolve after standing up to the Canuck who refused to give way on streets of Londonderry: "On my way home I met a Canadian sailor in a narrow part of the pavement who made no effort to move, and so I stopped and said, 'Who is going to get out of the way – you or I?' He said, 'Well, as you are carrying a cane I guess perhaps I'd better.' Christ, there are times when I never want to see another Canadian."[12] Whether such incidents occurred at sea or on the streets of Londonderry, they got Layard's blood up in a nearly adversarial vein. As long as they did not occur too often, and as long as he could see himself as the superior quality, which he always did, the conflict was probably beneficial to his psyche.

Layard's walk through the streets of old Londonderry illustrates another way he coped with tension: whenever possible, he sought diversions. During layovers he went for long walks or tried to avail himself of the local culture, be it visiting cathedrals or going to the theatre. He also loved informal get-togethers, tipping a glass with friends or associates while enjoying good conversation – he especially enjoyed a good debate on religion. At sea he always had a book going, and read biographies, novels, classics, and even Shakespeare. He also exercised and walked miles on deck. All these pursuits were of value, but the diary was the critical outlet. Quite simply, the diary was a release, a way to get things off his chest. Without it, his mental anguish might have become overwhelming.

In his excellent study of courage and morale among American and British aircrew in the Second World War, Mark Wells suggests that the ability to identify with a group was a key factor in overcoming combat stress.[13] That was certainly the case with Frank Layard. Identification with the long-established values and traditions of an officer in the Royal Navy was probably the key factor enabling him to rise above the numerous challenges or obstacles thrown his way, including the strain of command. Although loyalty to an institution or a profession seems almost trite in the context of contemporary cynicism, it was a vital component of Layard's character.

More than anything, his long education and experience in the Royal Navy ingrained in him that duty was paramount. No matter how much his confidence waned and no matter how tired he became, his devotion to duty drove him to persevere and, along with his skill, formed the essence of his professionalism. Abstract concepts like duty are difficult to define in concrete terms, but three diary entries from the first months of the Second World War shed light on Layard's attitude. At that time he was serving ashore at the experimental department at Whale Island, and the war at sea had begun to take its grim toll. In October 1939 he learned that a colleague, Cdr. R.F. Jolly, RN, captain of the destroyer HMS *Mohawk,* though mortally wounded in an air attack, had succumbed to his wounds only after taking his ship safely into port. "Stories of that sort make an enormous impression upon me," he wrote. "It makes me wonder if I could ever be heroic like that."[14] A week later he volunteered for special service: "I hope I am not required as I don't think I'm brave enough, but I feel I must make an effort to do something better worth while than just sitting comfortably back here."[15] In late November 1939 came news of the sacrifice of the armed merchant cruiser HMS *Rawalpindi* in an attack by the German battle cruisers *Scharnhorst* and *Gneisenau,* as well as word that another friend had been killed when the destroyer *Gypsy* was mined. "With every fresh naval disaster," he agonized, "I get a return of this awful complex: 'How would I meet a similar circumstance.' Should I have done my duty bravely or should I have disgraced myself in a blind funk?"[16] To Layard, the pull of duty, which included living up to the vaunted fighting standards of the Royal Navy, was inexorable. He had been brought up in a service that expected officers to perform gallantly and to do the right thing. As hokey and idealistic as that may seem to subsequent generations, that outlook formed the foundation of his professionalism. Thus when fatigue began to take a heavy toll in the winter of 1944-5, although Layard probably would have gone ashore if asked, he would not be driven ashore.

A change of scenery also helped. At the end of March the remnants of E.G. 9 were transferred to Portsmouth to support convoys running up the English Channel to Le Havre. They now escorted convoys along scheduled routes, which lifted numerous command decisions from Layard's shoulders. He was also based almost literally on the doorstep of Harvest Lodge in Prinsted, where he could benefit from the full support of his family, especially Joan. In a sense he commuted to work. "What a bit of luck!!," Layard exclaimed.[17] The war continued its dreary progress, and E.G. 9's adventures continued even beyond VE Day, when they took the surrender of a large group of U-boats, but the pall of exhaustion and depression that had begun to shroud his mood lifted perceptively.

Wednesday, 28 March 1945 – Greenock/At sea

It rained and was v. foggy all the a.m. At 1000 a boat arrived and Hearn and I went ashore and a car took us to Marymount (N.C.S.O.), where we were supposed to meet Skinner and the Captain of the *Johan de Witt,* who we are escorting again to Belfast. The *Monnow* hadn't yet got in and the Captain of the *de Witt* was delayed, so we got a car to Bagatelle and went to see Ops. While there I spoke to Packington at Derby Ho. and asked him about the group. *Saint John* is leaving for her refit in Canada almost at once, and a new frigate is due to join the group about the 8th. *Nene* arrives Derry on the 30th having completed her repairs in the Tyne, and we are to continue doing local escort work from the Clyde until about 15th.

Got a car and a boat back to the ship for lunch. *Monnow* secured alongside us after oiling on arrival from Barrow with the *Amphion,* a new S/M, and Skinner came over and sat talking until nearly 1800. The sailing of the *de Witt* was delayed and eventually we passed the boom at 2300. *Monnow* was further delayed with engine defects and didn't catch us up till off the Clyde Lt. Vess. The weather had cleared quite a bit but we still got rain showers. The news is magnificent, and I listen to almost every hourly summary. Wrote to J. Saw from the latest fleet order that I got my M.I.D. for "leadership and skill in damage control." Presumably when *Matane* was bombed. Lucas and 2 ratings also got a mention.

Thursday, 29 March 1945 – At sea/Belfast

We arrived at Belfast and anchored in the Lough at 0600. I had had only about 1 hour's sleep owing to the delayed time of sailing. In the a.m. I held a flag hoisting exercise and signalled that an officers whaler's crew was to go away to exercise under oars and sail. It is about time some of these fat young men took some exercise. After lunch I had a bit of shut eye and then read and took some exercise on the upper deck and thought out some drills for tomorrow. Our advance in the West seems to go on more or less unopposed. The Russians have crossed the Austrian border and are only 20 miles from Vienna.

Friday, 30 March 1945 – Belfast/At sea

At 0930 I carried out General Drill with the 2 ships. *Monnow* was ahead of *Loch Alvie* in nearly all evolutions. After that we had a signal exercise. At 1230 we got under way, and after hanging about for a bit the *Johan de Witt* came down from Belfast and met us at the entrance buoys, and we escorted her back to the Clyde.

As we reached Ailsa Craig we decoded a signal saying the 9th E.G. was to be temporarily lent to C. in C. Portsmouth and we were to proceed there forthwith at our best speed, so we turned round and beetled off. A tremendous surprise. Couldn't suit me better if we can only get in for a day or two. *Nene* is to be sent on to join us when ready. We were down somewhere off K1 buoy by midnight. The advance in the West and East continues. A fine day, but fresh and rather cold W. wind.

Saturday, 31 March 1945 – At sea

The usual rather misty weather as we approached K4 buoy at 0800. We never saw it but turned off and took the inside route past Grassholm for which the visibility was quite good enough. Blowing quite hard from the S. We passed Lundy Island at about 1300 and got down into our old familiar waters off the Cornish coast. It was pretty thick all the way down and we were very thankful for Q.H. I made my E.T.A. Portland Bill, which is the limit of Portsmouth area, as I felt sure we would be detailed for some job as soon as we got there, but as time went by and we received no orders I thought perhaps we *would* go to Portsmouth, and so at midnight I made another E.T.A. Needles.[18] We rounded Longships just before dark.

Sunday, 1 April 1945 – At sea/Portsmouth

Our route was remarkably clear, but at about 0245 we picked up a fast American convoy on radar on opposite courses and I went up and pulled over a bit to starboard to keep clear. As we approached the Needles the visibility closed down to about ¾ mile. Our radar broke down, and when we went the wrong side of a buoy and suddenly saw the Needles close to starboard and breakers on the port side it was rather an unpleasant moment, but it was really alright and we soon got back into the Channel. The fog lifted a bit as we passed Hurst Castle at about 0830, but it was misty and rainy all the way up to Spithead. In spite of several signals we could not get any information as to what to do and eventually decided to go alongside the duty oiler at Spithead. Before we got there we were ordered to pass the O.S.B. at 1030 and proceed up harbour and secure at South Slip Jetty with *Monnow* inside and go to 12 hours' notice. What a bit of luck!! I could hardly believe it.

Went ashore to see Capt. D. as soon as we secured. He is one King,[19] an S.O. of a Western Approaches group not long ago. I gather we may be required p.m. tomorrow. Rang up J. and got a taxi and went home for lunch. Got a great welcome from the family. G. is home from school. Started to prune the roses and tried to continue after tea but it rained so hard I had to give up. J. has an airman Corporal and his wife by name of Lock as lodgers, but she has just gone to hospital. They have the drawing room and spare room. He seems a very nice man. It seems incredible that I should get home like this. Blowing half a gale in the night.

Monday, 2 April 1945 – Portsmouth

Still blowing quite a bit but fine and sunny. We got the car out and at about 1000 J. and I drove in to Portsmouth and I took her on board the *Loch Alvie*. I hear we are now staying in till tomorrow. Took J. down to the wardroom for a drink and so that she could meet the officers and then we had lunch in my cabin. At about 1330 we drove to the gate and J. did some telephoning, and then we drove up to Fort Southwick.[20] While J. went in to see some Wren friends I together with Skinner, Old, and several other of the officers went down the tunnel and called on Operations to find out what was what. The most interesting thing is that we are not going to work as the 9th E.G. We are definitely attached to Portsmouth and will work with the Portsmouth Flotilla taking the place of 3 French frigates which have been taken away. It seems there is now absolutely no job for me at all, so I think after our first spell of convoy work is over I'll see the Chief of Staff[21] and ask for leave.

We talked to various people for about an hour and then climbed up the thousands of steps to the surface again. J. and I then drove home leaving the others to return to the Dockyard. Shifted into plain clothes and went with Raymond and Mr. C. to Jane's to return something and then on to the Marshes for a bit and then home where I did some more pruning. Dodo, Allan, and Jane came in for drinks. We decided that my next job must be in command of the Danube Flotilla when we occupy Germany and Austria. It really looks as if the end might come any day now, as the Germans seem to be quite broken in the W. now. Clocks went on one hour for double summer time.

Tuesday, 3 April 1945 – Spithead/At sea

I had an early breakfast and caught the 0820 from Southbourne and walked to the Dockyard and got on board at about 0900. We slipped at 1000 and went out and anchored at Spithead, leaving *Monnow* still alongside with some engine defect. As we went out we passed *Nene* going up harbour. She has come straight on here after refitting and making good all her leaks in the Tyne. I spent the whole forenoon wading through signals and orders in preparation for our first escort job tonight. After lunch I asked the Captain of the *Hotham* to come over and give me some local information. We are escorting a fast personnel convoy to Le Havre, the escorts being *Loch Alvie, Hotham,* and *Tonkinois* and *Croix de Lorraine* (2 French frigates). At 1630 we weighed anchor again near the Ryde S.E. buoy and closed the Commodore of our convoy so that we could exchange information. As it was rather rough I did not go over to see him but did it all by signal.

I'm not at all happy about the officers in this ship, and I know I ought to deliver them a little speech, but I can't somehow formulate my ideas into words. I don't think there is the right sort of mutual understanding between officers and men. It would be so much easier if this was my own ship.

We weighed at 2215, picked up the rest of the escorts and went out ahead of our convoy of 3 ships. It is certainly nice to have Old to do the navigation on this first trip while I look out for the general organisation. Bright, sunny day but strong wind.

Wednesday, 4 April 1945 – At sea/Le Havre

The trip across to Le Havre was without incident, but Old and I were up pretty well all the way and we anchored just before daylight in the Roads at about 0615 and I had about an hour's sleep before breakfast. We lay at anchor all day. A beautiful calm, sunny day. I slept a bit in the p.m. and gave a lot of thought again to an address to the officers which I intend giving on discipline. Started to read one of Forrester's Captain Hornblower books. We got orders in the dog watches to take a return convoy to Spithead sailing at midnight. There are 9 ships this time, but it is a 14 knot convoy again. I weighed and took my 4 escorts out ahead of the Commodore at 2340. Some 120,000 Germans have been cut off in the Ruhr, which is now completely surrounded.

Thursday, 5 April 1945 – Le Havre/At sea/Le Havre

An uneventful trip. Old and I were up most of the night and we arrived and anchored at Spithead at about 0830. The convoy was v. badly handled by the Commodore, I thought, and the amount of chat that went on over the T.B.S. was remarkable. Q.H. on this run is very poor as it is generally only possible to get one station. A great pity. At about 1100 we got orders to raise steam forthwith and proceed back to Le Havre, but as we had a bit of our main engine down for repair we couldn't go till 1300, and so at 1130 I had the Captains of the *Hotham* and the French ship *Croix de Lorraine* over for a drink. The latter is a v. nice fellow. I spent some of the time on the trip back on my bunk getting some sleep.

I was annoyed at the way Old and his officers will hurriedly and quite unjustifiably classify A/S contacts as wreck or non sub. In my opinion it is quite impossible to tell without careful investigation, and if in a hurry everything should at least be attacked once. We arrived at Le Havre at about 1900. *Monnow, Nene, Watchman,* and *L'Escarmouche* (Frenchman) were here as escort and we took over S.O. and made a lot of signals. The fast V.W.P.[22] convoy sailed at midnight as usual. There were 6 ships, and this time the U.S. Commodore was better but still v. verbose.

Friday, 6 April 1945 – At sea/Spithead/At sea

Again an uneventful trip until we were nearing F buoy, which is about 5 miles S. of the Nab.[23] It was daylight by then and just before 0700 when we got a contact on the port side. There was the usual reluctance to do anything about it, but after some hesitation the Officer of the Watch turned to carry out a Squid attack but the Squid wasn't ready or the crew weren't there, and so they tried to drop a D/C. Then owing to some misunderstanding the ship swung almost 60° off the attacking course and then it was too late. As a result nothing was done, which showed deplorable unreadiness. I was just thinking what a very poor show it was when there was an explosion at the stern of the 2nd ship. Obviously a torpedo. I felt quite sick with dread and worry, and my brain was quite woolly with indecision. However, as we phoned the hit ship (the *Cuba*)[24] we got a good contact and carried out an attack, which brought up some oil and splintered wood. I told *Nene* to go and stand by the *Cuba,* who was abandoning ship and who sank in about ¾ hour. I put the Frenchman on to sweep down tide from my contact and told *Monnow* and *Watchman* to screen the rest of the ships into safe waters.

After 2 attacks our contact rather faded out and nothing much in the way of evidence appeared, and so on the return of *Monnow* and *Watchman* I reorganised a line abreast search across tide to the S., but as always happens it was almost impossible to get on with the search as all ships seemed to be continually falling out of contact. *Watchman* reported attacking a good echo but after buoying it he left it. We likewise buoyed and left ours.

We were reinforced later by *Hoste* and *Vidette* and then old Gwinner appeared in the *Balfour.* After sweeping S. and then back again I turned the whole line to the W. to sweep down tide and had just thankfully surrendered control to Gwinner when *L'Escarmouche* reported sighting bodies in the water which turned out to be 4 German officers and 4 men. The weight off my mind was terrific to know that U-boat had not escaped and, of course, we'd hoped and thought our 3 attacks had done it but as the bodies appeared near *Watchman*'s buoy and a contact with bubbles and oil rising was gained just near, it was obvious that *Watchman*'s one H/H attack had done the trick. Rather a bloody fluke, one can't help thinking, considering he left it so quickly. Prisoners were then sent in and all ships proceeded either to continue patrol and proceed into harbour, except ourselves who were ordered to remain with the contact to try and get E/S trace evidence.[25]

Later on about 1300 *Vidette* and *Hotham* were sent back to join us and we were then told to go to the wreck of the *Cuba,* fix it, and take soundings. While doing so we rescued a cat from one of the rafts floating about. *Nene,* before going in with survivors, reported only one man missing out of some 260. I had all officers on to the bridge and told them that in my opinion the deplorable unpreparedness of this ship had probably resulted in the torpedoing of the *Cuba.* We returned to the U-boat again but eventually about 1800 we were all allowed to return and we anchored in St. Helen's roads at 1900. I then had to make out the usual long signal about screening and sailing of the W.V.P. convoy,[26] and at 2240 we weighed with *Vidette* and rendezvoused with *Monnow* and *Nene* at the Nab and took up screening positions on the convoy as they came down the Channel. Old wasn't v. clever and we were badly astern and out of station for a long time. The *Tonkinois* joined us at EH3 buoy, where we turn S.

An exhausting day. I don't think I can really take much credit for this kill but thank God for it. Perfect calm weather helped us.

Saturday, 7 April 1945 – At sea/Le Havre/At sea

We arrived without incident and anchored in Havre roads at 0615. Got about an hour's sleep before breakfast. At 1130 I had the 4 C.O.s over for a drink and discussed the U-boat incident. The captain of the *Tonkinois* is another nice chap. I drank rather too much gin. After lunch I put in about 2 hours' good sleep and woke up feeling frightfully gummy. The convoy form and orders came on board and I made out the usual sheaf of sailing signals and did a bit of writing. Got in some more sleep after dinner. At 2330 we weighed and went out ahead of the V.W.P. convoy of 5 ships.

Saw in latest A.F.O.s that Stacey, Bradley,[27] and 2 or 3 ratings have got D.S.C. and Distinguished Conduct Medals. There are one or two mentions in addition for *Saint John*'s submarine off the Wolf on 1st Sept. I'm v. glad, but they have been long enough about it.

Sunday, 8 April 1945 – At sea/Spithead/At sea

A fine bright night and an uneventful trip. We had the *Loyal Ulsterman,* a White Ensign Landing Ship, who is much more efficient as Commodore. We got in and anchored at about 0830 off the Spit fort. *Loch Alvie* went to divisions and I walked round with Old. As usual a pretty scruffy lot. I spoke a word to them afterwards. At lunch time in the W.R. after 2 or 3 gins I talked rather garrulously to some of the officers about officer-like qualities and discipline. Slept a bit in the p.m. after making my usual sailing signals, and at 1630 we weighed and re-anchored in the convoy anchorage so as to be in touch with the Commodore. He, however, in his ship didn't arrive from Southampton till about 1900, and at 1930 I pulled over in the whaler and discussed the convoy organisation with the Commodore. There are only 3 ships and we have 5 escorts.

At 2100 Old reported capstan trouble which put it out of action, and so we signalled that we would probably be late and rigged deck tackle to weigh by hand. At 2200 it became apparent we would definitely be late and we signalled again. Then *Monnow* came up and reported her radar out of action and asked to remain behind, and anyhow if she sailed she wanted someone else to be S.O. I was v. worried. Eventually told her to sail, told *Nene* to take charge, and told C. in C. I thought *Monnow*'s radar *must* be put right. In the meantime I was undecided what we ought to do with a capstan completely out of action, and so I asked instructions and we were told to buoy and slip cable and proceed, which we did. We were an hour behind the convoy but we managed to catch them shortly after passing EA8 buoy.

Monday, 9 April 1945 – At sea/Le Havre/At sea

Arrived Le Havre at 0600 and after *Monnow* had anchored we went alongside as we couldn't anchor. All was well until about 1100 when suddenly a ground swell seemed to get up, and the 2 ships started to surge and bang about so alarmingly that *Loch Alvie* had to shove off. As we had all been invited to go over to *Watchman* for a drink at 1130, I hopped over to *Monnow* before the *Loch Alvie* shoved off and went over to *Watchman* with Skinner. The Captain is a V.R. 2½ called Clarke.[28] A v. nice chap. He told us all about his submarine. It was a pretty lucky business.

Shaw and I both went back on board *Monnow* for more drinks and lunch. In the p.m. it was really quite rough and I decided to remain in *Monnow* and had a bit of a zizz in the Captain's cabin. At 1600 I decided to stay and make the trip in *Monnow* and made all the necessary signals. Skinner took me round some of the ship. He is a nice old boy and really v. keen, but I deplore the way his officers wear high necked sweaters, scarves, etc., or open necked shirts all day long. After supper we had rather a good movie in the W.R. and at 2230 we weighed. The convoy (it was only 2 ships) left an hour earlier than usual for some reason. Rather interesting doing a trip in another ship. *Monnow* is certainly an efficient ship.

Tuesday, 10 April 1945 – At sea/Portsmouth

All went well and without incident until we neared F buoy where we met the slow Le Havre-Wight convoy also making up for the Nab, and for a bit there was a bit of confusion. I really got rather frightened at our turn and I thought Skinner was going to have a collision. The trouble was we had sailed an hour early, but in addition we'd somehow made up almost another hour and arrived at F buoy at 0500. On getting in we were told to anchor as usual in Area 28. *Loch Alvie* was sent alongside the *Albatross* (a small repair ship waiting off Ryde) to get her capstan put right, and after breakfast I went back on board her. Spent the whole forenoon writing out my report of Friday's happenings when the *Cuba* was torpedoed and *U-1195* subsequently sunk.

At about 1200 I went over to the *Albatross.* The Captain was on leave and I had a drink with the 1st Lieut., the Chief, and Old. In the p.m. I had some shut eye. Our capstan can't be ready until tomorrow at earliest, and so the W.V.P. convoy is sailing this evening without us and *Monnow* will be S.O. I turned in early so as to have a good night in. We have taken Hanover, are close to Leipzig, and the Russians have taken Vienna. I read a Portsmouth General Order which detailed what was to be done as soon as the announcement was made that Hostilities had ended in Europe!!! It looks as if in high places it was considered that the end was now v. near.

Wednesday, 11 April 1945 – Portsmouth/At sea

A really good night in. Hearn and I caught the 0900 drifter into the Dockyard. I went out and rang up J. and asked her to come in for lunch and then went to M. and Pounsford and got my M.I.D. palm leaf sewn on. Then had a hair cut at Gieves and then went back to the Dockyard to see Capt. D., with whom I broached the question of leave while working here. He told me 3 ships had already been detailed to relieve us so that we could go back to Western Approaches, and on ringing up Fort Southwick I was told instead of doing that we might be sent farther E. up Channel to the Dover area being either operated from there or here. In any case it does *not* look like the right moment to ask for leave.

I then went out to the Queens and met J. for lunch. Also met Isaac in the bar. J. told him that Letty[29] had told her about the U-boat and said the C. in C. and the whole staff were much excited and delighted. It was a perfectly lovely sunny morning, but it clouded over after lunch. J. and I went out and I did some shopping with her, and we looked in 2nd hand junk shops and finally just looked in to see Biddy. By then (1530) it had started to rain, so I put J. into a bus for home and trolleyed to the Dockyard and got v. wet walking to the steps, where I caught a 1630 boat off. Found our capstan job was finished. We were detailed for the usual nightly W.V.P. convoy with 2 D.E.s from the 1st E.G., and I made the usual crop of signals. We sailed earlier than usual and were at the Nab end buoy by 2130. It was otherwise without incident. The leave business is most disappointing. I don't believe I'll ever get it. It cleared up again before dark and we had another fine night.

Thursday, 12 April 1945 – At sea/Portsmouth/At sea

We arrived at HV3 buoy off Le Havre at about 0345, and in accordance with our orders we detached and turned round to return to Portsmouth. I hoped to get some sleep but it wasn't to be, as we got just one contact after another, which we attacked and classified in turn as non sub. Later on we ran into a number of floating mines and those in range had to be sunk. The inefficient way in which A/S and gunnery things are done infuriates and depresses me. It is, in my opinion, certainly the Captain's fault. He bawls and shouts at everyone but takes *no* further steps to enquire into and find out the reasons for errors and mistakes and only makes officers and men sore and angry. He neither drives nor leads and, nice as he is, he is just spoiling the ship and I don't know what to do about it.

After endless delays we arrived off the Nab at about 1300, and on reaching the gate we were told to proceed up harbour to a buoy and our anchor and cable would be sent to us. After rather a misty a.m. it turned out a most lovely afternoon and evening. We secured alongside a corvette at about 1430. I had a few winks in my chair but not nearly enough after rather a sleepless night last night. An R.A.F. Flight Lieut. arrived on board for a few days' visit. We slipped at 2000 and went out and closed and communicated with the Commodore of the W.V.P convoy. The escorts are *Monnow, Nene, Garlies,* and *Gore.* We all weighed at 2120 and were just shaping up for the gate when the fort told us the port was closed. After hanging about for a bit we anchored again and were told later on to weigh at 2345 and proceed, which we did, but no indication of what the delay was about in the first place.

Friday, 13 April 1945 – At sea/Le Havre

Just beyond the Nab we ran into thick fog and shortly after altering course round F buoy the Commodore reported he had been in collision with another ship. It was most unfortunate, as we'd seen this ship on our radar plan position indicator and it looked as though we might have to alter for him. Then we got a contact and ran in to drop a depth charge. The explosion threw our radar off and before we got it going again the collision had happened. The Commodore reported damage to his stern and said he thought he ought to turn back, so I told *Garlies* to screen him back and sent *Gore* to find out what damage had been done to the other ship. The remaining 3 escorts carried on with the other ship of the convoy. Our troubles weren't over even then, as we met and had to dodge 2 other convoys before getting much further. The fog was still v. thick at daylight but with Q.H. and radar we had no difficulty in making HV3 buoy, and then we conned our convoy into the roads and anchored him and then we anchored ourselves still in thick fog.

Heard on the news that President Roosevelt had died, which is a great loss to the Allies. The fog lifted in the p.m. and we got our sailing orders for the usual V.W.P. tonight, but later on it came in thick again and the whole thing was cancelled till tomorrow. I had a yarn with Old and tried to tell him how I thought he was failing in his handling of his officers, but I don't think he really understood. At 1930 Flight Lieut. Dyson, who is on board for a few days, gave a talk to the ship's company about Bomber Command. I had asked him to do this and it was most interesting. I still think it requires more guts to fly night after night over Germany than practically any other war job. Sat up talking in the wardroom quite late.

Saturday, 14 April 1945 – Le Havre/At sea

A lovely hot, sunny day. The fog had cleared away. At 1030 I went over to the *Nene* and walked round her. I was pleasantly surprised how clean she was. I addressed the ship's company and had a drink and then came back for lunch. A bit of shut eye after lunch. At 1800 the Captains of *Gore* and *Garlies* came over and had a drink with Old and me. We weighed (the 3 of us) at 1130 and went out with the V.W.P. convoy, which tonight consisted of 9 ships, which is the biggest we'd had so far. They were v. slow forming up into 2 columns, and there seemed to be no end to the non subs which were being plastered by all the escorts.

Sunday, 15 April 1945 – At sea/Portsmouth

As we approached EA5 buoy we found ourselves overtaking and slightly converging on a slow convoy which was miles off its proper route, and I had a v. worrying time getting round it and dealing with stragglers at the same time. Even then our troubles were not at an end, because on nearing F buoy we found another slow convoy converging and as it was then 0530 and still dark a good deal of confusion occurred, and it was a long time before I felt the group could safely proceed up harbour. On arrival we were told to proceed up harbour and secure to No. 4 trot with *Monnow* alongside us and *Nene* alongside the wall. 12 hours' notice and 48 hours' lay over.

We were secured by about 0800 and at 0900 I went ashore. Called in at Capt. D.'s office and then caught a train to Southbourne and arrived home at about 1030. Feeling v. tired as I had literally had no sleep at all last night, and so I went to bed and had a little shut eye before lunch. It was a most lovely really hot, summer like day. I worked in the garden and we had tea in the garden. At about 1830 we went round and drank beer with Miss Boldsworthy. Rachael Wildbore Smith was there. She has come down to sell her house, for which she is asking £5,000!!! We looked in on Jane before coming home and took a gin off her.

Monday, 16 April 1945 – Portsmouth

J. and I caught the 0845 [bus] to Portsmouth, and I went into the Dockyard and she went in to Southsea. Got a boat from Kings Stairs, looked at a few things on board, and then Hearn and I came ashore again and caught the 1100 routine car to Fort Southwick. On arrival at Operations we found the daily convoy conference was going on, which Mrs. Parker (the Wren officer who arranges escorts, etc.) invited us to attend. The Chief of Staff (Commodore Symons Taylor) and a number of other types were there. I mentioned Sunday morning's experience of convoys all converging off F buoy and made some suggestions. The idea that we should go and operate round Dover is apparently off. We are now just waiting for *Inver, Erne,* and *Snowdrop* to arrive, when we will return to Western Approaches. Date still unknown. I looked in on Letty Medley while in the tunnel. Caught a car back at 1220 and I dropped off at Cosham and picked up an Emsworth bus back. Found J. had arrived just ahead of me.

Another wonderful day. I worked hard in the garden in the p.m. The children went down to the Marshes and had a bathe with the Thews. After putting R. to bed J. and I went round to the Harvest Home and had a glass of beer. I rang up Capt. D.'s duty officer to find out what time I had to be on board tomorrow and was told the *Loch Alvie* was coming alongside for some boiler defects.

Tuesday, 17 April 1945 – Portsmouth

I caught the 0845 bus to Portsmouth but when I got into the Dockyard, in spite of having had my hair cut at Gieves first, the *Loch Alvie* was still manoeuvring with tugs in the harbour and it was some time before I could get on board. The brickwork in both boilers wants renewing, and we certainly won't go out till tomorrow. At about 1130 I walked round to the *Barfleur,* the first of our new super Battle class destroyers. Michael Townsend is Captain. I had hoped to see something of the ship, but before I could do so Ted LeMesurier and Ross arrived from Department Naval Ordnance Bath and we had to round with them. However, I had 2 v. good gins and a yarn. He is an awfully nice chap. From there I went to Capt. D.'s office, as I wasn't sure I oughtn't to transfer to *Monnow* or *Nene* as *Loch Alvie* was held up, but Stevenson the S.O.O. said one of their own frigates with a Commander was going out on tonight's convoy, and as he was senior to me there was obviously no point in my going out as a passenger, so I can stay in with a clear conscience.

After that I bussed to the Queens where I met J., G., and R., who had all come in by car for R's treatment. They were sitting in the lounge with Biddy and Mrs. Lawrence having drinks. We lunched there and after a bit of a sit down we took the children to the fair at the Clarence Pier and went on the dodgems and switchbacks. It is wonderful how unfrightened G. is now of those sort of things, considering how terrified she was of anything like that a few years ago. From there we took the car to the Dockyard and went on board *Loch Alvie* for tea, and I had a hot and exhausting time showing the children round. The ship being covered with wet paint didn't make it any easier. However, they loved it. We eventually got home at about 1800.

Yet another remarkable day with almost mid summer heat. I immediately got into my gardening clothes. The news when we left the ship was that we wouldn't be finished until p.m. Thursday, which is just too good to be true. I did some digging and played some sort of High Lokaman game with the children. Molly came for drinks. Heard that yet another ship – the *Cape Breton* – is detailed to join E.G. 9 shortly. How glorious it is to be at home at this most lovely time of the year, especially during this freak hot spell.

Wednesday, 18 April 1945 – Prinsted

Hearn rang up early to say p.m. tomorrow was still our completion date, and so I decided to take a day's leave. Unfortunately, G. had to go to London for a long standing dental appointment and they went off by taxi to Havant at 0810. I spent a most strenuous morning in the garden weeding and digging and getting very hot, as it was yet another day of summer temperature. Mrs. Lock, our lodger's wife, returned from hospital, and she, I, and Raymond all had lunch together. More gardening in the p.m. cutting grass. J. and G. returned at about 1445. We all had our early tea in the garden and then went round to Jane's, where we collected the Thew family and Hayes family, and all of us went down to the Marshes for the children to bathe. I actually bathed too and it was really lovely and quite warm, and most refreshing after all my efforts in the garden. On our way back we stopped for a drink at Jane's and then came home, and I carried on cutting the grass until the mower got so blunt I had to stop. In our absence the Garrett's "Bobby" had knocked over the rabbit's run and chased one rabbit into the field at the back of the house. We had given up all hope of seeing it again, but G. spotted it in the drain behind the kitchen and she and I caught it. Had a bath before supper and read to G. afterwards, who in the end was v. tearful about my departure. She loves me dearly without any doubt. In a life which I have always found difficult and frightening, my home and my family are like an oasis of comfort and happiness. I am v. lucky.

Thursday, 19 April 1945 – Portsmouth/At sea

My brief leave is over, alas, and I caught the 0845 bus into Portsmouth. I heard on getting on board that we were sailing at 1400, but later on it was put back to 1600. Bob Knight and Bird came on board for a drink and took me off back to Whaley for lunch. The Island was looking very trim and pre-war. After lunch Knight showed me over the X.P. and took me along to the American "Waller trainer," the last word in anti-aircraft training devices, a sort of super Dome teacher.[30] Bird eventually drove me back to the Dockyard. We slipped at 1600 and went out and anchored in Area 28. When we left we were told we would be at a ½ hour's notice but probably wouldn't be required till tomorrow evening, however we'd hardly anchored an hour when we were told to weigh at about 1800 and escort a fast ship to Plymouth. We finally got away with our American ship, the *Explorer,* at about 1830 just as *Monnow* and *Nene* arrived in. On clearing the Nab we went on to 16 kts. Nothing much for me to do but just being there made me feel I was responsible to a large extent, and so I was up and about the chart house and bridge most of the night. Another heavenly day. Wonderful visibility. Saw Chichester Cathedral plainly as we went out.

The advance continues rapidly in Germany. We are up to the Elbe. Magdeburg, Leipzig, and Nurnberg have all fallen, Bremen and Hamburg are threatened, and now the Russians in a final offensive against Berlin are across the Oder in force. However, it is obvious there is going to be no order to stop fighting and the Germans will continue to resist until every square mile is ours, and that includes Norway, and so it is still a long time before we can celebrate V. day.

Friday, 20 April 1945 – At sea/Portsmouth/At sea

We had to dodge round a couple of convoys and finally arrived off Plymouth at about 0415 and then we dropped our charge, turned round, and came back. Once headed back again I turned in in my cabin. In the forenoon watch I did a few drills with the Officer of the Watch, which might have been a great deal better. We passed through the Needles Channel and anchored at about 1330. I slept a bit, but somewhat uncomfortably owing to a twinge of lumbago, in my chair after lunch but I'm feeling worried and unhappy about this ship. I'm afraid if I go on as I am I shall be undermining the Captain's authority, but I see so many things I don't like that I can't keep my mouth shut.

Got orders for the usual W.V.P. convoy tonight with 8 escorts in all, which meant a lot of signals. I got Skinner and Shaw over at 1700 and told them what I wanted to do if we are in harbour at Le Havre all tomorrow in the way of drills, and I was going to walk round *Monnow,* but as we had received a signal telling us to land all our Portsmouth orders it looks as if we were off shortly. I feel I ought to have made more use of all this harbour time for inspections and drills.

Later on we got a signal telling us to return immediately on arrival at Le Havre, oil, and go to Plymouth, pick up 2 ships, and escort them to 45N en route Med and then return to Western Approaches. No more days at home now. Wrote to J. At 2000 we got under way and went up and anchored near the Commodore and gave him all the news. At 2220 we all weighed and went out. Our convoy consists of 5 ships all packed with troops, 3 French frigates, the *Zanzibar,* and *St. Helena,* in addition to the 3 of us in E.G. 9. At 2220 we all weighed and went out. Just to make things easier they sailed a slow convoy at exactly the same time. Sometimes I wonder whether they aren't all mad up in the tunnel at H.Q.

Saturday, 21 April 1945 – At sea/Portsmouth/At sea

It was unexpectedly misty as we approached the French coast and we never saw Cap d'Antifer Light and only just saw the buoy. It was blowing quite a bit and looked like a break in the weather. At HV3 buoy we detached (0615) with *Monnow* and *Nene* and shaped course to return to Pompey.[31] The day improved steadily and turned out nice and sunny again. Strained my eyes in the direction of home as we went in. Could see Chichester Cathedral, Stoke Clump, Kingley Vale, and the water tower at Thorney, but not Prinsted of course. Got through the boom at about 1200 but found both sides of the oiler full, and so we all anchored, but in about ½ hour it was clear and we all went alongside. I slept a bit after lunch. Feeling wretchedly depressed at leaving. Portsmouth with all its rather inefficient organisation is near enough home to feel v. much like home. *Nene* had about 260 tons to take in and the oiler was very slow, and it wasn't till 1730 that she finished and we were able to get away. We went out the Needles Channel and shaped course for Plymouth at 15½ knots. A lovely evening and a bright moonlight night. We had to do a certain amount of traffic dodging.

Sunday, 22 April 1945 – At sea

We arrived off Plymouth breakwater at about 0210, and a motor launch came alongside us and put our sailing orders on board. The 3 of us with *Holmes* (a D.E.) are escorting *Highway* and *Monowai,* who missed the last R.M.F. convoy, S. towards Gibraltar. *Highway,* who is one of those T.L.C. dock ships and is a white ensign job,[32] is S.O. of the party. The 3 of them left harbour at 0230 and we formed up as a screen and off we went at 15 knots. A bright clear moonlight night.

We passed about 12 miles off Ushant, which was clearly visible at noon. We got a lot of non sub echoes in the p.m. and were continually dropping single charges and Squid patterns. I've never known a ship so bad at classifying echoes, although when screening at this speed one more or less has to go for every contact as there is scarcely time for careful investigation. At about 1730 the Chief reported condenser trouble, and so we asked the Commodore to reduce to 12 knots. We stopped one engine and opened up the condenser, found the leak, stopped it, closed up, and were back on 2 engines at 15 knots in under 3 hours, which was I thought v. good work. Just before dark we ran into rain squalls and poor visibility. The Russians in their new and final drive are now in the outskirts of Berlin, and American and Russian troops are expected to meet any moment now S. of Berlin. At about 2100 when about in the middle of the Bay we altered to 270° on the rather zigzag route which we have been given.

Monday, 23 April 1945 – At sea

I had a pretty good night in. At 0615 the *Highway,* without any previous warning, altered about 45° to port to the new course, with the result that it was about ¾ hour before the screen was reformed. At the same time I discovered that *Highway* had been making a balls of aircraft homing, and although I'd specially told the W/T office to set watch and listen out to see whether this would happen they took no steps to answer for *Highway* or try and help the aircraft. I was v. annoyed. We were mostly in thick fog during the a.m., but it cleared up and turned out hot and sunny in the p.m. I spent some time writing out inspection reports on ships of the group, which according to Western Approaches Routine Orders have to be produced by S.O.s every quarter. I sent for Brown and asked him confidentially whether he noticed what a different atmosphere there was in this ship and *Nene,* compared to *Matane, Swansea,* and *Saint John.* I think the officers here are a poor bunch but also both Captains are v. largely to blame. At 2140 *Highway* detached the 9th E.G. and we turned round. Our orders are to go to Milford Haven, escort a ship from there to the Clyde, and then go to Londonderry for our lay over.

Tuesday, 24 April 1945 – At sea

Lots of sleep but the chart house bunk is v. hard. We carried out an exercise at 1030 dropping smoke floats, turning round and firing at them, and then throwing a depth charge at them. At 1700 we did another exercise firing close range at a shell burst in the sky. Calm but rather overcast.

Wednesday, 25 April 1945 – At sea

We arrived at the Wolf at about 0500 and got slightly mixed up with another escort group while rounding Land's End. Up along the old familiar beat along the Cornish coast. We arrived off the Milford Haven buoy at 1330 and found the *Richmond Castle* – a large fast merchant ship – waiting for us. We immediately formed up ahead of her and started off at 16 knots for the Clyde. After quite a warm day it turned really cold in the evening.

Thursday, 26 April 1945 – At sea/Londonderry

We arrived off the Mull of Galloway at about 0230, and I was up on the bridge until about 0400 when we were well on our way up the new Clyde swept channel. We left our charge on arrival at the Cumbraes at 0645 and turned back for Londonderry. We arrived at Moville at about 1400, embarked pilots, and proceeded straight up river. I had a bath while we were going up. Shortly after securing I went up to see Selby and get the news. It seems my relief has been nominated (one Plomer, a Canadian V.R. Commander),[33] but I shall have to do at least one more trip. The *St. Pierre* is keen to join the group but the *Cape Breton* is still working up in Bermuda, and until she arrives *Monnow* will not be released. It is hoped to get *Matane* here in time for me to get into her before we sail.

I then went in to see the Commodore, who was a bit tight and very talkative and kindly gave me 2 v. strong whisky and sodas. When I got back on board there was a big party going on in the wardroom and after withdrawing to my cabin with Old and Shaw, Skinner appeared dead drunk. Silly old bugger. So we turned him in on my bunk and in desperation sent for Hearn and said he must take me ashore for dinner. We went up to the club where we had a v. good evening, met a lot of chaps, and drank quite a lot. Got back on board at about 2300 and found to my relief that Skinner had gone. I was just turning in when he appeared again, now much sobered down, and we sat talking and arguing until nearly 0200. Max Horton has sent for him to give him a bit of a raspberry on account of his Courts of Enquiry. I'd give a lot to be in on the meeting, and I did my best to advise Skinner on how to behave. I rang up J. from the club and she is going to come up here, as with the *St. Pierre* and *Matane* I can't get away.

Friday, 27 April 1945 – Londonderry

Feeling none too well. At 0900 I went to the Customs Office and sent off the necessary wire to get J. over. Then I went to a meeting in the *Charlottetown* about this voluntary service in the Pacific for Canadians. The Canadian Government have said that they will provide a fleet of 2 cruisers, 2 light carriers, 6 destroyers, and 38 frigates for the Far East when the German war is over. They now say only volunteers will be sent out there, and as it is estimated that they will need about 40,000, or nearly 90% of the existing strength, and they are only likely to get about 10% volunteers, they are faced with a v. funny situation. It all sounds like a dirty political ramp. They are even allowing the regular R.C.N. to volunteer. This is likely to make their navy a laughing stock and is bitterly resented.[34]

When that was over we had our group conference. I met Tullis, the C.O. of the *St. Pierre,* an N.R. without much apparent personality.[35] As I am staying back I told Old he could go on leave. Trouble started right away, and I had to enquire into the reason for Wrens being on board these ships after 2100 last night. A long screed also arrived on dress and discipline and out of bounds regulations, which I reckoned ought to be read to the ship's company. At about 1730 I went ashore and booked a room at The Melville and then went to the club and read the papers. The illustrated papers showing our advance into Germany are most interesting. It was announced at 1800 that the Russians and Americans had joined up S. of Berlin. The Russians are now fighting in Berlin. Back on board for supper. Later on Shaw came over for a drink. He *is* a bore, but I can't make up my mind about him. Is he conscientious but ineffectual and quite a non-entity, or is he really rather good? Cold, raw day.

Saturday, 28 April 1945 – Londonderry

At 0800 Mallet[36] cleared lower deck and I read out to the ship's company the Commodore's memo on dress and discipline. I said a few words in explanation. At 1100 I went on board *St. Pierre* and had a yarn with the Captain and then went into the wardroom and met the officers and spoke to them. After lunch I went up to the offices but found everybody out, and so I walked along to the Anchor Line offices and had talk with [Pay] Captain Vaughan about slops and kit, which seems a bit difficult to come by. From there to the club for tea and a look at the papers. Back on board for supper and then I wrote to G. and read a bit and then went to bed. A very cold wind with showers and intervals of sunshine.

Sunday, 29 April 1945 – Londonderry

Another beastly day with a bitter wind and alternate periods of sunshine and hail and sleet showers. There was a big Canadian church parade with parties from all ships and the whole lot marching to church with *Niobe*'s band, which is very good. I went. The service was in the Presbyterian church, which is a v. austere place with altar, but the service I thought was short and to the point and a good sermon. After church I walked up to the old American Yard to call on the S.O. of the American group who are here working with C. in C. W.A., but having got there I found he was out of the ship and so I walked back on board and went across to *Monnow* and had a drink in their wardroom. Went ashore for a bit of a walk after lunch and finished up at the club for tea. The latest *Illustrated London News* has horror pictures of the scenes found at some concentration camps, which have recently been liberated in Germany. Quite frightful. Back on board, shifted, and then went to drink with the Selbys. Shared a service car up there with Finch Noyes. Quite a big party. Afterwards the Base T. officer drove F.N. and me to the

Officer's Club, where we had a v. late supper and rather a lot of beer. Mussolini has been captured and shot by Italian patriots.

Monday, 30 April 1945 – Londonderry

At about 0800 there was quite a heavy snow squall, and the snow lay for about 2 or 3 hours. I went up to see the Chief of Staff thinking I had a justifiable moan about some defects in *Loch Alvie,* but he managed to show me I was quite wrong and I came away feeling an awful fool. Later on I went to the clothing store and got some slops. That awful bore Squadron Leader Amery came on board and stayed to lunch, but anyhow he kindly drove me to the station at 1515 to meet J. His wife was also arriving. After rather a cold wait the Larne train came in but no J. I immediately came to the conclusion that she had caught the Belfast train from Larne, which proved to be right when about ¼ hour later the Belfast train came in with J. and, of course, some naval officer who she had picked up on the way and had been helping along. We drove to the Melville. J. had had a v. comfortable trip with a sleeper. Lovely to see her. We took a little walk in the town after having tea. Bright sunshine in the p.m. but a bitter wind still blowing.

There are all sorts of reports of offers of unconditional surrender from Himmler, which have been officially denied in New York and London, but it is pretty certain *something* is in the wind pointing to the end coming in Europe any day now. If only it would come before we have to sail again!!

Tuesday, 1 May 1945 – Londonderry

I gave myself a day's leave. I thought a trip to Buncrana might be rather nice, but a cold wind with hail and rain squalls was not conducive to excursions and so we called it off. Did a short shopping trip in the morning and had some coffee. After lunch we went to a cinema and saw quite an amusing film, and then at about 1700 we went on board to hear the news as Churchill was speaking in the House and we wondered if he had said anything about peace offers. He said he had nothing to tell the House on the question. We had some tea and later on went down to the wardroom for a drink. Back to the hotel for dinner, and then we went to the Navy Hall to watch some boxing in aid of King George's Fund for Sailors. It was pretty poor boxing but there was one all-in wrestling bout. I've never seen it before and I don't think I want to see it again. A pretty filthy sort of sport, where kicking and gouging are allowed.

Wednesday, 2 May 1945 – Londonderry

The paper announced that the Germans in Italy had surrendered unconditionally. Great news! I went on board in the a.m. but came back to the hotel for lunch. Out again after lunch as I wanted to see some fighter direction training, but it all came to nothing. Shaw came on board with an awful moan about having been told by the Commodore that the no Wrens were to be allowed on board *Nene* till July. Tried to soothe him down. Back to the hotel and took J. out to tea. While we were shifting preparatory to going out to dinner, Wing Commander Harrison rang up to ask me to lecture to the air force course at Maydown on support groups.[37] I couldn't well say no but was far from pleased at the idea and v. worried, as lecturing is not my forte and I have no time to think the subject up. J. and I went to the club for dinner. Mallet joined us afterwards, as did Skinner and one or two others. Skinner just back from seeing the C. in C. (Max Horton) at Derby House, who apparently was v. nice to him.

Thursday, 3 May 1945 – Londonderry

I went on board fairly early and referred to some old reports of proceedings for some information for my lecture. At about 1000 Harrison picked me up and drove me to Maydown. I had to talk to a mixed class of R.A.F. and Fleet Air Arm who are on a course. I got on much better than I expected, and in fact Harrison said it was one of the best lectures given by S.O.s. I feel awfully bucked with myself. He drove me back to the Dockyard and I went to see Allen at the tactical table then on board for a drink and then, Harrison having driven me to the Melville, he came in and had another drink with J. and me. We discussed the news, which is all v. exciting with the German Army surrendering in millions and Hamburg and other big towns being declared open cities. We thought of going to Buncrana or Moville for the afternoon, but the weather again wasn't sufficiently settled. However, after lunch we took ourselves for quite a long walk behind the town and finished up on board at about 1800 for the news, but nothing new came through. Shaw and Mallet had a drink with us, and then we went back to our hotel for dinner and early to bed.

Friday, 4 May 1945 – Londonderry

Went on board. After a v. uncomfortable night in our lousy bed we decided we must change our room. Who should appear almost as soon as I got on board but John Band, now Captain of the *Stonetown* in a C group which has just arrived. Grand seeing him again. Had to dash off with Hearn to the ferry and go across to Ebrington to watch *St. Pierre* at the N.E.A.T. They did really well. I came back on board for lunch and stayed till about 1500 doing paper work. Just before I left the ship Old arrived back off leave. Went back to the hotel and found J. established in a v. much nicer room. At about 1830 J. and I went on board *Stonetown,* where we were royally entertained by Band and he and J. met at last. Later on the 3 of us went up to the club for the usual Friday evening dance. It was rather empty and much quieter than usual, but we enjoyed it and gathered quite a party round us in the end. After the dance we all went down on board the *Antigonish* for a short time, but J. could not stick it long. She has had a tummy upset and was feeling a bit queasy.

Saturday, 5 May 1945 – Londonderry

A car came for me at 0900 and took me to Ebrington Barracks to sit on a court martial. Joe Selby was President and I and 3 other Commanders sat on the court. The prisoner was a Canadian Able Seaman charged with sticking [i.e., stabbing] two Petty Officers and direct disobedience. He first of all pleaded guilty, but after some discussion we decided we couldn't accept the plea as in mitigation he was pleading drunkenness, which had to be proved, and so the trial went forward. We finally found him guilty and in view of his previous record we dismissed him with disgrace. The sentence was not easy to decide on.

I got back to the Melville soon after 1300 and had lunch with J. It rained pretty hard in the p.m. I went up to Operations and the Exercise office to find out the form for our departure. I find *Matane* is to arrive here about 1100 on Monday, and I shall go to her then. I then went down on board and did some work. Old amazed me by his attitude of moan and complaint but taking no steps himself to put things right. Back to the hotel at about 1700, and at 1730 J. and I caught a bus and called on the Allens for a brief moment and then walked on to the Selbys for dinner. Afterwards they took us to a concert at the Navy Hall (another Navy Week show). It was really awfully good, and I thoroughly enjoyed it. Another unconditional surrender of German armies in Denmark and N.W. Germany.

Sunday, 6 May 1945 – Londonderry

Went on board in the a.m. and was prevented from doing my work by Skinner, who came over and wanted to talk. At 1130 I went up to see Joe Selby to make out a joint training report on the group. Feeling tired and depressed I went back to the Melville for lunch. After lunch I lay down in our room but did not manage to sleep, and at about 1530 J. and I went out. We took a bus to Ebrington and then walked down to the river edge and sat there for a bit watching the ships and finally came back by ferry to the hotel. After a showery a.m. and early p.m. it turned out warm and sunny. We went down on board the ship at 1800 and I supervised some packing. At 1830 we went down to the wardroom where I threw a small drinking party. I asked the Commodore but he couldn't come. Carne, Naftel,[38] and Skinner were there in addition to ships' officers. At 2000 when none of my guests made a move, J. and I got up to go, but when we got back to the hotel at 2030 all food was off, and so we went to the club where we had some v. nice cold salmon. After supper we sat with the Mays and finally went in behind the bar to drink beer. Instead of an early evening it was about midnight before we left, and I badly needed a good long night in. There are rumours of total surrender but nothing official, yet. Heard at Operations that after our Group Training Period we are going on the next Russian convoy.

Monday, 7 May 1945 – Londonderry/At sea

J. had breakfast with me and then I went on board. *Loch Alvie* was due to slip at 1030, and as by 1015 *Matane* had not arrived and as my gear was all packed and off the *Loch Alvie,* I went ashore and had a hair cut. *Matane* was alongside when I'd finished, and I went on board and so got back after 10 months to my original ship. The Captain, a 2 stripe V.R. called Jones,[39] seems a nice sort of chap. At 1200 I went to see the Commodore, as with Brown and Hearn there are 13 officers, not counting the C.O. and me, and only 9 bunks. I arranged to get rid of 2. Went back to the Melville for lunch and afterwards took J. to the station and saw her off for Larne. Perhaps not so bad as usual, with the war in Europe virtually over and long leave for me in sight. The Commodore told me that he had made a signal recommending me for a period of shore service when relieved at the end of this operational period.

Back on board with a heavy heart. The rest of the group is out doing gunnery exercises, and *Matane* is topping up with provisions, stores, and ammunition. We heard there was to be an important announcement at 1600. It seems the Germans have signed unconditional surrender, but it has not yet been decided when Mr Churchill's announcement will be made. We slipped at 1740 and went down to Moville and alongside the oiler, and at 2230 the group slipped and proceeded for Loch Alsh.

Feeling v. tired. Too many parties I guess during the time in harbour. I was amazed and delighted to find that at lunch the vegetables are handed round, instead of being put on the plate outside and thrown at you. This is the 1st Canadian ship I've found to do this.

Tuesday, 8 May 1945 – At sea/Lisahally

Just off Inishtrahull we met an E. bound convoy, which we had some little trouble avoiding owing to our defective T.B.S. We got a signal shortly after leaving saying today, the 8th, was V day and at about 0100 a signal from Com. D. telling us to return to Moville and so we turned back and anchored at about 0330, very nearly hitting the wreck off Dunagree Point as we came in. As by 0730 there was no further signal for us I told all ships, except *Loch Alvie* who was full, to proceed alongside the tankers at 0930 and complete with fuel. After we were alongside and secured, the Captain cleared lower deck and read prayers – very badly I thought – and then I addressed the ship's company also rather badly.

I was having a V day glass of beer in the wardroom before lunch when we got a signal to embark pilots and proceed up to Lisahally and give leave to one watch.

This we did, arriving about 1400. As soon as I'd fixed up about sentries, patrols, leave trains, etc. I lay down on my bunk for a sleep but didn't get much. At 1500 Churchill broadcast to the nation that the war with Germany was over and the Admiralty ordered "Splice the Main Brace." From then on most everyone in the ships was tight. After that I went ashore for a walk. It was a lovely hot, sunny day, but my walk was spoilt by worrying about the drunks. As I came on board I passed 3 men carrying jugs to the canteen with the intention of bringing beer back on board for the watch on board. I found Skinner half tight in my cabin, but he gave me some good advice and calmed me down just as I was thinking of putting sentries and patrols everywhere. Really there was nothing for it but to prevent booze coming on board and otherwise let them be.

Our wardroom in the evening was full of Wrens who had bicycled over. I had a good many drinks but didn't enjoy myself. Thank God V. day only comes once in a lifetime, but oh, am I thankful it has come.[40] Instructions have been broadcast to all German U-boats telling them to surface and surrender and make for certain ports by certain routes. I expect we will be employed escorting them in.

Wednesday, 9 May 1945 – Lisahally

There were v. few absentees, and taken all in all, in spite of my worries V day celebrations passed off very harmlessly. Reports have started to come in already of U-boats on their way to surrender. The C.O.s came over to my cabin and we discussed U-boat boarding parties. We were told to grant night leave, and so I suppose we are here until tomorrow. After lunch I had a short talk to the boarding officers of all ships and told them briefly what they should do if sent to board a surrendered U-boat. I then shifted and went ashore. I walked across Maydown aerodrome and finally finished up at 1600 at Hyde Smith's house. He is the C.O. of Maydown. They gave me some tea and then I stayed on to drinks. They had quite a party including the Selbys. I was sent back in a car at about 1930 and had a late meal on board. After that I wrote to J. and did some reading. At about 2130 John Band appeared, having got back from his Tactical Course at Liverpool, and we sat talking and drinking till about 0100. He is a nice chap. Joe Selby tells me we are going on our Russian convoy and will sail for Greenock tomorrow. Windy with some rain squalls.

Thursday, 10 May 1945 – Lisahally/At sea

I feel rather as if I'd been on the toot for about a week. At 1130 I went on board *St. Pierre* and spoke to the ship's company. I tried to get a little shut eye in my chair after lunch but was much disturbed by signals and latterly by the fact that, although I'd made a signal that no men were to leave the Dockyard, I saw lots going out with baseball bats and gloves and balls. After getting v. angry I found it was only with the permission of their own ships, who owing to a misunderstanding thought I'd given authority to do so. It started to rain at about 1900. The Commodore and some other big shots came over to look at the U-boat berths. 17 are coming here and are having to be secured alongside the inside of the jetty. So far, according to signals, about 15 U-boats are on their way to surrender. We slipped at 2100 and proceeded to sea after dropping pilots at Moville and shaped course for the Clyde at 15 knots. It cleared up after 2230.

Friday, 11 May 1945 – At sea/Greenock

I was on the bridge most of the night. Sufficient traffic to keep on dodging quite a bit until we got into line ahead in the Clyde swept channel. We passed through the gate at about 0715 and went alongside the oiler. Shoved off from there at 0930 and *Monnow, Nene,* and *Matane* all secured together to our buoy while *Loch Alvie* and *St. Pierre* anchored. I was feeling v. sleepy and had a bit of a snooze after lunch, but my cabin became terribly hot. After tea I put on a pair of grey flannels and had an hour's hard walk on the upper deck. A hot, stuffy, thundery day. Quite a lot of signals and orders about this Russian convoy came through. I think we are quite definitely committed to it. I had rather hoped the whole thing might be cancelled. At 1900 I went over to the *Onslow* at Hugh Browning's (D 17) invitation. He is S.O. of the convoy. E.G. 4, whose group is also on this convoy, should have been there but wasn't. We had a stand up supper in the wardroom. Back on board at 2220 to find Kilgour in the wardroom. He has come over to commission one of the new Canadian destroyers.[41]

Saturday, 12 May 1945 – Greenock/At sea

I went ashore at about 0915 with the other C.O.s and my staff and got a car to Marymount. At 1000 there was an escort conference followed at 1100 by a convoy conference. Garwood[42] is E.G. 4, and our convoy is J.W. 67 and possibly the last Russian convoy of all time. After the conference I went back with Hugh Browning to Bagatelle and saw the Staff Officer (Operations) and then called on the Admiral and took a drink off him. He is an awfully nice old boy (Hill by name). The arrival of the U-boats at Lisahally is apparently to be quite a show. C. in C. Western Approaches himself will take the surrender.

Back on board at about 1245 and after lunch I got fussed and worried about this and that. Charts and orders which haven't arrived, signals to be made, and so on, and the worry about the job ahead in general. Couldn't help comparing myself with Hugh Browning, with the responsibility of the whole thing on his shoulders and not apparently thinking about anything but his game of golf this afternoon. Being unruffled and unworried is certainly a sign of greatness. Slept a bit and read a bit. Had a short C.O.s meeting at 1800. At 2045 we slipped and proceeded, all except *Nene* who is to be on the close screen and sails later. Passed the gate at 2130 and pottered along down the swept channel keeping about 5 miles ahead of the convoy. According to our signals the U-boats continue to surrender in good numbers.

Sunday, 13 May 1945 – At sea

I got v. little sleep, being on the bridge most of the night. On reaching the end of the swept channel at about 0400 we formed line abreast. At daylight the convoy formed 4 columns, and when we had passed Oversay I detached *Monnow* and *Loch Alvie* to take position MM, and we and *St. Pierre* went out on the starboard bow to CC.[43] We rounded Skerryvore at about 1700, and as we got up towards the narrower part of the Minches our 2 divisions closed in together ahead of the convoy, which went back again into single line. At about 2230 we passed 8 U-boats being escorted S. to Lough Foyle by 2 escort groups, but they were rather a long way off. Just as we approached the narrows we overtook 3 tankers bound for Loch Ewe. At first I tried to hold back and keep behind them, but as they were only doing about 6 knots and as it was a v. light night I decided to pass them, which I did. We are getting up to the latitudes now where there are only a few hours of v. light darkness at this time of year.

Monday, 14 May 1945 – At sea

We got through the narrows at about 0200 and formed line abreast again ahead of the convoy, who at daylight proceeded to form a broad front, which brought us down to 7 knots for some hours before the manoeuvre was completed (there's 26 ships in the convoy). At about 1000 I sent the 2nd Div. out to MM and went over to CC with the 1st Div. We got an aircraft report of 2 surrendering U-boats, which we thought we might see, and sure enough at about 1130 just N. of Cape Wrath we sighted them making to the E. across the track of the convoy for Loch Eriboll, which is one of the main concentration places. I told *St. Pierre* to close one and we went over to the other one ourselves. Ours was *U-1010*. When it was clear that they were well out of the way of the convoy we rejoined. Quite exciting seeing them surrendering, but I'm afraid I can't help being sorry for them. Defeat and surrender must be very bitter.[44]

The day, which had been misty and rainy, cleared up but it blew quite fast from the W. and gave us quite a choppy beam sea. The great thing was that the visibility improved, and that is the important point when keeping station in the outer screen. It allows you to give the radar a rest. We turned to the N. at about 1500 to make up towards the E. of the Faeroes. It was still quite light at midnight.

Tuesday, 15 May 1945 – At sea

I had a pretty good night in. At about 1000 when level with the Faeroes we altered to 027°. Good visibility all day, and we were able to keep the convoy in sight comfortably at 7-8 miles. The light carrier *Queen*[45] joined up and took station in the convoy. An uneventful day with one contact, which we attacked before classifying fish. The signalled reports are a bit confusing, but it seems that 34 out of a possible 60 U-boats at sea when the surrender was made have been accounted for.

Wednesday, 16 May 1945 – At sea

Hazy and necessary to use radar from time to time for station keeping. At 0800 we altered to 046° and we crossed the Arctic Circle during the forenoon. At about noon we intercepted a signal from the Norwegian destroyer *Stord* reporting a German convoy of 5 ships and 14 U-boats in Vestfjord proceeding to Trondheim and asking if this was in order. Shortly afterwards Capt. D17 was told to detach one of his E.G. to intercept the convoy and bring the U-boats to Loch Eriboll, and he detailed us to detach. It put me in a flat spin of course. By 1430 we had formed up and were heading for Trondheim at 17 knots. It blew up quite a bit from the S., and it was cold and wet. My chief concern was whether we would be able to intercept, as in spite of 2 signals from C. in C. Home Fleet, one to *Stord* and one to the old 4 stacker *Broadway* who seemed somehow to be mixed up in the show, we could get no reply and no definite position, course, and speed. Later on I became worried about the minefields off the Norwegian coast and made a signal asking for information. Loran failed us after about 1600 and of course there was no sun. All very worrying.

Thursday, 17 May 1945 – At sea

A most ambiguous reply came back to my signal re: minefields, which left me no wiser at all, and so eventually at 0130 I decided to alter course to the N. round the pecked line danger area, although it seemed quite possible that by doing so the convoy would pass ahead of us into Trondheim. By now I wasn't too sure of my exact position but luckily the wind went right down, the mist dispersed, and there was extreme visibility when the sun rose at about 0400. We sighted mountain tops at about 40 miles but found the land difficult to identify. However at about 0530 we sighted the convoy on our port bow and so all was well. We went to action stations as we approached. It consisted of a couple of large armed yachts, 3 submarine depot ships, auxiliaries, and 15 U-boats.

We closed the leading yacht – obviously the S.O. – and the others closed the U-boats and the whole convoy was ordered to stop. I tried to give my orders by hailing but that was hopeless and so I lowered a boat and sent No. 1 over, who found a Captain on board who called himself S.O. Arctic and Barents Sea.[46] When he heard his U-boats had to go to England he was inclined to refuse, as it was contrary to the orders from his High Command, but No. 1 was v. firm and he soon saw he had to do as he was told. The chief thing was to get him to tell the U-boats how to form up, to find out if the surrender terms had been carried out, and such details as amount of fuel, numbers of the boats, etc. The Captain (Jones) terrified and infuriated me by the way he handled the ship, and I thought at one time we were going to hit the *Grilse,* which would have looked pretty.

At last it was all fixed up. *Loch Alvie* had meanwhile put an officer and signalman on board the senior U-boat, and at 0700 we started off with the submarines and told the 5 big ships to proceed in to Trondheim. The U/Bs were in 2 columns, *Matane* ahead and 2 escorts either side. My troubles weren't over then, however, for they started to straggle and develop engine trouble. Eventually I made a signal saying this was not in keeping with the known efficiency of the U/B service, and on arrival if there was any negligence C.O.s and any others concerned would be punished and would not return to Germany. We got settled down a bit better later on, but then from being a flat calm (thank God for it) when we met in the early morning, the wind got up from the W. and by the evening it was blowing really hard and we had to slow down. I don't think they look like giving any real trouble but it was a most exhausting and worrying day. If we get all of them in, anybody else can have all the rest of the surrendering they want.

Friday, 18 May 1945 – At sea

Blowing harder if anything in the morning. I can't see any reason for this blow as the glass, which has been steady as a rock, is now slowly rising. About 1000 there was a break in the clouds, and from then on the wind gradually veered to the W. and eased. The S/Ms must have taken a hammering as there was quite a big beam sea. No. 8 of the starboard column straggled badly all day, and *St. Pierre* couldn't get any reply to any signal. It was also extremely difficult to make the leaders understand that *Matane* was guide and that they had to adjust course and speed to keep one on each quarter. On calling for a fuel report I found 2 boats haven't got enough to reach Loch Eriboll, and so I made a signal saying they would have to go in to Lerwick.

In the evening I made a long signal to the group and the U-boats giving orders for detaching and how it was to be carried out on arrival off Lerwick tomorrow. It turned into a beautiful calm, clear evening and we sighted the N. top of the Shetlands at 38 miles. Still rather worried about my boats and thought of all the awful things that *might* happen and wondered what on earth I would do. It is no good, I can't be Prussian enough on these occasions. *Nene* has a German interpreter and they intercepted a W/T signal from the S.O. to the other U-boats saying it was all over, they had to bite the bitter apple, and there was only one thing left to do – to give up their boats. At first it crossed my mind that it was a reminder that they had to scuttle but on second thoughts they wouldn't say so *en clair;* however, I signalled the S.O. and told him we were reading what he made and told him no more signals on W/T without permission.

Saturday, 19 May 1945 – At sea/Loch Eriboll

After the short period of darkness it was a lovely still, calm morning as we came down the E. side of the Shetlands. When off the entrance to Bressay Sound I detached *St. Pierre* with 2 U-boats to fuel at Lerwick and carried on with the remainder through the Fair Island Channel and then W. of the Orkneys for Loch Eriboll. It blew quite fresh from the E. in the p.m., and by the time we got to the Loch entrance it was blowing about Force 8 with an almost cloudless sky. Having made elaborate arrangements to get into single line before arriving, S.O. Loch Eriboll (who is Evans with all his Loch Alsh group training team) [told me] to get them all inside the shelter before stopping, and so I quickly had to alter my orders and we approached in 2 columns. Unfortunately, we only have a v. small scale chart of the place.

As we approached we had aircraft overhead and press photographers. It was announced on the news that 15 U-boats were being escorted in by the Royal Navy. This made the Canadians awfully sore. I must say they might have found out or have been told that we were an R.C.N. group. When we got into the entrance at about 1915 I stopped the whole outfit, and harbour launches went alongside and put guards on board the U-boats, took the whole thing out of my hands, and we proceeded up the Loch to anchor. I must say it was a great relief to have got them in without incident. I had a late supper and a v. good whisky and soda with Jones. A Canadian press photographer came on board. As I am an R.N. officer and of no news value to him I was able, thank God, to avoid any personal photography, and I suggested it would be far more suitable if he featured Skinner heavily.

Sunday, 20 May 1945 – Loch Eriboll/At sea

I was awakened from time to time with reports of ships straggling, and at about 0200 a U-boat came alongside having broken away from another one. At about 0530 we began to drag and had to shift berth with the U-boat still alongside. The wind was fairly whistling down from the mountains, and the water is all v. deep and holding ground not too good. Jones again frightened me a lot the way he handled the ship, but eventually we managed to get a good hold of the bottom and I went down and had a bath and breakfast. I went over to see Martin Evans, who is S.O. Loch Eriboll living in the *Philante*. We discussed this and that and he gave me a drink. The impression seems to be that the surrender is nearly completed now.

Back on board for lunch. All the officers have been over the U-boat this morning, and as far as I can see there has been quite a bit of fraternization, but I can't see how anything short of a miracle can stop it if the boats are berthed alongside us. In the p.m. signals were flying to and fro, which I organised on departure. *St. Pierre* was sent off ahead to Greenock to land the Norwegian passengers which we *were* taking to Russia. Very heavy squalls continued all day but eased about 1800. I'm feeling tired and v. wind swept.

At 2000 the group weighed and proceeded with the 5 U-boats in which we have armed guards for Loch Alsh. Most amazing cloud formation in the evening. According to the news there is much bickering going on between us and Marshal Tito about the occupation of Trieste. What with this and the virtual deadlock with Russia over the Polish question, the future of the Peace is beginning to look v. rocky already.

Monday, 21 May 1945 – At sea/Loch Alsh/At sea/Lisahally

It rained a bit in the night but by dawn it was clear and it developed into a lovely calm, sunny day. We arrived at Loch Alsh at 0730 and our U-boats all went alongside 2 depot ships. After that we anchored and I had a bath and breakfast. Who should come on board just before we sailed but Mr. Bloody Brian Gourley, now Capt. Gourley, N.O.I.C. Loch Alsh. He was my Captain at the end of the last war in the *Sea Bear*.[47]

As soon as we'd all collected our armed guards we weighed and were off for Londonderry by 1015. Got a signal from Taylor (E.G. 5 and in charge of this surrender business here) saying there must have been fraternization, as English cigarettes had been found on some Germans. How the hell can you help fraternization if you berth U-boats alongside ships for 24 hours. As a matter of fact, it was v. bad in this ship and I had to get the Captain to do something about it.[48]

It was quite beautiful as we went through the narrows of the Kyles of Rhea. I remained in line ahead until we turned S. in open water, and then I got into line abreast but remained in close order. Quite like peace time, steaming about so close together. On arrival at Moville at 1830 we embarked pilots and went up to Lisahally to fuel. I had the C.O.s over and we talked for a long time, and I couldn't get rid of Skinner till nearly midnight. There are now about 18 surrendered U-boats here.

Tuesday, 22 May 1945 – Londonderry

The group slipped at about 0800, went up harbour and secured alongside. I went up to see the Commodore, Selby, and others and to learn our fate, which is as follows: *Matane* goes off tomorrow to join E.G. 16, *St. Pierre* sails for Canada on 25th, and the 3 others pay off over here and hand the ships back to the R.N. date unknown. The group finishes here and now, and I pack up and go on leave.

There has been a signal to the Commodore from N.O.I.C. Loch Alsh about the cigarettes, money, Canada badges, etc., found on the Germans, which must have come from the 9th E.G. To the very last we were true to form. Never out of trouble. On asking Coates, the 1st Lieut. who was the officer of the armed guard in *Matane*'s U-boat, he told me how the U-boat's crew were beaten up the hatch and abused by the R.N. officer who relieved him, and how when No. 1 protested this R.N. officer said, "I am in charge now and any how what do you know about it, you are only a Canadian V.R." Pretty deplorable behaviour.

With *Matane* going I have got to get busy getting out. Spent all the p.m. and dogs packing, tearing up letters and papers, and doing some writing. At about 1900 Jones and I went up to the club for dinner. Saw the Mays. She still hasn't had her baby, which must be v. overdue now. Drank a lot of Guinness and talked to Cann[49] after dinner about the difficulties of being a travelling S.O. It rained nearly all day.

Wednesday, 23 May 1945 – Londonderry

I got up early, completed my packing, and finished off some odd paper work. The *Matane* was sailing at 1100 and so I got all my gear out and across to *Loch Alvie.* At about 1130 I went round to the *Kokanee* to see Lucas, who is Captain there, and to take a cheque for £5 for King.[50] At 1300 I went along to the Savoy, where I'd been asked to a farewell lunch by the Commodore for the American group S.O. and C.O.s. Quite a good party. The Commodore told some *most* amusing stories. He is a v. good raconteur.

As soon as I could get away I went back on board *Loch Alvie,* where Hearn had produced a shorthand typist for me, and I dictated my report of proceedings, which took quite a bit of time. Montgomery took my heavy luggage to the station and I then went up to the Commodore's house, where I had been offered a bed for a night or two. Took Rutherford the secretary along to the Magee mess for a drink, and at 1930 I walked along to the club and met Hearn, Flavelle, Radcliffe, and Mallet and gave them dinner. Afterwards Brown and Kidd and the rest of my staff came along and I said good bye to them. They are going back to Canada tomorrow in the *Carlplace,* which is sailing with the *St. Pierre* and one other. Walked back to the Commodore's house at about 2300 and turned in.

Thursday, 24 May 1945 – Londonderry

After breakfast I went up to Naftel's office and started to write out my S206s. Went down on board the ships at about 1130 and then went to lunch with Sharky Armstrong in his destroyer. Allen from the Tactical Table was there too and a v.g. lunch. Back to Naftel's office after that, and in about an hour's time I finished my S206s and went over to the Commodore's house and lay down and had 40 winks on my bed. Later on I walked to the club where I met Skinner, Old, and Shaw and they gave me a farewell dinner. All these late nights and drinking are doing me no good.

Friday, 25 May 1945 – Londonderry/Belfast

I went down to the ships at about 0930. At 1000 the Commodore arrived and addressed all 2 ship's companies in *Loch Alvie,* and there was the usual cheering. Afterwards he had some beer. After he had gone I said some individual good byes and then pushed off, leaving my Canadian group for good. I am glad to be finished with it as I'm stale, but I'm glad I started and finished it myself.

The *Monnow, Loch Alvie,* and *Nene* left at 1100 for Sheerness, where they will turn the ships back to the R.N. and the crews will return to Canada. I went to the Pay office, collected my ticket and ration card, went to the station, and then returned to the offices where I found I had to alter my plans as the C. in C. had just made a signal that all S.O.s on leaving their groups were to come and see him, and so instead of Larne-Stranraer I had to go Belfast-Heysham. Joe Selby came and had a farewell drink with me at the club, and the Commodore and Cann lunched with me. Quite an amusing farewell meal.

I caught the 1540 to Belfast and on arrival I had a meal at the Station Hotel and then went on board the Heysham boat, and I was v. relieved to find I had a cabin, which it turned out I was sharing with one Thorold, another S.O. of a recently paid off group. He had with him his staff officer, a rather amusing but v. fatiguing young man, but between them had a v. good supply of booze, which we proceeded to drink with a Wren officer and her husband, by name McClelland.

Saturday, 26 May 1945 – Heysham/Prinsted

I was about the last off the boat at Heysham at 0730 without breakfast. The Liverpool train left at 0830 and we changed at Preston, and on arrival at Exchange Station I had to cloak room all my stuff and I had a considerable amount. From there I walked to Derby House, and in due course had an interview with Sir Max [Horton], who was v. nice and told me to insist on a long bit of leave. I went downstairs and saw Smithy, had a drink with Colville in the bar, and had an early lunch in the Officers' Mess, and then met the McClellands at the Exchange, where we'd fixed an R.N. truck to take our baggage across to Lime Street, and caught the 2:00 to Euston.

The train was packed and we could only find seats in a 3rd class. The McC.s got out at Rugby. An uncomfortable journey, but the train was pretty punctual at Euston at 1830. I had thought of spending the night in town but changed my mind and trundled all my stuff to Waterloo in a taxi and caught the 7:26 slow to Havant. Got an Army officer who got out at Guildford to telephone J. and ask her to fix a taxi, which was waiting, and I was home at about 2145. My God, it's wonderful to be home on some really worthwhile leave, and is it a relief to have finished with all that worry and responsibility.

Epilogue: Respite

Frank Layard never went to sea again. After taking the long rest recommended by Adm. Sir Max Horton, in July 1945 he joined the book writing department at Whale Island, where he oversaw the preparation of technical manuals for new gunnery equipment. "It took a bit of time to get the hang of the job," he reflected in his draft memoirs, "but when I had settled in I found it interesting and less exhausting than commanding a Canadian group of ships."[1] It was also a happy time domestically as he adjusted to peacetime ashore. His sisters, Katharine and Peggie, returned home safely from the Far East and he enjoyed the company of his young children. Not surprisingly, his long association with things naval sometimes influenced his child-rearing tactics: when young Raymond was frightened awake by a severe thunderstorm one night, Layard told him that it was just Nelson in the *Victory* firing his cannon as he chased the French up the Channel.

In early 1947 Layard left the book writing team to serve as area commander of the Scotland and Northern Ireland Sea Cadet Corps. Although it kept him in the navy, the hours were long and tiring, and Joan did not take to life in Scotland. When he finally moved on in 1949, he "was thankful to be shot of the job and I know that J. was only too glad to get away. I don't think ever before or since have I worked so hard."[2] That year, on Trafalgar Day, Layard finally took retirement after thirty-eight years in the navy. He briefly considered selling encyclopedias and even running a farm with his sister, but, apart from a return to the Admiralty during the Korean emergency, he lived out a long, quiet life as an English country gentleman. He passed away on 25 November 1999, just three days shy of his hundredth birthday. His beloved Joan joined him the following year.

Although he kept in touch with a few of the Canadians who had served under him right up until his death, Frank Layard's last formal contact with the Royal Canadian Navy came in June 1953. For Commonwealth navies like Canada's, the Coronation Review in Portsmouth was the highlight of the summer. Each sent warships to represent their country, and the RCN's Coronation Squadron – the aircraft carrier *Magnificent*, the cruisers *Ontario* and *Québec*, and the frigates *Swansea* and *La Hulloise*, under the command of Layard's former colleague Rear-Adm. Roger Bidwell – was among the most impressive. Festivities abounded, and many old friendships were rekindled among serving and retired officers at a special Coronation Dinner for senior Dominion officers at the Portsmouth Navy Club. Layard was honoured to be invited, and besides renewing acquaintance with Bidwell, he was introduced to the commanding officer of *Swansea,* who invited him to dine in his old ship. "Whenever I go on board a small ship," a sentimental Layard wrote after lunching with Lt.-Cdr. W.D.F. Johnston, RCN, "and particularly one which I have commanded, I get a wave of intense longing to do it again."[3]

If the requirement "to do it again" had arisen in the mid-1950s, the Canadian navy would not have needed Frank Layard. Although its leaders would have appreciated an officer of his talent and experience, they no longer had need of a *foreign* officer with those qualities. The RCN had grown and matured, and by that point in its history there were many Canadian officers, active and retired, professional and reservist, who had the ability to command an escort group – or squadron, as they were then known. That, of course, had not been the case in the midst of the Second World War. At that time of crisis and frenzied growth, there were simply not enough Canadian officers of Layard's calibre to fill the RCN's leadership void at sea. Somebody obviously would have taken E.G. 9 to war if he had not stepped forward, and Layard could have turned down the job – indeed, given his attitude towards things Canadian it is almost surprising that he did not – but one wonders if anyone could have matched the breadth of his professionalism. The reader will now appreciate that Layard poured all his considerable attributes as a naval officer, as well as his soul, into the job. To be sure there were faults and mistakes, but in the end he succeeded not just in running an effective support group that helped to win the inshore U-boat campaign, but also in providing a positive, to some even inspiring, example of leadership. His remarkable diary, which details that accomplishment in a day-by-day litany of challenge and survival, thus provides a lasting example of how a naval leader can cope with and surmount the extraordinary demands associated with command at sea in wartime.

Appendix 1:
Career Highlights of Commander A.F.C. Layard, DSO, DSC, RN

1899 (28 November)	Born at Southwick, England
1913	Entered RN College Osborne as a naval cadet
1914	Moved to RN College Dartmouth
1915	Rated midshipman and joined the battle cruiser HMS *Indomitable* in the Grand Fleet
1917	Promoted sub-lieutenant
1917-18	Served in the destroyers HMS *Vancouver* and *Sea Bear* in the Grand Fleet
1919-20	Sub-lieutenant's courses and two terms at St. John's College, University of Cambridge
1921-3	Served in the battleships HMS *Benbow* and *Emperor of India*
1923-4	Served in destroyer HMS *Velox* in the Atlantic Fleet
1924-8	First lieutenant of the destroyers HMS *Velox* in the Atlantic Fleet and *Verity* in the Mediterranean and Far Eastern Fleets
1928	Promoted lieutenant-commander
1928-30	Served in battleships HMS *Benbow* and *Emperor of India* of the Training Squadron
1930-3	In command of the destroyers HMS *Wakeful* and *Vivacious* in the Atlantic and Mediterranean Fleets
1932 (3 December)	Married Miss Joan Binning
1933	Attended Tactical School at Portsmouth
1933-4	In command of the destroyer HMS *Walpole* in the Atlantic Fleet
1935	Sports officer in the Reserve Fleet
1935-6	In command of the minesweepers HMS *Stoke* and *Harrow* in the Mediterranean Fleet
1936-41	Experimental Department, HMS *Excellent,* Portsmouth
1941-2	In command of the destroyers HMS *Chelsea, Firedrake,* and *Broke* in Western Approaches Command
1943	Miscellaneous Weapons Department of the Admiralty

1943	Promoted acting commander, appointed SO of the RCN support group W 10, and in command of the destroyer HMS *Salisbury*
1944-5	SO of the RCN support group E.G. 9, and in command of the frigates HMCS *Matane, Swansea,* and *Saint John*
1945-7	Book Writing Department, HMS *Excellent*
1947-9	Area officer sea cadets, Scotland and Northern Ireland
1949 (21 October)	Retired from the RN
1951-4	Recalled for service in the Directorate of Manning of the Admiralty
1999 (25 November)	Died in Chichester, England

Appendix 2
The Ships of EG 9

River Class Frigates

HMCS *Matane*	February-July 1944; May 1945
HMCS *Swansea*	February-November 1944
HMCS *Stormont*	April-December 1944
HMCS *Meon*	May-October 1944
HMCS *Saint John*	April 1944-February 1945
HMCS *Port Colborne*	April 1944-February 1945
HMCS *Monnow*	August 1944-May 1945
HMCS *Nene*	October 1944-May 1945
HMCS *St. Pierre*	April-May 1945

Loch Class Frigates

HMCS *Loch Alvie*	September 1944-May 1945

Flower Class Corvettes

HMCS *North Bay*	February-April 1944
HMCS *Frontenac*	February-April 1944
HMCS *Owen Sound*	February-April 1944
HMCS *Baddeck*	February-April 1944
HMCS *Atholl*	February-April 1944

Appendix 3
U-Boats Destroyed by Ships Attached to EG 9

U-845 10 March 1944 in the North Atlantic (48°20' N, 20°33' W) by HMCS *Swansea,* HMCS *Owen Sound,* HMCS *St. Laurent,* and HMS *Forester* (*St. Laurent* and *Forester* not in E.G. 9)

U-448 14 April 1944 in the North Atlantic (46°22' N, 19°35' W) by HMCS *Swansea* and HMS *Pelican* (*Pelican* not in E.G. 9)

U-311 22 April 1944 southwest of Ireland (52°09' N, 19°07' W) by HMCS *Matane* and HMCS *Swansea*

U-247 1 September 1944 in the English Channel (49°54' N, 05°49' W) by HMCS *Saint John* and HMCS *Swansea*

U-309 16 February 1945 in Moray Firth (58°09' N, 02°23' W) by HMCS *Saint John*

Source: Axel Niestlé, *German U-Boat Losses during World War II: Details of Destruction* (Annapolis: Naval Institute Press, 1998).

Notes

Prologue: Like Cutting Butter

1 Two modified US Coast Guard cutters mounted a similar operation at Oran. There, the subterfuge included a British naval officer trying to trick the French by using an American accent. See Rick Atkinson, *An Army at Dawn: The War in North Africa, 1942-1943* (New York: Henry Holt, 2002), 72.

2 A reference to a submerged contact detected by asdic, an early form of sonar.

3 Capt. H.L. St. J. Fancourt, RN, was the senior officer of Terminal, and Lt.-Col. E.T. Swenson commanded the 3rd.

4 *Malcolm* sustained heavy damage to her boilers and upper deck, and played no further role in the operation.

5 A Swiss-designed 20mm gun that was common equipment in Allied ships

6 The three young engineer officers were poised to lead boarding parties to ensure that French merchant ships anchored in Algiers were not scuttled to block the harbour. Such was the surprise of Terminal that no such effort was mounted.

7 Lt. A.M. Wickham, RN. Layard's departure from *Broke* was obviously without incident as his diary, presumably tucked safely away, survived unscathed.

8 Lt.-Cdr. S.E. Crewe-Read, RN.

9 Diary, 14 November 1942.

10 "Operation TORCH – Report of Proceedings," Naval Commander, Expeditionary Force, 30 March 1943, 3, Public Record Office, DEFE, 2/602.

11 Diary, 17 March 1943; *London Gazette,* 12 March 1943. Fancourt also received the DSO. Two other Brokes were awarded the Conspicuous Gallantry Medal, the highest gallantry award after the Victoria Cross, for remaining at their posts despite being wounded and under fire.

Introduction: An Officer and His Diary

1 Layard's twelve commands were the RN destroyers *Wakeful, Vivacious, Walpole, Chelsea, Firedrake, Broke,* and *Salisbury*; the RN minesweepers *Stoke* and *Harrow*; and the RCN frigates *Matane, Swansea,* and *Saint John.*

2 Cdre. G.W.G. Simpson evaluation, or "flimsy," of Cdr. A.F.C. Layard, 24 May 1945. Layard Papers in family possession. Flimsies were short personal assessment reports, consisting only of a few phrases. Longer, more detailed evaluations were called S206 for the name of the form.

3 Layard ms, vol. 4, 15. The Layard ms is a draft manuscript, based on the diary, that Layard wrote years after the war. There is no indication that he ever intended to have it published, and it remains in the family's possession. It was organized inconsistently, and thus some references are described by the year they are covering and others by a particular volume or page number.

4 Officers like Alan Easton, Donald Macintyre, and D.A. Rayner have described only portions of the inshore campaign in their memoirs, and none discuss 1945. D.E.G. Wemyss's *Walker's Group in the Western Approaches* is quite sketchy in his account of the campaign. Alan Easton,

50 North: An Atlantic Battleground (Toronto: Ryerson Press 1966); Donald Macintyre, *U-Boat Killer* (London: Weidenfeld and Nicholson, 1956); D.A. Rayner, *Escort: The Battle of the Atlantic* (London: William Kimber, 1955); D.E.G. Wemyss, *Walker's Groups in the Western Approaches* (Liverpool: Daily Post and Echo, 1948).

5 E.G. 6 narrowly missed out, proceeding overseas at about the same time as E.G. 9, but returning home in April 1945. E.G.s 11, 12, 16, 25, and 26 were the other RCN groups to take part.

6 Two examples of this veneer from the Second World War are Roger Hill's *Destroyer Captain: Memoirs of the War at Sea* (London: William Kimber, 1975) and Alan Easton's *50 North*.

7 Layard ms, 5.

8 C. Whayman interview with Cdr. A.F.C. Layard, 27 February 1992, oral history collections of the Royal Naval Museum; also cited in Ronald Spector, *At War at Sea: Sailors and Naval Combat in the Twentieth Century* (New York: Viking, 2001), 36.

9 Excerpts of Mrs. Layard's diary are in the Layard family papers.

10 Layard ms, vol. 1, 7.

11 Layard ms, vol. 1, 7.

12 Layard ms, vol. 1, 8.

13 Layard ms, vol. 1, 8.

14 Layard's grades are in Layard family papers.

15 Quoted in Max Arthur, *The True Glory: The Royal Navy, 1914-1939, A Narrative History* (London: Hodder and Stoughton, 1996), 71-6. Layard's account of Jutland and his other contributions to Arthur's book are based on a series of articles published in the *Naval Review*.

16 Layard "flimsy," 15 December 1917.

17 Layard ms, vol. 1, 37.

18 In the interwar period *Vancouver* was transferred to the RCN.

19 Diary, 26 June 1918.

20 Diary, 11 November 1918.

21 Layard ms, vol. 1, 41-2. In his biography of Cunningham, John Winton overlooks *Sea Bear*'s participation in the cruise, mentioning that the force included a cruiser and two destroyers, whereas there were actually three of the latter type. John Winton, *Cunningham: The Greatest Admiral since Nelson* (London: John Murray, 1998), 40-1.

22 Rudyard Kipling, "The Scholars," in *Rudyard Kipling's Verse: The Definitive Edition* (New York: Doubleday, 1940), 795-7.

23 Diary, 11 July 1930.

24 These reductions were instituted by the First Lord of the Admiralty, Sir Eric Geddes. In all, 200 junior officers voluntarily retired while another 350 were placed in retirement status. In 1929, Layard survived another program that reduced the number of lieutenant-commanders. See Stephen W. Roskill, *Naval Policy Between the Wars*, vol. 1, *The Period of Anglo-American Antagonism, 1919-1929* (London: Collins, 1968), 125.

25 Layard ms, vol. 1, 60.

26 Diary, 14 February 1926.

27 Diary, 26 August 1930. Layard was promoted lieutenant-commander on 15 February 1928.

28 Lieutenant-commanders entered the zone two years after their promotion to that rank and remained in it for four years; thus Layard was in the zone from 1930 to 1934.

29 Stephen King-Hall, *My Naval Life, 1906-1929* (London: Faber and Faber, 1952), 258.

30 Diary, 10 March 1933. The exercise was a fleet engagement, in which Layard was posing as rear-admiral destroyers of the "Red" force, or Japan.

31 Layard ms, vol. 1, 112-13; see also diary, 7 October 1931.

32 Diary, 30 September 1933.

33 Then lieutenant, but later admiral, Sir John Lee-Barber, RN.

34 Layard ms, vol. 1, 106.

35 Ibid., 73.
36 In an article recounting his experiences in Malta, Layard admitted that "as a bachelor I must say I sometimes got tired of it." A.F.C. Layard, "Malta: Some Memories," *Naval Review* 74, 4 (October 1986): 372.
37 Diary, 30 and 31 December 1934.
38 It appears that had Layard been promoted he would have been appointed to command one of the new "F" class destroyers.
39 Diary, 5 March 1935.
40 Cdr. C.H. Ringrose, Cdr. E.C. Thornton, and Lt.-Cdr. E.W. Reep, all fellow destroyer captains in the Mediterranean Fleet. The Sliema Club was a gathering place for destroyer officers, whose ships moored in nearby Sliema Creek.
41 Lt.(E) J.B. Newsom, RN, engineering officer of the destroyer *Vimiera,* and Mrs. Glasford, the wife of Lt. C.E. Glasford.
42 Diary, 28 June 1944.
43 Mr. John Connolly was the executive assistant to the Canadian naval minister, and Capt. H.S. Rayner, RCN, was the director of plans.
44 The Layards had two children: Gillian, born in 1935, and Raymond, who came into the world in January 1941 during the dark days of the blitz on Portsmouth.
45 Capt. A.J. Baker-Creswell, RN (ret'd), to Vice-Adm. Peter Gretton, RN (ret'd), 5 October 1981, National Maritime Museum, Greenwich, Gretton Papers, vol. 23, part 1, MS 93/008.
46 Diary, 24 September 1935.
47 The November 1937 Navy List indicates that of fourteen lieutenant-commanders at Whale Island, only Layard and another were not gunnery specialists.
48 Diary, 3 September 1939.
49 Diary, 28 July 1941.
50 Layard first briefly commanded the more modern destroyer HMS *Firedrake,* but after one North Atlantic convoy he was transferred to the World War One-vintage *Broke.* Layard suspected the change was made because the commander-in-chief Western Approaches Command, Adm. Sir Percy Noble, wanted an officer of the rank of commander in *Firedrake.* This suspicion was later confirmed by the Admiralty, "who blame C. in C. W.A. for my short stay in *Firedrake* and say he's always changing his mind about where he wants his Commanders." Diary, 5 May 1942.
51 For more on S.C. 94, see Anti-Submarine Warfare Division, "Analysis of U-Boat Operations in the Vicinity of Convoy S.C. 94. 31st July-13th August, 1942," 15 September 1942; Capt. D. Liverpool, "S.C. 94," 20 August 1942; and "Report of Proceedings Received from Commanding Officer HMS *Broke,*" n.d., all Public Record Office (PRO), ADM 199/2007. See also W.A.B. Douglas, Roger Sarty, and Michael Whitby, *No Higher Purpose: The Official Operational History of the Royal Canadian Navy in the Second World War, 1939-1943,* vol. 2, part 1 (St. Catharines, ON: Vanwell Publishing, 2003), 505-8; and Marc Milner, *North Atlantic Run: The Royal Canadian Navy and the Battle for the Convoys* (Toronto: University of Toronto Press, 1985), 142-7.
52 Diary, 9 August 1942.
53 HMS *Broke,* "Report of Attack on U-boat," n.d., National Archives of Canada (NAC), RG 24, vol. 11334, 8280-SC-94; *Befehlshaber der Unterseeboote* (German U-boat headquarters) war diary, 8-9 August 1942, Directorate of History and Heritage (DHH), National Defence Headquarters, Ottawa, 79/446; and Robert C. Fisher, "Fog of War: The Battle of the Atlantic, Summer 1942," July 1991, 98, unpublished ms, DHH, Naval History Collection, 2000/5.
54 Western Approaches' only criticism was that Layard should have reported the torpedo tracks to the other escorts. See Captain D. Western Approaches minute, n.d., PRO, ADM 199/2007.

55 See Peter Gretton, *Convoy Escort Commander* (London: Cassell, 1964); Macintyre, *U-Boat Killer;* and Alan Burn, *The Fighting Captain: Frederic John Walker RN and the Battle of the Atlantic* (London: Leo Cooper, 1993).

56 Layard ms (1943), 67

57 Lt.-Cdr. N.S. Norway, RNVR.

58 Layard ms (1943), 67-8.

59 Layard ms (1943), 68.

60 Diary, 12 June 1943.

61 Layard ms, vol. 1, 1.

62 John Band and Alan Easton, conversations with the editor.

63 Two Canadian historians, Marc Milner and Fraser McKee, both of whom interviewed Layard and wrote monographs that included reference to the events he was involved in, were apparently not informed of the diary's existence. See Marc Milner, *The U-Boat Hunters: The Royal Canadian Navy and the Offensive against Germany's Submarines* (Toronto: University of Toronto Press, 1994); and Fraser McKee, *HMCS Swansea: The Life and Times of a Frigate* (St. Catharines, ON: Vanwell Publishing, 1994). Milner misidentifies Layard as an officer of the Royal Naval Reserve, which would have greatly disturbed the old gentleman.

64 See diary entries for 25 October 1943 and 22 January 1944.

65 G.R. Miles papers, DHH, 98/23.

Chapter 1: One Does Get Tired of Them

1 For the early history of the RCN, see Marc Milner, *Canada's Navy: The First Century* (Toronto: University of Toronto Press, 1999); Michael Hadley and Roger Sarty, *Tin Pots and Pirate Ships* (Montreal: McGill-Queen's University Press, 1991); and John G. Armstrong, *The Halifax Explosion and the Royal Canadian Navy: Inquiry and Intrigue* (Vancouver: UBC Press, 2002).

2 For the wartime travails of the RCN, see W.A.B. Douglas, Roger Sarty, and Michael Whitby, *No Higher Purpose: The Official Operational History of the Royal Canadian Navy in the Second World War, 1939-1943,* vol. 2, part 1 (St. Catharines, ON: Vanwell Publishing, 2003); and Marc Milner, *North Atlantic Run: The Royal Canadian Navy and the Battle for the Convoys* (Toronto: University of Toronto Press, 1985).

3 Diary, 17 October 1943. Film historian Thomas Doherty calls *Corvette K 225* (Universal Studios 1943) "a good-neighborly nod to the Canadian Navy." Thomas Doherty, *Projections of War: Hollywood, American Culture and World War II* (New York: Columbia University Press, 1993), 153.

4 Diary, 1 December 1943.

5 For a study of wartime Halifax, see Steven Kimber, *Sailors, Slackers and Blind Pigs: Halifax at War* (Toronto: Doubleday Canada, 2002).

6 As Captain D (short for destroyers), Prentice handled the administration and training of RCN ships based on Halifax.

7 C-in-C CNA to NSHQ, 212020Z/August 1943, DHH, W-10 8440; "The First Year of Canadian Operational Control in the Northwest Atlantic," 5, DHH, Western Escort Force 8440-130.

8 "The First Year of Canadian Operational Control in the Northwest Atlantic," 5, DHH, Western Escort Force 8440-130; C-in-C CNA, "State of the Western Escort Force," 29 September 1943, DHH, Western Escort Force 8440-130.

9 For a good survey of these ships, see Arnold Hague, *The Towns* (Kendal, UK: World Ship Society, 1990).

10 Marc Milner, *Battle of the Atlantic* (St. Catharines, ON: Vanwell Publishing, 2003), 174-6; David Syrett, *The Defeat of the German U-Boats: The Battle of the Atlantic* (Columbia: University of South Carolina Press, 1994), 183 and throughout; Clay Blair, *Hitler's U-Boat War,*

vol. 2, *The Hunted, 1942-1945* (New York: Random House, 1998), ch. 6; and Eberhard Rössler, *The U-Boat* (Annapolis: Naval Institute Press, 1981), 144, 188, 335.

11 Diary, 22 September 1943.

12 Syrett, *Defeat of the U-Boats,* 227.

13 For U-boat operations in Canadian waters, see Douglas, Sarty, and Whitby, *No Higher Purpose*; W.A.B. Douglas, Roger Sarty, and Michael Whitby, *A Blue Water Navy: The Official Operational History of the Royal Canadian Navy in the Second World War, 1943-1945,* vol. 2, part 2 (St. Catharines, ON: Vanwell Publishing, 2004); and Michael L. Hadley, *U-Boats against Canada* (Montreal: McGill-Queen's University Press, 1985).

14 Diary, 7 September and 24 October 1943. The Second Sea Lord was responsible for RN officers' appointments.

15 *Mersey* was the training establishment in Liverpool.

16 Probably Lt. D.G.M. Gardner, RNVR, on the administrative staff at Derby House, the headquarters of Western Approaches Command.

17 Rear-Adm. J.S.M. Ritchie, RN (ret'd).

18 Lt.-Cdr. W.S. Thomas, RN, served under Layard in the early 1930s in *Vivacious* and *Walpole.*

19 Capt. Gilbert Roberts, RN. For more on this officer and the Western Approaches Tactical Unit, see Mark Williams, *Captain Gilbert Roberts and the Anti-U-Boat School* (London: Cassell, 1979).

20 Cdr. G.R. Cousins, RN (ret'd).

21 Air Cmdre. R.L. Ragg, senior air staff officer at No. 15 Group, Coastal Command.

22 On 25 August 1943 in the Bay of Biscay, the sloop HMS *Egret* blew up and sank after being hit by a glider bomb from an HE 177 bomber. The Canadian destroyer *Athabaskan* received heavy damage from another bomb. This was one of the first attacks with this weapon, which was essentially the equivalent of a modern cruise missile.

23 Lt.-Cdr. R.C. Blagg, RN (ret'd), was on the administrative staff at Derby House.

24 Commodore A.S. Russell, RN.

25 Lt.-Cdr. A.E. Wilmott, RNR.

26 Cdr. E.H. Chavasse had been appointed CO of the frigate HMS *Bentinck.*

27 This was the battleship *Roma,* sunk by a glider bomb while sailing to surrender to the Allies.

28 Cdr. Rolph C. Medley, RN. Medley commanded the destroyer HMCS *Saskatchewan,* so he may well have been complaining about the RCN and Canadians.

29 Moville, which the Irish pilot describes as "a small town on the shores of a shallow bay, with a small boat harbour protected by a stone quay," served as an anchorage, work-up base, and refuelling point for escorts working out of Londonderry. Admiralty, *Irish Coast Pilot* (London: HMSO, 1954), 454.

30 This was the battle for ONS 18/ON 202. HMS *Itchen,* HMS *Lagan,* and HMCS *St. Croix* were sunk by acoustic torpedoes. Only one sailor from each ship survived.

31 Cdr. A.M. McKillop, RN. He later became SO of the RCN support group E.G. 12.

32 A Coston gun fired a line over to another ship, allowing the transfer of light materials.

33 Capt. D.S. McGrath, RN.

34 The Admiralty estimated that some twenty-two U-boats were in the North Atlantic in the third week in September; there had been only five the previous month. David Syrett, ed., *The Battle of the Atlantic and Signals Intelligence: U-Boat Situations and Trends, 1941-1945* (Ashgate, UK: Naval Records Society, 1998), 230, 246.

35 Lt.-Cdr. R.J.C. Pringle, RCNVR.

36 Pay Cdr. F.M. Johnson, RN.

37 Secretary of the 3rd Destroyer Flotilla.

38 In 1813 the frigate HMS *Shannon,* commanded by Capt. Philip Broke, defeated USS *Chesapeake* off Boston in a famous battle, and took her to Halifax as her prize.

39 Point Pleasant Park retains its beauty and is the site of Canada's Sailors' Memorial.
40 Paymaster Capt. J.A.E. Woodhouse, RN.
41 Unlike the UK, Canadian cities had no blackout.
42 Lt. K.I. Hamilton, RN.
43 Lt.-Cdr. W.E.S. Briggs, RCNR.
44 Cdr. B.J. de St. Croix, RN.
45 Lt. (E) [Engineering] W. Wilcox, RN.
46 The October 1943 Navy List gives *Salisbury*'s wardroom as Lt. P.C.S. Black, RN; Lt. J. Oates, RNVR; Lt. R. Watson, RNR; Surgeon Lt. R.B.H. Tierney, RNVR; Surgeon Lt. L.G. Hisey, RCNVR; Commissioned Engineer H.K. Smith; Gunner P.A.L. Meeze; and Mids. K.W. Oxley, RNVR.
47 Lt. J.A. Ogilvie, RN.
48 The attack teacher and the night action table and tactical table mentioned later were simulators designed to train personnel in anti-submarine tactics and evolutions.
49 The close escort usually maintained station within a couple of hundred metres of the convoy while the extended screen was deployed out to horizon distance.
50 HMCS *Stadacona* was the main base facility in Halifax.
51 Cdr. M.M. Wilson, RN.
52 Lt.-Cdr. J.P. Stewart, DSC, RNR. Stephens was a young officer with Layard in *Broke*.
53 On Sunday Divisions the ship's company paraded formally for inspection and church services.
54 Almost certainly Lt.-Cdr. D.W. "Debbie" Piers, a well-known, affable RCN officer.
55 Capt. R.E.S. Bidwell, RCN.
56 "Grass widow" is navy slang for a wife whose husband is away at sea.
57 Cmdre. G.M. Hibbard, RCN.
58 *Niagara*'s CO was Lt.-Cdr. W.H. Willson, RCN.
59 HHX convoys were splinter convoys sailing from Halifax to join the main HX convoys from New York to the UK.
60 Under the Atlantic Convoy Instructions, no matter what their rank, SOs of the close escort of a convoy controlled the movements of support groups in company. This rule was reversed in September 1944 to give SOs more flexibility in the inshore campaign in UK waters.
61 Pound died on 21 October 1943 from the aftereffects of a stroke he had suffered in September 1943.
62 On the night of 9-10 October 1943, *U-220* laid sixty-six magnetic mines off St John's.
63 Lt.-Cdr. A.T. Morgan, RNVR.
64 Cdr. J.M. Rowland, DSO (and Bar), RN, who achieved fame early in the war when his ship HMS *Wolverine* destroyed two U-boats, including Günther Prien's *U-47*.
65 Cmdre. H.E. Reid, RCN, and Cmdre. C.R.H. Taylor, RCN.
66 Cdr. J. Phipps, RN, was a long-time friend, and Layard had been best man at his wedding.
67 Marginal note added by Layard in 1951, which demonstrates how he reviewed his diaries in later years, although he rarely made such notations.
68 The Crowsnest, established as the Sea-Going Officers Club by Capt. Rollo Mainguy, RCN, earlier in the war, still exists in St John's.
69 Sir Humphrey Walwyn was the governor of Newfoundland.
70 Lt.-Cdr. A.C. Price, RN.
71 Lt.-Cdr. G.H. Jones, RNR.
72 Fort Pepperill, the large US base outside St John's.
73 Cdr. G.A.V. Harrison, RN.
74 Cdr. M.B. Evans, RN, SO of the RN escort group B 3.
75 Cdr. P.W. Burnett, RN, SO of the RCN escort group C 2. He was evidently dubbed "Egg" for his impressive cerebral apparatus.

76 Asdic search equipment is located in a streamlined dome that extends beneath a ship's hull. In some ships, the domes are retractible to prevent damage.
77 Argentia was the US Navy escort base in Newfoundland.
78 Cdr. D.T. Dowler, DSC, RN.
79 Capt. F.J. Walker, RN. Layard knew Walker, having attended the RN Tactical Course with him in 1933. For more on Walker and E.G. 2's remarkable careers see Alan Burn, *The Fighting Captain: Frederic John Walker RN and the Battle of the Atlantic* (London: Leo Cooper, 1993).
80 Sub-Lt. Timothy Walker was lost in HMS *Parthian* on 10 August 1943.
81 Lt. F.L. Boyer, RN.
82 HMS *Canada* was the RN's manning and liaison establishment in Halifax.
83 A neighbour in Prinsted.
84 Cdr. J.V. Waterhouse, RN.
85 Cmdre. W.J.R. Beech, RCN.
86 Lt.-Cdr. B.D.L. Johnson, RCNR and Lt.-Cdr. A.H. Easton, RCNR.
87 Sir Oswald Moseley was leader of the fascist movement in the UK.
88 Lt.-Cdr. N.M.S. Seeger, RN.
89 Capt. E.R. Mainguy (pronounced "Mengy") was director of naval personnel at Naval Service Headquarters in Ottawa.
90 Logging is a mild rebuke whereby the officer's name and transgression are entered in the ship's deck log.
91 In operations in the Aegean Sea during October-November 1943, German air superiority cost the British and Greek navies four cruisers damaged, six destroyers sunk, and four others damaged. See Stephen W. Roskill, *The War at Sea, 1939-1945*, vol. 3, part 1 (London: HMSO, 1960), 191-203.
92 The Johnson scandal was a major *cause célèbre* in Halifax. The bodies of Johnson and his daughter were indeed recovered, but his motive was never ascertained, although people surmised he was reacting to his wife's infidelity. See Kimber, *Sailors, Slackers and Blind Pigs*, 191-93, 195-99, 215-18.
93 Lt.-Cdr. F.A. Large, RCNVR.
94 Lt.-Cdr. M.G. Stirling, RCN.
95 Capt. I.A.P. MacIntyre, RN.
96 Cdr. E.R.A. Smith, RN, a colleague from Whale Island.
97 The Knights were neighbours in Prinsted, and Bob Knight had worked with Layard at Whale Island.
98 Lt. C.R. Speak, RNVR.
99 Acting captain, and later vice-admiral, A.K. Scott-Moncrieff, DSO, RN, a talented destroyer officer and close friend.

Chapter 2: Shaking Down

1 RCN Narrative, "The First Year of Canadian Operational Control in the Northwest Atlantic," 3-5, DHH, Western Escort Force, 8440-130. See also W.A.B. Douglas, Roger Sarty, and Michael Whitby, *A Blue Water Navy: The Official Operational History of the Royal Canadian Navy in the Second World War, 1943-1945*, vol. 2, part 2 (St. Catharines, ON: Vanwell Publishing, 2005); and Marc Milner, *The U-Boat Hunters: The Royal Canadian Navy and the Offensive against Germany's Submarines* (Toronto: University of Toronto Press, 1994).
2 Figures compiled from Ken MacPherson and Ron Barrie, *The Ships of Canada's Naval Forces, 1910-2002* (St. Catharines, ON: Vanwell Publishing, 2002).
3 Diary, 26 March 1944.

4 In many conversations with the editor, Easton freely admitted his dislike of the sea and his strong reluctance to go back there in 1940.
5 Alan Easton, *50 North: An Atlantic Battleground* (Toronto: Ryerson Press, 1966), 271.
6 Ibid., 205.
7 Ibid., 211-12.
8 Ibid., 233.
9 Remarks of senior officer on form S206 by Cmdre. G.W.G. Simpson, 5 September 1944, NAC, PRC-0-39060. Biographical material on King is derived from RN and RCN records in his navy personnel file, cited above, and from Fraser McKee, *HMCS Swansea: The Life and Times of a Frigate* (St. Catharines, ON: Vanwell Publishing, 1994), 37-42.
10 It was thought at the time that the Q-ship SS *Merops* destroyed the submarine, but postwar research revealed no German loss on that day. King's DSC citation reveals no details of his role in the engagement. See *Supplement to the London Gazette*, 22 June 1917, 6254.
11 Diary, 8 February 1944.
12 Diary, 11 May 1944.
13 Layard remarks, form S206, 25 April 1944, NAC, PRC-O-39060.
14 Layard remarks, form S206, 11 August 1944, NAC, PRC-O-39060.
15 Cdr. J.V. Waterhouse, RN, "Working Up Programme – HMCS 'SAINT JOHN,'" 5 June 1944, 10-11, NAC, RG 24, vol 11726, CS 148-36-4.
16 Layard remarks, form S206, 9 March 1945; Simpson remarks, form S206, 20 March 1945, NAC, PRC-O-69360.
17 The date of Stacey's departure from *Saint John* has been inaccurately reported elsewhere. Both Joseph Schull's *The Far Distant Ships: An Official Account of Canadian Naval Operation in World War II* (Ottawa: Queen's Printer, 1950) and Ken MacPherson and Ron Barrie's *Ships of Canada's Naval Forces, 1910-2002* (St. Catharines, ON: Vanwell Publishing, 2003, and previous editions) say Stacey remained in command until 19 February 1945. In reality he left the ship on 11 November 1944, when Layard took over as CO until 19 February 1945.
18 Edward R. Paquette and Charles G. Bainbridge, eds., *Honours and Awards: Canadian Naval Forces, World War II* (Vancouver Island: E.W. Bickle, 1986), 501.
19 Murray remarks, form S206, 1 June 1943, NAC, PRC-O-67520.
20 Cmdre. G.O. Stephenson, "Working-up Report on HMCS *Monnow*," 22 April 1944, NAC, RG 24, vol. 11724, CS 148-23-4.
21 Layard remarks, form S206, 23 May 1945; Simpson remarks, form S206, 27 May 1945 both NAC, PRC-O-67520.
22 Diary, 23 and 26 February 1945.
23 Diary, 1 March 1945.
24 Band's conversations with the editor.
25 Joan served in the Women's Royal Navy Service until March 1944 but left the service when it became difficult to manage her family commitments.
26 Capt. Frank L. Houghton, RCN. SCNO(L) was located at 10 Haymarket Square, just around the corner from Piccadilly Circus and a short walk from the Canadian High Commission at Canada House on Trafalgar Square.
27 A popular hotel in Southsea. It was one of the Layards' favourite meeting places and is still open for business.
28 Scott-Moncrieff was awarded a bar to his DSO for "gallant and distinguished" service with Force H in the Mediterranean while CO of the destroyer *Faulknor.* See *London Gazette,* 18 January 1944.
29 Cdr. P.K. Wallace, Cdr. C.N.E. Currey, and Cdr. (E) R.W. Parker.
30 Cdr. C.V. Jack, RN (ret'd).

31 Group staff consisted of an escort staff officer who rode in the SO's ship, and H/F, radar, and torpedo specialists who were spread among the other ships in the group. The three watch keepers in the SO's ship in the rank of lieutenant were to include a specialized small "n" [navigation] and "s" [signals]. See Naval Staff Minutes, 22 January 1944, DHH, 81/520.
32 Long after the war Layard added a rare postscript in his diary: "In a book which Easton wrote after the war called *50 North: Canada's Atlantic Battleground* he tells of his arrival to take command of the group and what he thought about me *and* having the S.O. in his ship. He says some rather nice things and seemed to think that our relationship was good, and so perhaps the feeling I had at times that I was interfering too much was unfounded." In conversations with the editor, Easton confirmed that it was a tricky situation but he held no hard feelings towards Layard, for whom he held great respect.
33 Lieutenants W.D.H. Gardiner, G.C. Brown, and B. Hynes, respectively.
34 Cdr. E.A. Mount-Haes, RN.
35 The RN had to arrange "passage" crews to steam the American-built BDEs across the Atlantic. Canadian officers and men were sometimes assigned this duty.
36 Skipper Lt. J.M. Watson, RCNR.
37 Lt.-Cdr. E.T.P. Wennberg, RCNVR.
38 The wife of Lt.-Cdr. F.W.T. Lucas, RCNVR, who later served as Layard's first lieutenant in *Matane.*
39 Capt. A.N. Harrison, RN.
40 Acting Commander E.L. Armstrong, RCN, a retired British officer called up for service with the Canadians.
41 Bidwell was appointed to command the escort carrier HMS *Puncher.*
42 Although Layard makes no reference to it, 7 February 1944 was the date E.G. 9 was declared operational.
43 The operations plot displayed operational information for the theatre, including convoy positions, U-boat intelligence, and weather conditions.
44 "Blue" and "White" turns were formation manouevres.
45 Non-sub echoes were generally schools of fish, anomalies in the ocean, or, in shallow water, objects on the sea bottom such as rock formations or wrecks.
46 The chart house was a small, covered structure at the back of the bridge where the navigator had some shelter to do his calculations.
47 HMCS *Avalon* was the name of the base at St. John's.
48 The SS *Kelmscott* was sunk by *U-845* on 9 February 1944. For more detail see Michael L. Hadley, *U-Boats against Canada* (Montreal: McGill-Queen's University Press, 1985), 191, 201.
49 "Observant" was an asdic search pattern in which the ships searched on prearranged coordinates from a contact or datum point.
50 Sub-Lt. John Westwater, RCNVR.
51 Lt.-Cdr. George A. Myra, RCNR. When *Stormont* later joined E.G. 9, Myra became one of Layard's most dependable COs.
52 Layard's sisters, Katherine and Peggie, had returned to the Far East as adults. Although Peggie barely escaped when the Japanese entered Singapore, her husband, John, Katherine, and Katherine's husband, Peter, were taken prisoner.
53 Cdr. D.K. Laidlaw, RCN, head of the operations staff at *Stadacona.*
54 Lt.-Cdr. K.L. Dyer, RCN.
55 A Gamma search was a line-abreast hunt that usually extended sixty miles (97 kilometeres) along a U-boat's estimated line of advance. For more detail, see the editor's introduction to Chapter 4.
56 The creep attack was a tactic formulated by Walker's E.G. 2. One ship held the echo and directed the other over the target. The second ship approached quietly at a slow speed of

about five knots so as not to reveal its position to the U-boat and thus prevent it from taking avoiding action.

57 The British nautical history journal.

58 *Iroquois* was an RCN Tribal class destroyer returning to Canada for refit. At that time she was probably the most prestigious warship in the Canadian service, which may account for the preferential treatment.

59 Lt. C.M. Carruthers, RCNVR.

60 Canadian anti-acoustic torpedo gear was a noisemaker designed to lure acoustic homing torpedoes away from a ship's screws.

61 *Valleyfield*'s CO was Lt.-Cdr. D.T. English, RCNR, who died when the frigate was sunk by *U-548* on 7 May 1944.

62 *Matane* was thought by others in E.G. 9 to be an unhappy ship. John Band to editor, 20 September 2001.

63 Cdr. J.C. Hibbard, DSC, RCN.

64 This is according to the Beaufort wind scale, which was devised in 1805 by Rear-Adm. Sir Francis Beaufort to quantify the effects of the wind. Zero is calm and 12 is a hurricane. Force 9-10 is strong gale force winds of between 41 and 55 knots.

65 The latest version of high frequency direction finding set, which gave a visual display of fixes.

66 An old flame of Layard's from the early 1930s who devastated him when she broke off their relationship.

67 The SO of the escort group was Cdr. J. Byron, DSC, RNR.

68 For a good study of the weaknesses of RXC and Canadian naval radar development in general, see David Zimmerman, *The Great Naval Battle of Ottawa: How Admirals, Scientists and Politicians Impeded the Development of High Technology in Canada's Wartime Navy* (Toronto: University of Toronto Press, 1989).

69 This was *U-744*, sunk after a thirty-two-hour hunt, the second longest of the war. See Milner, *U-Boat Hunters*, 116-19.

70 Star shell was normally set to burst behind the target so as to create a silhouette. The step-aside procedure, whereby escorts approached datum points for U-boats from a broad angle on the bow, was intended to counter Gnats.

71 Cdr. R.A. Currie, RN.

Chapter 3: Overseas

1 Area Combined Headquarters, located at command headquarters like Halifax, Liverpool, Plymouth, and Portsmouth, had naval and airforce staffs working alongside each other. Naval commanders like Rear-Admiral Murray in Halifax and Admiral Sir Max Horton in Liverpool ran the overall operations while air force officers controlled air activities.

2 Stephen W. Roskill, *The War at Sea, 1939-1945*, vol. 1 (London: HMSO, 1954), 360.

3 The historiography of the Battle of the Atlantic is immense, but any interested reader will do well to start with the American, British, and Canadian official histories: Samuel E. Morison, *History of United States Naval Operations in World War II.* Vol. 1, *The Battle of the Atlantic, September 1939-May 1943* (Boston: Little, Brown, 1947); Roskill, *War at Sea;* and W.A.B. Douglas, Roger Sarty, and Michael Whitby, *The Official Operational History of the Royal Canadian Navy in the Second World War*, vol. 2, 2 vols. (St. Catharines, ON: Vanwell Publishing, 2003-4). Marc Milner's *Battle of the Atlantic* (St. Catharines, ON: Vanwell Publishing, 2003) is probably the best recent survey of the campaign, while Stephen Howarth and Derek Law, eds., *The Battle of the Atlantic, 1939-1945: The 50th Anniversary Naval Conference* (Annapolis: Naval Institute Press, 1994) contains scholarly articles on virtually every aspect of the battle.

4 Capt. A.J. Baker-Creswell, RN (ret'd) to Vice-Admiral Peter Gretton, RN (ret'd), 5 October 1981, National Maritime Museum, Greenwich, Gretton Papers, vol. 23, part 1, MS 93/008. Baker-Creswell was a navigation specialist. A British historian argues in a recent study that anti-submarine warfare was given more attention than has previously been acknowledged by historians such as Stephen Roskill. See G. Franklin, *Britain's Anti-Submarine Capability, 1919-1939* (London: Frank Cass, 2003).
5 It appears that hydrophones were *Vivacious*'s only anti-submarine detection system during Layard's time in command. The fitting of asdic in RN destroyers during the interwar period varied from class to class, see Willem Hackmann, *Seek and Strike: Sonar, Anti-Submarine Warfare and the Royal Navy, 1914-1954* (London: HMSO, 1984), 204-12.
6 Lt.-Cdr. R.J.R. Dendy. Diary, 2 March 1933.
7 Diary, 22 March 1933. Cdr. S.H.T. Arliss was CO of the destroyer *Thruster*, which, with *Salmon*, was attached to the First Anti-Submarine Flotilla based on Portland.
8 Diary, 10 May 1933.
9 Diary, 15 May 1933.
10 Diary, 31 May 1933.
11 Diary, 11/12 September 1933.
12 For more on Tobermory, see Richard Baker, *The Terror of Tobermory: An Informal Biography of Vice-Admiral Sir Gilbert Stephenson, KBE, CB, GMG* (London: W.H. Allen, 1972); and James Goldrick, "Work-up," in Howarth and Law, *Battle of the Atlantic*, 220-39. For overall anti-submarine training, see Malcolm Llewellyn-Jones, "The Pursuit of Realism: British Anti-Submarine Tactics and Training to Counter the Fast Submarine, 1944-1952," in *The Face of Naval Battle: The Human Experience of Modern War at Sea*, ed. John Reeve and David Stevens, 220-4. (Crows Nest, Australia: Allen and Unwin, 2003).
13 Diary, 4 August 1942. Scott was one of Layard's instructors at Osborne in 1913-14.
14 See also Mark Williams, *Captain Gilbert Roberts and the Anti-U-Boat School* (London: Cassell, 1979); and Goldrick, "Work-up," 227.
15 Diary, 11 September 1943. Interestingly, the great Capt. F.J. Walker, a prewar anti-submarine specialist, refused to attend the WATU.
16 Goldrick, "Work-up," 228.
17 See, for example, Marc Milner, *North Atlantic Run: The Royal Canadian Navy and the Battle for the Convoys* (Toronto: University of Toronto Press, 1985); Marc Milner, *The U-Boat Hunters: The Royal Canadian Navy and the Offensive against Germany's Submarines* (Toronto: University of Toronto Press, 1994); Roger Sarty, *Canada and the Battle of the Atlantic* (Montreal: Art Global, 1998); and Donald E. Graves, *In Peril on the Sea: The RCN and the Battle of the Atlantic* (Toronto: Robin Brass Studio, 2003).
18 For more on Horton, see Adm. W.S. Chalmers, *Max Horton and the Western Approaches* (London: Hodder and Stoughton, 1954), a favourable biography of the C-in-C.
19 Diary, 3 April 1944.
20 Simpson's memoirs, *Periscope View* (London: Macmillan, 1972), cover his career as a submariner but, unfortunately, include almost no mention of his time with Western Approaches.
21 Diary, 16 March 1944. "Anti-Gnat tactics" refers to manoeuvres and searches designed to counter the German naval acoustic torpedo, or Gnat.
22 Diary, 28 December 1944. This became a constant refrain of Layard's; in September 1944 he had made similar complaints about the brass in Plymouth.
23 Diary, 26 September 1944. This episode caused Layard great trepidation, as he was an extremely loyal officer; indeed, his diary rarely contains any criticism of senior officers.
24 Layard ms (1944), 71.
25 River class frigates had a displacement of 1,445 tons (standard) and endurance of 7,200 miles at twelve knots, and a top speed of about nineteen knots fully loaded. Their complement included about thirteen officers and 144 men. The "Q" attachment to type 144 asdic was a

crucial innovation that enabled target depth to be calibrated, while FH 3 and FH 4 displayed D/F bearings on a plan position indicator. Hedgehog was an anti-submarine warfare mortar that fired 24 contact-fused projectiles about 200 metres ahead of a ship. For details about anti-submarine sensors and weaponry at that stage of the war, see Milner, *U-Boat Hunters*, 86-93; and Hackmann, *Seek and Strike*.

26 Peter Elliott, *Allied Escort Ships of World War II: A Complete Survey* (London: Macdonald and Janes, 1977), 211-15. See also the foreword to Ken MacPherson's *Frigates of the Royal Canadian Navy, 1943-1974* (St. Catharines, ON: Vanwell Publishing, 1989) written by Ian Tate, an experienced frigate officer.

27 John Band, then *Swansea*'s first lieutenant, recalls asking a staff officer in Londonderry about what would happen to the RXC removed from his ship. The officer took him in a jeep outside the city and showed him a field full of junked RXCs rusting in the Irish air.

28 Diary, 31 October and 3 November 1944. Squid was an ahead-throwing anti-submarine weapon that enabled vessels to maintain contact during the run in to an attack. More powerful than hedgehog, its fuse was set to explode automatically at the depth relayed through an escort's type 147 depth-setting asdic set. See Hackmann, *Seek and Strike*, 309-10.

29 Diary, 21 March 1944.

30 Supt. J. Carpenter, WRNS.

31 Capt. W.H. Selby, RN.

32 Cdr. (E) R.R. Shorto, RN.

33 Capt. J.B. Glencross, RN (ret'd).

34 The main anti-Gnat tactic was the step-aside procedure.

35 Rather than surfacing in inshore waters to recharge their batteries, the Admiralty suspected U-boats escaped the heavy air patrols by slipping into the waters of neutral Eire.

36 The Easy Item or EI manoeuvre was an ASW search turn developed by Capt. F.J. Walker's E.G. 2. For an explanation, see the editor's introduction to Chapter 4. See Alan Burn, *The Fighting Captain: Frederic John Walker RN and the Battle of the Atlantic* (London: Leo Cooper, 1993), 197.

37 Lt. H.P. Duchesneau, RCNVR.

38 The River Foyle runs between the southern end of Lough Foyle and the city of Londonderry. The river is about 20 feet (6 metres) deep and the narrowest section of the channel is about 300 feet (90 metres), with about double that at Londonderry. Admiralty, *Irish Coast Pilot* (London: HMSO, 1954), 461-3.

39 Adm. Sir Max Horton, C-in-C Western Approaches Command.

40 Lt. George S. Miller, RCNVR.

41 Cdr. C.B. Allen, RN.

42 Acting Lt.-Cdr. George A. Myra, RCNR.

43 Lt. John W. Telfer, RCNVR. David Kilgour noted that Telfer "was so slow and confused that if he ever had to fire at a sub on the surface, by the time he gave the order to fire it would have been too late." Kilgour to Alan Easton, 6 July 1993, DHH, 94/169.

44 "Red" signifies port and "green" starboard.

45 This was *U-448*, destroyed with twenty-five survivors.

46 Cdr. D.M. MacLean, RNR.

47 Lt.(E) A. MacIntosh, RCNR.

48 Lt.(L) F.R. Hunt, RCNVR.

49 Layard's self-recrimination proved unjustified; after the war *Matane* and *Swansea* were credited with the destruction of *U-311*.

50 Lt.(n) David G. Kilgour, RCNVR. Upon learning of Layard's opinion after reading parts of the diary, Kilgour noted that "he never said anything to me at the time and so this voice from fifty years ago came as a pleasant surprise." Kilgour to Alan Easton, 2 July 1993, DHH, 94/169.

51 Lt.-Cdr. F.W.T. Lucas, RCNVR, who joined from HMCS *Haida*.

52 Lt. P.C.H. Cooke, RCNVR, the new group ASW officer.
53 On 3 May 1942, Layard and his friends dressed in tails, hired a horse and cart, and headed into the Republic for a party.
54 Lt.-Cdr. D. Copelin, RCNR, Commodore Simpson's staff officer (administration) and the Canadian escort liaison officer in Londonderry.
55 Prentice was appointed SO of the RCN support group E.G. 11.
56 Lt.-Cdr. A.M. Lee, RNVR.
57 Acting Cdr. E.W. Finch-Noyes, RCN. HMCS *Montreal* was in the escort group C4.
58 Although Layard seldom mentions it, perhaps because he was comfortable financially through his father's estate, the RCN paid its personnel at a considerably higher rate than the RN. Thus British officers on loan to the Canadian service stood to receive a relatively substantial raise.
59 *Valleyfield* was sunk by *U-548* on 7 May, about 50 miles (80 kilometres) southeast of Cape Race. For an account of her tragic loss, which claimed 125 lives, see Michael L. Hadley, *U-Boats against Canada* (Montreal: McGill-Queen's University Press, 1985), 210-19.
60 Lt.-Cdr. R.D. Freaker, a long-time friend.
61 Cdr. G.W. Gregorie, RNR.
62 This was actually Capt. E.R. Mainguy, RCN. HMS *Uganda* was later substituted for *Minotaur.*
63 Lt.(g) J.L. Lewtas, RCNVR.
64 A/S Ps were anti-submarine warfare training evolutions, often involving a live submarine.
65 Capt. H.V. King, RN.
66 Naval slang for a carpenter.
67 TBS was a short-range communications system that enabled ships' COs to speak directly with one another.
68 Actually, this was combined convoy KMS 50G, which was made up of OS 76 and KMS 50, bound for Gibraltar and Freetown, respectively. See Arnold Hague, *The Allied Convoy System, 1939-1945: Its Organization, Defence and Operation* (St. Catharines, ON: Vanwell Publishing, 2000), 164-9.
69 The RN and RCN were replacing amatol with more powerful minol as explosive in depth charges.
70 Lt.-Cdr. St. Clair Balfour, RCNVR.
71 Lt.-Cdr. C.J. Angus, RCNR, and Lt.-Cdr. William R. Stacey, RCNR.
72 Gunner (T) S.J.C. Guppy, RN. Gunner (torpedo) was a warrant officer.
73 Lt.-Cdr. R.C. Gwinner, RN, was SO of E.G. 1.

Chapter 4: The Great Endeavour

1 Admiralty, Director of Naval Operational Research Memo, "The Case for Increasing the Number of A/S Escorts Involved in OVERLORD," April 1944, PRO, ADM 219/120. See also F.H. Hinsley et al., *British Intelligence in the Second World War,* vol. 3, part 2, *Its Influence on Strategy and Operations* (London: HMSO, 1988), 95-7.
2 W.A.B. Douglas, Roger Sarty, and Michael Whitby, *A Blue Water Navy: The Official Operational History of the Royal Canadian Navy in the Second World War, 1943-1945,* vol. 2, part 2 (St. Catharines, ON: Vanwell Publishing, 2005), ch. 16; Marc Milner, *The U-Boat Hunters: The Royal Canadian Navy and the Offensive against Germany's Submarines* (Toronto: University of Toronto Press, 1994); and Bill McAndrew, Donald E. Graves, and Michael Whitby, *Normandy 1944: The Canadian Summer* (Montreal: Art Global, 1994), 92.
3 The other escort groups were the Royal Navy's EGs 1, 2, 5, and 15, and the Royal Canadian Navy's E.G. 6. The escort carriers were *Fencer, Emperor,* and *Pursuer.* PRO, ADM 199/1723.
4 Cdr. D.E.G. Wemyss, RN, who commanded the sloop *Wild Swan,* described the operations as "hard slogging ... We patrolled and we searched. We moved from one patrol area to an-

other, without making contact." D.E.G. Wemyss, *Walker's Groups in the Western Approaches* (Liverpool: Daily Post and Echo, 1948), 136-7. For a similar sentiment see Donald Macintyre, *U-Boat Killer* (London: Weidenfeld and Nicholson, 1956), 153.

5 Confidential Admiralty Fleet Order (CAFO) 753/41, from 1941, instructed escorts operating inshore to drop at least one depth charge pattern on any wreck they contacted to confirm that it was indeed a wreck.

6 Diary, 28 June 1944.

7 For the inshore campaign, see Douglas, Sarty, and Whitby, *Blue Water Navy,* ch. 18; Marc Milner, *Battle of the Atlantic* (St. Catharines, ON: Vanwell Publishing, 2003), 197-207; Milner, *U-Boat Hunters*; McAndrew, Graves, and Whitby, *Normandy 1944;* Lt.-Cdr. D.M. McLean, "The Last Cruel Winter: RCN Support Groups and the U-Boat Schnorchel Offensive" (MA thesis, Royal Military College of Canada, 1992); and Günter Hessler, *The U-Boat War in the Atlantic* (London: MOD, 1989).

8 Diary, 9 September 1944.

9 Diary, 30 December 1944.

10 Diary, 6 July 1944.

11 Minutes of the RCN-RCAF Anti-submarine Warfare Committee, 23 November 1945, App. 2, DHH, 181.009 (D 3188). A Gamma search utilizing two support groups could cover a ninety-mile-wide channel. See Admiralty, Anti-U-boat Division, "Asdic Barrier Patrols-Effectiveness," 11 June 1944, PRO, ADM 199/1787.

12 Alan Burn, *The Fighting Captain: Frederic John Walker RN and the Battle of the Atlantic* (London: Leo Cooper, 1993), 197.

13 Diary, 12 February 1944.

14 E.G. 9 is credited with destroying *U-247* on 1 September 1944 and *U-309* on 16 February 1945, but the group was also involved in the hunt that resulted in the sinking of *U-1195* by HMS *Watchman* on 6 April 1945.

15 Cdr. Donald Macintyre, RN, Cdr. J.D. Birch, RNR, and Acting Cdr. R.C. Gwinner, RN. Like Layard, Birch was on loan to the RCN as SO of E.G. 6.

16 Acting Capt. D.V. Peyton-Ward, RN, Capt. I.A.P. MacIntyre, RN, and an unknown officer.

17 *Matane*'s signal officer, Sub-Lt. J. Westwater, RCNVR.

18 Although Adm. Sir Bertram Ramsay, Layard's old commander in *Benbow,* was the naval commander for Overlord, the C-in-Cs of the Home commands retained the authority to control operations in their area. Thus C-in-C Plymouth, Adm. Sir Ralph Leatham, was responsible for anti-submarine operations in the immediate southwest approaches to the English Channel, while C-in-C Western Approaches was responsible for the area to seaward.

19 Lt.-Cdr. J.P. Stewart, RNR.

20 Lt. A.A. Terry, RNR.

21 Layard is upset that the crew were not all wearing the proper uniform, in this case No. 3s, the standard working dress.

22 Acting Capt. H.R. Graham, RN.

23 David Kilgour recalled that Layard was trying to bring the sailboat in smartly, dropping the sails at the last minute to stop right alongside: "Instead, when he gave the order to let down the sails, his crew (including me) of officers completely buggered things up, the sails didn't come down, and the whaler smacked straight into the side of the ship to the laughter of everybody watching." Kilgour to Alan Easton, 6 July 1993, DHH, 94/169.

24 In 1934 Layard had briefly commanded a destroyer subdivision based on Queenstown, in what was then known as the Irish Free State.

25 The buzzers informed the depth charge crew on the quarterdeck when to release their charges.

26 This was the major destroyer action fought off Ile de Batz between four German and eight Allied destroyers, including the Canadian *Haida* and *Huron.* Layard's information was overly

optimistic; the Germans lost the destroyers *ZH-1* (sunk) and *Z-32* (forced aground), while *Z-24* and *T-24* suffered damage but made it to Brest.

27 Rear-Adm. Edward Renouf had been Layard's superior at the Miscellaneous Weapons Department at the Admiralty in 1943.

28 Simpson was correct; King received a DSC for his role in the destruction of *U-448*.

29 Stacey's MID was in recognition of his service on the east coast of Canada prior to taking over *Saint John*.

30 The Layard family home in Tunbridge Wells. Its name is derived from Sri Lanka.

31 This refers to the first strategic bombing attack launched from bases in the newly captured Marianas Islands.

32 Cdr. L.B.A. Majendie, RN.

33 This refers to Bishop's Rock off the Isles of Scilly, and Lizard Point, the westernmost significant headland on Britain's Channel coast. Both are prominent navigation points.

34 Adm. Sir George Edward-Collins, RN, was FOIC Falmouth, with Capt. A.D. Cochrane, RN, as chief of staff.

35 This was the great gale of 19-21 June 1944. It not only seriously disrupted the movement of supplies to the beachhead, but also forced aground scores of small ships and landing craft.

36 The Admiralty "U-boat Trend" for the period 12-21 June 1944 reported evidence of "half a dozen" U-boats operating in the English Channel. See David Syrett, ed., *The Battle of the Atlantic and Signals Intelligence: U-Boat Situations and Trends, 1941-1945* (Ashgate, UK: Naval Records Society, 1998), 400.

37 Wolf Rock off the Isles of Scilly.

38 At Defence Watch all guns and other weapons are manned, whereas at Cruising Watch only some are.

39 Probably a reference to sonobuoys.

40 This would have been the wreck of the German destroyer *Z-32*, forced aground on Ile de Batz by the Canadian destroyers *Haida* and *Huron* in the destroyer action on 8/9 June.

41 His officers had an idea of how he would react. According to David Kilgour, "Jim Lewtas and I joked at the time, since we knew he had been reading a life of Nelson and had a deep sense of duty, that if he had sighted an enemy destroyer he would have headed straight for it in order to carry out Nelson's order 'to engage the enemy more closely' regardless of the odds." Kilgour to Alan Easton, 6 July 1993, DHH, 94/169.

42 Acting Capt. R.F. Morice, RN.

43 Capt. D. Orr Ewing, RN.

44 Rear-Adm. H.E. Reid, RCN. Layard had met Reid in October 1943 when he was flag officer Newfoundland.

45 Eddystone Light, just south of Plymouth.

46 A series of rocks and shoals in the Channel Islands just west of Alderney.

47 This refers to Spring tides, i.e., the stronger tides during the full and new moon.

48 The Smalls are a group of islands off the coast of Pembrokeshire, Wales.

49 Lt. H.G. Grieve, RNVR, and Acting Lt.(E) W.E. Garner, RN.

50 Acting Capt. P.B. Cross, RCNVR.

51 Lt. John T. Band, RCNVR.

52 On 6 July, *Ottawa*, HMCS *Kootenay*, and HMS *Statice* destroyed *U-678* in the Channel south of Portsmouth.

Chapter 5: Exasperation Inshore

1 Robert W. Love and John Major, eds., *The Year of D-Day: The 1944 Diary of Admiral Sir Bertram Ramsay* (Hull: University of Hull Press, 1994), 108. *U-672* scuttled herself north of

the Channel Islands after being attacked by the frigate HMS *Balfour.* Jürgen Rohwer and Gerd Hümmelchen, *Chronology of the War at Sea, 1939-1945* (Annapolis: Naval Institute Press, 1992), 291; and Axel Niestlé, *German U-Boat Losses during World War II: Details of Destruction* (Annapolis: Naval Institute Press, 1998), 81.

2 Layard ms, 1944.

3 Ibid.; diary, 20-21 July 1944.

4 Diary, 15 August 1944.

5 Somerville and Ramsay were, respectively, CO and commander of the battleship *Benbow* in the early 1920s, Cunningham was Captain D of the 1st Flotilla when Layard was in the destroyer *Velox* during the mid-1920s, Rawlings was commander of the battleship *Emperor of India* in the late 1920s, and Burrough was gunnery officer in *Indomitable* during the First World War.

6 Layard ms, vol. 1, 49.

7 Ibid., 65.

8 John T. Band, conversation with editor.

9 Ibid.

10 Lt. J.R. Bradley to Layard, 14 May 1945, Layard papers. Officers in *Broke* expressed similar sentiments to Layard after her loss.

11 G.N. Brewer cited in John Winton, *Cunningham: The Greatest Admiral since Nelson* (London: John Murray, 1998), 43. Like Layard, Brewer was a successful escort group commander during the Second World War.

12 Cdr. Clive Gwinner, RN.

13 De Havilland Mosquito fighter-bombers often provided cover for maritime operations in the Bay of Biscay.

14 Cdr. R.A. Currie, RN.

15 Main armament gun mountings in RN and RCN warships were designated "A," "B," "X," and "Y" from bow to stern, and thus "Y" gun was *Matane*'s sternmost four-inch mounting.

16 The captain's cabin serves as a secondary aid station in emergency situations.

17 Lt.-Cdr. C.G. Weller, RCNR. The CNAA, or Canadian naval administrative authority, was the liaison officer in Plymouth.

18 Acting Cdr. R.H. Mallinson, RN.

19 Capt. C. Caslon, RN.

20 Cdr. S.J.S Boord, RN, a term mate of Layard's at Osborne.

21 An interesting comment, given that earlier in his career Layard considered the stuffy professional atmosphere in battleships to be rigid and stifling. Perhaps he just missed the RN.

22 HMCS *Niobe* was the RCN manning establishment in the UK.

23 Lt.-Cdr. R.B. Ford, RN (ret'd).

24 Flimsies were short personnel assessment reports.

25 Noting Layard's comment David Kilgour added, "And we did." Kilgour to Alan Easton, 6 July 1994, DHH, 94/169.

26 Lt.(E) F. St. J. LeFlufy, RN.

27 This was *U-736,* destroyed by the Squid-equipped frigate HMS *Loch Killin* and the sloop HMS *Starling.*

28 They were awaiting passage with a convoy to North Russia.

29 Lt. (AIS) L.W. Earl, RCNVR, who replaced Cooke as the group ASW officer.

30 Lt.-Cdr. H.J. Beverley, RNR.

31 Capt. G.C.F. Ryan, RN (ret'd). "Dugout" was the term used to describe an officer brought out of retirement.

32 Plymouth Command had mounted a close blockade of the major ports along the Biscay coast. Coastal Command patrol and strike aircraft as well as surface and escort groups were

used to catch ships and submarines attempting to escape the US Army onslaught into southwest France.

33 German M-class minesweepers were armed with 4.1-inch guns and other light weapons. Layard's anxiety likely stemmed from the fact that a number of minor surface actions had been fought in the area in recent weeks.

34 He later died.

35 Force 27 was carrying out antishipping sweeps off German-occupied ports.

36 Nothing untoward happened because the force of Bristol Beaufighter fighter-bombers that Layard observed – a Coastal Command strike wing comprising squadrons No. 236 RAF and No. 404 RCAF – destroyed *Z-24* and *T-24*, the only operational German destroyers remaining in the Biscay area. See Brereton Greenhous et al., *The Crucible of War, 1939-1945: The Official History of the RCAF*, vol. 3 (Toronto: University of Toronto Press, 1994), 465; and Christina J.M. Goulter, *A Forgotten Offensive: RAF Coastal Command's Anti-Shipping Campaign, 1940-1945* (London: Frank Cass, 1995), 224-30.

37 Cdr. Edgar George Skinner, RCNR, became E.G. 9's second-in-command. *Monnow* joined from the RCN midocean group C 2.

38 Lt. S.E. Hausard of the US Army Air Force's 181st Fighter Squadron. See Fraser McKee, *HMCS Swansea: The Life and Times of a Frigate* (St. Catharines, ON: Vanwell Publishing, 1994), 114.

39 The Directorate of Torpedoes and Mining, the Admiralty section responsible for antisubmarine weaponry.

40 *Bickerton* was sunk off North Cape by *U-354* on 22 August 1944. See Donald Macintyre, *U-Boat Killer* (London: Weidenfeld and Nicholson, 1956), 220-7.

41 It was a kill; *Saint John* and *Swansea* were later credited with the destruction of *U-247*. Thanks to Malcolm Llewellyn-Jones for sharing his research on the last cruise of *U-247*. Layard's admitted reluctance to stay in the area of the contact is in stark contrast to McKee and Darlington's account, which gives a large measure of the credit for the kill to Layard's stubborn persistence to stay in the area. Fraser McKee and Bob Darlington, *Canadian Naval Chronicle* (St. Catharines, ON: Vanwell Publishing, 1994).

42 The Admiralty's Operational Intelligence Centre thought three U-boats were operating off North Cornwall at this time. David Syrett, ed., *The Battle of the Atlantic and Signals Intelligence: U-Boat Situations and Trends, 1941-1945* (Ashgate, UK: Naval Records Society, 1998), 448.

43 Regulations gave leave only to those sailors who had next of kin in England or Scotland with whom they could stay. That obviously excluded a great number of Canadians, which was the reason for Layard's request.

44 Layard's confusion is understandable, as USS *Humboldt*, a small 840-ton seaplane tender, had lines similar to a sloop. See Paul Silverstone, *US Warships of World War Two* (London: Ian Allen, 1971).

45 HMCS *Prince Robert* was an auxiliary anti-aircraft cruiser.

46 Capt. A.M. Hope, RCN.

47 Chaplain I.R. Edwards, RCNVR.

48 Lt.(g) J.A. Falconer, RCNVR.

49 This was HX 307. Dividing the convoy into Irish Sea and English Channel sections facilitated the movement of supplies and materiel to the continent. See Arnold Hague, *The Allied Convoy System, 1939-1945: Its Organization, Defence and Operation* (St. Catharines, ON: Vanwell Publishing, 2000), 41.

50 Vice-Adm. P.W. Nelles, RCN, former Canadian chief of naval staff, then serving as senior Canadian naval officer in the UK.

51 Phoenixes were the large concrete caissons used to form breakwaters in the Mulberry artificial harbours off Normandy.
52 Lt.-Cdr. E.G. Old, RCNR.

Chapter 6: Deep Open Waters

1 See Andrew Lambert, "Seizing the Initiative: The Arctic Convoys, 1944-45," in *Naval Power in the Twentieth Century*, ed. N.A.M. Rodger (Annapolis: Naval Institute Press, 1996), 151-62.
2 Clay Blair, *Hitler's U-Boat War*, vol. 2, *The Hunted, 1942-1945* (New York: Random House, 1998), 645.
3 For more on the attack on *Chebogue*, see W.A.B. Douglas, Roger Sarty, and Michael Whitby, *A Blue Water Navy: The Official Operational History of the RCN in the Second World War 1943-1945*, vol. 2, part 2 (St. Catharines, ON: Vanwell Publishing, 2005), ch. 19. Although *Chebogue* was towed safely to the UK, the frigate was paid off as a constructive loss.
4 David Syrett, ed., *The Battle of the Atlantic and Signals Intelligence: U-Boat Situations and Trends, 1941-1945* (Ashgate, UK: Naval Records Society, 1998), 465.
5 Admiralty, Naval Historical Branch, *Arctic Convoys, 1941-1945*, 3, PRO, ADM 234/369. This staff history was written by Cdr. L.J. Pitcairn-Jones, RN, and published internally in 1954.
6 Admiral of the Fleet Sir Dudley Pound to Adm. E.J. King, USN, 18 May 1942. Cited in R. Ruegg and Arnold Hague, *Convoys to Russia: Allied Convoys and Naval Surface Operations in Arctic Waters, 1941-1945* (Kendal, UK: World Ship Society, 1992), an excellent statistical summary of the Murmansk run. See also B.B. Schofield, *The Arctic Convoys* (London: Macdonald and Janes, 1977); Richard Woodman, *The Arctic Convoys, 1941-1945* (London: John Murray, 1994); and Correlli Barnett, *Engage the Enemy More Closely: The Royal Navy in the Second World War* (London: W.W. Norton, 1991).
7 Outbound United Kingdom-North Russia convoys were intitally designated "P.Q." and the return convoys, "Q.P." In December 1942 the designations were changed to "J.W." and "R.A." respectively.
8 Adm. Sir Max Horton to Adm. Sir Bruce Fraser, 31 May 1944, PRO, ADM 199/237, also cited in Lambert, "Seizing the Initiative."
9 SO EG 9, Report of Proceedings, 19 December 1944, 1, DHH, 81/520 8440 EG 9 vol. 2.
10 Cdr. Hon. H.A. Pakington, RN.
11 Balfour was appointed senior officer of the support group E.G. 27, which operated in Canadian waters out of Halifax. After reading portions of the diary in 2001, Balfour, like many others, was staggered by Layard's lack of confidence. "If he, a career officer, lacked confidence in himself – which certainly was not evident to those of us who served under his command – you can imagine how I felt. I'm thankful that I had those months of being part of E.G. 9 under someone whom I thought competent and a leader whom I respected." St. Clair Balfour to John Band, 6 March 2001.
12 This refers to the signal Layard sent to the C-in-C Western Approaches on 10 September 1944 requesting that his ship's boiler clean in Plymouth instead of Londonderry so that his sailors would not face leave restrictions.
13 Lt. J.L.F. Bonnet, RCNVR.
14 Officers who had passed a short specialized gunnery course included a lower case "g" after their rank. Those who passed the more rigorous long course at Whale Island used an upper case "G."
15 HMS *Philante* was the Western Approaches anti-submarine training vessel based at Larne.
16 Operation SCABBARD was a special search procedure developed to counter the problem of bottomed U-boats.

17 Months later Admiral Horton passed along a message from the senior destroyer officer in the *Card* hunter-killer group: "The Division Commander wishes to comment on the most cordial and efficient co-operation of H.M. Escort Group 9 during the subsequent search." Admiralty to C-in-C Western Approaches, 22 March 1945, Layard papers.

18 Flag officer Gibraltar and Mediterranean Approaches, Vice-Adm. Sir Harold Burrough, KBE, CB, DSO, RN, whom Layard had served under in *Indomitable* and in Operation Terminal.

19 The Admiralty U-Boat Situation Report for the week ending 23 October concluded, "After a fairly promising start the hunt by USS *Card* and E.G. 9 for the 740 tonner making for the western approaches to the Straits of Gibraltar failed to produce any result and the last trace of the quarry was an inconclusive radar contact early on the 16th. It is probable that the U-boat has persisted in its advance and may now be beginning its patrol in approximately latitude 10°00'W." Syrett, *Signals Intelligence*, 473.

20 This would be the first reports of the Battle of Leyte Gulf.

21 The Admiralty's skepticism was appropriate. Despite several close calls *U-1227* eluded E.G. 9 and the *Card* task group and made it back to port. See Blair, *Hitler's U-Boat War*, vol. 2, 645-6.

22 Fifteen British Escort class anti-submarine vessels were supplied by the United States to the RN through the lend-lease program.

23 Presumably *Card*'s call sign.

24 "DF" refers to a destroyer flotilla, not an escort group like E.G. 9, but this was probably a sentimental slip on Layard's part.

25 Capt. S. Boucher, RN, a term mate and old friend of Layard's.

26 Lt.-Cdr. M.N. Tufnell, RN.

27 Lt.-Cdr. E.D.J. Abbott, RN, an old flotilla mate of Layard's.

28 John Band, *Swansea*'s No. 1, recalls an amusing day trying to slip his captain, who was first somewhat tight and later groggy from the anaesthetic, past suspicious officers at the hospital and headquarters. At one point Layard had to be propped up in the jeep as they drove past FOGMA HQ. David Kilgour recalled that the crew was amused by the incident and that "the whole group thought Layard was gradually becoming Canadian." Kilgour to Alan Easton, 2 July 1993, DHH, 94/169.

29 Perhaps Lt.-Cdr. M.C. Morris, RN.

30 HMS *Cormorant* was the depot ship at Gibraltar.

31 Layard could not have known, but the Battle of Leyte Gulf included the action in Surigao Strait, which was the last ever engagement between opposing battleships.

32 The battleship HMS *King George V* was on passage out to the Pacific.

33 E.G. 26 was another RCN support group.

34 E.G. 9's tasking was in response to intelligence that two U-boats were patrolling north of Ireland close by the approaches to the North Channel. One of these boats, *U-438*, torpedoed HMS *Whitaker*. See Syrett, *Signals Intelligence*, 480; and Jürgen Rohwer, *Axis Submarine Successes, 1939-1945* (Annapolis: Naval Institute Press, 1983), 185.

35 Gwinner's call sign was evidently a sentimental choice, as he joined the navy in 1922, six years after the Battle of Jutland.

36 This was HMCS *Skeena*, wrecked on Videy Island off Reykjavik on 25 October 1944. Prentice's group was composed of old RN C-class destroyers built in the early 1930s that had seen hard service on the North Atlantic and in the Channel. See Douglas, Sarty, and Whitby, *Blue Water Navy*, ch. 19.

37 Lt.-Cdr. E.R. Shaw, RCNR.

38 An area off Loch Eriboll on the north coast of Scotland.

39 I.F.F., or identification friend or foe, was a transponder that gave a "friendly" signal to allied radar transmissions.
40 A listening watch meant keeping A/S silence by using only the passive hydrophones as opposed to the active asdic.
41 Shark was a low-velocity projectile fired from a four-inch gun and designed to penetrate a U-boat's hull below the waterline.
42 Acting Cmdre. R.M.J. Hutton, RN, an old friend and term mate of Layard's.
43 There were no docking facilities at Scapa Flow and observing destroyers and other ships secure to buoys – a difficult evolution at the best of times, but immensely more challenging when at the mercy of the perpetual gales that howled through the Orkneys – was a favourite spectator sport at the anchorage. See, for example, Roger Hill's fine memoir *Destroyer Captain: Memoirs of the War at Sea* (London: William Kimber, 1975).
44 HMS *Tyne* was the tender for Home Fleet destroyers.
45 Lt.-Cdr. R.H.R. Moodie, RN.
46 Acting Cdr. R.M. Spencer, RN.
47 Rear-Adm. R.R. McGrigor, RN, Capt. H.W.S. Browning, RN, and an unidentified officer. Following RN custom, Layard refers to McGrigor as C.S. 1 in the entries covering the convoy.
48 Lt. C.G. McIntosh, RCNR.
49 Lt. H.B. Blanchard, RCNVR, and Lt. J.L. Panabaker, RCNVR, two of *Saint John*'s officers.
50 Under *King's Regulations and Admiralty Instructions* junior personnel could not present gifts to their superiors.
51 Electrical Lt. G.R. MacDougall, RCNVR.
52 Cdr. D.M. MacLean, RN.
53 The senior officer of the 6th Destroyer Flotilla.
54 Intelligence reports indicated that some twenty U-boats were patrolling in the White Sea or off Kola Inlet at this time. Syrett, *Signals Intelligence*, 498-501.
55 Cdr. G.A. Thring, RN, in HMS *Tavy* was SO E.G. 20.
56 Capt. C.F.W. Norris, RN, an old colleague of Layard's.
57 The destroyer *Cassandra*'s bow was blown off by a torpedo from *U-365*. After temporary repairs at Kola Inlet she sailed back to the UK.
58 Through Ultra decrypts of German messages, the Admiralty was able to provide Rear-Admiral McGrigor with warning of the air attacks. See F.H. Hinsley et al., *British Intelligence in the Second World War*, vol. 3, part 2, *Its Influence on Strategy and Operations*, (London: Her Majesty's Stationery Office, 1988), 490-3.
59 Some seventy JU-88 torpedo bombers were based in northern Norway with KG 26 at this time. In this attack they failed to score any hits and lost two aircraft. See A.R.A. Claasen, *Hitler's Northern War: The Luftwaffe's Ill-Fated Campaign, 1940-1945* (Lawrence: University of Kansas Press, 2001), 247; and Jürgen Rohwer and Gerd Hümmelchen, *Chronology of the War At Sea, 1939-1945* (Annapolis: Naval Institute Press, 1992), 318.
60 The aircraft commander, who spoke halting English, described how he had lost contact with the rest of his force but had flown towards flak sighted on the horizon: "as he zoomed down through an opening below low-lying clouds he came into direct range of MONNOW's guns. He added that he never saw the ship until flak started bursting in the plane." CNMO, "Murmansk Convoy," 23 April 1945, DHH, 81/520 *Monnow* 8000.
61 Nine U-boats were hunting RA 62 but only *U-365*, the boat that torpedoed *Cassandra*, managed to establish contact. That proved her undoing, as on 13 December she was destroyed by two Swordfish aircraft from *Campania*. See Rohwer and Hümmelchen, *Chronology of the War at Sea*, 318.

62 Not surprisingly, in this report Layard vented about the difficulty in keeping distant station on a convoy during near-perpetual darkness while under radio silence.
63 These would be the first reports of the Battle of the Bulge, the German offensive in the Ardennes.
64 Layard's moniker for Cdr. Edgar Skinner, CO of *Monnow.*

Chapter 7: Wreck to Wreck, Contact to Contact

1 Admiralty, Trade Division, Monthly Chronological History and Merchant Ship Casualties, October 1944, PRO, ADM 199/2090. This section is based on W.A.B. Douglas, Roger Sarty, and Michael Whitby, *A Blue Water Navy: The Official Operational History of the RCN in the Second World War, 1943-1945,* vol. 2, part 2 (St. Catharines, ON: Vanwell Publishing, 2004), ch. 19, which was researched and written by the editor. See also Marc Milner, *Battle of the Atlantic* (St. Catharines, ON: Vanwell Publishing, 2003), ch. 9.
2 Admiralty, Trade Division, Monthly Chronological History and Merchant Ship Casualties, November 1944, PRO, ADM 199/2090.
3 Steaming almost exclusively with schnorchel, U-boats made slow progress between Norway and the UK, and the voyage sometimes took as long as three weeks.
4 Clay Blair, *Hitler's U-Boat War,* vol. 2, *The Hunted, 1942-1945* (New York: Random House, 1998), 636.
5 Director Anti-U-Boat Division, "Anti-U-boat Results Inshore in Western Approaches Command for the Period 1st September, 1944, to 31st January, 1945," 4 February 1945, 1, PRO, ADM 205/44; Admiralty, Trade Division, Monthly Chronological History and Merchant Ship Casualties, December 1944, PRO, ADM 199/2090.
6 First Sea Lord to Prime Minister, 30 December 1944. When informed of these measures, Churchill responded, "This is very interesting. You are absolutely right to reinforce strongly." PM to First Sea Lord, 9 January 1945, PRO, ADM 205/43.
7 Admiralty, Trade Division, Monthly Chronological History and Merchant Ship Casualties, December 1944, PRO, ADM 199/2090.
8 Cabinet Anti-U-Boat Warfare Committee, "Minutes of the Meeting held in the Cabinet War Room, on Friday, 26th January, 1945 at 11.30 am," 1, PRO, PREM 3/414/1.
9 Ibid., 2.
10 V.E. Tarrant, *The Last Year of the Kriegsmarine* (London: Arms and Armour Press, 1996), 190.
11 C-in-C WA to AIG 32, 1903/13 September 1944, DHH, 81/520 Support Groups (General) 8440; D.M. McLean, "Confronting Technological and Tactical Change: Allied Anti-Submarine Warfare in the Last Year of the Battle of the Atlantic," *Canadian Military History* 7, 3 (Summer 1998): 29; C-in-C WA, "Orders for Anti U-Boat Operations in Coastal Waters of the Western Approaches Command (Short Title: 'Operation CE')," 11 October 1944 and 15 February 1945, PRO, ADM 199/50.
12 Admiralty, Anti-U-Boat Division, "Asdic Detection of U-boats Inshore," 30 October 1944, PRO, ADM 205/36.
13 United Kingdom, Admiralty, *Defeat of the Enemy Attack on Shipping: A Study of Policy and Operations* (London: Historical Section, 1957), 129.
14 Thanks to Jan Drent for these figures.
15 Malcolm Llewellyn-Jones, "British Responses to the U-Boats, Winter 1943 to Spring 1945" (MA thesis, King's College, London, 1997), 18.
16 "Minutes of a Meeting Held at ACHQ Liverpool on 3rd October 1944 to Discuss a Programme of Schnorkel and other Trials and Practices," 4 October 1944, PRO, ADM 1/16121, cited ibid., 18.
17 Later, the submarines *Satyr* and *Scepter* were also converted. See Malcolm Llewellyn-Jones, "Trials with HM Submarine *Seraph* and British Preparations to Defeat the Type XXI U-boat,

September-October 1944," *Mariner's Mirror* 86, 4 (November 2000): 434-51; and Malcolm Llewellyn-Jones, "The Pursuit of Realism: British Anti-Submarine Tactics and Training to Counter the Fast Submarine, 1944-1952," in *The Face of Naval Battle: The Human Experience of Modern War at Sea,* ed. John Reeve and David Stevens (Crows Nest, Australia: Allen and Unwin, 2003), 224-5.

18 Diary, 4 February 1945.

19 SO EG 9, Report of Proceedings, 3 March 1945, DHH, 81/520 EG-9 8440 vol. 2.

20 Layard ms, vol. 4, 9.

21 *Port Colborne* fell victim to "condenseritis," but the others suffered from extensive hull leakage caused by damage from depth charges.

22 SO EG 9, Report of Proceedings, 3 March 1945. The River class destroyers of EGs 11 and 12 were also worn down by the heavy toll, and had to be amalgamated into one group before being disbanded altogether.

23 Intelligence estimates concluded that two U-boats were operating off the south coast of Ireland while two others were in the same area on transit into the English Channel. David Syrett, ed., *The Battle of the Atlantic and Signals Intelligence: U-Boat Situations and Trends, 1941-1945* (Aldershot, UK: Naval Records Society, 1998), 515.

24 According to the entry on 19 December 1944, *Saint John*'s coxswain had been drunk at sea, a most serious offence.

25 A slow Gibraltar-UK convoy.

26 A fast Gibraltar-UK convoy.

27 SO E.G. 5 was Cdr. B.W. Taylor, RN.

28 Cdr. G.W. Burrell, RN (ret'd).

29 Capt. A.F. Campbell, Capt. T. Harland, Cdr. D.E.G. Wemyss, Cdr. A.A.F. Talbot, and Cdr. J.V. Waterhouse, RN.

30 Start Point, south of Torquay.

31 This was *U-1055,* which actually sank three ships in the Irish Sea on 11 January.

32 Lt. J.R. Bradley, RCNVR.

33 *Vimy*'s CO was Lt.-Cdr. K.H.J.L. Phibbs, RN.

34 Lt.-Cdr. J.S. Davis, RCNVR.

35 CU convoys, in this case CU 54, transported oil from the United States to the UK. See Arnold Hague, *The Allied Convoy System: Its Organization, Defence and Operation* (St. Catharines, ON: Vanwell Publishing, 2000), 183-4.

36 A Thames-Bristol convoy.

37 Capt. W.Y. Beverley, RN.

38 The destroyer HMS *Icarus* and the corvette HMS *Mignonette* killed *U-1199.*

39 De St. Croix was Layard's predecessor in command of HMS *Salisbury,* and apparently created much ill will in Halifax with his criticisms of the RCN. See entry for 9 October 1943.

40 The Goodliffe's were old friends of Layard who lived in the Republic.

41 Slt. M.B.E. Clarkson, RCNVR.

42 Vice-Adm. G.C. Jones, RCN, Mr. John Connolly, and Capt. H.S. Rayner, DSC, RCN. Jones was Chief of the Naval Staff and Rayner the Director of Plans. Connolly was actually executive secretary to the minister, a political appointment.

43 Acting Cdr. H. Freeland, RCNR, was SO of C 2.

44 Acting Capt. H.R.H. Vaughan, pay captain on the staff at Londonderry.

45 It is surprising that Layard did not take up the matter of his replacement with either Jones or Rayner, who would have been in a better position to act. One can only surmise that Layard did not want to seem to be complaining about his own position to a senior officer.

46 HMS *Ferret* was the tender for the naval HQ at Londonderry.

47 Capt. E.A.B. Stanley, RN (ret'd).

48 Intelligence identified this as *U-483*. See Syrett, *Signals Intelligence*, 540.
49 SO E.G. 10 was Cdr. P.B. Burnett, RN.
50 This was Operation VERITABLE, the offensive launched into the Rhineland by 1 Canadian and 30 British Corps.
51 The Admiralty, citing the success of E.G. 10, which destroyed three U-boats in the same area, criticized Layard for relying solely on hedgehog and not taking advantage of *Loch Alvie*'s Squid. Anti-U-boat Division minute, 30 March 1945, PRO, ADM 199/198. The attack was assessed "G," or "no damage to a submarine believed to have been present."
52 This was the Yalta Conference.
53 The initial intelligence report described this as a "promising attack," but there was some suspicion that it was a "dead" U-boat that had actually been destroyed previously. When it was confirmed that *Saint John* had destroyed a U-boat, there was some confusion over which one it was, but it was later identified as *U-309*. See Anti-U-boat Division minute, 30 March 1945, PRO, ADM 199/198; and Syrett, *Signals Intelligence*, 543, 547-8.
54 Acting Cdr. R.H.R. Moodie, RN, on the staff of *Vindictive*, the repair ship at Scapa Flow.
55 The site where ships of the German High Seas Fleet, including the battle cruiser *Derflinger*, scuttled themselves in 1919.
56 Cdr. G.A.C. Williams, RN (ret'd).
57 Capt. G.C. Colville, RN, Chief Staff Officer (Operations) at Western Approaches.
58 Cdr. C.W. McMullen, RN.
59 In other words, as senior officer of the group but not commanding officer of the ship.
60 Cdr. J.G.C. Gibson, RN (ret'd), responsible for support group operations at Rosyth.
61 River class frigates displaced about 1,445 tons, with an overall length of 301 feet six inches and a breadth of 36 feet six inches. The slightly larger Loch class displaced about 1,430 tons, with an overall length of 307 feet and a breadth of 38 feet six inches. See Peter Elliott, *Allied Escort Ships of World War II: A Complete Survey* (London: Macdonald and Janes, 1977), 211, 229.
62 Lt. D.N. Radcliffe, RCNVR.
63 Capt. J.H. Ruck-Keene, RN.
64 Adm. Sir William Whitworth.
65 Capt. H.W. Faulkner, RN.
66 Lt. G.F. Hearn, RCNVR, Earl's relief.
67 Lt. J.D. Flavelle, RCNVR.
68 Cdr. A.M. McLaron, RCNR.
69 Lt.-Cdr. H.E. McArthur, RCNVR, CO of the frigate HMCS *Capilano* of the RCN group C 2.
70 Cdr. W.P. Carne, RN.
71 S206s are rated on a scale of 1 (poor) to 9 (excellent).
72 Lt.-Cdr. W.D. Ely, RN (ret'd).
73 Vice-Adm. Sir Richard A.S. Hill, KBE, CB, RN.
74 Presumably a gale warning.
75 Some twenty U-boats were reported to be patrolling British waters. Syrett, *Signals Intelligence*, 561.
76 Lt. D.G. Smeeton, RN.
77 See entry for 25 March 1945.
78 Capt. J.H. Jauncey, RN.
79 Capt. J.R. Hunter, RCNVR.
80 This is indeed what occurred. *New Glasgow* literally ran over *U-1003* while it was schnorcheling, inflicting fatal damage that eventually forced the crew to scuttle their boat.

Chapter 8: Oasis of Comfort and Happiness

1 Diary, 1 September 1942.

2 Layard made the calculations on a calendar in his 1944 diary, where he also counted up twenty-nine days of leave at Prinsted. The fact that he made the effort to make these calculations – something he had not done before – indicates that the strain was beginning to tell.

3 D.A. Rayner, *Escort: The Battle of the Atlantic* (London: William Kimber, 1955), 230. Thanks to Gil Lauzon for alerting me to Rayner's account.

4 Diary, 8 November 1944; see also Marc Milner, *The U-Boat Hunters: The Royal Canadian Navy and the Offensive against Germany's Submarines* (Toronto: University of Toronto Press, 1994), 188.

5 HMCS *New Glasgow* to C-in-C Plymouth, 4 March 1945, DHH, EG-26 8440 vol 1. Simmons was replaced by Cdr. R.M. Aubrey, RN, another "retread" like Layard.

6 Douglas M. McLean, "The Last Cruel Winter: RCN Support Groups and the U-Boat Schnorchel Offensive" (MA thesis, Royal Military College of Canada, 1992).

7 Diary, 27 March 1945.

8 Diary, 29 January 1945.

9 I had the good fortune to become friends with two former captains of Canadian escorts on the North Atlantic run, Alan Easton and Louis Audette. Both said that they suffered from ulcers, and that many of their colleagues suffered from the same affliction.

10 Capt. J.A. McCoy, RN, was Capt. D. Western Approaches when Layard returned to sea in July 1941.

11 Diary, 20 July 1941. Lt.-Cdr. N.V.J.T. "Pug" Thew, RN, was CO of the destroyer HMS *Jupiter* and a neighbour of Layard. He was treated roughly by the Japanese as a prisoner after *Jupiter* was sunk in the Battle of the Java Sea, and was ultimately invalided out of the navy.

12 Diary, 7 March 1945.

13 Mark K. Wells, *Courage and Air Warfare: The Allied Aircrew Experience in the Second World War* (London: Frank Cass, 1995), 61.

14 Diary, 19 October 1939. The incident took place in British waters on 16 October 1939. Despite a horrible stomach wound, Jolly remained on the bridge giving steering orders for the eighty minutes it took to get the ship into the Firth of Forth. He collapsed only after saluting the flagship and died later in hospital. He was awarded the Empire Gallantry Medal. See Martin Brice, *The Tribals: Biography of a Destroyer Class* (London: Ian Allen, 1971), 180.

15 Diary, 26 October 1939.

16 Diary, 25 November 1939.

17 Diary, 1 April 1945.

18 The Needles is a narrow, rugged peninsula in the western approaches to the Isle of Wight.

19 Capt. H.V. King, RN.

20 The location of Portsmouth Command Headquarters.

21 Cmdre. S. Taylor, RN.

22 VWP convoys ran from France to the Isle of Wight. See Arnold Hague, *The Allied Convoy System, 1939-1945: Its Organization, Defence and Operation* (St. Catharines, ON: Vanwell Publishing, 2000), 114.

23 Nab Light marked the entrance to the deep-water channel for Portsmouth and Southampton.

24 The *Cuba* was a large, 11,420-ton troop ship.

25 Sole credit for killing *U-1195* indeed went to *Watchman*, although it seems clear that *Loch Alvie* could have received an assist.

26 WVP convoys ran from the Isle of Wight to France. Hague, *Allied Convoy System*, 114.

27 Lt. James Bradley, RCNVR, *Saint John*'s asdic control officer, received a bar to this DSC for his role in the destruction of *U-309* in February 1945.

28 Lt.-Cdr. J.R. Clarke, RNVR.
29 The wife of Layard's colleague, Cdr. Rolph Medley, RN.
30 XP was the experimental department at Whale Island, where Layard worked from 1936 to 1941. Developed by Mr. Fred Waller, formerly responsible for special effects at Paramount Pictures, the Waller trainer reproduced aircraft attacks on a large concave movie screen and allowed realistic training for gunners. See *Popular Science,* September 1943.
31 Pompey is naval slang for Portsmouth.
32 H.M.S. *Highway* was US Navy Casagrande class landing ship (dock) that had been transferred to the RN.
33 Cdr. J. Plomer, RCNVR, an escort commander with considerable experience in the Battle of the Atlantic.
34 It did and it was. This was a political dodge by Prime Minister Mackenzie King. See W.A.B. Douglas, Roger Sarty, and Michael Whitby, *A Blue Water Navy: The Official Operational History of the Royal Canadian Navy in the Second World War, 1943-1945,* vol. 2, part 2 (St. Catharines, ON: Vanwell Publishing, 2004), ch. 22.
35 Lt.-Cdr. J.A. Tullis, RCNR.
36 Lt. J. Mallet, RCNVR.
37 Maydown was the satellite field to the RAF and Fleet Air Arm station at Eglinton.
38 Lt.-Cdr. F.R.K. Naftel, RCNVR.
39 Lt. F.J. Jones, RCNVR.
40 This is a curious statement, considering that Layard had celebrated the end of the Great War by toasting victory with champagne in the wardroom of the destroyer HMS *Sea Bear.*
41 The RCN had agreed to acquire eight CR class destroyers for its Pacific Task Force, but with the sudden conclusion to the war only two, *Crescent* and *Crusader,* were commissioned.
42 Cdr. R.C.S. Garwood, RN.
43 Position MM was on the port bow of the convoy, and CC was on the starboard bow.
44 Layard had the same reaction when he witnessed the surrender of the German High Seas Fleet at Scapa Flow in 1918. For more on E.G. 9's experience with the surrender of the U-boats, see Milner, *U-Boat Hunters,* 265-7.
45 Not to be confused with the light fleet carriers (CVL) then being commissioned into the RN, *Queen* was an escort carrier (CVE).
46 The first lieutenant of *Matane* was Lt. J.J. Coates, RCNVR, while *Kapitän zur See* R. Suhren was senior German officer in the yacht *Grilse.*
47 Layard's unpleasant reaction stemmed from the fact that Gourley had been an extremely harsh, unpopular captain. See editor's introduction to Chapter 6.
48 The rules regarding fraternization were quite strict: the C-in-C Home Fleet, to whom Layard reported in this instance, instructed personnel that "friendliness or familiarity is not permitted and an attitude of stern courtesy adopted. The attitude of Allied personnel is to be just but firm making clear that immediate compliance with order and instructions will be enforced." C-in-C Home Fleet to Home Fleet, 191054B May 1945, DHH, Prentice papers. In response to the criticism Layard suggested, "It is indeed difficult to prevent English or Canadian personnel from displaying those small acts of kindness and good will which is our National characteristic." SO EG 9, Report of Proceedings, 23 May 1945, DHH, 81/520 EG-9 8440 vol. 2.
49 Lt.-Cdr. D.M. Cann, RN (ret'd).
50 Lucas had been Layard's first lieutenant in *Matane* during the summer of 1944. The £5 was payment of a wager that Layard had made with Cdr. Clarence King that the European war would end in 1944.

Epilogue: Respite

1 Layard ms, vol. 4, 17.

2 Layard ms, vol. 4, 21.

3 Diary, n.d. June 1953. Strangely, there is no mention of Layard's visit to *Swansea* in Johnston's detailed report of the Coronation ceremonies. DHH, 81/520 Swansea 8000.

Selected Bibliography

Baker, Richard. *The Terror of Tobermory: An Informal Biography of Vice-Admiral Sir Gilbert Stephenson, KBE, CB, GMG.* London: W.H. Allen, 1972.

Barnett, Correlli. *Engage the Enemy More Closely: The Royal Navy in the Second World War.* London: Norton, 1991.

Blair, Clay. *Hitler's U-Boat War.* 2 vols. New York: Random House, 1996-8.

Chalmers, W.S. *Max Horton and the Western Approaches.* London: Hodder and Stoughton, 1954.

Douglas, W.A.B., Roger Sarty, and Michael Whitby. *No Higher Purpose: The Official History of the RCN in the Second World War, 1939-1943.* Vol. 2, part 1. St. Catharines, ON: Vanwell Publishing, 2003.

–. *A Blue Water Navy: The Official Operational History of the Royal Canadian Navy in the Second World War, 1943-1945.* Vol. 2, part 2. St. Catharines, ON: Vanwell Publishing, 2005.

Easton, Alan. *50 North: An Atlantic Battleground.* Toronto: Ryerson Press, 1966.

Elliott, Peter. *Allied Escort Ships of World War II: A Complete Survey.* London: Macdonald and Janes, 1977.

Franklin, G. *Britain's Anti-Submarine Capability, 1919-1939.* London: Frank Cass, 2003.

Goldrick, James. "Work-up." In *The Battle of the Atlantic, 1939-1945: The 50th Anniversary International Naval Conference,* ed. Stephen Howarth and Derek Law, 220-39. Annapolis: Naval Institute Press, 1994.

Graves, Donald E. *In Peril on the Sea: The RCN and the Battle of the Atlantic.* Toronto: Robin Brass Studio, 2003.

Greenhous, Brereton, S. Harris, W. Johnston, and W. Rawling. *The Crucible of War: The Official History of the RCAF,* vol. 3. Toronto: University of Toronto Press, 1994.

Gretton, Peter. *Convoy Escort Commander.* London: Cassell, 1964.

Hackmann, Willem. *Seek and Strike: Sonar, Anti-Submarine Warfare and the Royal Navy, 1914-1954.* London: HMSO, 1984.

Hadley, Michael L. *U-Boats against Canada.* Montreal: McGill-Queen's University Press, 1985.

Hague, Arnold. *The Allied Convoy System, 1939-1945: Its Organization, Defence and Operation.* St. Catharines, ON: Vanwell, 2000.

–. *The Towns.* Kendal, UK: World Ship Society, 1990.

Hill, Roger. *Destroyer Captain: Memoirs of the War at Sea.* London: William Kimber, 1975.

Hinsley, F.H., with E.E. Thomas, C.F.G. Ransom, R.C. Knight. *British Intelligence in the Second World War.* Vol. 3, part 2, *Its Influence on Strategy and Operations.* London: HMSO, 1979-90.

Howarth, Stephen, and Derek Law, eds. *The Battle of the Atlantic, 1939-1945: The 50th Anniversary International Naval Conference.* Annapolis: Naval Institute Press, 1994.

Lambert, Andrew. "Seizing the Initiative: The Arctic Convoys, 1944-45." In *Naval Power in the Twentieth Century,* ed. N.A.M. Rodger, 151-62. Annapolis: Naval Institute Press, 1996.

Layard, A.F.C. "Algiers – 8 November 1942." *Naval Review* 66, 2 (April 1978): 156-61.

–. "Coal Ship." *Naval Review* 65, 1 (January 1977): 66-9.

–. "Malta: Some Memories." *Naval Review* 74, 4 (October 1986): 372-5.

Llewellyn-Jones, Malcolm. "The Pursuit of Realism: British Anti-Submarine Tactics and Training to Counter the Fast Submarine, 1944-1952." In *The Face of Naval Battle: The Human Experience of Modern War at Sea,* ed. John Reeve and David Stevens, 219-39. Crows Nest, Australia: Allen and Unwin, 2003.

–. "Trials with HM Submarine *Seraph* and British Preparations to Defeat the Type XXI U-boat, September-October 1944." *Mariner's Mirror* 86, 4 (November 2000): 434-51.

McAndrew, Bill, Donald E. Graves, and Michael Whitby. *Normandy 1944: The Canadian Summer.* Montreal: Art Global, 1994.

McAndrew, Bill, Bill Rawling, and Michael Whitby. *Liberation: The Canadians in Northwest Europe.* Montreal: Art Global, 1995.

Macintyre, Donald. *U-Boat Killer.* London: Weidenfeld and Nicholson, 1956.

McKee, Fraser. *HMCS Swansea: The Life and Times of a Frigate.* St. Catharines, ON: Vanwell Publishing, 1994.

McLean, D.M. "Confronting Technological and Tactical Change: Allied Anti-Submarine Warfare in the Last Year of the Battle of the Atlantic," *Canadian Military History* 7, 3 (Summer 1998): 29-34.

–. "Muddling Through: Canadian Anti-Submarine Doctrine and Practice, 1942-1945." In *A Nation's Navy: In Quest of Canadian Naval Identity,* ed. Michael L. Hadley, Rob Huebert, and Fred W. Crickard. Montreal: McGill-Queen's University Press, 1996.

MacPherson, Ken, and Ron Barrie. *The Ships of Canada's Naval Forces, 1910-2002.* St. Catharines, ON: Vanwell Publishing, 2002.

Milner, Marc. *Battle of the Atlantic.* St. Catharines, ON: Vanwell Publishing, 2003.

–. *Canada's Navy: The First Century.* Toronto: University of Toronto Press, 1999.

–. *North Atlantic Run: The Royal Canadian Navy and the Battle of the Convoys.* Toronto: University of Toronto Press, 1985.

–. "The Royal Canadian Navy and 1943: A Year Best Forgotten?" In *1943: The Beginning of the End,* ed. Paul D. Dickson, 123-36. Waterloo, ON: Canadian Committee for the History of the Second World War, 1995.

–. *The U-Boat Hunters: The Royal Canadian Navy and the Offensive against Germany's Submarines.* Toronto: University of Toronto Press, 1994.

Niestlé, Axel. *German U-Boat Losses during World War II: Details of Destruction.* Annapolis: Naval Institute Press, 1998.

Paquette, Edward R., and Charles G. Bainbridge, eds. *Honours and Awards: Canadian Naval Forces, World War II.* Vancouver Island: E.W. Bickle, 1986.

Reeve, John, and David Stevens, eds. *The Face of Naval Battle: The Human Experience of Modern War at Sea.* Crows Nest, Australia: Allen and Unwin, 2003.

Roskill, Stephen W. *Naval Policy between the Wars.* 2 vols. London: Collins, 1968-76.

–. *The War at Sea, 1939-1945.* 3 vols. London: HMSO, 1954-61.

Ruegg, R., and Arnold Hague. *Convoys to Russia: Allied Convoys and Naval Surface Operations in Arctic Waters, 1941-1945.* Kendal, UK: World Ship Society, 1992.

Sarty, Roger. *Canada and the Battle of the Atlantic.* Montreal: Art Global, 1998.

Schofield, B.B. *The Arctic Convoys.* London: Macdonald and Janes, 1977.

Schull, Joseph. *The Far Distant Ships: An Official Account of Canadian Naval Operations in World War II.* Ottawa: Queen's Printer, 1950.

Syrett, David, ed. *The Battle of the Atlantic and Signals Intelligence: U-Boat Situations and Trends, 1941-1945.* Ashgate, UK: Naval Records Society, 1998.

–. *The Defeat of the German U-Boats: The Battle of the Atlantic.* Columbia: University of South Carolina Press, 1994.

Tarrant, V.E. *The Last Year of the Kriegsmarine.* London: Arms and Armour Press, 1996.

United Kingdom, Admiralty. *The Defeat of the Enemy Attack on Shipping, 1939-1945: A Study of Policy and Operations.* London: Historical Section, 1957.

Whitby, Michael. "The Seaward Defence of the British Assault Area, 6-14 June 1944." *Mariner's Mirror* 80, 2 (May 1994): 191-207.

–. "The Strain of the Bridge: The Second World War Diaries of Commander A.F.C. Layard, RN." In *The Face of Naval Battle: The Human Experience of Modern War at Sea,* ed. John Reeve and David Stevens, 200-18. Crows Nest, Australia: Allen and Unwin, 2003.

Williams, Mark. *Captain Gilbert Roberts and the Anti-U-Boat School.* London: Cassell, 1979.

Winton, John. *Cunningham: The Greatest Admiral since Nelson.* London: John Murray, 1998.

Woodman, Richard. *The Arctic Convoys, 1941-1945.* London: John Murray, 1994.

Zimmerman, David. *The Great Naval Battle of Ottawa: How Admirals, Scientists and Politicians Impeded the Development of High Technology in Canada's Wartime Navy.* Toronto: University of Toronto Press, 1989.

Index